LEARNING AND TEACHING EARLY MATH

D1599747

The third edition of this significant and groundbreaking book summarizes current research on how young children learn mathematics and illustrates how best to develop foundational knowledge to realize more effective teaching.

Using straightforward, practical language, early math experts Douglas Clements and Julie Sarama show how *learning trajectories* help teachers understand children's level of mathematical understanding and lead to better teaching. By focusing on the inherent delight and curiosity behind young children's mathematical reasoning, learning trajectories ultimately make teaching more joyous: helping teachers understand the varying levels of knowledge exhibited by individual students allows them to better meet the learning needs of all children.

This thoroughly revised and contemporary third edition of *Learning and Teaching Early Math* remains the definitive, research-based resource to help teachers understand the learning trajectories of early mathematics and become confident, credible professionals. The new edition draws on numerous new research studies, offers expanded international examples, and includes updated illustrations throughout.

This new edition is closely linked with *Learning and Teaching with Learning Trajectories*—

$[LT]^2$–an open-access, web-based tool for early childhood educators to learn about how children think and learn about mathematics. Head to LearningTrajectories.org for ongoing updates, interactive games, and practical tools that support classroom learning.

Douglas H. Clements is Distinguished University Professor, the Kennedy Endowed Chair in Early Childhood Learning, and co-Executive Director of the Marsico Institute of Early Learning, at the University of Denver.

Julie Sarama is Distinguished University Professor, the Kennedy Endowed Chair in Innovative Learning Technologies, and co-Executive Director of the Marsico Institute of Early Learning, at the University of Denver.

Studies in Mathematical Thinking and Learning
Alan H. Schoenfeld, Series Editor

Artzt/Armour-Thomas/Curcio *Becoming a Reflective Mathematics Teacher: A Guide for Observation and Self-Assessment, Second Edition*

Artzt/Armour-Thomas/Curcio/Gurl *Becoming a Reflective Mathematics Teacher: A Guide for Observation and Self-Assessment, Third Edition*

Baroody/Dowker (Eds.) *The Development of Arithmetic Concepts and Skills: Constructing Adaptive Expertise*

Boaler *Experiencing School Mathematics: Traditional and Reform Approaches to Teaching and Their Impact on Student Learning*

Carpenter/Fennema/Romberg (Eds.) *Rational Numbers: An Integration of Research*

Chazan/Callis/Lehman (Eds.) *Embracing Reason: Egalitarian Ideals and the Teaching of High School Mathematics*

Cobb/Bauersfeld (Eds.) *The Emergence of Mathematical Meaning: Interaction in Classroom Cultures*

Cohen *Teachers' Professional Development and the Elementary Mathematics Classroom: Bringing Understandings to Light*

Clements/Sarama *Learning and Teaching Early Math: The Learning Trajectories Approach*

Clements/Sarama/DiBiase (Eds.) *Engaging Young Children in Mathematics: Standards for Early Childhood Mathematics Education*

English (Ed.) *Mathematical and Analogical Reasoning of Young Learners*

English (Ed.) *Mathematical Reasoning: Analogies, Metaphors, and Images*

Fennema/Nelson (Eds.) *Mathematics Teachers in Transition*

Fennema/Romberg (Eds.) *Mathematics Classrooms That Promote Understanding*

Fernandez/Yoshida *Lesson Study: A Japanese Approach to Improving Mathematics Teaching and Learning*

Greer/Mukhopadhyay/Powell/Nelson-Barber (Eds.) *Culturally Responsive Mathematics Education*

Kaput/Carraher/Blanton (Eds.) *Algebra in the Early Grades*

Kitchen/Civil (Eds.) *Transnational and Borderland Studies in Mathematics Education*

Lajoie *Reflections on Statistics: Learning, Teaching, and Assessment in Grades K-12*

Lehrer/Chazan (Eds.) *Designing Learning Environments for Developing Understanding of Geometry and Space*

Li/Huang (Eds.) *How Chinese Teach Mathematics and Improve Teaching*

Ma *Knowing and Teaching Elementary Mathematics: Teachers' Understanding of Fundamental Mathematics in China and the United States, Anniversary Edition*

Martin *Mathematics Success and Failure Among African-American Youth: The Roles of Sociohistorical Context, Community Forces, School Influence, and Individual Agency*

Martin (Ed.) *Mathematics Teaching, Learning, and Liberation in the Lives of Black Children*

Petit/Laird/Marsden *A Focus on Fractions: Bringing Research to the Classroom*

Petit/Laird/Marsden/Ebby *A Focus on Fractions: Bringing Research to the Classroom, Second Edition*

Petit/Laird/Wyneken/Huntoon/Abele-Austin/Sequeira *A Focus on Ratio and Proportions: Bringing Mathematics Research to the Classroom*

Reed *Word Problems: Research and Curriculum Reform*

LEARNING AND TEACHING EARLY MATH

The Learning Trajectories Approach

Third Edition

Douglas H. Clements and Julie Sarama

Routledge
Taylor & Francis Group

NEW YORK AND LONDON

Third edition published 2021
by Routledge
52 Vanderbilt Avenue, New York, NY 10017

and by Routledge
2 Park Square, Milton Park, Abingdon, Oxon, OX14 4RN

Routledge is an imprint of the Taylor & Francis Group, an informa business

© 2021 Douglas H. Clements and Julie Sarama

The right of Douglas H. Clements and Julie Sarama to be identified as authors
of this work has been asserted by them in accordance with sections 77 and 78
of the Copyright, Designs and Patents Act 1988.

All rights reserved. No part of this book may be reprinted or reproduced or
utilised in any form or by any electronic, mechanical, or other means, now
known or hereafter invented, including photocopying and recording, or in any
information storage or retrieval system, without permission in writing from the
publishers.

Trademark notice: Product or corporate names may be trademarks or
registered trademarks, and are used only for identification and explanation
without intent to infringe.

Second edition published by Routledge, 2014
First edition published by Routledge, 2009

British Library Cataloguing-in-Publication Data
A catalogue record for this book is available from the British Library

Library of Congress Cataloging-in-Publication Data
Names: Clements, Douglas H., author. | Sarama, Julie, author.
Title: Learning and teaching early math : the learning trajectories approach /
Douglas H. Clements and Julie Sarama.
Description: Third edition. | New York, NY : Routledge, 2021. | Series: Studies in
mathematical thinking and learning | Includes bibliographical references and index.
Identifiers: LCCN 2020029015 | ISBN 9780367538552 (hardback) |
ISBN 9780367521974 (paperback) | ISBN 9781003083528 (ebook)
Subjects: LCSH: Mathematics-Study and teaching (Early childhood) |
Educational psychology. | Child development. | Curriculum planning.
Classification: LCC QA135.6 .C55 2021 | DDC 372.7/049-dc23
LC record available at https://lccn.loc.gov/2020029015

ISBN: 978-0-367-53855-2 (hbk)
ISBN: 978-0-367-52197-4 (pbk)
ISBN: 978-1-003-08352-8 (ebk)

Typeset in Interstate
by River Editorial Ltd, Devon, UK

Visit the author hosted companion website: www.LearningTrajectories.org

We wish to dedicate this book to those who taught us, including the thousands of children and teachers who shared their lives and thinking with us, and to our closest teachers, our families. We also thank our graduate students, post-doctoral fellows, and colleagues who provided valuable feedback.

CONTENTS

PREFACE

Who dares to teach must never cease to learn.

(John Cotton Dana, 1856-1929)

Mathematics is, in its way, the poetry of logical ideas.

(Albert Einstein, 1879-1955)

Think of the biggest number you can. Now add five. Then, imagine if you had that many Twinkies. Wow, that's five more than the biggest number you could come up with!

(Child, age 6)

Everyone knows that effective teaching involves "meeting the students where they are" and helping them build on what they know. But that's easier said than done. Which aspects of math are important, which less so? How do we diagnose what a child knows? How do we build on that knowledge—in which directions, and in what ways?

We believe that "learning trajectories" help answer these questions and help teachers become more effective professionals. Just as importantly, they open up windows to seeing young children and math in new ways, making teaching more joyous because the mathematical reasoning of children is both impressive and delightful.

Learning trajectories have three parts: (a) a specific mathematical goal, (b) a path along which children develop to reach that goal, and (c) a set of instructional activities fine-tuned for each step along said path that help children reach the following step. So, teachers who understand learning trajectories understand the math, the way children think and learn about math, and how to help children learn it better.

Learning trajectories connect research and practice. They connect children to math. They connect teachers to children. They help teachers understand the level of knowledge and thinking of their classes *and* the individuals in their classes as key in serving the needs of all children. (Equity issues are important to us and to the nation. This entire book is designed to help you teach *all* children, but equity concerns are discussed specifically and at length in Chapters 14, 15, and 16.) *Learning and Teaching Early Math* will help you understand the learning trajectories of early math in order to become a quintessential professional.

Learning and teaching, of course, take place in a context. For the last two decades, we have had the honor and advantage of working with several hundred early childhood teachers who have worked with us on creating new ideas for teaching and have invited us into their class-rooms to test these ideas with the children in their charge. We wish to share with you a bit about this collaborative work.

Background

In 1998, we began a 4-year project funded by the National Science Foundation (NSF). The purpose of "Building Blocks–Foundations for Mathematical Thinking, Pre-Kindergarten to Grade 2: Research-Based Materials Development" was to create and evaluate math curricula for young children based on a theoretically sound research and development framework. Based on theory and research on early childhood learning and teaching, we determined that Building Blocks' basic approach would be *finding the mathematics in*, and *developing mathematics from, children's activity*. To achieve this, all aspects of the Building Blocks project have been based on learning trajectories. Teachers have found this combination of the Building Blocks' approach and learning trajectories to be a powerful teaching tool.

More than 20 years later, we are still finding new opportunities for exciting research and development in early math. Funding from the U.S. Department of Education's Institute of Education Sciences (IES), National Science Foundation (NSF), Heising-Simons Foundation, Bill & Melinda Gates Foundation, and Office of Special Education Programs (OSEP) has allowed us to work closely with thousands of teachers and tens of thousands of children. All of these agencies and individuals have contributed ideas to this book and its companion. In addition, these projects have increased our confidence that our approach, based on learning trajectories and rigorous empirical testing at every step, can, in turn, make a contribution to all educators in the field of early math. The model for working with educators in all positions–from teachers to administrators, trainers to researchers–has been developed with IES funding to our TRIAD (Technology-enhanced, Research-based Instruction, Assessment, and professional Development)[1] project.

The "Companion" Books

We believe that our successes are due to the people who have contributed to our projects, as well as to our commitment to grounding everything that we have done in research. Because the work has been so drenched in research, we initially decided to publish two books. The companion to the first edition of the present book–*Early Childhood Mathematics Education Research: Learning Trajectories for Young Children* (Sarama & Clements, 2009)–reviews extensively the research underlying our original learning trajectories, emphasizing the research that describes the paths of learning; that is, children's natural progressions in developing the concepts and skills within a certain domain of math (most research citations for these are in the companion book, although we have added recent ones to this edition). The present book describes and illustrates how these learning trajectories can be implemented in the classroom *and* brings the research and the learning trajectories up to date.

What's New and Different about this Edition

Early childhood math education continues to be of great interest, so there are abundant new research and resources, all of which we share in this edition. International work is particularly highlighted. We appreciate the suggestions our readers have provided, and we tried to put every one into practice.

One of the most important enhancements to this book is our incorporation of our new *Learning and Teaching with Learning Trajectories* tool (www.LearningTrajectories.org). Readers can now see videos of children's thinking at *each level* of each topic or learning trajectory, and of *classroom* and home videos of teachers and caregivers helping children *learn* that topic. Along with hundreds of other resources, this will revolutionize the way one can learn about and use learning trajectories. See more about this tool on pp. 11-14.

Reading this Book

In straightforward, no-nonsense language, we summarize what is known about how children learn and how to build on what they know. In Chapter 1, we introduce the topic of math education for very young children. We discuss why people are particularly interested in engaging young children with math. Next, we describe the idea of learning trajectories in detail. We end with an introduction to the Building Blocks project and explain how learning trajectories are at its core.

Most of the following chapters address one math topic, and we describe how children understand and learn about that topic. These descriptions are brief summaries of the more elaborate reviews of the research that can be found in the aforementioned companion book, *Early Childhood Mathematics Education Research: Learning Trajectories for Young Children* (Sarama & Clements, 2009), as well as updates to those bodies of research. Next, we describe how experiences—from the beginning of life—and classroom-based education affect children's learning of the topic. Chapters 2 to 11 then culminate in a detailed description of learning trajectories for the chapter's topic.

Read more than the topic chapters, even if you just want to teach a topic! In the last three chapters, we discuss issues that are important for putting these ideas into practice. In Chapter 14, we describe how children think about math and how their feelings are involved. Equity concerns complete that chapter. In Chapter 15, we discuss the contexts in which early childhood education occurs and the curricula that are used. In Chapter 16, we review what we know about specific instructional practices. The topics of these three chapters are unique to this book. Because there are no corresponding chapters in the companion book for these three important chapters, we review more research in this book. We have made the implications for practitioners clear.

To teach children with different needs, and to teach effectively, make sure you read Chapters 14, 15, and especially 16. Some readers may wish to read those chapters immediately after having read Chapter 1! Whichever way you choose, please know that the learning trajectories that describe children's learning and effective teaching for each topic are only *part* of the story—the other, critical part is found in those final three chapters.

This is not a typical book of "cute teaching ideas." (OK, many of the teaching ideas and activities, and especially children's reactions to them, are very cute!) We believe, however, that it may be the most practical book that you, as a teacher of early math, could read. The many teachers with whom we have worked claim that, once they understood the learning trajectories and ways to implement them in their classrooms, they—and the children they teach—were changed for the better forever. Moreover, they also changed their beliefs, shedding the unfortunate misconceptions that many teachers hold about early math education, such as:

1. Young children are not ready for mathematics education.
2. Mathematics is for some bright kids with mathematics genes.
3. Simple numbers and shapes are enough.
4. Language and literacy are more important than mathematics.
5. Teachers should provide an enriched physical environment, step back, and let the children play.
6. Mathematics should not be taught as a stand-alone subject matter.
7. Assessment in mathematics is irrelevant when it comes to young children.
8. Children learn mathematics only by interacting with concrete objects.
9. Computers are inappropriate for the teaching and learning of mathematics.

(From Sun Lee & Ginsburg, 2009)

Note

1 Like many acronyms, TRIAD *almost* works … we jokingly ask people to accept the "silent p" in "professional development."

ACKNOWLEDGMENTS

Appreciation to the Funding Agencies

We wish to express our appreciation for the funding agencies that have not only provided financial support but also intellectual support, in the form of guidance from program officers (most notably and recently, Caroline Ebanks and Christina S. Chhin from the IES and Edith S. Gummer and Finbar "Barry" Sloane from the NSF), as well as opportunities to collaborate with other projects and attend conferences to exchange ideas with colleagues.

The ideas and research reported here have been supported by all of the following grants. Any opinions, findings, and conclusions or recommendations expressed in this material are those of the authors and do not necessarily reflect the views of the funding agencies.

Grants

Barrett, J., Clements, D. H., & Sarama, J. *A longitudinal account of children's knowledge of measurement.* Awarded by the NSF (Directorate for Education & Human Resources (EHR), Division of Research on Learning in Formal and Informal Settings (DRL)), award no. DRL-0732217. Arlington, VA: NSF.

Barrett, J., Clements, D. H., Sarama, J., & Cullen, C. *Learning trajectories to support the growth of measurement knowledge: Prekindergarten through middle school.* Awarded by the NSF (EHR, DRL), award no. DRL-1222944. Arlington, VA: NSF.

Clements, D. H. *Conference on standards for preschool and kindergarten mathematics education.* Supported in part by the NSF (EHR, ESIE) and the ExxonMobil Foundation, award no. ESI-9817540. Arlington, VA: NSF. In Clements, D. H., Sarama, J., & DiBiase, A.-M. (Eds.). (2004). *Engaging young children in mathematics: Standards for early childhood mathematics education.* Mahwah, NJ: Lawrence Erlbaum Associates.

Clements, D. H., & Sarama, J. *Building blocks—Foundations for mathematical thinking, prekindergarten to Grade 2: Research- based materials development.* Awarded by the NSF (EHR, Division of Elementary, Secondary & Informal Education (ESIE), Instructional Materials Development (IMD) program), award no. ESI-9730804. Arlington, VA: NSF.

Clements, D. H., & Sarama, J. *Scaling up TRIAD: Teaching early mathematics for understanding with trajectories and technologies—Supplement.* Awarded by the IES as part of the Interagency Education Research Initiative (IERI) program, a combination of the IES, the NSF (EHR, Division of Research, Evaluation and Communication (REC)), and the National Institutes of Health (NIH) (National Institute of Child Health and Human Development (NICHD)). Washington, D.C.: IES.

Clements, D. H., & Sarama, J. *Deepening and Extending the Learning and Teaching with Learning Trajectories Tool ([LT]^2).* Awarded by the Heising-Simons Foundation. Grant #2015-157. 6/1/16 – 5/31/18. ($510,401).

Clements, D. H., & Sarama, J. *Learning and Teaching with Learning Trajectories ([LT]^2).* Awarded by the Bill & Melinda Gates Foundation. Grant #OPP1118932. 12/1/14 – 11/30/16. (24 months; $679,550).

Clements, D. H., & Sarama, J. *Math and Executive Function Project (EF).* Awarded by the Heising-Simons Foundation. Grant #2014-156 (through Stanford University, #60875796-118042). 12/1/14 – 6/30/16. (19 months; $114,136).

Clements, D. H., & Sarama, J. *Preschool-Elementary-Coherence Project (COHERE).* Awarded by the Heising-Simons Foundation. Grant #2014-156 (through Stanford University, #60875796-118042). 12/1/14 – 6/30/1. (19 months; $1,968,961).

Clements, D. H., & Sarama, J. *Scalable Professional Development in Early Mathematics: The Learning and Teaching with Learning Trajectories Tool.* Awarded by the Heising-Simons Foundation. Grant #2013-79. 11/25/13 – 5/31/16. ($500,000).

Clements, D. H., Sarama, J., & Baroody, A. J. *Background Research for the NGA Center Project on Early Mathematics.* Awarded by the National Governors Association. 7/22/2013-11/30/2013. (4 months; $25,000).

Clements, D. H., Sarama, J., Baroody, A. J., & Purpura, D. *Evaluating the Efficacy of Learning Trajectories in Early Mathematics.* Awarded by the U.S. Department of Education, IES (Institute of Education Sciences). Grant No. R305A150243. 8/1/2015. (4 years; $3,500,000).

Clements, D. H., Sarama, J., Bodrova, E., & Layzer, C. *Increasing the efficacy of an early mathematics curriculum with scaffolding designed to promote self-regulation.* Awarded by the IES, Early Learning Programs and Policies program, award no. R305A080200. Washington, D.C.: NCER, IES.

Clements, D. H., Sarama, J., Klein, A., & Starkey, P. *Scaling up the implementation of a pre-kindergarten mathematics curricula: Teaching for understanding with trajectories and technologies.* Awarded by the NSF as part of the IERI program, a combination of the NSF (EHR, REC), the IES, and the NIH (NICHD). Arlington, VA: NSF.

Clements, D. H., Sarama, J., & Layzer, C. *Longitudinal study of a successful scaling-up project: Extending TRIAD.* Awarded by the IES (Mathematics and Science Education program), award no. R305A110188. Washington, D.C: National Center for Education Research (NCER), IES.

Clements, D. H., Sarama, J., & Lee, J. *Scaling up TRIAD: Teaching early mathematics for understanding with trajectories and technologies.* Awarded by the IES as part of the IERI program, a combination of the IES, the NSF (EHR, REC), and the NIH (NICHD). Washington, D.C.: IES.

Clements, D. H., Sarama, J., & Ready, D. *Learning Trajectories as a Complete Early Mathematics Intervention: Achieving Efficacies of Economies at Scale*. Awarded by the U.S. Department of Education, IES (Institute of Education Sciences). Grant No. 1908889. July 1, 2019 – June 30, 2024. (5 years, $4,575,683).

Clements, D. H., Sarama, J., & Tatsuoka, C. *Using rule space and poset-based adaptive testing methodologies to identify ability patterns in early mathematics and create a comprehensive mathematics ability test*. Awarded by the NSF, award no. 1313695 (previously funded under award no. DRL-1019925). Arlington, VA: NSF.

Clements, D. H., Watt, D., Bjork, E., & Lehrer, R. *Technology-enhanced learning of geometry in elementary schools*. Awarded by the NSF (EHR, ESIE), Research on Education, Policy and Practice (REPP) program. Arlington, VA: NSF.

Sarama, J., & Clements, D. H. *Planning for professional development in pre-school mathematics: Meeting the challenge of Standards 2000*. Awarded by the NSF (EHR, ESIE), Teacher Enhancement (TE) program, award no. ESI-9814218. Arlington, VA: NSF.

Sarama, J., Clements, D. H., Day-Hess, C. A., & Watt, T. W. *Evaluating the Efficacy of an Interdisciplinary Pre-school Curriculum (EPIC)*. Awarded by the U.S. Department of Education, IES (Institute of Education Sciences). Grant No. R305A190395. 7/1/2019. (4 years; $3,295,431).

Sarama, J., Clements, D. H., Duke, N., & Brenneman, K. *Early childhood education in the context of mathematics, science, and literacy*. Awarded by the NSF, award no. 1313718 (previously funded under award no. DRL-1020118). Arlington, VA: NSF.

Starkey, P., Sarama, J., Clements, D. H., & Klein, A. *A longitudinal study of the effects of a prekindergarten mathematics curriculum on low-income children's mathematical knowledge*. Awarded by the Office of Educational Research and Improvement (OERI), U.S. Department of Education, as Preschool Curriculum Evaluation Research (PCER) project. Washington, D.C: OERI.

Vinh, M., Lim, C., Sarama, J., & Clements, D. H. *Special Education Educational Technology Media, and Materials for Individuals with Disabilities*. Office of Special Education Programs (OSEP, U.S. Dept. of Education). Federal Award No: H327G180006 Subaward No: 5112267, $1,968,961 for subcontract from University of North Carolina). 1/1/2019 – 12/31/2023.

APPRECIATION TO SRA/MCGRAW-HILL

The author and publisher wish to express appreciation to SRA/McGraw-Hill for kindly giving permission for the many screen shots provided by them for use throughout this title.

WHAT IS *LEARNING AND TEACHING WITH LEARNING TRAJECTORIES–[LT]^2?*

- [LT]^2 is a web-based tool for early childhood educators to learn about how children think and learn about mathematics, and how to teach mathematics to young children "their way" (birth to age 8).
- [LT]^2 allows teachers, caregivers, and parents to see the learning trajectories for math as they view short video clips of classroom instruction and children working on math problems in a way that clearly reveals their thinking.

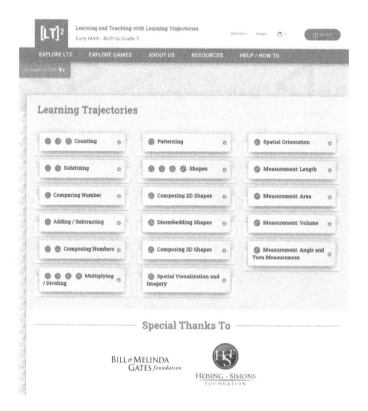

[LT]² is a new open-access tool for early math teaching and learning, *closely linked to this book* and developed thanks to funding from the Heising-Simons Foundation and the Bill and Melinda Gates Foundation, along with decades of research conducted by professors Julie Sarama and Douglas H. Clements. Large-scale studies show that the learning trajectories and [LT]² work, as validated by the "What Works Clearinghouse" and praised on the cover of *The New York Times* and in the *Wall Street Journal*. Read about two teachers' use of [LT]² - **https://bit.ly/2oQ1Yq4** & **https://bit.ly/2veu83O**.

[LT]² runs on all technological platforms, addresses new ages–birth to age 8 years–and includes alignments with standards and assessments, as well as software for children. [LT]² enables teachers to help children find the mathematics in–and develop the mathematics from–their everyday activities, including art, stories, puzzles, and games. Head to **Learning Trajectories.org** for on-going updates, interactive games, and practical tools that support classroom learning.

1 Young Children and Mathematics Learning

Snow was falling in Boston and preschool teacher Sarah Gardner's children were coming in slowly, one bus at a time. She had been doing high-quality math all year, but was still amazed at her children's ability to keep track of the situation: The children kept saying, "Now, 11 are here and 7 absent. Now, 13 are here and 5 absent. Now ...."

Why have so many people become interested in math for very young children lately? Because early math is *surprisingly important*.

First, math is increasingly important in a modern global economy, but math achievement in many countries has not kept up. Our own country, the USA, has fewer high-performing and more low-performing students than many other countries, especially in math (http://ncee.org/pisa-2018-les sons/). These differences appear as early as first grade, kindergarten ... and even preschool (Gerofsky, 2015b; Mullis, Martin, Foy, & Arora, 2012b; OECD, 2014). Although some high-performing countries are showing improvements, many like the USA are not (Mullis et al., 2012b). This is one reason interest in improving early childhood math education has emerged from around the globe, such as in Africa, South and Latin America, and Asia. These increased interests are often paired with a special focus on children who have not been provided opportunities to learn (McCoy et al., 2018b).

Many young children do not even get the *chance* to learn the more advanced math taught in many other countries. If each child is given such opportunities, *all people in each country bene-fit*, economically and socially, because everyone contributes more to social and technological advancements.

> *During most of the 20th century, the United States possessed peerless mathematical prowess—not just as measured by the depth and number of the mathematical specialists who practiced here but also by the scale and quality of its engineering, science, and financial leadership, and even by the extent of mathematical education in its broad population. But, without substantial and sustained changes to its educational system, the United States will relinquish its leadership in the 21st century.*
>
> The National Mathematics Advisory Panel[1] (NMP, 2008, p. xi)

Second, these early childhood years have been found to be *surprisingly important for develop-ment through life*. That is, what math children know when they *enter* kindergarten predicts their math achievement for years to come (Duncan et al., 2007). Math also predicts later success in *read-ing* (Duncan et al., 2007; Duncan & Magnuson, 2011), so, *math appears to be a core component of cognition*. Further, knowledge of math in the early years is the best predictor of graduating high school (McCoy et al., 2017; Watts, Duncan, Siegler, & Davis-Kean, 2014). One more argument for early childhood math is that number and arithmetic knowledge at age 7 years predicts socioeco-nomic status at age 42 (even controlling for all other variables, Ritchie & Bates, 2013).

These predictions may show that *math concepts and skills are important to all of school and life*. Math provides a new way to see the world, the beauty of it, and the way you can solve problems that arise within it. However, math is much more: *Math is critical thinking* and *problem solving*, and high-quality *math experiences also promote social, emotional, literacy, and general brain development* (Aydogan et al., 2005b; Clements, Sarama, Layzer, Unlu, & Fesler, 2020a; Dumas, McNeish, Sarama, & Clements, 2019; Sarama & Clements, 2019b; Sarama, Lange, Clem-ents, & Wolfe, 2012b)! No wonder they predict later success.

Third, although the math-achievements gap between countries is troubling, an even larger and more damaging gap lies between children growing up in higher- and lower-resource com-munities. Both the income gap and the achievement gap have been increasing for decades (Bachman, Votruba-Drzal, El Nokali, & Castle Heatly, 2015; Reardon, 2011). Children shouldn't be at a disadvantage just because their communities lack resources to provide *charging stations* for learning math—and they do not have to be. They would think and learn just as well if they have the same *opportunities* to learn math early. That's why we are working to make good early math learning resources available to children in all communities.

Fourth, if our country's children have limited math knowledge initially and achieve less later in school compared to children in other countries, can there possibly be bright spots? Yes. From their first years, children have boundless interest and curiosity in math … *and* the ability to learn to think like mathematicians. In high-quality early childhood education programs, young children can engage in surprisingly deep investigations of math ideas. They can learn skills, problem solv-ing, and concepts in ways that are natural and motivating to them. This brings us to the main reason to engage young children in math: *Young children love to think mathematically*. They become exhilarated by their own ideas (like the 6-year-old quoted at the beginning of the preface) and the ideas of others. To develop the *whole* child, we must develop the *mathematical child*.

Fifth, teachers enjoy the reasoning and learning that high-quality math education brings forth from their children. High-quality math throughout early childhood does not involve pushing elem-entary arithmetic onto younger children. Instead, good education allows children to experience math as they play in and explore their world. A higher proportion of children are in early care and education programs every year. We teachers are responsible for bringing the knowledge and intel-lectual delight of math to all children, especially those who have not yet had many high-quality educational experiences. Good teachers can meet this challenge with research-based "tools."

Most children acquire considerable knowledge of numbers and other aspects of mathemat-ics before they enter kindergarten. This is important, because the mathematical knowledge that kindergartners bring to school is related to their mathematics learning for years thereafter—in elementary school, middle school, and even high school. Unfortunately, most children from low-income backgrounds enter school with far less knowledge than peers from middle-income backgrounds, and the achievement gap in mathematical knowledge progressively widens throughout their pre-K-12 years.

The National Math Advisory Panel (NMP, 2008, p. xvii)

Fortunately, encouraging results have been obtained for a variety of instructional programs developed to improve the mathematical knowledge of preschoolers and kindergartners, especially those from low-income backgrounds. There are effective techniques—derived from scientific research on learning—that could be put to work in the classroom today to improve children's mathematical knowledge.

The National Math Advisory Panel (NMP, 2008, p. xvii)

These tools include specific guidance on how to help children learn in ways that are both appropriate and effective. In this book, we pull that knowledge together to provide a core tool: "learning trajectories" for each major topic in early math.

What are Learning Trajectories?

Children follow natural developmental progressions in learning and development. As a simple example, they learn to crawl, then walk, then run, skip, and jump with increasing speed and dexterity. These are levels in the developmental progression of movement. Children follow natural developmental progressions in learning math, too, by learning math ideas and skills in their own way.

Teachers who understand these developmental progressions for each major domain or topic of math, and base their instruction on them, build math learning environments that are particularly developmentally appropriate, effective, and meaningful (Figure 1.1). These developmental paths are the basis for this book's *learning trajectories*. Learning trajectories help us answer several questions: What goals or objectives should we hold? Where do we start? How do we know where to go next? How do we get there?

Learning trajectories have three parts: (a) a math goal, (b) a developmental path along which children progress to reach that goal, and (c) teaching practices, including the educational environment, interactions, and activities, *matched* to each of the levels of thinking in that path, that help children develop ever-higher levels of thinking. Let's examine each of these three parts.

Goals: The Big Ideas of Math

The first part of a learning trajectory is a math goal. Our goals include the "big ideas of math": clusters of concepts and skills that are mathematically central and coherent, consistent with children's thinking, and generative of future learning. These big ideas come from mathematicians, researchers, and teachers (CCSSO/NGA, 2010; Clements, 2004; NCTM, 2006; NMP, 2008). They include math content but *also research on students' thinking about and learning of math*. As an example, one big idea is that *counting can be used to find out how many in a collection*.

Figure 1.1 Carmen Brown encourages a preschooler to "mathematize"

Development Progressions: The Paths of Learning

The second part of a learning trajectory consists of levels of thinking, each more sophisticated than the last, through which children develop on their way to achieving the math goal. That is, the developmental progression describes a typical path that children follow in developing an understanding and skill about that math topic.

Humans are born with a fundamental sense of quantity.

(Geary, 1994, p. 1)

This development of math abilities begins when life begins. As we will see, young children have certain math-like competencies in number, spatial sense, and patterns from birth. However, young children's ideas and their interpretations of situations are uniquely different from those of adults. For this reason, good early childhood teachers are careful not to assume that children "see" situations, problems, or solutions the way adults do. Instead, good teachers interpret what the child is doing and thinking and attempt to see the situation from the child's point of view. Similarly, when they interact with the child, these teachers also consider the environment, activities, and their own actions from the child's point of view so they can help the child develop the next level of thinking. This makes early childhood teaching both demanding and rewarding.

Our learning trajectories provide simple labels and examples for each level of each developmental progression. The "Developmental Progression" column in Table 1.1 describes three main

Table 1.1 Samples from the Learning Trajectory for Counting (the full text for each level, the full learning trajectory, and links to resources are described in Chapter 3)

Age (years)[2]	Developmental Progression	Instructional Activities
1	**Number Word Sayer: Foundations** *Verbal* No verbal counting. Names some number words with no sequence.	*Number Talk*: Associate number words with quantities and as components of the counting sequence. *Diez Amigos Finger Play* and *Two Little Butterflies Finger Play*: Finger plays like this one are a fun way to teach children about counting and numbers.
1-2	**Chanter** *Verbal* Chants number words in "singsong" fashion and may run them together. The number words may be indistinguishable from one another. After watching and adult put one to six "food tokens" into an animal puppet, imitates the puppet-feeding with attention to number.	*Verbal counting, songs, finger plays, and more*: Repeated experience with the counting sequence in varied context. This can include songs; finger plays, such as "This Old Man"; counting going up and down stairs; and just verbal counting for the fun of it (how high can you go?)! *Counting with Maracas and More*, Use maracas or other percussion instruments to support the development of number concepts and counting.
3	**Reciter (10)** *Verbal* Verbally counts to ten with some correspondence with objects but may either continue an overly rigid correspondence or exhibit performance errors (e.g., skipping, double counting). "One [points to first], two [points to second], three [starts to point], four [finishes pointing, but is now still pointing to third object], five, ... nine, ten, eleven, twelve, 'firteen,' fifteen ..."	*Count, Clap, and Stomp*: Have all children count from one to ten or an appropriate number, making motions with each count. For example, say, "one" [touch head], "two" [touch shoulders], "three" [touch head], etc.
4	**Counter (Small Numbers)** Accurately counts objects in a line to five and answers the "how many" question with the last number counted, understanding that this represents the total number of objects (the cardinal principle).	*Mr. MixUp*: The puppet Mr. MixUp makes a lot of counting mistakes such as saying the wrong word for "how many" after counting; children help Mr. MixUp by catching his mistake.

levels of thinking in the counting learning trajectory. Under the descriptions are examples of children's thinking and behavior for each level.

Teaching Practices: The Paths of Teaching

The third part of a learning trajectory consists of a set of teaching practices, including educational environments,[3] interactions, and instructional activities, linked to each of the levels of thinking in the developmental progression. These tasks are designed to help children learn the ideas and skills needed to *construct the next level of thinking*. That is, as teachers, we can use these tasks to promote children's growth from the previous level to the goal level. The last column of Table 1.1 provides example instructional activities. (Again, the complete learning trajectory in Chapter 3 includes not only all the developmental levels but also *many more* instructional tasks for each level.)

How do activities help children build each level of thinking? Although teaching and learning resist simple descriptions, we try to embody the *mental* "actions on objects" that enables thinking at a level in children's actions with manipulatives or their bodies (again, Chapter 3 will have more detail; the following are but brief examples). *Count All Day!* in Table 1.1 develops verbal counting with enjoyable activities such as counting in books, songs, finger plays, and clapping or marching up steps. Each allows children to actively produce the verbal counting sequence, with most illustrating the notion of counting-words-as-indicators-of-increasing-quantity (more fingers or higher stairs). The actions are producing number words from an ordered list along with physical action of clapping or marching.

Kitchen Counter's actions include verbal counting, but the computer supports that—the child can focus on the goal of clicking on each object once and only once—an action of attention (like pointing) directed at physical items. The "bite" out of the piece of food *and* error messages as necessary ("You already took a bite out of that one!") to scaffold this one-to-one correspondence activity.

The **Counter (Small Numbers)** level includes a more challenging concept: The last number word reached while counting a set *tells you how many in the set.* Adults find this "obvious," but the concept—*cardinality,* or "how-manyness" in counting—is a significant insight that children must construct. Let's examine the activity *How Many in My Hand?* in more detail (see Figure 1.2). For comparison, first consider that many teachers practice counting with a group by laying out, say, four cubes and asking children to "count with me," leading them in verbal counting as they point to each block, "1, 2, 3, 4." Children do get practice with verbal counting, but the one-to-one correspondence is done by the teacher and may not be noticed by children, and the notion of cardinality is nowhere to be found.

[LT]²   ☑ Whole Group   ☑ Small Group | Center | Computer Center

How Many in a Hand?

Trajectory: Counting
Level: Counter (Small Number)

✓ **Quick Description:** Children learn that counting tells how many (that the last number word tells how many in a group. (Adapted from: *Building Blocks*)

Activity

- Secretly put about four inch cubes in one hand and hide it behind your back.
- Tell children you saw the wooden inch cubes and you thought, "I wonder how many I can hold in one hand?"
- Ask children to count aloud with you to find out how many.
- Remove just one of the cubes, and place it where children can see and focus on it. Say "one" with the children.
- Repeat until you have counted and displayed all four cubes. Then show your empty hand.
- Ask children how many cubes there are in all (gesture around them). If they reply with the correct number, agree, gesture around the group of cubes again, and reiterate that, together, you counted 4 cubes.
- Tell children you put the inch cubes in a learning center (or on the tables), and challenge them to find out, during free time, how many *they* can hold in one hand.
- Repeat with a different number of cubes and/or different size objects on subsequent days.

Materials

✓| wooden inch cubes or other similar size objects (an adult should be able to hold 4 or 5 of the objects in one hand)

Notes

1. We start with a hidden handful so there is a quantitative question—how many *are there?* —the goal of counting.
2. We lay the cubes out one at a time to help children *use* their ability to *subitize (recognize the number in)* small sets to understand the "cardinality principle" or how-manyness idea of counting. That is, when we say "two" we *see* two and so forth for "three" and "four."

Figure 1.2 The "How Many in My Hand?" activity

In contrast, *How Many in My Hand?* engages children with the concept of cardinality and the cardinality principle in counting (last counting word is "how many") in several ways (see Figure 1.2):

1. Starting by hiding cubes behind the teacher's back immediately makes children curious about cardinality: How many *are* back there?
2. Removing the cubes one at a time evokes children's recognition of small numbers (See Chapter 2). When they count "one" they *see one,* and when they count "two," they *see two,* so the "last number counted" is telling the number they see.
3. The teacher gestures *around* the set and repeats: "Yes, I could hold *four.*" Again, reinforcing the notion that the last number word tells how many were counted.
4. The teacher challenges the children to try it themselves, motivating them to figure out how many *they* can hold and making them, not the teacher, the main actors. (They will be motivated—one way or the other—to hold more than four!)

These simple but powerful characteristics of the *How Many in My Hand?* activity help children build the cardinality concept: They learn the mental actions of *unifying* the group (understanding the objects *as* a group) and assigning a number to the group—*quantifying* it.

In summary, learning trajectories describe the goals of learning, the thinking and learning processes of children at various levels along the developmental progression, and the learning activities in which they might engage. People often have several questions about learning trajectories. You may wish to read our responses to those questions that interest you now and return to this section after you have read more about specific learning trajectories in the chapters that follow.

Frequently Asked Questions (FAQ) about Learning Trajectories

Why Use Learning Trajectories? Learning trajectories allow teachers to support the *math of children—the thinking of children as it develops naturally.* Because the trajectories are formed on research of children's natural thinking, we know that all the goals and activities are within the developmental capacities of children. We also know that each level provides a natural *developmental building block* to the next level. We know that the activities provide the *mathematical building blocks* for school success because the research on which they are based typically involves more children who have had the educational advantages that allow them to do well at school.

When are Children "At" a Level? Children are identified to be "at" a certain level when most of their behaviors reflect the thinking—ideas and skills—of that level. Usually, they show a few behaviors from the next and previous levels as they learn. *And we have new empirical evidence that the learning trajectories approach is more effective than other approaches* (Clements, Sarama, Baroody, & Joswick, 2020a; Clements, Sarama, Baroody, Joswick, & Wolfe, 2019).

Can Children Work at More Than One Level at the Same Time? Yes, although most children work mainly at one level (and are starting to learn the next one; of course, if they are tired or distracted, they may operate at a lower level). Levels are not "absolute stages." They are "benchmarks" of complex growth that represent distinct ways of thinking. So, another way to think of them is as a sequence of different *patterns* of thinking and reasoning. Children are continually learning within levels and then moving from one level to the next.

Can Children Jump Ahead? Yes, especially if there are separate "subtrajectories" within a trajectory. For example, we have combined many counting competencies into one "counting" sequence with subtrajectories, including verbal counting and object counting. Many children learn to count to 100 at age 6 after learning to count objects to ten or more; however, some may learn that verbal skill earlier. The subtrajectory of verbal counting skills would still be followed. There is another possibility: Children may learn deeply and thus appear to jump ahead several "levels" after a rich learning experience.

Are all Levels Similar in Nature? Most levels are *levels of thinking*–a distinct period of time of qualitatively distinct ways, or patterns, of thinking. However, a few are merely "levels of attainment," similar to a mark on a wall to show a child's height; that is, a couple signify simply that a child has gained more knowledge. For example, consider reading numerals such as "2" or "9." Children do follow a learning trajectory of first matching, then recognizing, then naming numerals (Wang, Resnick, & Boozer, 1971). However, once they have reached that level, children must learn simply to name (and write) more numerals, which usually does not require deeper or more complex thinking. Thus, some trajectories are more tightly constrained by natural cognitive development than others. Often a critical component of such constraints is the mathematical development in a domain; math is a highly sequential, hierarchical domain in which certain ideas and skills often have to be learned before others.

How are Learning Trajectories Different from just a Scope and Sequence? They are related, of course. But they are *not* lists of everything children need to learn, because they don't cover every single "fact" and they emphasize the "big ideas." Further, they are about children's levels of thinking, not just about the ability to answer a math question. So, for example, a single math problem may be solved *differently* by students at *different* (separable) levels of thinking, even if they all get it right (or wrong!).

Does Every Trajectory Represent Just "One Path"? As mentioned, some trajectories have "subtrajectories." In some cases, the names make this clear. For example, in Comparing and Ordering, some levels are about the "Comparer" levels and others about building a "mental number line." Similarly, the related subtrajectories of "Composition" and "Decomposition" are easy to distinguish. Sometimes, for clarification, subtrajectories are indicated with a note in italics after the title. For example, in Shapes, "Parts" and "Representing" are subtrajectories within the Shapes trajectory. Some children may be further ahead in one subjectory that another.

A more complex question is *whether there is one path every child follows*. Generally, children develop similarly through these broad levels of thinking (they are *not* narrow "lockstep" movements!). However, there are many factors, from cultural to individual, that may account for some children altering that path, usually in small ways (e.g., level 5 before 4).

Frequently Asked Questions (FAQ) about Using Learning Trajectories

How Do These Developmental Levels Support Teaching and Learning? The levels help teachers (as well as curriculum developers) understand children's thinking; the ability to create, modify, or sequence activities. *Teachers who understand learning trajectories (especially the developmental levels that are at their foundation) are more effective, efficient, and fun for everyone.*

Through planned teaching and also by encouraging informal, incidental math, teachers help children learn *at an appropriate and deep level.*

There are Ages in the Charts. Should I Plan to Help Children Develop Just the Levels that Correspond to my Children's Ages? No! The ages in the table are typical ages at which children develop these ideas. But these are rough guides only—children differ widely. Furthermore, the children achieve *much later levels* with high-quality education. So, these are approximate "starting levels," not goals. Children who are provided high-quality math experiences are capable of developing to levels one or more years beyond their peers.

Are the Instructional Tasks the Only Way to Teach Children to Achieve Higher Levels of Thinking? No, there are many ways. In some cases, however, there is some research evidence that these are especially effective ways. In other cases, they are simply illustrations of the kind of activity that would be appropriate to reach that level of thinking. Further, teachers need to use a variety of pedagogical strategies in teaching the content, presenting the tasks, guiding children in completing them, and so forth.

Are Learning Trajectories Consistent with Teaching the Common Core? Unfortunately, some people have interpreted that "teaching the Common Core" means only teaching each standard directly and then moving on. But learning is not an all-or-nothing acquisition of knowledge or skills (Sarama & Clements, 2009c; Sophian, 2013). The Common Core goals are benchmarks, but good curricula and teaching always work *up to those goals* and weave the learning opportunities throughout children's lives. They learn the ideas at higher levels of sophistication and generality. Finally, *when we wrote the Common Core, we started by writing learning trajectories–at least the goals and developmental progressions.* Thus, learning trajectories are at the *core* of the Common Core. And learning trajectories are *not* based on the idea to "directly teach it once and drop it."

Before we leave the Common Core, we note that misconceptions and misinformation about the CCSSM standards abound, *especially* the erroneous idea that they are "developmentally appropriate" for the youngest children. We know if children have opportunities to learn, they can meet and exceed all those standards. If you need accurate information about the CCSSM, please see our many articles on the topic (Clements, Fuson, & Sarama, 2017a; 2017b, 2019; Fuson, Clements, & Sarama, 2015).

Other Critical Goals: Strategies, Reasoning, Creativity, and a Productive Disposition

Learning trajectories are organized around topics, but they include far more than concepts, facts, and skills. Processes, or math practices, and attitudes are important in every one. Chapter 13 focuses on general processes, such as problem solving and reasoning. But these and other general processes are also an integral part of every learning trajectory. Also, specific processes are involved in every learning trajectory. For example, the process of composition–putting together and taking apart–is fundamental to both number and arithmetic (e.g., adding and subtracting) and geometry (shape composition).

Finally, other general educational goals must never be neglected. The "habits of mind" mentioned in the box include curiosity, imagination, inventiveness, risk-taking, creativity, and persistence. These are some of the components of the essential goal of *productive disposition.*

Children need to view math as sensible, useful, and worthwhile and view themselves as capable of thinking mathematically. Children should also come to appreciate the beauty and creativity that is at the heart of math. Remember Albert Einstein's quote at the beginning of the preface: "Mathematics is, in its way, the poetry of logical ideas."

All these should be involved in a high-quality early childhood math program. These goals are included in the suggestions for teaching throughout this book. Further, Chapters 14, 15, and 16 discuss how to achieve these goals. These chapters discuss different learning and teaching contexts, including early childhood school settings and education, equity issues, affect, and instructional strategies.

As important as mathematical content are general mathematical processes such as problem solving, reasoning and proof, communication, connections, and representation; specific mathematical processes such as organizing information, patterning, and composing, and habits of mind such as curiosity, imagination, inventiveness, persistence, willingness to experiment, and sensitivity to patterns. All should be involved in a high-quality early childhood mathematics program.

(Clements, 2004, p. 57)

Learning Trajectories and the "Building Blocks" Project

The "Building Blocks" project was funded by the National Science Foundation (NSF)[4] to develop pre-kindergarten (pre-K) to Grade 2 software-enhanced, math curricula. Building Blocks was designed to enable all young children to build math concepts, skills, and processes. The name "Building Blocks" has three meanings (see Figure 1.3). First, our goals are to help children develop the main *mathematical building blocks*—that is, the big ideas described previously. Second is the related goal to develop *cognitive building blocks*: general cognitive and metacognitive (higher-order) processes such as moving or combining shapes to higher-order thinking processes such as self-regulation. The third is the most straightforward: Children should be using building blocks for many purposes, but one of them is for learning math.

Based on theory and research on early childhood learning and teaching (Bowman, Donovan, & Burns, 2001; Clements, 2001), we determined that Building Blocks' basic approach would be *finding the mathematics in, and developing mathematics from, children's activity*. To do so, all aspects of the Building Blocks project are based on learning trajectories. Many of the examples of learning trajectories stemmed from our work developing, field-testing, and evaluating curricula from that project. Praised on the cover of *The New York Times* and the *Wall Street Journal* and validated by the "What Works Clearinghouse," this project was the genesis of this book as well as the web-based tool that we turn to next.

The overriding premise of our work is that throughout the grades from pre-K through 8 all students can and should be mathematically proficient. [p. 10]

Mathematical proficiency ... has five strands:

1 *conceptual understanding–comprehension of mathematical concepts, operations, and relations*
2 *procedural fluency–skill in carrying out procedures flexibly, accurately, efficiently, and appropriately*
3 *strategic competence–ability to formulate, represent, and solve mathematical problems*
4 *adaptive reasoning–capacity for logical thought, reflection, explanation, and justification*
5 *productive disposition–habitual inclination to see mathematics as sensible, useful, and worthwhile, coupled with a belief in diligence and one's own efficacy.*

(Kilpatrick, Swafford, & Findell, 2001, p. 5)

The Learning and Teaching with Learning Trajectories Tool

To help teachers understand and teach the Building Blocks curriculum, we created an Internet site that featured descriptions and videos of children's thinking and instructional activities that developed it (e.g., see Sarama & Clements, 2003). Teachers found it so useful that we created a new site, the *Learning and Teaching with Learning Trajectories*[5]

| *Manipulative* **Building Blocks** | *Mathematical* **Building Blocks** | *Cognitive* **Building Blocks** |

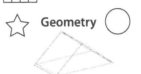

Copying, creating, and combining numbers and shapes.

Figure 1.3 The Building Blocks project was named because we wanted to use manipulatives like children's building blocks (on and off the computer) to help children develop mathematical and cognitive building blocks–the foundations for later learning (see http://building blocksmath.org)

tool at www.LearningTrajectories.org. There you can see videos of children's thinking at *each level* of each topic (learning trajectory) as in Figure 1.4, as well as *classroom* and home videos of teachers and caregivers helping children *learn* that level of thinking. Each instructional activity has PDF files, that you can print out and use, fully describing the activity, along with materials (e.g., shape printouts) to accompany the activities, *and* links and notes on how to make sure *all* children, including children with disabilities, can fully engage in each activity. [LT]² also features an extensive Resource section with videos, articles, and links on teaching and on particular topics and issues of teaching (e.g., dual language learners).

(a)

Figure 1.4 The *Learning and Teaching with Learning Trajectories* (LTLT, OR [LT]²) tool at www.Lear ningTrajectories.org. (a) presents the home screen of [LT]²

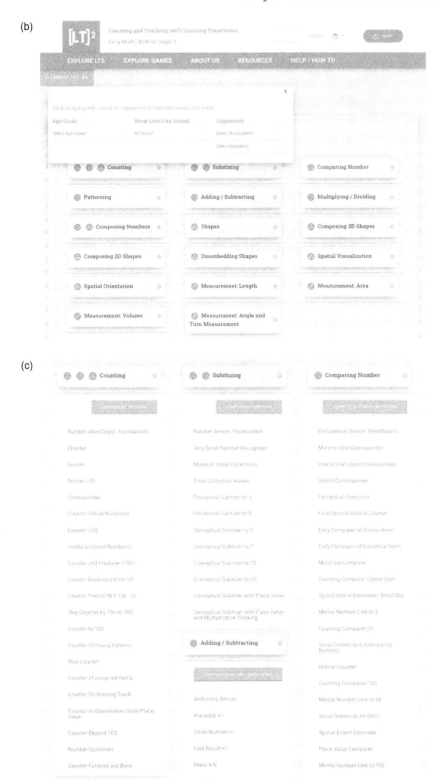

Figure 1.4 (continued) (b) [LT]² includes full research–validated learning trajectories for all topics in early math and alignments with many national and state standards and assessments. (c) For each topic, once "opened" a "Learn about ..." section teaches users about the goal, and a full list of levels of the developmental progression

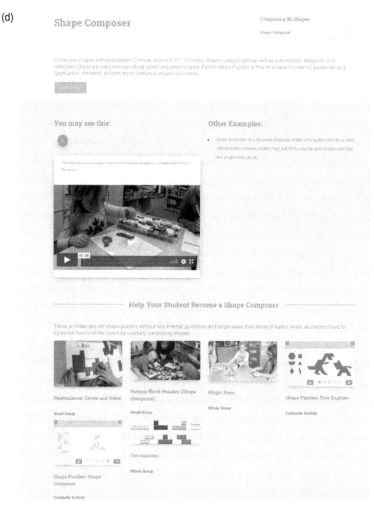

Figure 1.4 (continued) (d) For each level, [LT]² provides a definition, one or more videos, and descriptions of children's thinking for each level of each developmental progression, and then instructional activities that teach that level

We encourage you, as you read about each level, to go to [LT]² and see videos of children that illustrate that level of thinking and then see (and use!—when appropriate) videos and other resources for instructional activities that help children build that level of thinking.

Final Words

Against this background, let us explore the learning trajectories in Chapters 2 through 12. Chapter 2 begins with the critical topic of *number*. When do children first understand number? *How* do they do it? How can we help children's initial ideas develop? Throughout, we emphasize math processes, or practices, and attitudes. Further, the last few chapters provide guidance regarding understanding children, communities, and cultures, and tools such as effective teaching strategies. You may want to at least skim Chapter 13 before reading the following chapters on learning trajectories.

Figure 1.4 (continued) (e) For each of instructional activity, $[LT]^2$ provides directions, videos, and a set of downloadable, carefully formatted PDF files of the activity as well as materials for the activities in English and Spanish

Remember, we encourage you to go to $[LT]^2$ at LearningTrajectories.org and actually **see** children at each level of development and the activities that helped them develop each level.

Before we move forward, let's review the reasons early math is surprisingly important.

The Surprising Importance of Early Math: A Summary

1   *Math is important, but math teaching and learning has not improved in the USA, including in the youngest children. Better early math for all helps everyone: strong math skills = social progress.*

2   *Early math learning, from birth, is critical for all future learning … and living. Early math promotes math, but also social, emotional, literacy, and general brain development. There is much to gain and nothing to lose from high-quality early mathematics.*

3   *All children deserve fair opportunities to learn. We need powerful "charging stations" for math in all communities. Math should be purposeful, relevant, and fun for all children, not passive, irrelevant, and tedious for some.*

4   *From their first years, children have boundless interest in and curiosity for math … and the ability to learn to think like mathematicians. Math is a language best learned early. And young children love to think mathematically, to see the world through a mathematical lens in new and powerful ways.*

5   *Teachers and families enjoy all that high-quality math brings to their children. And research provides the tools math makes math easier, more effective, and more enjoyable.*

Figure 1.4 (continued) (f) [LT]² provides a variety of resources for all users, including videos about various issues and topics for a variety of users, guides for professional developers, and so forth

Notes

1 One of the authors, Douglas Clements, was a member of the NMAP and co-author of the report, which can be found at www.ed.gov/about/bdscomm/list/mathpanel/.

2 The ages in the tables are typical ages at which children develop these ideas. However, children vary widely and just as important, *with high-quality education*, children achieve much later levels.

3 Environments and interactions are important—for infants and toddlers, foundations for math are embedded in rich materials and structures in the environments and interesting, everyday interactions with adults and peers. This continues throughout early childhood education but the role of intentional activities increases as developmentally appropriate—engaging, meaningful, challenging-but-achievable!

4 The "Building Blocks—Foundations for Mathematical Thinking, Prekindergarten to Grade 2: Research-based Materials Development" project was funded by the NSF (award no. ESI-9730804; granted to D. H. Clements and J. Sarama) to create and evaluate math curricula for young children based on a theoretically sound research and development framework. We describe the framework and research in detail in Chapter 15. For the purposes of full disclosure, note that we have subsequently made this curriculum available through a publisher and thus receive royalties. All research was conducted with independent assessors and evaluators.

5 Funded by the Heising-Simons Foundation and the Bill and Melinda Gates Foundation, *Learning and Teaching with Learning Trajectories* is also known by its initials, LTLT, or, therefore, as $[LT]^2$ (one of those "math jokes" almost totally devoid of actual humor).

2 Quantity, Number, and Subitizing

Three pictures hang in front of a 6-month-old child. The first shows two dots, the others show one dot and three dots. The infant hears three drumbeats. Her eyes move to the picture with three dots.

Before you read further, what do you *make* of this startling research finding? *How* in the world could such a young child *do* this? At some intuitive level, this infant has recognized number and a change in number. When developed, and connected to verbal number names, this ability is called *subitizing*–recognizing the numerosity of a group quickly, from the Latin "to arrive suddenly." In other words, people can see a small collection and almost instantly tell how many objects are in it. Research shows that this is *one of the first and main abilities very young children should develop* (Aunio & Räsänen, 2015a; Baroody & Purpura, 2017a; Clements, Sarama, & MacDonald, 2019; Hannula-Sormunen, Lehtinen, & Räsänen, 2015). Children from low-resource communities and those with special needs often lag in subitizing ability, harming their math development. This is why the first learning trajectory we discuss involves children's "approximate number system" (ANS) and subitizing.

The Development of Quantity, Number, and Subitizing

The Earliest Number Competence: The ANS

Both animals and people can represent number across senses without language. For example, monkeys and birds can be trained to discriminate both large and small sets (of visual dots or sounds) that differ in a 1:2 (or greater) ratio (but not 2:3) (Starr, Libertus, & Brannon, 2013). For example, they can determine if there are more white or gray dots in Figure 2.1. Even more interesting and fun, see the video from these researchers' laboratory on [LT]² in the Number Senser: Foundations level for Subitizing.

Baby chicks, shown four objects going behind a screen on the right, then one going beyond a screen on the left, then one moved from the right to the left, go immediately to the screen on the right (Vallortigara, 2012).

Most children without specific disabilities (e.g., Williams syndrome) have these competencies, which form one of the innate abilities that support later numerical knowledge. Six-month-olds can discriminate the 1:2 ratio (as in Figure 2.1) but by 9 months of age, they can also distinguish sets in a 2:3 ratio (e.g., 10 compared to 15). ANS correlates with math competencies in

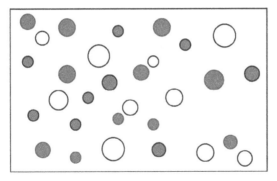

Figure 2.1 The task is to say whether there are more white or gray dots

preschoolers, even with age and verbal ability controlled (Libertus, Feigenson, & Halberda, 2011a; Mazzocco, Feigenson, & Halberda, 2011). This effect is stronger for those who are low in math knowledge (Bonny & Lourenco, 2013). Nevertheless, studies show these abilities can be developed (e.g., by special video games in which children make similar comparisons).

However, we do not know a lot about *how* the ANS supports later math and *what* math it supports. It may only support intuitive math (Baroody & Purpura, 2017a). Also, it may be that measures of ANS are tapping into other abilities, such as executive functions (Baroody & Purpura, 2017a). Yet another possibly is that ANS is a sign of, and ANS training leads to, greater *interest* and *engagement* in math-related activities or heightened attention to math-related learning opportunities, which in turn improve math abilities (Libertus, 2019) or increase the ability to focus on number instead of conflicting stimulus features. (Fuhs, McNeil, Kelley, O'Rear, & Villano, 2016).

Types of Subitizing

Recognition of number and subitizing differ from the ANS in that the goal is to determine the *exact* number of items in a set. When you "just see" how many objects are in a very small collection, you are using *perceptual subitizing* (Clements, 1999b). For example, you might see three dots on a die and quickly say "three." You perceive the three dots intuitively and simultaneously.

How is it you can see an eight-dot domino and "just know" the total number, when evidence indicates that this lies above the limits of perceptual subitizing? You are using *conceptual subitizing*—seeing the parts and putting together the whole. That is, you might see each side of the domino as composed of four individual dots and as "one four." You see the domino as composed of two groups of four and as "one eight." All of this can happen quickly—it is still subitizing—and often is not conscious.

Another categorization involves the different types of things people can subitize. Spatial patterns such as those on dominoes are just one type. Other patterns are temporal and kinesthetic, including finger patterns, rhythmic patterns, and spatial-auditory patterns. Creating and using these patterns through conceptual subitizing helps children develop abstract number and arithmetic strategies. For example, children use temporal patterns when counting on. "I knew there were three more so I just said, nine ... *ten, eleven, twelve*" (rhythmically gesturing three times, one "beat" with each count). They use finger patterns to figure out addition problems. For example, for 3 + 2, a child might put up a finger pattern they know as three, then put up two more (rhythmically–*up, up*) and then recognize the resulting finger pattern as "five." Children who cannot subitize conceptually are handicapped in learning such arithmetic processes. Children may be limited to subitizing small numbers at first, but such actions are useful "stepping stones" to the construction of more sophisticated procedures with larger numbers.

Subitizing and Mathematics

The ideas and skills of subitizing start developing very early, but they, as every other area of math, are not just "simple, basic skills." Subitizing introduces basic ideas of cardinality–"how many," ideas of "more" and "less," ideas of parts and wholes and their relationships, beginning arithmetic, and, in general, ideas of quantity. Developed well, these are related, forming webs of connected ideas that are the building blocks of math through elementary, middle, and high school, and beyond. Early ANS supports early calculation, and subitizing supports counting (Soto-Calvo, Simmons, Willis, & Adams, 2015).

   As we discuss the details of children's initial learning of subitizing, let's not lose the whole–the big picture–of children's math future. Let's not lose the wonderment over the fact that children so young can think, profoundly, about math.

Moving along the Learning Trajectory

Increasing the Number

A 5-year-old walking with her mother, casually notes, "That truck had seven apples on it." Mom just barely caught the picture on the side of the truck as it zoomed out of sight. "Oh, yes! *How* did you count that so fast?"

   "I didn't count. I subitized."

   Mom: "You *what?*"

An important, even if obvious, factor in determining the difficulty of subitizing tasks is the size of the collection. Children begin this phase even before 2 years of age, distinguishing between collections with one and more than one objects and naming the number in very small sets. For some time, this applies mainly to the word "two," a bit less to "one," and with considerably less frequency, "three" (Clements et al., 2019).

   Such early attention to "two" served preschool-age children's ability to begin attending to subgroups of "two" when conceptually subitizing larger sets of items (e.g., four, five, MacDonald, 2015; MacDonald & Shumway, 2016; MacDonald & Wilkins, 2017). Symmetrical orientations and orientations with a large space between subgroups of "two" seemed to afford these children opportunities to attend to both subgroups. Symmetrical orientations freed children's working memory resources, as they only needed to describe one "two" when building towards the total set of four. Individual's subitizing activity has been found to be affected by the space between the items in an orientation and was found to support young children's attention to the subgroups of the entire group of items (Gebuis & Reynvoet, 2011; MacDonald & Wilkins, 2017). That is, space between groups of "twos" and "threes" afforded individuals more effective subitizing of four or more items. By 4 or 5 years of age, most children recognize collections up to four, and then subitizing and counting become connected, a point to which we return in Chapter 3.

Arrangement of the Objects

Another factor is the spatial arrangement of objects. In general, for young children, objects in a line spaced *separately* and not too close together (and in different colors at the beginning, only for perceptual separation) are easiest, next easiest are rectangular (pairs of objects in rows), then "dice," or "domino" arrangements, then scrambled arrangements (Kim, Pack, & Yi, 2017). Further, when items are not arranged in rectangular or canonical arrangements, and the items increase in their relative size, children and adults have more difficulties subitizing these items accurately (Leibovich, Katzin, Harel, & Henik, 2016). More specifically, children make fewer errors for ten dots than for eight with the "domino five" arrangement, but fewer errors for eight dots for the "domino four" arrangement. We will illustrate these in the learning trajectory at the end of this chapter.

Experience and Education

> Two preschoolers are watching a parade. "Look! There's clowns!" yells Paul. "And three horses!" exclaims his friend Nathan.

Both friends are having a good experience. But only Nathan is having a *mathematical* experience at the same time. Other children see, perhaps, a brown, a black, and a dappled horse. Nathan sees the same colors, but also sees a quantity—*three* horses. The difference is probably this: At school and at home, Nathan's teachers and family notice and talk about numbers. Although children are sensitive to quantity, *interactions with others is essential to learning subitizing*, it does not develop "on its own" (Baroody, Li, & Lai, 2008). Children who *spontaneously* focus on number and subitizing number are more advanced in their number skills (Edens & Potter, 2013; Hannula-Sormunen et al., 2015; Nanu, McMullen, Munck, & Hannula-Sormunen, 2018b).

Let's first discuss the sensitivity to quantity, such as the ANS. Making judgments of the number in sets of all sizes (including number of movements, tones, etc.) will probably help strengthen children's ANS systems (Libertus, Feigenson, & Halberda, 2013; Wang, Odic, Halberda, & Feigenson, 2016). These are usually not labeled with number words but, rather, with vocabulary such as "more" and "fewer" (for dots) or "more" and "less" (for lengths of distance or durations of time—see Chapter 4). For the youngest children, intersensory redundancy—for example, you see a ball bouncing more times, it takes longer, you hear more noises—helps focus attention on number (Jordan, Suanda, & Brannon, 2008). Computer activities in which children indicate which of two displays has more may also be useful (Park, Bermudez, Roberts, & Brannon, 2016; Van Herwegen & Donlan, 2018), and may be especially important for children from low-resource communities who may not have had many learning opportunities (Fuhs et al., 2016; Szkudlarek & Brannon, 2018). *However*, there is also research that shows that learning number words while subitizing and count- ing (Chapter 3) predicts later ANS *more* than ANS predict counting and subitizing (Mussolin, Nys, Content, & Leybaert, 2014)! Similarly, symbolic skills play a more potent and long-lasting role than non-symbolic skills (Toll & Van Luit, 2014b). Once children know numerals, learning more about exact numbers and numerals promotes ANS, but *not* the reverse (Lyons, Bugden, Zheng, De Jesus, & Ansari, 2018). And time spent on specific ANS-type activities is time *not* spent in learning number words (Baroody & Purpura, 2017a). So, we recommend the everyday experiences but are more cautious toward virtual games targeted to ANS-type comparisons.

Next let's talk about subitizing as naming the exact number in sets. Parents, teachers, and other caregivers should begin naming very small collections with numbers after children have established names and categories for some physical properties such as shape and color (Sandhofer & Smith, 1999). Numerous experiences naming such collections help children build connections between quantity terms (number, how many) and number words, then build word-cardinality connections ("two" is ˙ ˙), and finally build connections among the representations of a given number. Nonexamples are important, too, to clarify the boundaries of the number (Baroody, Lai, & Mix, 2006). For instance, "Wow! That's *not* two horses. That's *three* horses!" For children who are less interested and competent in math, it is especially important for teachers to talk to them about number; for example, extending their interest in manipulating objects to include math ideas such as number and shape (Edens & Potter, 2013).

In contrast to this research-based practice, mis-educative experiences (Dewey, 1938/1997) may lead children to perceive collections as figural arrangements that are not exact. Richardson (2004) reported that for years she thought her children understood perceptual patterns, such as those on dice. However, when she finally asked them to *reproduce* the patterns, she was amazed that they did not use the same number of counters. For example, some drew an "X" with nine dots and called it "five" (see Figure 2.2) Thus, without appropriate tasks and close observations, she had not seen that her children did not even accurately imagine patterns, and their patterns were certainly not numerical. Such insights are important in understanding and promoting children's math thinking.

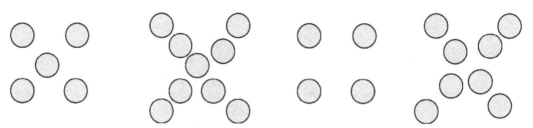

Typical arrangement   *Not* fives: "X" and square arrangements children made
of five

Figure 2.2 Children had only seen a single pattern for five—on the left. When asked to make a pat- tern of five, some incorrectly produced arrangements like those on the right (e.g., "X" and square)

Textbooks and "math books" often present sets that discourage subitizing. Their pictures combine many inhibiting factors, including complex embedding, different units with poor form, lack of symmetry, and irregular arrangements (Carper, 1942; Dawson, 1953). For example, they may show five birds, but have different types of birds spread out on a tree with branches, leaves, flowers, a sun shining overhead–you get the idea. Such complexity *hinders* conceptual subitizing, increases errors, and encourages simple one-by-one counting.

Due to their curriculum, or perhaps their lack of knowledge of subitizing, most teachers do not do sufficient subitizing work. One study showed that children *regressed* in subitizing from the beginning to the end of kindergarten (Wright, Stanger, Cowper, & Dyson, 1994). How could that be? Probably, the following type of interaction was common. A child rolls a die and says "five." Looking on, the teacher says, "Count them!" The child counts them by ones. What has happened? The teacher thought her job was to teach counting. But the child was using subitizing– which is more appropriate and better in this situation! However, the teacher is unintentionally telling the child that her way is not good, that one must always count.

In contrast, research provides guidelines for helping children develop subitizing. Naming small groups with numbers, before counting, helps children understand number words and their cardinal meaning ("how many") without having to shift between ordinal (counting items in order) and cardinal uses of number words inherent in counting (cf. Fuson, 1992a). Briefly, such naming of small, subitized groups can more quickly, simply, and directly provide a wide variety of examples and contrasting counterexamples for number words and concepts (Baroody, Lai, & Mix, 2005). These can be used to help infuse early counting with meaning (see Chapter 3 on counting). So, teachers who say, "Count them!" inappropriately not only hurt children's subitizing, but they also hurt their development of counting and number sense.[1]

Another benefit of number recognition and subitizing activities is that different arrangements suggest different views of that number (Figure 2.3).

Developing Early Number Recognition–Foundations of Subitizing

For everyone, but especially teachers of toddlers and 3-year-olds, do you want to hear the easiest, but most important "activity" you can do to help children recognize numbers of objects? *Use small number words in your everyday interactions as frequently as you can.* Instead of saying, "Clear the cups off the table so we have room for this," simply say, "We need more area on the table for this, would you please take those *three* cups off the table?" There is no need to be "artificial" in this kind of talk. Simply use number words up to about five *every* time it makes sense. And give your children's parents the same advice. Such simple but powerful

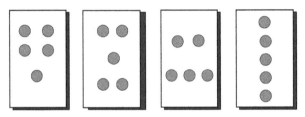

Figure 2.3 Arrangements for conceptual subitizing that may suggest 5 as 4 + 1, 2 + 1 + 2, 2 + 3, or 5

interactions also increase children's *spontaneous focus on number* (Rathé, Torbeyns, Hannula-Sormunen, De Smedt, & Verschaffel, 2016).

Other activities include *Numbers On Me* (only one and two) and *Numbers Me* (one to about four) in which the teacher asks children how old they are. They might respond by saying the number and showing that many fingers. Then ask children how many arms they have. Have them wave their arms. Repeat with hands, fingers, legs, feet, toes, head, nose, eyes, and ears. Include motion when possible, such as "Wiggle your ten fingers," and have fun! Make silly, incorrect statements. For example, "I have four ears ... three feet ... five eyes." Mix them with correct statements. Have children say whether or not you are correct. When children disagree, ask: How many do I have? *How do you know?*

Specific Subitizing Activities

Many number activities can promote perceptual and then conceptual subitizing. Perhaps the most direct activity is known as "Quickdraw" (Wheatley, 1996) or "Snapshots" (Clements & Sarama, 2007a) or simply "Subitize!" As an example, tell children they have to quickly take a "snapshot" of how many they see—their minds have to take a "fast picture." Show them a collection of counters for 2 seconds or less, and then cover it. Then, ask children to construct a collection with the same number or say the number. If you have them say the number, have them think-pair-share. This is an important teaching strategy that we use *all the time*, but due to space constraints won't write it into every activity in the book.

Think-pair-share goes like this. You ask a question or pose a problem. Children think silently by themselves first. Then they "pair up" and each share their answer and solution strategy (when there is one—for perceptual subitizing, there isn't) with their partner. That is the important sharing, but the teacher can select a couple children to share with the whole group or just summarize what they heard.

Back to Snapshots: Consistent with what research shows, first use straight lines of objects, then rectangular arrangements, and then dice arrangements, all with small numbers. Separating these typical dice arrangements with a large space promotes children's attention to subgroups for Perceptual Subgroup Subitizing (Kim et al., 2017). As children learn, use different arrangements and larger numbers.

What type of objects? This is tricky. Children may answer more quickly if the objects are different colors and shapes (Clements et al., 2019; Kim et al., 2017). However, we do not want children to try to "memorize" items as individuals—we want them to see them as a *number* of items in a *collection*. So, move to simple, high-contrast items as soon as possible (e.g., black dots on white paper plates).

There are many worthwhile variations of the "Snapshots" activity.

- Have students construct a quick–image arrangement with manipulatives (and watch for any misconceptions such as shown in Figure 2.2).
- Play Snapshots on the computer (see [LT]² software for multiple subitizing levels; several levels are show in Figure 2.4).
- Play finger-placement game on the computer. For example, pieces of fruit are shown briefly and the child has to place that many fingers on the screen with one or two hands

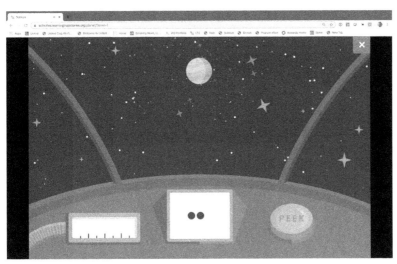

Figure 2.4a An early level of the activity "Subitize" from [LT]². First, children are shown an arrangement of dots for 2 seconds

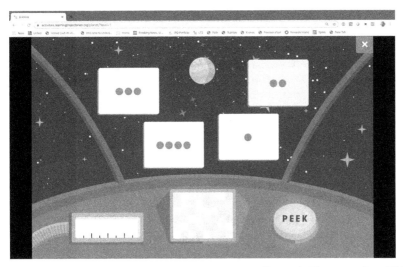

Figure 2.4b They are then asked to click on the corresponding set. They can "peek" for 2 more seconds if necessary. They are given feedback verbally, the planet gets closer, and the gauge showing them their progress advances

(Barendregt, Lindström, Rietz-Leppänen, Holgersson, & Ottosson, 2012; Sedaghatjou & Campbell, 2017).

- Play a matching game. Show several cards, all but one of which have the same number. Ask children which does not belong (this also teaches early classification; see Chapters 12 and 13).

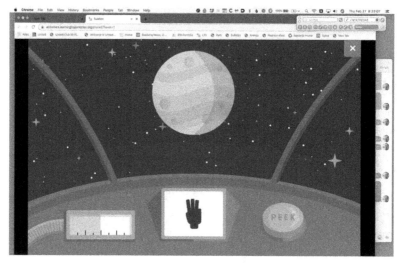

Figure 2.4c Several representations are offered, such as finger patterns

- Play concentration-type games (we call them "memory" games) with cards that have different arrangements for each number and a rule that you can only "peek" for 2 seconds. (See the resource, "Introducing and Using Games" on [LT]².)
- Give each child cards with zero to ten dots in different arrangements. Have students spread the cards in front of them. Then announce a number. Students find the matching card as fast as possible and hold it up. Have them use different sets of cards, with different arrangements, on different days. Later, hold up a written numeral as their cue. Adapt other card games for use with these card sets (see Clements & Callahan, 1986). Familiarity and interest in numerals is a significant predictor of later math abilities (Rathé, Torbeyns, De Smedt, & Verschaffel, 2019b).
- Place various arrangements of dots on a large sheet of poster board. With students gathered around you, point to one of the groups as students say its number as fast as possible. Rotate the poster board on different sessions.
- Challenge students to say the number that is one (later, two) more than the number on the quick image. They might also respond by showing a numeral card or writing the numeral. Or, they can find the arrangement that matches the numeral you show.
- Encourage students to play any of these games as a free-time or station activity.
- Remember that patterns can also be temporal and kinesthetic, such as rhythmic and auditory patterns. A motivating subitizing and numeral writing activity involves auditory rhythms. Scatter children around the room on the floor with individual chalkboards. Walk around the room, then stop and make a number of sounds, such as ringing a bell three times at a steady beat. Children should write the numeral 3 (or hold up three fingers as in Figure 2.5) on their chalkboards and hold it up. These can also develop conceptual subitizing. For example, how many claps: <clap>, <clap>, <clap> [pause], <clap>, <clap>, <clap>? (See *Hearing Numbers* at the "Perceptual Subitizer to 5" and "Conceptual Subitizer to 5" in Table 2.1 and in [LT]².)

Figure 2.5 Children hear three bell tones and hold up three fingers

Table 2.1 A Learning Trajectory for Recognition of Number and Subitizing

Age (years)[4]	Developmental Progression	Instructional Activities (Designed to Help Children Achieve this Level)
0–1	**Number Senser: Foundations:** Has inborn specific "sensers" for number from the first months of life without explicit knowledge of number. Intuitively distinguishes between groups of one and of two (and possibly two and three). Also shows sensitivity to ratios of quite large numbers. (Approximate Number System, or ANS). These are pre-math, foundational abilities. Shown many groups of three, a child "habituates" to them (i.e., becomes uninterested, relaxed) but immediately shows interest when then shown a group of two.	Number Peekaboo, [LT][2]: Peekaboo is a classic infant-caregiver interaction because young children enjoy the novelty of slight variations after becoming comfortable with one interaction. While children will enjoy seeing one toy over and over, they may find it particularly funny when the one toy changes to two toys. *Noticing collections:* Besides providing a rich sensory, manipulative environment, use words such as "more" and perform actions of adding objects, which direct attention to comparisons of numbers.
1–2	**Very Small Number Recognizer** Begins connecting small quantities to number words to form an explicit idea of cardinality, or "how-many-ness." Following the child's first birthday, the number words "one" and "two" are often learned. Other general terms such as "more" and "less" usually follow. Only over time do they begin to understand that all groups labeled with the same number word have the same amount. Shown a pair of shoes, a 2-year old says, "Two shoes."	*Numbers On Me*, [LT][2]: See main text, p. 24. Only one and two. Move parts of their body. *Naming Numbers*, [LT][2]: Gesture to a small group of objects (one or two). Say, "There are two balls. Two!" When the children are able, ask them how many there are. This should be a natural part of interaction *throughout* the day at school and at home.
2–3	**Maker of Small Collections** Makes a small collection (usually one to two and possibly three) with the same number as another collection (via mental model; i.e., not necessarily by matching–for that process, see *Compare Number*). Might also be verbal but often is not. May not recognize spatial structures at first, and may count this (Nes, 2009). When shown a collection of three, makes another collection of three in the same arrangement.	*Get the Number*, [LT][2]: Ask children to get the right number of crackers (etc.) for two to three children. *Make Groups*, [LT][2]: Lay out a small collection, say two blocks. Cover them. Ask children to make a group that has the same number of blocks as your group has. After they have finished, hide their version as well. Then uncover both groups, yelling "Ta-da!" Compare the two groups and ask children if they are the same. Name the number (e.g., "Both have three!").

(Continued)

Table 2.1 (Cont.)

Age (years)[4]	Developmental Progression	Instructional Activities (Designed to Help Children Achieve this Level)
2–3	**Small Collection Namer** Names groups of one, two, and three with increasing accuracy. Most children of about 34–39 months of age can accurately name groups of one, two, and three. Many children learn to recognize and name groups of four about 6 months later. For a Maker of Small Collections (the previous level), the child may rely on matching strategies to make their small collection. In Small Collection Namer, the child is actually able to recognize small groups without relying on a model or matching strategy. Three dogs walk by, child says, "Three doggies!"	*Numbers On Me (Small Collection Namer)*, [LT][2]: See main text, p. 24. Only one and two. Move parts of their body Small Collection Namer. *I See Numbers*, [LT][2]: Gesture to a small group of objects (one to three whenever the children are capable). When the children are able, ask them how many there are. This should be a natural part of interaction *throughout* the day at school and at home. Name collections as "two." Also include nonexamples as well as examples, saying, for instance, "That's not two. That's three!" Or, put out three groups of two and one group of three and have the child find out "the one that is not like the others." Discuss why. *Board Games–Small Numbers*, [LT][2]: Play board games with a special die (number cube) or spinner that shows only one, two, and three dots (then add zero to it). *See the resource, "Introducing and Using Games" on* [LT][2]. *Start Subitizing Small Sets*: Make your own groups in canonically structured arrangements–such as the following for three–and see how fast children can name them. 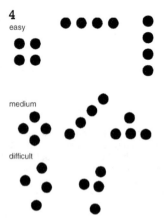
3–4	**Perceptual Subitizer to 4** Instantly recognizes collections up to four briefly shown and verbally names the number of items. When shown four objects briefly, says "four."	*Snapshots (to 4)*, [LT][2]: Play "Snapshots" with collections of one to four objects, arranged in line or other simple arrangement, asking children to think-pair-share and respond verbally with the number name. Use any of the bulleted modifications on pp. 24–25. Start with the smaller numbers and easier arrangements, moving to those of moderate difficulty only as children are fully competent and confident. **4** easy medium difficult *Subitize! Planets: Perceptual Subitizer to 4*, [LT][2]: Play on the computer with matching items as in Figures 2-4.

Table 2.1 (Cont.)

Age (years)[4]	Developmental Progression	Instructional Activities (Designed to Help Children Achieve this Level)
4	**Perceptual Subitizer to 5** Instantly recognizes briefly shown collections up to five and verbally names the number of items. Recognizes and uses spatial and numeric structures beyond the situations in which they were already experienced (i.e., in which they were initially learned). Shown five objects briefly, says "five."	*Snapshots (Perceptual Subitizer to 5)*, [LT][2]: Play with dot cards, starting with easy arrangements, moving to more difficult arrangements as children are able. 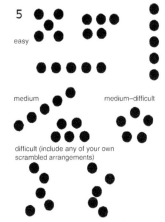 *Fantastic Five (Tricky Two)*, [LT][2]: Children subitize the number of counters hidden under a moving container. *Hearing Numbers*, [LT][2]). See p. 26. *Subitize! Planets: Perceptual Subitizer to 5)*: Play [LT][2] 's "Subitize" on computer with matching dots to numerals with groups up to and including five. 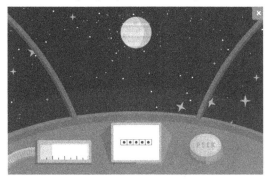
4	**Conceptual Subitizer to 5** Verbally labels all arrangements to about five, shown only briefly, by seeing the parts and quickly knowing the whole. Conceptual subitizing refers to the ability of children to identify a whole quantity as a result of composing smaller quantities (recognized through perceptual subitizing) that make up the whole. "Five! Why? I saw 3 and 2 and so I said five."	*Snapshots (Conceptual Subitizer to 5)*, [LT][2]: Use different arrangements of the various modifications of "Snapshots" to develop conceptual subitizing and ideas about addition and subtraction. The goal is to encourage children to see the addends *and* the sum as in "two olives and two olives make four olives" (Fuson, 1992b, p. 248). With conceptual subitizing, their think-pair-share discussion can provide their answer *and* how they knew, as in the example to the left.

(Continued)

Table 2.1 (Cont.)

Age (years)[4]	Developmental Progression	Instructional Activities (Designed to Help Children Achieve this Level)
		  Hearing Numbers, [LT][2]). See p. 26. *Subitize! Planets: Conceptual Subitizer to 5*, [LT][2]'s Play on computer with matching dots to numerals.
4-6	**Conceptual Subitizer to 7** Verbally labels all arrangements to six, then seven, when shown only briefly. "Seven! Cause five and that two are seven."	*Snapshots (to 7)*, [LT][2]: Use different arrangements of the various modifications of "Snapshots" to develop conceptual subitizing and ideas about addition and subtraction.
5-6	**Conceptual Subitizer to 10** Verbally labels most briefly shown arrangements of all numbers two to ten. Children may know some familiar ones ("five and five make ten" is common) early, but this level is reached when most combinations of all numbers up to ten are recognized (e.g., seven and two *seen* as nine; five and three *seen* as eight; etc.). Uses structures such as tens frames to recognize larger quantities. "In my mind, I made a group of six and then a group of three there, so ...nine."	*Snapshots to 10*, [LT][2]: Play "Snapshots," showing five to ten large dots in different arrangements to suggest all pairs of numbers and asking children, "How many dots in *this* picture?" *Subitize! Planets: Conceptual Subitizer to 10*, [LT][2]'s Play on computer with matching dots or fingers to numerals. The computer version's feedback emphasizes that "three and four make seven." 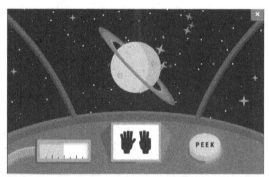
6-7	**Conceptual Subitizer to 20** Verbally labels structured arrangements of to 20, shown only briefly, by seeing the parts and quickly knowing the whole. Spontaneously makes use of a top-down strategy to subitizing large quantities (Nes, 2009). Children may know some familiar ones ("ten and ten make 20" is common) early, but this level is reached when *most all* combinations of numbers from one to ten are recognized (e.g., seven and nine is *seen* as 16). "I saw three fives, so ten and five ... 15"	*Subitize Dots to 20*, [LT][2]: Use a fives and tens frame to help children visualize addition combinations, but also move to mental arithmetic. (Make sure children can reproduce such frames on their own, as well. See "spatial structuring" in Chapters 11 and 12.) 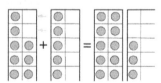 *Subitize! Planets: Conceptual Subitizer to 20*, [LT][2]: Play on computer with matching dots to numerals.

Table 2.1 (Cont.)

Age (years)[4]	Developmental Progression	Instructional Activities (Designed to Help Children Achieve this Level)
7	**Conceptual Subitizer with Place Value** Verbally labels structured arrangements, shown only briefly, using groups, skip counting, and place value. "I saw two groups of tens and three groups of twos, so 40 … 46!"	*Subitize! Planets: Conceptual Subitizer Place Value*, [LT][2]: Play on computer with matching dots to numerals. 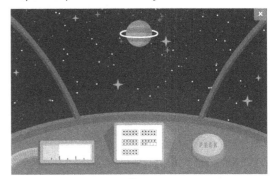 *Snapshots (to 50)*, [LT][2]: Play Snapshots with structured groups that support the use of increasingly sophisticated mental strategies and operations, such as asking children, "How many dots in the following picture?"
8	**Conceptual Subitizer with Place Value and Multiplicative Thinking** Verbally labels structured arrangements, shown only briefly, using groups, multiplicative thinking, and place value. This level builds on the previous level, such that children are able to use the base-ten system to conceptually subitize larger numbers. Children are able to verbalize the quantity of tens they see. A child sees a group of 62 dots and says, "I saw groups of tens and threes, so I thought, 5 tens is 50 and 4 threes is 12, so 62 in all."	*Snapshots*, [LT][2]: Play "Snapshots" with structured groups that support the use of increasingly sophisticated mental strategies and operations, such as asking children, "How many dots in the following picture?" 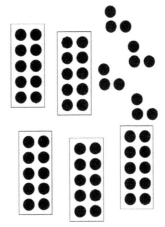 *Subitize! Planets: Conceptual Subitizer Place Value*, [LT][2]: Play on computer with matching dots to numerals.

Across many types of activities, from class discussions to textbooks, show children displays of numbers that encourage conceptual subitizing. Follow these guidelines to make groups: (a) groups should not be embedded in pictorial context; (b) simple forms such as homogeneous groups of circles or squares (rather than pictures of animals or mixtures of any shapes) should be used for the units; (c) regular arrangements should be emphasized (most including sym-metry, with linear arrangements for preschoolers and rectangular arrangements for older stu-dents being easiest); and (d) good figure-ground contrast should be provided.

To develop strong conceptual subitizing, go beyond simply showing pictures. Have children experience many real-life situations such as finger patterns, arrangements on dice and dominoes, egg cartons (for "double-structures"), arrays (rows and columns—see an extended discussion in Chapter 11), and other structures. Have them *discuss* and especially *build* arrangements to "make it easy to see how many." Such thoughtful, interactive, constructive experiences are effective ways of building spatial sense and connecting it to number sense (Nes, 2009). For example, they might draw flowers with a given number of petals or draw or build pictures with manipulatives of houses with a certain number of windows so that they and others can subitize the number.

Encourage and help students advance to more sophisticated addition and subtraction (see also Chapters 5 and 6 for more on this, and also for learning trajectories that address this more advanced conceptual subitizing). For example, a student may add by counting on one or two, solving 4 + 2 by saying "4, 5, 6," but be unable to count on five or more, as would be required to solve 4 + 5 by counting "4, 5, 6, 7, 8, 9."

Counting on two, however, gives them a way to figure out how "counting on" works. Later, they can learn to count on with larger numbers by developing their conceptual subitizing or by learning different ways of "keeping track." Eventually, students come to recognize number pat-terns as both a whole (as a unit itself) and a composite of parts (individual units). At this stage, a student is capable of viewing number and number patterns as units of units (Steffe & Cobb, 1988). For example, students can repeatedly answer what number is "ten more" than another number. "What is ten more than 23." "33!" "Ten more?" "43!"

In later chapters (12 and beyond), we discuss the importance of children seeing *patterns* (including spatial patterns) and *structures*—and these extend our discussions of subitizing.

Meeting Special Needs

Special populations, including children with disabilities, find subitizing particularly difficult and deserve special attention to subitizing. Only a minority (31%) of children with moderate mental handicaps (chronological ages 6 to 14 years) and a slight majority (59%) of children with mild mental handicaps (ages 6 to 13) successfully subitize sets of three and four (Baroody, 1986b; see also Butterworth, 2010). Some children with learning disabilities could not subitize even at 10 years of age (Koontz & Berch, 1996). Early deficits in spatial pattern recognition may be the source of difficulty (Ashkenazi, Mark-Zigdon, & Henik, 2013b). Subitizing in preschool is a better predictor of later math success for children with ASD (autism spectrum disorder) than for typic-ally developing children (Titeca, Roeyers, Josephy, Ceulemans, & Desoete, 2014).

Because conceptual subitizing often depends on accurate enumeration skill, teachers should remedy deficiencies in both perceptual subitizing and counting early (Baroody, 1986b). Teachers should cultivate familiarity of regular patterns by playing games that use number cubes or dominoes and avoid taking basic number competencies, such as subitizing, for granted in special populations.

Pattern recognition of fives and tens frames, such as illustrated in Figure 2.7, can assist stu-dents with mental handicaps and learning disabilities as they learn to recognize the five- and ten-frame configuration for each number. "These arrangements ... help a student first to

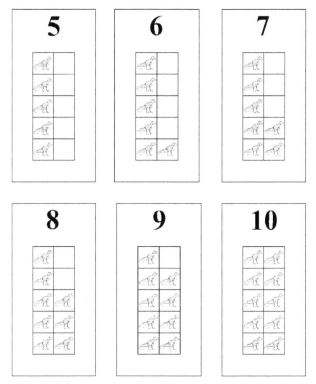

Figure 2.7 Pattern recognition of fives and tens frames

recognize the number and use the model in calculating sums. It is this image of the number that stays with the student and becomes significant" (Flexer, 1989). Visual-kinesthetic finger patterns can similarly help, especially with the critical number combinations that sum to ten.

Learning Trajectory for Recognition of Number and Subitizing: Putting It All Together

The learning trajectory for subitizing is fairly straightforward. However, because subitizing is often a *neglected* quantifier, it is often not well represented in standards. For example, the CCSSM does not emphasize subitizing as much as we believe it should, although you can find this clear statement in the introduction to Kindergarten: "Students choose, combine, and apply effective strategies for answering quantitate questions, *including quickly recognizing the cardinalities of small sets of objects*" (CCSSO/NGA, 2010, p. 9, emphasis added). Head Start's Early Learning Outcomes Framework (ELOF) has more extensive coverage of subitizing, but even here, they do not mention it soon enough (as we saw, it begins in the first year of life, and children learn their first number words by *18 months*), and they do not mention conceptual subitizing with larger numbers. Remember, to see how CCSSM, ELOF, and many other standards and assessments align with the learning trajectories, use the alignment tool in [LT]² as illustrated in Figure 2.8. Notice that *learning trajectories not only* give far more details for each level, but they also provide *levels in between* those of the ELOF—essential for guiding children's educational experiences.

Therefore, we state our own goal simply here: *Children recognize and then subitize (recognize quickly) the number in a group without counting.* This starts from the first years and develops to multidigit numbers in the primary grades.[2] *Subitizing is for all young children.*

To meet that goal, Table 2.1 provides the two additional components of the learning trajectory, the developmental progression and the instructional tasks. (Note that the ages in all the learning trajectory tables are only approximate, especially because the age of acquisition usually depends heavily on experience. Children who receive high-quality education progress one or more years beyond the "typical" ages in these learning trajectories.) Using the "Snapshots" activity described above as one basic instructional task, the learning trajectory shows different number and arrangements of dots that illustrate instructional tasks designed to promote that level of thinking. Although the activities in the learning trajectories presented in this book constitute a research-based core of an early childhood curriculum, a complete curriculum includes more (e.g., relationships between trajectories and many other considerations; for example, see Chapter 15).

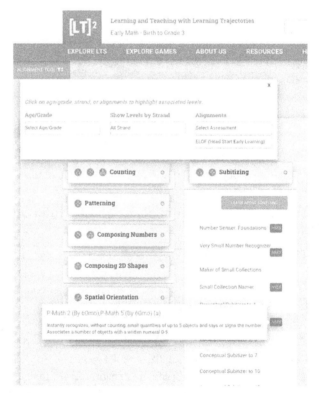

Figure 2.8 Click on the green alignment tool and select a standard (or assessment—here we selected the ELOF) to see how learning trajectory levels align with those standards. Then hover your cursor over one to see the specific standard or click on a level to see it on that level's page

We strongly recommend that you fully read and study the learning trajectory in Table 2.1. If you simply "glance through it," you will miss the *key knowledge* that is packed into the levels of thinking and the tightly related instructional activities.

Just as important, remember to go to our new tool, the *Learning and Teaching with Learning Trajectories*[3] tool at LearningTrajectories.org. There you can see videos of children's thinking at *each level* of subitizing as well as *classroom* and *home* videos of teachers and caregivers helping children *learn* that level of thinking. There are many additional instructional activities on [LT][2] as well.

Extending the Subitizing Learning Trajectory

As an extension, later primary-grade students can improve numerical estimation with modifications of "Snapshots." For example, show students arrangements that are too large to subitize exactly. Encourage them to use subitizing in their estimation strategies. Emphasize that using good strategies and being "close" is the goal, not getting the exact number. Begin with organized geometric patterns but include scrambled arrangements eventually. Encourage students, especially those in higher grades, to build more sophisticated strategies: from guessing to counting as much as possible and then guessing to comparing ("It was more than the previous one"), to grouping ("They are spread about four in each place. I circled groups of four in my head and then counted six groups. So, 24!"). Students do perform better, using more sophisticated strategies and frames of reference, after engaging in such activities (Markovits & Hershkowitz, 1997). For these and for all subitizing activities, stop frequently to allow students to share their strategies. *If students do not quickly develop more sophisticated strategies based on place value and arithmetic operations, estimation activities may not be a good use of instructional time.* "Guessing" is not math thinking. (See Chapter 4.)

Final Words

"Subitizing is a fundamental skill in the development of students' understanding of number" (Baroody, 1987a, p. 115) and must be developed. However, it is not the only way to quantify groups. In many ways, counting is a more general and powerful method, and we turn to this topic in Chapter 3.

Notes

1   "Number sense" includes a large number of competencies, including composing and decomposing numbers, recognizing the relative magnitude of numbers, dealing with the absolute magnitude of numbers, using benchmarks, linking representations, understanding the effects of arithmetic operations, inventing strategies, estimating, and possessing a disposition toward making sense of numbers (Sowder, 1992b).

2   Later grades use subitizing in many ways, such as in supporting the development of counting concepts and skills and solving arithmetic problems. These goals will be highlighted in subsequent chapters.

3   Funded by the Heising-Simons Foundation and the Bill and Melinda Gates Foundation, *Learning and Teaching with Learning Trajectories* is also known by its initials, LTLT, or, therefore, as [LT][2] (one of those "math jokes" almost totally devoid of actual humor).

4   The ages in the table are typical ages at which children develop these ideas. However, children vary widely and just as important, *with high-quality education*, children achieve much later levels. See p. 9 in Chapter 1.

3 Verbal and Object Counting

Before her fourth birthday, Abby was given five train engines. She walked in one day with three of them. Her father said, "Where's the other ones?" "I lost them," she admitted. "How many are missing?" he asked. "I have 1, 2, 3. So [*pointing in the air*] foooour, fiiiive ... two are missing, 4 and 5. [*Pauses*] No! I want these to be [*pointing at the three engines*] 1, 3, and 5. So, 2 and 4 are missing. Still two missing, but they're numbers 2 and 4."

Abby thought about counting and numbers—at least small numbers—abstractly. She could assign 1, 2, and 3 to the three engines, or 1, 3, and 5! Moreover, she could *count* the *numbers* (not just the engines). That is, she applied counting ... to counting numbers! What *are* the ideas and skills that develop in such sophisticated counting? What do most young children know about counting? What more might they learn?

Changing Views of Counting

In the middle of the 20th century, Piaget's research on number strongly influenced views of early math. Among the many positive influences were an appreciation for children's active role in learning and the depth of the math ideas they constructed. One unfortunate influence was the belief that, until children can *conserve* number, counting is meaningless. For example, asked to give themselves the same number of "candies" as an interviewer has, 4-year-olds might use matching as shown in Figure 3.1.

But, when the interviewer spreads their objects out, as in Figure 3.2, the children may claim that the interviewer now has *more*. Even asking children to count the two collections may not help them determine the correct answer.

The Piagetians believed that children needed to develop the logic that underlies conservation of number before counting was meaningful. This logic consists of two types of knowledge. First was "hierarchical classification," such as knowing that, if there are 12 wooden beads, eight blue and four red, there are more wooden beads than blue beads. What does that have to do with *number* and counting? To understand counting, Piagetians argued, children must understand that each number *includes* those that came before, as illustrated in Figure 3.3.

The second type of logical knowledge is "sequencing." Children have to both properly produce number words in sequence and sequence the objects they count, so that they count each object exactly once (no easy task for young children, especially if faced with an unorganized group). Also, children have to understand that each counting number is *quantitatively* one more

Figure 3.1 After an adult makes the bottom row of "candies" and asks the child to give herself the same number, the child uses one-to-one correspondence

Figure 3.2 The adult spreads his "candies" out, and the child now states that he has more than she does

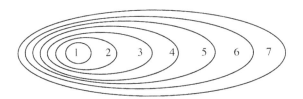

Figure 3.3 The hierarchical inclusion of numbers (cardinality, or "how many?" property)

than the one before, as shown in Figure 3.4. However, children have inborn capabilities to build on. In fact, so do other animals—in some tasks, such as see numerals 0 to 8 for less than an eye blink, trained chimpanzees do *better than people* (Angier, 2018).

Both these notions have much truth in them. Children must learn these ideas to understand number well. However, *children learn much about counting and number before they have mastered these ideas.* And, in fact, rather than requiring these ideas before counting is meaningful, counting

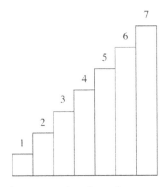

Figure 3.4 The ordinal, or sequencing, property of numbers

may help children make sense of the logical ideas. That is, counting can help *develop* knowledge of classification and seriation (Clements, 1984).

The Development of Counting

Verbal Counting

The Mathematics of Verbal Counting

Although counting to small numbers is universal in human cultures, counting to large numbers requires a *system* to keep track. Our Hindu-Arabic numeral system is based on two ideas (Wu, 2011). First, there are only ten symbols called "digits" (0, 1, 2, 3, 4, 5, 6, 7, 8, 9). Second, all possible counting numbers are created by using those ten digits in different places—the concept of "place value." Any number, then, is the *sum* of the *products* of each "face" (digit) and its "place"; for example, 1,926 is 1 *thousand*, 9 *hundreds*, 2 *tens*, and 6 *ones*. When we count, we get up to 9, and then signify the next number with the digit 1 in the tens place and the digit 0 as a "placeholder" in the ones place: 10. Then, we work through ten digits in the ones place, 10 to 19, at which point we run out again, so we put in the tens place: 20. Twenty one means we cycled through 0 to 9 twice, so we knew we counted 20 times plus one more time.

Children's Development of Verbal Counting

This brief mathematical description suggests why we use the term "verbal counting" rather than "rote counting"—after 20, children need to use mathematical patterns and structures, not just "rote memory." Further, children who can count starting at any number performed better on all numerical tasks, so fluent verbal counting is not rote, but, rather, is based on their *recognition* of the structure of numbers—the *patterns* of verbal counting. After 71 ... is *72* ... children recognize the pattern of "one ... *two*" and apply it here.

There are other reasons verbal counting is not rote. Without verbal counting, *quantitative* thinking does not develop. As an example, children who can continue counting when starting at any number are better on *all* number tasks. Children learn that numbers derive order and meaning from their embeddedness in a system, and they learn a set of relationships and rules that allows the generation, not recall, of the appropriate sequence. Even in the "rote" portion of verbal counting—1 to 20 (in English and Spanish)—*children recognize that numbers that come later are "bigger"* (they don't think that when reciting the ABCs).

Language is important. As an example, people who are deaf and sign, but do not have access to a usable model for language, spoken or signed, do not consistently extend the correct number of fingers when communicating about sets greater than three, nor do they always correctly match the number of items in one set to a target set when that target set is greater than three (Spaepen, Coppola, Spelke, Carey, & Goldin-Meadow, 2011). Similarly, cross-cultural studies indicate that learning of counting varies with the language in which the number system is learned (see the companion book). For example, Chinese, like many East Asian languages, has a more regular sequence of number words than English. In both English and Chinese, the numbers 1 through 10 are arbitrary and the numbers after 20 follow a regular pattern of naming the decade name and then the digit name (e.g., "twenty-one"). However, in Chinese (and in many

Asian languages), there are two important differences. First, the tens numbers directly mirror the single-digit number names ("two-tens" rather than "twenty"; "three-tens" rather than "thirty") and the numbers from 11 to 20 also follow a regular pattern (comparable to "ten-one," "ten-two," etc.) instead of the obscure "eleven, twelve ...." Through 3 years of age, children in the various cultures learn 1 through 10 similarly; however, those learning English learn the "teens" more slowly and with more errors, especially with 13 and 15. Only US children make errors such as "twenty-nine, twenty-ten, twenty-eleven ..."; Chinese children do not make that kind of mistake. (See place value in Chapter 6.) But also note that there are many intertwined factors, such as cultural practices. For example, in China, relatives are known as "Brother No. 1, Brother No. 2 ...," days are labeled "Weekday No. 1, Weekday No. 2, Weekday No. 3 ...," and so forth (Ng & Rao, 2010).

Second, Asian number words can be pronounced more quickly, providing another significant cognitive advantage (Geary & Liu, 1996). They do not provide the same burden on working memory that English and Spanish words do (Ng & Rao, 2010), and they may make learning one-to-one correspondence easier in object counting. Dutch children are one group that has it even more difficult than English children: Their "twenty-two" is translated to "two and twenty," putting the ones first through the number sequence.

Learning verbal counting occurs over years. At first, children can only say some numbers in words, but not necessarily in sequence. Then, they learn to count verbally by starting at the beginning and saying a string of words, but they do not even "hear" counting words as separate words (children similarly might say "l-m-n-o-p" as one word). (Interestingly, around this level they can duplicate a series of actions with attention to number without verbal counting, another early foundation for object counting, Sella, Berteletti, Lucangeli, & Zorzi, 2016.) Then, they do separate each counting word and they learn to count up to 10, then 20, then higher. Only later can children start counting from any number, what we call the "Counter from *N* (*N* + 1, *N* – 1)" level. Even later, they learn to skip count and count to 100 and beyond. Finally, children learn to count the number words themselves (e.g., to "count on"; see Chapter 4). These levels are summarized in Table 3.2.

Object Counting

As shown in Chapter 2, naming how many items are in small configurations of items requires experiences in which the configurations are labeled with a number word by adults or older children ("Here are two blocks"), which enable children to build meaning for number words: They tell how many. The earliest levels of counting, even object counting, do not have that meaning for children.

An important milestone in early numerical knowledge is achieved when children connect the counting of objects in a collection to the number of objects in that collection. Initially, children may not know how many objects there are in a collection after counting them. If asked "How many are there?" they typically count again, as if the "how many?" question is a directive to count rather than a request for how many items are in the collection. Children must learn that the last number word they say when counting refers to how many items have been counted. This is more complex than simply "repeating" that last counting word. When children enumerate, it's about ordering: Keep the objects in order, keep the counting words in order, follow the procedure of enumeration one-by-one in sequence… However, at the *end* of counting, children have to switch from the order of individuals to the cardinality, or "how-manyness" of the *whole group*. This is the count to cardinal transition, and it's not obvious.

Thus, to count a set of objects, children must not only know verbal counting, but also learn (a) to coordinate verbal counting with objects by pointing to or moving the objects and (b) that the last counting word names the cardinality of ("how many objects in") the set. This process is illustrated in Figure 3.5.

Understanding the cardinal principle is necessary to develop the later levels of counting (Spaepen, Gunderson, Gibson, Goldin-Meadow, & Levine, 2018), as well as other LTs such as Comparing Number and Adding/Subtracting. More striking, research shows that *acquiring the cardinal principle by kindergarten is too late! Preschoolers* need to gain this knowledge and skill (Geary et al., 2017).

Meaningful counting such as this is basic in many ways. It is the method for quantifying groups larger than small subitizable collections. It is the necessary building block for all further work with number.

Also, *counting is the first and most basic and important algorithm*. That is, most everything else in number, algebra, and beyond depend in some way on counting. Why is it an algorithm—a word usually used for ways to represent and process arithmetic with multidigit numbers (e.g., "column addition")? Because an algorithm is a step-by-step procedure that is guaranteed to solve a specific category of problems. Counting is the first step-by-step procedure that children learn that solves certain problems—determining how many elements are in a finite set. *The math of object counting*, therefore, is that every set that yields the same "last counting word" has the *same number of items* in it.

The easiest type of collection for 3-year-olds to count has only a few objects arranged in a straight line that can be touched as children proceed with their counting. Between 3 and 5 years of age, children acquire more skill as they practice counting, and most become able to cope with numerically larger collections.

There are many additional counting skills children need to learn. They need to produce a collection of a given number, that is, "count out" a group. To adults, that may seem to be no more difficult than counting a collection. However, to produce 4, children have to keep track of the number word they are on, and keep one-to-one correspondence, *and* compare the number word they said to the 4 with each count. Before they reach that level of competence, they often just keep going!

Next, children learn to count objects in different arrangements, keeping track of which they have and have not yet counted. They learn to count collections without needing to touch or

"one… two… three… four… five… six… seven… Seven in all!"

Figure 3.5 Object counting, including one-to-one correspondence and cardinality ("how many uses?")

move objects during the act of counting. Eventually, they have to count objects they cannot see! As an example, researcher Les Steffe was working with 5-year-old Brenda. He showed her three squares and told her four more were covered under a cloth. He asked her how many squares there were in all. Brenda tried to raise the cloth. Steffe stopped her. Brenda counted the three visible squares.

Brenda:	One, two, three. (*Touches each visible item in turn.*)
Les Steffe:	There's four here (*tapping the cloth*).
Brenda:	(*Lifts the cloth, revealing two squares.*) Four, five. (*Touches each and puts cloth back.*)
Les Steffe:	OK, I'll show you two of them. (*Shows two.*) There's four here, you count them.
Brenda:	One, two ... (*then counts each visible*) three, four, five.
Les Steffe:	There's two more here (*taps the cloth*).
Brenda:	(*Attempts to lift the cloth.*)
Les Steffe:	(*Pulls back the cloth.*)
Brenda:	Six, seven (*touches the last two squares*).

Brenda's attempt to lift the cloth indicates that she was aware of the hidden squares and intended to count the collection. But she could not count because she did not *experience* them. She could take *perceived* items as being countable but could not count *imagined* items. Later, she counted the interviewer's fingers instead of six items he was hiding. When he pointed out he had six marbles hidden, Brenda said, "I don't see no six!" Later in development, children can *mentally produce items to count*. Brenda had not yet reached that level.

Finally, don't neglect numerals as representing a count! Children's knowledge of symbols such as "3" or "9" is more predictive of later success in math than other aspects of counting (Martin, Cirino, Sharp, & Barnes, 2014). Indeed, children's *spontaneous* attention and interest in numerals is important (Rathé et al., 2019), and reading numerals is completely developmentally appropriate for even 3- and 4-year-olds. So, playing a game such as "Number Jump", teachers might display figures (see Figure 3.6) *or* numerals.

Counting Strategies

Children also learn to quickly tell how many there are in a collection if one is added or removed by counting up or down. That is, knowing there are four balls in a box, when another one is put in, they learn to say "five"–the next counting number. Perhaps that seems obvious to adults, but it is a watershed moment in children's understanding of number (Baroody & Purpura, 2017). That is, it leads to children learning sophisticated counting strategies, such as "counting on" or "counting backward" to solve arithmetic problems (we discuss this in detail in Chapter 4).

Children learn to *modify* the acts of counting in multiple ways, from counting on to counting "counts" (remember Abby's engines) to skip counting and much more. These are counting strategies and will be the focus of *using* counting in many of the forthcoming chapters.

Figure 3.6 Counting events as well as objects. In "Number Jump," children count or subitize the number of fingers they see, and then count as they jump up that many times

---

Whether they are at the higher object counting or counting strategies levels, children should be supported in developing more advanced levels of counting, as only the advanced levels predict later math achievement.

(Nguyen et al., 2016)

Zero and Infinity

Five-year-old Dawn was changing the speed of moving objects on the computer screen by entering commands. The command "SETSPEED 100" made them go fast. "SETSPEED 10" made them go slower. She tried speed limits such as 55 and very slow speeds like 5 and 1. Suddenly, she excitedly called her friend and then her teacher. Visitor Seymour Papert and the teacher were confused. What was exciting? Nothing was happening.

They found out that *"Nothing" was* happening. Zero! She had entered "SETSPEED 0" and the object stopped. Dawn talked about how it was "moving," but the speed was zero. Zero was a number! Not "none" or "nothing," but a real number. Papert concluded that such discoveries lie at the heart of learning math. This story also reveals that zero is *not* an obvious concept. It was invented by people far later than were the counting numbers. However, even children as young as 3 or 4 years of age can learn to use zero to represent the absence of objects.

Children think about zero in different ways and build special rules to account for this exceptional number. The same attributes that make zero difficult may also make it serve children's math development. Zero may play a special role in children's increasingly algebraic knowledge of

[handwritten margin note: Zero is Nothing]

number. Because they have to be conscious of the rules for zero, such experiences may build a foundation for the creation of generalized rules in the structures of arithmetic.

During dinner, a father asked his second grader what he had learned in school:

Son:	I learned that if you multiply or divide by zero, the answer is always zero.
Dad:	What would be the answer if you multiplied two by zero?
Son:	Zero.
Dad:	What if you divided two by zero?
Son:	Zero.
Dad:	What is two divided by two?
Son:	One.
Dad:	What is two divided by one? How many ones are there in two?
Son:	Two.
Dad:	What is two divided by one-half? How many halves are there in two?
Son:	Four.
Dad:	What is two divided by one-quarter?
Son:	Eight.
Dad:	What seems to be happening as we divide by numbers closer to zero?
Son:	The answer is getting bigger.
Dad:	What do you think about the idea that two divided by zero is zero?
Son:	It's not right. What is the answer?
Dad:	It doesn't look like there is an answer. What do you think?
Son:	Daddy, wouldn't the answer be infinity?
Dad:	Where did you learn about infinity?
Son:	From Buzz Lightyear.

(adapted from Gadanidis, Hoogland, Jarvis, & Scheffel, 2003)

Asked to count backward, label a number line, and so forth, first graders showed different ideas of zero (Bofferding & Alexander, 2011). Some treated zero as an endpoint, refusing to label marks to the left of zero or labeling all marks to the left with zeros. Others left zero off the number line. Such results suggest we need better conversations such as the one above about zero and negative numbers (even if they are not emphasized in standards until later grades).

Summary

Early numerical knowledge includes several *interrelated* aspects, including recognizing and naming how many items are in a small configuration (small number recognition and, when done quickly, subitizing), learning the names of and eventually ordering list of number words to ten and beyond, enumerating objects (i.e., saying number words in correspondence with objects), understanding that the last number word said when counting refers to how many items have been counted, and learning counting strategies to solve problems. Children learn these aspects, often separately through different kinds of experiences, but *gradually* connect them during the preschool years (cf. Linnell & Fluck, 2001; Nunes, Bryant, Evans, & Barros, 2015; Reikerås, 2016). For example, very young children may learn to focus on the number in small groups and, separately, learn verbal counting while enumerating these and other groups (initially without accurate correspondence) as a verbal string. As these abilities grow, they motivate the use of each type of quantification, and become increasingly interrelated, with recognition motivating verbal counting, as well as building subitizing ability that supports object counting skills of correspondence and cardinality (Batchelor & Gilmore, 2015; Eimeren, MacMillan, & Ansari, 2007). Skilled object counting then motivates and supports more advanced perceptual and conceptual subitizing abilities. Each of the four aspects begins with the smallest numbers and gradually includes larger numbers. In addition, each includes significant developmental levels.

For example, small number recognition moves from nonverbal recognition of one or two objects, to quick recognition and discrimination of one to four objects, to conceptual subitizing of larger (composed) groups. As children's ability to subitize grows from perceptual to conceptual patterns, so too does their ability to count and operate on collections grow from perceptual to conceptual.

Experience and Education

Many early childhood teachers, working with the youngest children[1] through first-grade students and beyond, underestimate children's ability to do, and to learn more about, interesting counting. Too often, children learn little or nothing about counting from preschool to first grade. Textbooks "introduce" counting skills that children already possess and spend considerable time on one number, such as 3, eventually moving to 4, then 5 ... usually neglecting numbers above 10. Some also teach these topics by rote. A study showing that Finland's preschoolers knew much more about counting than those in Iran also showed that only Finns learned counting meaningfully with objects and connections to real life (Aunio, Korhonen, Bashash, & Khoshbakht, 2014). Research suggests several positive alternatives to limited scope and rote memorization.

Verbal Counting

Initial verbal counting involves learning the list of number words that—from one to ten and usually twenty—is an *arbitrary* list for speakers of English and Spanish. There are few salient patterns (Fuson, 1992a). Initially, the counting words are a "song to sing" (Ginsburg, 1977). Children learn at least some of this list as they do general language or the ABCs. Thus, rhythms and songs can play a role, although attention should be given to separating the words from each other and understanding each as a counting word (e.g., some children initially tag two items with the two syllables of "se-ven").

If the words are arbitrary, why did we say that we do not like the term "rote counting"? Because verbal counting should be meaningful and part of a *system* of number, even for young children (Pollio & Whitacre, 1970). Children can learn to recognize that counting words reference how in an intuitive way, that the higher you count, the "more you have" or "larger" the number is, and so forth, *even with numbers up to 20*. Beyond these, the patterns and structure of verbal counting should be emphasized by making the base-ten, place value, and structure of number names more accessible to young children (Miller, Smith, Zhu, & Zhang, 1995). Familiarize

U.S. children with Arabic numerals at an earlier age than is expected at present. Further, both anecdotal reports and a study (Van Luit & Van der Molen, 2011) support counting with English words *and*, once in a while, English translations of East Asian structures ("ten-one [for 11], ten-two, ten-three … two-tens, two-tens-one [21], two-tens-two …"). Research shows this helps children map the single-digit to decade terms (Magargee, 2017; Van Luit & Van der Molen, 2011), both to facilitate the counting sequencing and to mitigate potential harmful effects on children's belief systems if they experience this early math task as being confusing and arbitrary, demanding mostly memorization (Fuson, 1992a). Indeed, research suggests that language effects are not all-pervasive (Mark & Dowker, 2015); instead, high-quality teaching of challenging tasks (e.g., counting up or down; see "Counter from N ($N + 1$, $N - 1$)") is *more* important than the language used in counting (Laski & Yu, 2014).

If children make mistakes, emphasize the importance of accuracy and encourage students to count slowly and carefully (Baroody, 1996). Invite children to count with you. Then ask them to do it (the same task again) alone. If necessary, have the child mirror you, number by number. "Say each number after I say it. 'One'" (pause). If they do not respond, repeat "one" and then tell the children to say "one." If children say "two," then say "three" and continue, allowing them to mirror you or continue your counting. If children still make the mistake when counting on their own, mark this as a special "warm-up" exercise for the child every day.

Language Before Object Counting

Number words play a role in naming very small collections (recall subitizing in Chapter 2) and orienting children to attend to numerical aspects of situations. They bring number to conscious awareness. For example, a girl was sitting with her dog when another dog wandered into the yard. She says, "Two doggie!" She then asked her mother to give her "two treats" and gave one to each. As another example, researcher Grayson Wheatley was interacting with a 4-year-old with dominoes. The child would build and make shapes with them but did not attend to the number of dots. Wheatley began to talk as he put pieces together, saying, "These two go together because there are three dots on each." After doing this for a while, as he was still building, he began to attend to the dots and put together pieces that had the same number of dots. He had made a start at abstracting the idea of "three." Research suggests provision of multiple experiences such as these before any major focus on object counting.

Subitizing and Object Counting–A Great Relationship

When trying to develop subitizing concepts, consciously try to connect experiences with counting and subitizing. Young children may use perceptual subitizing to make units for counting and to build their initial ideas of cardinality. For example, their first cardinal meanings for number words may be labels for small sets of subitized objects, even if they counted the sets first (Fuson, 1992b; Steffe, Thompson, & Richards, 1982).

Use many ways to link counting objects to children's recognition of the numbers in small collections. One effective teaching activity, "How Many in a Hand?" emphasizes that counting tells "how many" (from Clements & Sarama, 2007a–see [LT][2], Counter (Small Numbers)). With four counters out of sight in your hand behind your back, tell children you saw some wooden inch cubes (or another similar size item) and you thought, "I wonder how many I can hold in one hand?" Tell them you put as many as you can hold in the hand behind your back. Ask children to help you *count to find out how many* cubes you have hidden in your hand. Remove one with the other hand, placing it in front of the children so they see and focus on this one (keep the others hidden). Repeat until you have counted out all four cubes. Display your now-empty hands. Gesture around all the cubes and ask children how many there were in all. Agree that "There are four [gesturing again]! We counted and there are four." Notice that children hear each counting word as it is spoken in enumeration *while observing the corresponding collection containing that number of objects—a number you have already taught them to subitize.* So, a child who does not yet know the cardinality principle will see: When we say one, I *see* one. When we say "two," I know that's two! ... and so forth, so at four, that idea has been clearly illustrated (that's why we bring out one at a time, instead of pointing to them in a visible line). Also, gesturing around them and repeating "There are four" reinforces that important idea. We then challenge children to see how many fit in *their* hand during play time, saying, "Your hand is smaller, I don't think you can hold as many as me."

Are there other characteristics that make this activity better than rote-like counting of object in a line? Yes, we *start* with a question, "How many in my hand?", that *counting answers*. Also, asking children to do it *themselves* is more motivating and meaningful (and, we bet you can guess, will lead to counting higher than 4, as they struggle to beat the teacher).

Another technique would be to ask children to count a collection they can subitize, then add or subtract an object and have the children count again. In both activities, *subitizing helps imbue counting with cardinality.*

Counting can also support subitizing. Children can use many processes, including perceptual subitizing, counting, and patterning abilities, to develop conceptual subitizing. This more advanced ability to quickly group and quantify sets in turn supports their development of number sense and arithmetic abilities. A first grader explains the process for us.

Seeing a 3 by 3 pattern of dots, she says "nine" immediately. Asked how she did it, she replies, "When I was about four years old, I was in nursery school. All I had to do was count. And so, I just go like 1, 2, 3, 4, 5, 6, 7, 8, 9, and I just knew it by heart and I kept on doing it when I was five too. And then I kept knowing 9, you know. Exactly like this [she pointed to the array of nine dots].

(Ginsburg, 1977, p. 16)

Object Counting, Continued

Of course, children also need substantial experience counting along with others and counting by themselves. Counting objects takes considerable practice to coordinate and can be facilitated by having children touch objects as they count and by counting objects organized into a row. However, children are also well prepared for such coordination, especially if rhythm is introduced, although they must concentrate and try hard to achieve continuous coordination throughout the whole counting effort. Such effort increases their accuracy substantially (Fuson, 1988) and asking children to "slow down" and "try very hard to count just right" should be the first intervention to use when you observe an error in counting. Parents and some teachers may discourage pointing at objects or assume that when children use correspondence in simple tasks, they do not need help using it in more complex tasks (Linnell & Fluck, 2001). However, errors increase when the indicating act is eye fixations and such errors may be internalized. Therefore, allow—and encourage parents to allow—children to point to objects, and encourage it as another early intervention when counting errors are observed (Fuson, 1988, 1992a; Linnell & Fluck, 2001). Emphasize finger counting—it is fundamental to representing number and teaching counting and arithmetic concepts (Crollen & Noël, 2015)! Encourage children with special difficulties, such as learning disabilities, to work slowly and carefully and to move objects to a new location (Baroody, 1996).

Cardinality is one of the most frequently neglected aspects of counting instruction, and its role may not be appreciated explicitly by teachers or parents (Linnell & Fluck, 2001). *Develop subitizing ability first for small numbers* (Paliwal & Baroody, 2020). Then use the "How Many in a Hand?" approach, which was designed to emphasize the ordinal-cardinal connection in several ways. In addition, when observing children, teachers are often satisfied by accurate enumeration and do not ask children "how many?" following enumeration. Use this question when teaching and assessing to help prompt children to make the count to cardinal transition. Have them count first and then ask them how many (Paliwal & Baroody, 2020). Seek to understand your children's conceptualizations and the benefits of discussing counting and its purposes and creating opportunities for both adult- and child-generated situations that require counting.

To develop these concepts and skills, children need extensive experience in contexts where they have to know "how many." Parents may ask, "How many?", but only as a request to enumerate, *not* to address the count-to-cardinal transition (Fluck, 1995; Fluck & Henderson, 1996). Expert teachers notice that difference—and that makes a big difference (Anantharajan, 2020). Then they engage children in activities such as those in Table 3.2, which emphasize the cardinal value of the counted collection. The activities demand that the cardinality be known, and some of the activities hide the objects so the request to tell "how many" will not be misinterpreted as a request to recount the collection.

Many teachers and parents use counting books, but many have problems. The books give children limited opportunity to learn the number 0 and numbers beyond 10, as well as limited exposure to multiple representations of number (number words, "twenty"; numerals, "20"; and quantities, 20 pictures) necessary to build strong number understanding and counting skills. *Use high-quality books* (see a list in [LT]^2's Resources).

An important caution: Children can learn counting *procedures* without the critical concepts. For example, they may identify that skipping an object or starting a count with 2 or 3 (on the first object) are "incorrect" but still maintain that the last number word tells how many in the set (Nunes et al., 2015). *Don't assume* that counting behaviors indicate understanding, *engage in math talk to assess and develop those meaningful concepts.*

Research from the field (Baroody, 1996; Baroody & Purpura, 2017) and from the Building Blocks project suggests the following teaching strategies are useful when children make errors. See Box 3.1.

Box 3.1 Teaching Strategies for Specific Counting Errors

- *One-to-one errors (includes keeping-track-of-what's-been-counted errors)*: Emphasize the importance of accuracy and encourage the children to count slowly and carefully to "count each item exactly once." When relevant, explain a keeping-track strategy. If moving objects is possible and desirable in the activity, suggest the strategy of moving items to a different pile or location. Otherwise, explain making a verbal plan, such as "Go from top to bottom. Start from the top and count every one"–then carry out the plan together.If the children return and re-count objects (e.g., in a circular arrangement):

- Stop and tell them they counted that item already. Suggest that they start on one they can remember (e.g., one at the "top" or "the corner" or "the blue one"–whatever makes sense in the activity; if there is no identifier, highlight an item in some way).

- Ask the children to click on items as they count in the computer activity "Kitchen Counter" (see Table 3.2, p. 36), providing highlighting to the object, marking it. If they click on a highlighted item, the character immediately says they counted that item already.Playing board games, if children start counting the space their token starts on as "one" or make other one-to-one errors:

- Stop and remind them that they are counting *jumps*–move the token with them making an exaggerated jump as you count "onnnnne..." and so forth.

- Tell children that they (their token) is on zero. Say "zero" and then make the jump and say "one" and so forth.

- Help children realize that if they are "passing" another player, they have to count the space the other player's token occupies.

- Use straight paths rather than long, curved paths and, if necessary, give each child their own game board.

- Have children count out, or produce, counters (disks) for the number they rolled and place them on the path ahead of their token, *then* move the token to the last counter.

- For the easiest game, have students count out, or produce, counters (disks) for the number they rolled and fill the spaces on their own game board, organized into a grid, such as two rows of five (Moomaw, 2015).

Cardinality (the "how many?" rule) errors: Ask the children to re-count. Demonstrate the cardinality rule on the collection. That is, count the collection, pointing to each item in turn, stretch out the last counting word ("One, two, three, four, fiiiivvve") then gesture at them all, saying, "Five in all!" (Note: You have to count and then say how many in the set–doing one or the other doesn't help, Baroody & Purpura, 2017.) Demonstrate the cardinality rule on a small (subitizable) collection in an easily recognizable arrangement (see the Snapshots activities in

Chapter 2). Use the "How many in my Hand?" activity in [LT]² at the level Counter (Small Numbers).

- *Cardinality errors (production tasks—knowing when to stop)*: Remind the children of the goal number and ask to re-count. Count the collection, say that is not the requested number, and ask the children to try again. If there were too few, count the existing collection quickly and ask the children to put on another object, saying when that has been done, "And that makes—." Allow the children to add more than one as long as this does not exceed a total. If there were too many, ask the children to remove one or more items, and then re-count. So, count the existing collection quickly and say, "There are too many. Take some away so that we have—." Demonstrate.
- *Guided counting sequence (when the above are not sufficient)*: Ask the children to count out loud as they point to each object. Suggest a keeping-track strategy if necessary. If there are still errors after this remediation, say, "Count with me," and name the keeping-track strategy you will model. Have the children point to each item and say the correct counting word, thus walking the children through the counting. Demonstrate the cardinality rule—repeat the last counting number, gesture in a circular motion to all the items, and say, "That's how many there are in all." For "Counter to" activities, emphasize the goal number, saying, "[Five!] That's what we wanted!"
- *Skip Counting*:

  Say: "Try again." (*Remind them of the goal number.*)
  Say: "Count with me. Count by [tens]." (*If you are counting items, move the appropriate amount with each count.*)
  Say: "Count by [tens] like this: (*demonstrate*). Now, count with me."

Solving Problems and Counting Strategies

Why count? To find out how many. *Why*? Too often, children do it because someone asked them to! Much more meaningful, and educationally powerful, is to count to solve problems. Some involve only object counting, such as "Get Just Enough" activities, for example, in which children count the number of children at their table and get that many napkins (see [LT]² Producer (Small Numbers) and Counter and Producer (10+)). But even here, *there is a purpose for counting*. Further, there is *natural feedback*—if you counted correctly, when you return to the table, you can give everyone exactly one napkin and have none left over.

Children should especially count when there is a purpose for counting. Asking children to get you four pens, and so on, are situations that emphasize awareness of plurality, a particular cardinal goal, and the activity of counting. In this way, most counting tasks should emphasize the situation and goal and the cardinal result of counting, not just the procedures of counting (Steffe & Cobb, 1988). How many chairs are at the table (so how many kids can sit there)? How many kids are at the block center?

Of course, children love to count even when adults do not (quite!) see the purpose. They love to count how many steps they climb and especially how many times they can "do something"—such as keeping a ball in the air by hitting it up to each other. How many blocks can we count? How many bricks in that wall? One study indicated that collaborative counting, in which pairs of kindergartners counted a set of materials, contributed to individual cognitive progress by allowing an expansion of the range and sophistication of the children's strategies, such as a heightened explicit awareness of the need to keep track of one's counting acts when counting items of a hidden collection (Wiegel, 1998). An important feature of the tasks was that they were designed on a research-based developmental progression of counting.

Similarly, Japanese preschools teach children counting and other math effectively by embedding it in everyday activities, such as signing, arts and crafts, taking attendance, and exercising. The following is an example involving crafts (many more are in the article).

The teacher walks around the classroom distributing red strips of paper (crab feet) to each child. The teacher asks the children, "How many feet are each of you supposed to receive? Please count the number of crab feet that you have received." One boy reports to the teacher, "I have eight!" and confirms this by counting the feet one by one, "one, two, three...eight." ... After all children have received their materials, the teacher addresses the whole class: "Well, let me ask you. Who has five feet? Who has six?" Only a few children hold up their hands. When the teacher asks, "Who has eight?" many children cheerfully raise their hands...

(Sakakibara, 2014, p. 22)

Critical however, is this author's concluding statement: "the teacher must be sensitive to the children's current state of mathematical development" (Sakakibara, 2014, p. 24). *Everyday activities will not effectively teach math unless learning trajectories and the children's levels of thinking are known and used.* Once you do know the levels, though, talk math! At home and especially at school, the more math talk you engage in the better children do in counting, including at more advanced levels (Ramani, Rowe, Eason, & Leech, 2015).

Approaches to math education differ for East Asian countries other than Japan. In China, teaching math is planned and intentional (Li, Chi, DeBey, & Baroody, 2015). For example, compared to 27% of U.S. teachers who did not set any goals and 20% who did not use a curriculum or any resources for math, only 3% of Chinese teachers were in these categories.

The following section also emphasizes counting for a *reason* and developing *counting strategies*. As mentioned, more on teaching counting strategies is provided in the next couple of chapters.

Language, Numbers, and Object Counting

Subitizing and counting rely on careful and sustained application of number words. Seeing multiple examples of the same number that differ in all aspects except numerosity, and nonexamples, is particularly helpful (Baroody et al., 2006).

Similarly, using *numerals* ("1" or "4") meaningfully helps children develop number concepts. Children may begin to use written representations for number as early as 3 years of age or as late as 6 years, depending on the home and preschool environments (Baroody et al., 2005). Number and numeral games such as "Tins" are motivating for children and emphasize representations of number. A different number of objects is placed in each of four covered tins, which are scrambled. The child must find the tin with the number of objects the teacher states. Soon after introducing the game, the teacher introduces a new feature: Children can write on sticky notes to help themselves find the correct tin (Hughes, 1986). Children can use iconic representations or, better, numerals.

Indeed, several curricula use games of various types to develop counting abilities in young children (see Chapter 15). Children as young as 3 years of age can successfully play such games with peers after they have been introduced by an adult (Curtis, 2005). Instruction in counting and naming numerals can help children transfer their knowledge to other areas, such as addition and subtraction (but may not transfer to other skills such as comparison, Malofeeva, Day, Saco, Young, & Ciancio, 2004). Therefore, include "racing" or board games and other activities in your counting learning trajectory (see also Chapter 4).

Are such board games useful because "children practice counting"? Yes, but that is *not* their most important contribution. Consider all that happens when a child rolls a five on a die. They first have to count (or subitize) the dots (or read and understand the numeral "5" if that is the cube they are using). Then they have to move that many, counting the *jumps*, not the spaces (about a third of children incorrectly count the space they start on as "one," Moomaw, 2015). They have to stop when they reach five jumps. *Also, consider how that experience differs if they roll a three.* They see and count fewer dots for three than five. They jump fewer times. They move a shorter distance on the path, and all this takes less time. *That's a powerful set of experiences comparing five to three.* Children not only count different things (dots and jumps) but build *intuitive relationships between quantities of five and quantities of three.* So, again include "racing" or board games and other activities in your counting learning trajectory and encourage families to play them as well.

Two more tips. First, if you are working in small groups, and can provide substantial scaffolding to children, consider *Race to Space* at the Mental Number Line to 10 (and 100) level(s) of the Comparing LT as an introduction to games using a straight path. Second, *please see the resource, "Introducing and Using Games" on* [LT]².

Computer activities are another effective approach (Moyer-Packenham et al., 2015). After introducing numerals with games similar to "Tins," the computer activities can ask children to respond to questions by clicking on a numeral (numerals are written on "cards" that initially have fives-and-tens frame dot representations as well), or read a numeral to know what size collection to produce (see computer activities on [LT]²). Children using these and other activities outperformed comparison groups that also were taught numerals (Clements & Sarama, 2007a). For kindergartners and older children, the use of Logo activities has a similar facilitative effect on the use of numerals, including connecting them to quantitative concepts (Clements, Battista, & Sarama, 2001; Clements & Meredith, 1993).

There are four pedagogically significant characteristics of these activities. First, the symbols have a quantitative meaning that children understand, and they build upon verbal representations. Second, children create their own representations initially. Third, the symbols are useful in the context of the activity. Fourth, children can translate from the situation to the symbols and back again.

Written numerals can play a valuable role in focusing children on representing and reflecting on numbers. The use of symbols with understanding may have an impact on number concepts through its role in providing a common cognitive model that facilitates communication about number, especially between young children and older people, and possibly in becoming part of the child's cognitive model of number (Munn, 1998). However, children probably should have considerable experience with concrete situations and verbal problem solving with numerical operations, such as adding and subtracting, before relying on symbols as the sole communicative tool. Slow, informal, meaningful uses in pre-K are more effective than traditional school methods, which lead to procedural approaches with less quantitative meaning (Munn, 1998).

Therefore, help children explicitly connect verbal and written symbols to each other and to "sensory-concrete" (see p. 380 in Chapter 16) quantitative situations. Encourage them to use numerals as symbols *of* situations and symbols *for* reasoning. The emphasis should always be on thinking mathematically, using symbols to do so when appropriate.

Teaching Zero

Education can make a difference in children's learning of zero. For example, one university preschool, compared to others, increased children's development of idea about zero by one full year (Wellman & Miller, 1986). Because situations and problems involving zero are often solved differently by young children (Evans, 1983), specific use of the term "zero" and the symbol "0," connected to the development of the concept—discussions of real-world knowledge of "nothing" or the number in set with no elements—should begin early. Activities might include counting backward to zero, naming collections with zero (a time for the motivation of silliness, such as the number of elephants in the room), subtracting concrete objects to produce such collections, and discussing zero as the smallest whole number (non-negative integer). Eventually, such activities can lead to a simple generalized rule, such as adding zero does not change the value, and an integration of their knowledge of zero with knowledge of other numbers. Remember Dawn's SETSPEED 0, which was a powerful educational experience.

Learning Trajectory for Counting

The learning trajectory for counting is more complex than that for subitizing in Chapter 2. First, there are many conceptual and skill advancements that make levels more complicated. Second, there are *subtrajectories* within counting. That is, the three subtrajectories for counting are verbal counting, object counting, and counting strategies. These are related but can develop somewhat independently. For example, if a child was taught and asked by her parents only to count verbally, she may be well advanced in verbal counting ("I can count to 300!") but not skilled in counting objects with understanding. Most of the levels deal with counting objects (and thus are not labeled further), but those that are mainly verbal counting skills are labeled "*Verbal*," and those that tend to begin as mainly verbal skills but also can be applied to object counting situations are labeled "*Verbal and Object*." Those labeled "*Strategy*" are particularly important in supporting comparison (Chapter 4) and arithmetic skills and become increasingly integrated with (even identical to) the arithmetic strategies described in Chapter 5 (counting is a main predictor of children's arithmetic competence; see Passolunghi, Vercelloni, & Schadee, 2007; Spaepen et al., 2018; Stock, Desoete, & Roeyers, 2009).

The importance of the *goal* of increasing children's ability to count verbally, count objects meaningfully, and learn increasingly sophisticated counting strategies is clear. See Table 3.1, which describes the standards from the CCSSM, but also *remember to see how CCSSM, ELOF, and many other standards and assessments align with the learning trajectories, use the alignment tool in* [LT]². Notice that *learning trajectories not only give far more details for each level*, but they also provide *levels in between* those of the standards—essential for guiding children's educational experiences.

Table 3.1 Goals for Counting the Common Core State Standards (CCSSM)

Counting and Cardinality (K.CC in CCSSM)

Know number names and the count sequence.

1. Count to 100 by ones and by tens.
2. Count forward beginning from a given number within the known sequence (instead of having to begin at 1).
3. Write numbers from 0 to 20. Represent a number of objects with a written numeral 0–20 (with 0 representing a count of no objects).

Count to tell the number of objects.

1. Understand the relationship between numbers and quantities; connect counting to cardinality.

   (a)   When counting objects, say the number names in the standard order, pairing each object with one and only one number name and each number name with one and only one object.
   (b)   Understand that the last number name said tells the number of objects counted. The number of objects is the same regardless of their arrangement or the order in which they were counted.
   (c)   Understand that each successive number name refers to a quantity that is one larger.

2. Count to answer "how many?" questions about as many as 20 things arranged in a line, a rectangular array, or a circle, or as many as ten things in a scattered configuration; given a number from 1–20, count out that many objects.

Measurement and Data (K.MD in CCSSM)

Classify objects and count the number of objects in each category.

1. Classify objects into given categories; count the numbers of objects in each category and sort the categories by count. [Limit category counts to be less than or equal to 10.]

Operations and Algebraic Thinking (1.OA in CCSSM)

Add and subtract within 20.

1. Relate counting to addition and subtraction (e.g., by counting on 2 to add 2).
2. Add and subtract within 20, demonstrating fluency for addition and subtraction within 10. Use strategies such as counting on; making ten (e.g., $8 + 6 = 8 + 2 + 4 = 10 + 4 = 14$); decomposing a number leading to a ten (e.g., $13 + 4 = 13 + 3 + 1 = 10 + 1 = 9$); using the relationship between addition and subtraction (e.g., knowing that $8 + 4 = 12$, one knows $12 + 8 = 4$); and creating equivalent but easier or known sums (e.g., adding $6 + 7$ by creating the known equivalent $6 + 6 + 1 = 12 + 1 = 13$).

Number and Operations in Base Ten (1.NBT in CCSSM)

(Continued)

Table 3.1 (Cont).

Extend the counting sequence.

1. Count to 120, starting at any number less than 120. In this range, read and write numerals and represent a number of objects with a written numeral.

Operations and Algebraic Thinking (2.OA in CCSSM) Work with equal groups of objects to gain foundations for multiplication.

2. Determine whether a group of objects (up to 20) has an odd or even number of members, e.g., by pairing objects or counting them by twos; write an equation to express an even number as a sum of two equal addends.

Number and Operations in Base Ten (2.NDT in CCSSM) Understand place value.

3. Count within 1,000; skip count by fives, tens, and hundreds.

With those as the goals, Table 3.2 provides the two additional components of the learning trajectory, the developmental progression and the instructional tasks. (Note that the ages in all the learning trajectory tables are only approximate, especially because the age of acquisition usually depends heavily on experience.)

Table 3.2 Learning Trajectory for Counting

Age (years)	Developmental Progression	Instructional Activities

1	**Number Word Sayer:** **Foundations** *Verbal* No verbal counting.
	
	Names some number words with no sequence.
		Number Talk, [LT]²: Associate number words with quantities (see the initial levels of the "Recognition of Number and Subitizing" learning trajectory in Chapter 2 and [LT]²) and as components of the counting sequence.
		    Diez Amigos Finger Play and *Two Little Butterflies Finger Play*, [LT]²: Finger plays like this one are a fun way to teach children about counting and numbers.
		    Counting Books (Foundation), [LT]²: Books help build familiarity with counting words and beginning concepts.

1–2	**Chanter** *Verbal* Chants number words in "sing-song" fashion and may run them together. The number words may be indistinguishable from one another ("onetwothree," Fuson, 1988).
	    May begin a nonverbal object "counting" such as copying an adult's item-by-item placement of objects (Sella et al., 2016).
	
	After watching an adult put one to six 'food tokens' into an animal puppet, imitates the puppet-feeding with attention to number.
		Verbal counting, songs, finger plays, and more: Repeated experience with the counting sequence in varied context. This can include songs; finger plays, such as "This Old Man"; counting going up and down stairs; and just verbal counting for the fun of it (how high can you go?)!
		    Counting with Maracas and More, [LT]²: Use maracas or other percussion instruments to support the development of number concepts and counting.
		    Feel the Beat, [LT]²: Children count beyond the numbers they already know while doing a variety of rhythmic motions as they count.

"LMNOP"

(Continued)

Table 3.2 (Cont).

Age (years)	Developmental Progression	Instructional Activities
2	**Reciter** *Verbal* Verbally counts with distinct words, not necessarily in the correct order above "five." "One, two, three, four, five, seven." If knows more number words than number of objects, rattles them off quickly at the end; if more objects, "recycles" number words (inflexible list exhaustion). Uses number words ("My dad is 20 years.") Puts objects, actions, and words in many-to-one (age 1; 8; i.e., about 1 year, 8 months) or overly rigid one-to-one correspondence (age 2; 6).	*Acting Out Songs and Finger Plays*, [LT]²: Children act out songs as they sing along to practice counting groups of objects/animals. See *When I Was One* in [LT]². *Catch the Mistake (to 5)*, [LT]²: The teacher asks the children to help a puppet, Mr. MixUp, correct his verbal counting mistakes.
3	**Reciter (10)** *Verbal* Verbally counts to ten with *some* correspondence with objects but may either continue an overly rigid correspondence or exhibit performance errors (e.g., skipping, double counting). "One [points to first], two [points to second], three [starts to point], four [finishes pointing, but is now still pointing to third object], five, … nine, ten, eleven, twelve, 'firteen,' fifteen …" Asked for 5, counts out 3, saying, "one, two, *five*."	*Note*: All the activities from the previous levels can be adapted for this level by counting to 10. Also, see [LT]² for finger plays and songs (*Baker's Truck, This Old Man*). *Count, Clap, and Stomp*, [LT]²: Have all children count from 1 to 10 or an appropriate number, making motions with each count. For example, say, "one" [touch head], "two" [touch shoulders], "three" [touch head], etc.

	Corresponder Keeps one-to-one correspondence between counting words and objects (one word for each object), at least for small groups of objects laid in a line.
	
	  • • • •
	"1, 2, 3, 4"
	
	May answer a "how many?" question by re-counting the objects or violate 1-1 or word order to make the last number word be the desired or predicted word.
		Rhythmic Counting (Corresponder), [LT]²: Children count using different rhythms and movements for each count. This is similar to earlier verbal counting activities *but* move *slowly and deliberately* so the children *do* maintain the correspondence.
		   Simon Says, [LT]²: Children play *Simon Says* with every command involving a number (tap your head three times). The game also develops the executive function of inhibition.
		   Ding Clink Bam, [LT]²: Children practice one-to-one correspondence by counting to the chimes of a xylophone or another repeated sound.
		   Counting Wand (Corresponder), [LT]²: Children use a counting wand to count the number of children in a group, focusing on the one-to-one correspondence.
		   Kitchen Counter: In this Building Blocks activity, children click on objects one at a time while the numbers from 1 to 10 are counted aloud. For example, they click on pieces of food and a bite is taken out of each as it is counted.

(Continued)

Table 3.2 (Cont).

Age (years)	Developmental Progression	Instructional Activities

4	**Counter (Small Numbers)** Accurately counts objects in a line to 5 and answers the "how many" question with the last number counted, understanding that this represents the total number of objects (the cardinal principle).
	
	• • • •
	"1, 2, 3, 4 ... *four!*"
		How Many in My Hand? See pp. 6-7 and [LT]². *This relies on subitizing so make sure subitizing of small numbers is developed first* (Paliwal & Baroody, 2020).
		    Shake Them Up, [LT]²: Children predict whether the number of counters stays the same when they are hidden in a bag.
		    Cubes in Boxes, [LT]²: Have the child count a small set of cubes. Put them in the box and close the lid. Then ask the child how many cubes you are hiding. If the child is ready, have him/her write the numeral (otherwise, write it yourself) on a sticky note and label the box. Dump them out and count together to check. Repeat with two boxes and two different sets. After both are labeled, ask children to "Find the box with three cubes." Say "Three! Ta-da!" once the correct box is opened.
		    Which Color Is Missing?, [LT]²: Assign each child in a small group a different color. Have each choose *five* crayons of that color. Once they have checked each other, have them put their crayons into the same large container. Then choose one child to be the "sneaky mouse." With everyone's eyes closed, the sneaky mouse secretly takes out one crayon and hides it. The other children have to count their crayons to see which color the mouse has hidden.
		    Help the Turtle Get Home: Counter (Small Numbers), see [LT]²: Students identify number amounts (from 1 through 5) on a die (physical game board) or dot frame (computer version shown here) and move forward a corresponding number of spaces on a game board. *Always play every board game off-computer, too.*
		    Option: Make a cube with *shapes* on it and children count the sides of the shapes.
		
		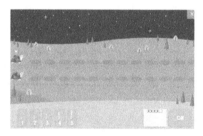
		
		    Mr. MixUp (Counter (Small Numbers)), [LT]²: Mr. MixUp makes a lot of counting mistakes such as saying the wrong word for "how many" after counting; children help Mr. MixUp by catching his mistake.
		    Note: See [LT]² for many more activities.

	Counter (10) Counts arrangements of objects to 10 with understanding of the cardinal principle. May be able to read and write numerals to represent 1-10.	*Note:* [LT]² has many more activities than just those listed here. *Counting Towers (Up to 10),* [LT]²: A day before, read *Shape Space.* Ask what shapes work well in which part of a tower (e.g., would the "tip on the triangle

(Continued)

Table 3.2 (Cont).

Age (years)	Developmental Progression	Instructional Activities
	Accurately counts a line of nine blocks and says there are nine. May be able to tell the number just after or just before another number, but only by counting up from 1. What comes after 4? "1, 2, 3, 4, 5. *Five!*" Verbal counting to 20 is developing.	block" make it a good base?). Set up stations with different objects to stack. Encourage children to stack *as many as they can*, and to *count them to see how many they stacked*.  *Counting Books*: Read good counting books, such as *Anno's Counting Book* by Mitsumasa Anno. Ask children if they ever count how many blocks they can stack in a tower. Have children work at a station and build a tower as high as they can. Ask them to estimate how many blocks are in their tower. Count the blocks with them before they knock it down. Try to get a larger number in the tower. Read *One Was Johnny* by Maurice Sendak. Talk about how the room is getting crowded, because when you count each number, one more is added to the room (and then subtracted later in the book). Act out the story with groups of children. *Counting Jar (Counter 10)*, [LT][2]: A "counting jar" holds a specified number of items for children to count without touching the items. Use the same jar all year, changing its small amount of items weekly. Have children spill out the items to count them. They may wish to write and post their count on sticky notes. *Help the Turtle Get Home: Counter (10)*, [LT][2]: Students play a board game up to 10 with a friend (on the [LT][2] computer activity with a friend or the computer).  *Dino Shop 1*: Students identify the numeral that represents a target number of dinosaurs in a number frame.

(*Continued*)

Table 3.2 (Cont).

Age (years)	Developmental Progression	Instructional Activities

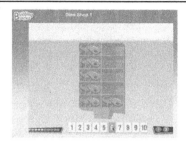

Concentrate!: Counting Cards to Counting Cards 1-6, [LT][2]: Children match counting cards (each with a numeral and corresponding dot cluster) within the framework of a "Concentration" card game. Notice children have to say if they match or not, unlike many computer games that just encourage random clicking because the computer decides! Also play these games off-computer.

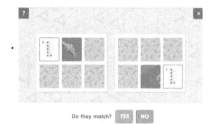

Concentrate: Tens Frame to Numeral 1-6, [LT][2]: Similar game, now matching dots to numerals. Rewards include a filled-in picture.

Number Line Race: Give children number lines of different colors. Player 1 rolls a die and asks the banker for that many counters. The banker gives that number and Player 1 places the counters in order along his/her number line while counting. S/he then moves his/her playing piece along the counters, counting out loud again, until the piece is on the last counter. Ask children who are closest to the goal, and how they know it. *Note*: [LT][2] has many more activities than just those listed here.

Producer (Small Numbers) Counts out objects to 5. Recognizes that counting is

(Continued)

Age (years)	Developmental Progression	Instructional Activities
	relevant to situations in which a certain number must be placed. Produces a group of four objects.	*Number Moves*, [LT]²: While waiting during transitions, have children count how many times you jump, clap, or some other motion. Then have them do those motions the same number of times. Initially, count the actions with children. Later, do the motions but model and explain how to count silently. Children who understand how many motions will stop, but others will continue doing the motions. *Help the Turtle Get Home: Producer (Small Numbers)*, [LT]²: Building on the earlier computer activities, children have to move the turtle to a space, which helps give them the idea of producing a set.  *Cookie Game–Math Plus!*, [LT]², a special activity that also develops executive function, see [LT]² for many more details: Children play in pairs. Player 1 rolls a number cube and puts that many toppings (counters) on his/her plate. Player 1 asks Player 2, "Am I right?" Player 2 must agree that Player 1 is correct. At that point, Player 1 moves the counters to the circular spaces for chocolate chips on his/her cookie. Players take turns until all the spaces on their cookies are filled.  *Shopkeeper Fill Orders to 5*, [LT]²: One child is the shopkeeper, while the other children come to the shop to purchase items with play money. The shopkeeper matches the order by giving each shopper the correct number of items.
5	**Counter and Producer** (**10**+) Counts and counts out objects accurately to 10, then beyond (to about 30). Has explicit understanding of cardinality (how numbers tell how many). Keeps track of objects that have and have not been counted, even in different arrangements. Writes or draws to represent 1 to 10 (then, 20, then 30).	*Note*: [LT]² includes three *"Math Plus!"* activities for this level. These are rich, multiple-session activities that promote math at this level *and* executive function. They are worth a close look: 1 *Cookie Game–Math Plus!*, [LT]² 2 *Magician's Trick–Math Plus! !*, [LT]² 3 *Change Game–Math Plus! !*, [LT]²

Table 3.2 (Cont).

Age (years)	Developmental Progression	Instructional Activities
	Counts a scattered group of 19 chips, keeping track by moving each one as they are counted.	*Knock It Down (Beyond 10)*, [LT][2]: (See basic directions above.) To allow children to count to 20 and beyond, have them make towers with other objects, such as coins. Children build a tower as high as they can, placing more coins, but not straightening coins already in the tower. The goal is to estimate and then count to find out how many coins are in your tallest tower. To count higher, have children make pattern "walls." They build a pattern block wall as long as they can. This allows them to count to higher numbers.
	Gives next number (usually to 20s or 30s). Separates the decade and the ones part of a number word and begins to relate each part of a number word/numeral to the quantity to which it refers.	
	Recognizes errors in others' counting *and* can eliminate most errors in own counting (point-object) if asked to try hard.	Variations:

<u>Variations:</u>

1   Pairs can play a game in which they take turns placing coins.
2   Roll a number cube to determine how many coins to put on the tower.
3   Adopt this activity to any number of settings. For example, how many cans of food, such as soup (or other heavy objects) can two children hold when each holds two corners of a towel? Repeat this with very large or small cans. With your guidance, they could also try to make a tower of the cans (ordering them by size, with the largest on the bottom).

Number Jump with Numerals: Hold up a numeral card and have children first say the numeral. Together, children do a motion you pick (such as jump, nod head, or clap) that number of times. Repeat with different numerals. Be sure to use 0 (zero).
Mr. MixUp Counting: Use a somewhat goofy puppet called "Mr. MixUp."

(Continued)

Table 3.2 (Cont).

Age (years)	Developmental Progression	Instructional Activities
		Tell children that Mr. MixUp frequently makes mistakes. Ask children to help Mr. MixUp count. They listen to Mr. MixUp, catch his mistake, correct him, and then count with him to help him "get it right." Have Mr. MixUp make mistakes such as the following, in approximately this developmental order: *Verbal counting mistakes* Wrong order (1, 2, 3, 5, 4, 6) Skipping numbers (...12, 14, 16, 17) Repeat numbers (...4, 5, 6, 7, 7, 8) *Object counting mistakes* One-to-one mistakes, such as skipping objects; count-point, i.e., saying one number word but pointing twice or vice versa (but points are 1-1 with objects); point-object, i.e., pointing once but indicating more than one object or pointing more than once to one object (but counting words are 1-1 with pointing) *Cardinality/Last number mistakes* Saying the wrong number as the "final count" (e.g., counting three objects, counting "1, 2, 3 [correctly, but then saying], there's 4 there!") *Keeping-track-of-what's-been-counted mistakes* Double counting, i.e. "coming back" and counting an item again. Skipping objects when counting objects not in a line. *Concentrate* [LT]²: Children match different representations of number, on-computer (pictured here) and off. There are *Concentrate* games at this level: ççç and *Tens Frame to Domino Patterns 1-12*.

Concentrate: Counting Cards to Counting Cards 1-12   Concentrate: Tens Frame to Numeral 1-12   Concentrate: Tens Frame to Domino Patterns 1-12

Age (years)	Developmental Progression	Instructional Activities
	Counter Backward from 10 *Verbal and Object* Counts backward from 10 to 1, verbally, or when removing objects from a group. "10, 9, 8, 7, 6, 5, 4, 3, 2, 1!"	*Count and Move—Forward and Backward*: Have all children count from 1 to 10 or an appropriate number, making motions with each count, and then count backward to zero. For example, they start in a crouch, then stand up—bit by bit—as they count up to 10. Then they count backward to zero (sitting all the way down). *Blast Off!*: Children stand and count backward from 10 or an appropriate number, crouching down a bit with each count. After reaching zero, they jump up yelling, "Blast off!" See the similar activities, all on [LT]², such as *Growth Spurt, Blooming Flowers*, and others. *Countdown Game*, [LT]² : Children play a version of "Duck, Duck, Goose" by counting down from 5, then 10. *No More Monkeys Jumping on the Bed!*: The classic finger play, from 5, but also down from 10. *Magician's Trick—Math Plus!*, [LT]²: Focus on counting backwards.
6	**Counter from *N* (*N* + 1, *N* − 1)** *Verbal and Object* Counts verbally and with objects from numbers other than 1 (but does not yet keep track of the *number* of counts).	*How Many in the Box Now?* [LT]²: Have the children count objects as you place them in a box. Ask, "How many are in the box now?" Add one, repeating the question, and have children think-pair-share (see

(Continued)

Table 3.2 (Cont).

Age (years)	Developmental Progression	Instructional Activities
	Asked to "count from 5 to 8," counts "5, 6, 7, 8!" Immediately determines numbers just after or just before. Asked, "What comes just before 7?" says, "Six!"	Chapter 2, p. 24). Then check the children's responses by counting all the objects. Repeat, checking occasionally. (See also, *How Many Now? Sneaky Swiper* in [LT]².) <u>Variations</u>: Place coins in a coffee can. Declare that a given number of objects is in the can. Then have the children close their eyes and count on by listening as additional objects are dropped in. *I'm Thinking of a Number*: Using counting cards, choose and hide a secret number. Tell children you hid a card with a number and ask them to guess which it is. When a child guesses correctly, excitedly reveal the card. Until then, tell children whether a guess is more or less than the secret number. As children become more comfortable, ask why they made their guess, say "I knew 4 was more than the secret number and 2 was less, so I guessed 3!" Repeat, adding clues, such as your guess is two more than my number. Do this activity during transitions.  *Magician's Trick–Math Plus!*, [LT]²: See Chapter 4. *Build Stairs*: Build stairs with connecting cubes first, then have children close their eyes and hide one. Children identify the missing step. 

Table 3.2 (Cont).

Age (years)	Developmental Progression	Instructional Activities
	Skip Counter by tens to 100 *Verbal and Object* Skips counts by tens up to 100 or beyond with understanding; e.g., "sees" groups of ten within a quantity and counts those groups by ten (this relates to multiplication and algebraic thinking; see Chapters 7 and 13). "10, 20, 30 … 100."	*Skip Counting Ourselves*, [LT]²: Children, one at a time, raise their arms above their head while the class chorally yells, "two" (then four, six …). Repeat showing one hand at a time for skip counting by fives (or both hands simultaneously for skip counting by tens). *Busy Beaver 10s*, [LT]²: Children count by tens to 100 using bundles of ten sticks.
	Counter to 100 *Verbal* Counts to 100. Makes decade transitions (e.g., from 29 to 30) starting at any number. "… 78, 79 … <u>80</u>, 81 …"	*Count the Days of School*, [LT]²: Each day of school, add a numeral to adding machine tape, taped to the wall, which will eventually surround the classroom. Count from 1 each day and then add that day's numeral. Write the multiples of 10 in red. Some days (e.g., on day 33), count just these red numerals—10, 20, 30 … and then continue with the final "ones"—31, 32, 33. Count the red numbers two ways: "ten, twenty, thirty, forty …" *and*, sometimes, as "one ten, two tens, three tens, four tens." *Numbers with Pizzazz (to 100)*, [LT]²: Children practice skip counting by tens, counting by ones, and counting on from any number, both with and without a hundreds chart. *Number Flip (to 100)*, [LT]²: Children count forward and backward through the decade transitions as they flip numeral cards in sequence.
	Counter On Using Patterns *Strategy* Keeps track of counting acts, but only by using numerical patterns (spatial, auditory, or rhythmic) for adding 1 to about 3. "How much is 3 more than 5?" Child feels three "beats" as they count, "5 … 6, 7, 8!"	*How Many in the Box Now? (Patterns)*, [LT]²: Main directions above, but now add 2, 3, or even 4. Repeat this type of counting activity in a variety of settings, adding more objects at a time (starting with 0 to 3). Use story settings for the problems; for example, sharks eating small fish (children can be "sharks" eating actual fish crackers at the snack table), toy cars and trucks parking on a parking ramp, a superhero throwing bandits in jail, etc. *Teacher Suggestion*: Act incredulous, saying, "How do you *know* that? You can't even *see* them?" Have children explain. *Teaching Note*: If they need help, suggest that children count and keep track using their fingers. *Help the Turtle Get Home: Counter On Using Patterns*: Students are given a numeral and a frame with dots. They count on from this numeral to identify the total amount, and then move forward a corresponding number of spaces on the game board.  *Follow Me*, [LT]²: Children follow teacher in counting up from a given number.

Age (years)	Developmental Progression	Instructional Activities

Skip Counter *Verbal and Object* Counts by fives and twos with understanding.

  Child counts objects, "2, 4, 6, 8 ... 30."

Counter On Keeping Track *Strategy* Counts forward or back from a given number keeping track of counting acts numerically, first using objects, then by "counting counts."

  How many is 3 more than 6? "6 ... 7 [puts up a finger], 8 [puts up another finger], 9 [puts up third finger]. 9." What is 8 take away 2? "8 ... 7 is one, and 6 is two. 6."

Skip Counting, [LT]^2: Besides counting by tens, count groups of objects with skip counting, such as pairs of shoes by twos, or number of fingers in the class by fives. See also *Skip Counting with Cubes*, [LT]^2.

Count on with Objects, [LT]^2: The teacher shows counters (say five), covers them, and puts out (say four) more. Children use counting strategies to continue counting on from a given number, at first by laying out four objects and counting up ("fiiivvvee ... 6, 7, 8, 9!"), then with mental counting strategies.

  Easy as Pie: On a (any) game board, using numeral cubes, students add two numerals to find a total number (sums of 1 through 10), and then move forward a corresponding number of spaces on a game board. The game encourages children to "count on" from the larger number (e.g., to add 3 to 4, they would count "4 ... 5, 6, 7!").

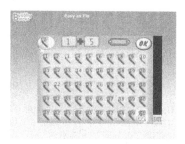

  Eggcellent: On a (any) game board, students use strategies to identify which two of three numbers, when added together, will enable them to reach the final space on a game board in the fewest number of moves. Often, that means the sum of the largest two numbers, but sometimes other combinations allow you to hit a positive or avoid a backward action space.

Counter of Quantitative Units/Place Value Understands the base-ten numeration system and place value concepts, including ideas of counting in units and multiples of hundreds, tens, and ones. When counting groups of ten, can decompose into 10 ones if that is useful.

How Many Eggs?, [LT]^2: Using plastic eggs that break into halves, show some whole eggs and some halves and ask "how many?" Repeat in "play store" settings, with different materials (e.g., crayons and broken crayons, and so forth).

  Buying Candy Bars (Counter of Quant), [LT]^2: Children use varying currencies ($1, $5, $10) to pretend to buy items.

(Continued)

Table 3.2 (Cont).

Age (years)	Developmental Progression	Instructional Activities
	Understands value of a digit according to the place of the digit within a number. Counts by tens and ones to determine the total. Counts unusual units, such as "wholes" when shown combinations of wholes and parts. Shown three whole plastic eggs and four halves, counts and says there are five whole eggs.	
	Counter Beyond 100 *Verbal and Object* Accurately counts beyond 100, recognizing the patterns of ones, tens, and hundreds. "After 159 comes 160 because after 5 tens comes 6 tens."	*Count the Days of School*, [LT]²: Extend the previous activity (p. 63). *Beavers and Sticks*, [LT]²: Children count bundles of sticks by ten past 100 emphasizing good decade and hundred transitions.
7	**Number Conserver** Consistently conserves number (i.e., believes number has been unchanged), even in face of perceptual distractions such as the spreading out of objects in a collection. Counts two rows that are laid out across from each other and says they are the same. Adult spreads out one row. Says, "Both still have the same number; one's just longer."	*The Tricky Fox*, [LT]²: Tell a story using stuffed animals. The fox is tricky and tells the other animals that they should take the row of food with the most—and he spreads one row out, but not the other, actually more numerous, row. Ask children how to avoid being tricked.

	Counter Forward and Back *Strategy* Counts "counting words" (single sequence or skip counts) in either direction. Recognizes that decades sequence mirrors single-digit sequence.
	
	What's 4 less than 63? "62 is 1, 61 is 2, 60 is 3, 59 is 4 ... so, 59."
	What is 15 more than 28? "2 tens and 1 ten is 3 tens. 38, 39, 40, and there's 3 more ... 43."
	
	Switches between sequence and composition views of multidigit numbers easily.
	
	Counts backward from 20 and higher with meaning.
		(*See Chapter 5 for most activities for this competence.*)
		    Adding Subtracting Hundreds Chart, [LT]²: Children use a "hundreds chart" to add (and later subtract) multidigit numbers using the structure of the hundreds chart and place value. (See full directions and materials on [LT]².)
		    Jumping on Number Line, [LT]²: Children use the "open number line" to count forward and back using place value. (See Chapter 5 and full directions and materials on [LT]².)
		    Figure the Fact: Students add numeric values from 1 through 10 to values from 0 through 99 to reach a maximum total of 100. That is, if they are "on" 33 and get an 8, they have to enter 41 to proceed to that space because the spaces are not marked with numerals, at least until they move through them.
		
		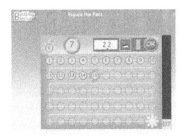
		
		Jumping on Number Line, [LT]²: Children use a number line to add (and later subtract) multidigit numbers.

We strongly recommend that you carefully read the learning trajectory in Table 3.2. Counting is a key competence, and these learning trajectory tables go far beyond simply "presenting activities." They summarize the *key knowledge* of the levels of thinking in counting and the tightly related instructional activities. Study the developmental progression and think about *why* each activity will help children develop each level of thinking.

Also, remember to go to our new tool, the *Learning and Teaching with Learning Trajectories* tool at LearningTrajectories.org. *We encourage you, as you read about each level, to go to* [LT]² *and see videos of children that illustrate that level of thinking and then see (and use!—when appropriate) the instructional activities that help children build that level of thinking.* There are many additional instructional activities on [LT]² as well.

Final Words

Counting is the first and most basic mathematical algorithm children learn. Early counting predicts later mathematic success and even later *reading* fluency (Koponen, Salmi, Eklund, & Aro, 2013). Every child should be helped to learn counting—in all its complex splendor—early and well (Geary et al., 2017). Remember, *advanced*, not basic, counting predicts later school success (Nguyen et al., 2016).

Subitizing and counting are the main ways children determine the number of a collection of objects. In many situations, they need to do more, including comparing, using number relationships, and place value (Chapter 4), as well as using counting *strategies* for arithmetic (Chapter 5).

Note

1 Research confirms recommended practice: Math education should start from the *earliest* years (Hojnoski, Caskie, & Miller Young, 2018).

4 Comparing, Ordering, and Estimating

Jeremy and his sister Jacie were arguing about who had more dessert. "She has more!" declared Jeremy. "I do not!" said Jacie, "We have the same." "No. See, I have one, two, three, four, and you have one, two, three, four, five." "Listen, Jeremy. One of my cookies broke in half. You can't count each half. If you're counting pieces, I could break all yours in half, then you would have *way* more than me. Put the two halves back together and count. One, two, three, four. Four! We have the same."

Jacie went on to argue that she would prefer one whole cookie to the two broken halves anyway, but that's another story. Which "count"—Jeremy's or Jacie's—do you think was better, and why? In what situations should you count separate things, and in what situations might that lead you astray?

Chapter 2 introduced the notion that children possess or develop some ability to compare amounts in the first year of life. However, accurately comparing can be challenging in many situations, especially those in which people might think of either discrete quantities (items countable with whole numbers) or continuous quantities (magnitudes that are divisible, such as length or the amount of matter, see Chapter 10, especially footnote 1), as in Jeremy and Jacie's cookie debate. In this chapter, we discuss comparing, and two closely related actions, ordering— in which one must compare multiple quantities to sequence them from least to greatest—and estimating discrete quantity, in which one must compare a quantity to a benchmark or an intuitive sense of a discrete number of objects (Chapters 10 and 11 discuss continuous quantity).

The Mathematics of Ordering Numbers and Ordinal Numbers

Ordering numbers is the process of determining which of two numbers is "larger than" the other. Formally, given two whole numbers a and b, b is defined as larger than a if, in counting (see Chapter 3) a precedes b. One relationship must pertain to any such two numbers: $a = b$, $a < b$, or $b < a$. *Equals* in this case means *equivalent*, that is, not necessarily "exactly the same" (some comparisons are equal in that sense, such as $6 = 6$), but at least equal in value ($4 + 2$ is equivalent in value to 6). This relationship of equivalence is *reflexive* (something equals itself, $x = x$), *symmetric* ($x = y$ means that $y = x$), and *transitive* (if $x = y$ and $y = z$ then $x = z$).

We can also define (and think about) ordering numbers on a "number line"—a line on which points are uniquely identified with numbers. This gives a geometric/spatial model for number. Usually, the number line is constructed with a horizontal straight line, with a point designated

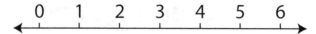

Figure 4.1 A section of a number line

as zero. To the right of 0, equally spaced points are labeled 1, 2, 3, 4 … such as on a ruler. The whole numbers are identified with these points (see Figure 4.1). The line segment from 0 to 1 is called the "unit segment" and the number 1 is called the "unit." Once we have determined this, all the whole numbers are fixed on the line (Wu, 2011b).

Thus, $a < b$ also means that the point a on the number line is to the left of b as we define the number line. Statements such as $a < b$ and $b > a$ are called "inequalities." When whole numbers are used to put items in order, or in a sequence, they are "ordinal numbers." Often, we use the ordinal terms "first, second, third …," but not always: A person who is "number 5" in a line is labeled by a word that is no less ordinal in its meaning because it is not expressed with the word "fifth."

Relating ordering numbers to counting (see Chapter 3), we can see that if a and b are whole numbers and b has more digits than a, then $a < b$ (so, 99 < 105). If a and b have the same number of digits, then moving from the left, if for the first digit in which they do not agree, a's digit $<$ b's digit, then $a < b$ (215 < 234).

The ability to use this type of reasoning explicitly develops over years, and, of course, children do not necessarily use the procedure we just described to do the comparisons. But they can and do learn a lot about comparing and ordering.

The Development of Comparing, Ordering, and Estimating

Comparing and Equivalence: Two Quantities

As we saw in Chapter 2, infants begin to construct relationships between numbers. For example, as long as the numbers differ enough (in a 1:2 or 2:3 ratio), the infants are sensitive and attracted to differences in large numbers. See this by watching the video in [LT]² from Libertus and Brannon's laboratory again in the Comparing Number learning trajectory at the "Comparison Senser: Foundations" level. Infants also build equivalence relations between very small sets, possibly by intuitively establishing correspondences, as early as the first year of life.

Later, they learn to compare the number of objects in two sets by matching them one to one. They also learn to explicitly tell which of two sets has more perceptually ("just by looking") as long as one set is considerably more than the other.

This ability develops considerably, especially as children learn number words, subitizing, and then counting. For example, they can explicitly compare sets as early as 2 or 3 years of age in certain everyday situations but show only the beginnings of such competence on teacher-given tasks at 2½ to 3½ years of age. They do this even before they count the sets with understanding (i.e., know the "cardinality principle" in Chapter 3) *if* they can recognize or subitize the numbers in the collections (Batchelor & Gilmore, 2015a). Most children learn to answer questions such as "Which is more, 6 or 4?" by age 4 or 5 years. All children must learn to reason that if the counts of two collections are 9 and 7, the collection with 9 has more *because* 9 comes later in the counting sequence than 7. The complexity of math thinking is highlighted in research that shows that in comparing sets of dots, the further apart they are, the faster people can say which is larger. But with numerals, they are faster if the numerals are closer, suggesting that people use different systems for these two types of comparisons (Mulligan et al., 2018).

On number conservation tasks that involve comparing two sets (see p. 36 of Chapter 3), even asking children to count the two sets may not help them determine the correct answer. Or, if children deal out items to two puppets, and the teacher counts out one set, they still may not know how many the other puppet has. Such tasks may overwhelm their "working memory," and children may not know how to use counting for comparisons. Only in the primary school grades do many children achieve success across such a wide range of tasks.

As we saw in previous chapters, both non-symbolic (e.g., comparing two sets of dots) and symbolic (comparing two number words such as "four" said out loud or symbols such as "4") comparison competencies are important for math learning. They support each other and help children learn other math competencies (Toll, Van Viersen, Kroesbergen, & Van Luit, 2015). However, of the two, the symbolic comparisons are more important and should be encouraged (rather than considered "developmentally inappropriate").

Another set of symbols that are often confused in later grades are relational symbols: =, <, and >. Equals (=) is sometimes understood with simple examples (4 = 4) but less often in more complicated number sentences (3 + 6 = _ - 5), which we will discuss in later arithmetic chapters. But the greater than (>) and less than (<) symbols challenge many people. Even teachers are confused by distractions; for example, which symbol to put between 4 and 6 (Hassidov & Ilany, 2017). People also get confused about "which way is the symbol supposed to go." Teachers often use the "mouth" metaphor (the "crocodile wants to eat the biggest number," so the mouth is open toward the bigger number, 4 < 6). We have two suggestions. First, research shows that children are far more accurate saying "4 is smaller than 6" or "6 is bigger" than placing the correct symbol between them. If *understanding* is our goal, why spend a lot of time with placing the symbol in the early grades? Second, once the symbols do become important, Herb Gross suggests first talking about the equal sign (=): Why was it chosen? Two equal length lines ... parallel so equal distant apart! What if one side was smaller? Perhaps ... we bring the lines together: Ah! 4 < 6.

Ordering and Ordinal Numbers: Multiple Numbers

Ordering Numbers

A female chimpanzee called Ai has learned to use Arabic numerals to represent numbers. She can count from zero to nine items, which she demonstrates by touching the appropriate number on a touch-sensitive monitor, and she can order the numbers from zero to nine in sequence.

(Kawai & Matsuzawa, 2000)

Well, the ability to order or sequence numbers is certainly not too developmentally advanced for preschoolers! As they learn to count, they can learn to order multiple quantities (e.g., on dot cards) or numerals.

However, if denied high-quality learning experiences, even 5- and 6-year-olds may be unable to do so or to figure out which number, 6 or 2, is closer to 5 (Griffin, Case, & Siegler, 1994). They may not have developed the "mental number line" representation of numbers as well as their more advantaged peers. (Although some have claimed that mental number lines are innate, "bootstrap" abilities, this does not seem to be the case. We have a sense of quantity, not all of which is spatial, but must build the mental number line through experiences; Núñez, 2011; Núñez, Doan, & Nikoulina, 2011)

Subtle, but important: We use the common phrase "mental number line" but it is not a *mathematical* number line for children for many years. That being said, it is *astounding* how early the foundations for it develop. For example, 7-month-old infants prefer sequences of arrays that are in order *and* left to right (McCrink & de Hevia, 2018)! This is then affected by culture and experience, but even in the preschool years, it is really a mental number *path* or *list* in that it includes sets of a discrete number of objects, not continuous quantities (e.g., all fractions), as described at the beginning of the chapter.

Finding out *how many* more (or fewer) there are in one collection than another is more demanding than simply comparing two collections to find which has more. Children have to understand that the number of elements in the collection with fewer items is contained in the number of items in the collection with more items. That is, they have to mentally construct a "part" of the larger collection (equivalent to the smaller collection) that is not visually present. They then have to determine the "other part" or the larger collection and find out how many elements are in this "left-over amount."

Ordinal Numbers

Ordinal numbers, usually (but not necessarily) involving the words "first, second ..." indicate position in a series or ordering. As such, they have different features (e.g., their meaning is connected to the series they describe). Most children in typical U.S. circumstances learn terms such as "first," "second," and "last" early, but learn others only much later. East Asian languages use the same terms for cardinal and ordinal numbers which may help those children learn the *names* sooner (Ng & Rao, 2010), but they may understand the *difference between* ordinal and cardinal meanings later.

Estimation

An estimation is not merely a "guess"—it is at least a mathematically *educated* "guess." Estimation is a process of solving a problem that calls for a rough or tentative evaluation of a quantity. There are many types of estimation, which—along with the common confusion between an estimate and (often wild) "guesses"—has resulted in poor teaching of this skill. The most common types of estimation discussed are measurement, numerosity, and computational estimation (Sowder, 1992a). Measurement estimation, such as "about how wide is this room?"

will be addressed in Chapters 11 and 12. Computational estimation, such as "about how much is 17 × 22?" has been most widely researched (see Chapter 6).

Numerosity estimation often involves procedures similar in ways to measurement and computational estimation procedures. To estimate the number of people in a theater, for example, a person might take a sample area, count the people in it, and multiply by an estimate of the number of such areas in the theater. Early numerosity estimation may involve similar procedure (e.g., try to "picture ten" in a jar then count by tens as you visually "mark off" each group), or even a straightforward single estimate based on benchmarks (10 "looks like this"; 50 "looks like that") or merely intuition.

One more type of estimation is "number line estimation"; for example, the ability to place numbers on a number line of arbitrary length, given that the ends are labeled (say, 0 to 100). The ability to build such a mental structure appears particularly important for young children, so we begin with this estimation type.

Number Line (Path) Estimation

Building an increasingly sophisticated "mental number line" is an important math goal. Such competencies support development and performance of arithmetic, estimation, and other math processes. The first skill after learning a mental number *list*—the first and critical step—may be to form a linear representation of numbers. But most people tend to exaggerate the distances between numbers at the lower end of a given number line—numbers that are more familiar—and underestimate the distances between numbers at the high end. So, rather than represent numbers as on a number line, such as shown in Figure 4.1, they tend to represent them as shown in Figure 4.2, below, due to the greater experience and thus familiarity with smaller numbers. (Think how "far apart" one thousand and one million are for you; are one billion and one trillion similarly spaced or are they each just "very big numbers"?) People need to become fluent with the numbers in the sequence and develop strategies for partitioning it to improve their number line estimates (Hurst, Monahan, Heller, & Cordes, 2014).

Improving children's number line estimation may have a broad beneficial effect on their representation, and therefore knowledge, of numbers. Further, the estimates of preschoolers from low-resource communities often reveals a lack of experience with numerical magnitudes, so facilitating their learning of number line estimation is particularly important.

Estimation of Numerosities

Once children learn to subitize (Chapter 2) and count (Chapter 3), can they then estimate the number of objects in a collection? Perhaps surprisingly, not well. Children may need to learn

Figure 4.2 Children initially internally represent smaller numbers as "further apart" than larger numbers

such foundation skills well and build mental images of both numbers and "benchmark" collections (e.g., what "ten objects" looks like) to perform numerosity estimation accurately. That is, children need to be able to subitize or count to the number to be estimated to have some sense of it; so, early numerosity estimate may have to wait for those competencies to develop to avoid meaningless guessing.

Experience and Education

Comparing Two Quantities or Numbers

Very early conversations about "which is more" can be beneficial for all ages. Comparing the quantities in sets of all sizes strengthens children's ANS systems and informal number sense, and should be a regular part of informal, incidental experiences (Libertus, Feigenson, & Halberda, 2011b). Vocabulary such as "more" and "fewer" (for dots) or "more" and "less" (for lengths of distance or durations of time) should be used and developed. Intersensory redundancy—for example, you see a ball bouncing more times, it takes longer, you hear more noises—helps the youngest children attend to and build strong quantitative *foundations* for number (Jordan et al., 2008).

To compare *numbers*, young children need to learn other competencies. For example, inviting 3-year-olds to play with containers that provoke one-to-one correspondence (wiffle balls and a muffin tin) improves their abilities on challenging number-matching tasks (matching a card with two flowers to one with two turtles, *not* the card with three flowers) more than free play with the balls without the muffin tin (Mix, Moore, & Holcomb, 2011).

Children also need to learn about the significance of the results of counting. To help them generalize, provide a variety of meaningful tasks (i.e., familiar, everyday comparisons such as the number of treats) and situations in which counting is a relevant strategy and inferences must be made. Prompt children to count in these comparing situations and then *verify* that counting led to correct judgments.

Of course, children also have to realize how to use counting to compare the number in two collections. They must be able to think, "I counted six circles and five squares, so there are more circles, because 6 comes after 5 when we count." To do this, children also must understand that each counting number is quantitatively one more than the one before (recall the "Counter from N ($N + 1$, $N - 1$)" level in Chapter 3, pp. 39, 61-62).

Language, even in supposedly "simple" situations, can be surprisingly complex but—used well—supportive of learning. A 5-year-old was told she had 7¢ and asked what she could buy (Lansdell, 1999). Later, she used the phrase "one more"; that is, an item costing 8¢ was "one more" than she had. Then, for an item costing one less cent, she said she had "one more less." She thought she could buy that item (for 6¢) with her 7¢. The teacher gave her the 7¢ to hold, and the girl talked herself into thinking that it was OK, she could buy the item. Then the teacher introduced the term *change*: "You'd have 1 penny left, wouldn't you. One penny change. So that would be nice...." The teacher then asked about a 5¢ purchase, and the girl said, "I'd have 2 pennies change."

The next day she confused this terminology, but not the concept. The teacher corrected her use of language, confirming her computational accuracy, but mirroring the correct language.

Soon thereafter, *change* was used to mean changing pennies to other coins. Impressively, the girl was still able to use *change* correctly in both senses, with increased confidence.

The researcher claimed that the informal talk and language were the most important aspects of these interactions, but the clarification or introduction of math terminology is also important. Many math terms may be ambiguous, usually due to their having non-mathematical meanings, and the teacher's closed questions and direct statements helped the child agree on specific new mathematical meanings. In addition, open questions helped the teacher understand the child's meanings and concepts.

Thus, we teachers need to be aware of such potentially ambiguous words, introduce new words and meanings after concepts are understood, and be careful and consistent in our use of the words. To do this, we should observe children's use of the words, build on the child's own language, and negotiate new meanings through practical experiences (Lansdell, 1999).

Order and Ordinal Numbers

Ordinal number words are potentially more confusing than the verbal counting words, and the two series are often difficult to relate. However, some repeated experiences with everyday activities are easy to implement, such as who is first, second, third … in lining up. Also, explicitly discuss the correspondences (e.g., "Who's second? 'Second' means number two in line") and plan activities that invite such connections. For example, in the Building Blocks curriculum (Clements & Sarama, 2007c), children build and label stairs with connecting cubes and, on the computer, with squares and numerals. They also insert missing steps. These activities encourage children to note that the second step is number 2 (has two cubes), and so forth. Summative evaluations revealed strong positive effects on children's understanding and skill with ordinal relations and sequencing.

Children may also learn about ordinal relations from observing the consequences of adding and taking away objects (Cooper, 1984; Sophian & Adams, 1987). This suggests that multiple experiences adding and subtracting small numbers (especially repeated additions/subtractions of 1) will help build ordinal relations as well as arithmetic competencies. For children who have difficulty, including those with learning disabilities, analogies are helpful. For example, if children cannot identify which of two collections is more, relate the numbers to children's ages, as in, "Who is older, Jack who is 7 years old or Sue who is 5? … How do you know?"

Finally, experiences such as these help children understand and practice conservation of number. Surprisingly, strategy diversity (using different strategies to find a solution) also typifies children's approach to this task (Siegler, 1995b). This study included three training conditions; correctness feedback, feedback with requests to justify one's reasoning, and feedback with requests to justify the *researcher's* reasoning. The last was the most effective (although order of feedback/explanation were confounded, as were, in the last condition, seeing another's perspective and explaining a correct response). Children use multiple types of explanations, and those explaining the researcher's reasons gave a greater variety than those who explained their own reasons. Again, then, the benefits of verbalizations and strategy diversity are evident.

Number Line Estimation

Having children place numerals on a number line may be helpful for first and second graders, but it can be confusing for younger children. Playing board ("racing") games can develop *all* children's ability to do number line estimation, as well as to order magnitudes, count, and recognize numerals. Encourage parents to play such games at home as well. Board games ("racing" type board games such as Candyland or Chutes and Ladders) may be beneficial because they provide multiple cues to both the order of numbers and the numbers' magnitudes (Siegler & Booth, 2004). In such games, the greater the number in a square, the greater the distance that the child has moved the token, the greater number of discrete moves the child has made, the greater number of counting words the child has spoken, and the greater amount of time since the game began—intersensory redundancy again. Board games can be easily and successfully integrated into classrooms as young as preschool (Ramani, Siegler, & Hitti, 2012).

But wait! Before you pull out Candyland, learn this: *The usual way we play these games can be near useless!* For Candyland especially, one spins a spinner, gets a color and moves to that color. *No math is learned* (Siegler & Booth, 2004). Further, even if you use dice or spinners with dots or numerals, mental number lines do *not* develop well unless there are numerals on the board's path (as in Chutes and Ladders). *And* this is the most difficult to "re-learn." You can't play the usual way: If you are on 14, and roll a 3, you count "1, 2, 3...." This does little to promote reading numerals (children ignore them) and develop a mental number line. Instead, children *must read the numerals as they move over them*, as in "15, 16, 17!" (Laski & Siegler, 2014). This is odd to most of us as adults, but it is necessary for developing number relationships and the mental number line. See "Race to Space Game" as an example at three different levels in Table 4.2 and especially on [LT]². See the resource, "Introducing and Using Games" on [LT]² too.

The goal is to build *number sense*, which includes but is not limited to placing numbers on a line or playing a board game. For one, involve children's whole bodies: First graders who estimated the position of target numbers on a 0-100 number line by *walking* to the estimated position improved in both number line estimation and addition more than those who estimated distances on a screen (Link, Moeller, Huber, Fischer, & Nuerk, 2013). Further, many competencies help build a mental number line, especially children's *familiarity* with numbers in the range considered; for example, their ability to spontaneously subitize (Chapter 2, Nanu et al., 2018b) or to be a "Counter from *N* (*N* + 1, *N* - 1)" (Chapter 3, Ebersbach, Luwel, & Verschaffel, 2015).

Finally, building number sense through number line estimation is *not the same as having children work with "number lines"* or to solve problems using number lines. That model can actually be difficult for children to use, perhaps because children are confused by the dual representation of number as points and distances (or vectors) (Gagatsis & Elia, 2004). Using a printed number line is not an easy or obvious tool for kindergartners (Skoumpourdi, 2010).

And, in fact, it may be that solving arithmetic problems in a given range is another, possibly most effective, way of developing number line estimation. Incrementing and decrementing numbers may build that kind of number sense (Laski & Yu, 2014c, see Chapters 5 and 6).

Estimation of Numerosities

Although some have claimed success in promoting numerosity estimation through activities, the limited effects of others suggest caution in devoting much time to these activities in the earliest years. Any time that is given, probably in the primary grades, might best follow several guidelines. First, ensure that subitizing, counting, and especially number line (like a board game path) estimation skills are well developed. Subitizing skills should be developed at least for small numbers, and counting and number line estimation skills should be developed at least up to the numbers to be estimated. Second, help children develop and understand benchmarks well ("I know what ten counters looks like"). Again, benchmarks might be beneficially developed in number line estimation tasks initially, and then expanded to include images of collections of objects of those sizes (in different arrangements, see Chapter 2). Third, within a short instructional unit, expect development to occur more within a level of the learning trajectory. Fourth—and this is important for arithmetic as well—make sure children learn to connect quantities to numerals. This skill appears to be important for developing increasingly sophisticated strategies for basic arithmetic combinations ("facts") (Vanbinst, Ghesquiere, & Smedt, 2012). Note, again, that both exact recognition (perceptual and conceptual subitizing) and approximate estimation contribute to later arithmetic learning (Obersteiner, Reiss, & Ufer, 2013).

Learning Trajectory for Comparing, Ordering, and Estimating Numbers

The learning trajectory for comparing, ordering, and estimating numbers, like that for counting, is complex because there are many conceptual and skill advancements and, more obviously, there are *subtrajectories* for each subdomain.

Table 4.1 Goals for Comparing, Ordering, and Estimating Numbers from the Common Core State Standards (CCSS)

Counting and Cardinality (K.CC in CCSS)

Compare numbers.

1. Identify whether the number of objects in one group is greater than, less than, or equal to the number of objects in another group, e.g., by using matching and counting strategies. [Include groups with up to ten objects.]
2. Compare two numbers between 1 and 10 presented as written numerals.

Number and Operations in Base Ten (1.NBT in CCSS)

Understand place value.

3. Compare two two-digit numbers based on meanings of the tens and ones digits, recording the results of comparisons with the symbols >, =, and <.

Number and Operations in Base Ten (2.NBT in CCSS)

Understand place value.

4. Compare two three-digit numbers based on meanings of the hundreds, tens, and ones digits, using >, =, and < symbols to record the results of comparisons.

Measurement and Data [2.MD in CCSS]

Measure and estimate lengths in standard units.

5. Estimate lengths using units of inches, feet, centimeters, and meters.

The importance of *goals* for this domain is clear for comparing, ordering, and at least some aspects of estimation (see Chapter 6 for more on comparison of multidigit numbers and Chapter 10 for length). The places these goals appear in the CCSS are shown in Table 4.1. Remember, to see how CCSSM, ELOF, and *many other* standards and assessments align with the learning trajectories, use the alignment tool in [LT]^2.

This learning trajectory is a bit complex, so we added something new to our learning trajectory table. We don't want you "lose the forest for the trees." So, we have added a column that encourages you to think of the *big picture*, the broad levels of thinking. Keep these broad level in mind and you will not let the "trees"—the instructional important but numerous!—levels distract you from the major developments your children will make.

With the goals stated above, then, Table 4.2 shows the two additional components of the learning trajectory, the developmental progression and the instructional tasks. (Note that the ages in all the learning trajectory tables are only approximate, especially because the age of acquisition usually depends heavily on experience.)

Final Words

In many situations, people wish to compare, order, or estimate the number of objects. Another common type of situation involves putting collections—and the numbers of these collections—together and taking them apart. These operations of arithmetic are the focus of Chapter 5.

Table 4.2 Learning Trajectory for Comparing, Ordering, and Estimating Numbers

Age	Broad	Developmental Progression	Instructional Activities
0–1		**Comparison Senser: Foundations**: From the first months of life, children are sensitive to a change in the number, either of a change of very small collections, such as 1 vs. 2, or large changes in larger collections, such as double the number. Therefore, we know infants have an unconscious, innate sensitivity to such simple equivalence comparisons.	Activities encourage explorations of and talk, often first modeled by an adult, about quantities (many, only one, more, fewer, less, etc.) everywhere possible in natural conversations. See examples in [LT]^2.
1	**Object Matching–Visual, Physical**	**Many-to-One Corresponder** *Comparing*: Recognizes that two very small collections have the "same number" by intuitively making a correspondence between the items in each collection. At this level, in certain situations, children may also put objects, words, or actions in one-to-one or many-to-one correspondence or a mixture. Puts one or a couple blocks in each muffin tin.	*Informal matching*, [LT]^2. Provide rich sensory, manipulative environments that include objects that provoke matching. Activities encourage children to match sets intuitively, as in putting clothes on each doll, and discussing what they are doing.
2		**One-to-One Object Corresponder** *Comparing*: Puts objects into one-to-	*One-to-one correspondences*: Discuss the correspondences the child makes or could make.

(Continued)

Table 4.2 (Cont.)

Age	Broad	Developmental Progression	Instructional Activities
		one correspondence when it is clear the materials are a physical "pair." In other situations, such as setting the table, may start to do one-to-one, but then may keep on passing out items until they are all dispersed, or may skip some (due to the lack of clear matching, such as cups "near" plates) (Tirosh, Tsamir, Levenson, & Barkai, 2020).	"Does every doll have a block to sit on?" "Does every child have a drink?" Put out identical simple cut-out pictures of an animal (e.g., eight ducks), and have children put one rubber duck on each one.

		Puts one block in each muffin tin but is disturbed that some blocks remain so finds more tins to put every last block in something. Implicitly sensitive to the relation of "more than/less than" involving very small numbers (from 1 to 2 years of age). Uses words to include "more," "less," or "same."	*Put Them Together* [LT][2]: Children put just enough of one group of objects to match another group where the relationship is clear as in *one-to-one provoked correspondences*, such as an egg carton and plastic eggs that fit exactly or objects inside others (Tirosh et al., 2020). See research on the benefits and another example about wiffle balls and muffin tins on p. 72 (Mix et al., 2011). *One-to-one puzzles*, [LT][2]: Provide knob or simple shape puzzles in which each shape is to be placed inside a corresponding hole in the puzzle.
2–3		**Object Corresponder** *Comparing*: Puts objects into one-to-one correspondence, although may not understand that this creates equal groups (age 2; 8).	*Put Them Together* [LT][2], see above, is also useful as needed. *Match Them Up*, [LT][2]: Children get enough of one group of objects to match another group, such as setting the table. *Setting the Table*, [LT][2]: Children give one item to each person at a small table. If children have difficulties, joining the play and talking about the one-to-one correspondence can be helpful. Also, use only 3–4 to begin with (Tirosh et al., 2020).
		Put a straw in each carton (doesn't worry if extra straws are left) but doesn't necessarily know there are the same number of straws and cartons.	
		Perceptual Comparer *Comparing*: Compares collections that are quite different in *number* (e.g., one is at least twice the other).	*Which Has More?* and *Who Has More?*, [LT][2]: Show two sets and ask children to judge which has more (or less).
		Shown ten blocks and 25 blocks, points to the 25 as having more.	
	Visual Comparison	Compares similar collections but only involving very small numbers. Compares collections using number words "one" and "two" (age 2; 8).	
		Shown groups of two and four, points to the group of four as having more.	
3		**First-Second Ordinal Counter** *Ordinal Number*: Identifies the "first"	*Who's Up First?*, [LT][2]: Discuss who wishes to be first and second in line (or up to bat, etc.).

(Continued)

Age	Broad	Developmental Progression	Instructional Activities
		and often "second" objects in a sequence.	Gradually extend this to higher ordinal numbers.
3		**Early Comparer of Similar Items** (1–4 items) *Comparing*: Compares collections of 1–4 items verbally or nonverbally ("just by looking"). The items must be the same. May compare the small collections using number words "two" and "three" (approximately age 3; 2), and "three" and others (age 3; 6). Some do this before they can accurately count by using recognition of number/subitizing for these quantities. May transfer an ordering relation from one pair of collections to another. Identifies ••• and ••• as equal and different from •• or • •.	*Is it Fair? (Similar)*, [LT][2]: Show children a small number of similar objects given to two people (dolls, stuffed animals …) and ask if it's fair–if they both have the same number. *Compare Snapshots (Similar Items)*, [LT][2]: Secretly place two counters on one plate and four counters on another plate. Using a dark cloth, cover the plate that has four counters. Show children both plates, one covered. Tell children to watch carefully and quietly, keeping their hands in their laps, as you quickly reveal the covered plate so they can compare it to the other plate. Ask children: "Do the plates have the same number of counters?"
3–4		**Early Comparer of Dissimilar Items** *Comparing*: Matches small, equal collections consisting of different items, showing that they are the same number. Matches collections of three shells and three dots, then declares that they "have the same number."	*Is it Fair? (Dissimilar)*, [LT][2]: As above with dissimilar items.
4		**Matching Comparer** *Comparing*: Compares groups of 1–6 by matching. Gives one toy bone to every dog and says there are the same number of dogs and bones.	*Comparing by Matching*, [LT][2]. Ask children to determine whether there are the same number of spoons as plates, rocks in two piles (and many other similar situations). Provide feedback as necessary. Talk to them about how they knew "for sure" and how they figured it out. Talk with children to begin to develop the idea that one-to-one matching creates equal groups: "If you know the number in one of the groups, then you know the number in the other." *Goldilocks and the Three Bears*: Read or tell *Goldilocks and the Three Bears* as a flannel board story. Discuss the one-to-one correspondence of bears to other things in the story. Ask: "How many bowls are in the story?" "How many chairs?" "How do you know?" Then ask, "Were there just enough beds for the bears? How do you know?" Summarize that one-to-one match can create equal groups. That is, "If you know the number of bears in one group, then you know the number of beds in the other group." Tell children they can retell the story and match props later in center time. *Party Time 1*: Students practice one-to-one correspondence by matching party utensils to placemats. Discuss how *many* there are of each.

(Continued)

Table 4.2 (Cont.)

Age	Broad	Developmental Progression	Instructional Activities
	Counting Comparison	**Counting Comparer (Same Size)** *Comparing*: Accurately compares via counting, but only when objects are about the same size and groups are small (up to about five). Counts two piles of five blocks each, and says they are the same. Not always accurate when the larger collection's objects are smaller in size than the objects in the smaller collection. Accurately counts two equal collections, but, when asked, says the collection of larger blocks has more.	*Flip to Compare*, [LT]²: A game like "War," in which two players compare the card they flipped over. *Compare Snapshots (Same Size)*, [LT]²: Similar to the above, but with two important differences. 1. Higher numbers are used, up to 5 and more as children gain confidence. 2. We *use counting to check* explicitly. For example: Secretly place three counters on a plate and five counters on another plate. Using a dark cloth, cover the plate that has five counters. Show children both plates, one covered. Tell children to watch carefully and quietly, keeping their hands in their laps, as you quickly reveal the covered plate so they can compare it to the other plate. Uncover the plate for 2 seconds and cover it again. Ask children: "Do the plates have the same number of counters?" Because the answer is "no," ask: "Which plate has more?" Have children point or say the number on the plate. "Which plate has fewer counters?" If needed, repeat the reveal. Uncover the plate indefinitely. Ask children how many counters are on each plate. Confirm that five is more than three because five comes after three when counting. *Compare Game*: For each pair of children playing, two or more sets of counting cards (1-5) are needed. Teach children to mix the cards (e.g., by mixing them all up when they are face down), and then deal them evenly (one to the first player, then one to the second player ...) and face down to both players. Players simultaneously flip their top cards and compare to find out which is greater. The player with the greater amount says, "I have more," and takes the opponent's cards. If card amounts are equal, players each flip another card to determine a result. The game is over when all cards have been played, and the "winner" is the player with more cards. 

(Continued)

Age	Broad	Developmental Progression	Instructional Activities
			Use cards with dot arrays and numerals at first, then just dot arrays. Start with small numbers and slowly add larger numbers. Play the game on computers, too (as below).
5		**Spatial Extent Estimator–Small/ Big** *Numerosity Estimation:* Estimates which set is more or less if the differences are clear (e.g., one is double the other). Names a "small number" (e.g. from 1-4) for sets that cover little space and a "big number" (10-20 or more) for sets that cover a lot of space. Children classify numbers "little"/"big" idiosyncratically, and this may change with the size of the to-be-estimated objects.	*The Estimating Jar (Small/Big)*, [LT]²: Put objects in a clear plastic jar and secure the lid. Tell children this is an "Estimating Jar," and that they will estimate how many items are in it, recording their estimates and their names on self-sticking notes to post by the jar. At the end of the week, spill the items out, count them, and compare the counts to the estimates.
		Shown nine objects spread out for 1 second, and when asked, "How many?", responds, "Fifty!"	
5		**Counting Comparer (5)** *Comparing:* Compares with counting, even when larger collection's objects are smaller. Later, figures out *how many* more or less.	*Get Just Enough (Counting Comparer 5)*, [LT]²: Children get just enough of one group of objects to match another group; e.g., a pair of scissors for each child at their table. At this level, make sure they have to go across the room to get the scissors, so they have to count. The same can be done with "Setting the Table" (see above)—make sure counting is necessary.
		Accurately counts two equal collections, and says they have the same number, even if one collection has larger blocks.	*Memory Game–Number:* For each pair of children, one set of dot cards and one set of numeral cards are needed. Place card sets face down in two separate arrays. Players take turns choosing, flipping, and showing a card from each array. If the cards do not match, they are returned face down to the arrays. If they match, that player keeps them.

			Concentrate!: Counting Cards to Counting Cards 1-6, [LT]²: Children match counting cards (each with a numeral and corresponding dot cluster) within the framework of a "Concentration" card game. Notice children have to say if they match or not, unlike many

(Continued)

Table 4.2 (Cont.)

Age	Broad	Developmental Progression	Instructional Activities
			computer games that just encourage random clicking because the computer decides!
			Find the Number–Compare: Before children get to the center, conceal several pizzas (paper plates), each under its own opaque container and each with a different number of pepperoni slices (round counters) under its container. Display one pizza with three to five pepperoni slices. The goal is for children to find the hidden match to the pizza on display.
4		**Mental Number Line to 5** *Number Line Estimation*: Uses knowledge of counting number relationships to determine relative size and position when given perceptual support. Shown a 0 at one end of a line segment and a 5 at the other, places a "3" approximately in the middle.	*Who is Older?*, [LT]^2: Ask children who is older, a 2-year-old or a 3-year-old. Provide feedback as necessary. Ask them to explain how they know. *Help the Turtle Get Home: Counter (Small Numbers)*, see [LT]^2: See Chapter 3, p. 56. *Race to Space (5)*, [LT]^2: Make a board game with numbers 1 to 10 in consecutively numbered, linearly arranged, equal-size squares ([LT]^2 has full directions and resources for this). Children roll or spin a "1" or a "2." They move that many *while* they say each number their token lands on (e.g., if they are on the numeral "5" and rolled a "2" they would move and say "Six, seven!" Also see the two sections on games in the Resources, for guidelines for introducing/teaching and using games. *What's the Missing Step?*, [LT]^2: Show children a growing and shrinking cube staircase tower (1, 2, 3, 4, 3, 2, 1). Have children close their eyes while you remove the first tower of three cubes. Now ask them which step they think is missing. Ask why they selected that step. Did they count? Did they just know? Show the missing step and count the cubes. Repeat, but, this time, remove the second tower of three cubes. Ask for their answers; ask why they think that.
	Mental Number Line		
		Serial Orderer to 5 (Comparing Number) *Comparing/Ordering*: Orders quantities (dots) or numerals up to 5. Similarly orders lengths marked into units. Given cards with 1 to 5 dots, puts in order. Given towers of cubes, puts in order (1 to 5).	*Crowded Room!*, [LT]^2: Children order, or seriate, five lengths with countable connecting cubes. *Order Cards (5)*, [LT]^2: Place dot cards 1 to 5 so they are left to right from the children's perspective. Ask children to describe the pattern. Tell children to keep counting out loud, predicting the next number as you continue to lay out the next dot card in the pattern. *Then* have children mix up these cards and then put them in order on their own (including in centers). They can work together or race to put two sets of cards in order and so forth.
5		**Ordinal Counter** *Ordinal Number*: Identifies and uses ordinal numbers from "first" to "tenth." Can identify who is "third in line."	*Ordinal Construction Company*: Students learn ordinal positions (first through tenth) by moving objects between the floors of a building.

(Continued)

Age	Broad	Developmental Progression	Instructional Activities
5		**Counting Comparer (10)** *Comparing:* Compares with counting, even when larger collection's objects are smaller, up to 10. Accurately counts two collections of nine each, and says they have the same number, even if one collection has larger blocks.	*Mr. MixUp–Comparing*, [LT]²: Tell children that Mr. MixUp needs help comparing. Compare collections of objects of different sizes. For example, show four blocks and six much smaller items, and have Mr. MixUp say, "The blocks are bigger so that's the bigger number." Ask children to count to find out which group really has more items and explain to Mr. MixUp why he is wrong. *Flip to Compare*, [LT]²: For each pair of children playing, two or more sets of counting (with dots and numerals, and, soon thereafter, just dots) cards (1–10) are needed. Mix and deal cards evenly face down. Players simultaneously flip their top cards and compare to find out which is greater. The player with the greater amount says, "I have more," and takes the opponent's card. If card amounts are equal, players each flip another card to determine a result. The game is over when all cards have been played.   

(Continued)

Table 4.2 (Cont.)

Age Broad	Developmental Progression	Instructional Activities
		Cube Towers–Which Has More, Which Has Fewer?, [LT]²: Show two towers: one made of eight identical blocks on the floor and another made of seven similar identical blocks on a chair. Ask children which tower is taller. Discuss any strategies they invent. Summarize that, although the tower on the chair is higher, from the bottom of the tower to the top of the tower it is shorter because it consists of fewer blocks than the tower on the floor.
	Mental Number Line to 10 *Number Line Estimation*: Uses internal images and knowledge of number relationships to determine relative size and position. Which number is closer to 6: 4 or 9?	*Race to Space (10)*, [LT]²: See the directions above but especially the complete directions and set of resources on [LT]². *I Have More (Flip to Compare)*, [LT]²: See above. *What's the Missing Step?*, [LT]²: As above, 1–10. *Help the Turtle Get Home: Counter (10)*, [LT]²: See Chapter 3, Counter (10), p. 56. *I'm Thinking of a Number (Number Line to 10)*, [LT]²: Using counting cards from 1 to 10, choose and hide a secret number. Tell children you hid a card with a number and ask them to guess which it is. When a child guesses correctly, excitedly reveal the card. Until then, tell children whether a guess is more or less than the secret number. As children become more comfortable, ask why they made their guess; for example, "I knew 4 was more than the secret number and 2 was less, so I guessed 3!" Repeat, adding clues, such as, "Your guess is two more than my number." Do this activity during transitions. *Rocket Blast 1*: Students estimate the placement of a tick mark on a 1–20 number line to the nearest whole number. 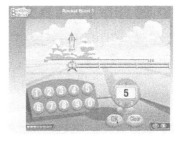
6	**Serial Orderer to 6+ (Number)** *Comparing/Ordering*: Orders quantities (dots) or numerals to 6 and beyond. Similarly orders lengths marked into units. Given cards with 1 to 12 dots, puts in order. Given towers of cubes, puts in order (1 to 10).	*Build Stairs (6+)*: Have children make "stairs" with connecting cubes. Encourage them to count each step. Ask them to describe the numbers. Extensions: Have someone hide one of the stairs and you figure out which one is hidden, then you insert it. Have them mix up the steps and put them back in order.

Age	Broad	Developmental Progression	Instructional Activities

Order Cards (6+), [LT]² : In small groups or centers, challenge students to put dot cards 1 to 10 (or more) in order. They can work together or race to put two sets of cards in order and so forth.

Magician's Trick, [LT]² (this is a rich, Math + (math + executive function) activity; please see the extensive resources on [LT]²): Place counting cards 1 to 10 in numerical order so that children see them in left-to-right order and count them with children. Then place the cards face down, still in order. Ask a volunteer to point to any of the cards. Using your "math magic" (really, counting from 1 to the chosen card), tell children which card it is. The volunteer flips the card to show you are correct, and then replaces it face down.

Ask children to use their math magic in a similar manner after you point to one of the cards. Remind them where "1" is, then point to "2." Have children spontaneously say what they think the card is. Turn it over to check. Have children take turns playing independently.

(Continued)

Age	Broad	Developmental Progression	Instructional Activities
			Variations: This variation encourages counting forward and backward from numbers. Start as before. Tell children this is a new way to play, by keeping the cards *showing* after they are guessed. Play with them, and after one card is left face up, point to the next card right after the face-up card. Ask children to use their "math magic," and then to tell how they figured it out. Discuss that you could count forward from the face-up card. Keeping both cards face up, repeat with a face-down card that comes right before another card. Have children take turns playing independently.
		Spatial Extent Estimator *Numerosity Estimation*: Extends sets and number categories to include "small numbers," which are usually subitized, not estimated; "middle-size numbers" (e.g., 10–20); and "large numbers." The arrangement of the to-be-estimated set affects the difficulty. Shown nine objects spread out for 1 second and asked, "How many?", responds, "Fifteen."	*The Estimating Jar*, [LT][2]: Put 5-15 objects in a clear plastic jar and secure the lid. Tell children this is an "Estimating Jar," and that they will estimate how many items are in it, recording their estimates and their names on self-sticking notes to post by the jar. At the end of the week, spill the items out, count them, and compare the counts to the estimates. Start with large items so 5–10 fit in the jar, then move to smaller (and thus more numerous) items. Talk to children about their strategies as they are estimating and at the end of the week. *Estimate How Many (Spatial Extent)*, [LT][2]: In specifically designed instructional situations (e.g., a whole-group lesson in which a large chart is covered with a number of dots) or other setting (e.g., noting a large flock of birds on the playground), ask children to estimate the number. Discuss strategies, having someone demonstrate each, then challenge children to apply them to new situations. Encourage them to use benchmarks ("I know 10 is about this many, so I thought, 10, 20, 30 …").
7		**Place Value Comparer**[1] *Comparing*: Compares numbers with place value understandings. "63 is more than 59 because 6 tens is more than 5 tens even if there are more than 3 ones."	*Equal Shmequal and Balance Scales*, [LT][2]. Read *Equal Shmequal* by Virginia Kroll, in which animals try different properties (e.g., meat-eating or not) to find a fair way to play tug-of-war and decide on weight. While reading it, put a balance scale on the table. Have children put base-ten blocks on the trays to represent the plot (e.g., 3 ones for 3 small animals vs. 3 tens for 3 large animals). Then have children compare other multidigit numbers and explain their reasoning, making connections to the story and to the balance scale. (This is adapted from Larson & Rumsey, 2018, who include many other books and ideas.) *Which Number is Greater?*, [LT][2]: Write two numbers, such as 64 and 47 or 35 and 58, on the board. Ask children which number is greater than the other. Write another pair of two-digit numbers on the board. Cover up the tens place with a note card or piece of

Table 4.2 (Cont.)

Age	Broad	Developmental Progression	Instructional Activities
			construction paper. Discuss and encourage them to explain their strategies. Repeat with the ones place hidden. *What is the Largest/Smallest Number I Can Make?*, [LT]²: Using numeral cards, students construct numbers from 0–99 and determine which number combination makes the greatest number and which number combination makes the smallest number (see [LT]² for full instructions). *Snapshots Compare* with place value models. See also activities in Chapter 6 dedicated to place value (pp. 128–130).
		Mental Number Line to 100 *Number Line Estimation*: Uses knowledge of number relationships and mental images, including how ones can be embedded in tens, to determine relative size and position. Asked, "Which is closer to 45: 30 or 50?", says, "45 is right next to 50, one five away, but 30 isn't."	*Race to Space (100)*, [LT]²: See the directions above but especially the complete directions and set of resources on [LT]². (Laski & Siegler, 2014). *I'm Thinking of a Number (100)*, [LT]²: As above, but done verbally or with an "empty number line"—a line segment initially labeled only with 0 to 100, filled in with each of the children's estimates. *Rocket Blast (100)*, [LT]²: Students estimate the placement of a tick mark on a 1–100 number line to the nearest whole number. The activities in Chapter 6 dedicated to place value (pp. 128–130) and those at the higher levels of the learning trajectories in that chapter develop these abilities as well.
7		**Scanning with Intuitive Quantification Estimator** *Numerosity Estimation*: Scans a group of objects and relates the results to a mental number line to perform a useful numerosity estimation. Shown 40 objects spread out for 1 second and asked, "How many?", responds, "About thirty."	*Estimate How Many (Scanning)*, [LT]²: See above.
7–8		**Mental Number Line to 1000** *Number Line Estimation*: Uses internal images and knowledge of number relationships, including place value, to determine relative size and position. Asked, "Which is closer to 3500: 2000 or 7000?", says, "70 is double 35, but 20 is only 15 from 35, so 20 hundreds, 2000, is closer."	*I'm Thinking of a Number (1000)*, [LT]²: As above, 0 to 1000. *Rocket Blast (1000)*, [LT]²: Students estimate the placement of a tick mark on a 1–1000 number line to the nearest whole number. Some computer games give useful feedback on guesses. 

(Continued)

Table 4.2 (Cont.)

Age	Broad	Developmental Progression	Instructional Activities
8		**Benchmarks Estimator** *Numerosity Estimation*: Counts a portion of the to-be-estimated collection and uses that as a benchmark from which an estimate is made, intuitively or using repeated addition or multiplication. Scanning can be linked to recalled benchmarks. Shown 11, says, "It looked closer to 10 than 20, so I guess 12." Shown 45 objects spread out for 1 second and asked, "How many?", responds, "About 5 tens—fifty."	*Estimate How Many (Benchmark)*, [LT][2]: (see above) Emphasize strategies at this level or the next.
		Composition Estimator *Numerosity Estimation*: Decomposes or partitions the to-be-estimated set into convenient subset sizes, then recomposes the numerosity. Initially, this is done with regular arrangements using repeated addition or multiplication. Later, the process can be done with irregular arrangements and children more consistently use multiplication skills to recompose. Shown 87 objects spread out and asked for an estimate responds, "That's about 20—so, 20, 40, 60, 80. Eighty!"	*Estimate How Many (Composition)*, [LT][2]: (see above) Emphasize strategies at this level.

Note

1 See Chapter 6 for much more information about place value.

5 Arithmetic
Early Addition and Subtraction and Counting Strategies

Alex is 5 years old. Her brother, Paul, is 3. Alex bounds into the kitchen and announces:

> Alex: When Paul is 6, I'll be 8; when Paul is 9, I'll be 11; when Paul is 12, I'll be 14 (*she continues until Paul is 18 and she is 20*).
>
> Father: My word! How on earth did you figure all that out?
>
> Alex: It's easy. You just go "three-FOUR-five" (*saying the "four" very loudly, and clapping hands at the same time, so that the result was very strongly rhythmical, and had a soft-LOUD-soft pattern*), you go "six-SEVEN-[clap]-eight," you go "nine-TEN-[clap!]-eleven.
>
> (Davis, 1984, p. 154)

Is this small, but remarkable, scene a glimpse at an exceptional child? Or, is it an indication of the potential *all* young children have to learn arithmetic? If so, how early could instruction start? How early *should* it start?

The Earliest Arithmetic

We saw that children have a sense of quantity from birth. Similarly, they appear to have some sense of arithmetic. For example, they appear to expect that, if you add one, you have one more. Figure 5.1 illustrates an experiment that provides an example of this. After seeing a screen hide one doll, and a hand places another doll behind the screen, 5-month-olds look longer when the removal of the screen reveals an incorrect, rather than a correct, outcome (a violation-of-expectations procedure; Wynn, 1992).

Research on subitizing (Chapter 2) and early arithmetic suggests that infants intuitively represent a small collection (e.g., 2) as individual objects that they "track," but not as a group. In contrast, they represent large numbers (e.g., 10) as groups, but not as individual objects. However, they can combine images of such groups and intuitively expect a certain outcome. For example, shown two groups of five dots combined—picture for yourself five dots appearing in place of the doll in Figure 5.1, then another five dots added, slipping behind the screen—they discriminate between the outcome of 5 (incorrect, like the "impossible" outcome in Figure 5.1) and 10 (correct). Also, by 2 years of age, children show signs

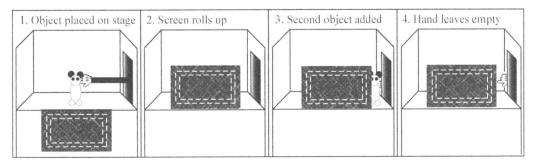

Then either…

Figure 5.1 An experiment revealing 5-month-olds' sensitivity to adding one object

of understanding that adding increases, and taking away decreases, quantity. The intuitive quantity estimators they use may be innate, and facilitate later-developing, explicit arithmetic. However, they do not appear to directly lead to and determine this explicit, accurate arithmetic.

Across many studies, research suggests that children develop an initial *explicit* understanding of addition and subtraction with small numbers by about 3 years of age. However, it is not until 4 years of age that most children can solve addition problems involving even slightly larger numbers with accuracy (Huttenlocher, Jordan, & Levine, 1994).

Most children do not solve larger-number problems without the support of concrete objects until about 5½ years of age. However, *this is not so much an age, or biological, limitation, as an experiential, limitation.* That is, with experience, preschoolers and kindergartners can learn "counting-all" and even basic "counting-on" strategies.

Arithmetic: Mathematical Definitions and Properties

Mathematically, we can define addition in terms of counting (Wu, 2011b). This connects arithmetic to counting (especially incrementation, also known as the successor operation, the addition of 1 to a number). The *sum* 3 + 8 is the whole number that results from counting eight numbers starting at 3: *3* … 4, 5, 6, 7, 8, 9, 10, 11 (Wu, 2011b). One would not welcome the task, but the sum 37 + 739 is the number that results from counting 739 numbers starting at 37: *37* … 38, 39 … 774, 775, 776. In general, for any two whole numbers *a* and *b*, the sum *a* + *b* is the number that results by counting *b* more numbers starting at the number *a* (Wu, 2011b).

We can also skip count. If we do skip counting by tens *ten times*, we have 100. Similarly, skip counting by 100s *ten times* results in 1000, and so forth. All this is consistent with what we learned about counting in Chapters 3 and 4. Thus, 47 + 30 can be solved by skip counting by tens: 47 ... 57, 67, 77. Place value is fundamental to arithmetic, which we discuss in more detail in Chapter 6.

From the earliest levels, arithmetic depends on two properties:

1. *The associative law of addition:* (*a* + *b*) + *c* = *a* + (*b* + *c*). For example, this allows a mental addition strategy that simplifies some computations, such as: 4 + 4 + 6 = 4 + (4 + 6) = 4 + 10 = 14.
2. *The commutative law of addition: a* + *b* = *b* + *a*. Illustrating commutativity, think how odd it would be if the number of toy vehicles you put in an empty toy box depended on whether you put the trucks or the cars in first.

Young children usually do not know these laws explicitly but learn to use them intuitively. However, some studies indicate that children do understand the concept of commutativity when using it in counting strategies (Canobi, Reeve, & Pattison, 1998).

Subtraction does not follow these laws. Subtraction is defined mathematically as the inverse of addition; that is, subtraction is the *additive inverse—a* for any *a*, such that *a* + - *a* = 0. Or, for 8 - 3, the difference is the number that, when added to 3, results in 8. So, *c* - *a* = *b* means that *b* is the number that satisfies *a* + *b* = *c*. Thus, although it seems cumbersome, one can think of (8 - 3) as ((5 + 3) - 3) = 5 + (3 - 3) = 5 + 0 = 5. Or, since we know that subtraction and addition are inverses of each other, saying:

8 - 3 = □

means the same as:

8 = 3 + □

That is, asking "What is 8 - 3?" means the same as "What number added to 3 gives 8?"

Subtraction can also be intuitively understood through counting: The *difference* 8 - 3 is the whole number that results from counting *backward* 3 numbers starting at 8 - 8 ... 7, 6, 5. This process is consistent with the "take away" notion of subtraction. All of these notions are equivalent, and to us they seem natural. For students coming to grips with subtraction, seeing them all as the "same thing" takes time and many experiences.

Addition and subtraction can therefore be understood through counting, and that is one way in which children come to learn more about these arithmetic operations. This way of understanding arithmetic is the focus of this chapter.

Addition and Subtraction Problem Structures (And Other Factors that Affect Difficulty)

In most cases, the larger the whole numbers, the more difficult the problem. This is so even for single-digit problems, due to the frequency one has experienced the arithmetic computations and the strategies one must use. For example, children use a more sophisticated strategy to solve subtraction combinations whose minuend (the "whole" from which a part is subtracted) are larger than 10 than for those that are smaller than 10.

Beyond the size of the number, it is the *type*, or *structure* of the word problem that mainly determines its difficulty. Type depends on the *situation* and the *unknown*. There are four different situations, shown in the four rows of Table 5.1. The names in quotation marks are those some people consider useful in classroom discussions. For each of these categories, there are three quantities that play different roles in the problem, any one of which could be the

Table 5.1 Addition and Subtraction Problem Types

Category	Start/Part Unknown	Change/Difference Unknown	Result/Whole Unknown
Join ("Change Add To") An action of joining increases the number in a set.	*Start Unknown* ___ + 6 = 11 Al had some balls. Then he got 6 more. Now he has 11 balls. How many did he start with?	*Change Unknown* 5 + ___ = 11 Al had 5 balls. He bought some more. Now he has 11. How many did he buy?	*Result Unknown* 5 + 6 = ___ Al had 5 balls and gets 6 more. How many does he have in all?
Separate ("Change Take Away") An action of separating decreases the number in a set.	*Start Unknown* ___ − 5 = 4 Al had some balls. He gave 5 to Barb. Now he has 4. How many did he have to start with?	*Change Unknown* 9 − ___ = 4 Al had 9 balls. He gave some to Barb. Now he has 4. How many did he give to Barb?	*Result Unknown* 9 − 5 = ___ Al had 9 balls and gave 5 to Barb. How many does he have left?
Part-Part-Whole ("Collection") Two parts make a whole, but there is no action—the situation is static.	*Part ("Partner") Unknown* [diagram: 10 over □ and 6; tree 10 → □, 6] Al has 10 balls. Some are blue, 6 are red. How many are blue?	*Part ("Partner") Unknown* [diagram: 10 over 4 and □; tree 10 → 4, □] Al has 10 balls; 4 are blue, the rest are red. How many are red?	*Whole ("Total") Unknown#* [diagram: □ over 4 and 6; tree □ → 4, 6] Al has 4 red balls and 6 blue balls. How many balls does he have in all?
Compare The numbers of objects in two sets are compared.	*Smaller Unknown* [diagram: 7; □ with 2 fewer] Al had 7 balls. Barb has 2 fewer balls than Al. How many balls does Barb have? (More difficult language: "Al has 2 more than Barb.")	*Difference Unknown* [diagram: 7; 5 with ___] "Won't get": Al has 7 dogs and 5 bones. How many dogs won't get a bone? Al has 6 balls. Barb has 4. How many more does Al have than Barb? (Also: How many fewer balls does Barb have?)	*Larger Unknown* [diagram: □; 5 with 2 more] Al has 5 marbles. Barb has 2 more than Al. How many marbles does Barb have? (More difficult language: "Al has 2 marbles less than Barb.")

unknown. In some cases, such as the "parts" of Part-Part-Whole problems, there is no real difference between them. In others, such as the Result Unknown, Change Unknown, or Start Unknown of Join problems, the differences in difficulty are large. Result Unknown problems are easy, Change Unknown problems are moderately difficult, and Start Unknown are the most difficult. This is due in large part to the increasing difficulty children have in modeling, or "acting out," each type. Study these problem types so that you can reliably classify any word problem.

The Development of Arithmetic Counting Strategies

Most people can invent strategies for solving such problems. The strategies of young children are notably creative and diverse. For example, preschool to first-grade children can invent and use a variety of covert and overt strategies, including counting fingers, finger patterns (i.e., conceptual subitizing, see Chapter 2), verbal counting, retrieval ("just knowing" a combination), derived combinations ("derived facts"; e.g., "doubles plus 1": $7 + 8 = 7 + 7 + 1 = 14 + 1 = 15$). Children are flexible strategists, using different strategies on problems they perceive to be easier or harder. This chapter focuses on counting-based strategies.

Children's Modeling and Counting Strategies

Strategies usually emerge from children's modeling the problem situation. That is, children as young as preschool and kindergarten can solve problems using concrete objects or drawings (see the section *Manipulatives and "Concrete" Representations* in Chapter 16). Children with fewer experiences engaging in math have more difficulty solving verbally presented problems.

Counting Strategies

Preschoolers, 3 and 4 years of age, were told stories in which they were asked, for example, to help a baker. They were shown an array of goods, which they counted. Then the array was hidden, and one, two, or three more goods were added or subtracted. Children were asked to predict, and then count to check. Even the 3-year-olds understood the difference between predicting and counting to check a prediction. All were able to offer a number that resulted from an addition or subtraction that was consistent with the principles that addition increases numerosity and subtraction decreases numerosity. They made other *reasonable* predictions. Their counts were usually correct and children preferred them to their predictions (Zur & Gelman, 2004).

Developmentally, most children initially use a "counting-all" strategy. As illustrated in Figure 5.2, given a situation of 5 + 2, such children count out objects to form a set of five items, then count out two more items, and, finally, count all those starting again at "one" and—if they make no counting errors—report "7." These children naturally use such counting methods to solve story situations as long as they understand the language and situation in the story.

After children develop such methods, they eventually *curtail* them. On their own, 4-year-olds may start "counting on"; for example, solving the previous problem by counting, "Fiiiive … six, seven. Seven!" The elongated pronunciation may be substituting for counting the initial set one by one. It is *as if* they counted a set of five items. Some children first use transitional strategies, such as the "shortcut-sum" strategy, which is like counting-all strategy, but involves only one

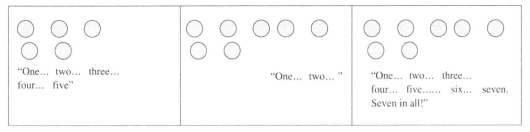

Figure 5.2 Using the "counting-all" procedure to solve an addition problem (5 + 2)

count; for example, to solve 4 + 3, 1, 2, 3, 4..., 5, 6, 7 and answer 7. Importantly, children pass through an intermediate stage in which they can count on in situations only when prompted (Tzur & Lambert, 2011). They have to construct the ability to *anticipate* the counting actions of starting at the number in one set and to stop after counting on the number in the second set (especially if items are not present).

Children then typically move to the "counting-on-from-larger" strategy, which is preferred by most children once they invent it. Presenting problems such as 2 + 23, where counting on saves the most work, often prompts children to invent or adopt this strategy. Thus, counting skills–especially sophisticated counting skills–play an important role in developing competence with arithmetic. Counting easily and quickly predicts arithmetic competence in kindergarten and later. Knowing the next number ("Counter from *N* (*N* + 1, *N* - 1)," in Chapter 3) predicts arithmetic achievement and addition speed in Grades 1 and 2.

"Counting on" when increasing collections, and the corresponding "counting-back-from" when decreasing collections, are powerful numerical strategies for children. However, they are only beginning strategies. In the case where the amount of increase is unknown, children use "counting-up-to" to find the unknown amount. If six items are increased so that there are now nine items, children may find the amount of increase by counting, "Siiiix; 7, 8, 9. Three." And if nine items are decreased so that six remain, children may count from 9 down to 6 to find the unknown decrease (Separate Change Unknown), as follows: "Nine; 8, 7, 6. Three." However, counting backward, especially more than three counts, is difficult for most children unless they have high-quality instruction in this skill.

Instead, children in many parts of the world learn "counting-up-to" the total to solve a subtraction situation because they realize that it is easier. For example, the story problem "8 apples on the table. The children ate 5. How many now?" could be solved by thinking, "I took away 5 from those 8, so 6, 7, 8 (raising a finger with each count), that's 3 more left in the 8." When children fully realize that they can find the amount of decrease (e.g., 9 - □ = 6) by putting the items back with the 6 and counting from 6 up to 9, they begin to establish that subtraction is the inversion of addition and can use addition instead of subtraction. This understanding develops over several years but may emerge in the preschool years and can be used by kindergartners with good instruction.

Metacognitive Strategies and Other Knowledge

There is much more to solving even simple word problems than just knowing counting strategies. Children must understand the language, including the semantics and the syntax, and be familiar with the situations the language represents. Also, solutions of word problems occur in various social-cultural contexts and those, too, affect children's solutions. For example, some teaching acts can lead to children using unproductive "coping strategies," or may even involve direct teaching of unfortunate strategies that limits children's problem-solving abilities. As an example, some children come to use, or are taught to use, "key-word" approaches, such as finding the word "left" or "less" in a problem and then subtracting a small from a larger number they find in the text. This does not work, of course, if the problem is: Frank gave away 3 cookies and still has 7 left. How many did he have to start with? Even children not taught to use the flawed key-word approach need to avoid that trap, using the executive function of *inhibitory control* (Chapter 14).

When children consider problems for which they have no immediate strategy, they often do *not* apply "heuristics," or general strategies or representations that may serve as guides. Teaching of heuristics such as "make a drawing" or "break the problem down into parts" have not been remarkably successful. However, *metacognitive* or self-regulatory teaching, often including heuristics, shows more promise (Verschaffel, Greer, & De Corte, 2007). Chapter 13 focuses on such problem-solving processes.

Summary

Babies are sensitive to some situations that adults see as arithmetical. They may be using an innate ANS or subitizing ability that is limited to very small numbers, such as 2 + 1. Or they may be individuating and tracking individual objects. In any case, they possess a far richer foundation for arithmetic than traditional Piagetian accounts suggested.

Only later in preschool can children solve problems with larger numbers (but not yet large; e.g., 3 + 2), using concrete objects and subitizing and/or counting. Later again, children develop more sophisticated counting and composition strategies as curtailments of these early solution strategies. That is, children learn to count from a given number (rather than starting only from one), generate the number before or after another number, and eventually embed one number sequence inside another. They think about the number sequence, rather than just saying it (Fuson, 1992a). Such reflection empowers counting to be an effective and efficient representational tool for problem solving. Thus, educators must study the processes children use as well as the problems they can solve to understand both their strengths and limitations at various ages. Learning involves a complex development of knowledge, understanding, and skill, usually involving the use of a mix of strategies. More sophisticated strategies are learned, strategies are selected more effectively, and speed and accuracy of executing these strategies increases (NMP, 2008).

Experience and Education: Arithmetic Counting Strategies

At *every* age, children need opportunities to learn arithmetic. In the U.S., virtually all children need *better* opportunities than those presently provided to solve addition and subtraction problems, building on their competencies with subitizing, modeling, and counting. Because this unfortunate state of affairs is so common, we begin this section by discussing roadblocks to high-quality instruction (see also Davenport, Henry, Clements, & Sarama, 2019b).

Roadblocks to High-quality Experience and Education

Limiting Beliefs

Children can learn arithmetic from 3 years of age, and, in limited contexts, even earlier. Yet most preschool teachers and other professionals do not believe arithmetic is appropriate, and do not believe very young children can think arithmetically. Thus, it is unsurprising that young children do not receive high-quality educational experiences with arithmetic.

Typical Instruction

Instruction often helps students perform arithmetic procedures, but *at the expense of conceptual understanding*. Children are initially competent at modeling different problem types. Schooling makes them ask, "What do I do, add or subtract?" and makes them perform more wrong-operation errors. Instead, informal modeling and understanding the situations need to be encouraged and instruction needs to build on informal knowledge (Frontera, 1994). *Children need experience with all problem types* (Artut, 2015a).

Textbooks

In too many traditional U.S. textbooks, only the simplest meanings are given for addition and subtraction problems Join or Separate, Result Unknown (Stigler, Fuson, Ham, & Kim, 1986). Indeed, both curricula and teachers in many countries present only the simplest problem types (Saribaş & Arnas, 2017). That is unfortunate, because (a) most kindergartners can already solve these problem types and (b) other countries' first-grade curricula include *all* the types in Table 5.1 (p. 91).

Textbooks also do little with subitizing or counting, automatization of which aids arithmetical reasoning, and de-emphasize the use of sophisticated counting strategies. The younger the children, the more problematic these instructional approaches become. No wonder that American schooling has a weak positive effect on children's accuracy on arithmetic, but an inconsistent effect on their use of strategies.

In addition, textbooks offer an inadequate presentation of problems with anything but small numbers. In one kindergarten text, only 17 of the 100 addition combinations were presented, and each of these only a small number of times.

Teaching Arithmetic Counting Strategies

There are other reasons to believe that present practice is inadequate with regard to teaching arithmetic counting strategies. For example, longitudinal studies suggest that in spite of the gains many younger children make through adopting efficient mental strategies for computation in the first years of school, a significant proportion of them still rely on inefficient counting strategies to solve arithmetical problems mentally in the upper years of primary school (Carr & Alexeev, 2011; Clarke, Clarke, & Horne, 2006; Gervasoni, 2005; Perry, Young-Loveridge, Dockett, & Doig, 2008). Early use of more sophisticated strategies, including fluency and accuracy in second grade, appears to influence later arithmetical competence. Children using manipulatives continue to need to use manipulatives (Carr & Alexeev, 2011).

How might we do better? Teachers want children to advance in their sophistication, but effective advances usually do not involve replacing initial strategies with school-based algorithms, such as "column addition" (see Chapter 6). Instead, *effective teaching helps children curtail and adapt their early inventions and strategies.*

General Approaches

As we shall see repeatedly, one of the main lessons from research for arithmetic is to *connect children's learning of skills, facts, concepts, and problem solving.* So, work with children to pose problems, make connections, and then work out these problems in ways that make the connections visible. Encourage children to use increasingly sophisticated counting strategies, seek patterns, and understand the relationship between addition and subtraction (cf. Davenport et al., 2019b; Gervasoni, 2018b).

Other studies confirm the advantages in children inventing, using, sharing, and explaining *different strategies* for more demanding arithmetic problems. *The number of different strategies children understand and employ predicts their later learning.*

Counting On

Encourage children to invent new strategies. To begin, help children learn the "Counter from N ($N + 1$, $N - 1$)" level of counting well. This helps because children often use the knowledge that $n + 1$ tasks can be solved by the "number-after" strategy (the counting word after n is the sum) to invent the counting-on strategy. If children, especially those with a learning disability, need help with the number-after skill, provide and then fade a "running start." All children benefit from instruction that targets discovering rules for $n + 1$ and $1 + n$ as well as for $n + 0 = n$ and $0 + n = n$, and this can be delivered with computers (Baroody, Eiland, Purpura, & Reid, 2012, 2013). Also, to spur children to start using the counting-on-from-larger strategy, pose problems in which its use would save considerable effort, such as $1 + 18$. Children originally can count on only when prompted—initially by others and then sometimes by their own self-reflection ("Oops! I already knew how many in that group!") and may revert to counting all. Providing children with tasks such as these (e.g., $8 + 1$ to get started on $n + 1$; or $3 + 21$ to encourage them to use counting on in more problems) and prompt them to use counting on ("Can you start with 21 and count up for a faster way?"). This will serve to support their internalization and improved understanding of the process and their knowledge that such strategies yield the same answer as counting all with increased efficiency (Tzur & Lambert, 2011).

If some children do not then invent "counting on" for themselves and always use "counting all," encourage understanding of the connection between counting and arithmetic by emphasizing the successor principle—adding 1 gives a total that is "the next counting number." Children can often invent this concept and skill with good activities (see Chapter 3 for activities as well as Table 5.2) and minimal guidance (Baroody, Purpura, Eiland, & Reid, 2015).

If some children need more assistance, this is an admittedly time-consuming but very successful method: teach understanding and use of the subskills. For example, lay out numerals "6" and "4" and ask a child to lay out that number of counters. Ask him to count to find how many in all. As he is counting, right as he reaches "six," point to the last counter of the first group (the sixth object). When he counts that last counter, point to the numeral card and say,

Table 5.2 Goals for Addition and Subtraction (Emphasizing Counting Strategies) from the Common Core State Standards–Mathematics (CCSSM)

Operations and Algebraic Thinking [K.OA in CCSSM]

Understand addition as putting together and adding to and understand subtraction as taking apart and taking from.

1. Represent addition and subtraction with objects, fingers, mental images, drawings, sounds (e.g., claps), acting out situations, verbal explanations, expressions, or equations. [Drawings need not show details but should show the mathematics in the problem. (This applies wherever drawings are mentioned in the Standards.)]
2. Solve addition and subtraction word problems, and add and subtract within 10, e.g., by using objects or drawings to represent the problem.
3. For any number from 1 to 9, find the number that makes 10 when added to the given number, e.g., by using objects or drawings, and record the answer with a drawing or equation.

Operations and Algebraic Thinking [1.OA in CCSSM]

Represent and solve problems involving addition and subtraction.

1. Use addition and subtraction within 20 to solve word problems involving situations of adding to, taking from, putting together, taking apart, and comparing, with unknowns in all positions, e.g., by using objects, drawings, and equations with a symbol for the unknown number to represent the problem. [The CCSSM refers to their Glossary, Table 1, which has information very similar to this chapter's Table 5.1.]
2. Solve word problems that call for addition of three whole numbers whose sum is less than or equal to 20, e.g., by using objects, drawings, and equations with a symbol for the unknown number to represent the problem.

Understand and apply properties of operations and the relationship between addition and subtraction.

1. Apply properties of operations as strategies to add and subtract. Examples: If $8 + 3 = 11$ is known, then $3 + 8 = 11$ is also known. (Commutative property of addition.) To add $2 + 6 + 4$, the second two numbers can be added to make a ten, so $2 + 6 + 4 = 2 + 10 = 12$. (Associative property of addition.) [Students need not use formal terms for these properties.]
2. Understand subtraction as an unknown-addend problem. For example, subtract $10 - 8$ by finding the number that makes 10 when added to 8. Add and subtract within 20.

1. Relate counting to addition and subtraction (e.g., by counting on 2 to add 2).
2. Add and subtract within 20, demonstrating fluency for addition and subtraction within 10. Use strategies such as counting on; making ten (e.g., $8 + 6 = 8 + 2 + 4 = 10 + 4 = 14$); decomposing a number leading to a ten (e.g., $13 - 4 = 13 - 3 - 1 = 10 - 1 = 9$); using the relationship between addition and subtraction (e.g., knowing that $8 + 4 = 12$, one knows $12 - 8 = 4$); and creating equivalent but easier or known sums (e.g., adding $6 + 7$ by creating the known equivalent $6 + 6 + 1 = 12 + 1 = 13$).

Work with addition and subtraction equations.

1. Understand the meaning of the equal sign and determine if equations involving addition and subtraction are true or false. For example, which of the following equations are true and which are false? $6 = 6, 7 = 8 - 1, 5 + 2 = 2 + 5, 4 + 1 = 5 + 2$.
2. Determine the unknown whole number in an addition or subtraction equation relating to three whole numbers. For example, determine the unknown number that makes the equation true in each of the equations $8 + ? = 11, 5 = ? - 3, 6 + 6 = ?$.

Operations and Algebraic Thinking [2.OA in CCSSM]

Add and subtract within 20.

1. Fluently add and subtract within 20 using mental strategies. [See standard 1.OA.6 for a list of mental strategies.] By end of Grade 2, know from memory all sums of two one-digit numbers. [See the following chapter in this book.]

(Continued)

Table 5.2 (Cont.)

___

Work with equal groups of objects to gain foundations for multiplication.

1.   Determine whether a group of objects (up to 20) has an odd or even number of members, e.g., by pairing objects or counting them by twos; write an equation to express an even number as a sum of two equal addends.

Measurement and Data [2.MD in CCSSM]

Measure and estimate lengths in standard units.

1.   Measure to determine how much longer one object is than another, expressing the length difference in terms of a standard length unit.

Work with time and money.

1.   Solve word problems involving dollar bills, quarters, dimes, nickels, and pennies, using $ and ¢ symbols appropriately. *Example: If you have 2 dimes and 3 pennies, how many cents do you have?*

Represent and interpret data.

1.   Draw a picture graph and a bar graph (with single-unit scale) to represent a data set with up to four categories. Solve simple put-together, take-apart, and Compare problems using information presented in a bar graph. [The CCSSM refers to their Glossary, Table 1, which has information very similar to this chapter's Table 5.1.]

___

"See this is 6 also. It tells how many counters there are here." Have him count again, and interrupt him sooner, until he understands that when he reaches that object, he will have counted 6. Next, point to the first counter of the second group (addend), and say, "See, there were *six* counters here, so *this* one (exaggerated jump from last counter in the first addend to first counter in the second addend) gets the number *seven*." If need be, interrupt the child's counting of the first addend with questions: "How many here (first addend)? So, this dot (last of first) gets what number? And this one (first of second)?" Continue until the child understands these ideas and can answer easily.

Such teaching of counting strategies can be especially effective for children with math difficulties. It is most effective to follow the teaching with deliberate planned practice (Fuchs et al., 2010, who also promoted retrieval whenever possible).

"Counting all" and other strategies, such as "counting-up-to" and "counting-down-to," are not just good strategies for finding answers. They also develop Part–Part–Whole relationships more effectively than teaching paper-and-pencil algorithms (Wright, 1991).

Other arithmetic concepts are foundational to the development of children's strategies and to their math learning (Aunio & Räsänen, 2015a).

Adding Zero (Additive Identity)

This is simply the understanding that adding zero to any number results in that number, or $n + 0 = n$ (zero is called the additive identity). Children can learn this as a general rule, and thus do not need to practice combinations involving zero.

Commutativity often develops without explicit teaching. Presenting tasks such as 3 + 5 near the commuted problem 5 + 3, and doing so systematically and repeatedly, is useful.

Inversion

In a similar vein, children's use of arithmetical principles, such as the inverse principle, before formal schooling should be considered when planning curriculum and teaching (most curricula do not do so, Baroody, 2016a). Once kindergartners can verbally subitize small numbers and understand the additive and subtractive identity principle, they can solve inversion problems using 1 ($n + 1 - 1 = $ _?) and slowly work up to 4. A useful teaching strategy is to first add or take away the *same* objects, discuss the inversion principle, and then pose problems in which you add several objects, and take away the same number, but not the same objects. Research suggests that children do better on inversion problems than others, especially when the tasks use pictures to represent the problem (Gilmore & Papadatou-Pastou, 2009).

Research also suggests that discussing the inverse relationship between addition and subtraction explicitly with second and third graders helps them understand and use that concept (Nunes, Bryant, Evans, Bell, & Barros, 2011). Children saw a cartoon representation of story problems (e.g., a mail carrier had some letters, delivers 12, now has 29 left. How many did he start with?). They were then asked to show how they could solve the problem with a calculator, because this challenged children to apply inversion before doing any calculating. The children solved inversion problems better than a control group. Those who were taught with inversion and direct (non-inversion) problems mixed together performed better than those who were taught inversion problems in a block (Nunes et al., 2011).

Invention or Direct Instruction?

Some argue that children must invent their own arithmetic strategies. Others claim that *children making sense of mathematical relations is key*, but the exact teaching approach matters less. Research suggests the following:

- Challenge preschoolers to build subitizing, counting, and other competencies and then work on arithmetic problems in concrete settings.
- Later, ask children to solve semi-concrete problems, in which children reason about hidden but previously manipulated or viewed collections.
- Encourage children to invent their own strategies—with peers and with your *active* guidance—discussing and explaining their strategies.
- Encourage children to adopt more sophisticated, beneficial strategies as soon as possible.
- Avoid a dichotomy between child-invented ("constructivist") approaches and direct instruction. For some children, at some point in the learning process, presenting clear models, explicit math talk by the child and teachers, and practice of each new concept, strategy, or skill with immediate feedback is beneficial.

(Gersten et al., 2015)

Representations

Forms of representation are important factors in young children's arithmetic problem solving.

Representations in Curricula

Primary-grade students tend to ignore *decorative* pictures, such as a picture of a bus (and nothing else) with a word problem about the number of children getting on and off the bus. Children attend to, but are not always helped by, pictures containing information required for solution of the problem; that is, when they must also interpret a diagram to glean necessary information that is not in the text (these are more difficult; Elia, Gagatsis, & Demetriou, 2007). Decorative pictures should be avoided. Students should be taught to use informational pictures when that is an instructional goal.

Students often ignore, or are confused by, number line representations as well. If number lines are to be used to teach arithmetic, students should learn to move between number line and symbolic representations. One study suggested that carefully guided peer tutoring on using the number line to solve missing addend problems (e.g., 4 + _ = 6) was successful and was appreciated by both teachers and the students, who were first graders. The tutors were taught to use a teaching procedure, a shortened version of which follows.

1. What is the sign?
2. Which way do you go? [*on the number line*]
3. Is the blank before or after the equal sign? [*the former is "tricky"*]
4. What's the first number; put your pencil on it; it tells you where to start.
5. Identify the second number as the goal.
6. How many jumps?
7. Put that number in the blank and read the entire number sentence to check.

There are other important specifics. First, the intervention only helped when peer tutors demonstrated and guided use of the number line—the number line was not useful by itself. Also, the accuracy of children who just solved missing addend problems decreased, indicating that practicing errors is not helpful. There was anecdotal evidence that it was important for peers to give feedback to the students they were tutoring. Thus, present, typical instruction on use of representations, especially geometry/spatial/pictorial representations, may be inadequate for most students and should receive more attention.

Finally, successful models are more often number *paths* with *steps* (discrete, countable models) not number lines (see Chapter 4). In arithmetic, too, this kind of representation, guided by the teacher, can be very helpful to preschoolers just learning arithmetic (Banse et al., 2020).

Language: Always Important

Of course, a key representational tool is the child's oral language. It is useful to have children name the problem type. This takes time, but research indicates it is useful (Schumacher & Fuchs, 2012). Children can role play the situation, describe it in their own words, and use any of the representations discussed in this section (manipulatives, diagrams, etc.). They can then express the relationship in the problem with a math expression, such as $B - s = D$, where "B" is the bigger number, "s" the smaller number, and "D" the difference. Encourage children to describe problems and their solution strategies to each other and to the class. Reflect their ideas back to them, elaborating them with clear, consistent math vocabulary and, when appropriate, explanations.

Use *relational* language. This is especially important when discussing Compare problems. Teachers should provide explicit instruction on the meanings of relational terminology and the symmetrical relationship between more and less/fewer within a word-problem context (adapted from Schumacher & Fuchs, 2012). For example, after identifying Compare problem types, provide instruction on the specific meanings of "more," "less," and "fewer." Discuss how to identify which quantity is more or less. Consider the problem from Table 5.1, "Al had 7 balls. Barb has 2 fewer balls than Al. How many balls does Barb have?" The statement "Barb has 2 more than Al" should be simplified to "Barb has more than Al" to ensure the relation is understood. Also, teach children to say or write an alternative relational statement, so that "Barb has 2 fewer balls than Al" becomes "Al has 2 more balls than Barb."

In the study, second graders were taught this and then the following sequence. After identifying the problem type and the appropriate math expression, $B - s = D$, they identified the unknown in the Compare problem they were solving and placed "x" under that part of the expression. Next, the students identified and wrote in the other numbers. They then solved the problem by finding "x." These children outperformed others taught regularly and those in a special "calculation" intervention (Schumacher & Fuchs, 2012).

Manipulatives[1]

What about manipulatives, whether counters or fingers? Many teachers *view these strategies as crutches and discourage their use too soon* (Fuson, 1992a). Paradoxically, those who are best at solving problems *with* objects, fingers (Crollen & Noël, 2015b), or counting are *least* likely to use those less sophisticated strategies *in the future*, because they are confident in their answers and so move toward accurate, fast retrieval or composition (Siegler, 1993). Thus, help and encourage all children, and especially those from lower-income communities, to use these strategies until they are confident.

Trying to move children too fast to retrieval ironically makes this development slow and painful. Instead, move as soon as possible—but not sooner—to counting strategies, and discuss how and why strategies work and why a new strategy is desirable; this will help children build meaning and confidence.

For what period are manipulatives necessary? For children at any age they can be necessary at certain levels of thinking. Preschoolers initially need them to give meaning to arithmetical tasks and the number words involved. In certain contexts, older children require concrete representations as well. For example, Les Steffe asked first grader Brenda to count six marbles into his hand. Then he covered them up, showed one more, and asked how many he had in all. She said one. When he pointed out he had six marbles hidden, Brenda said adamantly, "I don't see no six!" For Brenda, there could be no number without things to count (Steffe & Cobb, 1988). Successful teachers interpret what the child is doing and are thinking and attempting to see the situation from the child's point of view. Based on their interpretations, they conjecture what the child might be able to learn or abstract from his or her experiences. Similarly, when they interact with the child, they also consider their own actions from the child's point of view. Brenda's teacher, for example, might hide four marbles and then encourage Brenda to put up four fingers and use them to represent the hidden marbles.

Fingers—the Best Manipulative?

Fingers are especially important (Crollen & Noël, 2015b). Teaching useful *finger* addition methods accelerates children's single-digit addition and subtraction as much as a year over traditional methods in which children count objects or pictures (Fuson, Perry, & Kwon, 1994). The particular strategy in this study was to use the non-writing hand to perform counting-on-keeping-track tasks (even for subtraction). The index finger represents 1, the middle finger 2, and so forth up to 4. The thumb represents 5 (all other fingers are raised), the thumb and index finger 6, and so forth. Children would then count on using fingers to keep track of the second addend. Most children moved to mental methods by second grade; more children from low-resource communities used the finger method throughout the second grade, but they were proud to be able to add and subtract large numbers. Educators should note that different cultures, such as traditional U.S., Korean, Latino, and Mozambican have different informal methods for representing numbers with fingers (Draisma, 2000; Fuson et al., 1994).

As we saw previously, if teachers try to eliminate use of fingers too soon, children just put them "under the desk" where they are not visually helpful, or they adopt less useful and more error-prone methods. Further, the most sophisticated methods are *not* crutches that held children back.

Moving beyond Manipulatives

Once children have established successful strategies using objects as manipulatives, they can often solve simple arithmetic tasks without them. To transition to more abstract strategies, ask children to count out five toys and place them into an opaque container, count out four more toys and place them into the container, and then figure out how many toys in all without peeking at them.

Drawings and diagrams that children produce are important representational tools. For example, to solve 6 + 5, children might draw 6 circles, then 5 circles, and then circle 5 of the 6 along with the second 5 to make 10, and then announce that the total is 11. As another example, consider the diagrams in Table 5.1 on p. 91. Karen Fuson found that the second diagrams for the "Collections" problem types were more useful for children (Fuson, 2018b). They called them "math mountains" and introduced them with stories of "Tiny Tumblers," some of whom tumbled down one side and some the other side of the mountain. They would draw dots in circles on each side and then make different combinations. Their number sentences for this problem type started with the total (e.g., 10 = 4 + 6) and would record all the combinations they could make (10 = 0 + 10; 10 = 1 + 9 ...). Chapter 13 presents other research on children's use of diagrams in problem solving, but those in Table 5.1 have been used successfully in hundreds of classrooms (Fuson, 2018b).

Use Numerals

Although worksheets of facts and time tests are not recommended for preschoolers (see Chapter 6), *numerals are helpful representations*. That is, numerals representing quantities to be added or subtracted, such as a "4" and a "5" (not necessarily as "4 + 5") help children remember and operate on those numbers (Alvarado, 2015). They should not be thought of as "too abstract" for young children. Another study found a similar benefit of "counting cards"—each of which has both a numeral and dots in a five-and-tens frame (Banse et al., 2020). Beyond just numerals, kindergartners can recognize the familiar number sentences (3 + 4 = 7) but may have a hard time producing them. First graders can do both, but recognition of *unfamiliar* number sentences (7 = 3 + 4) is challenging (Mark-Zigdon & Tirosh, 2017c).

Teaching Arithmetic Problem Solving

A main issue for teaching is knowing the sequence in which to present the problem types. The broad developmental progression is as follows.

1. *(a) Join, Result Unknown (change plus); (b) Part-Part-Whole, Whole Unknown; and (c) Separate, Result Unknown (change minus)*. Children can *directly model* these problems' actions, step by step. For example, they might solve a Join problem as follows: "Morgan had 3 candies (child counts out 3 counters) and then got 2 more (child counts out 2 more). How many does he have in all?" (The child counts the counters and announces "five.") Attention should be paid to the math vocabulary, for example, that "altogether" means "in all" or "in total."

2. *Join, Change Unknown and Part-Part-Whole, Part Unknown*. A three-phase developmental progression occurs leading to the ability to solve these types. First, children learn to solve the first two problems types (a and b in #1 above) with "counting on." Second, they learn to solve the last problem type (c in #1), Separate, Result Unknown problems, using "counting on" (thinking of 11 - 6 as 6 + □ = 11, and "counting-up-to" 11, keeping track of the 5 counts) or "counting back" (which students can do if they have well-developed skills in counting backward). In either case, intentional instruction is needed. The counting backward solution might work best if all early childhood teachers, preschool and up, developed that skill conscientiously. The "counting-up" method might work best if you explicitly help children see how to transform the subtraction to a missing-addend addition problem. This represents another advantage of this approach—the relationship between addition and subtraction is highlighted.

    Third, and finally, they learn to apply that strategy to solve these two new types; for example, counting on from the "start" number to the total, keeping track of the number of counts on the fingers, and reporting that number.

3. *"Start Unknown and Compare"* (Artut, 2015a). Children can use commutativity to change the Join, Start Unknown problems to those that yield to "counting on" (e.g., □ + 6 = 11 becomes 6 + □ = 11, and then count on and keep track of the counts). Or, they use reversal to change □ - 6 = 5 to 6 + 5 = □. At this point, all of these types of problems can be solved by new methods that use derived combinations (using a known combination, such as 5 + 5 = 10, to figure out another combination; such as 6 + 5 as "one more" or 11—discussed in detail in Chapter 6).

Compare type problems present children with several unique difficulties, including vocabulary challenges. Many children interpret "less" or "fewer" as synonyms for "more" (Fuson, 2018b). They hear the larger term in many situations (taller, longer) more frequently than the smaller term (shorter), so they need to learn several vocabulary terms. Comparisons can be expressed in several ways, and one way is easier. The order "Jonah has 6 candies" then "Juanita has 3 more than Jonah" is easier than "He has 3 fewer than Juanita" in figuring out how many candies Juanita has. Research shows that for "There are 5 birds and 3 worms," the question, "How many birds won't get a worm?" is easier than "How many more birds than worms are there?" (Hudson, 1983). Thus, such wording might be used to introduce these problems. Children can also be encouraged to draw matching diagrams, such as Figure 5.3.

Later, children could use the type of bar diagrams shown in Table 5.1 on p. 91, which have been successful in hundreds of classrooms (Fuson, 2018b). Similar wording changes in initial presentations of comparison problems help children, such as changing the question, "How many more does A have than B?" to "How many would B have to get to have the same number as A?" Eventually, ask students to rephrase questions, including changing a "fewer" to a "more" statement. Further, although textbooks often model the use of subtraction to solve comparison problems, more students think of comparisons using an unknown addend *count on* or *add on*. Counting or adding on models the comparison situation because the two addends (the small quantity and the difference quantity) are added on one side of the equation and they then balance the large quantity which is written alone on the other side of the equation.

Schema-based approaches are similar with explicit attention to naming the problem type, as in Table 5.1 (Jitendra, 2019). Students are taught to find the problem type, organize information in the problem using a schema diagram, plan how to solve the problem, and solve the problem. This has been shown to be useful for third graders with or without mathematical difficulties (Jitendra, 2019).

In summary, children benefit from instruction in two aspects of problems. First is understanding *situations*, including understanding "what's going on" in the contexts as well as the language used to describe them. Second is understanding the *math structure*, such as learning Part–Whole relationships via fact families or solving missing addend problems such as $\square + 3 = 8 - 2$. Children who are novices, poor performers, or who have cognitive impairments or learning difficulties,

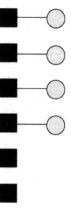

Figure 5.3 A matching diagram for comparison problems

may benefit particularly from situational training. More experienced and higher-performing children may profit more from math training. Such math training should be combined with help transferring their Part-Whole knowledge to problem settings by including both in the same instructional settings and discussing the similarities (e.g., "What do we know? Right, the whole and one part. How much in the whole? The part? What are we trying to find? Right! The other part. So, what strategy should we use? ...").

As a similar combination, specifically designed story contexts can help students develop an abstract understanding of Part-Whole problems (which most curricula do not do, Baroody, 2016a). For example, one teacher told stories about a grandfather who sent presents to his two grandchildren or, later, about the two children sending presents to him. Another story was about children who live on two islands and travel by boat to school. Children represented these with a Part–Part–Whole board (similar to the Part–Part–Whole diagrams in Table 5.1). They are guided to understand the complement principle in terms of Part-Whole relations; that is, if parts 5 and 8 make the whole 13, then subtracting one part from the whole leaves the other part (Baroody, 2016a).

Implications–A Brief Summary

Provide a full range of activities appropriate to the age (from at least 3 years on), covering subitizing, counting, counting strategies, and an increasing range of addition and subtraction situations (problem types), which should cover all problem types by the end of first grade. Emphasis should be on meaning and understanding, enhanced through discussions. Slow and inefficient learning occurs when principles are not understood. The tedious and superficial learning of school-age children is too often the product of not understanding the goals and relationships in arithmetic problems. *Meaning for the child must be the consistent focus*. A few additional implications are highlighted below and, of course, they are woven into the chapter's learning trajectory.

- The most important way to keep arithmetic meaningful, challenging, and enjoyable is, unsurprising–to *teach with learning trajectories*. In arithmetic, we have conducted *studies that show the advantage of teaching with learning trajectories* as compared to teaching the goal skills and procedures. (Clements et al., 2020a).
- For the youngest children, use physical objects related to the problem (rather than structured "math manipulatives"), which supports their use of informal knowledge to solve the arithmetic problems.
- Begin instruction with children's solution methods, ensuring initial semantic analysis of problems, that is, "What is happening in this situation?" and build more sophisticated numerical and arithmetic strategies in tandem with the development of conceptual understanding.
- Build multiple supporting concepts and skills. Subitizing is an important support to counting strategies such as counting on, and, as discussed in the following section, for small-number composition/decomposition approaches to addition and subtraction. Simple counting practice transfers to addition and subtraction, but counting skills should also include effortlessly counting forward and backward, counting in either direction starting with any number, naming the number before or after another number, "counting on using patterns," "counting on keeping track" of the number of counts, and eventually embedded quantities within counting sequences.

- Provide a variety of experiences, including children creating, using, sharing, and explaining different strategies to help children develop their adaptive expertise with arithmetic.
- Avoid pictures and illustrations that are merely decorative, as they are ignored by (or confuse) children and do not support problem solving, but only add to the length of textbooks (NMP, 2008).
- If children have difficulty with a certain problem type, use "you-language"; for example, instead of "Al had 7 balls. Barb has 2 fewer balls than Al. How many balls does Barb have?" pose it as "*I* have 7 balls. *You* have 2 fewer balls than me. How many balls do *you* have?" (Artut, 2015a).
- Provide instruction on the use of representations, especially geometry/spatial/pictorial representations.
- Ask children to explain and justify solutions rather than to merely "check" their work. Without guidance, requests to "check" are often not helpful to most young children, but justification, such as explaining to others "why you are right," both builds concepts and procedures and serves as a meaningful introduction to checking one's work.
- Here is an example of checking well done and a model for children's initial explorations. Briefly, having children explore problems on their own and then providing instruction was not as effective as first providing instruction (Loehr, Fyfe, & Rittle-Johnson, 2014b). *However*, asking children to explore problems, then providing instruction, *and then asking them to check their answers and mark if they were correct or put a new answer down was more effective than first providing instruction.* This is "productive failure" *followed* by an opportunity to *integrate* knowledge, think more deeply, and *apply* what was learned (Loehr et al., 2014b).
- Choose curricula that avoid the difficulties of too many U.S. textbooks; instruction should mitigate any limitations of any curriculum used.

In summary: Present children with a range of addition and subtraction types and encourage them to invent, adapt, use, discuss, and explain a variety of solution strategies that are meaningful to them. Most children can begin to do this even in pre-K, and most can develop such understandings and skills through the kindergarten and first-grade years. Children at the level of counting perceptual units may need to be encouraged to put two collections into one box and count all the items to establish the act of uniting and quantifying the sum. Most children can quickly learn to reprocess two collections and conceive of it as one quantifiable collection. They can then solve problems with an increasingly diverse range of strategies. Having them add one or two more to a collection encourages their awareness of increasing the number in a collection and encourages them to connect their counting and adding schemes (similar for counting backward, taking away, and subtraction). Some children need to re-count, but most, even in the pre-K year, can learn to count up with experience. In all cases, the emphasis should be on children's use of strategies that are meaningful to them. Approaches that emphasize understanding, meaningfulness, patterns, relations, and invention of strategies, if used consistently and patiently, also work with children with special needs (Baroody, 1996). Informal strategies such as knowing how to add 0 or 1 should be encouraged; research shows that, if paced appropriately, children classified as learning-disabled can be taught to use such patterns and strategies (see Chapters 15 and 16 for more on children with special needs). Additional specific implications are woven into the following learning trajectories in this and other chapters.

Table 5.3 Learning Trajectory for Addition and Subtraction (Emphasizing Counting Strategies)

Age	Developmental Progression	Instructional Activities
1	**Arithmetic Senser: Foundations** Very young children are sensitive to combining or separating perceptual groups. An infant may observe, point, or make sounds while someone else introduces a quantity of objects. They will notice the effects of increasing or decreasing small collections by one item and may also be sensitive to the results of combining larger groups. An infant, shown two groups of five dots hidden behind a screen one at a time, acts more surprised and interested when the screen is taken away to show only five dots (an incorrect amount) than if it is removed to reveal ten dots (a correct amount).	*Everyday foundational experiences with addition and subtraction situations, [LT]²*: Besides providing richly sensory, manipulative environments of quantities that change, use of words such as "more" and actions of adding objects directs attention to comparisons and combinations.
2-3	**Preverbal** +/- Adds and subtracts very small collections (totals up to 3), often making a collection rather than answering verbally. Shown 2 objects then 1 object going under a napkin, makes a set of 3 objects to "match."	*Solving nonverbal Join, Result Unknown or Separate, Result Unknown (take away) using the smallest numbers*: For example, children are shown 2 objects then 1 object going under a napkin, and then asked to show how many, [LT]².

4	**Small Number** +/- Finds sums for Join, Result Unknown and Separate, Result Unknown problems with totals up to 5 by "counting all" with objects.
	
	Asked, "You have 2 balls and get 1 more. How many in all?" counts out 2, then counts out 1 more, then counts all 3: "1, 2, 3 ... 3!"
		Word Problems, [LT]²: Have children solve simple Join, Result Unknown or Separate, Result Unknown (take away) problems with toys that represent the objects in the problems. Use totals up to 5. Ask children how they got their answer.
		    Tell children you want to buy 3 toy Triceratops and 2 toy Tyrannosauruses. Ask how many dinosaurs that is altogether.
		    Finger Word Problems, [LT]²: Challenge children to solve simple problems with their fingers. Children should place their hands in their laps between each problem.
		    Children show 3 fingers on one hand and 2 fingers on the other and count them to find how many altogether.

4-5	**Find Result** +/- Finds sums for Join, Result Unknown problems ("You had 3 apples and get 3 more, how many do you have in all?") and Part–Part–Whole ("There are 6 girls and 5 boys on the playground, how many children were there in all?") problems by *direct modeling, counting all, with objects*.
	
	Asked, "You have 2 red balls and 3 blue balls. How many in all?", counts out 2 red, then counts out 3 blue, then counts all 5.
	
	Solves take-away problems by separating with objects.
	
	Asked, "You have 5 balls and give 2 to Tom. How many do you have left?", counts out 5 balls, then takes away 2, and then counts remaining 3.
		Word Problems, [LT]²: Children solving all the above problem types using manipulatives or their fingers to represent objects.
		    Separate, Result Unknown (take away) problems, [LT]²: "You have 5 balls and give 2 to Tom. How many do you have left?" Children might count out 5 balls, then take away 2, and then count remaining 3.
		    Part–Part–Whole, Whole Unknown problems, [LT]²: They might solve, "You have 2 red balls and 3 blue balls. How many in all?"
		    Note: In all teacher-guided activities, present commuted pairs one after the other, 5 + 3 then 3 + 5. With such experiences, most children learn to incorporate commutativity into their strategies. Also, encourage children who can to use the shortcut-sum strategy (to solve 5 + 3, "1, 2, 3, 4, 5 ... 6, 7, 8 ... 8!"), which serves as a transition to "counting on."
		    Places Scenes (Addition) - Part-Part-Whole, Whole Unknown Problems, [LT]²: Children play with

(Continued)

Table 5.3 (Cont.)

Age Developmental Progression	Instructional Activities
	toy on a background scene and combine groups. For example, they might place 4 Tyrannosauruses and 5 Apatosauruses on the paper and then count all 9 to see how many dinosaurs they have in all.

Compare Game (Adding), [LT]²: For each pair of children, use two or more sets of counting cards (1–10). Mix and deal cards evenly, face down. Players simultaneously flip two cards to add, and then compare which is greater. The player with more says, "I have more!" and takes the opponent's cards. If cards are equal, each player flips another card to break the tie.

The game ends when all cards have been played, and the winner is the player with more cards.

Variation: Play this game without a winner by not allowing players to collect cards. *See the resource, "Introducing and Using Games" on* [LT]².

Find a Five, [LT]²: Children make groups of 1 to 5 beans then hide them under cups. Then, they mix up the cups. In pairs, children try to find 2 cups that equal 5. When ready, increase to a higher sum.

Make It *N* Adds on objects to "make one number into another," without needing to count from 1. Does not (necessarily) represent how many were added (this is not a requirement of this intermediate-difficulty problem type) (Aubrey, 1997).

Make it Right, [LT]²: Children solve problems such as, "This puppet has 4 balls, but she should have 6. Make it 6."

Note that "I'm Thinking of a Number" in Chapter 3 helps develop the relevant counting skills.

Asked, "This puppet has 4 balls, but she should have 6. Make it 6," puts up 4 fingers on one hand, immediately counts up from 4 while putting up 2 more fingers, saying, "5, 6."

Find Change +/- Finds the missing addend (e.g., 5 + _ = 7 or 9 - _ = 3) to solve Join and Separate, Change Unknown problems by adding on or taking away objects.

Solve Join, Change, Unknown problems such as, "You have 5 balls and then get some more. Now you have 7 in all. How many did you get?"

Join-to, count-all groups: Asked, "You have 5 balls and then get some more. Now you have 7 in all. How many did you get?", counts out 5, then counts those 5 again starting at 1, then adds more, counting "6, 7," then counts the

Solve Part-Part-Whole, Part Unknown problems, [LT]²: "There are 6 children on the playground. 2 are boys and the rest are girls. How many are girls?"

This problem type may be more difficult for most students, and not solvable independently until the next level because it requires keeping the

(Continued)

Table 5.3 (Cont.)

Age	Developmental Progression	Instructional Activities
	balls added to find the answer, 2. (Some children may use their fingers, and attenuate the counting by using finger patterns.) *Separate-to, count-all groups*: Asked, "Nita had 8 stickers. She gave some to Carmen. Now, she has 5 stickers. How many did she give to Carmen?", counts 8 objects, separates until 5 remain, counts those taken away. Compares by matching in simple situations. *Match, count rest*: Asked, "Here are 6 dogs and 4 balls. If we give a ball to each dog, how many dogs won't get a ball?", counts out 6 dogs, matches 4 balls to 4 of them, then counts the 2 dogs that have no ball.	added-on objects separate from the initial objects. Children might use fingers and finger patterns. They might use "adding-on" if they make one part first, or "separating from" if they count out 6, then remove 2, then count the remaining objects. With supportive phrasing and guidance, however, many children can learn to solve them. For example, using "boys and girls" in the above problem helps. So does saying "and the rest are." Finally, saying the known sum first helps, too.

5–6	**Counting Strategies** +/– Finds sums for joining ("You had 8 apples and get 3 more …") and Part–Part–Whole ("6 girls and 5 boys …") problems with finger patterns and/or by counting on.
	
	Counting on: "How much is 4 and 3 more?" "Fourrrrr … five, six, seven [*uses rhythmic or finger pattern to keep track*]. Seven!"
	
	Counting-up-to: May solve missing addend (3 + _ = 7) or Compare problems by counting up; e.g., counts "4, 5, 6, 7" while putting up fingers, and then counts or recognizes the 4 fingers raised.
	
	Asked, "You have 6 balls. How many more would you need to have 8?", says, "Six, seven [*puts up first finger*], eight [*puts up second finger*]. Two!"
		How Many Now? Have the children count objects as you place them in a box. Ask, "How many are in the box now?" Add 1, repeating the question, then check the children's responses by counting all the objects. Repeat, checking occasionally. When children are ready, sometimes add 2, and eventually more objects.
		    Variation: Place coins in a coffee can. Declare that a given number of objects are in the can. Then have the children close their eyes and count on by listening as additional objects are dropped in.
		    More Toppings, [LT]²: Children use cut-out "pizzas" and brown disks for toppings. The teacher asks them to put 5 toppings on their pizzas, and then asks how many they would have in all if they put on 3 more. They count on to answer, then actually put the toppings on to check.
		    Double Compare, [LT]²: Students compare sums of cards to determine which sum is greater. Encourage children to use more sophisticated strategies, such as counting on.
		
		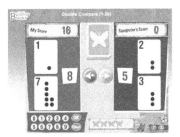
		
		Solve Join, Result Unknown and *Part–Part–Whole, Whole Unknown problems*, [LT]²: "How much is 4 and 3 more?"
		    Encouraging the use of counting on: Children often will start using counting on instead of direct

Table 5.3 (Cont.)

Age	Developmental Progression	Instructional Activities

		modeling (counting-all strategies) when the former is particularly easy to apply, such as when first addend is very large (23) and second one very small (2).
		    Teaching counting-on skills, [LT]²: If children need assistance to use counting on, or do not spontaneously create it, explicitly teach the subskills as on pp. 92–93.
		    Word Problems, [LT]²: Students solve word problems (totals to 10) off and on the computer.
		    Turn Over Ten and *Make Tens*, [LT]²: See Chapter 6. Many children will, especially at first, use counting strategies to solve the tasks in these games.

6	**Part-Whole** +/–: Has initial Part-Whole understanding and can solve all previous problem types using flexible strategies. May use some known combinations, such as 5 + 5 is 10. Sometimes can do Start Unknown (e.g., _ + 6 = 11), but only by trial and error.
	
	    Asked, "You had some balls. Then you get 6 more. Now, you have 11 balls. How many did you start with?", lays out 6, then 3 more, counts and gets 9. Puts 1 more with the 3 ... says, "Ten," then puts 1 more. Counts up from 6 to 11, then re-counts the group added, and says, "Five!"
		Solve Separate, Result Unknown problems, [LT]²: "You have 11 pencils and give 7 away. How many do you still have?" Encourage children to use counting down–or, especially with the numbers in this example, counting up–to determine the difference. Discuss when each of these and other strategies would be most efficient. Also, Join, Change Unknown, Part-Part-Whole, Part Unknown, and Compare, Difference Unknown (e.g., "Nita has 8 stickers. Carmen has 5 stickers. How many more does Nita have than Carmen?").
		    Hidden Objects, [LT]²: Hide 4 counters under the dark cloth and show students 7 counters. Tell them that 4 counters are hidden and challenge them to tell you how many there are in all. *Or*, tell them that there are 11 in all and ask how many are hidden. Have them discuss their solution strategies. Repeat with different sums.

6–7	**Numbers in Numbers** +/– Recognizes when a number is part of a whole and can keep the part and whole in mind simultaneously; solves Start Unknown (e.g., _ + 4 = 9) problems with counting strategies.
	
	    Asked, "You have some balls, then you get 4 more balls, now you have 9. How many did you have to start with?", counts, putting up fingers: "Five, six, seven, eight, nine." Looks at fingers and says, "Five!"
		Solve Start Unknown problems, [LT]²: "You have some balls, then you get 4 more balls, now you have 9. How many did you have to start with?"
		    Flip the Cards, [LT]²: Take turns. Students roll 2 numeral cubes (1–6), add them, and flip over numeral cards 1 to 12. Students can flip over any combination of cards whose sum equals the cube sum. Students continue until they cannot flip over any cards. Then, the sum of the cards still face-up is recorded. The lowest final sum wins. Available commercially as *Wake Up Giants* or *Shut the Box*.
		    Guess My Rule, [LT]²: Tell the class that they have to guess your rule. Students give a number (e.g., 4), then the teacher records:
		    $4 \rightarrow 8$
		 Students might guess the rule is "doubling." However, as the game continues:
		    $4 \rightarrow 8$
		    $10 \rightarrow 14$
		    $1 \rightarrow 5 \ldots$
		 The students then guess the rule is "add 4." *But they cannot say this*. If they think they know, *they* try to give the number to the right of the arrow.

(Continued)

Table 5.3 (Cont.)

Age Developmental Progression	Instructional Activities

The teacher records it if they are right. Only when (most) all of the students can do this do they discuss the rule.

Function Machine 1, [LT]²: Students identify a math function ("rule") by observing a series of operations that apply a consistent addition or subtraction value (+ 2, - 5, etc.).

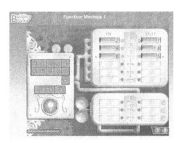

Deriver +/- Uses flexible strategies and derived combinations (e.g., 7 + 7 is 14, so 7 + 8 is 15) to solve all types of problems. Includes "Break Apart to Make Ten" (BAMT; explained in Chapter 6). Can simultaneously think of 3 numbers within a sum, and can move part of a number to another, aware of the increase in one and the decrease in another.

Asked "What's 7 plus 8?", thinks: 7 + 8   7 + [7 + 1]   [7 + 7] + 1 = 14 + 1 = 15.

Or, using BAMT, thinks: 8 + 2 = 10, so separate 7 into 2 and 5, add 2 and 8 to make 10, then add 5 more, so 15.

May solve simple cases of multidigit addition (sometimes subtraction) by counting by tens and/or ones.

"What's 20 + 34?" Student uses connecting cube to count up 20, 30, 40, 50 plus 4: 54.

All types of single-digit problems.

Tic-Tac-Total, [LT]²: Draw a tic-tac-toe board and write the numbers 0 2 4 6 8 0 and 1 3 5 7 9 nearby. Players take turns crossing out one of the numbers and writing it on the board. One player uses only even numbers, the other only odd numbers. Whoever makes 15 first as a sum of three numbers in a row (column, diagonal) wins (Kamii, 1985). Change the total to 13 for a new game.

21, [LT]²: Card game in which an ace is worth either 1 or 11, and 2 to 10 are worth their values. Dealer gives everyone 2 cards, including themselves.

On each round, each player, if sum is less than 21, can request another card, or "hold."

If any new card makes the sum more than 21, the player is out. Continue until everyone "holds."

The player whose sum is closest to 21 wins.

Variation: Play to 15 at first.

Multidigit addition and subtraction, [LT]²: "What's 28 + 35?" (See Chapter 6.)

7   **Problem Solver** +/- Solves all types of problems, with flexible strategies and known combinations.

Asked, "If I have 13 and you have 9, how could we have the same number?", says, "9 and 1 is 10, then 3 more to make 13. 1 and 3 is 4. I need 4 more!"

Multidigit may be solved by incrementing tens and ones by counting (latter not used for Join, Change Unknown).

"What's 28 + 35?" Incrementer thinks: 20 ... 30, 40, 50; then 58, 59, 60, 61, 62, 63.

Solve all types of problem structures for single-digit problems, [LT]²: See Chapter 6 for multidigit problems.

Learning Trajectories for Adding and Subtracting (Emphasizing Counting Strategies)

The learning trajectory for adding and subtracting is complex because there are many conceptual and skill advancements required. The importance of *goals* for this domain is clear: Arithmetic is a main focus of elementary education. Table 5.2 shows where these goals appear in the CCSSM. Given that children can use different strategies to solve problems, it is somewhat arbitrary whether to list standards here, in the next chapter, or both. Notice how arithmetic is reflected in the standards from several domains.

Based on those goals, Table 5.3 provides the two additional components of the learning trajectory, the developmental progression and the instructional tasks. Remember that the ages in all the learning trajectory tables are only approximate, especially because the age of acquisition usually depends heavily on experience. A final important note: *Most strategies will be used successfully for smaller numbers (totals 10 or less) a year or more before they are used successfully for larger numbers* (Frontera, 1994). *This should be considered when constructing tasks for children.*

We strongly suggest that you study Table 5.2 and Table 5.3 with the intent to understand and remember the learning trajectory. These are *not* illustrations to skim: *Teachers need to master the knowledge summarized here to be true professionals.* Complement this reading with

Table 5.4 Connections of the Number and Arithmetic Learning Trajectories

Broad Levels	Subitizing	Counting	Comparing, Ordering	Adding and Subtracting
Visual/ Percep- tual Thinker	Perceptual Subitizing	Counting with Cardinality	Matching Comparison	Small #s, Direct Modeling
	• Number Senser: Foundations • Very Small Number Recognizer • Maker of Small Collections • Small Collection Namer • Perceptual Subiti- zer to 4 • Perceptual Subiti- zer to 5	• Number Word Sayer: Foundations • Chanter • Reciter • Corresponder • Counter (Small Numbers) • Counter (10) • Producer (Small Numbers) • Counter and Pro- ducer (10+) • Counter Backward from 10	• Comparison Senser: Foundations • Many-to-One Corresponder • Object Corresponder • Perceptual Comparer • Early Comparer of Similar Items • Early Comparer of Dissimilar Items • Matching Comparer	• Arithmetic Senser: Foundations • Preverbal +/- • Small Number +/- • Find Result +/- • Make It *N*
Numer- ical/ Model- ing Thinker	Conceptual Subitizing	Counting Strategies	Numerical Comparison	Flexible Strategies
	• Conceptual Subiti- zer to 5 • Conceptual Subiti- zer to 7 • Conceptual Subiti- zer to 10 • Conceptual Subiti- zer to 20	• Counter from *N* (*N* +1, *N-1*) • Counter On Using Patterns • Counter On Keep- ing Track • Counter of Quanti- tative Units/Place Value	• Counting Com- parer (Same Size) • Counting Com- parer (5) • Mental Number Line to 5	• Find Change +/- • Counting Strat- egies +/- • Part-Whole +/- • Numbers in Num- bers +/- • Deriver +/-:

video examples of the developmental levels—so important to make them "real" and memorable, and descriptions, resources, and often videos of activities at [LT]² (LearningTrajectories.org).

Another "Forest and Trees" Structure to Help You

Now that we have covered most of number and arithmetic (more arithmetic follows in the next chapter), we wish to offer another table that is a very simple "forest"—only two broad levels, but that *also shows the linkages between the learning trajectories.* We have tried to make it clear how closely they are related, but Table 5.4 shows how very closely they are connected. We present just some of the relevant levels for illustration (especially, as you know, the learning trajectories go higher than the examples in the table).

Final Words

In Chapters 2 and 3, we saw that children quantify groups with different processes, such as subitizing and counting. They can also solve arithmetic tasks with different processes. This chapter emphasized a counting-based approach to arithmetic. Chapter 6 describes a composition-based approach, including conceptual subitizing. Children often use both, and even combine them, as has been suggested by the more sophisticated strategies already described (e.g., Deriver +/-).

Note

1 Several important and complex issues regarding manipulatives are discussed at length in Chapter 16.

6 Arithmetic
Composition of Number, Place Value, Multidigit Addition and Subtraction, Multiplication and Division, and Fractions

> I find it easier *not* to do [simple addition] with my fingers because sometimes I get into a big muddle with them [and] I find it much harder to add up because I am not concentrating on the sum. I am concentrating on getting my fingers right ... which takes a while. It can take longer to work out the sum than it does to work out the sum in my head. [*By "in my head," Emily meant that she imagined dot arrays. If that's what she liked, why didn't she just use those images? Why did she use fingers? She explains:*] If we don't use our fingers, the teacher is going to think, "Why aren't they using their fingers? ... They are just sitting there thinking." ... We are meant to be using our fingers because it is easier ... which it is not.
>
> (Gray & Pitta, 1997, p. 35)

Do you think the teacher should have Emily use concrete objects? Or should she encourage children such as Emily to use increasingly sophisticated arithmetic reasoning? For example, should she allow Emily to use mental images and then help Emily decompose and recompose numbers, such as using "doubles-plus-one" (7 + 8 is solved as 7 + 7 = 14, and 14 + 1 = 15)? This chapter discusses four topics involving increasingly sophisticated composition of number: arithmetic combinations ("facts"), place value, multidigit addition and subtraction, and multiplication and division, including fractions.

The Development of Composing Number

Composing and decomposing numbers is another approach to addition and subtraction, one that children can productively use alongside counting strategies, as the "doubles-plus-one" strategy illustrates. The "doubles" part is composition of number (putting together the parts, two 7s, to make 14) and the adding 1 part is based on counting. Conceptual subitizing *is* an important case of composition of number (see Chapter 2).

Initial Competencies with Part-Whole Relationships

Toddlers learn to recognize Part-Whole relations in intuitive, perceptual situations and can (usually nonverbally) represent parts that make a specific whole (e.g., •• and •• make ••••). Between 4 and 5 years of age, children learn from everyday situations that a whole is made up of smaller parts and thus is bigger than its parts; however, they may not always accurately quantify that relationship.

That is, they learn the idea of Part–Part–Whole non-numerically a bit before they learn it numerically (Langhorst, Ehlert, & Fritz, 2012). However, the two are "subtrajectories" that develop in parallel; one is not a prerequisite to learning the other.

Toddlers learn to recognize that sets can be combined in different orders (even if they do not explicitly recognize that groups are composed of smaller groups). Preschoolers show intuitive knowledge of commutativity (adding a group of three to a group of one yields a group with the same number as adding the group of one to a group of three) and, later, associativity (adding a group of four to a group of two, and then adding that group to a group of one, yields a group with the same number as adding the group of four *after* combining the two and one).

Then children learn that these same ideas apply in more abstract contexts, including specific arithmetic problems (Langhorst et al., 2012), for example, that "two" and "two" make "four." At that point, children can develop the ability to recognize that the numbers 2 and 3 are "hiding inside" 5, as are the numbers 4 and 1 (Fuson, 2018b). That is, they can develop explicit knowledge of Part–Whole relations at 4 or 5 years of age. They can eventually solve even "Start Unknown" problems (recall Table 5.1) with this complete Part–Part–Whole scheme.

In brief, children develop an early, primitive understanding of commutativity, then additive composition (large groups are made up of smaller groups), commutativity of combined groups, and then associativity. So, at least by 5 years of age, children are ready to solve problems that require Part–Whole reasoning, such as Join or Separate, Change Unknown problems. However, teachers may need to help children see the relevance in and apply their understandings of Part–Whole relationships to these types of problems.

Building on their Part–Whole understandings, children can learn to separate a group into parts in various ways, producing (eventually, all of) the number combinations composing a given number; for example, 8 as 7 + 1, 6 + 2, 5 + 3, and so on. This approach to arithmetic combinations builds on and complements the counting-based strategies of the previous chapter.

Learning Basic Combinations ("facts") and Fluency[1]

Recommendations for high-quality math education have never ignored the need for children to eventually become fluent in knowledge of basic number combinations, such as 4 + 7 = 11. That does not mean that the exact nature of the goal and when and how it might best be achieved garner similar agreement. Let's examine what the research tells us.

Getting Your Facts Straight: Misconceptions That Harm Children

World-wide research shows that the way most people in the U.S. think about arithmetic combinations and children's learning of them, and the language they use, *may harm more than help*. For example, we hear about "memorizing facts" and "recalling your facts." This is misleading regarding what goes on in the learning process (this section) and the teaching process (the following section). As we saw in Chapters 2 and 5, children move through a long developmental progression to reach the point where they can compose numbers. Further, they also should learn about arithmetic properties, patterns, and relationships, *and* intuitive magnitude as they do so. *All the knowledge is ideally learned simultaneously and in an integrated fashion with knowledge of arithmetic combinations.*

Research suggests that producing basic combinations is not just a simple "look-up" or rote memorization process. Retrieval *is* an important part of the process, but many brain systems help. For example, systems that involve working memory, executive (metacognitive) control, and even spatial "mental number lines" support knowledge of arithmetic combinations (Gathercole, Tiffany, Briscoe, Thorn, & The, 2005; Geary, 2011; Geary, Hoard, & Nugent, 2012; Passolunghi et al., 2007; Simmons, Willis, & Adams, 2012b). Further, for subtraction calculations, both the region specializing in subtraction *and* that specializing in addition are activated. So, when children *really know* 8 − 3 = 5, they also know that 3 + 5 = 8, 8 − 5 = 3, and so forth, and all these "facts" are *related in their minds*. This leads research to conclude that the *primary cause of problems with the basic combinations, especially among children at risk for or already experiencing learning difficulties, is the lack of opportunity to develop number sense during the preschool and early school years* (Baroody, Bajwa, & Eiland, 2009b, p. 69).

Implications for the next section are that children need considerable practice, distributed across time. Also, because counting strategies did not activate the same systems, we need to guide children to move to more sophisticated composition strategies. Finally, practice should not be "meaningless drill" but should occur in a context of making sense of the situation and the number relationships. Multiple strategies help build that number sense, and children who are strong in calculations know and use multiple strategies. If ever educators needed an argument against teaching "one correct procedure," this is it. There are other misconceptions about instruction that harm children, discussed in the following section.

Experience and Education: Composing Number

So, children should be able to reason strategically, adapting strategies for different situations and easily and quickly retrieving the answer to any arithmetic combination when that is appropriate. What do we know about facilitating such *adaptive expertise* (Baroody & Dowker, 2003b)? Making sense of arithmetic problems and number relationships, inventing and using new strategies, and discussing them yields educational gold. But first, what doesn't work?

What Does Not Work?

There are three main teaching misconceptions:

1.   *Arithmetic facts are single, disconnected items that must be learned separately.*

To many people, the term "fact" often means a piece of disconnected information. Some of us learned arithmetic at a time when some psychologists warned that 4 + 9 = 13 must be studied separately from 13 − 4 = 9 or even from 9 + 4 = 13. But meaningful teaching connects these and many other relationships.

Perhaps the word "fact" is just a term, not to be overly concerned about. However, it is important that educators understand and agree that students need to learn *related* facts, as the mathematician Poincaré points out at the beginning of this chapter. And they also should learn about arithmetic properties, patterns, and relationships as they do so. And that knowledge, along with intuitive magnitude and other knowledge and skills, ideally is learned simultaneously and in an integrated fashion with knowledge of arithmetic combinations. Thus, knowing an arithmetic combination well, *fluently*, means far more than knowing a simple, isolated piece of information. For example, students notice that the sum of n and 1 is simply the number after n in the counting sequence, resulting in an integration of knowledge of combinations with the well-practiced counting knowledge. Students who have learned all this have *adaptive expertise*—meaningful knowledge that can be flexibly applied to new, as well as familiar, tasks (Baroody & Dowker, 2003b).

2. *"Learning your facts" means rote memorization.*

Some readers might argue, "Then you have to memorize each fact and the connections between the facts. That's just *more* memorization." That is indeed a psychological viewpoint that is more than 100 years old. In this view, each fact is stored separately, such as in a verbal statement, "Four plus nine equals thirteen" (Baroody et al., 2009b). Counting to figure out a fact is viewed as an immature strategy that must be stamped out. Instead, "memorizing the math facts" has always and continues to be a central focus of the math curricula and textbooks, with pages and pages of worksheets asking students to memorize the answers (Fuson, 2003).

But wait: Didn't most of *us* learn by rote memorization? Didn't that work? No, most of us, especially those who succeeded in school, learned far more than just the rote verbalization. We learned to make sense of the *quantities* and *relationships* among combinations. Thus, we "know from memory"—but that is based on a deep network of understandings and skills. We call knowing from memory in this way *fluency*: accurate knowledge and concepts and strategies that promote adaptive expertise. *Students who achieve this kind of fluency can reconstruct combinations, use them to solve new types of problems, and more.* We do believe that retrieval—as a *part* of the learning and teaching process—is a very good thing. This is especially so when it is based on relationships and not just rote memorization—"knowing from memory" based on understanding.

Indeed, research has shone light on the dark side of teaching memorization only, and it's not pretty. Let's take a look at one "natural" study that happened in California. California used to have standards consistent with those of NCTM, with balanced consideration of concepts, skills, and problem solving. After pressure from conservative groups, they accelerated addition and subtraction basic-facts memorization (Henry & Brown, 2008b). That is, children were supposed to know all the basic addition and subtraction facts by the end of first grade. Further, "knowing" those facts was restricted to memorization. They passed laws that any textbooks purchased for California in 2008 had to teach children to memorize all the facts in first grade, with little guidance for second grade. Textbooks and teachers were thus to directly teach memorization using practices such as timed tests and flash cards. All these requirements and recommendations may have stemmed from a misunderstanding of the educational practices of high-performing countries such as Korea, China, Taiwan, and Japan (Henry & Brown, 2008b).

How did that work out for the teachers and students? Not well. Only 7% demonstrated adequate progress. Even among students from the highest performing schools, fewer than 11% made progress toward the memorization standard equivalent to their progress through the school year. Barely a fourth of the students demonstrated retrieval of 50% or more of addition and subtraction facts.

3. *The best way to master facts and build is through lots of rote practice (flash cards, work-sheets) and timed tests.*

In the California results, two instructional practices were *negatively* related to basic-facts retrieval:

•   Use of California-State-approved textbooks demanding retrieval in first grade.
•   Timed tests.

Students whose teachers relied on the basic-facts-memorization textbooks knew *fewer* facts. Indeed, they achieved about a third as well on basic facts as those who relied less heavily on these textbooks. Students whose teachers followed the advice of these textbooks not only didn't retrieve the facts, but they relied most heavily on low-level counting skills.

Similarly, students whose teachers used timed tests knew *fewer* facts. It may be surprising to find that practicing exactly what you think is the outcome skill works *against learning that skill.*

This is all counter-intuitive to many people. If you want students to memorize, *teach them to memorize.* Right? *Wrong*—at least in a limited sense of direct teaching of *rote* memorization—it doesn't work. At best, it develops only *routine expertise* (Baroody & Dowker, 2003b). At worst, it doesn't even do that well.

Other practices were neither helpful nor harmful. Flash card use didn't hurt but didn't support students' learning either. Neither did extensive work on small sums. Presenting easier arithmetic problems far more frequently than harder problems isn't a good idea. The opposite is the case in countries with higher math achievement, such as East Asian countries (National Mathematics Advisory Panel, 2008).

What happened? What does this study teach us? *Memorization without understanding, drill without developing concepts and strategies, is not an effective way to teach or learn arithmetic facts, much less the edifice that is mathematics.*

Even the *format* of arithmetic "fact" practice can interfere with present and future learning. Consider how reasonable these tasks seem.

$$3 + 4 = \underline{}$$
$$5 + 9 = \underline{}$$
$$6 + 0 = \underline{}$$
$$8 - 7 = \underline{}$$
$$9 - 5 = \underline{}$$
$$5 - 2 = \underline{}$$

Let's say that these tasks are done *after* students develop the concepts and strategies of arithmetic. What harm could come from such traditional practice of addition and subtraction facts?

Once again, research is clear. The more children do such traditional practice exercises, the *lower* their scores on equivalence problems such as 2 + 6 + 3 + 4 + 6 = 3 + 4 + __. U.S. students as a whole get *worse* on such problems from 7 to 9 years of age. Shockingly, even *undergraduates* given such traditional arithmetic practice get *worse* on equivalence problems (McNeil, 2008b; McNeil, Fyfe, & Dunwiddie, 2015; McNeil, Fyfe, Petersen, Dunwiddie, & Brletic-Shipley, 2011).

A steady diet of such types of tasks teach students limited patterns of thinking. They learn unfortunate rules such as "The equals sign means compute and put in the answer."

What Does Work?

The California study found that some approaches were successful, such as using thinking strategies. Such strategies include the following.

Conceptual Subitizing: The Earliest Addition

Teachers of children as young as 4 years can use "conceptual subitizing" to develop composition-based ideas about addition and subtraction (see Chapter 2). A benefit of subitizing activities is that different arrangements suggest different views of that number. Children can come to see all of the different number combinations for a given number by working with objects (e.g., five objects). Within a story context (e.g., animals in two different pens), children can separate the five objects into different partners (4 and 1; 3 and 2). Similarly, children can make "number pictures"—as many different arrangements of a given number as possible, with the subsets labeled (Baratta-Lorton, 1976).

Learning Reasoning Strategies

Effective teachers attend explicitly and directly to the important conceptual issues students are likely to encounter. They help students develop important conceptual understandings, as well as procedural skills (Hiebert & Grouws, 2007b). Students learn combinations better if they invent, use, share, and explain different strategies (Baroody & Rosu, 2004). Indeed, the number of different strategies children show predicts their later learning (Siegler, 1995b).

What are the "best" strategies? Research is clear that effective strategies include counting strategies (such as "doubles plus one" and counting on), conceptual subitizing, and Break-Apart-to-Make-Ten, or BAMT (Baroody, 1987b; Baroody et al., 2009b; Henry & Brown, 2008b; Murata, 2004b; Murata & Fuson, 2006). We discuss each of these, and other helpful approaches, below.

Commutativity and Associativity

Preschool and kindergarten teachers can develop foundational understanding of these important arithmetic properties by posing problems that children model with manipulatives, ensuring that a problem such as "3 and 2 more" is followed by "2 and 3 more." Many activities in which children separate sets of a given number in many different ways and name the subsets may be particularly helpful. For example, children lay four cubes along their line of sight and use a clear plastic sheet to "hide" one and then read "one *and* three." They then hide three and read "three *and* one" (Baratta-Lorton, 1976).

Discuss that the sum of 6 and 3 is 9 no matter what the order of the addends. Many children will build these understandings and strategies for themselves. Others will if the curriculum and teacher present problems in commuted pairs (6 + 7 and then, immediately after 7 + 6, as mentioned previously for small numbers). Still others may need explicit instruction on the property.

Help children relate their physical understandings, based on equivalence of groups of objects in various combinations and orders, to the *manipulations* of them that resulted in this different arrangement, and then to explicit numerical generalizations. In any of these forms, such instruction may help children develop more sophisticated strategies and thus relate their knowledge of arithmetic properties and their problem solving, which they often do not do. Especially fruitful might be ensuring children understand that larger groups are additively composed of smaller groups and using commutativity to learn to count on from a larger addend.

Whether they are subitizing, or subitizing and counting, children as young as kindergarten age benefit from finding all the decompositions for a number—all pairs of numbers "hiding inside" other numbers. Listing them can help children see patterns *and* can illustrate a way of representing equations that expands the traditional, limited, view of an equal sign as meaning "the answer comes next" (Fuson, 2009; Fuson, 2018b).

$$6 = 0 + 6$$
$$6 = 1 + 5$$
$$6 = 2 + 4$$
$$6 = 3 + 3$$
$$6 = 4 + 2$$
$$6 = 5 + 1$$
$$6 = 6 + 0$$

Indeed, just in case you still believe that it's better to always use the form $5 + 1 = 6$, note that *only using that form limits children's thinking and leads them to make more errors* (McNeil, 2008b). Children should learn to both recognize and produce a variety of legitimate number sentences (Mark-Zigdon & Tirosh, 2017b).

"Doubles" and the "N + 1" Rule

Special patterns can be useful and easy for children to see. One of these involves "doubles" ($3 + 3$, $7 + 7$), which can also allow access to combinations such as $7 + 8$ ("doubles-plus-one"). Children can learn the doubles (e.g., $6 + 6 = 12$) surprisingly easily. They appear to develop doubles plus (or minus) one ($7 + 8 = 7 + 7 + 1 = 14 + 1 = 15$) on their own or from brief discussions or practice using software. However, ensure that rules such as $n + 1$ (adding one to any number is simply the next counting word) are well established *first*. Also important is understanding that children may see "double" as both an operation (doubling a number) *and* a relationship (the number and its "double" are *equal* parts making a whole) (Björklund, 2015). Teachers may find discussing that there are "equally many" as in the "original whole unit" and that we "doubled the whole unit" helpful.

Fives and Tens Frames

Another special pattern is the spatial one of "fives and tens frames." These encourage decomposition into fives and tens (e.g., 6 made as $5 + 1$, 7 as $5 + 2$), as illustrated in Figure 6.1.

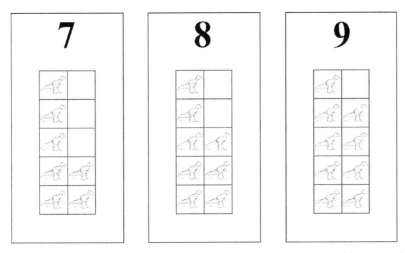

Figure 6.1 Fives and tens frames can help children decompose numbers and learn combinations

Break-Apart-to-Make-Ten (BAMT) Strategy

Japanese students often proceed through the same general developmental progression as U.S. students, and other researchers have identified moving from "counting all" to "counting on" and to derived combinations and decomposing-composing strategies. However, their learning trajectory at that point differs. They come together around a single strategy, an approach to strategy development supported by multiple studies (Clements, Vinh, Lim, & Sarama, 2020; Murata & Fuson, 2006): Break-Apart-to-Make-Ten (BAMT), which was also the most powerful strategy identified in the California study (Henry & Brown, 2008b).

Before these lessons, children work on several *related* learning trajectories. They develop solid knowledge of numerals and counting (i.e., progress along the counting learning trajectory). This includes the number structure for teen numbers as 10 + another number, which, as we learned, is more straightforward in Asian languages ("thirteen" is "ten and three"), although research suggests that experiences are more important than language (Laski & Yu, 2014c; Mark & Dowker, 2015a). They learn to solve addition and subtraction of numbers with totals less than 10 (i.e., Find Result +/− in the learning trajectory in Chapter 5), often chunking numbers into 5 (e.g., 7 as 5-plus-2, as Figure 6.1 illustrates).

With these levels of thinking established, children develop several levels of thinking within the composition/decomposition developmental progression (what we call Composer to 4, then 5 ... up to Composer to 10 in the learning trajectory at the end of this chapter). For example, they work on "break-apart partners" of numbers less than or equal to 10. They solve addition and subtraction problems involving teen numbers using the tens structure (10 + 2 = 12; 18 − 8 = 10), and addition and subtraction with three addends using tens (e.g., 4 + 6 + 3 = 10 + 3 = 13 and 15 − 5 − 9 = 10 − 9 = 1).

At this point the BAMT strategy is developed. The entire process (to fluency) follows four instructional phases. In Phase 1, teachers elicit, value, and discuss child-invented strategies and encourage children to use these strategies to solve a variety of problems. Supports to connect visual and symbolic representations of quantities are used extensively and curtailed and phased out as children learn. For example, in step 1, the teacher poses a problem such as 9 + 4. Then, she shows nine counters and four counters, and asks, "What do I need to make the 9 into a 10?" Children already *know* their break-apart partners to 10, so they say "one." The teacher moves one from the four to make a group of ten. Next, she highlights the three left. She reminds children that the 9 and 1 made 10 and guides them to see ten counters and three counters and think ten-three (remember they learned this too). Later, representational drawings serve this role, in a sequence such as shown in Figure 6.2, which reviews this instructional sequence.

In Phase 2, the teacher focuses on math properties and advantageous methods, especially BAMT. After many problems involving 9 plus another number, problems involving 8 and posed (then 7 … etc.). In Phase 3, children gain fluency with the BAMT (or other) methods. In Phase 4, distributed practice increases retention and efficiency and helps children generalize the use of the method in additional contexts and as a component of more complex methods.

Of the strategies for assisting students in Tharp and Gallimore's model (1988), this teacher uses questioning and cognitive restructuring extensively, and uses feeding back, modeling, instructing, and managing to a lesser extent. She also uses an additional strategy, engaging and involving. Phase 1 lessons are based first on children's ideas and contributions.

All strategies are accepted and appreciated. Students are expected to try to express their ideas and strategies as well as understand those of others. Strategies are often named for the students who created them. Children then vote for the "most useful" strategy; the majority like the BAMT strategy.

In Phase 2, the teacher reviews different methods, compares the methods mathematically, and votes on the best method. New problem types (e.g., adding to 8) are connected to previously solved problems (adding to 9). The teacher also moved her conceptual emphasis from the initial to later steps in the BAMT process (as illustrated in Figure 6.2). For homework, children review that day's work and preview the work to come the following day, supported by families.

In Phase 3, children practice the BAMT method to achieve fluency. "Practice" in Japanese means "kneading" different ideas and experiences together to learn. Children do not just drill but engage in whole-group (choral responding), individual-within-whole-group, and independent practice. In individual-within-whole-group practice, individual students answer, but then asked the class, "Is it OK?" They shout their response back. All practice emphasizes conceptual links.

The line slants between the numbers, indicating that we need to find a partner for 9 to make 10.

Four is separated into two partners, 1 and 3.

The ring shows how the numbers combine to make 10.

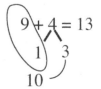

Ten and 3 are shown to add to 13.

Figure 6.2 Phases of instruction to teach the BAMT strategy

"Kneading knowledge" to learn was always about fluency *and* understanding. Phase 4 is distributed practice. This is not rote learning or rote practice but a clear, high-quality use of the concepts of learning trajectories. For example, children solve more sophisticated problem types using more sophisticated strategies.

Combined Strategies

Learning a variety of such strategies is good for children of all ability levels. Further, although BAMT is a powerful strategy and more helpful than others for later multidigit computation, it should not be the only strategy children learn. "Doubles + 1" and other strategies are also worthwhile learning objectives.

Helping students see linkages between strategies is also powerful. Recall the use of number paths to add in Chapter 5. One first-grade class was solving 7 + 5 (Lai, Carlson, & Heaton, 2018). Katie solved it by decomposing 5 into 3 and 2, adding the 3 to 7 to make 10, and then adding the 2 to make 12. Other students used a number path, starting at 7, and making 5 single-space jumps. The teacher *connected* the two strategies, helping children see that putting Katie's solution on the number line would mean "big jumps" (jump 3 to 10, then 2 to 12). She then asked students to represent another student's strategy with such big jumps. The teacher thus linked different strategies to show how they were structurally similar, helping children become not only more strategic, but increasing their understanding as well—concepts connected to procedures. She moved them from counting singles to breaking apart numbers—representing BAMT on a number path. In so doing, she also emphasized the role of tens, laying the foundation for the use of place value in arithmetic (Lai et al., 2018).

Good strategies should all work together, of course, to form adaptive expertise. For example, see the activity in Chapter 2 for the level "Conceptual Subitizer to 20" (p. 30). Notice how the fives and tens frames are used to give imagistic support for what is, basically, the BAMT strategy—all while encouraging conceptual subitizing.

Achieving Full Fact Fluency

To achieve true fluency, children must practice their arithmetic strategies. This is not drill, but repeated experiences combining different ideas and experiences to learn and internalize them. Children might engage in whole-group (choral responding), individual-within-whole-group, or practice independently. In individual-within-whole-group practice, individual students answer, but then ask the class, "Is it OK?" The class calls their response back. All this practice needs to emphasize conceptual links, synthesizing knowledge for fluency and understanding. They then can begin distributed practice (practicing a variety of combinations and strategies over time, rather than practicing one thing at a time for long periods). This is not rote learning or rote practice but a clear, high-quality use of skills and understandings to solve a variety of problems.

Educational technology can be an effective way to help children develop fluency, *once they understand, having progressed to that point in the learning trajectory* (Sarama & Clements, 2019b). A caveat is that drills should be used carefully and usually in moderation, especially with the youngest children and those who may be less motivated to perform academic work or less creative following a steady diet of only drills. Practice with technology may not generalize as well as paper-and-pencil work (Sarama & Clements, 2019b). Having children practice about 20% of the time on paper and pencil seems to solve that generalization limitation (Rich, Duhon, & Reynolds, 2017). In contrast, practice that encourages the development and use of strategies provides different contexts (supporting generalization), and promotes problem solving that may be more appropriate than drills or may be best used in combination with it (Sarama & Clements, 2019b). As one example, developing two strategies, subtraction-as-addition (for 8 − 5 think, "What added to 5 makes 8?") and using 10 (similar to BAMT) were developed successfully with computer programs, outperforming regular classroom instruction *and* computer-based drill (Baroody, Purpura, Eiland, Reid, & Paliwal, 2016a). Another note on former strategy: Six widely used U.S. curricula do *not* address critical levels of the learning trajectory for the meaningful learning of the subtraction-as-addition strategy: (a) reverse operations (adding 8 is undone by subtracting 8); (b) common Part-Whole relations (5 + 8 and 13 − 8 share the same whole 13 and parts 5 and 8); and (c) the complement principle in terms of Part-Whole relations (if parts 5 and 8 make the whole 13, then subtracting one part from the whole leaves the other part, Baroody, 2016a). Teachers need to step in and ensure children learn these levels.

See Chapter 16, pp. 387–401 for much more on educational technology. Chapter 16 has many more details on practice (pp. 377–378) and teaching. Also see a full book we co-authored on this issue, called *No More Math Fact Frenzy* (Davenport et al., 2019b). For now, we summarize some research-based tips.

Tips for Achieving Fluency

Research establishes several guidelines for helping children achieve fluency with arithmetic combinations; that is, correct and accurate knowledge *and* concepts and strategies that promote *adaptive expertise*.

1   Follow learning trajectories so that children develop the concepts and strategies of the domain first. Understanding (along with procedures) should precede practice.
2   Ensure practice is distributed, rather than massed (Ericsson, Krampe, & Tesch-Römer, 1993b). For example, rather than studying 4 + 7 for 30 seconds, it is better to study it once, then study another combination, then return to 4 + 7. Further, practice on all combinations is best done in short but frequent sessions. For long-term memory, a day or more should eventually separate these sessions.
3   Use contingent reinforcement in short, frequent sessions. As a simple example, children look at a written combination, then cover, copy, and compare and gain a reward for beating a previous score (Methe, Kilgus, Neiman, & Chris Riley-Tillman, 2012). For example, the reward might be Earning Free Time (see Codding, Hilt-Panahon, Panahon, & Benson, 2009b).
4   Other simple research-based strategies include "audio-recorded problems" and "incremental rehearsal" (Codding et al., 2009b):

   • Audio-recorded problems—problems are recorded, then a time delay allows children to write their answer, then the answer is read.
   • Incremental rehearsal—first, the teacher identifies which combinations the child knows. The child is told one unknown. Then the unknown combination is rehearsed nine times by folding the unknown combination in with nine known combinations.

5   In all cases, make sure the instructional strategy matches the students' needs. As one example, children who are accurate but slow may benefit from timed practice; however, this may harm children who are struggling to be accurate, whereas the strategies in #3 and #4 above would be helpful (Codding et al., 2009b).

6   Although timed tests are often done badly (Henry & Brown, 2008b), practice for speed, done well, is useful and important. Tutoring with speeded practice is more effective than tutoring with unspeeded practice (Fuchs et al., 2013). Combined with instruction on number knowledge and relationships, including emphasis on retrieval but also with efficient counting strategies for correcting any mistakes, speeded practice leads to fluency and competency in complex calculations (Fuchs et al., 2013). Children who are accurate but slow may benefit from timed practice, but such timed practice may harm children who are struggling to be accurate (Codding et al., 2009b). Once children are accurate and competent with strategies, game-like, *self-motivated* practice for speed is an excellent complement. Such practice should be short, frequent, stress-free, and fun, with each student engaged in improving their own performance.

7   Similarly, use practice software that includes research-based strategies.

8   Ensure practice continually develops relationships and strategic thinking. For example, at least some practice should occur on all forms of all possible combinations. This may help children understand properties, including commutativity, additive inverse, and equality, as well as supporting students' retrieval of basic combinations:

$$5 + 3 = 8 \qquad 3 + 5 = 8 \qquad 8 - 5 = 3 \qquad 8 - 3 = 5$$
$$8 = 5 + 3 \qquad 8 = 3 + 5 \qquad 3 = 8 - 5 \qquad 5 = 8 - 3$$

As an illustration, teachers make "math mountain" cards such as those in Figure 6.3 (Fuson, 2018b). Students cover any of the three numbers and show them to their partner, who tells what number is covered. Other representations show the Part–Part–Whole relationship, also shown in Figure 6.3.

This suggests that it is not just the arithmetic combinations that should be automatic. *Students should also be fluent with the related reasoning strategies.* For example, the Building Blocks software not only provides the drill problems following these guidelines but also presents each group of combinations based on the strategy that is most helpful in a particular type of solution. As a specific illustration, the software initially groups together all those combinations that yield nicely to the BAMT strategy.

Intensive Interventions for Children at Risk

At several points in this book, we argue that some children fail to make progress in the learning trajectories in Chapter 5 and in this chapter. Here, we emphasize that, if children are not making progress in Grade 1 and, especially, Grade 2, they need intensive interventions (see Chapters 14, 15, and 16 and [LT]^2, which also has many resources on teaching children with disabilities of many types).

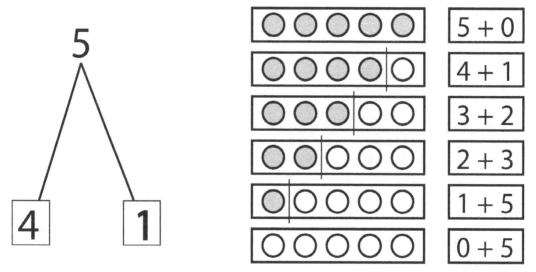

Figure 6.3 "Math Mountain" (made into cards for practicing arithmetic combinations) and other Part-Part-Whole representations

Learning and Teaching Combinations: Final Words

An important goal of early math is students' growth of flexible, fluent, accurate knowledge of addition and subtraction combinations. Learning these combinations is not about rote memorization. The learning trajectory progresses from (a) building foundational concepts of number and arithmetic and learning to figure out simple combinations with counting and visually-based strategies, to (b) learning reasoning strategies to determine combinations more efficiently, and *then* to (c) achieving full facts fluency (Baroody et al., 2009b; Sarama & Clements, 2009c). Seeing and using patterns, and building relationships, can free children's cognitive resources to be used in other tasks. Children generalize the patterns they learn and apply it to combinations that were not studied (Baroody & Tiilikainen, 2003). Number combination instruction that focuses on encouraging children to look for patterns and relations can generalize to problem-solving situations and can free attention and effort for other tasks.

> Science is facts; just as houses are made of stones, so is science made of facts; but a pile of stones is not a house and a collection of facts is not necessarily science.
>
> (Jules Henri Poincairé)

The Development of Grouping and Place Value

What determines children's development of base-ten understandings? Not so much age as *experience*. Use of the BAMT strategy, for example, helps children group into tens to solve addition and subtraction problems and to develop place value concepts. Place value has been a part of the learning trajectories of Chapters 2, 3, 4, and 5, but here we focus directly on the concepts of grouping and place value.

Extending the Math

Grouping underlies multiplication and measuring with different units. A special grouping organizes collections into groups of ten. That is, a numerical collection can be measured using units of one, ten, one hundred, or one thousand, and, in a written multidigit numeral, the value of a digit depends on its position in the numeral. For example, the digit 5 in 53 indicates 50 (5 units of ten) but in 1,508 the 5 indicates 500 (5 units of one hundred). To build understanding of numbers greater than 10, children must build on their early numerical knowledge and decomposing/composing to understand even the teen numbers as 1 ten and some extras and later to understand numbers above 19 as some number of groups of ten and some extras. Beginning with the teen numbers, the written numerals and the number words both refer to groups of ten (e.g., 11 is 1 group of ten and 1 one).

From what we saw about counting, comparing, and addition in Chapters 3, 4, and 5, we know that 35 is the number that results from counting 5 more than 30. Similarly, 435 is the number that results from counting 35 more than 400. So, 435 = 400 + 30 + 5 (Wu, 2011b). The symbol "435" illustrates a deep idea in the Hindu-Arabic number system: Each digit represents different magnitudes, depending on its *place* in the symbol. The *place value* of the digit means its value, or magnitude, as in "4" meaning "400" in "435" (but "4" means "40" in "246"). The sum of 400 + 30 + 5, used to represent the separate place value of each digit, is called the number's *expanded notation*.

Children's Knowledge of Grouping and Place Value

Preschool children begin to understand the process of making groups with equal numbers of objects. Such grouping, and knowledge of the special grouping into tens, appears not to be related to counting skill. However, experience with additive composition does appear to contribute to knowledge of grouping and place value.

Children's development of place-value understandings faces many challenges. The language is not consistent (in many languages)—"fourteen" puts the four first vs. "14" and, of course, "teen" does not mean "ten" to many children. Further, 14 and 41 have the same symbols but mean quite different numbers (cf. Mix, Smith, & Crespo, 2019).

Teachers often believe that their students understand place value because they can, for example, put digits into "tens and ones charts." However, ask these students what the "1" in "16" means and they are as likely to say "one" (and mean 1 singleton) as they are to say, "one ten." Or, they may exchange a dime for 10 pennies and add 6 pennies to a dime to make 16, but refuse to subtract 6 pennies from a dime, because they *do* believe that a dime and 10 pennies are *not* fundamentally the same quantity. These are just two of many tasks that illustrate the difference between children with little, and children with developing or strong, knowledge of place value.

Several classifications systems have been used to describe the levels of thinking children develop from moving from little or no knowledge, to strong knowledge of place value. The following is a synthesis (Fuson, Smith, & Lo Cicero, 1997; Fuson et al., 1997; Herzog, Ehlert, & Fritz, 2019; Rogers, 2012).

- Students who say only "one" have little or no knowledge of place value. They will usually make a group of 16 objects to represent "16," but they do not understand the place value of the numeral.
- Students understand that "26" means a group of 20 cubes along with a group of 6 cubes, but for "twenty-six" might write "206." May recognize and use equivalent representations like 3 hundreds = 30 tens = 300 ones.
- Students create a group of 26 cubes by counting two groups of 10 (10, 20), and then counting up by ones (21, 22, 23, 24, 25, 26).
- Students count "1 ten, 2 tens…" (or even "1, 2 tens") and then count the ones as before.
- Students connect the number words (twenty-six), numerals (26), and quantities (26 cubes) without the support of manipulatives; they understand that 546 is equal to 500 plus 40 plus 6 and can use a variety of strategies for solving multidigit number problems.
- Students understand the exponential nature of number systems (we'll return to this idea in the later section on multiplication).
- Students can apply their knowledge to problems with other bases.

Students may be at a higher level for small numbers (e.g., up to 100) than they are for numbers with which they are less familiar (e.g., numbers to 1000). Students eventually need to understand that 500 is equal to 5 times 100, 40 is equal to 4 times 10, and so forth. They need to know that all adjacent places have the same exchange values: exchange 1 unit to the left for 10 units to the right and vice versa.

Language and Place Value

As we saw previously, English has thirteen rather than "threeteen" or, better, "ten-three"; twenty rather than "twoty" or, better, "two tens." Other languages, such as Chinese, in which 13 is read as "ten-three," are more helpful to children (although, as we said, experiences are more important than the language spoken!, Laski & Yu, 2014c; Mark & Dowker, 2015a). Also, neither "teen" nor "ty" *say* ten, although they mean ten in different ways. The written numbers are clearer in their pattern, but the written numerals are so succinct that they mislead children: a 52 looks like a 5 and a 2 side by side, without suggesting fifty or five tens to the beginner. It is especially unfortunate that the first two words following ten do not even feature the "teen" root at all. Instead, "eleven" and "twelve" stem from Old English words meaning "one left" (after ten) and "two left." The following section suggests ways to help children meet these challenges.

Experience and Education: Grouping and Place Value

Children learn to understand the ten-structured groupings named by our number words and written numbers as they see and work with quantities grouped into tens linked to number words and to written numbers. That is, they need to attend to unitizing (grouping and considering that group as a unit), relative position of numerals in a multidigit number, and language

(Brendefur, Strother, & Rich, 2018). They may count 52 blocks into their own units of tens and ones but counting and stacking blocks cannot take the place of working with the ideas and the symbols. Children have to think about and discuss these ideas. They might pretend to make stacks of blocks, while counting, "11 is one ten and one, 12 is one ten and two … 20 is two tens" and so forth. They have to engage in many experiences to establish ten as a benchmark and, more important, as a new unit (1 ten that contains 10 ones). Regular tens and ones words (52 is "five tens, two ones") used along with the ordinary words can help establish a language that symbolizes decomposing and composing. Further, solving simple addition problems in the pre-K and kindergarten years helps form a foundation for understanding place value. Following the counting, comparing, and addition learning trajectories in Chapters 3, 4, and 5 is consistent with these findings.

The diverse content of those chapters may suggest that there are two complementary approaches to learning grouping and place value. The first focuses directly on learning place value for numbers of a certain range (the teens, or numbers to 100). The second is using arithmetic problem solving as a good context for the learning of place value, which we discuss in the following section.

In the first approach, students work with place value ideas before arithmetic. For example, they might draw "bar" diagrams by tracing around a connecting cube with no gaps to compose a 5, then a 10 (Brendefur et al., 2018). The teacher asks what the bar would look like for quantities of 12, 8, or 20 and emphasized equal intervals (Chapter 10). She then shows children a cube bar of 10, wrapped in table, and says, "Now we have a unit of size 10" and shows drawing with numbers 0 to 10 marked and one with only 0 and 10 marked, to emphasize 10 as unit (of units). Discussion and new tasks emphasizes that one could draw 12 with 12 ones or one 10 bar and 2 ones. This is extended to larger two-digit numbers using bars, then "empty" number lines, as well as comparing numbers and arithmetic.

As another example, children could play "banking" games in which they roll two number cubes and take that many pennies (or single-dollar bills from a set of play money), *but* if they have 10 or more pennies, they have to trade 10 pennies for a dime before their turn is over. The first one to get to 100 wins. Students could take an inventory of classroom supplies, count chairs for an assembly, get ready for a party, or conduct a science experiment—in each case, grouping items to be counted into tens and ones. Similar games can involve throwing a ring or other object onto a target and accumulating scores.

Important here is to make *consistent connections between different representations*: spoken number words, grouped objects, numerals, number lines, one grouped set to another set of different materials and structure (e.g., bundled sticks to base-ten blocks) and so forth (Mix et al., 2019). For the number words, recall the recommendation in Chapter 3 that children sometimes count with English translations of East Asian structures ("ten-one [for 11], ten-two, ten-three … two-tens, two-tens-one [21], two-tens-two…") (Magargee, 2017; Van Luit & Van der Molen, 2011). For matching different materials, use gestures and even color coding (ones in one color, tens in another) to help children see how the structures are the same in both (Mix et al., 2019).

In one project, students also represented tens and ones with cardboard or paper "penny stripes" with 10 pennies separated into two groups of five on the front and 1 dime on the back (base-ten blocks were deemed too expensive). Eventually, students used drawings to solve problems. They drew columns of ten circles or dots, counted them by tens and by ones, and then

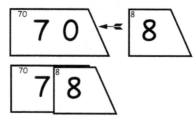

Figure 6.4 Place value "secret code cards"

connected the columns of ten by a 10-stick (or quick-ten). When they understood the 10-sticks as meaning ten ones, they just drew the 10-sticks and ones. Tens and ones were drawn using 5-groups to minimize errors and help students see the numbers at a glance. A space was left after the first five 10-sticks, and five 1-circles (or dots) were drawn horizontally and then the rest of the 1-circles drawn below these in a row.

During this work, the teacher called 78 "seventy-eight" but *also "7 tens, 8 ones."* Some children still viewed and operated on digits in a multidigit number as if they were singletons; therefore, "secret code cards" were introduced such as have been used by many educators. They were placed in front of each other to illustrate the place value system, as shown in Figure 6.4.

High-quality instruction often uses manipulatives or other objects to demonstrate and record quantities. Further, such manipulatives are used consistently enough that they become tools for thinking (see Chapter 16). They are *discussed* to explicate the place value ideas. They are used to solve problems, including arithmetic problems. Finally, they are replaced by mental strategies and symbols.

The Development of Multidigit Addition and Subtraction

Almost all, who have ever fully understood arithmetic, have been obliged to learn it over again in their own way.

(Warren Colburn, 1849)

Conceptual knowledge, especially of the base-ten system, influences how students understand, learn, and use strategies and algorithms for multidigit arithmetic (Hickendorff, Torbeyns, & Verschaffel, 2019). Recall that an algorithm is a step-by-step procedure that is guaranteed to solve a specific category of problems. A computation algorithm is a cyclic algorithm that solves computational problems, such as arithmetic problems, in a limited number of steps. Efficient, accurate, multidigit computation methods use the decomposition of the numbers into their place value quantities (they are "cyclic" because they then operate on one place, then the next ...), the commutative and associative properties in adding or subtracting like values, and, again, composition and decomposition whenever there are too many (when adding) or not enough (when subtracting) of a given value. (Recall the discussion in *Arithmetic: Mathematical Definitions and Properties*, Chapter 5, pp. 89-90.)

Strategies involving counting by tens and ones (see Chapter 3) can be altered along with children's developing understanding of numeration and place value to lead up to explicit multidigit addition and subtraction knowledge. Altering students' increasingly sophisticated counting strategies is a natural site for developing their understanding of place value in arithmetic. Rather than count by tens and ones to find the sum of 38 and 47, children might decompose 38 into its tens and ones and 47 into its tens and ones. This encourages the children to reason with ten as a unit like the unit of one and compose the tens together into 7 tens, or 70. After composing the ones together into 15 ones, they have transformed the sum into the sum of 70 and 15. To find this sum, the children take a 10 from the 15 and "give it" to the 70, so the sum is 80 and 5 more, or 85. Strategies such as this are modifications of counting strategies involving tens and ones just as certain strategies for finding the sum of 8 and 7 (e.g., take 2 from 7 and give it to 8, then add 10 and 5) are modifications of counting strategies involving only counting by ones.

To use such strategies, students need to conceptualize numbers both as wholes (as units in themselves) and composites (of individual units). Composites are "units of units" like 100 is 1 hundred, but also 10 tens (each of which are 10 ones of course). Students who have these concepts can, for example, repeatedly answer what number is "ten more" than another number. "What is ten more than 23?" "33!" "Ten more?" "43!" (see "Counter Forward and Back" in Chapter 3).

This, then, is the second approach to moving along the developmental progression for learning explicit place values, along with multidigit arithmetic. Like other developmental progressions, the levels of understanding of place value are not absolute or lockstep. Students might use a strategy based on a flexible combination of decomposition-composition strategies and counting-based, or sequence, strategies when solving a horizontally formatted arithmetic problem, such as 148 + 473. For example, they might say, "100 and 400 is 500. And 70 and 30 is another hundred, so 600. Then 8, 9, 10, 11 ... and the other 10 is 21. So, 621."

However, these same students may regress to an earlier level when solving problems in a vertical format, making mistakes such as the following.

$$\begin{array}{r} 148 \\ +473 \\ \hline 511 \end{array}$$ (*The student ignored the numbers that needed to be regrouped.*)

The vertical format can lead students to just think of each number as singles, even if they understand place value in other contexts. The historical work on "bugs" in algorithms provides many additional examples, such as the following.

$$\begin{array}{r} 73 \\ -40 \\ \hline 34 \end{array}$$ (*The student subracted the smaller from the larger digit in each case.*)

$$\begin{array}{r} 802 \\ -47 \\ \hline 665 \end{array}$$ (*The studen ignored the zero, borrowing from the 8 two times.*)

These examples have several lessons for us. Teaching arithmetic is much more than teaching procedures. It involves relationships, concepts, and strategies. Indeed, *if taught conceptually, most students will not make these types of errors.* But recall that the *end* goal is for students to be able to perform these algorithms *automatically, easily, without having to think too much about them.* However, if errors happen (we're all human), *if taught conceptually, most students catch these types of errors.* Further, they can *find their mistakes and fix them because they know both how and <u>why</u> the algorithm works.*

Finally, teaching arithmetic *well* does more than teach "computation"—it lays the groundwork for much of future math, including algebra (Mark-Zigdon & Tirosh, 2017b, see also Chapter 12). This is important: For all the warnings of "things that can go wrong" with teaching of algorithms, we must remember this:

> In training teachers and teaching pupils it cannot be emphasized strongly enough what an achievement our modern algorithms are and how much they contribute to our facility for calculations.
>
> (Mathematician Edward Barbeau, personal communication, 2020)

Algorithms are the culmination of eons of intellectual achievements.

Experience and Education: Multidigit Addition and Subtraction

The previous section showed that possessing strong knowledge of the properties and processes of counting, place value, and arithmetic helps students use algorithms adaptively and transfer their knowledge to new situations. Without this knowledge, children often make errors such as subtracting the smaller from the larger digit regardless of which is actually to be subtracted from which. Many of these errors stem from children's treatment of multidigit numbers as a series of single-digit numbers, without consideration of their place value and role in the math situation (Fuson, 1992b). Too many U.S. children learn to carry out the steps of algorithm, but do not develop conceptual understanding of place value. This is a problem.

Some have argued that "the standard algorithm" is actually *harmful* to children. For example, in classrooms where the standard algorithm was *not* taught, second and third graders performed better on problems such as mental addition of 7 + 52 + 186 than students in classrooms in which the standard algorithm was taught, *even when the latter were fourth-grade students* (Kamii & Dominick, 1997, 1998). Further, when they did make errors, the non-algorithm students' answers were more reasonable. The fourth-grade algorithm classes gave answers that were nonsensical (to those with conceptual knowledge and number sense), with sums above 700 or even 800. They also gave answers such as "four, four, four," indicating they thought about the numbers not as having place value, but, rather, just as a series of separate digits. The researchers argue that the standard algorithm is harmful because it encourages children to cease their own thinking and because it "unteaches" place value.

However, children's conceptual limitations and mistakes may be due to poor curricula or teaching of algorithms by rote—impeding children's opportunity for conceptual thinking. As traditionally taught, divorced from children's own strategies and from conceptual understanding, algorithms appear to replace quantitative reasoning. Algorithms purposefully work on one "column" after another without a concern for the place value of the numbers—and not having to "think" about them too much is a good thing—*after you understand them*. Too often, teachers directly teach standard algorithms regardless of their students' developmental progressions in fundamentals such as counting strategies, allowing the students to perform prescribed procedures *unconnected* to their understandings of number concepts.

In contrast, *curricula and teaching that emphasize both conceptual understanding simultaneously with procedural skill, and flexible application of multiple strategies that children invent or choose initially, lead to equivalent skill, but more fluent, flexible use of such skills, as well as superior conceptual understanding* (Hickendorff et al., 2019). Such teachers often ask children how they solved a problem and why their solutions worked.

Basically, at the start, follow the *curiosity path* (see more in Chapter 14 and https://make mathmoments.com). Use a guided discovery approach to help children invent and use their own strategies first to solve problems.

In general, then, high-quality teaching addresses concepts, procedures, and connections, but *also* emphasizes *students' sense-making*. For example, the use of visual representations of quantities and explication of the relationships between concepts and skills can be important. Teachers say, "Here, 8 tens and 7 tens are 15 tens. This equals 1 *hundred* and 5 *tens*," modeling with base-ten manipulatives as necessary. Such teaching is often necessary, but alone is not sufficient. *Students need to make sense of the procedures.* They need to describe and explain what they are doing in natural and then math language. At certain levels of understanding, especially, they need to be able to adapt procedures.

This is one of the main reasons that some argue that students should create their own strategies to solve multidigit arithmetic problems before formal instruction on algorithms. That is, children's informal strategies may be the best starting points for developing both place value and multidigit arithmetic concepts and skills. These strategies differ significantly from formal, paper-and-pencil algorithms. For example, children prefer working left to right, whereas the formal addition and subtraction algorithms work right to left (Kamii & Dominick, 1997, 1998). The reason for this is not just that it encourages children's creative thinking—although that *is* a remarkable finding of this research. As previously stated, one group of researchers believes that algorithms harm students' thinking. As another example, one teacher gave her class *only* problems in which one addend ended with "99" or "98" (e.g., 366 + 199). For most of the session, all the students used the standard algorithm. One student, who had not been taught these algorithms in previous grades, said that he changed 366 + 199 to 365 + 200 and then added to find 565. However, only three students adopted such methods—all the rest kept "lining up the digits" and computing each of these problems digit by digit.

Kamii blamed standard algorithms for students' reticence to *think* about problems. When the teachers stopped showing them algorithmic steps, the differences were called "astounding" (Kamii & Dominick, 1998). For example, one year after teachers stopped teaching standard algorithms and relied on students' thinking, correct answers on 6 + 53 + 185 went from three of 16 students, all of whom used the standard algorithm, to only two using the standard algorithm (both incorrectly) and 18 using their own strategies, with 15 of the 18 getting the correct answer.

Thus, Kamii is convinced that, at least for whole number addition and subtraction, algorithms introduced early do more harm than good. But what, many ask, if children make mistakes? Kamii's argument is that the reasoning of the students about these situations, is adequate for the class to *self*-correct any such errors. One second-grade class was asked to add 107 and 117. A first group of students added from the right and got 2114. A second said 14 was a two-digit numeral and could not be written in the ones place; you should only write the 4 there, so the answer is 214. A third group said the 1 in 14 should be written because it was more important, so answer was 211. The fourth group added the tens and said the answer was 224. Students discussed and argued for their point. The group using each approach defended it. At the end of the 45-minute period, the only thing the class could agree on was that it was impossible to have four different correct answers. (This is the point at which many teachers hearing the story worry the most—isn't it unethical to send them home without the right answer?)

Over the next session, *all* students in this class constructed a correct algorithm. They occasionally made mistakes, but were encouraged to defend their opinion until they were convinced that the procedures they had used were wrong. They learned by modifying their ideas, not just "accepting" a new procedure. These and similar studies support the notion that inventing one's own procedures is usually a good first phase (Baroody, 1987b; Clements et al., 2020). They also illustrate the approach, mentioned previously, of teaching place value in the context of solving multidigit addition and subtraction problems (Fuson & Briars, 1990).

Is student invention necessary? Some contend that invention at this level is not the critical feature. Rather, they argue for the importance of the *sense*-making in which students engage whether or not they invent, adapt, or copy a method.

Sense-making is probably the essence; however, we believe *the bulk of research indicates that initial student invention develops multiple interconnecting concepts, skills, and problem solving* (Clements et al., 2020). This does not mean that children must invent every procedure, but that conceptual development, adaptive reasoning, and skills are developed simultaneously, and that initial student invention may be a particularly effective way of achieving these goals. Finally, we believe that student invention is a creative act of math thinking that is valuable in its own right.

Mental Procedures Before Algorithms

Many researchers believe that use of written algorithms is introduced too soon and that a more beneficial approach is the initial use of mental computation. Kamii's writings and research exemplify this approach. Standard written algorithms intentionally relieve the user of thinking about where to start, what place value to assign to digits, and so forth. *This is efficient for those who already understand, but often has negative effects on initial learning.* In comparison, mental strategies are derived from and support underlying concepts. Conventionally taught students usually take a long time to master algorithms and often never master them. Students learn better if mental computation is taught and performed before written algorithms (and practiced throughout education), along with appropriate work with concrete materials and drawings.

Such mental computation creates *flexible* thinkers (Nunes, Dorneles, Lin, & Rathgeb-Schnierer, 2016). Inflexible students mostly use mental images of standard paper-and-pencil algorithms. For 246 + 199, they compute as follows: 9 + 6 = 15, 15 = 1 ten and 5 ones; 9 + 4 + 1 = 14, 14 tens = 1 hundred and 4 tens; 1 + 2 + 1 = 4, four hundreds; so, 445. Unsurprisingly, they frequently make errors.

Flexible students instead might compute as follows: 199 is close to 200; 246 + 200 = 446, take away 1; 445. The flexible students also used strategies such as the following to compute 28 + 35 (Hickendorff et al., 2019):

- *Compensation*: 30 + 35 = 65, 65 − 2 = 63 (or 30 + 33 = 63).
- *Decomposition*: 8 + 5 = 13, 20 + 30 = 50, 63.
- *Jump*, or "begin-with-one-number": 28 + 5 = 33, 33 + 30 = 63 (28 + 30 = 58, 58 + 5 = 63).

Compensation and decomposition strategies are aligned with base-ten blocks and other such manipulatives, whereas the jump strategy is aligned with 100s charts or number lines (especially the empty number line, discussed later in this chapter). For many students, the jump strategies are more effective and accurate. For example, in subtraction, students using standard algorithms often show the "smaller-from-larger" bug, as for 42 − 25, giving the answer 23.

Games can give targeted practice with the jump strategy. For example, in "The 11 Game," students spin two spinners (partially unbent paper clips can be spun around a pencil point). If they get what is illustrated in Figure 6.5, for example, they must subtract 11 from 19. See the resource, "Introducing and Using Games" on [LT]².

They then can put one of their counters on the result, 8 (which appears in two locations)–as long as one is open. Their goal is to be the first to get four in a row (horizontal, vertical, or oblique). The emphasis on adding or subtracting only 1 ten and 1 one helps children understand

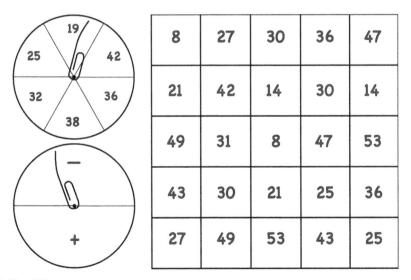

Figure 6.5 The "11" game

and establish a strong use of the jump strategy. Many variations are, of course, possible, such as changing 11 to 37 or adding or subtracting only multiples of 10. Try playing this game with a student or friend.

In a similar vein, a buying-and-selling situation embodied in a modified game of lotto was used successfully as a context to motivate and guide first graders in two-digit subtraction (Kutscher, Linchevski, & Eisenman, 2002). Students transferred their knowledge to the classroom context.

The Dutch more recently have promoted the use of the "empty number line" as a support for the jump strategies. Use of this model has been reported as supporting more intelligent arithmetical strategies. The number line is "empty" in that it is not a ruler with all numbers marked but simply keeps the order of numbers and the size of "jumps" recorded (not to scale), such as shown in Figure 6.6.

Other researchers believe that both the decomposition and jump strategies are worthwhile, and neither has to be learned first (Wright, Stanger, Stafford, & Martland, 2006). The jump strategy is preferred as a *mental arithmetic* strategy, with the empty number line as a recording, not a computational, device. From this view, students should use the empty number line to record what they have already done mentally, so it becomes a written representation and a way to communicate their thinking to their peers and the teacher.

Students also create combinations of these strategies. For example, students might first decompose a bit and then jump: 48 + 36 − 40 + 30 = 70; 70 + 8 = 78; 78 + 2 = 80; 80 + 4 = 84. They might also use compensation or other transformational strategies, such as: 34 + 59 → 34 + 60 − 1, so 94 − 1 = 93 (Wright et al., 2006).

Encourage students to use both strategies, but also help students *connect* them. For example, the jump strategy may de-emphasize decade structures but maintain number sense. Decomposition strategies emphasize place value but may lead to errors. Using and connecting both, intentionally addressing the math they each develop and using one to check the other, may be the most effective approach.

Other spinner games can provide substantial and enjoyable practice with these strategies. For example, "Spin Four" is similar to the "The 11 Game" except that the second spinner shows the amount added or subtracted from the number spun on the first spinner. This can be done in many ways. Figure 6.7 features subtraction with no regrouping (try it!). Other games can easily be constructed to feature subtraction with regrouping, addition with and without regrouping, or a combination of addition and subtraction.

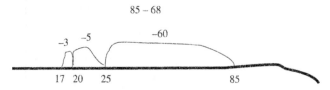

Figure 6.6 The empty number line supporting arithmetic

"Four in a Row" is a similar game, but here each player has 12 chips of one color ("see-through" if possible). Each chooses two numerals in the square on the left, summing them and covering them (just for this turn) with chips (see Figure 6.8). The player also covers the sum on the square on the right (this chip stays). The first to make four in a row with his/her chips is the winner (from Kamii, 1989, who credits Grayson Wheatley and Paul Cobb for this version; Kamii's books include many other games).

78	47	52	65	57
57	72	14	22	44
36	31	53	57	43
34	22	61	65	26
5	26	13	53	35

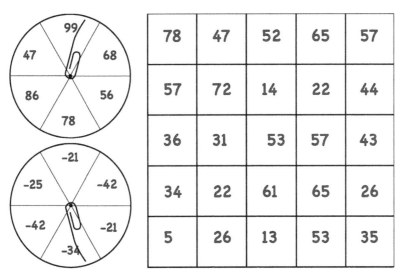

Figure 6.7 The "Spin Four" game

5	6	7
8	9	10
11	12	13

16	21	18	13	18
19	20	12	20	23
22	24	19	21	16
17	11	23	22	14
14	15	15	17	25

Figure 6.8 The "Four in a Row" game

Before we leave this topic, we note that it may be inaccurate to say a child "uses" a "jump" strategy when strategies are just barely forming (i.e., the youngest child). That is, they may not be deliberately choosing and applying strategies but basing computations on their familiarity with certain numbers' relations. A second grader may add 39 + 6 by deciding to add one to 39, then the "rest" of the 6 (i.e., 5) to the 40 to get 45, without conscientiously thinking—or even knowing about, "jump strategies." Such explicit knowledge and decision-making might emerge *from* repeated experiences using number relationships. At first these are "theorems-in-action" (Vergnaud, 1978) and are explicit strategies until they are mentally redescribed. Instructionally, this would imply that the initial goal is not so much to teach the strategies as to develop schemes of number relationships and then use them to construct strategies, discussing these strategies to highlight the math properties involved.

Which Algorithms?

There are many arguments about whether to teach *the* standard algorithms. Too often, such arguments have generated more heat than light, for several reasons:

- There is no single standard algorithm—if you mean exact steps one takes. Many different alterations of the standard *idea* have been used in the U.S. and around the world (e.g., see algorithms *a* and *b* in Table 6.1). All of these are mathematically valid, and even equivalent (Kilpatrick et al., 2001).
- What are taken as different "standard" algorithms by teachers and lay people are often *not* viewed as different by mathematicians, who believe they are all just simple *modifications* (often in the way numbers are recorded) of general place-value-based algorithms. That is, the algorithms in Table 6.1 all subtract in same-place-value columns and compose/decompose as necessary; they just do these processes and notate them in slightly different ways.

Several such modifications of the standard U.S. algorithm (Table 6.2) are useful (Fuson, 2009, 2020). For beginners, or those having difficulty, recording each addition showing its full place value, as in Table 6.2b, can develop their understanding and skill. Once this is attained, the accessible and mathematically desirable algorithm shown in Table 6.2c is superior to the standard shown in Table 6.1a for several reasons. First, the numeral (e.g., "13") is written with the digits close to each other, maintaining for the children the origin of the "13." Second, with students "adding from the top," the (usually larger) numerals are added first, freeing students' memory from holding an altered numeral (which was added to the "carried" 1). Instead, the larger numerals are added first, and the easy-to-add "1" is added last.

Similarly, notice the subtraction algorithm in Table 6.1c (compared to Table 6.1a). Regrouping everywhere *first* helps students concentrate *just* on the need to regroup and the regrouping itself. Once that has been completed, then the subtraction operations are performed one after the other. *Not* having to "switch" between the two processes allows better focus on each one.

Table 6.1 "Different" Standard Algorithms

a. Decomposition–U.S. traditional

$$\begin{array}{r} 4\ 5\ 6 \\ -1\ 6\ 7 \\ \hline \end{array}$$

$$\begin{array}{r} 4 \\ 4\ 5^1\ 6 \\ -1\ 6\ 7 \\ \hline \end{array}$$
Add 10 to 6 ones, "borrowing" from 5 tens.

$$\begin{array}{r} 4 \\ -4\ 5^1\ 6 \\ -1\ 6\ 7 \\ \hline 9 \end{array}$$
Subtract 16 − 7.

$$\begin{array}{r} 3^1\ \ 4 \\ -4\ 5^1\ 6 \\ -1\ 6\ 7 \\ \hline 9 \end{array}$$
Add 10 tens to 4 tens, borrowing from 4 hundreds.

$$\begin{array}{r} 4\ 5\!\!\!\diagup\ 6 \\ -1\ 6\ 7 \\ \hline 2\ 8\ 9 \end{array}$$
Subtract 14 − 6 (tens) and 3 − 1 (hundreds).

b. Equal addends–European and Latin American

$$\begin{array}{r} 4\ 5\ 6 \\ -1\ 6\ 7 \\ \hline \end{array}$$

$$\begin{array}{r} 4\ 5^1\ 6 \\ -1^1\ 6\ 7 \\ \hline \end{array}$$
Add 10 to 6 ones to make 16 ones, and 1 ten to 6 tens (here it is 1 *plus* 6 tens, *not* 16 tens).

$$\begin{array}{r} 4\ 5^1\ 6 \\ -1^1\ 6\ 7 \\ \hline 9 \end{array}$$
Subtract 16 − 7.

$$\begin{array}{r} 4^1\ 5^1\ 6 \\ -1^1\ 6\ 7 \\ \hline 9 \end{array}$$
Add 10 tens to 5 tens, 1 hundred to 1 hundred.

$$\begin{array}{r} 4^1\ 5^1\ 6 \\ -1^1\ 6\ 7 \\ \hline 2\ 8\ 9 \end{array}$$
Subtract 15 − 7 (tens) and 4 − 2 (hundreds).

c. Accessible and mathematically desirable–a modification of the U.S. algorithm (Fuson, 2009)

$$\begin{array}{r} 4\ 5\ 6 \\ -1\ 6\ 7 \\ \hline \end{array}$$

$$\begin{array}{r} 3^1\ \ 4 \\ 4\ 5^1\ 6 \\ -1\ 6\ 7 \\ \hline \end{array}$$
Regroup everywhere needed.

$$\begin{array}{r} 3^1\ \ 4 \\ 4\ 5^1\ 6 \\ -1\ 6\ 7 \\ \hline 2\ 8\ 9 \end{array}$$
Subtract everywhere.

These "accessible and mathematically desirable algorithms" are simple variations of the standard U.S. algorithms. However, they can significantly help students build both skill and understanding (Fuson, 2009).

For any variation, base-ten manipulatives and drawing can support the learning of composition and decomposition methods–especially in maintaining a connection between concepts and procedures. Use of drawings is illustrated in Tables 6.2b and c. (Notice there are two basic differences between the two, the order in which values are grouped and the way they are grouped.) Manipulatives or drawings help illustrate that different place value quantities need to be added separately and that certain quantities need to be composed to make a unit of a higher place value.

Research shows that the key is *teaching for meaning and understanding* and then moving to automaticity. Instruction that focuses on flexible application of a variety of strategies helps students build robust concepts and procedures. They learn to adaptively fit their strategies to the characteristics of the problems. In contrast, instruction that focuses only on routines results in students blindly following those routines. Understanding the math, and students' thinking about math, including the varied strategies and algorithms they might use, helps students create and use adaptive calculations. If students invent their own strategies first, they have fewer errors than students who were taught algorithms from the start.

Conceptually-based Instruction Supports Mathematical Proficiency

Teach conceptual knowledge first, and alongside, procedural knowledge. Have students develop their own methods first, the earlier in their educational lives the better. When standard

Table 6.2 Variations on the Standard Addition Algorithm

a. U.S. traditional

456 +167	1 456 +167 3	11 456 +167 23	11 456 +167 623
	Add 6 + 7, enter 3 in ones place, "carry" the 10 ones to create 1 ten.	Add 6 + 5 + 1 (tens), enter 2 in tens place, "carry" the 10 tens to create 1 hundred.	Add 1 + 4 + 1 (hundreds), enter 6 in hundreds place.

b. Transitional algorithm—write all totals (Fuson, 2009)

456 +167	456 +167 500	456 +167 500 110	456 +167 500 110 13 623

c. Accessible and mathematically desirable algorithm—a modification of the U.S. algorithm (Fuson, 2009)

456 +167	456 +167 3	456 +167 12^13	456 +167 6^12^13
	Add 6 + 7, enter "13" but with the 3 in the ones place and the 1 ten *under* the tens column.	Add 5 + 6 + 1 ten, enter "2" in the tens place and the 1 hundred under the hundreds column.	Add 4 + 1 + 1 hundred.

algorithms are developed, connect them to students' informal strategies and reasoning. The modified algorithms we present here can help children build concepts and procedures simultaneously. On that note, let us turn to this chapter's learning trajectories.

To support problem solving, use powerful representations. For example, "strip" or "tape" diagrams are used extensively in East Asian countries (Singapore, Japan), to serve as a consistent, beneficial representation of problem situations (Murata, 2008). A simple version of these was used in Table 5.1 (p. 91) to illustrate the problem types. Figure 6.9 shows in more detail how teachers and students might represent some of those problem types.

Keep children reasoning! Even after developing written algorithms, make sure you keep playing games such as "Close to 100" (or 1000) to ensure children are *thinking* about place value in arithmetic. Children play in pairs. From a deck of numeral cards (0-9), they deal each person 6.

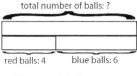

total number of balls: ?

red balls: 4 blue balls: 6

Al has 4 red balls and 6
blue balls. How many
balls does he have in all?

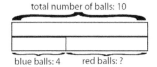

total number of balls: 10

blue balls: 4 red balls: ?

Al has 10 balls; 4 are blue,
the rest are red. How
many are red?

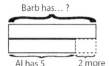

Barb has... ?

Al has 5 2 more

Al has 5 marbles. Barb has 2
more than Al. How many
balls does Barb have?

Figure 6.9 Strip diagrams used as a problem-solving tool

They pick 4 of the 6 and put them into a two-digit addition form in an attempt to get as close to 100 as possible. For example, a child who is dealt 5 3 0 3 6 9 1 might make:

$$\begin{array}{r} 86 \\ +13 \\ \hline \end{array}$$

That yields 99, so her score is 1. Whoever gets the closest (if your sum is 102, your score is "2"–so the "1" would win) gets a point. Such games sharpen mental math and keep algorithms infused with meaning. (The game is more challenging if you are only given 4 cards; further, older children can play close to 1,000.)

Inverse Operations and Checking One's Work

Because addition and subtraction are inverse operations, a good way for students to check the accuracy of their work is to do the related inverse operation–to check subtraction (503 - 384 = 119), add the subtrahend (384) and the difference (119).

Learning Trajectory for Composing Number and Multidigit Addition and Subtraction

The importance of the *goal* of increasing children's ability in these arithmetic abilities is clear. Table 6.3 shows where these goals appear in the CCSSM. Many of these are shared with those in the previous chapter, of course, because children can use different strategies to solve most problems. Again, notice how arithmetic is reflected in the standards from several domains.

With those goals, Table 6.4 provides the two additional components of the learning trajectory, the developmental progression and the instructional tasks. There are three important notes on this learning trajectory:

1 Unlike other learning trajectories, Table 6.4 is split into two parts, first composing, and then multidigit addition and subtraction. This was done to emphasize that the second part is a *copy* of the developmental progression already included in the learning trajectory in Chapter 5, enhanced with the instructional tasks from this chapter.

Table 6.3 Goals for Addition and Subtraction and Place Value (Emphasizing Composition, Fluency, Place Value, and Multidigit Arithmetic) from the CCSSM

Operations and Algebraic Thinking [K.OA in CCSSM]

Understand addition as putting together and adding to and understand subtraction as taking apart and taking from.

1   Represent addition and subtraction with objects, fingers, mental images, drawings, sounds (e.g., claps), acting out situations, verbal explanations, expressions, or equations. [Drawings need not show details but should show the math in the problem. (This applies wherever drawings are mentioned in the Standards.)]
2   Decompose numbers less than or equal to 10 into pairs in more than one way, e.g., by using objects or drawings, and record each decomposition by a drawing or equation (e.g., 5 = 2 + 3 and 5 = 4 + 1).
3   For any number from 1 to 9, find the number that makes 10 when added to the given number, e.g., by using objects or drawings, and record the answer with a drawing or equation.
4   Fluently add and subtract within 5.

Operations and Algebraic Thinking [1.OA in CCSSM]

Represent and solve problems involving addition and subtraction.

1   Use addition and subtraction within 20 to solve word problems involving situations of adding to, taking from, putting together, taking apart, and comparing, with unknowns in all positions, e.g., by using objects, drawings, and equations with a symbol for the unknown number to represent the problem. [The CCSSM refers to their Glossary, Table 1, which has information very similar to this book's Table 5.1.]
2   Solve word problems that call for addition of three whole numbers whose sum is less than or equal to 20, e.g., by using objects, drawings, and equations with a symbol for the unknown number to represent the problem.

Understand and apply properties of operations and the relationship between addition and subtraction.

1   Apply properties of operations as strategies to add and subtract. Examples: if 8 + 3 = 11 is known, then 3 + 8 = 11 is also known. (Commutative property of addition.) To add 2 + 6 + 4, the second two numbers can be added to make a ten, so 2 + 6 + 4 = 2 + 10 = 12. (Associative property of addition.) [Students need not use formal terms for these properties.]
2   Understand subtraction as an unknown-addend problem. For example, subtract 10 - 8 by finding the number that makes 10 when added to 8.

Add and subtract within 20.

1   Add and subtract within 20, demonstrating fluency for addition and subtraction within 10. Use strategies such as counting on; making ten (e.g., 8 + 6 = 8 + 2 + 4 = 10 + 4 = 14); decomposing a number leading to a ten (e.g., 13 − 4 = 13 - 3 - 1 = 10 - 1 = 9); using the relationship between addition and subtraction (e.g., knowing that 8 + 4 = 12, one knows 12 − 8 = 4); and creating equivalent but easier or known sums (e.g., adding 6 + 7 by creating the known equivalent 6 + 6 + 1 = 12 + 1 = 13).

Work with addition and subtraction equations.

1   Understand the meaning of the equal sign, and determine if equations involving addition and subtraction are true or false. For example, which of the following equations are true and which are false? 6 = 6, 7 = 8-1, 5 + 2 = 2 + 5, 4 + 1 = 5 + 2.
2   Determine the unknown whole number in an addition or subtraction equation relating to three whole numbers. For example, determine the unknown number that makes the equation true in each of the equations 8 + ? = 11, 5 = ? − 3, 6 + 6 = ?.

Number and Operations in Base Ten [1 .NBT from CCSSM]

Use place value understanding and properties of operations to add and subtract.

(Continued)

Table 6.3 (Cont.)

1   Add within 100, including adding a two-digit number and a one-digit number, and adding a two-digit number and a multiple of 10, using concrete models or drawings and strategies based on place value, properties of operations, and/or the relationship between addition and subtraction; relate the strategy to a written method and explain the reasoning used. Understand that in adding two-digit numbers, one adds tens and tens, ones and ones; and sometimes it is necessary to compose a ten.

2   Given a two-digit number, mentally find ten more or ten less than the number, without having to count; explain the reasoning used.

3   Subtract multiples of 10 in the range 10–90 from multiples of 10 in the range 10–90 (positive or zero differences), using concrete models or drawings and strategies based on place value, properties of operations, and/or the relationship between addition and subtraction; relate the strategy to a written method and explain the reasoning used.

Operations and Algebraic Thinking [CCSSM 2.OA]

Represent and solve problems involving addition and subtraction.

1   Use addition and subtraction within 100 to solve one- and two-step word problems involving situations of adding to, taking from, putting together, taking apart, and comparing, with unknowns in all positions, e.g., by using drawings and equations with a symbol for the unknown number to represent the problem. [The CCSSM refers to their Glossary, Table 1, which has information very similar to this Chapter 5's Table 5.1.]

Add and subtract within 20.

1   Fluently add and subtract within 20 using mental strategies. [See standard 1.OA.6 for a list of mental strategies.] By end of Grade 2, know from memory all sums of two one-digit numbers.

Work with equal groups of objects to gain foundations for multiplication.

1   Determine whether a group of objects (up to 20) has an odd or even number of members, e.g., by pairing objects or counting them by twos; write an equation to express an even number as a sum of two equal addends.

2   Use addition to find the total number of objects arranged in rectangular arrays with up to five rows and up to five columns; write an equation to express the total as a sum of equal addends.

Number and Operations in Base Ten [2.NBT in CCSSM]

Use place value understanding and properties of operations to add and subtract.

1   Fluently add and subtract within 100 using strategies based on place value, properties of operations, and/or the relationship between addition and subtraction.

2   Add up to four two-digit numbers using strategies based on place value and properties of operations.

3   Add and subtract within 1000, using concrete models or drawings and strategies based on place value, properties of operations, and/or the relationship between addition and subtraction; relate the strategy to a written method. Understand that in adding or subtracting three-digit numbers, one adds or subtracts hundreds and hundreds, tens and tens, ones and ones; and sometimes it is necessary to compose or decompose tens or hundreds.

4   Mentally add 10 or 100 to a given number 100–900, and mentally subtract 10 or 100 from a given number 100–900.

5   Explain why addition and subtraction strategies work, using place value and the properties of operations. [Explanations may be supported by drawings or objects.]

Measurement and Data [2.MD in CCSSM]

Measure and estimate lengths in standard units.

1   Measure to determine how much longer one object is than another, expressing the length difference in terms of a standard-length unit.

Relate addition and subtraction to length.

1   Use addition and subtraction within 100 to solve word problems involving lengths that are given in the same units, e.g., by using drawings (such as drawings of rulers) and equations with a symbol for the unknown number to represent the problem.

(Continued)

Table 6.3 (Cont.)

---

2   Represent whole numbers as lengths from 0 on a number line diagram with equally spaced points corresponding to the numbers 0, 1, 2, … and represent whole-number sums and differences within 100 on a number line diagram.

Work with time and money.

1   Solve word problems involving dollar bills, quarters, dimes, nickels, and pennies, using $ and ¢ symbols appropriately. *Example: If you have 2 dimes and 3 pennies, how many cents do you have?*

Represent and interpret data.

1   Draw a picture graph and a bar graph (with single-unit scale) to represent a data set with up to four categories. Solve simple put-together, take-apart, and compare problems using information presented in a bar graph. [The CCSSM refers to their Glossary, Table 1, which has information very similar to this Chapter 5's Table 5.1.]

---

2   Note that place value is fundamental to all number domains, so it is embedded in the learning trajectories in Chapters 2, 3, 4, and 5, as well as this one. This chapter simply has the most specific focus on place value.

3   Recall again that the ages in all the learning trajectory tables are only approximate, especially because the age of acquisition usually depends heavily on experience.

The Development of Multiplication and Division, and Fractions

Also related to grouping and place value is the idea of multiple "equal groups"… leading to multiplication and division. Grouping seems clear. Most of us learned that 2 × 3 means "two groups of three" or six in all. But place value? Yes: When we discussed "52 is 'five tens, two ones,'" well, five tens is 5 × 10. We can *define* multiplication as: 5 × 10 = 10 + 10 + 10 + 10 (Wu, 2011b).

Further, we did not fully explain one high level of place value understanding (p. 128): "Students understand the exponential nature of number systems." We know that 1,234 in expanded notion is 1000 + 200 + 30 + 4. But that can get tedious. For example, a recent estimate of the U.S. population was 321,526,816 or 300,000,000 + 20,000,000 + 1,000,000 … and so forth. Exponential notion puts it more succinctly: $3 \times 10^8 + 2 \times 10^7 + 1 \times 10^6$ … where 10^8 simply means 10 times 10 … eight times (100,000,000 − 1 with 8 zeros).

Now, that is far up this learning trajectory … let's get back to the beginning. Research has shown that very young children can learn *equipartitioning*–the main researcher in this area, Jere Confrey, also calls it *splitting* (Confrey, Maloney, Nguyen, & Rupp, 2014, see this for far more detail about this LT)–about the same time as they learn to count (see also Young-Loveridge & Bicknell, 2018). Equipartitioning has the goal of producing equal-sized groups. At the earliest ages, children give some, but not the same number, to each person. That is, they pass out objects (e.g., dolls) to different people but they just "dump" the objects, without appreciation of equal numbers to each (Miller, 1984b).

They begin with basic notions of "fairness" to build equal groups and to share objects equally among, first, two people, and later, larger numbers of people. To find the size of the fair share in equipartitioning problems, children typically use "partitive strategies," dealing one to each person in turn (Hunting, 2003). At first, this is dealing out small numbers to only two people, then more, but still without necessarily explicitly understanding that equal groups are

Table 6.4 Learning Trajectory for Composing Number and Multidigit Addition and Subtraction

Age	Developmental Progression	Instructional Tasks
0-1	**Actor on Parts: Foundations** Displays actions that show intuition about parts and wholes such as gathering objects together. Only nonverbally recognizes parts and wholes. Recognizes that sets can be combined in different orders but may not explicitly recognize that groups are additively composed of smaller groups.	*Block Party*, [LT][2]: Children explore parts and wholes by separating blocks of different colors, then re-organizing them as a whole.
1-3	**Parts Combiner** Recognizes that sets can be combined in different orders but may not explicitly recognize that groups are additively composed of smaller groups. The toddler also recognizes Part-Whole relations in nonverbal, intuitive, perceptual situations and can nonverbally represent parts that make a whole. When shown four red blocks and two blue blocks, intuitively appreciates that "all the blocks" include the red and blue blocks, but when asked how many there are in all, may name a small number, such as 1.	*Parts Combiner Finger Plays*, [LT][2]: Finger plays that include adding additional pieces throughout or showing how a whole can include parts support learning about number composition.
3-4	**Inexact Part-Whole Recognizer** Knows that a whole is bigger than parts but may not accurately quantify (label with numbers). (May show intuitive knowledge of commutativity, and, later, associativity with physical groups, later in more abstract contexts, including numbers.) When shown four red blocks and two blue blocks and asked how many there are in all, names a "big number," such as 5 or 10.	*Toy Bag: Parts in a Whole*, [LT][2]: Students explore quantities of toys in a bag. With support from a teacher to identify the number of toys, children practice thinking about how parts make up a whole. *Note*: Experiences in learning trajectories from other chapters are appropriate to developing these abilities. Especially relevant are subitizing (Chapter 2), counting (Chapters 3 and 5), comparing (Chapter 4), and sorting (Chapter 12).
4-5	**Composer to 4, then 5** Knows number combinations. Quickly names parts of any whole, or the whole given the parts. Shown four, then one is secretly hidden, and then is shown the three remaining, quickly says "one" is hidden.	*Finger Games*: Ask children to make numbers with their fingers (hands should be placed in their laps between tasks). These sessions should be short and fun, and repeated, spread out over many days.  Ask children to show 4 with their fingers. "Think, pair, share: Tell your partner how you did it. Now in a different way. Tell your partner." "Now make 4 with the same number on each hand."

(Continued)

Table 6.4 (Cont.)

Age	Developmental Progression	Instructional Tasks
		"Make 5 with your fingers," and discuss: "Did you use one hand only or two?" "Can you do it a different way?", and so on. Ask children to repeat the above tasks, but say, "You can't use thumbs." Challenge children by asking them to show 3 or 5 using the same number of fingers on each hand. Discuss why it cannot be done.
		Bunny Ears on, [LT]²: In this modification, have children make the numbers as "bunny ears"—holding their hands above their heads to make numbers 1 to 5 in different ways. Thus, they can see others' solutions, but have to make mental images of their own. *Up and Down*, [LT]²: In another session, ask children to show 4 on one hand. Ask how many fingers are up and how many are down (all on one hand only). Repeat with 0, 1, 2, 3, and 5 across several days and weeks. *Snap! (to 5)*, [LT]²: Agree on a number from 3 to 5. Make a train of that number of connecting cubes, all of one color. Put them behind your back and snap off some. Show the rest. Have students determine how many are behind your back. Discuss their solution strategies.
		Students work in pairs playing "Snap!", taking turns making the connecting cube train and snapping. Students should ask their partner to guess how many you have, then show them to check.
		Subitize!, [LT]: Students identify an image that correctly matches a target image from four multiple-choice selections.

5–6	**Composer to 7** Knows number combinations to totals of 7. Quickly names parts of any whole, or the whole given parts. Doubles to 10.	*Snap! (to 7)*, [LT]²: See above, but up to 7. *Make a Number*, [LT]²: Children decide on a number to make, say 7. They then get three decks
	Shown six, then four are secretly hidden, and shown the two remaining, quickly says "four" are hidden.	of cards and take out all the cards numbered 7 or more, shuffling the remaining cards. The children take turns drawing a card and try to make a 7 by combining it with any other face-up card—if they can, they can keep both cards. If they can't, they must place it face up beside the deck. When the deck is gone, the player with the most pairs wins. Play again by changing the number to make. *Note:* See Conceptual Subitizer to 7 on p. 30. See also many activities above and below (adapted for this level's numbers) on [LT]², including *Finger Games, Cookie Game, Break and Make,* and *Dump and Sing.*

Table 6.4 (Cont.)

Age	Developmental Progression	Instructional Tasks
	Composer to 10 Knows number combinations to totals of 10. Quickly names parts of any whole, or the whole given parts. Doubles to 20. "9 and 9 is 18."	*Finger Games*: Ask children to make numbers with their fingers (hands should be placed in their laps between tasks). Ask children to show 6 with their fingers. "Tell your partner how you did it." "Now in a different way. Tell your partner." "Now make 6 with the *same number* on each hand." Repeat with other even numbers (8, 10). Ask children to show 7 with their fingers and discuss responses. Can they do it a different way? Ask children to repeat the above tasks, but say, "You can't use thumbs." ("Can you make 10?") Challenge children by asking them to show 3, 5, or 7 using the same number of fingers on each hand. Discuss why it cannot be done. *Bunny Ears*: In this modification, have children make the numbers as "bunny ears"—holding their hands above their heads to make numbers 6 to 10 in different ways. *Up and Down*, [LT]²: Ask children to show 6. Ask how many fingers are up and how many are down (all on one hand only). Repeat with all numbers 0 to 10 across many days. *Turn Over Ten*, [LT]²: The goal of this card game is to accumulate the most pairs of cards that sum to 10. Provide each group of children with three collections of 0-10 cards. Ten cards are dealt to each player, who assembles them in one pile, face down. The remaining cards are placed face down in a "pick-up pile" between the two players. The top card of this pile is flipped over, face up. Player 1 turns over his/her top card. If this card forms a sum of 10 together with the card in the pick-up pile, that player takes and keeps the pair. (Whenever the card on top of the pick-up pile is used, a new one is turned over.) If the sum of 10 is not reached, the player places this top card next to the pick-up pile, so that these cards can be seen and used by players in subsequent turns (therefore, there may be a row of "discards" face up between the two players). In either case (pair formed or card discarded) the turn passes to the next player, who turns over his/her top card. If any of the cards showing can be used to form a pair of 10, the player keeps that pair. If a player sees a pair of cards showing that form 10, he can choose that pair during his/her turn instead of turning over the top card in his/her pile. Turns alternate until each player has turned over all of his or her cards. The player with the most pairs accumulated is the winner. *Make Tens*, [LT]²: The goal is to make tens with all your cards and avoid being left with the extra card. Provide each group of children a deck of cards made of two collections plus one other card of any number

Table 6.4 (Cont.)

Age	Developmental Progression	Instructional Tasks
		between 0 and 10 (this will eventually be the "Old Maid" card that cannot make a 10). For example, use one of the following:

1 Two collections of number cards (0–10) with dots and numerals, with one extra 5 card.
2 Collections of numeral (only) cards (0–10) with one extra 5 card.

Variation (two-player game): The entire deck is dealt out to both players. Both players first form all possible pairs of 10 in their own hands and set these pairs aside in their score pile. They keep the extras in their hand. They take turns choosing (without looking) one card from the other player's hand. If they can use it to make 10, they place that pair in their score pile. If they cannot use it, the card remains in their hand. At the end of the game, one player will be left with the odd card.

Slap a Ten, [LT][2]: The goal is to make tens with all your cards and be the first one "out." Provide each group of children with a deck of cards made of four decks of 1–10 cards.

Variation (two- to four-player game): Six cards are dealt out to each player. The remaining cards are placed in the middle, face down.
One player turns the top card over. The other players quickly determine if they can make a 10 with that and one card in their hand. If they can, they slap the card. The player who slaps it first must use it to make a ten. If they cannot, they keep the card and must take another card off the pile.
Players take turns turning over the top card.
The game ends when player goes "out" or the pile is gone. The player who went "out" or the one with the fewest cards in their hand wins.

Variation (if children are having a problem trying to slap the card at the same time):

If they can make a 10 with the card shown, they slap their own card down. The player who slapped it down first will ask "Is it 10?"
All players must agree that the two cards make 10.

Tens Memory Game:

For each pair of children, two sets of numeral cards (1–9) are needed.
Place card sets face down in two separate three-by-three arrays. Players take turns choosing, flipping, and showing a card from each array.
If the cards do not sum to 10, they are returned (face down) to the arrays. If they do, that player keeps them.
Use more cards to make a longer game.

Subitize!, [LT]: Students identify an image that correctly matches a target image from four multiple-choice selections.

Table 6.4 (Cont.)

Age	Developmental Progression	Instructional Tasks

7	**Composer with Tens and Ones** Understands two-digit numbers as tens and ones; count with dimes and pennies; two-digit addition with regrouping. "17 and 36 is like 17 and 3, which is 20, and 33, which is 53."	*Note*: All games above involving tens can be played with larger sums to extend children's knowledge of arithmetic combinations. *Make the Sum*, [LT]²: Six 1-10 decks of numeral cards are mixed and dealt out to players. Three number cubes are thrown by one player, who announces the sum. All players try to make this sum in as many ways as possible. The first player to use up all her or his cards wins. *Salute! (Composing Numbers)*, [LT]²: With a deck of cards with the face cards removed, and ace as 1, cards are dealt to two of the three players (Kamii, 1989). The two players sit facing each other with their cards face down. The third player says, "Salute!" and the two players take the top card from their piles and hold them on their foreheads so that the other two players can see them, but they cannot. The third player announces the sum of the two cards. Each of the other players tries to be the first to announce the value of their *own* cards. The person who is first takes both cards. The winner is the person who collects the most cards. *Hiding Cubes*, [LT]²: Show students connecting cubes—4 tens and 3 ones—for 2 seconds only (e.g., hidden under a cloth). Ask how many they saw. Discuss how they knew. Repeat with new amounts. Tell students you have a real challenge for them. Tell them there are 2 tens and 17 ones hidden. How many are there in all? Once they tell you, uncover them to check. Place four blue tens, one red ten, and four red singles. Tell students you have 54 cubes in all, and 14 are red. Ask them how many are blue. *Note*: From this point, the most important activities are included in the subitizing learning trajectory. See Chapter 2, p. 31, "Conceptual Subitizer with Place Value" and "Conceptual Subitizer with Place Value and Multiplicative Thinking."
6-7	**Deriver** +/− Uses flexible strategies and derived combinations (e.g., 7 + 7 is 14, so 7 + 8 is 15) to solve all types of problems.	*Multidigit Addition and Subtraction*: *All types* of single-digit problems, using derived and, increasingly, known combinations.

(Continued)

Table 6.4 (Cont.)

Age	Developmental Progression	Instructional Tasks
	Includes Break Apart to Make Ten (BAMT). Can simultaneously think of three numbers within a sum, and can move part of a number to another, aware of the increase in one and the decrease in another. Asked, "What's 7 plus 8?", thinks: $7 + 8 \rightarrow 7 + [7 + 1]$ $[7 + 7] + 1 = 14 + 1 = 15$. Or, using BAMT, thinks, $8 + 2 = 10$, so separate 7 into 2 and 5, add 2 and 8 to make 10, then add 5 more: 15. Solves simple cases of multidigit addition (and, often, subtraction) by incrementing tens and/or ones. "What's 20 + 34?" Student uses connecting cube to count up 20, 30, 40, 50 plus 4: 54.	(Note: Students should have achieved the level of "Skip Counter by 10s to 100" and "Counter to 100" before the following tasks; see Chapter 3's learning trajectory, starting on p. 54.) *Ten Spot (Composing Numbers)*, [LT]²: Present problems such as 40 + 10, initially by using separate fives and tens frames or connecting cubes in trains of 10. Ask how many dots (cubes) are there? How many tens? Add a ten and ask again. Progress to adding more than 1 ten at a time. *Repeat and fade*: Repeat as above until the students are fluent. Model the solution process yourself if necessary. As soon as possible, *hide* those placed out so children build visual, *mental* models. Eventually, present the problems only orally. Then, take away tens (e.g., 80 – 10). *Decade Spin (Composing Numbers)*, [LT]²: Present problems such as 70 + 3 and 20 + 7. Use the same strategy as above, placing 2 tens and then 7 ones out. If students need additional assistance, lay the ones out one at a time while counting by ones. Note the result ("27 … that means 2 tens and 7 ones") and encourage students to solve another one in a faster way. *Adding and subtracting multiples of 10s off the decade*: Present problems such as 73 + 10 and 27 + 20. Use the same strategy as above, placing 7 tens and 3 ones out, then adding tens one (or more) at a time. *Adding and subtracting within decades*: Present problems such as 2 + 3, then 22 + 3, then 72 + 3, and so forth (include 12 + 3 once the pattern is well established). Repeat.
7	**Problem Solver** +/- Solves all types of problems, with flexible strategies and known combinations. Asked, "If I have 13 and you have 9, how could we have the same number?", says, "Nine and one is ten, then three more to make 13. One and three is four. I need four more!" Multidigit may be solved by incrementing or combining tens and ones (latter not used for Join, Change Unknown). "What's 28 + 35?" Incrementer thinks: 20 + 30 = 50; +8 = 58; 2 more is 60, 3 more is 63. Combining tens and ones: 20 + 30 = 50. 8 + 5 is like 8 plus 2 and 3 more, so, it's 13. 50 and 13 is 63.	Solve all types of problem structures for single-digit problems. *Span Decades (Composing Numbers)*, [LT]²: Present problems that bridge decades, such as 77 + 3 and 25 + 7. As above, use manipulatives and modeling as necessary, until children can solve this mentally, or with drawings such as the empty number line. *Repeat and fade*: as above. *Subtracting across decades*: Present problems that bridge decades, such as 73 + 7 and 32 – 6. As above, use manipulatives and modeling as necessary, until children can solve this mentally, or with drawings such as the empty number line. *Adding and subtracting 10s and 1s with manipulatives*: Present addition problems using fives and tens frames or connecting cubes. Show 1 ten and 4 ones. Ask how many dots (cubes) are there? Add a ten *and* 3 ones and ask again. Continue to add 1–3 tens and 1–9 ones each time until you are close to 100. Then ask, "How many do we have in all? How many would we need to reach 100?" Use different manipulatives, such as imitation currency or coins.

Table 6.4 (Cont.)

Age	Developmental Progression	Instructional Tasks
		Talk it out with the empty number line (Composing Numbers), [LT][2]: Present addition (and then subtraction) problems under an empty number line (see top "35 + 57" figure below) and have students "talk aloud" to solve the problem, representing their thinking on the empty number line (see bottom "35 + 57" figure).

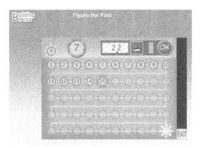

Move from problems such as 45 + 10 to 73 – 10, then 27 + 30 and 53 – 40, then move to …

Adding tens and ones: Present addition problems under an empty number line, as above. Start with problems without regrouping, such as 45 + 12, 27 + 31, and 51 + 35, then move to … problems with regrouping (e.g., 49 + 23, 58 + 22, 38 + 26) and problems that suggest transformations, such as compensation (e.g., 57 + 19   56 + 20 or 57 + 20 – 1; 43 + 45 (44 + 44); 22 + 48; and so forth).

Allow students to use strategies that "work" for them but encourage them to move from counting singles to more sophisticated strategies.

Present similar problems with place value manipulatives or drawings, such as base-ten blocks, or drawings of them (see Table 6.2).

Use different manipulatives, such as imitation currency or coins.

Repeat and fade: As above.

Subtracting tens and ones: Present subtraction problems under an empty number line, as above. Start with problems without regrouping (e.g., 99 – 55, 73 – 52, 59 – 35), then move to … problems with regrouping (e.g., 81 – 29, 58 – 29, 32 – 27, and so on) and problems that suggest transformations, such as compensation; e.g., 83 – 59 (84 – 60, or 83 – 60 + 1), 81 – 25, 77 – 28, and so forth.

Watch for "subtract smaller digit from larger digit" errors (e.g., in 58 – 29, subtracting 9 – 8 rather than the correct 8 – 9).

Present similar problems with place value manipulatives or drawings, such as base-ten blocks, or drawings of them (see the text).

Use different manipulatives, such as imitation currency or coins. *The 11 Game*: See p. 135 and Figure 6.7.

(Continued)

Table 6.4 (Cont.)

Age	Developmental Progression	Instructional Tasks
7-8	**Multidigit** +/– Uses composition of tens and all previous strategies to solve multi-digit +/– problems. Asked, "What's 37 – 18?", says, "I take 1 ten off the 3 tens; that's 2 tens. I take 7 off the 7. That's 2 tens and zero … 20. I have one more to take off. That's 19." Asked, "What's 28 + 35?", thinks, 30 + 35 would be 65. But it's 28, so it's 2 less: 63.	*Hidden 10s and 1s*: Tell students you have hidden 56 red connecting cubes and 21 blue cubes under a cloth. Ask them how many there are altogether. Progress to problems with regrouping, such as 47 + 34. Move to problems with subtraction without (85 – 23), then with (51 – 28) regrouping. *Spin Four*: See p. 136 and Figure 6.7. *Four in a Row*: See p. 137 and Figure 6.8. Variations: Make the game "Five in a Row" and to use larger addends. Variation: Have two small squares, one with larger numerals, the other with smaller. Students subtract. *Jumping to 100*, [LT]²: Using numeral cubes, one with the numerals 1 to 6 and the other with 10, 20, 30, 10, 20, 30, two teams take turns throwing the cubes and–starting at 0–adding that number to their position on an empty number line. Whoever reaches or passes 100 first wins. Variation: Jump down from 100 to 0. *Make Me 100*, [LT]²: One student (or team) enters a two-digit number. The other has to enter a single addition that will make the display "100." Points can be kept. Variation: Students (or teams) can only add a number from 1 to 10. They take turns, and the winner is the first team to display 100. *Higher-digit addition and subtraction*: Pose problems such as, "What's 374 – 189?" and "What's 281 + 35?"

produced. that is, they may make equal shares and yet not explicitly recognize that if there are seven in one share, there are seven in the other share(s) (Bryant, 1997; Miller, 1984b). Over time, they become more systematic, giving each person an object, checking that each has one, and repeating (Hunting & Davis, 1991).

Next, children can equipartition a single whole, such as circles or rectangles (see the "Geometry" domains in Table 6.5, which is where the CCSSM puts both partitioning and early fractions).

In later levels they do understand that that fair sharing of evenly divisible collections produces equal-sized groups (mathematically, the size of a fair share can be described as $1/n^{th}$ of the whole collection or as a particular number of elements out of the total).

Thus, early equipartitioning strategies eventually evolve into division as most of us think of it. On their way, children develop through levels of multiplication of division that are similar to those for adding and subtracting–moving from concrete modeling (and this happens earlier than typical schooling, Young-Loveridge & Bicknell, 2018), to the use of increasingly

Table 6.5 Goals for Multiplication and Division (And Fractions) from the CCSSM

Geometry [1.G in CCSSM]

Reason with shapes and their attributes.

1   Partition circles and rectangles into two and four equal shares, describe the shares using the words halves, fourths, and quarters, and use the phrases half of, fourth of, and quarter of. Describe the whole as two of, or four of the shares. Understand for these examples that decomposing into more equal shares creates smaller shares.

Operations and Algebraic Thinking [K.OA in CCSSM]

Work with equal groups of objects to gain foundations for multiplication.

1   Determine whether a group of objects (up to 20) has an odd or even number of members, e.g., by pairing objects or counting them by twos; write an equation to express an even number as a sum of two equal addends.
2   Use addition to find the total number of objects arranged in rectangular arrays with up to five rows and up to five columns; write an equation to express the total as a sum of equal addends. Geometry [2.G in CCSSM].

Reason with shapes and their attributes.

1   Partition a rectangle into rows and columns of same-size squares and count to find the total number of them.
2   Partition circles and rectangles into two, three, or four equal shares, describe the shares using the words halves, thirds, half of, a third of, etc., and describe the whole as two halves, three thirds, four fourths. Recognize that equal shares of identical wholes need not have the same shape.

---

sophisticated strategies, to combinations and multidigit. Indeed, our names for the levels in Table 6.6 are purposely modeled on the levels for adding and subtracting.

Children first model small-number multiplication problems by building each of the groups (Carpenter, Fennema, Franke, Levi, & Empson, 2014). They see multiplication as multiple "groups of" (Young-Loveridge & Bicknell, 2018). They can solve division or sharing problems with informal strategies, using concrete objects, now up to 20 objects and from two to five people. Some share one object to each person—"dealing them out"—even up to 9 years of age (Miller, 1984b). Others distribute groups such as giving two to each person again and again. Still others might count out equal groups, such as five to each person, then checking if the sum equals the product, and adjust as needed.

Children also learn to use count-based strategies, such as skip counting, to solve multiplication and measurement division problems. In measurement division, you know the total number, such as 28 candies, and how many you wish to give out to each person, such as four candies, and the question is: How many people will get a share? Children may solve 4×5 by skip counting by fives and using their fingers to keep track of the counts: 5, 10, 15, 20. Note that counting strategies are not used nearly as early for these operations as they are for addition and subtraction.

Eventually, children learn some facts, especially doubling ("times 2"). They then invent derived facts, such as solving 7×6 by knowing that five 7s is 35 (from previous skip counting or other experiences), so 7 more is 42. They learn to work with arrays—area models in rows and columns, extending their ability to use skip counting and multiplication in different contexts.

Table 6.6 Learning Trajectory for Multiplication and Division, and Fractions

Age	Developmental Progression	Instructional Tasks
0-2	**Nonquantitative Sharer: Foundations** Gives some, but not necessarily an equal number to each person.	*Numbers at Home*, [LT]²: Sharing in many contexts.
3	**Beginning Grouper and Distributive Sharer** Makes small groups (fewer than five). Shares by "dealing out," but usually only between two people. May not appreciate the numerical result.	*Tea Party Sharing*, [LT]²: Children explore multiplication and division by sharing pretend food and drink.
4-5	**Grouper and Distributive Sharer** Makes small equal groups (fewer than six) when in a context of "fair shares." Deals out equally between two or more recipients, but may not understand explicitly that equal quantities are produced (Confrey et al., 2014).	*Feeding Time at the Zoo*, [LT]²: Children determine how to feed the animals so that each one gets the same amount of fruit.
5	**Concrete Modeler X/÷** Solves small-number multiplying problems by grouping—making each group and counting all. Solves division/sharing problems with informal strategies, using concrete objects; up to 20 objects and 2-5 people. May justify results by equipartitioning using counting, arrays, or patterns (Confrey et al., 2014).	*Buying Candy Bars (Concrete Modeler)*, [LT]²: Children use varying currencies ($1, $5, $10) to buy candy bars.
6	**Parts and Wholes X/÷** Predicts qualitatively the inverse relation between divisor and quotient in simple, concrete situations. Can re-assemble equal groups or parts to make the collection or the single whole as "*n* times as many (much)" (Confrey et al., 2014).	*Buying Candy Bars (Parts and Wholes)*, [LT]²: Children use varying currencies ($1, $5, $10) to buy candy bars. They explore differences of results when dividing whole quantities among different numbers of friends.
7	**Skip Counter X/÷** Uses repeated adding, additive doubling, or skip counting to solve multiplication and for measurement division (finding out how many groups) problems. Uses trial and error for partitive division (finding out how many in each group). Predicts, demonstrates and justifies outcomes of equipartitioning collections (Confrey et al., 2014).	*Skip Counting with Cubes (Multiplying/Dividing)*, [LT]²: Children use skip counting strategies to count stacks of cubes.
8-9	**Deriver X/÷** Uses strategies, patterns, de/composition ($12 \times 2 = 10 \times 2 + 2 + 2$) and derived combinations, such as multiplying × 9 as $10 - 1$ or 7×8 from $7 \times 7 + 7$. Solves multidigit problems by operating on tens and ones separately. Quantitatively predicts the effects of changes in the number of people sharing one the size of the shares (inverse variation, Confrey et al., 2014). (See higher levels on [LT]² .)	*Multiplication Relation*, [LT]²: Children use their knowledge of one problem to solve one in a fact family. (Uses $2 \times 3 = 6$ to figure out 4×3.)

Fractions

Age	Developmental Progression	Instructional Tasks
0-2	**Foundations: Early Proportional Thinker** Has an intuition about proportions (Resnick & Singer, 1993). Shown a toy buried on the other side of a sandbox, and carried to the other side, moves to approximately the proportion of the sandbox to start to dig (Huttenlocher, Newcombe, & Sandberg, 1994).	*Half and half*, [LT]²: Break things into equal parts. When a child has language, talking about "Here's half for you and half for your sister" and so forth. Also discuss the whole, such as cutting an apple in half, narrating, "Is this the whole apple? No! Just a half! [Putting the two halves back together ...] *This* was the whole apple ..." and so forth. Experiences with equipartitioning (above for discrete) and from all previous chapters, especially spatial, geometric, and measurement, contribute to this developing intuition.

(Continued)

Table 6.6 (Cont.)

Age	Developmental Progression	Instructional Tasks
3–4	**Shape Equipartitioner** Can equipartition a whole shape, such as a circle or rectangle (Confrey et al., 2014).	*Share the Cake!*, [LT][2]: Children draw lines on paper "cakes" to share equally with a friend. Discuss that they are "exactly the same" (if congruent —same size and shape) or "the same amount" if they are halves that are not the same shape. Challenge them to make halves of a differently-shaped cake. Similar situations may occur if two children both want to color on the same piece of paper. Discuss the whole paper, that we could cut into parts, and to be fair they should be the *same size*, so we cut it into *halves*. Do the same for food, with which children *very* much want it to be equal (fair). Other contexts might be splitting playdough into halves, *or* thirds or fourths. *Symmetric Halves*, [LT][2]: Observe in the environments, and especially in children's building or drawing, *or* make (e.g., paper hearts) symmetric figures. Discuss the two halves: "Look, they are the same" (placing them on top of each other when possible).
4–5	**Half Recognizer** Recognizes "halves" at least in continuous (e.g., area) representations, especially in the context of fair shares (Wilkerson et al., 2014). Recognition of the need for ½ when sharing an odd number of objects. Intuitively and visually combines regions that are a part of a whole, showing initial foundations for addition (Mix, Levine, & Huttenlocher, 1997). **Unit Fraction Recognizer** Recognizes unit fractions in simple discrete (countable) and maybe continuous (e.g., area) representations for ½, ⅓, and ¼ and understands intuitively that they are formed by dividing a whole into equal parts. Names these shares (Confrey et al., 2014).	*Feed the Dogs Halves*, [LT][2]: Show children two identical stuffed dogs who like bread (or do chocolate bars and share between two dolls), showing a construction paper rectangle of "bread." We want to give them the same amount of bread. Show a plate with similar "bread" cut into two parts and ask children if it is fair to give the dogs these parts. Repeat with a variety of plates, including correct halves (e.g., parallel to the sides or diagonally corner to corner) and *incorrect, not cut into halves, but cut into two pieces that are not halves* (one part is bigger). Discuss which are "fair" and emphasize a fraction is a *number*, not "pieces." *Shape Puzzle Fractions*, [LT][2]: At children's level of 2D shape composition (e.g., Picture Maker), have them work on composing shape puzzles, describing their work with fractional language. Extend the language, such as asking how many halves make a whole. See Table 9.2.
7	**Fraction Recognizer** Recognizes simple (small number denominators) fractions in familiar continuous and discrete contexts. **Fraction Maker from Units** Creates a fraction representation with equal parts and the correct number of repetitions of a unit fraction (Steffe & Olive, 2010). Labels that fraction with written fraction notation. Compares fraction representations and states which is the larger number.	*Feed the Dogs Fractions*, [LT][2]: Show children two identical stuffed dogs who like bread, showing a construction paper circle "bread." We want to give them the same amount of bread. Show two plates, one with circular bread cut into halves and the other cut into fourths. Give one dog ½ and ask the child to figure out how to give the other dog the same amount of bread (from the fourths) (McMullen, Hannula-Sormunen, & Lehtinen, 2014). *Fractions of Rectangles*, [LT][2]: Children use two colors of square tiles to make different shapes of rectangles, some showing halves and some not. They start with six tiles and are asked to show different ways to show halves and *not* halves. Try halves with seven tiles (impossible). Have them make halves with other numbers of tiles they choose. As a challenge, have them name the fractions of the *non-halves* constructions. Repeat the basic activity, using colored tiles to make fourths and thirds of rectangles. Children copy their creations onto squared paper for discussions and

Age	Developmental Progression	Instructional Tasks
		displays. For example, they start with eight times, two of each of four colors. (Akers, Battista, Goodrow, Clements, & Sarama, 1997). *Shape Fractions*, [LT]²: At children's level of 2D shape composition, have them work on composing and decomposing shape puzzles, describing their work with fractional language. Extend the language, such as asking if ⅓ or ½ is larger. See Table 9.2 Learning Trajectory for the Composition and Decomposition of 2D Shapes.
8+	**Fraction Maker** Creates a fraction representation with equal parts and the correct number of repetitions of a unit or non-unit fraction (as long as they are not greater than a whole—fraction may be only a "part-of-a-whole"). Compare simple common fractions using physical models. **Fraction Repeater** Creates fraction representations with repetitions of unit and non-unit fractions, including results greater than a whole. Moves beyond fraction as a "part-of-a-whole" to fraction as a number with a relation to the reference whole. Understands that fractions with the same denominator can be added or subtracted using the units of the unit fraction. Compares simple common fractions using models such as the number line—understands that two fractions are equal when they represent the same portion of a whole or have the same length on the number line. **Fraction Arithmetic ✛** Adds and subtracts simple common fractions using physical models. **Fraction Arithmetic X/÷** Multiplies simple common fractions using rectangle array model. **Fraction and Integer Sequencer** Represents simple ratios as percentages, fractions, and decimals. Orders integers, positive fractions, and decimals.	*Number Hop, Fraction Crawl*, [LT]²: *Setup*: With a large number line (e.g., in chalk outsides), children pretend to be rabbits who can easily jump from one number to another. Then pretend they are turtles who crawl slowly. When a child is halfway to 1, ask, "Where are you now?" One-half! Next, introduce where a unit fraction (¼ or ½) is on a number line as illustrated (Hamdan & Gunderson, 2017). 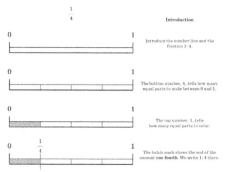 Give children a pre-segmented number line (all available on [LT]²) and have them shade the correct number of segments, place the fraction by drawing a hatch mark, and write the fraction above the hatch mark. As soon as possible, give children an unsegmented number line, and asked to segment, shade, and place the fraction at the correct location. Keep number lines for each denominator on the board separately, displaying them vertically so the 0 and 1 line up. Later, return to this display as children compare fractions. *Shape Fraction Combinations*, [LT]²: At the highest level of 2D shape composition, have children describe their work with fractional language. Extend the language, such as asking to describe the many ways they can fill a hexagon (6 sixths, 3 thirds, 2 halves, but also 1 half and 3 sixths, 2 sixths and 2 thirds, and so forth). See Table 9.2. *Share Brownies*, [LT]²: Children cut up rectangular "brownies" to make fair shares among four, eight, three, and six people. They fold paper into the same fractions, showing the unit fraction on each part. They then develop "fraction facts," such as ¼ + ¼ = ½ and ½ + ¼ + ¼ = 1. They cut out

Table 6.6 (Cont.)

Age Developmental Progression	Instructional Tasks
	both unit and non-unit pieces to compare fractions, such as comparing ⅔ to ½ or to ¾. They also share more than one brownie, figuring out that three friends sharing two brownies, each gets $\frac{2}{3}$, and if the two friends share three brownies, each gets 1 ½ (Tierney & Berle-Caman, 1997).

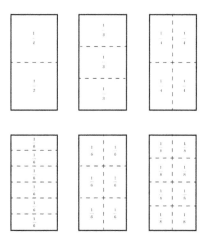

Hanging Fractions on a Number Line, [LT]²: Using (or making by folding) representations of fractions with rectangular areas and symbols, children cut them out and put them in order on the floor face down (not showing the symbols), first only unit fractions. They then name each fraction, turning the card over the check. They notice a number pattern (the larger the fraction, the small the denominator). They repeat, adding *non-unit* fractions. They then hang the fractions on a wire or wall (Tierney & Berle-Caman, 1997). See full instructions and materials on [LT]².

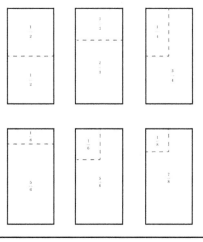

Then, ideally, children continue to use such reasoning strategies, using the commutative and associative properties (informally). For example, they might say "9 × 2 is nine 2s, but it's the same as two 9s, so 18." They also find and use patterns in the multiplication table, which promotes much easier and faster fluency with multiplication facts (Fuson, 2003). Think of the nines facts (9, 18, 27, 36, 45 …).

Also, similar to addition and subtraction, division and multiplication are inverse operations (e.g., the whole collection is *n* times as large as one person's share) that link to different ways in which one asks questions about a given situation. If a student is asked to determine the fair share when six cookies are shared among three people, a problem that results in two cookies per person, this is coded as the division statement: 6 ÷ 3 = 2. However, if a child is asked how many cookies were in the whole collection that results in three children each of whom has a fair share of two cookies, then this is coded as multiplication: 3 × 2 = 6.

As with equipartitioning, multiplicative thinking starts with whole numbers, then deals with continuous material (e.g., length) and ultimately fractions. The development of conceptual and procedural knowledge of fractions is *critical* for children. Children of all ages show they do not have foundational knowledge of fractions, such as confusion between whole numbers and fractions (Hunting & Davis, 1991) leading to their belief that ¼ is larger than ½ because 4 is larger than 2. Others add numerators and denominators, such as ¾ + 1/3 yielding 4/6, not noticing that 4/6 is less than ¾. At an even more basic level, children without high-quality educational experiences may claim that the shaded part of a circular region is "one-half" but asked what the *unshaded* part is, declare, "I don't know. Nothing!" However, children can and do build intuitions about fractions such as one-half (Hunting & Davis, 1991).

The learning trajectory for fractions in Table 6.6 provides ages, but like all these estimates, children vary considerably. For example, some primary school students do not understand even ½ fully (Gupta, 2014). Perhaps especially with fractions, *learning opportunities* are key, and they differ considerably for different children.

Experience and Education: Multiplication and Division and Fractions

Of course, children can learn a lot about "passing things out" and "fair shares" at an early age. Did each person get a napkin? Did each doll get a hat? Books are available for the very young (Lin, 2020b). You find activities for the first three levels of the learning trajectory in Table 4.2. Children should also experience "groups of" objects larger than one early on in their schooling. For example, discuss groups of two, using familiar contexts such as pairs of socks, shoes, gumboots, and mittens (Young-Loveridge & Bicknell, 2018).

Similarly, long before it is introduced formally, children can solve problems involving multiplication and division (e.g., sharing). Place value is based on these ideas, but there are many more experiences. One important one is the measurement of area, so much of our discussion of this topic is in Chapter 11.

Further, children can solve many multiplicative problems, presented meaningfully. For example, "Three children each have a pair of shoes. How many shoes do the children have altogether?" (Young-Loveridge & Bicknell, 2018, p. 265). A recent study suggests that certain types of problems are better than others. Typically, teachers introduce multiplication through repeated addition. For example, Tom has three and then Mike gives him three more, and so forth, how many are there in all? Although some problems of all types are useful, researchers showed that *many-to-one* correspondence problems are more effective in helping children learning multiplicative reasoning (Nunes, Bryant, Evans, & Bell, 2010). For example, Tom wants to put three flowers in each of these (illustrated) four pots. How many flowers will he need to buy? Deaf children often enter school with less knowledge of multiplication, but similar teaching strategies can help them learn multiplicative reasoning (Nunes et al., 2009).

Teachers can help build their students' fluency in multiplication and division by emphasizing the use of skip counting, reasoning strategies, commutativity (4 × 7 = 7 × 4), and the search for patterns.

Most of the teaching strategies for addition and subtraction apply to helping students be fluent with multiplication facts as well. Wait … why not division facts? Many people don't actually know "division facts"–for 56 ÷ 7, they think "What times 7 is 56? … 8!" Further, 2 × 8 is, of course, related to 8 + 8. Mathematics is a system and a structure. These are related to each other. Therefore, division facts may best be learned in relation to the multiplication fact. For example, 48 ÷ 6 = __ can be solved by recalling 6 × 8 = 48.

Also similar for multiplication and division, feature different formats of multiplication sentences. Students should learn and use all of the different symbols for division as well, including (24/8, 24 ÷ 8, $\frac{24}{8}$, and the reversed).

For many more suggestions on teaching multiplication and division, see our book, *No More Math Fact Frenzy* (Davenport et al., 2019b) and [LT][2]. Key activities are shown in Table 5.5.

Children need manipulative-based, conceptual experiences with fractions, even repeated activities involving halves (Gupta, 2014; Perry & Lewis, 2017; Wilkerson et al., 2014). Care must be taken to distinguish between whole-number and fraction concepts (e.g., thinking ¼ is larger than ½ because 4 is larger than 2). Children should work with discrete (e.g., counters) and continuous (circles) models, but a combination, such as "candy bars" marked with individual units may be the most understandable initially (Wing & Beal, 2004).

Math-talk-rich experiences are important, with careful introduction of symbols (e.g., ¼) after verbal language has been established (Gupta, 2014). Again, East Asian languages have helpful phases: ¾ is "out of four, three" instead of the more confusing "three fourth" (Siegler, 2017). Herb Gross suggests the "adjective-noun" notion: The noun is the "fourths" (denominator) and the adjective is "how many fourths" (e.g., three fourths in ¾). In such discussions, emphasize a fraction is a *number*, not just "pieces" (Perry & Lewis, 2017). Number line representations can be helpful for second and third graders (Hamdan & Gunderson, 2017), especially because they help children *see fractions as numbers that can be compared*–an important but often overlooked concept and skill. Measurement activities such as those in Chapters 10 and 11, can be particularly helpful.

Learning Trajectory for Multiplication and Division and Fractions

The entire domain of multiplicative thinking and rational numbers is a complex and important (Watts et al., 2015) topic, with many concepts, one that could be described in seven related learning trajectories: equipartitioning, multiplication and division, fraction-as-number, length and area, ratio and rate, similarly and scaling, and decimals and percent (Confrey et al., 2014). In this chapter we present multiplication and division and fraction-as-number, with equipartitioning involved in both—recognizing that the equipartioning in division is fundamental to the development of fraction knowledge. Later chapters involve length, area, and aspects of the other topics.

Table 6.5 details where these goals appear in the CCSSM.

Final Words

To this point, our discussions have emphasized number. Especially in early number, however, there appeared to be a strong spatial component. For example, some studies suggest that children's earliest quantification is *spatial* at its core. And this chapter's manipulatives such as base-ten blocks and representations such as the number line are also spatial. Just as or more important, knowledge of space and shape is important for its own sake. Spatial thinking is addressed in Chapter 7, and more specific geometric thinking in Chapters 8 and 9.

Note

1 We use the term "combination" instead of the common term "fact" for two reasons. First, "facts" implies they are verbal knowledge to be memorized by rote. We believe they are number relationships that are understood in a variety of ways that must be constructed by the child. Second, in contrast, "combination" implies that two numbers are decomposed to make another number, and that there are many related combinations (3 + 2 = 5; 2 + 3 = 5; 5 = 2 + 3; 5 − 2 = 3, etc.).

7 Spatial Thinking

Before reading on, when you read the title of this chapter, what did you think "spatial think-ing" would involve? How do you "think spatially" in a typical week? Which of those might you consider "mathematical"?

Spatial thinking is important because it is an essential human ability that contributes to math ability (Gilligan, Flouri, & Farran, 2017; Manginas, Nikolantonakis, & Papageorgioy, 2017; Mix et al., 2016; Verdine, Golinkoff, Hirsh-Pasek, & Newcombe, 2017). For example, preschoolers' spa-tial skills predict later math knowledge, even controlling early math knowledge (Rittle-Johnson, Fyfe, & Zippert, 2018b). However, spatial thinking is also important to science, engineering, and technology (the first three subjects of "STEM") as well as to literacy (Hawes, LeFevre, Xu, & Bruce, 2015; McGarvey, Luo, & Hawes, 2018; Simmons et al., 2012b; Verdine et al., 2017).

However, the relationship between spatial thinking and math is not straightforward. Some-times, "visual thinking" is "good" but sometimes it is not. For example, many studies have shown that children with specific spatial abilities are more mathematically competent (e.g., The Spatial Reasoning Study Group, 2015c).

However, other research indicates that students who process math information by verbal-logical means outperform students who process information visually (Clements & Battista, 1992a). Also, *overly specific* imagery in math thinking can cause difficulties. As we shall discuss in more detail in Chapter 8, an idea can be *too* closely tied to a single image. For example, con-necting the idea of "triangles" to a single image such as an equilateral triangle with a horizontal base restricts young children's thinking.

Therefore, spatial ability is important in learning many topics of math. The role it plays, how-ever, is elusive and, even in geometry, complex. Two major abilities are spatial orientation and spatial visualization (Bishop, 1980; Harris, 1981; McGee, 1979). We first discuss spatial orienta-tion, which involves an extensive body of research, then spatial visualization and imagery.

Spatial Orientation

Dennis the Menace is shown on a map where his family has driven. He looks aghast, and says, *"Two days? Just to go three inches?"*

(from Liben, 2008, p. 21)

Spatial orientation is knowing where you are and how to get around in the world; that is, understanding relationships between different positions in space, at first with respect to your own position and your movement through it, and eventually from a more abstract perspective that includes maps and coordinates. This essential competence is not only linked to learning math (Gunderson, Ramirez, Beilock, & Levine, 2012; Leavy, Pope, & Breatnach, 2018b; Van den Heuvel-panhuizen, Elia, & Robitzsch, 2015) but also how we *remember* things.

Like number, spatial orientation has been postulated as a core domain with some abilities present from birth. For example, infants focus their eyes on objects and then begin to follow moving objects. Toddlers use geometric information about the overall shape of their environment to solve location tasks. And, like number, we share some of these abilities with animals. For example, baby chicks can use geometric information from their surrounds to reorient themselves in space (Lee, Spelke, & Vallortigara, 2012; Vallortigara, 2012; Vallortigara, Sovrano, & Chiandetti, 2009). Again, as with number, such early competencies develop with experience, and sociocultural influences. What can young children understand and represent about spatial relationships and navigation? When can they represent and, ultimately, mathematize this knowledge?

The Development of Spatial Orientation

Spatial Location and Intuitive Navigation

What kind of "mental maps" do young children possess? Neither children nor adults actually have "maps in their heads"–that is, their "mental maps" are not like a mental picture of a paper map. However, people do build up private and idiosyncratic knowledge as they learn about space. They do this by developing two categories of spatial knowledge. The first based on their own bodies–a self-based system. The second is based on other objects–an external-based reference system. As children develop, these systems become better linked. Within each category, there is an early-developing type and a later-developing type. Let's look at each in turn.

Early Self- and External-based Systems

Self-based spatial systems are related to the child's own position and movements. The early-developing type is *response learning*, in which the child notes a pattern of movements that have been associated with a goal (Newcombe & Huttenlocher, 2000). For example, the child might get used to looking to the left from a highchair to see a parent cooking.

External-based reference systems are based on landmarks in the environment. The landmarks are usually familiar and important objects. In *cue learning*, children associate an object with a nearby landmark, such as a toy on a couch. Children possess both self- and external-based systems in the first months of life.

Later-developing Self- and External-based Systems

The later-developing type of self-based systems is *path integration*, in which children record the approximate distance and direction of their own movements. That is, they remember the "path they walked." As early as 6 months, and certainly by 1 year of age, children can use this strategy with some accuracy when they move themselves. Young school children can draw a simple land-mark map from home to school (Thommen, Avelar, Sapin, Perrenoud, & Malatesta, 2010).

The more powerful type of external-based systems, *place learning*, comes closest to people's intuition of "mental maps." Children store locations by remembering distances and directions to landmarks. For example, children might use the walls of a room as a frame of reference to find a toy.

This illustrates an early, implicit foundation for later learning of coordinate systems. This ability first develops during the second year of life and continues to be refined through life. As children develop, they get better at using—including knowing when to use—each of these types of spatial knowledge. They also *integrate* knowledge from each of these four types.

Spatial Thought

In their second year, children develop the critical capacity for *symbolic thought*. This supports many types of math knowledge, including explicit spatial knowledge. As one example, children learn to take others' perspectives in viewing objects. They learn to coordinate different view-points on objects, but also use an external frame of reference (as in place learning) to work out different viewpoints.

Navigation Through Large-scale Environments

Children also learn to navigate in large environments. This requires integrated representations as well, because one can see only some landmarks at any given point. Only older preschoolers learn scaled routes for familiar paths; that is, they know about the relative distances between landmarks. Even young children, however, can put different locations along a route into some relationship, at least in certain situations. For example, they can point to one location from another even though they never walked a path that connected the two.

Children as young as 3.5 years can learn to accurately walk along a path that replicates the route between their seat and the teacher's desk in their classroom. *Self-produced* movement is important. Kindergartners could not *imagine* similar movements or point accurately without moving, but they could imagine and recreate the movements and point accurately when they actually walked and turned. Thus, children can build mental imagery of locations and use this imagery, but they must physically move to show their competence. Preschoolers to first graders need landmarks or boundaries to succeed at such tasks. By third grade, children can use larger, encompassing frameworks that include the observer in the situation.

Thus, children develop these complex ideas and skills over years. However, even adults do not have perfectly accurate ideas about space. For example, all people intuitively view space as centered at one's home or other familiar place. They also view space as increasingly dense as they approach this center, so that distances seem larger the closer they get.

The Language of Space

Children learning English show a strong tendency to *ignore* fine-grained shape when learning novel *spatial* terms such as "on" or "in front of" or when interpreting known spatial terms. They show an equally strong tendency to *attend* to fine-grained shape when learning novel *object* names. For example, 3-year-olds shown an unusual object placed near a box and told, "This is acorp my box" tend to ignore the shape of the object and instead attend to its *location* relative to the box. They believe that "acorp" refers to a spatial *relation*. If they had instead been told "This *is* a prock" they would attend to the unusual object's *shape*.

The first spatial words English-speaking children learn are "in," "on," and "under," along with such vertical directionality terms as "up" and "down." These initially refer to transformations of one spatial relationship into other. For example, "on" initially does not refer to one object on top of another, but only to the act of making an object become physically attached to another.

Second, children learn words of proximity, such as "beside," "next to," and "between." Third, children learn words referring to frames of reference such as "in front of," "in back of," "behind." The words "left" and "right" are learned much later, and are the source of confusion for many years, usually not well understood until 6 to 8 years of age (although specific attention to those words helps preschoolers orient themselves).

By 2 years of age, children have considerable spatial competence on which language might be based. Further, in contrast to many who emphasize children's naming of objects, children use spatial relational words more frequently, and often earlier, than names. Moreover, the use of even a single-word utterance by a 19-month-old, such as "in," may reflect more spatial competence than it first appears when the contexts differ widely, such as saying, "in" when about to climb into the child seat of a shopping cart and saying "in" when looking under couch cushions for coins she just put in the crack between the cushions.

Models and Maps

At what age can children use and make representations of space? Even 2-year-olds can find their mother behind a barrier after observing the situation from above. But only by 2½ can then locate a toy when shown a picture of the space. By 3 years, children may be able to build simple, but meaningful, models with landscape toys such as houses, cars, and trees, although this ability is limited through the age of 6 years. For example, in making models of their classroom, kindergartners cluster furniture correctly (e.g., they put the furniture for a dramatic play center together) but may not relate the clusters to each other. In a similar vein, beginning about 3, and more so at 4 years of age, children can interpret arbitrary symbols on maps, such as a blue rectangle standing for blue couch or "x marks the spot." On another map they may recognize lines as roads ... but suggest that the tennis courts were doors. They can benefit from maps and can use them to guide navigation (i.e., follow a route) in simple situations.

To summarize, there are four spatial concepts for maps: Identification—what objects?, location—where?, direction—which way?, distance—how far? (Sarama & Clements, 2009). For identification and location, children from about 3-6 years of age can identify places on maps, landscape features on maps and aerial photographs, and can locate familiar places on maps. They might also use landmarks as a way to identify where places or items are located on a map, but they can easily confuse locations on maps if the map is not well aligned to their real world. Children aged 7-9 years more accurately locate places and landscape features on a map, although they perform better with familiar places and are inconsistent in using landmarks to identify locations. They begin to better understand grid or coordinate systems (Solem, Huynh, & Boehm, 2015, p. 15).

Regarding direction and distance, children aged 3-6 years understand relative distance, such as near, far, next to, and can begin using relative direction on maps if prompted. They may confuse direction if maps are not aligned to the world. Children aged 7-9 years better understand specific directions and distances (Solem et al., 2015, p. 15). More detail on year-to-year development is provided in Table 7.3.

Coordinates and Spatial Structuring

Even young children can use coordinates if adults provide the coordinates and guide children in their use. However, when facing traditional tasks, they and their older peers may not yet be able or predisposed to spontaneously make and use coordinates for themselves.

To understand space as organized into grids or coordinate systems, children must learn *spatial structuring*. Spatial structuring is the mental operation of constructing an organization or form for an object or set of objects in space. Children may first view a grid as a collection of squares, rather than as sets of perpendicular lines. They only gradually come to see them as organized into rows and columns, learning the order and distance relationships within the grid. For coordinates, labels must be related to grid lines and, in the form of ordered pairs of coordinates, to points on the grid. Eventually these, too, must be integrated with the grid's order and distance relationships to be understood as a math system.

Spatial Visualization and Imagery

Visual representations are central to our lives, including most domains of math. Spatial images are internal representations of objects that appear to be similar to real-world objects. People use four processes: generating an image, inspecting an image to answer questions about it, maintaining an image in the service of some other mental operation, and transforming an image.

Thus, spatial visualization abilities are processes involved in generating and manipulating mental images of two-and three-dimensional objects, including moving, matching, and combining them, with a goal of investigating and communicating ideas. Such visualization might guide the drawing of figures or diagrams on paper or computer screens. For example, children might create a mental image of a shape, maintain that image, and then search for that same shape, perhaps hidden within a more complex figure. To do this, they may need to mentally rotate the shapes, one of the most important transformations for children to learn. These spatial skills directly support children's learning of specific topics, such as geometry and measurement, but they can also be applied to math problem solving across topics (such as the use of the number line in arithmetic).

The Development of Spatial Visualization and Imagery

What Develops?

Children do have to develop the ability to move mental images, as early as 22 months of age (Örnkloo & von Hofsten, 2007b). That is, their initial images are not static, but dynamic. They can be mentally recreated, and even examined, but not necessarily transformed. Only dynamic images allow children to mentally "move" the image of one shape (such as a book) to another place (such as a bookcase, to see if it will fit) or mentally move (slide) and turn an image of one shape to compare that shape to another one. Slides appear to be the easiest motions for children, then turns and flips. However, the direction of transformation may affect the relative difficulty of turn and flip. Results depend on specific tasks, of course; even 4- to 5-year-olds can do turns if they have simple tasks and cues, such as having a clear mark on the edge of a shape and no "flipped" shape as a distractor. Competence in *mental* rotation are related to later arithmetic ability (Zhang & Lin, 2015). Others argue that imagery also supports later movement from arithmetic to algebra (The Spatial Reasoning Study Group, 2015c).

Probably due to reading instruction, first graders discriminate between mirror-image reversals (b vs. d) better than kindergartners. But they also treat orientation as a meaningful difference between *geometric shapes*, which it is not (a square does not "become" a diamond when rotated!—see Chapter 8). So, explicitly discuss when orientation is and is not relevant to calling a shape "the same" in different contexts.

From research, we know that the imagery of people who are congenitally blind is in some ways similar and some ways different from that of normally sighted people. For example, they can use touch and movement to build images of objects including spatial extent, or size. However, only sighted people visualize objects of different size at different distances, so the image will not overflow a fixed space. They image objects at distances so that the objects subtend the same visual angle. Thus, some aspects of visual imagery are visual, and not present in blind people's images, but some aspects of imagery may be evoked by multiple modalities (Arditi, Holtzman, & Kosslyn, 1988).

Equity issues arise with special skills. Children from low-resource communities, or those who are female or have low visual working memory, may benefit more than others from specific interventions to build spatial visualization (Carr et al., 2018)

Types of Images and Mathematical Problem Solving

There are different types of images, and they range from *helpful* to *harmful*, depending on their nature and the way children use them (cf. Toll & Van Luit, 2014b). High-achieving children build images with a conceptual and relational core. They are able to link different experiences and abstract similarities. Images of those with fewer opportunities to learn tend to be dominated by surface features. Instruction might help them develop more sophisticated images.

- *Schematic images* are thus more general and abstract. They contain the spatial relationships relevant to a problem and thus support problem solving (Hegarty & Kozhevnikov, 1999).
- *Pictorial images* of children do not aid problem solving and actually can impede success. They represent mainly the visual appearance of the objects or persons described in a problem.

For example, say the problem is, "At each of the two ends of a straight path, a man planted a tree, and then every 5 meters along the path he planted another tree. The length of the path is 15 meters. How many trees were planted?" The researchers found that high-achieving children reported math relationships in their schematic images, such as "I had a [mental] picture of the path, not the trees, and it had something 5 meters along, not trees, just something." Other children reported pictorial images, such as "I just saw the man going along planting trees." If children drew diagrams, they might differ as in Figure 7.1.

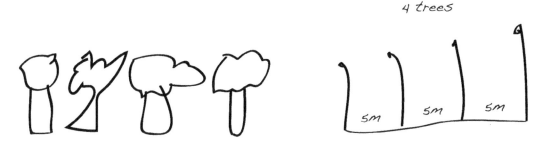

| Pictorial Representation | Schematic Representation |

Figure 7.1 Schematic versus pictorial images for the "path and trees" problem

Experience and Education

Spatial competencies should show major development in the early years, but "developmental rates and the competencies achieved are highly dependent on access to spatial activities, spatial language, and learning opportunities at home and at school" (National Research Council, 2009, p. 78). Unfortunately, in home and schools, many children have little access to good spatial experiences (Verdine et al., 2017).

Further, just in case any readers have encountered the notion that people either "have it or they don't" (Newcombe, 2010), spatial reasoning *can be taught and learned*–effectively! People of all ages, including young children, develop considerably with a variety of focused spatial experiences (Uttal et al., 2013). Impressively, interventions show an effect that would double the number of people with the spatial skills that engineers use (Uttal et al., 2013).

Spatial Orientation, Navigation, and Maps

For children of all ages, but especially the youngest, moving oneself around leads to later success in spatial thinking tasks. This suggests the benefit of maximizing such experience for all young children and may seem obvious, but there may be opportunities that are not presently pursued. In some communities, for example, young girls are allowed to play only in their yard, but same-age boys are allowed to explore the neighborhood. So, it's important to consider all possibilities, such as those for the youngest children in Table 7.1.

To develop children's spatial orientation, plan school environments that include interesting layouts inside and outside classrooms. Provide large-scale apparatuses that toddlers and preschool children can explore in many ways, including large cardboard boxes, planks, and blocks to build structures big enough to get into. Also provide activities that support developing spatial sense such as climbing up ladders and over obstacles (Meaney, 2016); crawling through tunnels, and pushing or riding carts, tricycles, and other wheeled vehicles around and between other objects (Leavy et al., 2018b). In so doing, provide just enough (not too much!) support (see a wonderful narrative and discussion in Meaney, 2016). Also include incidental and planned experiences with landmarks and routes, and frequent discussion about spatial relations on all scales, including distinguishing parts of children's bodies and spatial movements (forward, back), finding

Table 7.1 Opportunities for Unrestricted Movement, for Infants and Up (Adapted from Leavy et al., 2018b)

• playing on floor	• pulling themselves to sit
• grasping interesting objects hanging overhead	• lift their heads on tummies to see interesting objects
• providing soft blocks to climb over as they become more adept crawlers	• lying on backs reaching for their feet (trying to suck toes!)
• sitting, later jumping, in ball pools	• trying to roll over and back again
• rolling and chasing after different size and textured balls or water bottles filled with different ingredients such as rice or varying volumes of water with the addition of glitter, drops of food coloring	• crawling through tunnel or open cardboard box • pushing a baby trolley with wooden blocks (not sitting in baby walkers with castors) • pull selves up to stand near mirror
• pushing and pulling toys, miniature shopping carts	• driving tricycles or other vehicles with a trailer so that they can transport objects (older toddlers)

a missing object ("under the table that's next to the door"), putting objects away, and finding the way back home from an excursion. Rich language is important.

Children need specific instruction to learn about models and maps. School experiences are limited and fail to connect map skills with other curriculum areas, including math. Most students do not become competent users of maps even beyond their early childhood years. A "treasure hunt" with the school is a fruitful setting for getting children to draw their own maps.

Research provides suggestions to help children make those connections. Provide instruction on using maps that explicitly connects real-world space and maps, including one-to-one connection between objects and icons on the map, helps children understand maps–and symbols. Using oblique maps, on which tables are shown with legs, helps preschoolers' subsequent performance on plan ("bird's-eye view") maps. Telling very young children that a model was the result of putting a room in a "shrinking machine" helped them see the model as a symbolic representation of that space.

Informally, too, encourage children working with model toys to build maps of the room with these toys. Children might use cut-out shapes of a tree, swing set, and sandbox in the playground and lay them out on a felt board as a simple map. These are good beginnings, but models and maps should eventually move beyond overly simple iconic picture maps, and challenge children to use geometric correspondences. Help children connect the "abstract" and "sensory-concrete" meanings of map symbols (Clements, 1999a; see also Chapter 16 for a discussion of these terms).

Similarly, many young children's difficulties do not reflect misunderstanding about space but the conflict between such sensory-concrete and abstract frames of reference. Guide children to (a) develop abilities to build relationships among objects in space, (b) extend the size of that space, (c) link primary and secondary meanings and uses of spatial information, (d) develop mental rotation abilities, (e) go beyond "map skills" to engage in actual use of maps in local environments (Bishop, 1983), and (f) develop an understanding of the math of maps.

Work with children to raise the four mathematical questions: Direction–which way?, distance–how far?, location–where?, and identification–what objects? To answer these questions, children need to develop a variety of skills. Children must learn to deal with mapping processes of abstraction, generalization, and symbolization. Some map symbols are icons, such as an airplane for an airport, but others are more abstract, such as circles for cities. Children might first build with objects such as model buildings, then draw pictures of the objects' arrangements, then use maps that are "miniaturizations" and those that use abstract symbols. Some symbols may be beneficial even to young children. Over-reliance on literal pictures and icons may hinder understanding of maps, leading children to believe, for example, that certain actual roads are red (Downs, Liben, & Daggs, 1988). Similarly, children need to develop more sophisticated ideas about *direction* and *location*. Young children should master environmental directions, such as above, over, and behind. They should develop navigation ideas, such as front, back, "going forward," and turning. Older children might represent these ideas in simple route maps within the classroom.

Children can develop navigation ideas, such as left, right, and front, and global directions such as north, east, west, and south, from these beginnings. Perspective and direction are particularly important regarding the alignment of the map with the world. Some children of any age will find it difficult to use a map that is not so aligned. Also, they may need specific experiences with perspective. For example, challenge them to identify block structures from various viewpoints, matching views of the same structure that are portrayed from different perspectives, or to find the viewpoint from which a photograph was taken. Such experiences address such confusions of perspective as preschoolers "seeing" windows and doors of buildings in vertical aerial photographs (Downs & Liben, 1988). Introduce such situations gradually. Realistic Mathematics Education in geometry makes extensive use of interesting spatial and map tasks (Gravemeijer, 1990), but, unfortunately, research on the effects of this specific strand is lacking.

Primary-grade students can approach map creation mathematically, learning to represent position and direction. One third-grade class moved from initial, intuitively based drawings to the use of polar coordinates (determining a position by an angle and a distance) in creating a map of their playground (Lehrer & Pritchard, 2002). Walking encouraged characterization of length in a direction and drawing the maps led students to render space. Students learned about the usefulness of concepts such as origin, scale, and the relationship of multiple locations.

Combining physical movement, paper-and-pencil, and computer work can facilitate learning of math and map skills. Such spatial learning can be particularly meaningful because it can be consistent with young children's way of moving their bodies (Papert, 1980). For example, young children can abstract and generalize directions and other map concepts working with the Logo turtle (Sarama & Clements, 2019b). Giving the turtle directions such as forward ten steps, right turn, forward five steps, they learn orientation, direction, and perspective concepts, among others. For example, Figure 7.2 shows a "scavenger hunt" activity in which children are given a list of items the turtle has to get. From the center of the grid, they commanded the turtle to go forward 20 steps, then turn right 90 degrees, then go forward 20 more steps—that's where the car was. They have the car now and will give the turtle other commands to get other objects. Preschoolers to primary-grade students can similarly benefit with programmable robots designed for their age (Palmér, 2017) as well as other route-based games (Lin & Hou, 2016).

Walking paths and then recreating those paths on the computer help them abstract, generalize, and symbolize their experiences navigating. For example, one kindergartner abstracted the geometric notion of "path," saying, "A path is like the trail a bug leaves after it walks through purple paint" (Clements et al., 2001). Logo can also control a floor turtle robot, which may have special benefits for certain populations. For example, blind and partially sighted children using a computer-guided floor turtle developed spatial concepts such as right and left and accurate facing movements.

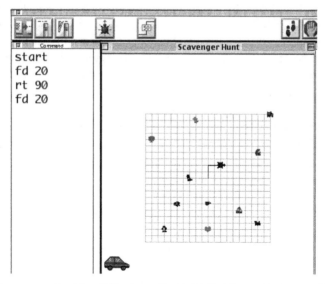

Figure 7.2 The "Scavenger Hunt" activity from *Turtle Math* (Clements & Meredith, 1994)

Many people believe that maps are "transparent"–that anyone can "see through" the map immediately to the world that it represents. This is not true. Clear evidence for this is found in children's misinterpretations of maps. For example, some believe that a river is a road or that a pictured road is *not* a road because "it's too narrow for two cars to go on."

Coordinates

Students should learn to understand and eventually quantify what grid labels represent. To do so, they need to connect their counting acts to those quantities and to the labels. They need to learn to mentally structure grids as two-dimensional (2D) spaces, demarcated and measured with "conceptual rulers" ("mental number lines"–see Chapter 10). That is, they need to understand coordinates as a way to organize 2D space by coordinating two perpendicular number lines–every location is the place where measures along each of these two number lines meet.

Real-world contexts can be helpful in teaching coordinates initially, but math goals and perspectives should be clearly articulated throughout instruction and the contexts should be faded from use as soon as students no longer need them (Sarama, Clements, Swaminathan, McMillen, & González Gómez, 2003). Computer environments can additionally aid in developing children's ability and appreciation for the need for clear conceptions and precise work. Turning the coordinate grid on and off can help children create a *mental* image of coordinates. Coordinate-based games on computers, such as versions of "Battleship," can help older children learning location ideas (Sarama et al., 2003). When children enter a coordinate to move an object, but it goes to a different location, the feedback is natural, meaningful, non-evaluative, and so particularly helpful.

Indeed, Logo can help children learn both "path" (self-based systems based on one's own movement and the routes one follows) and "coordinate" (external-based) concepts, as well as how to differentiate between them. One way to move the Logo turtle is to give it commands such as "forward 100" and "right 90." This path perspective is distinct from coordinate commands, such as "setpos [50 100]" (set the position to the coordinates (50, 100)). Figure 7.3 below shows Monica's layer cake project.

She is not only competent at using both path-based commands, including her "rect" procedure, but she shows understanding of the connection between each command and its graphic effect, the effects of changing each coordinate, and the distinction between path and coordinate commands. Monica initially struggled to differentiate between regions and lines, made erroneous, perceptually based judgments of path length, and interpreted two coordinate pairs as four separate numbers. So, her work on the layer cake project represented a substantial mathematical advance.

This study also suggests cautions regarding some popular teaching strategies. For example, phrases such as "over and up" and "the x-axis is the bottom," which we recorded on numerous occasions, do not generalize well to a four-quadrant grid. The "over and up" strategy also may hinder students' integration of coordinates into a coordinate *pair* representing *one* point (Sarama et al., 2003).

Building Imagery and Spatial Visualization

As early as the preschool years, U.S. children perform lower than children in countries such as Japan and China on spatial visualization and imagery tasks. There is more support for spatial thinking in these countries. For example, they use more visual representations and expect

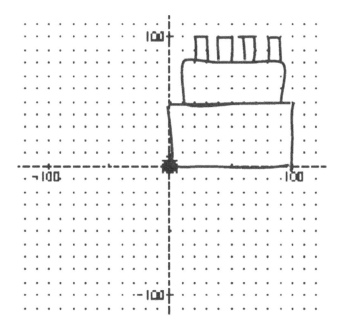

Monica chose the layer cake task as her project. She drew a plan on dot paper, as shown.

She wrote a rectangle procedure for the layers and the candles without any problems, counting the spaces on the dot paper to determine the lengths and widths.

After drawing the bottom layer on the computer, she tried the commands jumpto [0 10] and jumpto [0 50], saying, "I've always had a little problem with that." She carefully counted by tens and figured out that she needed a jumpto [10 50].

Figure 7.3 Continued next page

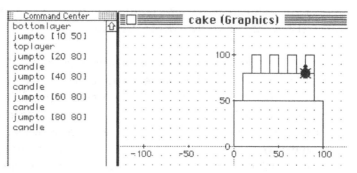

At this point she switched the grid tool on, saying, "Now it's gonna be hard." She had planned `jumpto [10 70]`, but seeing where the turtle ended up, she changed the input to `[10 80]` and then to `[20 80]`.

She entered her `candle` procedure. She looked back at her figure and decided that she did not like the way her candles were spread apart on the paper and decided not to do it like in her drawing. She counted on from (20, 80), entered `jumpto [40 80]` then her candle procedure. The teacher asked her if she could figure out the next jumpto from her commands without counting. She said that it would be `jumpto [80 80]`, probably adding 40 to her previous `jumpto`. But when she saw it, she changed the input to `[70 80]` and then to `[60 80]`. A final `jumpto [80 80]` and candle completed the first cake.

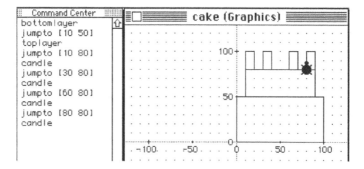

She wasn't satisfied with the location of her candles and wanted to move two over. She moved directly to the correct `jumpto` commands, changing the inputs to `[10 80]` and `[30 80]`. Her confidence indicated that she understood the connection between each command and its effect.

Figure 7.3a Monica's use of path and coordinate logo commands

children to become more competent in drawing. It is important, then, to encourage families to develop young children's spatial visualization. As another example, fathers' higher spatial *concept* support during block building predicted superior math achievement for first graders, especially girls (Thomson, Casey, Lombardi, & Nguyen, 2018c). Specifically, higher support included: (a) specific (e.g., using gestures or other words to clarify a concept) and wide-ranging concepts (e.g., saying "that goes in front, next to the other block"); (b) encouragement of the child's use of spatial concepts (e.g., using questions or suggestion that prompt the child's own use of a spatial concept); and (c) enriched explanations (e.g., "Even though it doesn't show all of them in the back, it shows enough of them so that it looks like it's symmetrical ... Do you know what symmetrical is?"). A study of Finnish parents showed the importance of both parents, with positive effects on children's spatial skills with more cognitive guidance, including encouraging children's independence and autonomy, but also assisting and guiding subtly based on the child's level of development (e.g., along a developmental progression, Sorariutta & Silvén, 2018).

So, we can and should do more. Opportunities in Table 7.1 can develop early spatial visualization. Also, for infants who can sit up, but are not yet mobile, use treasure baskets (Goldschmeid & Jackson, 1994). Over 14 in. (35 cm) in diameter, and 4 to 5 inches high, flat-bottomed with no handles and strong enough for an infant to lean on, the treasure basket is filled with natural household items (no plastic). Items are safe to mouth and stimulate a variety of senses; for example, large cloth ball and other balls, lemon, large pinecone, wooden spoon, and large wooden curtain rings. Children are in control, exploring the items' properties through a variety of senses. These experiences can be extended for toddlers, especially providing multiple copies of the same items (Leavy et al., 2018b).

Use manipulatives such as unit blocks, puzzles, and tangrams–intelligently (see Chapter 16). Encourage children to play with blocks and puzzles at school and home. Encourage girls to play with (the unfortunately termed) "boys' toys," helping them to develop higher visual-spatial skills. Also, talk to them about such play. Most teachers spend more time with boys than girls, and usually interact with boys in the block, construction, sand play and climbing areas, and with girls in the dramatic play area (Ebbeck, 1984). Watch for that in your own teaching–help all children to build a full range of competencies. Finally, encourage all children to use gestures when they are explaining, as this improves their spatial visualization skills (Ehrlich, Levine, & Goldin-Meadow, 2006b; Elia, 2018c).

Use geometric "Snapshot" activities to build spatial visualization and imagery. Children see a simple configuration for 2 seconds, then try to draw what they saw. They then compare their drawings and *discuss* what they saw. In Figure 7.4, different children see three triangles, "a sailboat sinking," a square with two lines through it, an envelope, and a "y in a box." The discussions are especially valuable in developing vocabulary and the ability to see things from other points of view. Encourage children to rotate the image to see how that changes their perspective. Younger children can view combinations of pattern blocks for 2 seconds and then construct a copy with their own pattern blocks.

From preschoolers to first graders, research supports *Snapshots* as a recommended activity. For example, first graders who drew and discussed what they saw made significant improvements in mental rotation (Tzuriel & Egozi, 2010).

These also generate good discussions, emphasizing the *properties* of shapes. Such imagistic/memory tasks also engender interesting discussions revolving around "what I saw." (Clements & Sarama, 2013; Razel & Eylon, 1986, 1990; Wheatley, 1996; Yackel & Wheatley, 1990). Having children use many different media to represent their memories and ideas with the "hundred languages of children" (Edwards, Gandini, & Forman, 1993) will help them build spatial visualization and imagery. Teachers, of course, should use both spatial language and gestures as much as

Figure 7.4 "Snapshots"–geometry

possible (Verdine et al., 2017). Gesture helps ground language in the world and its spatial rela-tionships. *These are easy habits to start and maintain, and they do a lot for your children's spatial development.* Interact during play too—scaffolding children's learning generates more spatial language, spatial problem solving, and spatial learning than open-ended free play (Verdine et al., 2017).

Tactile kinesthetic tasks ask children to identify, name, and describe objects and shapes placed in a "feely box" (Clements & Sarama, 2013). In a similar vein, executing geometric motions on the computer helped children as young as kindergartners learn these concepts (Clements et al., 2001). Activities that involve motion geometry—slides, flips, and turns—whether doing puzzles (see Chapter 9 and Lin & Chen, 2016) or Logo, improve spatial perception. Constructing shapes from parts with multiple media builds imagery as well as geometric concepts (see Chapter 8). Com-posing and decomposing 2D shapes and 3D shapes (e.g., block building) is so important that Chapter 9 is dedicated to these processes.

Building spatial abilities early is effective and efficient. For example, Grade 2 children bene-fited more than Grade 4 children from lessons taught to develop spatial thinking (Owens, 1992). In 11 lessons, children described the similarities and differences of shapes, made shapes from other shapes, made outlines using sticks, compared angles, made pentomino shapes, and found their symmetries. Those children outperformed a control group in a randomized field trial on a spatial thinking test, with differences attributable to the Grade 2 children. No difference was found between groups that worked cooperatively or individually, with whole-class discussions. Nearly all interactions that lead to heuristics about what to do or to conceptualizations were between the teacher and the student, not between students (Owens, 1992). So, teach actively.

Also, teach actively with manipulatives and multimedia. In a study with first graders, the group that used manipulatives or multimedia scored higher than those who didn't use either. The highest-performing group used both multimedia and manipulatives (Thompson, 2012).

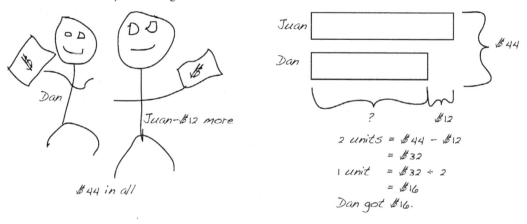

Problem: Juan and Dan shared $44 between them. Juan got $12 more than Dan. How much money did Dan get?

Pictorial Representation   Schematic Representation

Figure 7.5 Pictorial (not useful) versus schematic (useful) representations

The instruction developed spatial skills but was organized around three-dimensional (solid) shapes. Children discussed their attributes, had hands-on experience with them, determined which could stack, slide, or roll, and built them from two-dimensional patterns or nets (see Chapter 9), developing mental rotation abilities.

Mental rotation can also be developed through the use of puzzles, from insert puzzles in preschool to jigsaw and shape composition puzzles (Chapter 9). Puzzle games on computers have also proven effective (Lin & Hou, 2016).

An intervention targeting spatial skills as an integral feature of regular math in a K-2 classroom developed a range of competencies, compared to the control group, including spatial language, visual-spatial reasoning, 2D mental rotation, and symbolic number comparison (Hawes, Moss, Caswell, Naqvi, & MacKinnon, 2017). The spatial visualization and geometric activities were not an "add-on" but a part of the regular schedule, making the results especially impressive (the activities are incorporated into the learning trajectories in this book and [LT]^2).

An important domain in developing spatial skills in these ways is *engineering*. Projects in which children build make strong contributions to spatial skills (English, 2018b; Lippard, Riley, & Lamm, 2018; McGarvey et al., 2018; Portsmore & Milto, 2018). Also called *constructive play*, especially initially, this includes building with blocks (see Chapter 9), LEGO™ bricks, and other toys for building. Interestingly, it is not just time in such play, but the *quality, both accuracy and complexity*, of the building that seems to matter (The Spatial Reasoning Study Group, 2015c). For example, children who were given goals for block building, especially encased in a narrative, made greater gains in spatial competencies and block building skills that those who engaged only in free play with the blocks (Casey et al., 2008b). Extensive benefits, on math but also on executive function (see Chapter 14), came from a year-long intervention for at-risk kindergartners and first graders. In an after-school program, these children constructed and copied designs made from a variety of materials including LEGOs®, Wikki Stix®, and pattern blocks (Grissmer et al., 2013).

Remember children who haven't had high-quality learning opportunities often use pictorial images that do not aid problem solving and actually can impede success. They represent mainly the visual appearance of the objects or persons described in a problem. Instead, we want all children to use the schematic images often used by high-achieving children. As an example, see the representations in Figure 7.5. Schematic drawings such as that on the right side are more useful.

Thus, it may not be at all useful to encourage children to "visualize" just using pictures or diagrams. These are more general and abstract. They contain the spatial relationships relevant to a problem and thus support problem solving (Hegarty & Kozhevnikov, 1999). The diagrams for arithmetic in Chapters 5 (e.g., Table 5.1, p. 91) and 6 (e.g., Figures 6.3 and 6.7, pp. 126 and 137) illustrate such schematic images and thus are useful in many mathematics contexts. Teachers should help students develop and use specific types of schematic images.

Importantly, high-quality geometry activities also develop spatial visualization. See Chapters 8 and 9.

Finally, although research is limited, some studies show that developing children's spatial abilities also develops their *math*. For example, three approaches to spatial training for 3-year-olds were all successful in increasing their 2D and 3D visualization, with modeling and feedback and gesture feedback the most effective (Bower et al., 2020). In five sessions, children saw the nine shapes and then children had to manipulate shapes to match a model. Especially for low-resource learners, *the training also improved their math*, particularly simple arithmetic problems (Bower et al., 2020).

Also striking, a single session of mental rotation training improved 6- to 8-year-olds' *arithmetic calculations*, notably on Join, Change Unknown problems such as 6 + _ = 13 (Chapter 5). What was this training? Children saw two halves of a symmetric figure, such as one of the possibilities in Figure 7.6a (i.e., a1 *or* a2 *or* a3 *or* a4). They had to first *visually* choose which whole figure (Figure 7.6b) these halves would make when re-joined. Next, children confirmed the accuracy of their response by putting together actual "cut-outs" of the symmetric shapes. In this way, children were given immediate feedback about the accuracy of their mental transformations. This improved their *calculations* especially on Join, Change Unknown problems such as 6 + _ = 13 (Chapter 5), possibly because it helped them see the parts and wholes (Cheng & Mix, 2012).

One study gave 7 days of professional development to preschool to second-grade teachers "rug activities" involving drawing, building, copying, and visualization exercises such as those in Table 7.2, right up to the "Mental Mover" level. After a year, children demonstrated improvements on all of the spatial measures, including spatial language, 2D mental rotation, and visual-spatial geometric reasoning, *and*, remarkably, on a test of symbolic magnitude comparison (Moss, Hawes, Naqvi, & Caswell, 2015). *Do more spatial thinking activities!*

Learning Trajectories for Spatial Thinking

The *goal* of increasing children's knowledge of geometry and space is second in importance only to numerical goals and all these are (or should be) strongly interrelated (Moss et al., 2015). The places these goals appear in the CCSSM are shown in Table 7.2. Given the interrelatedness of topics in geometry and spatial thinking and across the grades, we present the goals for all

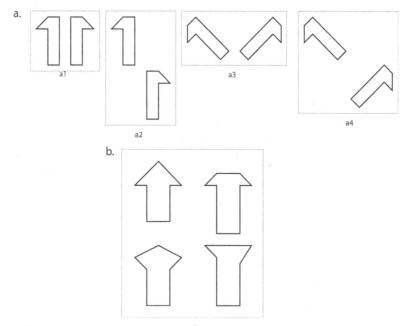

Figure 7.6 Put the Halves Back Together, [LT]² (mental rotation task adapted from Ehrlich et al., 2006b). The four types of halves, in order of increasing difficulty: a1 is a direct slide (translation), a2 a diagonal slide, a3 a direct rotation, a4 a diagonal rotation

these topics together, including goals for Chapters 7, 8, and 9, and also describe those for Grade 3. For this chapter, note especially the CCSSM standard K.G.1.

With those goals, Table 7.2 provides the two additional learning trajectory components, the developmental progression and the instructional tasks for *two* learning trajectories for spatial thinking: spatial orientation (maps and coordinates) and spatial visualization and imagery. The learning trajectory for maps becomes increasingly connected to children's development of *spatial structuring*, the ability to organize space into two dimensions, which is discussed in detail in Chapter 12 (because it is just as critical for understanding area, note standard 2.G.2 in Table 7.2). The reader may notice that the instructional tasks in this learning trajectory tend not to be specific activities, but global suggestions. This difference reflects our belief that (a) there is as yet too little evidence on the specific role of this learning trajectory in students' math development, (b) such activities may be conducted in other subject matter areas (e.g., social studies), and (c) these activities are often best done informally, as part of everyday activity.

However, these two learning trajectories represent only a small bit of the role of spatial thinking in mathematics, especially for spatial visualization, which we focused on geometric transformations and mental rotation. These abilities and dynamic imagery, *and* language for them, are important (Duval, 2014b; Elia, van den Heuvel-panhuizen, & Gagatsis, 2018b). However, we also saw that spatial and structural thinking is critical in conceptual subitizing (e.g., fives and tens frames), comparison and ordering (mental number line), counting strategies, and arithmetic (BAMT). Such spatial knowledge is central to geometry, measurement, patterns and structures, data presentation, and the other topics discussed in forthcoming chapters. Thus, attention to spatial thinking should be woven throughout the curriculum and is explicitly included in the learning trajectories in those chapters.

Learning Trajectories for Spatial Orientation and for Spatial Visualization and Imagery

The importance of the goal of increasing children's ability in spatial thinking and geometry is clear. Table 7.2 shows where these goals appear in the CCSSM. With those goals, Table 7.3 provides the two additional components of the learning trajectory, the developmental progression and the instructional tasks. Table 7.3 is split into two parts for the two types of spatial thinking. As always, complement this reading with video examples of the developmental levels—so important to make them "real" and memorable, and descriptions, resources, and often videos of activities at [LT][2] (LearningTrajectories.org).

Final Words

Visual thinking is thinking that is tied down to limited, surface-level, visual ideas. Children can learn to move beyond that kind of visual thinking to *flexible spatial thinking* that is linked to concepts, as they learn to manipulate dynamic images, as they enrich their store of images for shapes, and as they connect their spatial knowledge to verbal, analytic knowledge. In this way, instruction discussed in the next two chapters, on shapes and composing shapes, also makes a strong contribution to children's spatial thinking.

Table 7.2 Goals for Geometry and Spatial Thinking (For Chapters 7, 8, and 9) from the Common Core State Standards CCSSM

Geometry [K.E in CCSSM]

Identify and describe shapes (squares, circles, triangles, rectangles, hexagons, cubes, cones, cylinders, and spheres).

1. Describe objects in the environment using names of shapes, and describe the relative positions of these objects using terms such as *above, below, beside, in front of, behind*, and *next to.*
2. Correctly name shapes regardless of their orientations or overall size.
3. Identify shapes as two-dimensional (lying in a plane, "flat") or three-dimensional ("solid").

Analyze, compare, create, and compose shapes.

4. Analyze and compare two- and three-dimensional shapes, in different sizes and orientations, using informal language to describe their similarities, differences, parts (e.g., number of sides and vertices/ "comers") and other attributes (e.g., having sides of equal length).
5. Model shapes in the world by building shapes from components (e.g., sticks and clay balls) and drawing shapes.
6. Compose simple shapes to form larger shapes. *For example, "Can you join these two triangles with full sides touching to make a rectangle?"*

Geometry [1.G in CCSSM]

Reason with shapes and their attributes.

1. Distinguish between defining attributes (e.g., triangles are closed and three-sided) versus non-defining attributes (e.g., color, orientation, overall size); build and draw shapes to possess defining attributes.
2. Compose two-dimensional shapes (rectangles, squares, trapezoids, triangles, half-circles, and quarter-circles) or three-dimensional shapes (cubes, right rectangular prisms, right circular cones, and right circular cylinders) to create a composite shape, and compose new shapes from the composite shape. Students do not need to learn formal names such as "right rectangular prism."
3. Partition circles and rectangles into two and four equal shares, describe the shares using the words *halves, fourths,* and *quarters,* and use the phrases *half of, fourth of,* and *quarter of.* Describe the whole as two of, or four of the shares. Understand for these examples that decomposing into more equal shares creates smaller shares.

Geometry [2.G in CCSSM]

Reason with shapes and their attributes.

1. Recognize and draw shapes having specified attributes, such as a given number of angles or a given number of equal faces.[5] Identify triangles, quadrilaterals, pentagons, hexagons, and cubes.
2. Partition a rectangle into rows and columns of same-size squares and count to find the total number of them.
3. Partition circles and rectangles into two, three, or four equal shares, describe the shares using the words *halves, thirds, half of, a third of,* etc., and describe the whole as two halves, three thirds, four fourths. Recognize that equal shares of identical wholes need not have the same shape.

Geometry [3.E in CCSSM]

Reason with shapes and their attributes.

1. Understand that shapes in different categories (e.g., rhombuses, rectangles, and others) may share attributes (e.g., having four sides), and that the shared attributes can define a larger category (e.g., quadrilaterals). Recognize rhombuses, rectangles, and squares as examples of quadrilaterals, and draw examples of quadrilaterals that do not belong to any of these subcategories.
2. Partition shapes into parts with equal areas. Express the area of each part as a unit fraction of the whole. *For example, partition a shape into four parts with equal area, and describe the area of each part as 1/4 of the area of the shape.*

Table 7.3 Learning Trajectories for Spatial Thinking

Age	Developmental Progression	Instructional Tasks

a. Spatial Orientation (including maps and coordinates)

0–1	**Foundations of Spatial Orientation** Uses the earliest of two types of cognitive systems for spatial orientation—knowing where you are and how to get around in the world.
	
	1. *Response Learning*: Uses the first self-based system—that is, related to the child's own position and movements. Notes a pattern of movements that have been associated with a goal.
	
	   Looks to the left when in a high-chair, because that's where the food usually comes from.
	
	2. *Cue Learning*: Uses the first external-based systems, based on familiar landmarks.
	
	   Associates a toy bear with a small chair on which it often sits.
		Provide a rich sensory, manipulative environment, [LT]², and the freedom and encouragement to manipulate it and move through it. Infants who crawl more learn more about spatial relationships. See suggestions in Table 7.1 on p. 168.

0–2	**Path Integrater** Remembers and can repeat movements they have made including the approximate distances and directions.
	
	   Crawls to a place of their choice, navigating an obstacle to arrive at a destination within sight.
		Rich Environment, [LT]²: As above, see Table 7.1 on p. 168. Opting for walks for toddlers, rather than stroller rides, the use of low beds/cots instead of cribs, and seating that does not restrict movement also supports development in this area.
		   Use spatial vocabulary to direct attention to spatial relations: Once children have language, describe directions with words such as "there" (gesturing), "around," and "turn."

1–2	**Place Learner** Creates "mental maps" by storing locations, distances, and directions to landmarks and solves spatial problems. Uses the walls of a room as a frame of reference; uses spatial vocabulary, such as "in," "on," and "under," along with vertical directionality terms, such as "up" and "down."	*Rich Environment*, [LT]²: As above, see Table 7.1 on p. 168. Experiences in learning, remembering, and using landmarks build this ability. Discuss and ask children to go to, or retrieve something from, locations that are "in" or "under" objects in the room. *Use spatial vocabulary to direct attention to spatial relations*: Initially emphasize "in," "on," and "under," along with such vertical directionality terms as "up" and "down."

2–3	**Local-Self Framework User** Uses distant landmarks to find objects or location near them, even after they have moved themselves relative to the landmarks, *if* the target object is specified ahead of time. Orients a horizontal or vertical line in space (Rosser, Horan, Mattson, & Mazzeo, 1984). Uses spatial vocabulary to direct attention to spatial relations, including more difficult terms such as "beside" and "between."
	
	   3-year-olds recognize objects that guide them in walking from the front door of their school to their classroom.
		Walk different routes and discuss the landmarks you see: Ask children to point to where different landmarks are at various points along the path.
		   Use spatial vocabulary to direct attention to spatial relations: Emphasize words of proximity, such as "beside" and "between."
		   Ask 3-year-olds to find an object, shown a picture of its location.
		   Have children build with blocks to represent simple scenes and locations (see Chapter 9 for much more on block building). If children are interested, make a model of the classroom and point to a location in it that represents a place where a "prize" is hidden in the actual classroom. Use the notion of a "shrinking machine" to help them understand the model as a representation of the classroom space.
		   Going on a Bear Hunt, [LT]²: Read and discuss the book.

(Continued)

Table 7.3 (Cont.)

Age	Developmental Progression	Instructional Tasks
4	**Small Local Framework User** Locates objects after movement, even if target is not specified ahead of time. Searches a small area comprehensively, often using a circular search pattern. Uses words referring to frames of reference such as "in front of" and "behind" or "left" and "right." In meaningful graphing contexts, extrapolates lines from positions on both axes (like a coordinate grid) and determines where they intersect. Child searches a small area comprehensively, often using a circular search pattern. Extrapolates lines from positions on both axes and determines where they intersect in meaningful contexts.	*Use spatial vocabulary to direct attention to spatial relations*: Emphasize words referring to frames of reference such as "in front of" and "behind." Initiate the learning of "left" and "right." *Encourage parents to avoid pointing or showing when possible, but, instead, to give verbal directions* ("it's in the bag *on the table*"): Have students pose verbal problems for one another, such as finding a missing object ("under the table that's next to the door"), putting objects away, and finding the way back from an excursion. *Treasure Map*, [LT]²: During free time, challenge children to follow simple maps of the classroom or playground to find secret "treasures" that you have hidden. Interested children can draw their own maps. Start with oblique maps (e.g., in which chairs and tables are shown with legs). A good introduction to this activity is *Rosie's Walk* by Pat Hutchins. *Explore and discuss outdoor spaces*, permitting children (both sexes) as much freedom in self-directed movement as safely possible. Encourage parents to do the same. *Walk different routes and discuss different paths*, and which would be shorter, which would be longer. Ask *why* one path is shorter. *Introductory Barrier Game*, [LT]²: One student (the "designer") makes a design that is hidden from the partner, and the other student (the "builder") recreates the design based on the designer's verbal description.
5	**Local Framework User** Locates objects after moving, maintaining the overall shape of the arrangement of objects. Represents objects' positions relative to landmarks (e.g., about halfway in between two landmarks) and keeps track of own location in open areas or mazes. Uses spatial vocabulary to direct attention to spatial relations. Uses coordinate labels in simple situations such as games.	*Encourage children to build models of the room or playground* with toys. Plan and discuss different routes, and which would be the best route to take and why. Draw maps of routes, illustrating what will be "passed" or seen from different routes. *Treasure Hunt*, [LT]²: Children receive a letter with information about a mysterious treasure of ancient pirates hidden somewhere in their school, and the way to find it is to follow the indications/landmarks around the building, which help children to follow the correct route to reach the treasure. They follow the directions and draw a map. *Use spatial vocabulary to direct attention to spatial relations*: Emphasize all words listed previously, including the learning of "left" and "right." *Encourage children to make models of their classroom*, using blocks or play furniture to represent objects in the classroom. Discuss which ones go "near each other" and other spatial relationships. *Maps of the Playground*: Children might use cut-out shapes of a tree, swing set, and sandbox in the playground and lay them out on a felt board as a simple map. They can discuss how moving an item in the schoolyard, such as a table, would change the map of the yard. On the map, locate children shown sitting in or near the tree, swing set, and sandbox. In scavenger hunts on the playground, children can give and follow directions or clues. *Explore and discuss outdoor spaces*, permitting children (both sexes) as much freedom in self-directed movement as safely possible. Encourage parents to do the same. (This recommendation extends through the grades.)

(Continued)

Table 7.3 (Cont.)

Age	Developmental Progression	Instructional Tasks
		Encourage children to mark paths, such as a path from a table to the wastebasket with masking tape. With the teacher's help, children could draw a map of this path (some teachers take photographs of the wastebasket and door and glue these to a large sheet of paper). Items appearing alongside the path, such as a table or easel, can be added to the map. *Another (Bear) Hunt*, [LT]²: This activity is an extension of a popular children's book. Children create new verses to learn spatial vocabulary beyond the vocabulary featured in the original book. *Logo*: Engage children in age-appropriate *Turtle Math* environments (Clements & Meredith, 1994; Clements & Sarama, 1996). Have them tutor one another in those environments. *Ask children to solve two-dimensional matrices* (e.g., placing all objects where colors are sorted into rows and shapes are sorted into columns) or to use coordinates on maps.
6	**Map User** Locates objects using maps with pictorial cues. Extrapolates (extends) two coordinates, understanding the integration of them to one position, as well as use coordinate labels in simple situations.	*Use spatial vocabulary to direct attention to spatial relations*: Emphasize all words listed previously, and the various interpretations of "left" and "right." *Maps*: Continue the previous activities, but emphasize the four questions (see p. 186): direction, "Which way?"; distance, "How far?"; location, "Where?"; and identification, "What objects?" Notice the use of coordinates on maps. *Challenge students to find their house or school in Internet-based aerial photographs*, once you have accessed that location on the computer. *Ask students to plan routes* around the school using maps, then follow those routes. *Logo*: Engage children in age-appropriate *Turtle Math* environments (Clements & Meredith, 1994; Clements & Sarama, 1996). Have them tutor one another in those environments. *Use coordinates in all applicable situations*; for example, to label locations ("pegs") on geoboards as students build shapes. *Helicopter Ride*, [LT]²: Print out an aerial view of students' route from home to school. Talk about directions to school, distance from school, and landmarks along the way.
7	**Coordinate Plotter** Reads and plots coordinates on maps.	*Ask students to draw simple sketch-maps* of the area around their houses, classroom, playground, or the school. Discuss differences among representations of the same spaces. Present tasks in which maps must be aligned with the space. Showing children several maps and models, explicitly comparing them using language and visual highlights, helps build representational understandings. *"Battleship"-type games are useful*. Guide children in the following competencies in all coordinate work: • interpreting the grid structure's components as line segments or lines rather than regions; • appreciating the precision of location of the lines required, rather than treating them as fuzzy boundaries or indicators of intervals; • learning to trace closely packed vertical or horizontal lines that are not axes;

Table 7.3 (Cont.)

Age	Developmental Progression	Instructional Tasks
		• integrating two numbers into a single coordinate; • conceptualizing labels as signs of location and distance—(a) to quantify what the grid labels represent, (b) to connect their counting acts to those quantities and to the labels, (c) to subsume these ideas to a Part-Whole scheme connected to both the grid and to counting/arithmetic, and (d) to construct proportional relationships in this scheme (Sarama et al., 2003).
		Logo and coordinate computer games and activities benefit children's understanding and skills with coordinates (Clements & Meredith, 1994; Clements & Sarama, 1996).
8	**Route Map Follower** Follows a simple route map, with more accurate direction and distances.	*Engage students in practical map-using and map-making tasks* similar to "find the treasure" in an environment with which children are familiar, then less familiar. Include coordinate maps. (See pp. 128-132 of the present volume; Lehrer & Pritchard, 2002.) *Playground Geocache*, [LT]²: Rather than using a global positioning system, this geocaching game will use directions that teams create and provide to each other to find treasures on the playground.

	Framework User Uses general frameworks that include the observer and landmarks. May not use precise measurement even when that would be helpful, unless guided to do so.
	  Can follow and create maps, even if spatial relations are transformed.
		Spinning Map, [LT]²: Using grid paper to create a map with landmarks and coordinates, student give directions to someone who has only coordinates on their grid. They try to get from one location to another, spinning the map after every direction.
		  Find the Lost Pet, [LT]²: Students use a map and landmarks to find a lost item in the classroom.
		  Logo: Engage children in *Turtle Math* environments in which maps are translated to computer programs (Clements & Meredith, 1994; Clements & Sarama, 1996).

b. Spatial Visualization and Imagery

Age	Developmental Progression	Instructional Tasks
0-1	**Intuitive Mover: Foundations** Explores the size and shape of objects by observing them as they move in space, discovering how they move and fit into space, and eventually reproducing patterns of movement (without attempting different possible solutions). Such intuitive skills will eventually support future spatial visualization. A toddler plays with pattern blocks, moving them around in various ways to fit together in interesting ways.	*Play in a Rich Environment*, [LT]²: Manipulation of a wide variety of (safe) objects and containers—water play in rich environments provide children the strongest experience foundation for understanding spatial relationships. Describing children's actions with spatial words enhances these experiences.

1-2	**Concrete Slider, Flipper, Turner** Can move shapes to a location by physical trial and error.	*Play in a Rich Environment*, [LT]²: As above, enhanced with language.
		  Fill & Spill (Concrete Slider, Flipper, Turner), [LT]²: Children use a shape sorter to begin turning shapes to fit in a visually matching hole.
		  Make My Picture: Ask children to use blocks to duplicate a simple "picture."

3-4	**Simple Slider and Turner** Slides and turns objects accurately in easy tasks, guided by an early intuition that starts the motion and then	*Make My Picture—Hidden Version*: Ask children to use building blocks or pattern blocks to duplicate a simple "picture" that they see for 5 to 10 seconds and then is covered. (See also "Geometry Snapshots" in Chapter 8.)

(Continued)

Table 7.3 (Cont.)

Age	Developmental Progression	Instructional Tasks
	adjusts (the motion, direction, or amount[1]) in real time as the motion is carried out. Given a shape with the top marked with color, correctly identifies which of three shapes it would look like if it were turned "like this" (90° turn demonstrated) before physically moving the shape.	*Ask children to show how a circular object should be rotated to make it appear circular or elliptical*: Work with shadows to make a rectangle appear as a non-rectangular parallelogram ("rhomboid") or vice versa. *Putting the Pieces Together!*, [LT][2]: Have children solve jigsaw, pattern block, and simple tangram puzzles and discuss how they are moving the shapes to make them fit (see more in Chapter 8). Encourage parents to engage children in all types of puzzles and talk to them as they solve the puzzles (especially girls). *Feely Boxes*: Use "feely boxes" to identify shapes by touch (see more in Chapter 8). Challenge children to turn a well-marked shape to align it with another, congruent shape. *Snapshots–Geometry*: Students copy a simple configuration of pattern blocks shown for 2 seconds. (See Chapter 9 for more details.) *Shape Composition*: See activities at the early level Piece Assembler (see Chapter 9). Also see *Picture It, Then Turn, Turn, Turn*, [LT][2].
5	**Beginning Slider, Flipper, Turner** Uses the correct motions guided by more developed intuition, but not always accurate in direction and amount (adjusts these with trial and error). Knows a shape has to be flipped to match another shape but flips it in the wrong direction.	*Put the Halves Back Together* (Beginning Slider, Flipper, Turner), [LT][2]: See p. 176 and Figure 7.6. This level uses the a1 and a2 arrangements of halves. Discuss the symmetry of the figure. *Feely Boxes*: Use "feely boxes" to identify a wide variety of shapes by touch (see more in Chapter 8). *Tangram Puzzles*: Have children solve tangram puzzles and discuss how they are moving the shapes to make them fit (see more in Chapter 8). *Geometry Snapshots 2*: Shown a simple configuration of shapes for just 2 seconds, students match that configuration to four choices from memory (imagery). 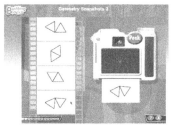 *Geometry Snapshots 3*: Students identify an image that matches the "symmetric whole" of a target image from four multiple-choice selections. 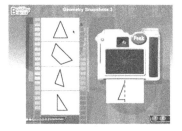 *Shape Composition*: See activities at the level Picture Maker (see Chapter 9). Also see *Piecing Pentominoes Together*, [LT][2].

(Continued)

Table 7.3 (Cont.)

Age	Developmental Progression	Instructional Tasks
6	**Slider, Flipper, Turner** Performs slides and flips, often only horizontal and vertical, using manipulatives but guided by mental images of these motions (of turns of 45, 90, and 180° and flips over vertical and horizontal lines). That is, they can mentally imagine the motion and the result of it. Knows a shape must be turned 90° to the right to fit into a puzzle.	*Put the Halves Back Together* (Slider, Flipper, Turner), [LT]^2: See p. 176 and Figure 7.6. This level uses the a3 and a4 arrangements of halves. Discuss the symmetry of the figure. *Snapshots–Geometry*: Students draw one or more shapes shown for 2 seconds. *Geometry Snapshots 4*: Students identify an image that matches one of four moderately complex configurations from memory (imagery). 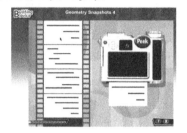 *Shape Composition*: See activities at the level Picture Maker (see Chapter 9). Also see *Pentomino Puzzle Perfection!*, [LT]^2 and *Shape Puzzles: Shape Composer*, [LT]^2.
7	**Diagonal Mover** Performs diagonal slides and flips as well as all motions from previous levels. Knows a shape must be flipped over an oblique line (45° orientation) to fit into a puzzle.	*Geometry Snapshots 6*: Students match geometric figures that differ on angle measure from memory (imagery). 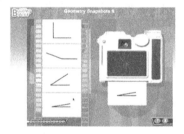
8	**Mental Mover** Predicts results of moving shapes using mental images (any direction or amount). "If you turned this 120°, it would be just like this one."	*Pattern Block Puzzles* and *Tangram Puzzles* at the Substitution Composer levels, [LT]^2: Ask students how many of a certain shape it would take to cover *another* shape (or configuration of shapes). Students predict, record their prediction, then try to check. (See Chapter 9 for more.)

Note

1 *Motion*: slide or turn. *Direction*: for slides, which way it is headed; for turns, clockwise or counterclockwise. *Amount*: for slides, how far, or turns, how much of a turn (in degrees).

8 Shape

One kindergartner impressed his teacher by saying he knew that a shape (Figure 8.1a) was a triangle because it had "three straight lines and three angles." Later, however, he said Figure 8.1b was *not* a triangle.

Teacher:	Doesn't it have three straight sides?
Child:	Yes.
Teacher:	And what else did you say triangles have to have?
Child:	Three angles. It has three angles.
Teacher:	Good! So...
Child:	It's *not* a triangle. It's upside down!

Did this kindergartner know triangles or not? What was *driving* his thinking about triangles, do you think? In general, how should we as educators help children develop the math of geometric shape? Why should we?

Shape is a fundamental concept in cognitive development. For example, infants mainly use shape to learn the names of objects (Smith, Jones, Landau, Gershkoff-Stowe, & Samuelson, 2002). Shape is also a fundamental idea in geometry, but in other areas of math, too (Dindyal, 2015). Unfortunately, geometry is one of U.S. students' weakest topics in math. Even in the preschool years, children in the USA know less about shape than children in other countries. Further, children from low-resource communities know less about shapes than those from higher-resource communities by 3 years of age (Chang et al., 2011). The good news is, children from diverse backgrounds know enough to build upon, and much like all children they can learn enough quickly and enjoy engaging with shapes (Clements, Sarama, Swaminathan, Weber, & Trawick-Smith, 2018a).

The Mathematics of 2D Shapes

Before we move on into young children's thinking and learning, let's take a side trip to define some geometric terms.[1] We use "attributes" to mean any characteristic of a shape. Some are "defining attributes." To be a square, a shape must have *straight* sides (mathematically, "sides"

 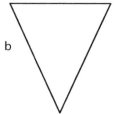

Figure 8.1 Two triangles ("a" and "b")

are line segments—always straight). Others are "non-defining attributes." A child might consider a shape "right side up" (if you turn a square, this child may say, "Now it's a diamond!") or describe it as "red" but neither of these attributes is relevant to whether the shape is a square or not. Some defining attributes describe the parts of a shape—as a square has *four sides*. Others are special attributes we call *properties*, which describe a *relationship between parts*. A square must have four *equal-length* sides. Equal describes the relationship amongst the sides. Similarly, the square's right angles depend on a different relationship between sides: They are *perpendicular*.

At the higher level of geometric thinking, then, students recognize and characterize shapes *by their defining attributes*. For instance, a child might think of a square as a plane (flat) figure that has four equal sides and four right angles. Properties are established by observing, measuring, drawing, and model-making. Not until later, often middle school or later, do students see relationships between *classes of figures* (see Figure 8.2). For example, most children incorrectly believe that a figure is not a rectangle because it is a square (whereas actually a square is a special type of rectangle).

Shape definitions

The following definitions are intended to help teachers both understand young children's development of specific math concepts and talk to them about these concepts. They are not formal definitions, but, rather, simple descriptions using a mixture of math and everyday vocabulary. The shapes in Box 8.1 are taken to be two-dimensional (plane) figures.

Relationships Between Shapes

The diagrams on p. 187 show the relationships between classes of shapes. For example, all the shapes in Figure 8.2a are quadrilaterals. A *proper subset* of them are parallelograms, all of which have two pairs of opposite parallel sides. Parallelograms in turn include other subclasses. If all of a parallelogram's sides are the same length, they are also called *rhombuses*. If all of a parallelogram's angles are the same, then they must all be right angles, and they are also called *rectangles*. If both are true—if they are rhombuses and rectangles—they are also called *squares*.

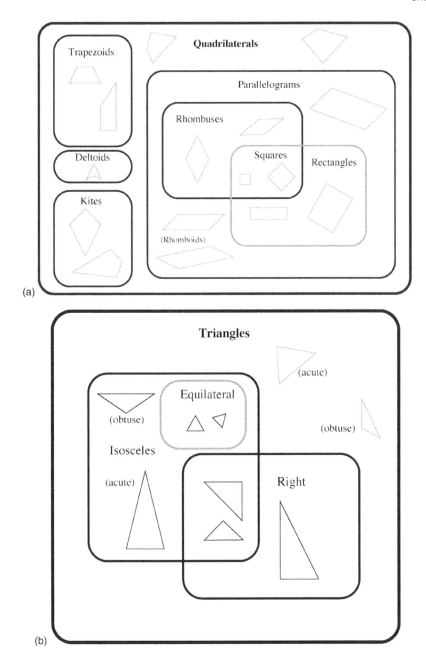

Figure 8.2 Venn diagrams of relationships between (a) quadrilaterals and (b) triangles

Children's Development of Geometry

Young Children's Learning about 2D Shapes

Children can match shapes from a very young age. They can insert shapes into the matching hole in a box consistently from 22 months of age, and make adjustments to the shapes' positions before their hands arrive at the holes (Örnkloo & von Hofsten, 2007b).

Although it may seem obvious that we learn about shapes by seeing them and naming them, some—such as Jean Piaget—say that isn't the whole story. It isn't even the main story. For Piaget, children do not "read off" of their spatial environment, but, rather, *construct* their ideas about shape by actively manipulating shapes in their environment and even by actively moving their eyes over its shape. Further, even if children can name a square, their knowledge might be limited. For example, if they cannot feel a hidden square and name it after exploring it with their hands, Piaget would claim they do not really understand the *concept* "square."

A husband-and-wife team of researchers, Pierre and Dina van Hiele, agreed that students construct their geometric ideas. They also describe *broad* levels of thinking through which students develop, which we have restructured (we return to these in Table 8.1). For example, at first children can match shapes but don't verbally distinguish between one shape and another: *Shape Sensers*. Later, they can, but only visually—they recognize shapes as wholes: *Visual Thinker*. They might call a shape a "rectangle" because "it looks like a door." They then develop to understand and talk about shapes in terms of their *parts*, such as "It's a triangle because it has three sides": *Parts Thinker*. Finally, they think about the defining attributes or *properties* of shapes: *Property Thinker*.

As we saw in Chapter 7, visualization is not a simple process, so developing into a *Visual Thinker* takes a *lot* of learning. It involves a growing (Dindyal, 2015) ability to apprehend and distinguish all of an object's characteristics: 3D, 2D, and 1D (line segments) aspects and their interrelationships, distinguishing the math properties that make it a real-world representation of an abstract math idea (Duval, 2014b; Elia et al., 2018b).

Thinking and Learning about Specific Shapes

Children are sensitive to shape from the first year of life. And they prefer closed, symmetric shapes, such as the *prototypes* of four classes of shapes in Figure 8.3. Most people from many cultures, even those with little or no exposure to other civilizations, prefer them too, so these are probably inborn preferences.

Culture influences these preferences. We conducted an extensive examination of materials that teach children about shapes from books, toy stores, teacher supply stores, and catalogues. With few exceptions (and with signs that this is changing in recent years), these materials introduce children to triangles, rectangles, and squares in rigid ways. Triangles are usually equilateral or isosceles and have horizontal bases. Most rectangles are horizontal, elongated shapes about twice as long as they are wide. No wonder so many children, even throughout elementary school, say that a square turned is "not a square anymore, it's a diamond" (Clements, Swaminathan, Hannibal, & Sarama, 1999b; Lehrer, Jenkins, & Osana, 1998b).

Table 8.1 Learning Trajectory for 2D Shapes

Age	Broad	Developmental Progression	Instructional Tasks

0-2		**"Same Thing" Comparer: Foundations** *Comparing* Compares real-world objects (Vurpillot, 1976). Judges two shapes the same if they are visually similar in any way.
		
		Says two pictures of houses are the same or different.
		
		Shape Matcher–Identical *Comparing* Matches familiar shapes (circle, square, typical triangle) with *same size and orientation*.
		
		Matches ☐ to ☐
			Shape & Spatial Talk, [LT]².
			    Match the Shapes (Shape Matcher–Identical), [LT]²: Sit in a circle with children. Using familiar (prototypical) shapes from the Shape Sets in two colors (see Figure 8.9 aux), give each child a shape from one color of the Shape Set. Choose a shape from the other color that otherwise exactly matches a child's shape. Ask children to say who has an exact match for your shape. After a correct response is given, follow up by asking how the child knows his or her shape is a match. The child might agree to fit his or her shape on top of your shape to "prove" the match. Have children show their shapes to others seated near them, naming the shape whenever they can. Observe and assist as needed. Repeat once or twice. Afterward, tell children they will be able to explore and match shapes later during Work Time.
			    Shape Pegs, [LT]²: Matching shapes, including number of holes in them.

	Shape Senser	**Shape Matcher–Sizes** *Comparing* Matches familiar shapes with *different sizes*. Matches ☐ to ▢	*Match the Shapes (Shape Matcher)*, [LT]²: As above, extended to different sizes and/or orientations. *Mystery Pictures 1*: Children build pictures by selecting shapes that match a series of target shapes. The skill children practice is matching, but the program *names* each shape so shape names are introduced. Shapes are familiar at this level.
		Shape Matcher–Orientations *Comparing* Matches familiar shapes with *different orientations*. Matches ☐ to ◇	

3		**Shape Recognizer–Typical** *Classifying* Recognizes and names a typical circle, square, and, less often, triangle. May physically rotate shapes in atypical orientations to mentally match them to a prototype.
		
		Names this a "square": ☐
		
		Some children correctly name different sizes, shapes, and orientations of rectangles, but also call some shapes "rectangles" that look rectangular but are not rectangles.
		
		Names these shapes "rectangles" (including the non-rectangular parallelogram):
			Circle Time!, [LT]²: Have children sit in the best circle they can make. Show and name a large, flat circle, such as a hula hoop. As you trace the circle with your finger, discuss how it is perfectly round; it is a curved line that always curves the same. Ask children to talk about circles they know, such as those found in toys, buildings, books, tri- or bicycles, and clothing. Distribute a variety of circles for children's exploration–rolling, stacking, tracing, and so on. Have children make circles with their fingers, hands, arms, and mouths. Review a circle's attributes: round and curves the same without breaks.
			    Find and Name the Twin (Typical), [LT]²: Like matching shapes (above) but asking children to *name* the shapes too.
			    Mystery Pictures 2: Children build pictures by identifying shapes that are *named* by the Building Blocks software program (i.e., at this level, children have to know the names; Mystery Pictures 1 is appropriate before this activity, as it teaches the shape names).

	Visual Thinker		

Table 8.1 (Cont.)

Age	Broad	Developmental Progression	Instructional Tasks

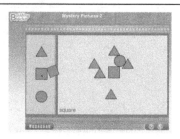

| 3-4 | | **Shape Matcher–More Shapes, Sizes & Orientations, Combinations** *Comparing* Matches a wider variety of shapes with *same size and orientation*.

Shape Matcher–Sizes and Orientations *Comparing* Matches a wider variety of shapes with *different sizes and orientations*.

Matches these shapes:

Shape Matcher–Combinations *Comparing* Matches *combinations* of shapes to each other.

Matches these shapes:
 | *Match and Name Shapes (Shape Matcher–More Shapes)*, [LT]²: As above, but using a wider variety of shapes from the Shape Sets in different orientations.

Match Blocks: Children match various block shapes to objects in the classroom. Have different block shapes in front of you, with all the children in a circle around you. Show one block and ask children what things in the classroom are the same shape. Talk children through any incorrect responses, such as choosing something triangular but saying it has the shape of a quarter circle.

Mystery Pictures 3: Children build pictures by selecting shapes that match a series of target shapes. The skill children practice is matching, but the program *names* each shape, so shape names are introduced. Shapes are more varied and include new (less familiar) shapes at this level.

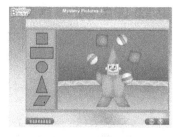 |
| 4 | | **Shape Recognizer–Circles, Squares, and Triangles** *Classifying* Recognizes some less typical squares and triangles and may recognize some rectangles, but usually not rhombuses (diamonds). Often doesn't differentiate sides/corners. May say two shapes are the same after matching only sides (Beilin, 1984) or comparing half of them.

Names these:
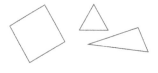 | *Concentrate: More Turned Shapes*, [LT]²: Online [LT]² game matching geometric shapes in different orientations.

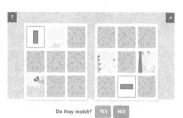

Feely Box (Match): Secretly hide a shape in the "Feely Box" (a decorated box with a hole large enough to fit a child's hand but not so large that you can see into the box). Display five shapes, including the one that exactly matches the one you hid. Have a child put his or her hand in the box to feel the |

(Continued)

Table 8.1 (Cont.)

Age Broad	Developmental Progression	Instructional Tasks

shape; that child should then point to the matching shape on display.

Circles and Cans, [LT]^2: Display several food cans, and discuss their shape (round) with children. Shift focus to the bottom and top, collectively the bases, of each can. Point out to children that these areas are circular; the edges are circles. Show the large sheets of paper on which you have traced the bases of a few cans that vary substantially in size. Trace one or two other cans to show children what you did, and then shuffle the papers and cans. Ask children to match the cans to the traced circles. For children who are unsure of their choice, have them place the can directly on the traced circle to check. Tell children they can all have a turn matching circles and cans during free time and store the activity's materials in a center for that purpose.

Is It or Not? (Circles), [LT]^2: Draw a true circle on a surface where the entire class can view it. Ask children to name it, and then tell them why it is a circle. Draw an ellipse (an oval) on the same surface. Ask children what it looks like, and then ask them to tell you why it is not a circle. Draw several other circles and shapes that are not circles but could be mistaken for them and discuss their differences. Summarize by reviewing that a circle is perfectly round and consists of a curved line that always curves the same.

Shape Show (Triangles), [LT]^2: Show and name a large, flat triangle. Walk your fingers around its perimeter, describing and exaggerating your actions: "Straaiiight side ... turn, straaiiight side ... turn, straaiiight side ... stop." Ask children how many sides the triangle has and count the sides with them.

Emphasize that a triangle's sides and angles can be different sizes; what matters is that its sides are straight and connected to make a closed shape (no openings or gaps). Ask children what things they have at home that are triangles. Show different examples of triangles. Have children draw triangles in the air. If available, have children walk around a large triangle, such as one marked with colored tape on the floor.

Shape Hunt (Triangles), [LT]^2:

- Finding shapes in the environment. Tell children to find one or two items in the room with at least one triangle face. For variety, hide Shape Set triangles throughout the room beforehand. When labeling them, do not just say the shape name, use the object's name and the shape's: "That clock is also a circle" (Verdine et al., 2016).
- Encourage children to count the shape's sides and, if possible, show the triangle to an adult, discussing its shape. For example, triangles have three sides, but the sides are not always the same length. After discussion, have the child replace the triangle so other children can find it.
- You may choose to photograph the triangles for a class shape book.

(Continued)

Table 8.1 (Cont.)

Age	Broad	Developmental Progression	Instructional Tasks
			Is It or Not? (**Triangles**): As above. Include variants (e.g., "skinny triangles") and distractors that are visually similar to triangles ("difficult distractors" or "foolers"), such as those in Figure 8.9b. *Feely Box (Name)*: Similar to "Feely Box (Match)", but now encourage the child to name the shape and explain how he or she figured it out.
		Constructor of Shapes from Parts—Looks Like *Parts* Uses manipulatives representing parts of shapes, such as sides, to make a shape that "looks like" a goal shape. May think of angles as a corner (which is "pointy"). Asked to make a triangle with sticks, creates this: 	*Build Shapes/Straw Shapes (Looks Like)*, [LT]²: Includes the naming of these shapes. In a small group lesson with the teacher, children use plastic stirrers, straws, or sticks of various lengths to make shapes they know. Ensure that they build shapes with correct attributes, such as all sides the same length and all right angles for squares. All stirrers should be "connected" (touching) at their endpoints. Discuss attributes as children build. If children need help, provide a model for them to copy or a drawing on which to place stirrers. Can they choose the correct amount and sizes of stirrers to make a given shape? If children excel, challenge them to get a shape "just right." (At *this* level of thinking, children make approximate representations.) *Build Shapes (Triangles)*, [LT]²: In a free-choice center, children use plastic stirrers to make triangles and/or to create pictures and designs that include triangles.
4–5 **Parts Thinker**		**Shape Recognizer—All Rectangles** *Classifying* Recognizes rectangles of all sizes, shapes, and orientations. Correctly names these shapes "rectangles": 	*Shape Show (Rectangles)* [and *Shape Show (Squares)*], both on [LT]²: Show and name a large, flat rectangle. Walk your fingers around its perimeter, describing and exaggerating your actions: "Straaiiight side … right turn, straaiiight side … right turn, another straaiiight side … right turn, long straaiiight side … stop." Ask children how many sides the rectangle has and count the sides with them. Emphasize that opposite sides of a rectangle are the same lengths, and all "turns" are right angles. To model this, you may place a stirrer that is the same length as one pair of sides on top of each of those sides and repeat for the other pair of opposite sides. To illustrate right angles, talk about the right angle —"like an uppercase L"—in a doorway. Make uppercase Ls with children using thumbs and index fingers. Fit your L on the angles of the rectangle. Ask children what things they have at home that are rectangles. Show different examples of rectangles. Have children walk around a large, flat rectangle, such as a rug. Once seated, have children draw rectangles in the air. Remember that squares are ("special") rectangles. *Mystery Pictures 3* (shown here) is appropriate before this activity, as it teaches the shape names. 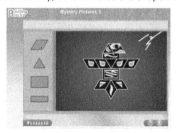

Table 8.1 (Cont.)

Age	Broad	Developmental Progression	Instructional Tasks
			Mystery Pictures 4: Children build pictures by identifying a wide variety of shapes that are *named* by the Building Blocks software program (i.e., children must know the names).

Shape Hunt (Rectangles): As above but involving rectangles.

Build Shapes/Straw Shapes: As above but involving rectangles.

Straw Shapes (Rectangles): As above but involving rectangles.

Is It or Not? (Rectangles), [LT]^2: As above with rectangles or squares.

I Spy, [LT]^2: Beforehand, "seed" the classroom with Shape Set shapes and other objects (especially those with less common shapes). Name the shape of something in the room. You may wish to start with something easily recognizable, such as "square" or "triangle." Have children guess the item or shape you are thinking about. If able, have the child who guessed correctly think of the next item or shape for you and get the class to guess.

Variation: Try the properties version, in which you describe a shape's attributes and see whether children can guess which item or shape you mean. This can also be done with Shape Sets, actual objects in the room, and/or other shape manipulatives.

Rectangles and Boxes, [LT]^2: Draw a large rectangle for the entire class to see, and trace it, counting each side as you go. Challenge children to draw a rectangle in the air as you count, reminding them that each side should be straight. Show a variety of boxes to children—such as toothpaste, pasta, and cereal boxes—and discuss their shape. Eventually, focus on the faces of the boxes, which should mostly be rectangles. Talk about the sides and right angles. On large paper, place two boxes horizontally and trace their faces. Have children match the boxes to the traced rectangles. Trace more boxes and repeat.

(Continued)

Table 8.1 (Cont.)

Age	Broad	Developmental Progression	Instructional Tasks
			Help children consider other box face shapes, such as triangles (candy and food storage), octagons (hat and gift boxes), and circles/cylinders (toy and oats containers). *Name Faces of Blocks*: During circle or free-play time, children name the faces (sides) of different building blocks. Ask children which classroom items also have fronts or faces of the same shape. *Don't Burn Your Feet–Math Plus!*, [LT]^2: ("Math Plus!" activities have been enhanced to also develop executive function. See all resource at [LT]^2.) Make large shapes on the floor/ground. Tell children to step only on a certain shape class (e.g., triangles) or characteristic (e.g., three sides). Ask children how they know the shape they are stepping on is correct. *Guess My Rule (Rectangles)*, [LT]^2: Tell children to watch carefully as you sort several Shape Set shapes into piles based on a "secret rule" (some attribute). • Ask children to silently ("in your heads") guess your sorting rule, such as "circles versus squares" or "four-sided shapes versus round." • Sort shapes one at a time, continuing until there are at least two to three shapes in each of the two piles. • Signal "shhh," and pick up a new shape, holding it between the two piles. With a look of confusion, gesture to children to encourage all of them to point quietly to which pile the shape belongs. • Place the shape in its correct pile. After all shapes are sorted, ask children what they think the sorting rule is. • Repeat with other shapes and new rules.
		Side Recognizer *Parts* Identifies sides as distinct geometric objects with attributes. May say two shapes are the same by comparing many of their attributes, but not all. Asked what this shape is △, says it is a "quadrilateral" (or has four sides) after counting each, running a finger along the length of each side.	*Exploring Shapes (Sides)*, [LT]^2: Children count the sides of shapes and then identify the shape based on the number of sides. *What Shape Am I Touching (Side Recognizer)*, [LT]^2: Children feel a shape without seeing it and name the shape by counting its sides. *True or False (Side Recognizer)*, [LT]^2: Children determine whether or not figures belong to a shape category using the shapes' sides. See also on [LT]^2: *True or False? Math Plus!*, an enhanced version to also teach executive function. *Shape Parts 1*: Students use shape parts to construct a shape that matches a target shape. They must place every component exactly, so it is a skill that is actually at the "Constructor of Shapes from Parts–Exact" level, but some children can begin to benefit from such *scaffolded* computer work at this level.

(Continued)

Table 8.1 (Cont.)

Age	Broad	Developmental Progression	Instructional Tasks

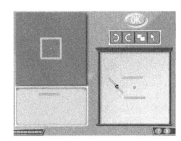

Most Attributes Comparer
Comparing Looks for differences in attributes, examining full shapes, but may ignore some spatial relationships.

"These are the same."

Corner (Vertex, Angle) Recognizer *Parts* Recognizes angles as separate geometric objects, at least in the limited context of "corners."

Asked why is this a triangle, says, "It has three angles" and counts them, pointing clearly to each vertex (point at the corner).

Feely Box (Describe): As above, but now children must describe the shape well enough without naming it that their peers can figure out the shape they are describing. Have children explain how he or she figured out which shape. They should describe the shape, emphasizing straightness of the sides and the number of sides and angles.

Explore Shapes and Angles, [LT]²: Children identify specific types of angles within shapes (e.g., right angles).
Feely Box (Describe): As above, emphasizing angles.
Shape Parts 1: As above, emphasizing angles.
True or False? Math Plus!, [LT]²: As above, emphasizing angles.
Don't Burn Your Feet–Math Plus!, [LT]²: As above, emphasizing angles.

5 | | **Shape Recognizer–More Shapes** *Classifying* Recognizes most familiar shapes and typical examples of other shapes, such as hexagon, rhombus (diamond), and trapezoid.

Correctly identifies and names all of these shapes:

Shape Step (More Shapes), [LT]²: Make shapes on the floor with masking or colored tape or chalk shapes outdoors. Tell children to step on a certain class of shapes (e.g., rhombuses) only. Have a group of five children step on the rhombuses. Ask the rest of the class to watch carefully to make sure the group steps on all the correct shapes. Whenever possible, ask children to explain why the shape they stepped on was the correct shape ("How do you know that was a rhombus?"). Repeat the activity until all groups have stepped on shapes.

Table 8.1 (Cont.)

Age	Broad	Developmental Progression	Instructional Tasks
			Mystery Pictures 4: Children build pictures by identifying a wide variety of shapes that are *named* by the Building Blocks software program (i.e., at this level, children have to know the names). This activity includes the hexagon, rhombus (diamond), and trapezoid.

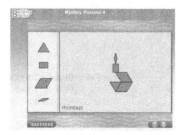

Geometry Snapshots 2: Shown a simple configuration of shapes for just 2 seconds, students match that configuration to four choices from memory (imagery). Off- or on-computer.

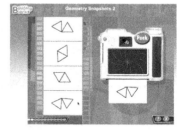

Find the Twin (More Shapes), [LT]² See above, emphasis on new shapes.
True or False (More Shapes), [LT]² See above, emphasis on new shapes.
Guess My Rule (More Shapes), [LT]²: As above, with "rules" appropriate for this level. For example: circles versus triangles versus squares (all different orientations), triangles versus rhombuses, trapezoids versus rhombuses, trapezoids versus "not

(Continued)

Table 8.1 (Cont.)

Age	Broad	Developmental Progression	Instructional Tasks
			trapezoids," hexagons versus trapezoids, triangles versus "not triangles," squares versus "not squares" (e.g., all other shapes), rectangles versus "not rectangles," rhombuses versus not "rhombuses."

6		**Shape Identifier** *Classifying* Names most common shapes, including, for example, rhombuses, hexagons, octagons, and trapezoids, without making mistakes, such as calling ovals "circles." Recognizes (at least) right angles, so distinguishes between a rectangle and a parallelogram without right angles.
		
		Correctly names all of the following shapes:
		
			Trapezoids and Rhombuses: Show pattern block shapes, one after another, having children name each one. Focus especially on the rhombus and trapezoid. Ask children what they could make with such shapes. Have children describe the properties of the shapes. A trapezoid has one pair of parallel sides (parallel–"go in the same direction"); a rhombus has two pairs of parallel sides all the same length.
			    Mr. MixUp (Shapes): Explain that children are going to help Mr. MixUp to name shapes. Remind children to stop Mr. MixUp right when he makes a mistake to correct him. Using Shape Set shapes, have Mr. MixUp start by confusing the names of a "square" and a "rhombus." After children have identified the correct names, ask them to explain how their angles are different (squares must have all right angles; rhombuses may have different angles). Review that all rhombuses and squares, which are actually a special kind of rhombus with all right angles, have four straight sides of equal length. Repeat with a trapezoid, a hexagon, and any other shapes you would like children to practice.
			    Geometry Snapshots 4: Students identify an image that matches one of four moderately complex configurations from memory (imagery).

7		**Angle Recognizer–More Contexts** *Parts* Recognizes and describe contexts in which angle knowledge is relevant, including corners (can discuss "sharper" angles), crossings (e.g., a pair of scissors), and, later, bent objects and bends (sometimes bends in paths and slopes). Only later can explicitly understand how angle concepts relate to these contexts (e.g., initially may not think of bends in roads as angles; may not be able to add horizontal or vertical to complete the angle in slope contexts; may even see corners as more or less "sharp" without representing the lines that constitute them). Often does not relate these contexts and may represent only some	*Mr. MixUp (Angles and Shapes)*, [LT][2]: As above, but this time confuse "sides" and "corners"; make sure children explain which is which. *Geometry Snapshots 6*: Students match geometric figures that differ in angle measure from memory (imagery). 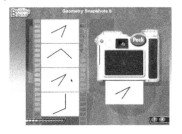

Table 8.1 (Cont.)

Age Broad	Developmental Progression	Instructional Tasks
	features of angles in each (e.g., oblique line for a ramp in a slope context).	
	Parts of Shapes Identifier *Classifying* Identifies shapes in terms of their components. "No matter how skinny it looks, that's a triangle because it has three sides and three angles." 	*What Shape Am I Touching (Parts of Shapes Identifier)*, [LT][2]: Teacher shows children a shape and asks children to name the shape and explain how they know it is that shape, emphasizing its sides and angles as defining attributes of the shapes. *Don't Burn Your Feet—Math Plus!*, [LT][2]: See above, now focusing on sides and angles.
	Congruence Superposer *Comparing* Moves and places objects on top of each other to determine congruence. Can also determine congruence by comparing all attributes and all spatial relationships. Says that two shapes are the same shape and the same size because they can be laid on top of each other. Says that two shapes are the same shape and the same size after comparing every one of their sides and angles.	*Shape Stacker (Superposer)*, [LT][2]: Children match identical shapes from the Shape Set, justifying why the shapes are congruent.

	Constructor of Shapes from Parts—Exact *Representing* Uses manipulatives representing parts of shapes, such as sides and angle "connectors," to make a shape that is completely correct, based on knowledge of components and properties—relationships between the components.
	
	Asked to make a triangle with sticks, creates
	
	△
		Warm-Up: *Snapshots and Straws (Shape Parts)*, [LT][2]: In preparation, secretly make a shape using straws, such as a rectangle, and cover it with a dark cloth. Give children a set of straws of various lengths. Tell children to look carefully and take a snapshot in their minds as you show your shape for 2 seconds, and then cover it again—immediately after—with a dark cloth. Have children build what they saw with their straws. Show your shape for 2 more seconds so children can check and change their shapes, if necessary. Then have children describe what they saw, and how they built their own. Repeat with other secret shapes, making them more complex as children's ability allows.
		    Build Shapes/Straw Shapes (Parts Exact), [LT][2]: As above, but now expecting children to represent all parts and properties correctly, as well as to make any of the shapes in the Shape Set, *or* a verbally named set of properties (e.g., make a shape that has (a) two pairs of adjacent sides the same length or (b) all four sides the same length but no right angles). Can they place pieces accurately and with little trial and error?
		    Give other challenges, such as: "Can you make a triangle with any three of these straws (lengths)?" (No, not if one straw is longer than the sum of the lengths of the other two.) "How many different shapes (classes) can you make with two pairs of straws the same length?"
		    Pentomino Symmetry Games, [LT][2]:
		    Children take turns to challenge each other to complete symmetrical puzzles/designs across a line of symmetry using pentominoes.

(Continued)

Table 8.1 (Cont.)

Age	Broad	Developmental Progression	Instructional Tasks
			Shape Parts 2: Students use shape parts to construct a shape that matches a target shape. They must place every component exactly. 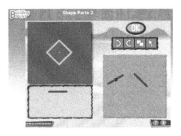
8+		**Angle Representer** *Parts* Represents various angle contexts as two lines, explicitly including the reference line (horizontal or vertical for slope; a "line of sight" for turn contexts) and, at least implicitly, the size of the angle as the rotation between these lines (may still maintain misconceptions about angle measure, such as relating angle size to the length of side's distance between endpoints, and may not apply these understandings to multiple contexts).	*Logo*: See Logo examples and suggestions in this and the previous chapter. *As the World Turns*, [LT]²: Have students estimate, then measure, draw, and label different real-world angle measures, such as a door opening, a radio control turning, a doorknob, head turning, turning a faucet on, and so forth. *Make me Double*, [LT]²: Children represent a larger angle out of straws by combining two smaller angles.
		Congruence Representer *Comparing* Refers to geometric properties and explains with transformations. "These must be 'congruent,' because they have equal sides, all square corners, and I can move them on top of each other exactly."	*Find My Pair*, [LT]²: Children have to prove that two shapes are the exact same size and shape.
	Property Thinker	**Shape Class Identifier** *Classifying* Uses class membership (e.g., to sort), not explicitly based on properties. "I put the triangles over here, and the quadrilaterals, including squares, rectangles, rhombuses, and trapezoids, over there."	*Guess My Rule (Shape Class Identifier)*, [LT]²: As above, with "rules" appropriate for this level, including all classes of shapes. *Shape Step (Classes)*, [LT]²: As above, with students told a shape class rather than a shape name (e.g., "All the rhombuses"—including squares!). Ask children to justify that the shape they selected is a member of that class. *Don't Burn Your Feet—Math Plus!*, [LT]²: See above.
		Shape Property Identifier *Classifying* Uses properties explicitly. Can see the invariants in the changes of state or shape but maintaining the shapes' properties. "I put the shapes with opposite sides parallel over here, and those with four sides but not both pairs of sides parallel over there."	*Shape Step (Properties)*, [LT]²: As above, with students told a property rather than a shape name (e.g., "All the shapes with all sides the same length" or "...at least one right angle"). Ask children to justify that the shape they selected has that property. *Guess My Rule (Shape Property Identifier)*, [LT]²: As above, with "rules" appropriate for this level, such as "has a right angles versus has no right angle," "regular polygons (closed shapes with all straight sides) versus any other shapes," or "symmetrical versus non-symmetrical shapes," etc.

(Continued)

Table 8.1 (Cont.)

Age	Broad	Developmental Progression	Instructional Tasks

I Spy (Property Identifier), [LT][2]: As above, but giving properties such as "I spy a shape with four sides and with opposite sides the same length, but no right angles."

What Shape Am I Touching (Shape Property Identifier), [LT][2]: Children identify shapes, even those with the same number of sides, through touch alone by figuring out all their properties (right angles, equal length sides, etc.).

Legends of the Lost Shape: Students identify target shapes using textual clues provided, such as having certain angle sizes.

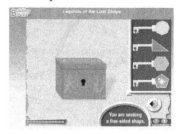

Property Class Identifier *Classifying* Uses class membership for shapes (e.g., to sort or consider shapes "similar") explicitly based on properties, including angle measure. Is aware of restrictions of transformations and also of the definitions and can integrate the two. Sorts hierarchically, based on properties.

"I put the 'equilateral triangles' over here, and 'scalene triangles' over here. The 'isosceles triangles' are all these ... they included the equilaterals."

Mr. MixUp (Property Class Identifier), [LT][2]: As above, but focus on class memberships and defining properties (e.g., Mr. MixUp says that "a rectangle has two pairs of equal and parallel sides, but [*erroneously*] could not be a parallelogram because it's a rectangle").

Which Shape Could It Be?, [LT][2]: Slowly reveal a shape from behind a screen. At each "step," ask children what class of shape it could be and how certain they are.

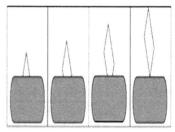

Shape Parts 3: Students use shape parts to construct a shape that matches a target shape, which is rotated, so the construction is at a different orientation. They must place every component exactly. Depending on the problem and the way it is approached, these activities can be useful at several levels.

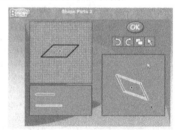

Shape Parts 4: As above, but with multiple embedded shapes.

Table 8.1 (Cont.)

Age	Broad	Developmental Progression	Instructional Tasks

Shape Parts 5: As above, but no model is provided.

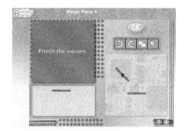

Angle Synthesizer *Parts* Combines various meanings of angle (turn, corner, slant), including angle measure.

"This ramp is at a 45° angle to the ground."

Straw Angles, [LT][2]: Ask children to make angles out of pipe cleaners and straws that have specific measures.

Shape Parts 6: As above, but the student must use sides and angles (manipulable "corners").

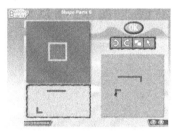

Shape Parts 7: As above, but with more properties/problem solving involved.

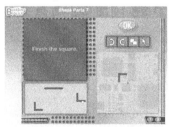

(Continued)

Table 8.1 (Cont.)

Age	Broad	Developmental Progression	Instructional Tasks

Logo: Using the Logo turtle to draw challenging shapes, such as creating an isosceles triangle in *Turtle Math* (Clements & Meredith, 1994).

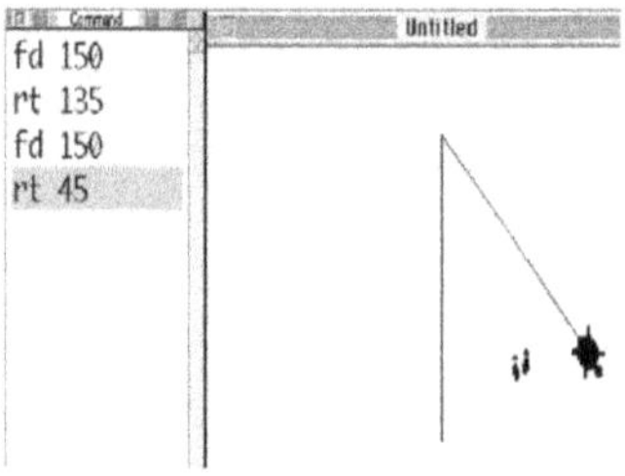

```
fd 150
rt 135
fd 150
rt 45
```

Box 8.1 2D Shapes

∠ *Angle*: Two lines that meet at a point, the vertex.

○ *Circle*: A two-dimensional figure that consists of all points a fixed distance from a point called its center. Circles are "perfectly round"; that is, they have a constant curvature.

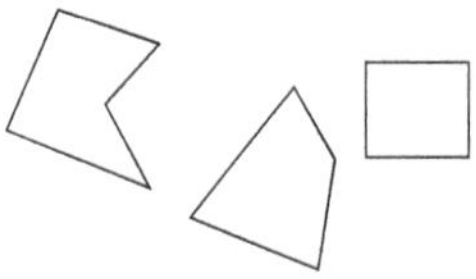

Closed: A two-dimensional figure is closed when it is made up of several line segments that are joined together; exactly two sides meet at every vertex, and no sides cross each other. (Similarly for curved figures.)

Congruent: Exactly alike in shape and size, so they can be superposed ("placed on each other" so they match).

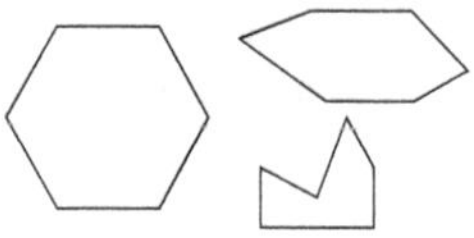

Hexagon: A polygon with six straight sides.

Kite: A four-sided polygon (quadrilateral) with two pairs of *adjacent* (touching) sides, each of which are the same length.

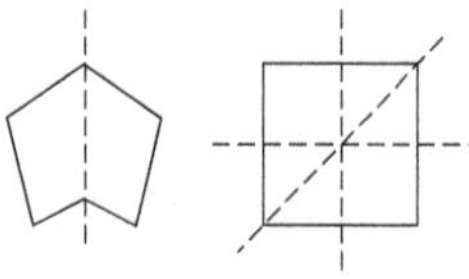

Line symmetry: Plane figures have line, or mirror, symmetry when their shape is reversed on opposite sides of a line. If the plane is folded at the line, the figures will be superposed.

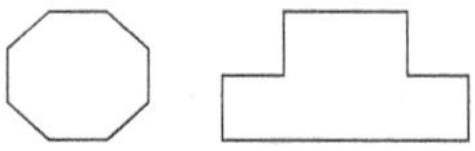

Octagon: A polygon with eight straight sides.

Orientation: How a figure is turned compared to a reference line.

Parallel lines: Lines that have the same orientation and remain the same distance apart (like railroad tracks).

Parallelograms: Quadrilaterals with two pairs of opposite parallel sides.

Pentagons: Polygons with five straight sides.

Plane: A flat surface.

Polygon: A closed plane figure bounded by three or more straight sides.

Quadrilateral: A polygon with four straight sides.

Rectangle: A polygon with four straight sides (i.e., a quadrilateral) and four right angles. As with all parallelograms, a rectangle's opposite sides are parallel and the same length.

Rhombus: A quadrilateral with four straight sides that are all the same length.

Right angle: Two lines that are perpendicular; that is, that meet like a corner of a typical doorway. Often informally called "square corner," right angles measure 90 degrees.

Rotational symmetry: A figure has rotational symmetry when it can be turned less than a full turn to fit on itself exactly.

Shape: Informal name for a geometric, two- or three-dimensional figure made up of points, lines, or planes.

Square: A quadrilateral that has four equal straight sides and all right angles. A square is both a special kind of rectangle and a special kind of rhombus.

Trapezoid: A quadrilateral with one pair of parallel sides. (Some insist trapezoids have *only* one pair of parallel sides; that is how they are categorized in Figure 8.2a. Others say they have to have *at least* one pair, which would then make all parallelograms a subset of the trapezoids.)

Triangle: A polygon with three sides.

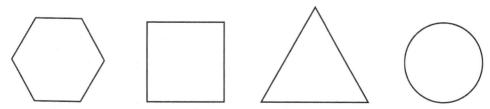

Figure 8.3 Exemplars of 2D figures that are closed and are symmetric, preferred by most people

So, children tend only to see only typical forms of each shape—what we will call *exemplars* (the shapes in Figure 8.3 are exemplars for each of four classes of shapes). They do not frequently see and discuss other members of the shape class, what we will call *variants*. *Nonexamples*—usually called *distractors* in assessments or instruction—are not members of that shape class. They are called *palpable distractors* if they have little or no *overall resemblance* to the exemplars and *difficult distractors* (for the children, we call them *foolers*) if they are highly visually similar to exemplars but lack at least one defining attribute. Figure 8.4 illustrates these for triangles.

One study found that at 25 months of age, children knew few shape names even of exemplars (Verdine, Lucca, Golinkoff, Newcombe, & Hirsh-Pasek, 2016). By 30 months, they had learned more shape names and were even correctly naming some variants.

A study of young children used the same line drawings previously used with elementary students for comparison purposes (Clements et al., 1999b); replication studies were conducted in Singapore (Yin, 2003) and Turkey (Aslan, 2004) and a similar study of preschoolers in Serbia (Maričić & Stamatović, 2017). What did we learn about visual prototypes and ideas young children form about common shapes?

Circles—which only have one basic prototype, because they can only vary in size—are the easiest shape for children to identify. From 92% of 4-year-olds to 99% of 6-year-olds accurately identified circles as those shown in Figure 8.5 (Clements et al., 1999b). Only a few of the youngest children chose the ellipse and another curved shape (shapes 10 and 11). Most children described circles as "round," if they described them at all. Thus, the circle was easily recognized but relatively difficult to describe for these children. They matched the shapes to a visual prototype. In a replication study, Turkish children showed the same pattern of responses (Aslan, 2004, Aktas-Arnas & Aslan, 2004; Aslan & Aktas-Arnas, 2007).

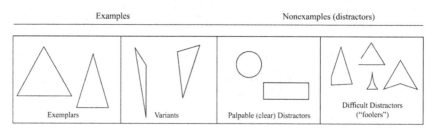

Figure 8.4 Exemplars, variants, palpable distractors, and difficult distractors for triangles

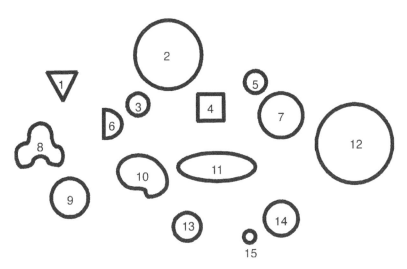

Figure 8.5 Students are to mark circles

Children also identified squares fairly well: 82%, 86%, and 91% for 4-, 5-, and 6-year-olds, respectively. Younger children tended to mistakenly choose non-square rhombi ("diamonds" such as shape 3 in Figure 8.6), 25% of 6-year-olds and 5% of 7-year-olds did so in Singapore. However, U.S. children were no less accurate in classifying squares without horizontal sides (shapes 5 and 11). This confusion—that turning a shape changes its name—can last until age 8 if not well addressed educationally. In Singapore, 7-year-olds were less likely to correctly identify

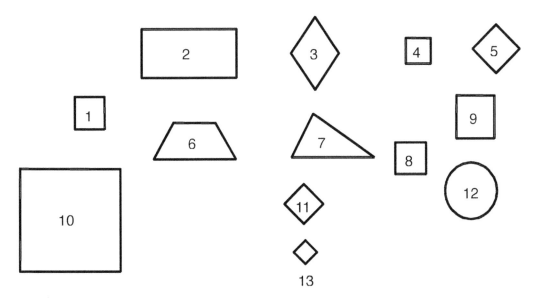

Figure 8.6 Students are to mark squares (adapted from Razel & Eylon, 1991)

these as squares than were 6-year-olds (Yin, 2003). Children in Serbia knew circles well, but squares less well (57%, Maričić & Stamatović, 2017). Children in all three countries were more likely to be accurate in their square identification when their justifications for selection were based on the shape's defining attributes. Children from Turkey did not give any property-based justifications until age 4; 41% did so by the age of 6 years (Aslan, 2004). Further, when children *did* use properties, they were correct most of the time (compare 70% correctness for visual responses to 91% for property responses). Children in Serbia knew circles well, but *not* squares (57%, Maričić & Stamatović, 2017).

   Children are less likely misled by orientation (the way a shape is "turned") when manipulatives are used, or when they walk around large shapes placed on the floor. Children are more likely to be accurate when their justifications for selection were based on the shape's defining attributes, such as the number and length of the sides.

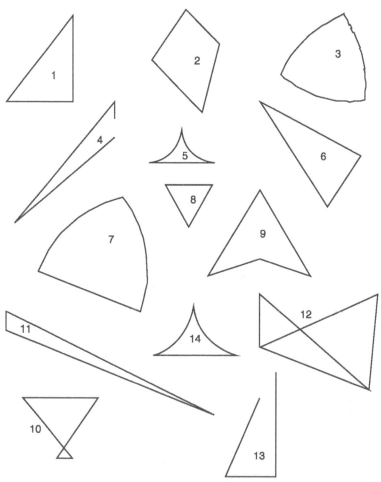

Figure 8.7 Student marks triangles (adapted from Burger & Shaughnessy, 1986,; Clements & Battista, 1991)

Children were less accurate at recognizing triangles and rectangles. However, their scores were not low; about 60% correct for triangles (Figure 8.7, but a bit better in Turkey and Serbia, where children identified these shapes only slightly less accurately, 68% and 78%, Aslan, 2004; Maričić & Stamatović, 2017). Across the years from 4 to 6, children go through a phase in which they accept many shapes as triangles, then another in which they "tighten" their criteria to reject some distractors but also some examples. The children's visual prototype seems to be of an isosceles triangle. Especially when not exposed to high-quality geometry education, they are misled by lack of symmetry or an aspect ratio—the ratio of height to base—not near one (e.g., a "long, skinny" triangle, such as shape 11).

Young children tended to accept "long" parallelograms or right trapezoids (shapes 3, 6, 10, and 14 in Figure 8.8) as rectangles. Thus, children's visual prototype of a rectangle is a four-sided figure with two long parallel sides and "close to" square corners.

Figure 8.8 Students are to mark rectangles (adapted from Burger & Shaughnessy, 1986; Clements & Battista, 1991)

Only a few children correctly identified the squares (shapes 2 and 7 in Figure 8.8) as rect-angles. Because they have all the properties of rectangles, these squares should be chosen. This is upsetting to many adults who have never been provided good geometry instruction themselves. But it is a good opportunity to encourage children to think *mathematically* and *logically*—even when the wider culture does not.

Although young children both in our study and those in the international studies were less accurate at recognizing triangles and rectangles, their performance shows considerable know-ledge, especially given the abstract nature of the test and the variety of shapes employed. Depressingly, they learn very little from these early years to sixth grade.

In their play, children showed interest and involvement with "pattern and shape" more fre-quently than any of the six other categories (Seo & Ginsburg, 2004). About 47% of these behaviors involved recognizing, sorting, or naming shapes. Finally, children do far more than just name shapes; they are an important part of much of children's play. Of course, that play involves three-dimensional (3D) shapes.

3D Figures

Babies only 1 or 2 days old can maintain object size despite changes in distance (and thus change in size of the retinal image, Slater, Mattock, & Brown, 1990). That is, they habituate in looking at a sphere of constant size that changes in distance from the new-born, but not when both this distance and the size of the sphere is changed so that the sphere fills the same angle on the retina (Granrud, 1987). In addition, infants can perceive 3D shapes, however, this is limited to continuously moving objects, rather than single or even multiple static views of the same object (Humphrey & Humphrey, 1995).

As with 2D figures, older children do not perform well in school-based tasks involving three-dimensional shapes, even into the intermediate grades (Carpenter, Coburn, Reys, & Wilson, 1976). South African first graders used different names for solids (such as "square" for cube) (Nieuwoudt & van Niekerk, 1997). U.S. students' reasoning about solids was much like that they used for plane figures; they referred to a variety of characteristics, such as "pointiness" and comparative size or slenderness (Lehrer et al., 1998b). Students also treated the solid wooden figures as malleable, suggesting that the rectangular prism could be transformed into a cube by "sitting on it." They use names for 2D shapes, probably indicating that they do not explicitly distinguish between two and three dimensions (Carpenter et al., 1976). Learning only plane fig-ures in textbooks during the early primary grades may cause some initial difficulty in learning about solids. Serbian children's most developed concepts are the cube (83%) and the sphere (76%); only 17% of children can recognize and name the rectangular prism (Maričić & Stamato-vić, 2017).

Two related studies asked children to match solids with their nets (a "pattern" or arrange-ment of 2D shapes that "fold up into" the 3D shape). Kindergartners had reasonable success when the solids and nets both were made from the same interlocking materials (Leeson, 1995). An advanced kindergartner had more difficulty with drawings of the nets (Leeson, Stewart, & Wright, 1997), possibly because he was unable to visualize the relationship with the more abstract materials.

The Mathematics of 3D Shapes

Definitions Related to Shapes. As with 2D shapes, the following definitions of 3D shapes are intended to help teachers both understand young children's development of specific math concepts and talk to them about these concepts. They are not formal math definitions, but, rather, simple descriptions mixing math and everyday vocabulary.

Box 8.2 3D Shapes

Cone: A 3D shape with one circular base (actually a *circular cone* because other curved shapes are possible bases) that is connected to a single point, the *vertex* that lies over the base, creating a curved surface.

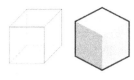

Cube: A special type of right prism whose faces are all squares.

Cylinder: A 3D shape that has two identical (congruent) parallel bases that are circles (or other shapes, usually curved) connected by a curved surface. (Most cylinders we deal with are right cylinders, but, as with prisms, they can be oblique.)

Prism: A 3D shape that has two identical (congruent) parallel bases that are polygons (2D shapes with straight sides), with corresponding sides of the bases connected with rectangles (these are *right prisms*, if connected with non-rectangular parallelograms, it is an *oblique prism*).

Pyramid: A 3D shape that has one base that is a polygon that is connected to a single point, the *vertex* that lies over the base, with triangles.

Sphere: A 3D shape that is a "perfectly round ball"; that is, all the points are at a fixed distance from a point called its center.

Congruence, Symmetry, and Transformations

Young children develop beginning ideas not just about shapes but also about symmetry, congruence, and transformations. As we saw, even infants are sensitive to at least some symmetric figures. Pre-schoolers often use and refer to rotational ⬠ ⬠ ⬠ ⬠ symmetry as much as they do line, or mirror ⬠⋯⬠, symmetry in working with pattern blocks, such as remarking that an equilateral triangle was "special, because when you turn it a little it fits back on itself" (Sarama, Clements, & Vukelic, 1996). They also produce symmetry in their play (Seo & Ginsburg, 2004). For example, preschooler Jose puts a double unit block on the rug, two unit blocks on the double unit block, and a triangle unit on the middle, building a symmetrical structure.

Many young children judge congruence (same shape, same size) based on whether they are, overall, more similar than different. However, children younger than kindergarten may not do an exhaustive comparison and may consider rotated shapes as "different." Until about 7 years of age, students may not attend to the spatial relationships of all the parts of complex figures. Not until later, at age 11, do most children perform as adults.

With guidance, however, even 4-year-olds and some younger children can generate strategies for verifying congruence for some tasks. They gradually develop a greater awareness of the type of differences between figures that are geometrically relevant and move from considering only some of the shapes' parts to considering the spatial relationships of these parts. In about first grade (sooner if well taught!), they begin to use superposition—moving one shape on top of another to see if it fits exactly.

In summary, teaching both shape recognition and transformations may be important to children's math development (see an extended and illuminating discussion in Howe, 2018). Traditional teaching of separate categories of "squares" and "rectangles" may underlie children's difficulties in relating these shape classes and their attributes. As an example, using a different transformation, increasing the shorter dimension of a rectangle bit by bit may allow children to develop dynamic intuition that a square may thus be produced.

Music and Geometry

Many people have conjectured that there is a relationship between music and math, but the evidence is scarce. One study, however, showed that intensive music training is associated with improved performance in geometry, such as detecting geometric properties and relating distance to numerical magnitudes (Spelke, 2008).

Experience and Education

> A toddler, 22 months old, puts a square peg into a square hole (Örnkloo & von Hofsten, 2007b). What does she know of shapes? What more will she learn in preschool and elementary school? What might she learn?

Is there time for spatial topics such as geometry and measurement when there is so much pressure to ensure children know number and arithmetic? Yes, for several reasons. First, the Common Core and other standards clearly indicate that geometry and measurement are essential math topics. Second, research is clear that engaging children in these spatial topics does not hurt other topics (Gavin, Casa, Adelson, & Firmender, 2013), but actually supports the learning of number and arithmetic (Sarama & Clements, 2009c, see also Chapter 7). We must do more: In many countries, from the U.S. to Poland (Klim-Klimaszewska & Nazaruk, 2017), there is little high-quality instruction in geometry in early childhood classrooms.

Shapes: 2D

Experiences and instruction play a large role in shaping children's knowledge of geometry. If they lack experience of shapes, and if the examples and nonexamples of shapes they do experience are rigid, not including a variety of variants of that shape class, children's mental images and ideas about that shape will also be rigid and limited. For example, many children learn to accept only isosceles triangles with a horizontal base as triangles, such as the "exemplars" in Figure 8.4. Others learn richer concepts, even at a young age; for example, one of the youngest 3-year-olds scored higher than every 6-year-old on the shape recognition tasks discussed previously.

This is important. *Children's ideas stabilize as early as 6 years of age* (Gagatsis & Patronis, 1990; Hannibal & Clements, 2010). So, *we must provide better, richer opportunities to learn about geometric figures* to all children between 3 and 6 years of age.

Directing attention to shapes and providing language are important for children of all ages, from infants and toddlers up. Their experiences can be so much richer than usual. In parents' everyday speech, shape names are only about 1/10 of 1% of words (Verdine et al., 2016)! This is a problem, considering they are sensitive to shape from their first year. Recall the treasure baskets from Chapter 7 (p. 173). Fill the baskets with those materials, all sizes and shapes of balls (Wait! Different shapes? Aren't balls all spheres? Mostly ... except for footballs and some leather balls, Leavy et al., 2018b), or new materials with very different 3D shapes and sizes for grasping, mouthing, dropping, rolling, and so forth.

Make all such experiments mathematical (Kinnear & Wittmann, 2018). Read shape books for the very young (e.g., Lin, 2020a), but *not those that mis-teach shapes* (Nurnberger-Haag, 2016)! In geometry as in other areas, all teachers need to use nuanced and adequate math language. For instance, teachers of toddlers can observe what a child is interested in and then introduce *variability* and *comparisons* of shapes.

As an example, read the following interaction between the teacher interested in promoting mathematics thinking and a toddler (Björklund, 2012). A 2-year-old toddler, Albin, is sorting blocks and balls.

Annette:	That's very nice, how many do you have, Albin?
Albin:	This many. (*Continues sorting.*)
Annette:	Shall we count? How many are there? I will help you count, what do we start with? One, and then two and then three (*pointing to one ball at a time*).
Albin:	No (*looks in another direction*).

(p. 223)

Noting the lack of interest in counting, the teacher quickly changes focus from number to other math concepts.

Annette: What do you call these? (*Points at one of two larger oval blocks.*)
Albin: ... A barrel.
Annette: Yes, it looks like a barrel ... you think there are any more barrels?
Albin: Yes (*puts the yellow block in another cup*).
Annette: Shall we look for some?
Albin: (*Rapidly picking up a black ball*): Black!
Annette: Black; is it a barrel, that one?
Albin: No, round (*shows it to Annette*). Ball.
Annette: Are there any more funny barrels?
Albin: (*Looks intensely into the box with blocks and balls and picks up a small block*): Here is one.

(p. 224)

The teacher found what the child was interested in and engaged the child in comparing shapes.

Of course, it is always important to get the language straight. "Straight" for example, means a line or path with no bends or turns, but informally, it can mean many things, including being exactly vertical or horizontal. As another example, many 4-year-olds say that they know triangles have "three points and three sides" (Clements et al., 1999b). Half of these children, however, were not sure what a "point" or "side" was! As with the number word sequence, the English language presents more challenges than others, such as East Asian languages. For example, in those languages, every "quadrilateral" is called simply "four-sided-shape." An acute angle is simply a "sharp angle." Those teaching in English or Spanish need rich discussions to bring these meanings to the fore. Language is more important to geometry than it is to the learning of most other math topics (Vukovic & Lesaux, 2013).

Further, although appearances usually dominate children's decisions, they are also learning and sometimes using verbal knowledge. Using such verbal knowledge accurately takes time and can initially appear as a step backward. Children may initially say a square has "four sides the same and four points." Because they have yet to learn about perpendicularity, some accept any rhombus as a square. Their own description convinces them even though they feel conflicted about the "look" of this "new square." With guidance, however, this conflict can eventually be beneficial, as they resolve it and build a firmer understanding of the properties of squares—that they *also* need four right angles.

So, *provide varied examples and nonexamples to help children understand attributes of shapes that are mathematically relevant as well as those (orientation, size) that are not.* Include "difficult distractors" of shapes such as triangles (e.g., Figure 8.4) and rectangles. *Discuss categories of shapes and what attributes each has.*

Doing this, you will be a welcome exception. U.S. educational practice usually does not reflect these recommendations. Children often know as much about shapes entering school as their geometry curriculum "teaches" them in the early grades. This is due to teachers and curriculum writers' assumptions that children in early childhood classrooms have little or no knowledge of geometric figures. Further, teachers have had few experiences with geometry in their own education. Thus, it is unsurprising that most classrooms exhibit limited geometry instruction. One early study found that kindergarten children had a great deal of knowledge about shapes and matching shapes before instruction began. Their teacher tended to elicit and verify this prior knowledge but did not add any content or develop new knowledge. That is, about two-thirds of the interactions had children repeat what they already knew in a repetitious format as in the following exchange:

Teacher:	Could you tell us what type of shape that is?
Children:	A square.
Teacher:	Okay. It's a square. (Thomas, 1982)

Even worse, when they did say something, teachers often make incorrect statements saying, for example, that every time you put two triangles together you get a square (Thomas, 1982). Instruction does not improve in the primary grades. Children actually *stop* counting the sides and angles of shapes to differentiate one from another vertices (Lehrer et al., 1998b). *Avoid these common poor practices.* Learn more about geometry and challenge children to learn more every year.

Families and the wider culture often do not promote geometry learning either. On a geometry assessment, 4-year-olds from America scored 55% compared to those from China who scored 84% (Starkey et al., 1999b). Recall the story about the two triangles (Figure 8.1) at the beginning of this chapter. This example illustrates the research finding on "concept images" that shows that certain visual prototypes can rule children's thinking. That is, even when they know a definition, children's ideas of shapes are dominated by mental images of a "typical" shape.

To help children develop accurate, rich concept images, provide experiences of many different examples of a type of shape. For example, Figure 8.9a ("examples") shows a rich variety of triangles that would be sure to generate discussion. Show nonexamples that, when compared to similar examples, help focus attention on the critical attributes. For example, the nonexamples in Figure 8.9b are close to the examples to their left, differing in just one attribute (can you name each attribute?). Use such comparisons to focus on each defining attribute of a triangle.

Mary Elaine Spitler's study of Building Blocks reveals that children felt quite *powerful* knowing and using definitions of triangles (Sarama & Clements, 2003). One preschooler said of the second figure from the top in Figure 8.9a, "That's not a triangle! It's too skinny!" But his Building Blocks friend responded, "I'm telling you, it *is* a triangle. It's got three straight sides, see? One, two, three! It doesn't matter that I made it skinny." Similar studies around the world confirm that children can learn much more than most people assume about geometry—at earlier ages.

Primary-grade children can extend these competencies, such as writing their solutions to challenging geometry problems. For example, they could be asked to determine whether four

Triangles

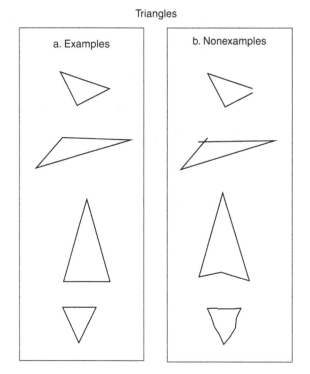

Figure 8.9 (a) Examples and matched (b) nonexamples of triangles

3-foot by 6-foot sleeping bags would fit inside a tent with floor space measuring 8 feet by 10 feet and explain why (Gavin et al., 2013). One second grader wrote, "... you can fit three but there is more sq. ft. left over enough to equal 18 just it wasn't a 3 × 6 it was a 9 × 2" (p. 484).

Second graders also might explore relationships among 2D and 3D shapes beyond identifying the shape of the faces of solids. As an example, they could write a paragraph comparing a square to a cube. As another example, they could build 3D shapes from two-dimensional shapes and study perspective by viewing 3D shapes from different positions and then drawing 2D representations (Gavin et al., 2013). Such drawing contributes to children's geometric learning—they learn new concepts, such as distinctions of 2D and 3D shapes, *while* drawing (Thom & McGarvey, 2015).

Seven Guiding Features of High-quality Teaching of Shapes

Summarizing, children can learn richer concepts about shape if their educational environment includes seven features.

First, ensure that children experience many different examples of a type of shape, so that they do not form narrow ideas about any class of shapes. *Use examplars* to bootstrap initial learning, and don't use common objects because they already have labels for them—use clear drawings or manipulatives. *However, examples should become more diverse as soon as possible.* Showing nonexamples and comparing them to similar examples helps focus children's attention on the critical attributes of shapes and prompts discussion. This is especially important for classes that have more diverse examples, such as triangles. See the illustration of the Building Blocks "Shape Set" in Figure 8.10 for an example of the variety of shapes children might explore.

Second, encourage children's descriptions while encouraging the development of language. Visual (prototype-based) descriptions should, of course, be expected and accepted, but attribute and property responses should also be encouraged (Clements et al., 2018a). They may initially appear spontaneously for shapes with stronger and fewer prototypes (e.g., circle, square). Again, they should be especially encouraged for shape categories such as triangles. Children can learn to explain why a shape belongs to a certain category—"It has three straight sides and is closed" or does not belong ("The sides aren't straight!"). Eventually, they can internalize such arguments; for example, saying, "It is a weird, long, triangle, but it has three straight sides and is closed!" Reading high-quality children's books on shapes can be fun and helpful (Flevares & Schiff, 2014). See the [LT]² Resource section for recommendations. If

Figure 8.10 Building Blocks' "Shape Set." Having two copies of each separate manipulable shape (each in two colors) allows children to explore, match, sort, analyze, and compose a rich variety of geometric figures

books make geometric mistakes, as they often do, children *love* to be "shape detectives," finding those mistakes!

Third, along with language, encourage *active processing*–feeling, gesturing (Elia, 2018c), and building.

Fourth, include a wide variety of shape *classes*. Early childhood curricula traditionally introduce shapes in four categories (in U.S. culture, considered "basic" shapes): circle, square, triangle, and rectangle. The idea that a square is not a rectangle is rooted by age 5. We suggest presenting many examples of squares and rectangles, varying orientation, size, and so forth, *including squares as examples of rectangles*. If children say, "That's a square," teachers might respond that it is a square, which is a special type of rectangle, and they might try double-naming ("It's a square-rectangle"). Older children can discuss "general" categories, such as quadrilaterals and triangles, counting the sides of various figures to choose their category.

Also, teachers might encourage them to describe why a figure belongs or does not belong to a shape category. Then, teachers can say that because a triangle has all equal sides, it is a special type of triangle, called an equilateral triangle. Children might also "test" right angles on rectangles with a "right-angle checker," (thumb and index finger held apart at 90°, or a corner of a piece of paper). Further, children should experiment with and describe a wider variety of shapes, including but not limited to semicircles, quadrilaterals, trapezoids, rhombi, and hexagons.

Use computer environments to engage and develop children's thinking about relationships between classes of shapes, including squares and rectangles. In one large study (Clements et al., 2001), some kindergartners formed their own concept (e.g., "It's a square rectangle") in response to their work with Logo. Many other models are possible such as software that presents the properties of "shape families" (Zaranis, 2018) or allows children to explore geometric motions (Seloraji & Eu, 2017). One "social assistive robot" engages children in geometric thinking through interactive play (Keren & Fridin, 2014). The visual and dynamic possibilities of computers makes them ideal for geometric explorations (see also Chapters 7, 9, and 16).

Fifth, challenge children with a broad array of interesting tasks. Experience with manipulatives and computer environments are often supported by research, if the experiences are consistent with the implications just drawn. Activities that promote reflection and discussion might include building models of shapes from components. Matching, identifying, exploring, and even making shapes with computers is particularly motivating (Clements & Sarama, 2003b, 2003c). Work with Logo's "turtle graphics" is accessible even to kindergartners (Clements et al., 2001), with results indicating significant benefits for that age group (e.g., more than older children, they benefited in learning about squares and rectangles). See Figure 8.11.

Sixth, use playful approaches and guided discovery teaching strategies. In a study comparing direct instruction, free play, and guided play, children learned more about geometry and shapes with guided play, where the teacher followed the children's lead and scaffolded the interaction (Fisher, Hirsh-Pasek, Golinkoff, & Newcombe, 2013). For example, a teacher observing children building a tower might ask, "What shapes do you have?" "Squares. See?" "What makes that a square?" and a bit later, "I wonder if it's possible to make a bigger square using the pieces you are holding up" (Hassinger-Das, Hirsh-Pasek, & Golinkoff, 2017).

Seventh, *teaching geometric reasoning too*. Geometry is a fruitful area for justification and reasoning (as research has shown). Consider the *Guess My Rule* activity ([LT]²). A teacher

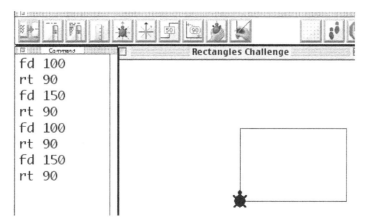

Figure 8.11 Using the Logo turtle to draw a rectangle in *Turtle Math* (Clements & Meredith, 1994)

(later, a child!) sorts about three shapes into each of two categories according to a secret rule (e.g., triangles vs. rectangles) in Figure 8.12, then ask children to silently identify, by pointing, how each additional shape should be sorted. Once most of the children are pointing correctly, the teacher asks them to think-pair-share to describe the rule.

This game starts simple, but shows its power for teaching math concepts *and* math practices (making and justifying conjectures) *and* executive function (cognitive flexibility, see Chapter 14). Because frequently children will think they guessed the sorting rule (e.g., rectangles vs. triangles) but then *the teacher puts a hexagon with the triangles.* **Now** what is the rule? Rectangles vs. non-rectangles? Or shapes with right angles vs. those without right angles. You have to "give up" on your first idea and see the next few shapes to make a new conjecture.

Eventually, the teacher may challenge children with a non-silent version of the game that include rules and shapes that are at the "intersection" of the two categories. For example, "All equal sides" and "All right angles" (Figure 8.13a). Then she holds up ... a square ... That goes in the *intersection* of the two, necessitating a new Venn diagram (Figure 8.13b).

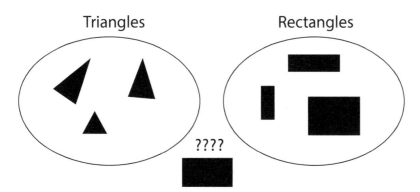

Figure 8.12 "Guess My Rule" with a very simple, starting rule

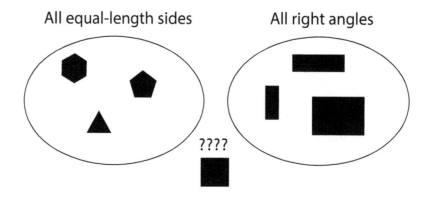

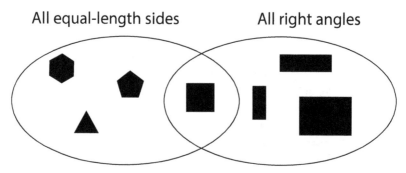

Figure 8.13a, 8.13b "Guess My Rule" with a new rule (a) and a challenging situation (b)

Shapes: 3D

Play and other activities with blocks is beneficial for many reasons. For geometric learning and to make the play more interesting and productive overall, mathematize children's play. Engage children in fruitful discussions of blocks and other solids, using specific terminology for solids, faces (including 2D shape names for them, of course), and edges for individual blocks, as well as terms for the overall structure, such as symmetry and horizontal, vertical, and oblique for the surfaces. Much more is known about building with blocks and other 3D shapes (see Chapter 9).

Exploring the attributes of 3D shapes can build spatial skills. Children should explore solids, feeling them and checking which would stack, slide, or roll and *why*. They should cut out and build 3D shapes from 2D nets. In the study, the group that used manipulatives or multimedia scored higher than those who didn't use either and the highest-performing group used both multimedia and manipulatives (Thompson, 2012).

Geometric Motions, Congruence, and Symmetry

Encouraging children to perform and discuss geometric motions improves their spatial skills. Computers are especially helpful, as the screen tools make motions more explicit. Exploratory environments can engage young children in investigations of symmetry (Chorney & Sinclair, 2018). Use computer environments to help children learn congruence and symmetry (Clements et al., 2001). There is undeveloped potential in generating curricula that seriously consider children's intuitions, preference, and interest in symmetry (Howe, 2018). Children's painting and constructions can be used as models in introducing symmetry, including 2D creations of painting, drawing, and collage, and 3D creations of clay and blocks.

Angle, Parallelism, and Perpendicularity

Angles are critical but often are not learned or taught well. Children have many varied and often incorrect ideas about what angles are. To understand angles, children must discriminate angles as critical parts of geometric figures, compare and match angles, and construct and mentally represent the idea of turns, integrating this with angle measure. These processes can begin in early childhood; for example, 5-year-olds can match angles. The long developmental process of learning about turns and angles can begin informally in early and elementary classrooms, as children deal with corners of figures, comparing angle size, and turns.

Computer-based shape manipulation and navigation environments can help mathematize these experiences. Especially important is understanding how turning one's body relates to turning shapes and turning along paths in navigation and learning to use numbers to quantify these turn and angle situations. For example, even 4-year-olds learn to click on a shape to turn it and say, "I need to turn it three times!" (Sarama, 2004, and Chapter 12).

Mitchelmore and his colleagues (Mitchelmore, 1993; Mitchelmore & White, 1998) have proposed the following sequence of tasks. Begin by providing practical experiences with angles in various contexts, including corners, bends, turns, openings, and slopes. The first examples for each should have two "arms of the angle" physically present, such as in scissors, road junctions, a corner of a table. Corners are the most salient for children and should be emphasized first. The other physical models can follow. Experience with bending (e.g., a chenille stick, aka "pipe cleaner") and turning (e.g., doorknobs, dials, doors) would be introduced last in this early phase.

Then help children understand the angular relationships in each context by discussing the common features of similar contexts, such as bends in lines or in paths on maps. Later, help students bridge the different contexts by representing the common features of angles in each context. For example, they can be represented by two line segments (or rays) with a common endpoint. Once turns are understood, use the dynamic notion of turning to begin measuring the size of the angles.

The Spirit of Math—A Final Logo Example

High-quality implementations of Logo experiences places as much emphasis on the spirit of math—exploration, investigation, critical thinking, and problem solving—as it does on geometric ideas. Consider first grader Andrew (Clements et al., 2001). At the final interview, he was quite sure of himself. When asked to explain something he thought clearly evident, Andrew would always preface his remarks with an emphatic, "Look!" On one item, he was asked, "Pretend you are talking on the telephone to someone who has never seen a triangle. What would you tell this person to help them make a triangle?"

Andrew:	I'd ask, "Have you seen a diamond?"
Interviewer:	Let's say that they said, "Yes."
Andrew:	Well, cut out a triangle. (*Pause.*) No, I made a mistake.
Interviewer:	How?
Andrew:	They have never seen a triangle. Well, cut it off in the middle. Fold it in the middle, on top of the other half, then tape it down, and you'll have a triangle. Then hang it on the wall so you'll know what a triangle is!
Interviewer:	What if they said they hadn't seen a diamond?
Andrew:	Make a slanted line over, then another slant the other way down, then another slanted line up, then another slanted line to the beginning.
Interviewer:	(*Thinks he is trying to describe a triangle*): What?
Andrew:	(*Repeats the directions. Then ...*): That's a diamond. Now, do what I told you before!

Andrew had done what mathematicians are so fond of doing. He had reduced the problem to one that was already solved! At the end, he asked, "Will this test be on my report card? 'Cause I'm doing really good!" Throughout the interview, it was apparent that Andrew was sure of his own reasoning and knowledge from his experience. Although Andrew is not typical of students in our project, it is important to note that students such as Andrew may later become mathematicians, scientists, and engineers. Andrew had been reflecting greatly on the ideas in the curriculum and relished the opportunity to discuss them so that he could demonstrate the results of his thinking.

Learning Trajectory for Shapes

As with others we have seen, the learning trajectory for 2D shapes is complex (the LT for 3D shapes follows, see Table 8.2). First, there are several conceptual and skill advancements that make levels more complicated. Second, there are four *subtrajectories* that are related, but can develop somewhat independently:

1. The *Comparing* subtrajectory involves matching shapes by different criteria in the early levels and determining congruence.
2. The *Classifying* subtrajectory includes recognizing, identifying ("naming"), analyzing, and classifying shapes.
3. The *Parts* subtrajectory involves distinguishing, naming, describing, and quantifying the components of shapes, such as sides and angles.
4. The closely related *Representing* subtrajectory involves building or drawing shapes.

The *goal* of increasing children's ability to name, describe, analyze, and classify geometric shapes and think spatially is second in importance only to numerical goals. The CCSSM include the goals already described in Table 7.2 (see p. 178, and especially K.G, 1-5; 1.G.1; 2. G.1; 3.G.1).

This is so complex, that we added a column that encourages you to think of the *big picture*, the broad levels of thinking we introduced on pp. 189-202: *Shape Senser, Visual Thinker, Parts Thinker*, and *Property Thinker*. Keep these broad levels in mind and you will not let the "trees" (the instructional important but numerous) levels distract you from the major developments your children will make.

Table 8.1, then, provides the learning trajectory to achieve the goals. Including the broad ("forest") levels, the developmental progression ("trees") and the instructional tasks. As we have stated in previous chapters, the ages in all the learning trajectory tables are only approximate, especially because the age of acquisition usually depends heavily on experience. This is especially true in the domain of geometry, where most children receive low-quality experiences.

Table 8.2 Learning Trajectory for 3D Shapes

Age	Developmental Progression	Instructional Tasks
0-2	**3D Perceiver: Foundations** Can perceive 3D shapes accurately from infancy, however, this competence is limited to continuously moving objects, rather than single or even multiple static views of the same object.	*Shape & Spatial Talk*, [LT]². Note: Explorations with 3D shapes are provided in the "Composing 3D Shapes" trajectory.
3-4	**3D Prototype Recognizer** Recognizes some prototypical 3D shapes, such as the sphere and cube, using formal or informal names. However, may use 2D vocabulary to name some 3D shapes and describe solids using a variety of informal characteristics, such as "pointiness" or "slenderness."	*Circles and Cans (3D)*, [LT]²: Children pair different sized cans with circles made by tracing the bases of the cans, connecting 2D shapes (circles) to 3D shapes (cylinders).
5-6	**3D Shape Recognizer** Recognizes more 3D shapes (solids), using informal and some formal names. Recognizes faces as 2D shapes.	*Rectangles & Boxes (3D)*, [LT]²: Children find shapes, especially rectangles, on boxes of various shapes and sizes, they trace all the faces of each box onto a separate piece of newsprint, shuffle them, and then try to match the boxes to the traces.
7	**3D Face Counter** Recognizes all faces of a solid as 2D shapes, counting faces accurately.	*What Kind of Box?*, [LT]²: Children examine boxes and talk about how many flat sides (faces) each has, as well as the type of faces.
8	**3D Shape Identifier** Identifies most solids, naming several of their attributes. Can identify the common solid created by a particular net.	*Comparing and Constructing 3D Shapes*, [LT]² : Students create 3D Shapes out of cardboard pieces, sharing the name of the shape and describing its attributes.
9+	**3D Shape Class Identifier** Identifies most solids, based on their properties.	*Guess My Rule (3D)*, [LT]²: Children guess the class of shapes (polyhedra or not; prism or not).

Final Words

As this chapter showed, children can learn a considerable amount about several aspects of geometric shapes. There is one more important competency, so important that we dedicate Chapter 9 to shape composition, both 2D and 3D.

Note

1 Relax and enjoy. Most of *us* were badly taught math, and especially geometry (Shahbari, 2017). Take your time and it *will* shape up for you!

9 Composition and Decomposition of Shapes

Zachary's grandmother was walking him out of preschool. He looked at the tiled walkway and yelled, "Look, grandma! Hexagons! Hexagons all over the walk. You can put them together with no spaces!"

(Figure 9.0.5)

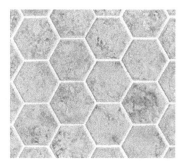

Figure 9.0.5 Hexagons tiled in a walkway

What does Zachary show he knows about shapes and geometry? Zachary and his friends have been working on the Building Blocks curriculum, which emphasizes putting shapes together. Children enjoy playing with puzzles and shapes, with challenges like tangram puzzles provide. If such experiences are organized into learning trajectories, students can benefit and enjoy these experiences even more. Teachers report such experiences can change the way children see their world.

The ability to describe, use, and visualize the effects of composing and decomposing geometric regions is important in and of itself. It also provides a foundation for understanding other math topics, especially number and arithmetic, such as Part-Whole relationships, fractions, area, and so forth. Also, such activity may develop executive function processes (Duran, Byers, Cameron, & Grissmer, 2018; Schmitt, Korucu, Napoli, Bryant, & Purpura, 2018).

In this chapter we examine three related topics. First, we discuss composition of 3D shapes in the restricted but important early childhood setting of building with blocks. Second, we discuss composition and decomposition of 2D shapes. Third, we discuss the disembedding of 2D shapes, such as in embedded (hidden) figures problems.

The Development of Composing 3D Shapes

Teachers are not surprised to learn that block play develops spatial language, creativity, symbolization (a cylinder as a can of food), language, and social-motional development (Cohen & Emmons, 2017; Cohen & Uhry, 2007).

However, many teachers *are* surprised to learn that building blocks were invented as an educational tool to develop children's *math* ideas (Aksoy & Aksoy, 2017, see the story of Patty Hill and Caroline Pratt in Chapter 15)[1].

Children initially build block structures one block at a time and only later explicitly put together these 3D shapes to create new 3D shapes. In their first year, they pound, clap together, or slide the blocks, or they use single blocks to represent an object, such as a house or vehicle. Children's first combinations are simple pairs. At about 1 year of age, they stack blocks, then make a "road." At about 2 years, they place each successive block congruently on or next to the one previously placed as shown in Figure 9.1. Around 2 to 3 years of age, children begin to expand their buildings to two dimensions, extending their construction in creating a floor or wall. At 3 to 4 years of age, children regularly build vertical and horizontal components within a building, even making simple arches.

At 4 or 5 years of age, children are developing *internal representations* of the spatial arrangements before and during building, which changes their constructions. At 4 years, they can use multiple spatial relations, extending in multiple directions and with multiple points of contact among components, showing flexibility in how they generate and integrate parts of the structure. For example, they produce more complex constructions, such as an enclosure, "+," and horizontal corner as in Figure 9.2, and make arches in two dimensions.

A small number of children will build a tower with all blocks; for example, by composing the triangular blocks to make rectangular blocks (Kamii, Miyakawa, & Kato, 2004). A 4-year-old built the tower in Figure 9.3, intuitively classifying the blocks by stability and ordering them by that categorization, using the more stable blocks at the bottom, combining triangular prisms in the layer near the top, and another triangular prism at the top, that is, in a position that leads to instability in the middle. By 5 years of age, their mental representations can organize substructures, allowing them to build, for example, eight arches on three levels, as in Figure 9.4.

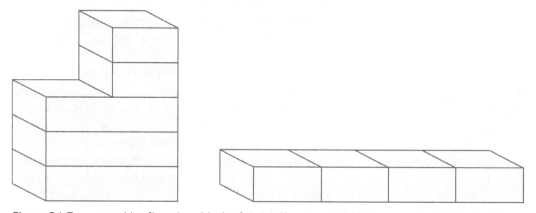

Figure 9.1 Two-year-olds often place blocks, frequently congruent blocks, on or next to each other

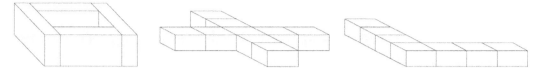

Figure 9.2 More complex arrangements

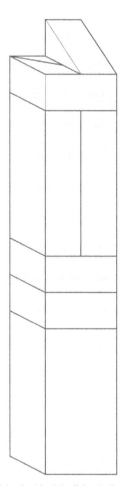

Figure 9.3 A 4-year-old building has blocks that build a tall and stable tower

The Development of Composing and Decomposing 2D Shapes

We have created and tested a developmental progression for the composition of 2D shapes. Briefly (see Table 9.1), children begin manipulating shapes as individuals, not really combining them to compose a larger shape. For example, children might use a single shape for a sun, a separate shape for a tree, and another separate shape for a person (see "Separate Shapes Actor: Foundations" in Table 9.1). They then place shapes next to each other to form pictures,

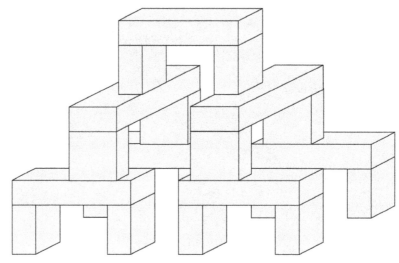

Figure 9.4 An arch of arches of arches (that's hierarchical thinking!)

often touching only at vertices (corners). In free-form "make-a-picture" tasks, for example, each shape used represents a unique role or function in the picture (e.g., one shape for one leg). Children can fill simple outline puzzles using trial and error but do not easily use turns or flips to do so; they cannot use motions to see shapes from different perspectives (Piece Assembler).

At the next level, children put shapes together with full sides touching to form pictures in which *several shapes play a single role* but use trial and error and do not anticipate creation of new geometric shapes (Picture Maker). An important level is attained when children develop the ability to combine shapes to make new shapes or fill puzzles with *intentionality* and *anticipation* ("I know what will fit"). They use angles as well as side lengths in their placing, and they use rotation and flipping intentionally to select and place shapes (Shape Composer).

A new type of ability develops as children learn to deliberately form composite units of shapes and to recognize and use substitution relationships (e.g., two trapezoid pattern blocks can make a hexagon, Substitution Composer). Soon after, they can construct and operate on composite units (units of units) intentionally. They can continue a pattern of shapes that leads to a "good covering" (Shape Composite Repeater). Children build and apply (iterate and otherwise operate on) units of units of units (Shape Composer–Units of Units).

The Development of Disembedding 2D Shapes

Over years, children develop in their ability to separate structures within embedded figures—that is, finding "hidden shapes" within more complex diagrams. Some 4-year-olds could find embedded circles or squares embedded in square structures; 5-year-olds were more likely to do so. Before 6 years of age, what children perceive is organized in a rigid manner into basic structures. That is, they can see *primary* structures but not *secondary* structures as shown in Figure 9.5. Children grow in the flexibility of the perceptual organizations they can create. They eventually integrate parts and can create and use "imaginary components." Of course, we all know that embedded

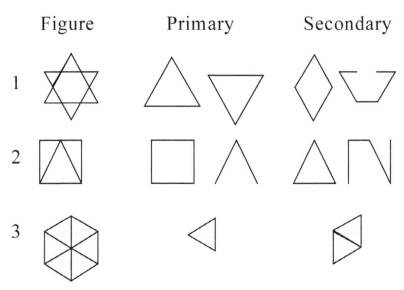

Figure 9.5 Primary and Secondary structures for figures. Rows 1 and 2 show contour, or *line* structures (row 1 overlapping, row 2 juxtaposed) and Row 3 shows area structures

pictures can be very complex and can stump people of any age who have to build them up piece by piece (were any secondary structures difficult for you?). The learning trajectory puts this body of research into a developmental progression.

Experience and Education

Composition of 3D Shapes

Block building has long been a staple of high-quality early childhood education (at least in theory). It supports children's learning of shape and shape composition ability, to say nothing of the general reasoning that it may help develop (The Spatial Reasoning Study Group, 2015c). Amazingly, block building in preschool predicts math achievement in high school (Wolfgang, Stannard, & Jones, 2001, although, like most research of this nature, this is "correlation, not necessarily causation"). Block building also helps develop spatial skills. For example, 9-year-olds who build a specific model out of LEGO blocks scored higher in spatial ability than those who did not complete the model (Brosnan, 1998). Further, 3D shape composition is a "natural" for many exciting projects. (McCormick & Twitchell, 2017). High-quality block play develops *all* the STEM domains: Science, Technology,[2] Engineering, and Mathematics (Bagiati & Evangelou, 2018; Chalufour, Hoisington, Moriarty, Winokur, & Worth, 2004; Gold, 2017).

Research provides several other useful guidelines, as follows:

*   Have younger children build with or alongside older preschoolers; in that context, they develop block-building skills more rapidly.
*   Provide materials, facilitative peer relationships, and time to build. Incorporate *planned, systematic* block building into the curriculum. Children should have open exploratory play *and*

solve semi-structured and well-structured problems, with intentional teaching provided for each. For example children build by duplicating models (of block buildings or of famous real-world buildings, Chalufour et al., 2004) or by listening to directions to build a shape with connecting cubes (The Spatial Reasoning Study Group, 2015c). This does not have to be direct instruction; see below for an example.

- Understand and apply children's developmental progressions in the levels of complexity of block building. More effective teachers provide verbal scaffolding for the children based on those levels (e.g., "sometimes people use a block to join ...") but avoid directly assisting children or engaging in block building themselves.
- Understand full learning trajectories—that is, the goal, developmental progression, *and* matched activities, to fully help children improve in block-building skills. Children of teachers who understand all three improve more than control groups who receive an equivalent amount of block-building experience during unstructured free-play sessions.
- Address equity. As with other types of spatial training, intentional instruction in block building may be more important for girls than boys. At the *least*, let's not let boys dominate the block center.
- Provide strong concept support, using math vocabulary (e.g., "I think the triangular block goes in front, next to the cylinder," see also Sæbbe & Mosvold, 2016) and gestures. This matters especially for girls (e.g., provided by their fathers, Thomson et al., 2018c).

Structured and sequenced block-building interventions will help provide boys and girls with equitable, beneficial opportunities to learn about the structural properties of blocks and thus spatial skills. For example, activities can be designed to encourage spatial and math thinking and sequenced to match developmental progressions. In one study, the first problem, based on a story, was to build an enclosure with walls that were at least two blocks high and included an arch (Casey et al., 2008a). This introduced the problem of bridging, which involves balanced measurement, and estimation. The second problem was to build more complex bridges, such as bridges with multiple arches and ramps or stairs at the end. This introduced planning and seriation. The third problem was to build a complex tower with at least two floors, or stories. Children were provided with cardboard ceilings, so they had to make the walls fit the constraints of the cardboard's dimensions.

Unit blocks also provide a window into the geometry of young children's play. These blocks allow children to explore a world where objects have predictable similarities and relationships. Children create forms and structures that are based on math relationships. For example, children have to struggle with length relationships in finding a roof for a building. Length and equivalence are involved in substituting two shorter blocks for one long block. Children also consider height, area, and volume. One of the inventors of today's unit blocks, Caroline Pratt (1948b), tells a story of children making enough room for a horse to fit inside a stable. The teacher told Diana that she could have the horse when she had made a stable for it. She and Elizabeth began to build a small construction, but the horse did not fit. Diana had made a large stable with a low roof. After several unsuccessful attempts to get the horse in, she removed the roof, added blocks to the walls to make the roof higher, and replaced the roof. She then tried to put into words what she had done. "Roof too small." The teacher gave her new words, "high" and "low," and she gave a new explanation to the other children.

Just by building with blocks, children form important ideas. These intuitive ideas can be fostered by teachers, such as Diana's, who discuss these ideas with children, giving words to their actions. For example, children can be helped to distinguish between different quantities such as height, area, and volume. Three preschoolers made towers and argued about whose was the biggest. Their teacher asked them if they meant whose was tallest (gesturing) or widest, or used the most blocks? The children were surprised to find that the tallest tower did not have the most blocks.

In many situations, you can help children see and discuss the similarities and differences among the blocks they use and the structures they make. You can also pose challenges that will focus children's actions on these ideas. At the right time, you might challenge the children to do the following:

- Put the blocks in order by length.
- Use other blocks to make a wall as long as the longest block.
- Use 12 half-units (square) blocks to make as many differently shaped (rectangular) floors as possible.
- Make a box that is four blocks square.

Learning Trajectory for Composition of 3D Shapes

The goals of increasing children's ability to compose geometric shapes and think spatially from the CCSSM were already described in Figure 7.6 (see p. ##). The learning trajectories for the composition of 3D geometric shapes are presented in Table 9.1. This is *only* for the set of unit blocks; composition of more complex and less familiar 3D shapes would follow a similar developmental progression but often at later ages and with more dependence on specific educational experiences.

Composition and Decomposition of 2D Shapes

Young children move through levels in the composition and decomposition of 2D figures. From lack of competence in composing geometric shapes, they gain abilities to combine shapes into pictures, then synthesize combinations of shapes into new shapes (composite shapes), eventually operating on and iterating those composite shapes. Early foundations for this learning appear to be formed in children's experiences. Few curricula challenge children to move through these levels. Our theoretical learning trajectory guides the selection of puzzles for children at different levels of the trajectory. The content and effects of one program illustrate the importance of shape and shape composition. An artist and collaborating educational researchers developed the Agam program to develop the "visual language" of children ages 3 to 7 years (Razel & Eylon, 1986). The activities begin by building a visual alphabet (lines, shapes, etc., at different orientations). For example, the activities introduce horizontal lines in isolation. Then, they teach relations, such as parallel lines. In the same way, teachers introduce circles, then concentric circles, and then a horizontal line intersecting a circle. The curriculum also develops verbal language but only following a visual introduction. Combination rules involving the visual alphabet and ideas such as large, medium, and small, generate complex figures. As words combine to make sentences, the

Table 9.1 A Learning Trajectory for the Composition of 3D Shapes

Age (years)	Developmental Progression	Instructional Tasks
0-1	**Separate Blocks Actor: Foundations** Either places blocks randomly or manipulates shapes as individuals, but does not combine them to compose a larger shape. May pound, clap together, or use slide blocks or single blocks to represent an object, such as a house or truck.	*Spatial Learning at Home*, [LT]²: Math happens all around the home for infants and toddlers. Experiences encourage explorations of and appropriate talk about blocks in many forms. Manipulating all kinds of blocks (pick up soft fabric or foam blocks, drop, repeat! or by 9 to 12 months, pick up two, bang together) and other objects builds foundations of fine motor and perceptual competencies from which all subsequent learning develops. Build towers for children and let them knock them down.
1	**Stacker** Shows use of the spatial relationship of "on" to stack blocks, although choice of blocks may be unsystematic.	*Stacking Numbers*, [LT]²: Children make stacks of blocks and compare the different ways that others make stacks. In general, encourage children to build with many kinds of blocks and other objects. Children naturally like to stack things on top of each other, especially when adults notice them doing so or model doing it themselves. In the illustration, a child tries to put a block on another, although it slides off. 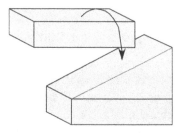
1½	**Line Maker** Shows use of relationship of "next to" to make a (one-dimensional) line of blocks.	*Build Roads*, [LT]²: Children are prompted to solve construction problems using any type of block, specifically build a road or other "line" constructions. That is, activities encourage children to build lines with many kinds of blocks. Children naturally like to organize blocks into lines, especially when adults notice them doing so or model doing it themselves to make something like a road for cars, a simple enclosure, or just a "really long line of blocks!" Accessories such as toy figures, animals, and vehicles can enhance play. 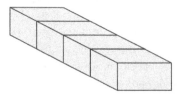
2	**Same Shape Stacker** Shows use of relationship of "on" to stack congruent blocks, or those that show a similarly helpful relationship to make stacks or lines.	*Block Stacker*, [LT]²: Children stack blocks on top of each other. Introduce this by reading *Crash! boom! A math tale* by Robie Harris (http://robieharris.com), illustrated by Chris Chatterton, or *Jack the Builder* by Stuart J. Murphy. Children naturally like to stack things on top of each other, especially when adults notice them doing so or model doing it themselves. Here adults may comment on

(Continued)

Table 9.1 (Cont.)

Age (years)	Developmental Progression	Instructional Tasks
		children making a tower of identical blocks, naming them and noticing how high it is. Discussing that the blocks are "all the same shape" provides more foundations for the later-developing concept of congruence. Introduce vocabulary such as *above*, *under*, and *next to*. Include large hollow blocks as well. 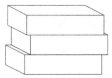
2-2.17	**Piece Assembler (3D)** Builds vertical and horizontal components within a building, but within a limited range, such as building a "floor" or a simple "wall." These, then, are two-dimensional structures.	*Making Things with Blocks*, [LT]²: Children are encouraged to represent and make objects using blocks, focusing on filling a two-dimensional area. The goal is creative construction with blocks, guided by the teacher noticing, describing, and encouraging types of 3D composition that are at this level (challenging, but achievable). Asking questions (do you need a wall there? are you making a big floor?) or even putting up pictures that illustrate the type of construction might motivate children to try that new way of composing 3D shapes (Chalufour et al., 2004). Copying each other's construction can be another helpful approach. You may wish to remove LEGOs temporarily to address STEM concepts such a shapes, stability, and balance with blocks that do not stick together (Chalufour et al., 2004). 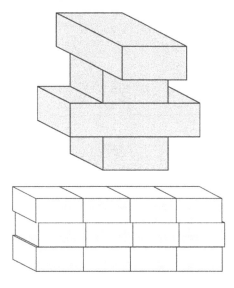
3-4	**Picture Maker (3D)** Uses multiple spatial relations, extending in multiple directions and with multiple points of contact among components, showing flexibility in	*Making Scenes with Blocks*, [LT]²: Children are prompted to solve construction problems using blocks. The goal is creative construction with blocks, with the teacher noticing, describing, and encouraging types of 3D

(Continued)

Table 9.1 (Cont.)

Age (years)	Developmental Progression	Instructional Tasks
	integrating parts of the structure. Starting at 30 months, produces arches/bridges, enclosures, corners, and crosses, although may use unsystematic trial and error and simple addition of pieces.	composition that are at this level for children (challenging, but achievable). Asking questions or even putting up pictures that illustrate the type of construction might motivate children to try that new way of composing 3D shapes. For example, can they build a fence so horses won't run away? Discuss the blocks they will use, such as "What block has the shape of the bottom of the house? How about the top, the roof?". 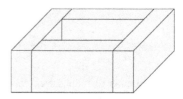
4-5	**Shape Composer (3D)** Composes shapes with anticipation, understanding what 3D shape will be produced with a composition of two or more other (simple, familiar) 3D shapes. Can produce arches (with vertical interior space), enclosures (with internal horizontal space), corners, and crosses systematically. Builds enclosures and arches several blocks high (Kersh, Casey, & Young, 2008). Later in this level, children add depth to make 3D structures, and they add roofs across structures multiple blocks high (but they may have no internal spaces) (Casey et al., 2008a).	*Building Shapes with Blocks*, [LT][2]: Children are prompted to solve construction problems using blocks. To engage children, have them create a play scene first, such as building a house or a town. Or tell a story in which the characters have a need for a construction ... that they might make! The goal of this level of thinking is to produce arches, ramps, enclosures, crosses, and to add depth to make 3D structures including roofs across structures multiple blocks high. So, consider the following if children build a simple rectangular enclosure (e.g., with four walls, three blocks high): "How will they see outside?" (Build an arch for a window.) "Is this a river? How will they get across?" (Build a bridge over it with ramps or steps to get up on the bridge.) If children have not made roofs, ask them how the people in the house can stay dry if it rains. If they have made a barn, introduce a tall animal that can't fit through the doorway and ask them how they could rebuild the barn to "let this tall horse in." 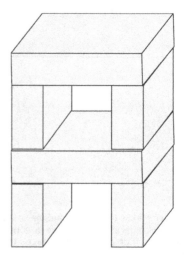

(Continued)

Table 9.1 (Cont.)

Age (years)	Developmental Progression	Instructional Tasks
5-6	**Substitution Composer and Shape Composite Repeater (3D)** Substitutes a composite for a congruent whole. Builds complex bridges with multiple arches, ramps, and stairs at the ends. Structures are 3D, often including roofs and multiple internal spaces.	*Build a Bridge*, [LT]²: Children look at images of bridges and then build a complex bridge using blocks. *Find Another Way*, [LT]²: Challenge children to put together blocks of different shapes and sizes to create the same shape as the original block. For example, two triangle blocks (triangular prisms) can make rectangle or square blocks (prism). Two-unit rectangular prisms make a longer rectangular prism. For example, ask them if there is another way they can build the same structure without using one of the types of blocks they have previously used (e.g., if they used up all the unit blocks, but could use two thinner rectangular prisms or two right triangular prism to fill the same space). Tell a story, such as about construction workers who want to build the exact same house but have run out of lumber of a specific size. For example, if children used long, rectangular prisms, remove that block from their building. Offer smaller blocks that can be composed together to make the same shape and size as the original rectangular prism. Asking questions (Can you build another rectangular prism the same size and shape with other blocks? How will we build a series of arches along this whole wall?) or even putting up pictures of actual buildings or block buildings that illustrate that type of construct might motivate children to try that new way of composing 3D shapes. Copying each other's construction can be another helpful approach. 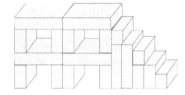
6-8+	**Shape Composer–Units of Units (3D)** Makes complex towers or other structures, involving multiple levels with ceilings (fitting the ceilings), and adult-like structures with blocks, including arches and other substructures.	*Build a Tower*, [LT]²: Using a problem narrative (Casey, Paugh, & Ballard, 2002) pictures of castles (Sarama, Brenneman, Clements, Duke, & Hemmeter, 2017), or a field trip, challenge children to create or recreate a variety of structures. 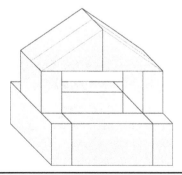

elements of the visual alphabet combine to form complex patterns and symmetric forms. The Agam approach is structured, with instruction proceeding from passive identification to memory to active discovery, first in simple form (e.g., looking for plastic circles hidden by the teacher), then in tasks that require visual analysis (e.g., finding circles in picture books). Only then does the teacher present tasks requiring reproduction of combinations from memory. The curriculum repeats these ideas in a large number of activities featuring multiple modes of representation, such as bodily activity, group activity, and auditory perception.

The results of using the program, especially for several consecutive years, are positive. Children gain in geometric and spatial skills and show pronounced benefits in the areas of arithmetic and writing readiness. Supporting these results, research in the U.S. has similar positive results (Clements et al., 2018a). The emphasis on the learning trajectory for composition of shape in the Building Blocks program (we borrowed heavily from the Agam program in designing Building Blocks) led to strong effects in this area—equivalent to benefits often found for individual tutoring. In a follow-up, large-scale randomized field trial with 36 classrooms, the Building Blocks curriculum made the most substantial gains compared to both a non-treatment and another preschool math curriculum, in shape composition (and several other topics). Especially because the other curriculum also included shape composition activities, we believe that the greater gains provided by the Building Blocks curriculum can be attributed to its explicit use of the sequenced activities following learning trajectories, as well as teachers' knowledge of trajectories. Other interventions also show the benefits of similar, sequenced shape composition activities (Casey et al., 2008).

Working with "polyominoes" is also engaging and mathematically rich. A polyomino is a plane geometric figure formed by joining one or more equal squares edge to edge. You may know the game "Tetris" which involves the geometric composition of … geometrically composed tetrominoes! (See also *Tetrominoes* in Table 9.2.) Trying to find all the distinct pentominoes (five squares) and in so doing, determining if shapes are congruent or not, is a rich math activity (Shiakalli & Zacharos, 2014). It also builds early concepts in other topics, such as area (see Chapter 11). Of course, the number of possible polyominoes increases considerably when adding each additional square (try it!).

There are many benefits of composing and decomposing shapes. Children learn math properties of shapes, they learn to solve problems and work creatively with forms, and they learn executive function processes. They also *see the beauty in mathematics* (Eberle, 2014). To maximize these benefits, help children move up the learning trajectory. Scaffold *just enough* to keep them developing. Use clear vocabulary to describe shapes and geometric motions (Clements et al., 2018a) and *use gestures* a lot in doing so (Elia, 2018c).

Learning Trajectories for the Composition and Decomposition of Geometric Shapes (2D)

The goals of increasing children's ability to compose geometric shapes and think spatially in the CCSSM were already described in Figure 7.6 (see p. ##, see especially Gr. 1, and Gr. 2; as well as the CCSSM standards K.G.6; 1.G, 2–3; 2.G, 2–3; 3.G.2). Because the learning trajectories for the composition and decomposition of 2D geometric shapes are closely connected, we present them together in Table 9.2.

Table 9.2 Learning Trajectory for the Composition and Decomposition of 2D Shapes

Age	Developmental Progression	Instructional Tasks
0-3	**Separate Shapes Actor: Foundations** Infants and toddlers manipulate shapes as individuals, but usually do not combine them to compose a larger shape. Make a picture: Toddlers may decompose, usually by trial and error. Given *only* a hexagon formed by two trapezoids, can break it apart to make this simple picture by random placement: 	*Block Play*, [LT]²: Children play with physical pattern blocks and other shape sets, often making simple pictures. Recall that the *Mystery Pictures* series (see p. ##) also sets the foundation for this learning trajectory and would be the first task for the following level. Children only match or identify shapes, but the *result* of their work is a picture made up of other shapes—a demonstration of composition.  In simple puzzles for this level, each shape is not only outlined, but often touches other shapes only at a vertex (corner), making the matching as easy as possible.
4	**Piece Assembler** Makes pictures in which each shape represents a unique role (e.g., one shape for each body part) and shapes touch. Fills simple puzzles in which all shapes are outlined, often using trial and error. Make a picture: 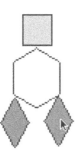	*Pattern Block Puzzles (Piece Assembler)*, [LT]²: Children match pattern blocks to the outlines to fill in puzzles. Pattern Block Puzzles 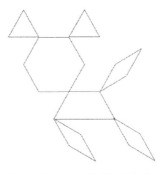 Then, the puzzles move to those that combine shapes by matching their sides, but each shape still mainly serves a separate role. Pattern Block Puzzles 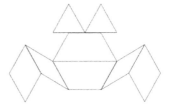

(Continued)

Table 9.2 (Cont.)

Age Developmental Progression	Instructional Tasks
	Shape Puzzles, [LT]² : There is a series of online games that provide these puzzles as well; see *Shape Puzzles: Piece Assembler* and *Shape Puzzles: Piece Assembler 2*.  *Shape Puzzles: Free Explore*, [LT]² is also engaging and important—Students make their *own puzzles* using pattern block shapes. Then they click on the "play" button (the right arrow) and it becomes a puzzle that a friend or family member can try to solve! *This is creative math play that all children should be doing.*  
5 **Picture Maker** Puts several shapes together to make one part of a picture (e.g., two shapes for one arm). Uses trial and error and does not anticipate creation of new geometric shape. Chooses shapes using "general shape" or side length. Fills "easy" "Pattern Block Puzzles" that suggest the placement of each shape (note that in the example on the right the child is trying to put a square in the puzzle where its right angles will not fit).	*Pattern Block Puzzles (Picture Maker)*, [LT]² : Children solve pattern block (or tangram) puzzles, truly combining shapes to make each part of the puzzle. Start with those where several shapes are combined to make one "part," but internal lines are still available. Use fractional language in discussing children's solutions (e.g., "You used two rhombuses to make that leg, half here [pointing] and half here!").

Table 9.2 (Cont.)

Age	Developmental Progression	Instructional Tasks

Make a picture:

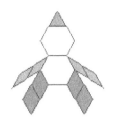

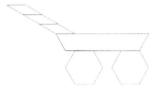

Later puzzles in the sequence require combining shapes to fill one or more regions, without the guidance of internal line segments.

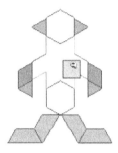

Shape Puzzles (Picture Maker), [LT]^2: Follows the same sequence online.

Shape Puzzles: Free Explore, [LT]^2 (see above) is beneficial at every level.

Put the Halves Back Together, [LT]^2: See p. ## and Figure 7.6. This level uses the a1 and a2 arrangements of halves.

See it, Build It, Check It, [LT]^2: Children are presented with an image composed of 2D shapes created with pattern blocks. They are then invited to recreate the image on their own. See also Duplicate the Design, [LT]^2.

Snapshots (Shapes): Give children pattern blocks. Secretly make a simple house with a square (foundation) and triangle (roof). Tell children to look carefully and take a snapshot in their minds as you show your house for 2 seconds, and then cover it immediately after with a dark cloth. Have children build what they saw with pattern blocks. Show your house for 2 more seconds so children can check and change their pictures, if necessary.

(Continued)

Table 9.2 (Cont.)

Age Developmental Progression	Instructional Tasks
	During the final reveal, have children describe what they saw and how they built their own. Repeat with other secret pictures, making them more complex as children's ability allows.
Simple Decomposer Decomposes ("takes apart" into smaller shapes) simple shapes that have obvious clues as to their decomposition. Given a hexagon, can break it apart to make this picture: 	*How Did I Make This?*, [LT]² : Children decompose a shape such as a pattern block (regular) hexagon into smaller shapes after seeing a model.

Shape Composer Composes shapes with anticipation ("I know what will fit!"). Chooses shapes using angles as well as side lengths. Rotation and flipping are used intentionally to select and place shapes. In the "Pattern Block Puzzles" below, all angles are correct, and patterning is evident.
 	
   Make a picture:

	Pattern Block Puzzles (Shape Composer) and online *Shape Puzzles: Shape Composer*, [LT]² : Children solve shape puzzles that have no internal guidelines and larger areas; therefore, children must compose shapes accurately. Use fractional language in discussing children's solutions (e.g., "You used a trapezoid to make half the body, and the half is three triangles, so one-sixth [pointing at each], one-sixth, and one-sixth!").

	Shape Puzzles: Free Explore, [LT]² (see above) is beneficial at every level.
	   Snapshots (Shapes): As above, but use several copies of the same shape so children have to compose mentally. Also, try simple outlines and see if they can compose the same shape with pattern blocks. Tangrams can provide additional challenges.
	   Can You Build This? and *Building with the Mind's Eye*, [LT]² : Build by duplicating models or by listening to directions to build a shape with connecting cubes (The Spatial Reasoning Study Group, 2015c).
	   Magic Keys, [LT]² : Children compose six different arrangements of five squares (pentominoes, see p. ##), creating "magic keys" to rescue a prince. See also *Tetrominoes*, [LT]² and *Pentominoes: Create and Solve*, in which children create *pentominoes puzzles* for other children to solve.
	   Put the Halves Back Together, [LT]² : See p. ## of Chapter 7, including Figure 7.6. This level uses the a3 and a4 arrangements of halves.

Table 9.2 (Cont.)

Age	Developmental Progression	Instructional Tasks
6	**Substitution Composer** Makes new shapes out of smaller shapes and uses trial and error to substitute groups of shapes for other shapes to create new shapes in different ways. Make a picture with intentional substitutions: 	*Can You Find Another Way?*, [LT]² : Children build pictures in different ways, substituting a new combination of shapes for an initial arrangement. Use fractional language in discussing children's solutions (e.g., "You used two trapezoids to make this hexagon, each is one half! Here the rhombuses are ... what? [thirds] And the triangles? [Sixths]"). 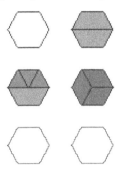  *Pattern Block Puzzles and Tangram Puzzles: New Ways*, [LT]² have children substitute shapes to fill an outline in different ways. It also challenges them to estimate how many of a certain shape it would take to cover another shape. After making predictions, they check their answers. *Shape Puzzles: Substitution Composer*, [LT]² is a fun version of this online series. *After* solving the puzzle the *first time*, the children's solution is shown in the bottom left-hand corner ... and the real task is to solve the same puzzle in *different ways*. 

Table 9.2 (Cont.)

Age	Developmental Progression	Instructional Tasks

Shape Decomposer (with help) Decomposes shapes using imagery that is suggested and supported by the task or environment.

Given regular hexagons, can break them apart to make these shapes:

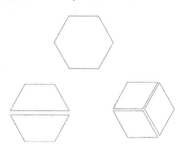

Super Shape! (Decomposer with Help), [LT]² : Starting with one large shape, students are challenged to find a solution to the puzzle by cutting the shape into smaller shapes and recomposing the pieces within the puzzle.

Super Shape 2 (and several additional levels) requires multiple decompositions in this Building Blocks software.

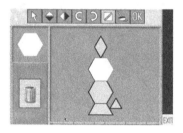

7 **Shape Composite Repeater** Constructs and duplicates units of units (shapes made from other shapes) intentionally; understands each as being both multiple small shapes *and* one larger shape. May continue a pattern of shapes that leads to tiling.

Children use a shape composition repeatedly in constructing a design or picture.

What Can You Make?, [LT]² : Children roll a die to determine what shapes they have to combine. Then they are asked to repeat the structure they have composed. See also *Make a Pair*, [LT]² .

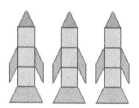

Paper Quilts, [LT]² : Children repeat the design of their quilt squares on the Paper Quilt sheet nine times to make their unique designed quilt.

Shape Decomposer with Imagery Decomposes shapes flexibly using independently generated imagery. That is, decomposition is intentionally specified by the child.

To break apart a square, the child may say that a cut needs to be made from angle to angle to make two right triangles.

Given hexagons, can break one or more apart to make shapes such as these:

Super Shape! (Imagery), [LT]² : Starting with one large shape, students are challenged to find a solution to the puzzle by cutting the shape into smaller shapes and recomposing the pieces within the puzzle. Ask children to describe their work using fractional language. The picture shows a Building Blocks software version.

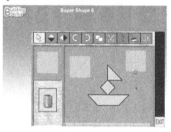

(Continued)

Table 9.2 (Cont.)

Age	Developmental Progression	Instructional Tasks

Geometry Snapshots 7: Students identify an image that matches one of four complex configurations from memory (imagery).

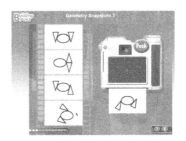

8   **Shape Composer—Units of Units** Builds and *applies* units of units (shapes made from other shapes). For example, in constructing spatial patterns, extends patterning activity to create a tiling with a new unit shape—a unit of unit shapes that they recognize and consciously construct.

   Builds a large structure by making a combination of pattern blocks over and over and then fitting them together.

Tiling Tetrominoes (Shape Composer Units of Units), [LT]^2: The child must repeatedly build and repeat superordinate units. That is, as in the illustration here, the child repeatedly built "Ts" out of four squares, used four Ts to build squares, and used squares to tile a rectangle.

Shape Decomposer with Units of Units Decomposes shapes flexibly using independently generated imagery and planned decompositions of shapes that themselves are decompositions.

Super Shape! (Units of Units), [LT]^2: Starting with one large shape, students are challenged to find a solution to the puzzle by cutting the shape into smaller shapes and recomposing the pieces within the puzzle. For units of units, challenge students to begin tiling by cutting small pieces of similar size

Table 9.2 (Cont.)

Age Developmental Progression	Instructional Tasks
Given only squares, can break them apart–*and then break the resulting shapes apart again*–to make shapes such as these: 	and fitting them together *in designs that solve the puzzle.* *Super Shape 7*: Children only get exactly the number of "super shapes" they need to complete the puzzle. Again, multiple applications of the scissors tool are required. A Building Blocks software version is show below. 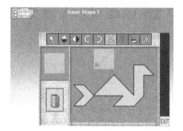 *Geometry Snapshots 8*: Students identify a configuration of cubes that matches one of four complex configurations from memory (imagery). 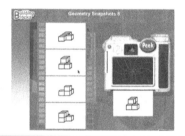

Disembedding 2D Shapes

More research is needed before suggesting a solid recommendation as to how much time to spend and how to approach the disembedding of 2D shapes. The motivating nature of disembedding activities (cf. "hidden pictures" activities in children's magazines) may indicate, however, that such activities may be interesting to children as extra work, such as might be added to learning centers or taken home.

The primary task we present in the learning trajectory is straightforward–to find figures in increasingly complex geometric figures, including embedded figures. It may be wise to have children embed figures themselves before finding already embedded figures.

Learning Trajectories for Embedded Geometric Figures (2D)

Table 9.3 presents a tentative learning trajectory for disembedding geometric shapes.

Table 9.3 A Learning Trajectory for the Disembedding of Geometric Shapes

Age	Developmental Progression	Instructional Tasks
3	**Intuitive Disembedder: Foundations** Can remember and reproduce only one or a small collection of non-overlapping (isolated) shapes.	See Chapters 7 and 8. *Finding Embedded Pictures*, [LT][2]: Reading with young children, in addition to supporting language development, also supports visual aspects of math thinking. When looking at picture books that are of interest to children, have conversations about objects, people, animals, etc. that can be found in the pictures.
4	**Simple Disembedder** Identifies frame of complex figure. Finds some shapes in arrangements in which figures overlap, but not in those in which figures are embedded within others. 	*Hidden Pictures*, [LT][2]: Children identify a simple primary structure that is part of a complex shape picture.  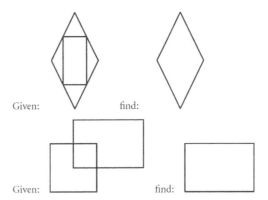 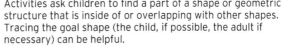
5-6	**Shapes-in-Shapes Disembedder** Identifies shapes embedded within other shapes, such as concentric circles and/or a circle in a square. Identifies primary structures in complex figures.	Activities ask children to find a part of a shape or geometric structure that is inside of or overlapping with other shapes. Tracing the goal shape (the child, if possible, the adult if necessary) can be helpful.

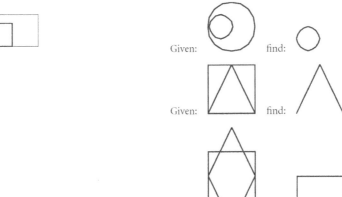

Table 9.3 (Cont.)

Age	Developmental Progression	Instructional Tasks
7	**Secondary Structure Disembedder** Identifies embedded figures even when they do not coincide with any primary structures of the complex figure. 	*Discover the Shape*, [LT][2]: Children attempt to immediately find a primary structure inside a complex figure. 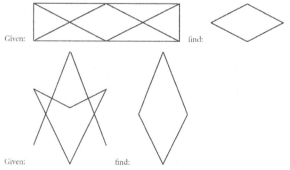
8	**Complete Disembedder** Successfully identifies all varieties of complex arrangements.	*Finding Funny Figures*, [LT][2]: Activities such as this ask children to find a geometric structure that may be a part of two or more different shapes, all of which are inside of a part of several overlapping shapes. Tracing the goal shape (the child, if possible, the adult if necessary) can be helpful. 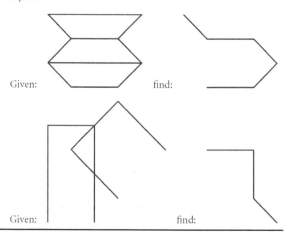

Final Words

The ability to describe, use, and visualize the effects of composing, decomposing, embedding, and disembedding shapes is an important math competence. It is relevant to geometry but also related to children's ability to compose and decompose numbers. Further, it underlies knowledge and skill with art, architecture, and the sciences. Thus, it helps people solve a wide variety of problems, from geometric proofs to the design of a floor space. Of course, such designs also require geometric measurement, the topic of the next two chapters.

Notes

1 This deflates the argument, "I don't want my children to have to learn math, I want them to play with blocks!" does it not?
2 Although commonly associated with computers, technology is at many levels, from the lower (wheels, hammers … blocks) to digital technologies.

10 Geometric Measurement
Length

First graders were studying math through measurement, rather than counting discrete objects. They described and represented relationships among and between quantities, such as comparing two sticks and symbolizing the lengths as "*A < B*." This enabled them to reason about relationships. For example, after seeing the following statements recorded on the board—if V > M, then M ≠ V, V ≠ M, and M < V—one first grader noted, "If it's an inequality, then you can write four statements. If it's equal, you can only write two."

(Slovin, 2007)

Do you think this (true) episode is of a gifted class? If not, what does it suggest about young children's math thinking? Do you think the context—thinking and talking about the length of sticks—contributes to these first graders' remarkable math insights?

The Importance, Challenges, and Potentials of Measurement Learning

Measurement is an important real-world area of math. In particular, we use lengths consistently in our everyday lives. Further, as the introductory story shows, measurement experiences also help develop other areas of math, including reasoning and logic. Also, by its very nature, measurement connects the two most critical domains of early math, geometry and number.

Unfortunately, typical measurement instruction in the U.S. does not accomplish these goals. Many children are taught to measure in a rote fashion. In international comparisons, U.S. students' performance in measurement is very low. By understanding measurement learning trajectories, we can do better for children.

And make no mistake: Our society doesn't promote much knowledge of measurement *outside* of classrooms either. People routinely walk into rug stores and choose a type of carpet. Asked, "What size for this carpet," they respond, "It's for our living room." "What measurements?" "Just the standard living room." *There is no single standard living room*. It's no surprise, then, that once they determine the linear measures (e.g., 20 feet by 26 feet) they still cannot calculate the price, which is by *area*, square feet in this case. We can do better. We must do better.

How early can we start? As in the domain of discrete number (as in Chapters 2 and 3), research shows that even infants are sensitive to continuous quantities.[1] At 3 years of age, children know that if they have some clay and then are given more clay, they have more than they did before. However, they cannot reliably make judgments about which of two amounts of clay is more. For example, if one of two equal amounts is rolled into a long "snake," they will say that it has "more clay."

Children also do not reliably differentiate between continuous and discrete quantity.[1] For example, they may try to share equally by dividing the number of cookie pieces rather than the amount of the cookies. Or, to give someone with fewer pieces of cookie "more," they may simply break one of that person's pieces into two smaller pieces!

Despite such challenges, young children can be provided with appropriate measurement experiences. They discuss amounts in their everyday play. They are ready to learn to measure, connect number to the quantity. In this chapter we discuss length. In the next chapter, we discuss other continuous quantities, such as area, volume, and angle size.

Length Measurement: Mathematical Definition and Concepts

Measurement can be defined as the process of assigning a number to a magnitude of some attribute—a continuous quantity—of an object relative to a unit. Length is a characteristic of an object found by quantifying how far it is between the endpoints of the object. "Distance" is often used similarly to quantify how far it is between any two points in space. The discussion of the number line (see Chapter 4) is critical here because this defines the number line used to measure length. Measuring length or distance consists of two aspects, then: identifying a unit of measure and *subdividing* (mentally and physically) the object by that unit, placing that unit end to end (*iterating*) alongside the object. Subdividing and unit iteration are complex mental accomplishments that are too often ignored in traditional measurement curriculum materials and instruction. Therefore, many researchers go beyond the physical act of measuring to investigate children's understandings of measuring as covering space (one-dimensional for length; see Chapter 11 for two and three dimensions) and quantifying that covering.

Let's lay out the concepts that children must learn (adapted from Clements & Stephan, 2004; Stephan & Clements, 2003).

Understanding of the attribute of length includes understanding that lengths span fixed distances.

Conservation of length includes understanding that as a rigid object is moved, its length does not change.

Transitivity is the understanding that, if the length of a white strip is greater than the length of a gray strip, and the length of the gray strip is greater than that of the black strip, then the white strip is longer than the black strip (even if you could not compare those two—Figure 10.1). A child with this understanding can use a third object to compare the lengths of two other objects.

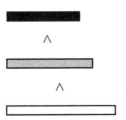

Figure 10.1 An illustration of the transitivity of length

Equal partitioning is the mental activity of slicing up an object into the same-sized units. This idea is not obvious to children. It involves mentally seeing the object as something that can be partitioned (or "cut up") into smaller lengths before even physically measuring. Some children who do *not* yet have this competence, for instance, may understand "5" as a single mark on a ruler, rather than as a length that is cut into five equal-sized units.

Units and unit iteration

In some ways the "other side of the coin" of equal partitioning, unit iteration is the ability to think of the length of a small unit such as a block as *part* of the length of the object being measured and count how many times you can place the length of the smaller block repeatedly, without gaps or overlaps, along the length of the larger object. This yields an equal partitioning of the larger object. Young children do not always see the need for *equal* partitioning and thus the use of *identical* units.

Accumulation of distance and additivity

"Accumulation of distance" is the understanding that, as you iterate a unit, the counting word represents the length covered by all units. Additivity is the idea that lengths can be put together (composed, including measuring around a perimeter) and taken apart.

Origin

"Origin" is the notion that any point on a ratio scale can be used as the origin (and that when available, we usually use "0"). Young children who lack this understanding may begin a measurement with the "1" instead of zero on a ruler or see a pencil that is laid between "2" and "10" and state that it is 10 (instead of 8) inches long.

Relation between number and measurement

Children must understand that the items they are counting to measure are continuous units. They make measurement judgments based upon counting ideas, often based on experiences counting discrete objects. For example, Inhelder and Piaget showed children two rows of matches. The matches in each row were of different lengths, but there was a different number of matches in each so that the rows were the same length (see Figure 10.2). Although, from the adult perspective, the lengths of the rows were the same, many children argued that the row with six matches was longer because it had more matches. They counted *discrete* quantities, but in measurement of *continuous* quantities, the size of the unit must be considered. Children must learn that the larger the unit, the fewer number of units in a given measure, that is, the inverse relation between the size of the unit and the number of those units.

Figure 10.2 An experiment to see if children focus more on discrete or continuous units

The Development of Length Measurement Concepts

Young children also learn to seriate objects—putting them in order—from early in life. Even children as young as 6 months of age can make simple judgments of length (Huttenlocher, Levine, & Ratliff, 2011). From 18 months of age, they know vocabulary such as "big," "small," and "more." By 2 or 3 years of age, they can compare numbers and number pairs on the basis of a common ordering relation. At 3 years, children can make paired comparisons, and 4-year-olds can make small series, but most do not seriate all objects. At about 5 years, children can put six lengths in order by length. Most 5-year-olds also can insert elements into a series.

However, even many primary-grade children do not yet explicitly conserve length or use transitive reasoning. As was the case with number, however, such logical ideas as conservation and transitive reasoning appear to be important for understanding some ideas, but their lack does not prohibit learning of beginning ideas. For example, students who conserve are more likely to understand the idea we just discussed, the inverse relation between the size of the unit and the number of those units. However, with high-quality education experience, even some preschoolers understand the inverse relation, so conservation may not be a rigid prerequisite, but rather a "supportive" idea. In a similar vein, children who conserve are more likely to understand the need to use equal length units when measuring. All in all, though, children can learn many ideas about comparing continuous quantities and measuring before they conserve. And early, high-quality measurement experiences will help develop those logical ideas.

Of course, this development is challenging and occurs over many years. The learning trajectory at the end of this chapter describes the levels of thinking that develop (Sarama, Clements, Barrett, Van Dine, & McDonel, 2011). Here we only briefly describe some common misconceptions and difficulties children have (Barrett, Clements, & Sarama, 2017a; Sarama, Clements, Barrett, Cullen, & Hudyma, 2019).

- To determine which of two objects is "longer," children may compare the objects at one end only.
- Children may leave gaps between units or overlap units when measuring.
- As old as 5 or 6 years, children may write numerals haphazardly to make a "ruler," paying little attention to the size of the spaces in between.
- Children may begin measuring at "1" rather than "0" or even measure from the wrong end of the ruler.
- Children may mistakenly think of marks on a ruler or heel-to-toe steps not as covering space but just a "point" that is counted.
- Some children believe it is necessary to have many copies of a unit to "fill up" the length of the object and will not iterate one copy of a unit (laying it down, marking where it ends, moving it, and so on).
- Some children will "fill up" the length of the object with a unit such as a ruler but will not extend the unit past the endpoint of the object they are measuring. In so doing, they always leave out any fractional part of the unit.
- Many children do not understand that units must be of equal size (e.g., measuring one object with paper clips of different sizes).
- Similarly, children may combine units of different size (e.g., 3 feet and 2 inches is "5 long").

Experience and Education

Young children naturally encounter and discuss quantities in their play (Ginsburg, Inoue, & Seo, 1999). Simply using labels such as "Daddy/Mommy/Baby" and "big/little/tiny" helps children as young as 2 or 3 years of age to become aware of size and to develop seriation abilities. However, teachers must be aware that even concepts such as "large" and "small" are *not* necessarily familiar to young children and easy to understand. Without a concrete reference, these terms can be difficult for toddlers (Björklund, 2012). A large object is only large compared to a smaller object, which has to be *a shared object of attention* for the children and the teacher (Björklund, 2018).

As an example, recall the interaction between teacher Annette and 2-year-old Albin (pp. 211–212). Let's re-join them as Annette guides the discussion to a comparison of sizes as well as shapes (Björklund, 2012). Annette inquired what Albin was calling the shapes.

Albin:	Small.
Annette:	Do you mean a small barrel?
Albin:	Yes. (*Places the block in an upright position.*) It can stand up.
Annette:	Can we compare them, Albin? Look, what is the difference? (*Takes the big yellow barrel from the cup and puts it standing beside the black barrel at the table.*)
Albin:	(*Looks closely at the two barrels, takes the smaller one, and places it on top of the bigger one. The blocks have holes going right through them.*)
Annette:	Yes, has it [the smaller block] room inside it [the bigger block]?
Albin:	(*Tries to put the smaller block inside the bigger one from both ends but with no success.*) No. (*Places the big yellow block to stand again and the black one on top of it.*)
Annette:	Can you find any more big barrels?
Albin:	(*Searches in the box and picks up another small black barrel. Holds the two black ones next to each other.*)
Annette:	Are they exactly the same?
Albin:	Yes, they are.
Annette:	Can you find a big barrel? (*Albin hesitates.*) It can be in another colour as well.
Albin:	(*Rapidly picks out an orange barrel.*) This one.
Annette:	Good, yes.

(p. 224)

Again, *comparisons* are critical for attending to and learning about math concepts, and this is especially true of size (continuous quantity).

Traditionally, the goal of measurement instruction has been to help children learn the skills necessary to use a conventional ruler. In contrast, research and recent curriculum projects suggest that, in addition to such skills, developing the conceptual *foundation* for such skills is critical to develop reliable procedures, concepts (understanding), *and* problem solving. Further, these foundations can be learned starting in preschool (e.g., Zacharos & Kassara, 2012) (Sarama et al., 2019). So, the following are research-based suggestions that are then formalized in the length learning trajectory in Table 10.2.

Many suggest an instructional sequence in which children compare lengths, measure with nonstandard units to see the need for standardization, incorporate the use of manipulative standard units, and measure with a ruler. For example, children might pace from one point to another. As they discuss their strategies, ideas concerning iterating units and using equal-length units emerge.

However, several studies suggest that early experience measuring with several different-sized (nonstandard) units may be the *wrong* thing to do. Until they *understand measurement and the role of the unit*, using different arbitrary units often confuses children. If they do not understand measurement well, or the role of *equal-length* units, switching units frequently—even if the *intent* is to show the need for *standard* units—may send the wrong message—that any combination of any lengths-as-"units" is as good as any other. In contrast, measuring with standard units—even on rulers—is less demanding and is often more interesting and meaningful for young children. Consistent use of these units may develop a model and a context for children's construction of the *idea* of and *need* for equal-length units, as well as the wider notion of what measurement is all about. Later, after they understand the idea of unit and the need for units to be equal in size (otherwise, they are not units!), different units can be used to emphasize the need for *standard* equal-length units (centimeters or inches).

We suggest a sequence of instruction based on recent research. With the youngest children, listen carefully to see how they are interpreting and using language (e.g., "length" as distance between endpoints or as "one end sticking out"). Also *use* language to distinguish counting-based terms, such as "a toy" or "two trucks," and measurement-based terms, such as "some sand" or "longer."

Once they understand these concepts, give children a variety of experiences comparing the length of objects. Once they can line up endpoints, children might use cut pieces of string to find all the objects in the classroom the same length as, shorter than, or longer than the height of their seat. Ideas of transitivity might be discussed.

Next, engage children in experiences that allow them to connect number to length. Provide children with both conventional rulers and manipulative units using *standard units* of length, such as edges of centimeter or inch cubes, specifically labeled "length units" and "centimeters/inches." As they explore with these tools, discuss the ideas of length-unit iteration (not leaving space between successive length units, for example), correct alignment (with a ruler), and the zero-point concept. Having children draw, cut out, and use their own rulers can be used to highlight these ideas.

In all activities, focus on the meaning that the numerals on the ruler have for children, such as enumerating lengths rather than discrete numbers. In other words, classroom discussions should focus on "What are you counting?" with the answer in "length units." Given that counting discrete items often correctly teaches children that the size of the objects does not matter (i.e., for counting discrete objects), plan experiences and reflections on the nature of properties of the length unit in various discrete counting and measurement contexts. Comparing results of measuring the same object with manipulatives and with rulers and using manipulative length units to make their own rulers helps children connect their experiences and ideas.

Children progress from counting paces to constructing a unit of units, such as a "footstrip" consisting of traces of their feet glued to a roll of adding-machine tape. Children may then confront the idea of expressing their result in different-sized units (e.g., 15 paces or 3 footstrips each of which has 5 paces). They also discuss how to deal with leftover space, to count it as a whole unit or as part of a unit. Measuring with units of units helps children think about length as a composition of these units. Furthermore, it provides the basis for constructing rulers with subdivisions (and the relationship between feet and yards or centimeters and meters).

In second or third grade, teachers might introduce the need for standard length units and the relation between the size and number of length units. The use of *multiple* nonstandard length units could be helpful *at this point*.

Instruction focusing on children's interpretations of their measuring activity can enable children to use flexible starting points on a ruler to indicate measures successfully. Without such attention, children often just read off whatever ruler number aligns with the end of the object into the intermediate grades.

Children must eventually learn to subdivide length units. Making one's own ruler and marking halves and other partitions of the unit may be helpful in this regard. Children could fold a unit into halves, mark the fold as a half, and then continue to do so, to build fourths and eighths.

Computer experiences also can help children link number and geometry in measurement activities and build measurement sense. Turtle geometry provides both motivation and meaning for many length measurement activities. This illustrates an important general guideline: Children should use measurement as a means for *achieving a goal not only as an end in itself*. Note that even young children can abstract and generalize measurement ideas working with computers if the interface is appropriate and activities well planned. In giving the turtle directions such as forward 10 steps, right turn 90°, forward 5 steps, they learn both length and turn and angle concepts. In Figure 10.3, children have to "finish the picture" by figuring out the missing measures (more challenging examples are shown in the learning trajectory at the end of the chapter).

Whatever the specific instructional approach taken, research has four general implications. *First, teach measurement as more than a simple skill*—measurement is a complex combination of concepts and skills that develops over years. Understand the foundational concepts of measurement so that you will be better able to interpret children's understanding and ask questions that will lead them to construct these ideas. For example, when children count as they measure, focus children's conversations on *what* they are counting—not "points" but equal-sized units of length. That is, if a child iterates a unit five times, the "five" represents five units of length. For some students "five" signifies the hash mark next to the numeral five instead of the amount of space covered by five units. In this way, the marks on a ruler "mask" the intended conceptual understanding involved in measurement. Children need to understand what they are measuring and why a unit on a ruler is numbered at its end, as well as the full suite of principles. Many children see no problem mixing units (e.g., using both paper clips and pen tops) or using different-sized units (e.g., small and large paper clips) as long as they covered the entire length of

Figure 10.3 "Missing measure" problem with the Logo turtle

the object in some way (Clements, Battista, & Sarama, 1998; Lehrer, 2003). Both research with children and interviews with teachers support the claims that (a) the principles of measurement are difficult for children, (b) they require more attention in school than they are usually given, (c) time needs first to be spent in informal measurement, where use of measurement principles is evident, and (d) transition from informal to formal measurement needs much more time and care, with instruction in formal measure always returning to basic principles (cf. Irwin, Vistro-Yu, & Ell, 2004).

Eventually, children need to create an abstract unit of length (Clements, Battista, Sarama, Swaminathan, & McMillen, 1997; Steffe, 1991). This is not a static image, but rather an interiorization of the process of moving (visually or physically) along an object, segmenting it, and counting the segments. When consecutive units are considered a unitary object, the children have constructed a "conceptual ruler" that can be projected onto unsegmented objects (Steffe, 1991). In addition, the general U.S. math curriculum does not adequately address the notion of unit, and measurement is a fruitful domain in which to turn attention away from separate objects and toward the unit we are counting (cf. Sophian, 2002).

Second, use initial informal activities to establish the attribute of length and develop concepts such as "longer," "shorter," and "equal in length" and strategies such as direct comparison. *Third, encourage children to solve real measurement problems, and, in so doing, to build and iterate units, as well as units of units.*

Fourth, help children closely connect the use of manipulative units and rulers. When conducted in this way, measurement tools and procedures become tools for math and tools for thinking about math (Clements, 1999c; Miller, 1984b, 1989). Well before first grade, children have begun the journey toward that end.

One last note: Explore children's learning of measurement with others. Professional learning communities or lesson study groups can be an exciting and effective way to enhance your teaching and reveal often surprising competencies of young children.

Learning Trajectory for Length Measurement

The importance of length measurement is shown by their frequent appearance in the CCSSM, as shown in Table 10.1.

Table 10.1 Goals for length measurement from the Common Core State Standards–Mathematics (CCSSM).

Measurement and Data [K.MD In CCSSM]

Describe and Compare Measurable Attributes.

1. Describe measurable attributes of objects, such as length or weight. Describe several measurable attributes of a single object.
2. Directly compare two objects with a measurable attribute in common, to see which object has "more of" or "less of" the attribute and describe the difference. *For example, directly compare the heights of two children and describe one child as taller/shorter.*

(Continued)

Table 10.1 (Cont.)

Measurement and Data [1.MD In CCSSM]

Measure Lengths Indirectly and by Iterating Length Units.

1. Order three objects by length; compare the lengths of two objects indirectly by using a third object.
2. Express the length of an object as a whole number of length units by laying multiple copies of a shorter object (the length unit) end to end; understand that the length measurement of an object is the number of same-size length units that span it with no gaps or overlaps. *Limit to contexts where the object being measured is spanned by a whole number of length units with no gaps or overlaps*

Measurement and Data [2.MD In CCSSM]

Measure and Estimate Lengths in Standard Units.

1. Measure the length of an object by selecting and using appropriate tools such as rulers, yardsticks, meter sticks, and measuring tapes.
2. Measure the length of an object twice, using length units of different lengths for the two measurements; describe how the two measurements relate to the size of the unit chosen.
3. Estimate lengths using units of inches, feet, centimeters, and meters.
4. Measure to determine how much longer one object is than another, expressing the length difference in terms of a standard length unit.

Relate Addition and Subtraction to Length.

1. Use addition and subtraction within 100 to solve word problems involving lengths that are given in the same units, e.g., by using drawings (such as drawings of rulers) and equations with a symbol for the unknown number to represent the problem.
2. Represent whole numbers as lengths from 0 on a number line diagram with equally spaced points corresponding to the numbers 0, 1, 2, ..., and represent whole-number sums and differences within 100 on a number line diagram.

Accepting those goals, Table 10.2 provides the two additional components of the learning trajectory, the developmental progression and the instructional tasks, most of which have been studied extensively and shown to be effective (Barrett et al., 2017a; Sarama et al., 2019).

Table 10.2 A Learning Trajectory for Length Measurement

Age	Developmental Progression	Instructional Tasks
2	**Length Senser: Foundations** Makes simple comparisons of length intuitively (similar to what we saw in Subitizing) as young as 6 months of age. However, may not recognize length as a distinct attribute (separate from general size, such as "small" and "big"). "This is long. Everything straight is long. If it's not straight, it can't be long."	*Everyday Length*, [LT]²: Children intuitively compare, order, and build with many types of materials. Encourage manipulation and exploration of their sizes. *Measurement talk*, [LT]²: Suggestions for talking about children's activities at this and the next level.
3	**Length Quantity Recognizer** Identifies length/distance as an attribute. May understand length as an absolute descriptor (e.g., all adults are tall), but not as a comparative (e.g., one person is taller than another).	*Building with Different Lengths*, [LT]²: Working with blocks not only inspires children to build and construct, but also to compare different features such as size and length. Engaging children in a building activity allows them to explore proportions using different

(Continued)

Table 10.2 (Cont.)

Age	Developmental Progression	Instructional Tasks
	"I'm tall, see?" May compare non-corresponding parts of shape in determining side length.	blocks such as cubes and rectangles to compare height or length. This is a guided play activity. *Talking at Length*, [LT]²: Teachers listen for and extend conversations about things that are "long," "tall," "high," and so forth. Encourage and discuss lengths whenever it is relevant, moving from global undifferentiated terms such as "big" to "tall" and "short" and "shorter" and "taller" or "wider" and especially "longer" and "length," and so forth. (Note: Many teachers work hard at "length" vs. "width" vs. "height"—but more important is recognizing that *these are all <u>length!</u>*)

4	**Length Direct Comparer** Physically aligns two objects to determine which is longer or if they are the same length. Uses terms: long, longer, longest.
	
	    Stands two sticks up next to each other on a table and says, "This one's bigger."
	
		Everyday Length Comparisons: In many everyday situations, children compare heights and other lengths directly (who has the tallest tower, the longest clay snake, etc.).
		    As Long As My Arm, [LT]²: Children cut a ribbon the length of their arms and find things in the classroom that are the same length.
		    Building Blocks & Measures, [LT]²: Block building can include rich experiences with length: Comparing the length of blocks, composing two blocks—see Composing Shape (3D)—to be the same length as other blocks, measuring the height of one's building, and so forth. See the full description and the delightful video on [LT]².
		    Compare Lengths: Teachers encourage children to compare lengths throughout the day, such as the lengths of block towers or roads, heights of furniture, and so forth.
		    Encouraging Comparison for Construction Activities, [LT]²: Children build items such as a house or a tower, and then they are asked to compare what they built to a tangible and visible item.
		    Measuring Our Shoes, [LT]²: Children compare the length of their shoes to determine if they are the same length in a narrative setting.
		    Line Up By Height: Children order themselves (with teacher's assistance) by height in groups of five during transitions.

4-5	**Length Indirect Comparer** Compares the length of two objects by representing them with a third object. Uses terms: long, longer, longest, short, shorter, shortest.
	
	    Compares length of two objects with a piece of string.
	
	When asked to measure, may assign a length by guessing or moving along a length while counting (without equal-length units).
	
	    Moves finger along a line segment, saying, "10, 20, 30, 31, 32."
	
	May be able to measure with a ruler, but often lacks understanding or skill (e.g., ignores starting point).
		Will the Table Fit?, [LT]²: Children solve everyday tasks that require indirect comparison, such as whether a doorway is wide enough for a table to go through. Children often *cover* the objects to be compared, so that indirect comparison is actually not possible. Give them a task with objects such as felt strips so that, if they cover them with the third object, such as a (wider) strip of paper (in which case, they will have to visually guess), they can be encouraged to then directly compare them. If they are not correct, ask them how they could have used the paper to better compare. Model laying it next to the objects if necessary.
		    The Helpful Elf (Length Indirect Comparer), [LT]²: Children ("elves" in this story setting) use an intermediate object to measure a "crack" in the castle wall so they can get the exact length of "supertape"

(Continued)

Table 10.2 (Cont.)

Age	Developmental Progression	Instructional Tasks

| | Measures two objects with a ruler to check if they are the same length but does not accurately set the "zero point" for one of the items. | needed to repair the crack. For other narrative settings, see *Ice Cream for Clifford* and *The Shorter Road to School* (*Length Indirect Comparer*), [LT][2]. |
| 4–5 | **Serial Orderer to 5 (Length)** Orders lengths, marked in one to five units. Also, can compare unmarked lengths that are clearly different using broad categories ("big" and "small") and so can order three to five such objects but only by trial and error. With an increase in working memory, begins to build a mental image of the final ordering in which the lengths increase "bit by bit" with each successive length the smallest increase. This leads to more accurate and somewhat more efficient ordering. (This level develops in parallel with "End-to-End Length Measurer.")

 Given towers of cubes, puts in order: 1 to 5. | *Build Stairs (Length to 5)*, [LT][2]: Children make "stairs" with connecting cubes and try to count the steps. They then mix them up and put them back in order.

 What's the Missing Step?: Children see stairs made from connecting cubes (physical manipulatives made into "steps" as in the previous activity). They cover their eyes and the teacher hides one step. They uncover their eyes and identify the missing step, telling how they knew.

 Build Stairs 3: Children should connect their knowledge of "number" to "length," as when they have to find the missing step in the stairs with connecting cubes or computer software (shown here). |

Line Up by Height, [LT][2]: Children order up to five lengths, first with connecting cubes (countable) and then with continuous lengths.

Age	Developmental Progression	Instructional Tasks
4–5	**End-to-End Length Measurer** Lays units end to end. May not recognize the need for equal-length units or be able to measure if there are fewer units than needed. The ability to apply resulting measures to comparison situations develops later in this level. **May use rulers with substantial guidance.** (This develops in parallel with "Serial Orderer to 5 (Length)".) Lays nine 1-inch cubes in a line beside a book to measure how long it is.	*Length Riddles*, [LT][2]: Give children connecting cubes and objects that are the length of three to six of these cubes, such as a book, crayon, pencil. Give children a clue, such as, "You write with me and I am seven cubes long. What am I?" Repeat with the other items.

Measure the Wooly Worm and many other activities, [LT][2]: In this and all activities, measure with physical or drawn units and focus on long, thin units, such as toothpicks cut to 1-inch sections. Explicit emphasis should be given to the *linear nature* of the unit. That is, children should learn that, when measuring with, say, centimeter cubes, it is the *length of*

(Continued)

Table 10.2 (Cont.)

Age	Developmental Progression	Instructional Tasks
		one edge that is the *linear* unit—not the area of a face or volume of the cube. *Workin' on the Railroad* (End to End), [LT]^2: In this motivating activity, children must get the train from the station to the city center by filling in the missing track pieces. They work together to measure using multiple units and find the correct pieces to fix the tracks. *Actual Size*, [LT]^2: After reading some of the book by Steve Jenkins, children measure animal body parts and measure to see how long the entire animal is. *Mr. MixUp's Measuring Mess*, [LT]^2 can be used at several levels. For example, have the puppet (Mr. MixUp) leave gaps between units used to measure an object, or overlap the units, or not align units with the starting and ending point (i.e., ends of the object). Measuring with rulers can begin. Making pictures of rulers and discussing key aspects of measurement that are or are not represented in these pictures can help children understand and apply these concepts. Children should also be asked to make a ruler using a particular unit, such as an inch or centimeter cube. They should learn to carefully mark each unit length and then add the correct numeral. Again, explicit emphasis should be given to the *linear nature* of the unit.
5-6	**Serial Orderer to 6+ (Length)** Orders lengths, marked in one to six units. Understands at least intuitively that any set of objects of different lengths can be placed into a series that always increases (or decreases) in length, so spontaneously seriates with few errors by selecting the shortest (or longest) object, then the next shortest (the one with the "smallest difference"), and so forth. Given towers of cubes, puts in order: 1 to 6.	*Build Stairs (Length to 6+)*, [LT]^2: Children make "stairs" with connecting cubes and count the steps. *Order By Length 6+*, [LT]^2: Children order from six to ten lengths, first with connecting cubes (countable) and then with continuous length that are not so "marked." They then can do the following. *What's the Missing Step?*: Children see stairs made from connecting cubes (physical manipulatives made into "steps"). They cover their eyes and the teacher hides one step. They uncover their eyes and identify the missing step, telling how they knew.
7	**Length Unit Relater and Repeater** Measures by repeating (iterating) a single unit and understands the need for equal-length unit. Repeatedly lays down a single inch unit to accurately measure an object. Relates the size and number of units (inverse relationship). "If you measure with centimeters instead of inches, you'll need more of them, because each one is smaller." Can add two lengths to obtain the length of a whole.	*Building Down to Iteration*, [LT]^2: Children learn iteration as the teacher carefully takes away the number of physical units (at the start—more than needed) used to measure until they iterate just one accurately and appreciating the need for precision and a placeholder when iterating. *Building Up to Iteration*, [LT]^2: In this approach, children try iteration with just one unit and the teacher adds to the number of physical units used to measure as necessary. *Treasure Box*, [LT]^2: Students check the size of a Treasure Box as it is carried home along a ruler-path, to see that the length of an object is the same no matter where it is on a ruler. *Length Riddles*, [LT]^2: Repeat this activity (see above), but provide fewer cues (e.g., only the length)

Table 10.2 (Cont.)

Age	Developmental Progression	Instructional Tasks
	"This is 5 long and this one is 3 long, so they are 8 long together."	and provide only one unit per child so they have to iterate (repeatedly "lay down") a single unit to measure.
	Often can use rulers with minimal guidance in straightforward situations.	*Workin' on the Railroad* (Length Unit Relater and Repeater), [LT]²: In this motivating activity, children must get the train from the station to the city center by filling in the missing track pieces. They work together to measure with a single unit and find the correct pieces to fix the tracks.
	Measures a book's length accurately with a ruler.	*Mr. MixUp's Measuring Mess*, [LT]² can be used at several levels. For example, have the puppet (Mr. MixUp) leave large gaps between iterations of the unit or fail to align the unit at the starting point (this is important with ruler use as well).
		Treats for Twins (Length Unit Relater and Repeater), [LT]²: Children use one or two manipulatives that are 1-inch long to measure a strip of fruit treat so they can get another strip that is exactly the same length at the "treat shop." They iterate units by "leapfrogging" two or using only one and marking the end of each unit. See also *The Helpful Elf (Length Unit Relater and Repeater)*, [LT]². They may also use a self-made ruler—see *The "Accidental" Ruler* and *Make a Ruler*, both in [LT]².
		Draw a Measure: Children may be able to *draw* a line to a given length before they measure objects accurately (Nührenbörger, 2001). Use line-drawing activities to emphasize how you start at the 0 (zero point), and discuss that to measure objects, you have to align the object to that point. Similarly, explicitly discuss what the intervals and the numbers represent, connecting these to end-to-end length measuring with physical units.
		More or Less?, [LT]²: A puppet, "Mr. Tricky," tries to convince children that if they use a larger unit they will need a larger number of them. The children discuss and figure out it is just the opposite, building the length unit *relater* concept of the inverse relation.
		Pirate Ropes, [LT]²: Children measure the length of different length ropes (units 2 and 4 times the length of the shortest unit) dropping from the side of a boat to the ocean floor in a picture, and chart and discuss the results.
		Spaceship Blueprints, [LT]²: Children confront measurement with different units and discuss how many of each unit will fill a linear space. They make an explicit statement that the longer the unit, the fewer are needed.
8	**Length Measurer** Measures, knowing need for identical units, relationship between different units, partitions of unit, zero point on rulers, and accumulation of distance. Considers the length of a bent path as the sum of its parts (not the distance between the endpoints). Begins to estimate.	*Broken Ruler*, [LT]²: Children use a broken ruler (the origin, or "zero point" is missing) to measure foam strips of different lengths. *Wobbly Roads*, [LT]²: Children use different units of measure, such as the edge of a cube, to determine the length of a non-linear road. See also *The Taxi Ride*, [LT]².

(Continued)

Table 10.2 (Cont.)

Age	Developmental Progression	Instructional Tasks
	"I used a meter stick three times, then there was a little left over. So, I lined it up from 0 and found 14 centimeters. So, it's 3 meters, 14 centimeters in all."	*Measure the Room*, [LT]²: To measure the dimensions of the classroom (or other measurement tasks) children create *units of units*, such as a "footstrip" consisting of traces of their feet glued to a roll of adding-machine tape. They measure in different-sized units (e.g., 15 paces or 3 footstrips each of which has 5 paces) and accurately relate these units. They also discuss how to deal with leftover space; that is, to count it as a whole unit or as part of a unit.
8	**Conceptual Ruler Measurer** Possesses an "internal" measurement tool. Mentally moves along an object, segmenting it and counting the segments. Operates arithmetically on measures ("connected lengths"). Subdivides a unit at least into halves. Estimates with accuracy. "I imagine one meter stick after another along the edge of the room. That's how I estimated the room's length is 9 meters."	*Yard Stick Visualization*, [LT]²: Children learn explicit strategies for estimating lengths, including developing benchmarks for units (e.g., an inch-long piece of gum) and composite units (e.g., a 6-inch dollar bill), and mentally iterating those units. *Missing Measures*: Students have to figure out the measures of figures using given measures. This is an excellent activity to conduct on the computer using Logo's turtle graphics (as shown here).

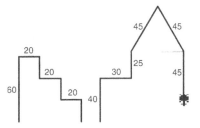

Imagine All the Pieces: In a variety of everyday activities, children find a need for more precision, requiring *subdivision* of the unit. In learning to subdivide units, children may fold a unit into halves, mark the fold as a half, and then continue to do so, to build fourths and eighths.

Final Words

This chapter addressed the learning and teaching of length measurement. Chapter 11 addresses other geometric attributes we need to measure, including area, volume, and angle.

Note

1 Compared to discrete quantities, which can be counted by whole numbers (exactly "4 dogs are here"), continuous quantities are those where there is no limit in how small the parts are into which it can be divided ("together the dogs weigh about 117.3 kg"). Scientific measurement with tools can give us only an approximate measure—to the nearest kilogram or pound, or the nearest 1/100th of a kg, but never an exact number.

11 Geometric Measurement[1]
Area, Volume, and Angle

I had a student who basically understood the difference between area and perimeter. I drew this rectangle on a grid. To figure the area, she counted down like this (Figure 11.1a), then she counted across like this (Figure 11.1b). Then she multiplied 3 times 4 and got 12. So, I asked her what the perimeter was. She said it was "the squares around the outside." She counted like this (Figure 11.1c). She understood the perimeter, she just counted wrong. She was always off by 4.

Do you agree with this teacher? Does the student understand area and perimeter and distinguish between them? What would you have asked the student to find out for sure?

Area Measurement

Area is an amount of two-dimensional surface that is contained within a boundary. Area is complex, and children develop area concepts over time. Sensitivity to area is present in the first year of life, as is sensitivity to number. However, infants' approximate number sense is more accurate than their corresponding sense of area. So, even infants find area challenging!

Area understandings do not develop well in typical U.S. instruction and have not for a long time. Young children show little explicit understanding of measurement. Primary graders, asked how much space a square would cover, used a ruler (once) to measure. Even with manipulatives, many measured a length of a side of a square, then moved the ruler to a parallel position slightly toward the

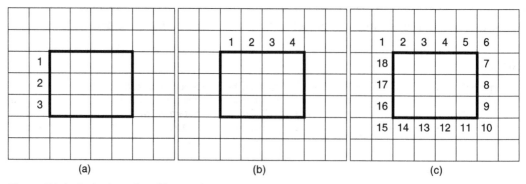

Figure 11.1 A student works with a perimeter problem

opposite side, and, repeating this process, added the values of the lengths (Lehrer et al., 1998b). Limitations in knowledge are also shown by preservice teachers, as the opening story illustrates.

To learn area measurement, children must develop a notion of what area is, as well as the understanding that decomposing and rearranging shapes does not affect their area. Later, children can develop the ability to build an understanding of two-dimensional arrays and then to interpret two lengths as measures of the dimensions of those arrays. Without such understandings and abilities, older students often learn a rule, such as multiplying two lengths, without understanding area concepts. Although area measurement is typically emphasized in the elementary grades, the literature suggests that there are some less formal aspects of area measurement that can be introduced in earlier years.

The Mathematics of Area Measurement

Understanding of area measurement involves learning and coordinating many ideas. Many of these ideas, such as transitivity and relation between number and measurement, are similar to those involved in length measurement. Other foundational concepts follow.

Understanding the attribute of area involves giving a quantitative meaning to the amount of 2D space, or surface. Children's first awareness of area can be seen in informal observations, such as when a child asks for more pieces of colored paper to cover their table. One way to intentionally assess children's understanding of area as an attribute is through comparison tasks. Preschoolers may compare the areas of two shapes by comparing only the length of their sides. With age or good experience, they move to valid strategies, such as one shape on top of the other.

To measure, a unit must be established. This brings us to the following foundational concepts.

Equal Partitioning

Equal partitioning is the mental act of "cutting" two-dimensional space into parts of equal area (usually congruent). Teachers often assume that "multiplying length times width" is the goal for understanding area. However, young children often cannot partition and conserve area, and use counting as a basis for comparing. For example, when it was determined that one share of pieces of paper cookie was too little, preschoolers cut one of that share's pieces into two and handed them both back, apparently believing that the share was now "more" (Miller, 1984b). These children may not understand any foundational concept for area; the point here is that, eventually, children must learn the concept of partitioning surfaces into equal units of area.

Units and Unit Iteration

As with length measurement, children often cover space, but do not initially do so without gaps or overlapping and tend to keep all manipulatives inside the surface, refusing to extend units beyond a boundary, even when subdivisions of the unit are necessary (e.g., using square units to measure a circle's area). They prefer units that physically resemble the region they are covering; for example, choosing bricks to cover a rectangular region and beans to cover an outline of their hands. They also mix shapes of different shape (and areas), such as rectangular and triangular, to cover the same region and accept a measure of "7" even if the seven covering shapes were of different sizes. These concepts have to be developed before they can use iteration of equal units to measure area with understanding. Once these problems have been solved, students need to structure two-dimensional space into an organized array of units to achieve multiplicative thinking in determining area.

Accumulation and Additivity

Accumulation and additivity of area operate similarly as they do in length. Primary-grade students can learn that shapes can be decomposed and composed into regions of the same area.

Structuring Space

Children need to *structure an array* to understand area as truly two-dimensional. That is, they need to understand how a surface can be tiled with squares that line up in rows and columns. Although this is taken as "obvious" by most adults, most primary-grade students have not yet built up this understanding. For example, consider the levels of thinking portrayed by different children as they attempted to complete a drawing of an array of squares, given one column and row, as illustrated in Figure 11.2 (discussed in detail in the companion book). At the lowest level of thinking, children see shapes inside the rectangle, but the entire space is not covered. Only at the later levels do all the squares align vertically and horizontally, as the students learn to compose 2D shapes in terms of rows and columns of squares.

Conservation

Similar to linear measurement, conservation of area is an important idea. Students have difficulty accepting that, when they cut a given region and rearrange its parts to form another shape, the area remains the same. A common response to Figure 11.3 is that the figure on the right takes up more space, either because it looks larger or it has six parts.

Experience and Education

Typical U.S. instruction does not build area concepts and skills well. One group of children were followed for several years (Lehrer et al., 1998b). They improved in space-filling and additive

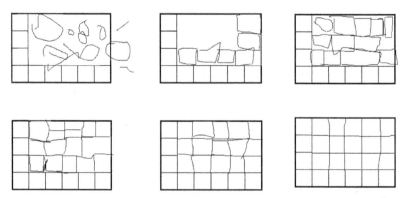

Figure 11.2 Levels of thinking for spatial structuring of 2D space

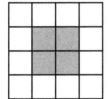 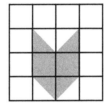

Figure 11.3 Which shape takes up more space?
(Barrett et al., 2017a; The Spatial Reasoning Study Group, 2015c)

composition by Grade 4, but not in other competencies, such as distinguishing area and length, using identical area-units, and finding measures of irregular shapes.

In comparison, research-based activities taught second graders a wide range of area concepts and skills (Lehrer et al., 1998). The teacher presented rectangles (1 × 12, 2 × 6, 4 × 3) and asked which covers the most space. After disagreeing initially, the students transformed the shapes by folding and matching and came to agreement that these rectangles covered the same amount of space. Folding the 4 by 3 rectangle along each dimension led to the recognition that the rectangle—and, ultimately, all three—could be decomposed into 12 squares (intentionally, these were the same as the unit squares in previous quilting activities). Thus, children moved from decomposition to measurement using area-units.

Next, the teacher asked students to compare the areas of "handprints," intending children to measure with squares in a counterintuitive context. Children tried superimposition first and then dismissed that strategy. Beans were used as the area-unit but were rejected as having inadequate space-filling properties (they "left cracks"). The teacher introduced grid paper. The children initially resisted using this tool, probably because they wanted units whose shape was more consistent with the shape of the hands. Eventually, however, the grid paper was adopted by the children. They created a notional system in which fractions of a unit were color-coded for the same denomination (e.g., 1/3 and 2/3 were the same color, and then could be combined into a single unit easily). Thus, they learned about space filling, the irrelevance of the resemblance of the unit shape and the object to be measured, notation, and non-integer measures.

The final task was to compare the area of zoo cages, given shapes (some rectangular, other composites) and their dimensions, but no internal demarcations (e.g., no grid paper). Children learned to build a multiplicative understanding of area. These children displayed substantial learning of all aspects of area measurement. Starting with approximately the same knowledge of measurement in second grade as the longitudinal children (Lehrer et al., 1998b), they surpassed, by the end of second grade, the performance of the longitudinal children, even when the latter were in their fourth grade year.

Thus, many more children could learn more about area, and learn formulas meaningfully, than presently do. Children should learn initial area concepts such as these, and also learn to structure arrays, laying the foundation for learning all area concepts and, eventually, learn to understand and perform accurate area measurement. As another approach, children could compare regions directly to see which covers more surface. Such enjoyable activities as paper folding, or origami, encourage the more sophisticated strategy of superposition—placing one shape on top of the other.

In meaningful contexts, have children explore and discuss the consequences of folding or rearranging pieces to establish that one region, cut and re-assembled, covers the same space (conservation of area). For example, for the oft-confused regions in Figure 11.3, children might compose the pieces on the left to make the figure on the right (using Shape Composition, Chapter 9). They might also use spatial visualization (Chapter 7), imaging that they move the triangular region in the bottom row of the left figure up into the space at the top of the figure. Importantly, all activities in the Shape Composition (Chapter 9) can be used to support children in understanding that different structures or arrangements of regions can have the same area. For example, in the polyominoes activities, children build arrangements of squares that appear very different, but *all have the same area*. Discussions of this can be quite fruitful (Bruce, Flynn, & Bennett, 2015).

Then challenge children to tile a region with a 2D unit of choice and, in the process, discuss issues of leftover spaces, overlapping units, and precision. Guide discussion of these ideas to lead children to mentally partition a region into subregions that can be counted. Counting equal area-units will move the discussion to area measurement itself. Help children realize that there are to be no gaps or overlapping and that the entire region should be covered. Returning to the problem in Figure 11.3, children might count *triangular* units in both or consider the right triangular regions in the figure on the left to be half-units.

Ensure children learn how to structure arrays. One study showed that helping children see and draw clear organizations of rectangular regions in rows and columns was most effective in developing their concepts of spatial structuring and area as in Figure 11.2 (Clements et al., 2018a). Playing with structured materials such as unit blocks, pattern blocks, and tiles can lay the groundwork for this understanding. Building on these informal experiences, children can learn to understand arrays and area explicitly in the primary grades.

In summary, the too-frequent practice of simple counting of units to find area (achievable by preschoolers) leading directly to teaching formulas is a recipe for disaster for many children (Lehrer, 2003). A more successful approach is building upon young children's initial spatial intuitions and appreciating the need for children to construct the idea of measurement units (including development of a measurement sense for standard units; for example, finding common objects in the environment that have a unit measure); experience covering quantities with appropriate measurement units and counting those units; and spatially structure the object they are to measure (e.g., linking counting by groups to the structure of rectangular arrays; building two-dimensional concepts), thus to build a firm foundation for formulas.

The long developmental process usually only begins in the years before first grade. However, we should also appreciate the importance of these early conceptualizations. For example, 3- and 4-year-olds can intuitively compare areas in some contexts.

Learning Trajectory for Area Measurement

The goals for area and volume are not well established for the early years, but some experiences, especially basic concepts of covering and spatial structuring, are probably important. For example, the CCSSM says, "Through building, drawing, and analyzing two-and three-dimensional shapes, students develop a foundation for understanding area, volume, congruence, similarity, and symmetry in later grades" (p. 9). Table 11.1 provides the two additional components of the learning trajectory, the developmental progression, and the instructional tasks.

Table 11.1 A Learning Trajectory for Area Measurement (modified based on new research from the Children's
          Measurement Project; levels from the companion book are in parentheses)

Age	Developmental Progression	Instructional Tasks
0-3	**Area Senser: Foundations** Even children in their first year are sensitive to area. However, they may not explicitly recognize area as an attribute (separate from general size, such as "small" and "big") for some time. If asked to fill in a rectangle, preschoolers may just draw approximations of circles (Mulligan, Prescott, Mitchelmore, & Outhred, 2005). Uses side matching strategies in comparing areas (Silverman, York, & Zuidema, 1984). Draws mostly-closed shapes and lines with no indication of covering the specific region. 	*Finger Paint the Area*, [LT]^2: Children cover surfaces with paint and learn vocabulary for specific dimensions. Such explorations build action-based foundation for understanding area. In many contexts, children can intuitively compare, order, and build with many types of materials, and increasingly learn vocabulary for covering and amount of 2D space.
4	**Area Quantity Recognizer** Perceives the amount of two-dimensional space and can make intuitive comparisons. However, when asked to compare, may compare lengths more than areas because lengths are salient and familiar to them (e.g., compare one side of one piece of paper to the side of another) or make estimates based on a "length plus (not times) width" intuition. However, may compare areas correctly if the task suggestions superposition (putting one on top of the other). Asked to partition a space into squares or copy an image of a rectangle partitioned into an array (rows and columns), may simply draw squares (usually!) inside the rectangle or other types of shapes or short paths on or around the rectangle. Asked which rectangular "candy" is the "same amount" as a bar 4 cm by 5 cm, one child chooses the 4 by 8 by matching the sides of the same length. Another child chooses the 2 by 7, intuitively summing the side lengths. Measures area with ruler, measuring a length, then moving the ruler and measuring that length again, apparently treating length as a 2D space-filling attribute (Lehrer et al., 1998b). Given square tiles and asked how many fit in a 4 by 5 area, child guesses 15. A child places one sheet of paper over the other and says, "This one."	*Turtle Cage*, [LT]^2: Children figure out which cage is bigger for Timmy the Turtle by comparing cages of different shapes and sizes. In other contexts, children might determine which piece of paper will let them paint the biggest picture.
4-5	**Physical Coverer and Counter** Prompted to measure, attempts to cover a rectangular space with physical tiles. However, doesn't organize or structure the 2D space without considerable perceptual support, such as a grid that outlines each individual unit. In drawing (or imagining and pointing to count	*Three Little Pigs*, [LT]^2: Children determine how many tiles are needed to cover a rectangular region (a floor of the pigs' houses) that has a grid of unit squares. To complement this, look for opportunities for children to cover a rectangular region with two-dimensional units of their choosing

Table 11.1 (Cont.)

Age	Developmental Progression	Instructional Tasks

squares as units of area), represents only certain aspects of that structure, such as approximately rectangular shapes next to one another. Makes comparison areas based on simple, direct comparisons (e.g., a child places one sheet of paper over another piece of paper to select the sheet that covers more space).

Covers a region with physical tiles and counts them by removing them one by one.

Draws within the region in an attempt to cover the region.

May fill only next to existing guides (e.g., sides of region).

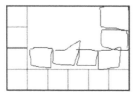

May attempt to fill region but leave gaps and not align drawn shapes (or only align in one dimension).

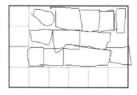

and, in the process, discuss issues of leftover spaces, overlapping units, and precision. Discussions of these ideas lead students to mentally partition a region into subregions that can be counted.

Is One Area the Largest?, [LT]²: Give children three rectangles (e.g., 1 ✚ 12, 2 ✚ 6, 4 ✚ 3) and asked which covers the most space. Guide them to transform the shapes by folding and matching and ultimately transforming them into 12 one-unit squares.

5 **Complete Coverer and Counter** Draws a complete covering of a specific region without gaps or overlaps and in approximations of rows. When provided with more than the total number of physical tiles needed, can build a region of specified area (e.g., build a rectangle with an area of 12 from a pile of 20 tiles).

Draws a complete covering, but with some errors of alignment. Counts around the border, then unsystematically in the interiors, counting some twice and skipping others.

Little Pigs' Brick House, [LT]²: Using tiles, children place squares on a rectangle with a partial grid to figure out how many squares cover the rectangular region (i.e., the area) for each wall of the pigs' brick houses.

Draw Little Pigs' Wall, [LT]²: Challenge children to draw a wall from *Little Pigs' Brick House* showing the bricks. Guide them to use the drawing strategy of using one line to represent the sides of two rows or columns. Discuss how to best represent a tiling, how there must be no gaps.

Area Unit Relater and Repeater Counts individual units, often trying to use the structure of rows. To

Rug Tiles, [LT]²: Children determine how many squares fit in rectangular regions such as

(Continued)

Table 11.1 (Cont.)

Age	Developmental Progression	Instructional Tasks

cover a region with physical units, repeats (iterates) an individual unit. Draws a complete covering based on an intuitive notion of rows and columns, making equal-sized units, but often draws them one at a time. That is, draws individual, mainly equal-sized units that are lined up but may not see groups of units making up individual rows or columns. Relates the size and number of units to cover a region, recognizing that differently sized units will result in different measures and that the larger the unit, the fewer will be needed. Compares areas by accurately counting units in each and comparing the resulting measures.

> Draws as above. Also, counts correctly, aided by counting one row at a time and, often, by perceptual labeling.

> For example, asked to compare shapes, states that they take up the same amount of space "because they both have 4."

a classroom rug by repeating, or iterating, a physical unit. They are guided to discuss, learn, and practice systematic counting strategies for enumerating arrays. At the end, they compare the areas of two differently shaped rugs.

Floor Tiles, [LT]^2: The teacher poses a problem: "Here is a model of the floor we have to tile. We would have to pay $1 for each of the smaller tiles and $2 for each of the larger tiles. Which is the better deal? Make a prediction." In figuring this out, children relate the size of an area unit to the number of units needed to measure a given rectangular region.

6   **Initial Composite Structurer** Identifies a square unit as both a unit and a component of a larger unit of units (a row, column, or group) and uses those structures in counting or drawing. However, needs figural support to structure the space themselves (this may include physical motions of some of the tiles or drawing some collections of units rather than from using the dimensions). At this level, usually does not coordinate the width and height and in measuring, may not use the dimensions of the rectangle to constrain the unit size. Makes reasonable estimates of areas.

> Draws and counts some, but not all, rows as rows. May make several rows and then revert to making individual squares but aligns them in columns. Does not coordinate the width and height. In measurement contexts, does not necessarily use the dimensions of the rectangle to constrain the unit size.

Measure Areas, [LT]^2: Children measure areas, with teacher guidance to use the structure of a row or column. For example, they are asked how many in a row (5–use a number that can easily be skip counted). The teacher sweeps their hand across the row, then sweeps across the next row and repeats the question.

Fill It In, [LT]^2: Children fill in missing squares. Once one or more rows are complete, the teacher uses gestures and language such as "bringing down" a row to focus on iterating rows and the number of units in them. Children learn that the units must be aligned in an array with the same number of units in each row by representing their actions of fitting successive squares into the rectangle. Apart from the squares along the edges of the rectangle, each additional square must match two of its sides to sides of squares already drawn. A child who uses a ruler to draw lines across the rectangle has surely become aware of the alignment of the squares but may still be unaware of the congruence of the rows, so discussion and checking may be important.

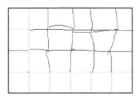

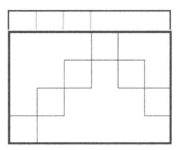

(Continued)

Table 11.1 (Cont.)

Age	Developmental Progression	Instructional Tasks
		Areas of Nonrectangular Regions, [LT]²: Children use squared paper to measure areas to reinforce the use of the unit square, as well as non-integer values.
7	**Area Row and Column Structurer** Decomposes and recomposes partial units to make whole units. For example, draws rows as rows making parallel horizontal lines and so forth. Begins conserving area and reasons about additive composition of areas (e.g., how regions that look different can have the same area measure) and recognizes the need for space filling in most contexts. Draws and counts rows as rows, drawing with parallel lines. Counts the number of squares by iterating the number in each row, either using physical objects or an estimate for the number of times to iterate. Those who count by ones usually do so with a systematic spatial strategy (e.g., by row). If the task is to measure an unmarked rectangular region, measures one dimension to determine the size of the iterated squares and eventually measures both, to determine the number of rows needed in drawing. May not need to complete the drawing to determine the area by counting (most younger children) or computation (repeated addition or multiplication). 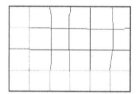	*Creating Grids*, [LT]²: To progress, children need to move from local to global spatial structuring, coordinating their ideas and actions so as to see squares as part of rows and columns. In this activity, children are encouraged to "fill in" open regions by mentally constructing a row, setting up a one-to-one correspondence with the indicated positions, and then repeating that row to fill the rectangular region. 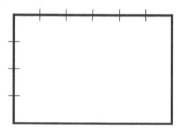 Children learn that the length of a line specifies the number of unit lengths that will fit along it, as when given rectangles with no markings. Discuss that, provided you put the zero mark against one end of the line, the number you read off the other end gives the number of units that would fit along the line. *Conserving Area and Shape Composition*, [LT]²: This is not a single activity, but a reminder that all activities in the Shape Composition (Chapter 9) support children in understanding that different arrangements can have the same area. For example, see *Magic Keys, Tetrominoes, Pentominoes: Create and Solve*, [LT]².
8	**Array Structurer** With linear measures or other similar indications of the two dimensions, multiplicatively iterates rows or columns to determine the area. Does not need to draw in the array to do so. Has an abstract understanding of the rectangular area formula. Understands and justifies that differently shaped regions can have the same areas. Compares regions with transitive reasoning (e.g., A is greater than B, B is greater than C, so I know A is greater than C). Drawings are not necessary. In multiple contexts, children can compute the area from the length and width of rectangles *and* explain how that multiplication creates a measure of area.	*Bricklayer*, [LT]²: Children estimate how large an area is based on a partially completed grid. Then they check their estimates and discuss their strategies. How did they know how many rows and columns there were? How did they calculate the number? Did they use multiplication or skip counting? Ideally, they would use multiplication to calculate the area and not have to draw in the entire triad, as they would be certain of their reasoning. Later, give children two rectangles (later, shapes made from several rectangles) and ask them how much more space is in one than the other.

Volume

Volume introduces even more complexity. First, the third dimension presents a significant challenge to students' spatial structuring, but the very nature of fluid materials that are measured with volume presents another complexity. This leads to two ways to physically measure volume, illustrated by "packing" a space such as a 3D array with cubic units and "filling" a 3D space with iterations of a fluid unit that takes the shape of the container. Filling is easier for children, about the same difficulty as measuring length. At first this might seem surprising, but we can see why, especially in the situation of filling a cylindrical jar in which the (linear) height corresponds with the volume.

On the other hand, "packing" volume is more difficult than length and area but also leads to more sophisticated understandings and to formulas for volume. Preschoolers may learn that fewer large objects will fit in a container than smaller objects. However, to understand packing volume, they have to understand spatial structuring in three dimensions. For example, understanding the spatial structure of one "layer" of a cube building is similar to understanding the spatial structure of the area of a rectangle. With many layers, the situation is complex, especially as some objects in a 3D array are "inside" and therefore hidden from view. Many younger students count only the faces of the cubes, often resulting in counting some cubes, such as those at the corners, multiple times and not counting cubes in the interior. Only a fifth of third graders in one study understood arrays of cubes as consisting of rows and columns in each of several layers.

Experience and Education

As with length and area, how students represent volume influences how they think of structuring volume. For example, compared to only a fifth of students without focused work on spatial structuring, *all* third graders with a wide range of experiences and representations of volume successfully structured space as a 3D array (Lehrer, Strom, & Confrey, 2002). Most even developed the conception of volume as the product of the *area* (i.e., length times width) and the height. One third grader, for example, used squared grid paper to estimate the area of the base of a cylinder, then found the volume by multiplying this estimate by the height of the cylinder "to draw it [the area of the base] through how tall it is." This indicates that a developmental progression for spatial structuring, including packing volume, could reasonably be far more progressive than some cross-sectional studies of students in typical U.S. instructional sequences would indicate.

Experiences with volume can start early, such as containers filled with balls (for unpacking, but also for filling!) or almost any container that can be filled and emptied. Sand and water tables, filled with non-breakable containers of different shapes and sizes, provide physical experiences and good conversation starters. Filling boxes with cubes (ideally boxes that "fit" the cubes well) and discussing how many fit in the bottom (layer) is motivating and interesting to children.

Learning Trajectory for Volume Measurement

Table 11.2 provides the two additional components of the learning trajectory, the developmental progression and the instructional tasks.

Table 11.2 A Learning Trajectory for Volume Measurement (modified based on new research from the Children's Measurement Project; levels from the companion book are in parentheses)

Age	Developmental Progression	Instructional Tasks
0–2	**Volume Senser: Foundations** Sensitive to volume even in the first year; however, they may not for some time explicitly recognize volume as an attribute (separate from general size, such as "small" and "big"). A toddler shows delight in filling up a pail with sand, dumping it out and saying "Big hill!"	*Water Table (Volume Senser)*, [LT]²: Water tables are a great way to introduce measurement concepts and use math vocabulary. As you play, point out math attributes like size and shape. *Fill and Spill* (Volume Senser), [LT]²: Toddlers fill a shape sorter full of shapes, then dump it all out! Repeat!
1–3	**Volume Quantity Recognizer** Identifies capacity or volume as attribute. Builds with blocks, associating more blocks with terms like "big" and fewer blocks with terms like "small." Says, "This box holds a lot of blocks!"	*Water Volume Play*, [LT]²: Fill tables with water or sand, but also with non-breakable containers of different shapes and sizes. Listen for and extend conversations about things that hold a lot (objects, sand, water). *Will I Fit? Box Play*, [LT]²: Children develop a sense of space by crawling in and out of boxes of various sizes. Caregivers label and question to support engagement in learning about space.
3–5	**Volume Filler** Can compare two containers by pouring one into the other (although can be confused at "which holds more" at first). Fills a container using another (smaller container) and counts the number needed to completely fill the larger container (but may not use accurately filled scoops and may not focus on quantifying the total volume or capacity). In packing situations, places cubes into a rectangular box to fill it. Eventually packs entire box with cubes in an organized way. Compares objects by physically or mentally aligning; refers to at least two dimensions of objects. May be able to compare two containers using a third container and transitive reasoning. Pours one container into another to see which holds more. Pours one container into two others, concluding that one holds less because it overflows, and the other is not fully filled.	In *Water Buckets*, [LT]²: Children compare how much sand or water about eight containers will hold. Ask children to show you which holds more and how they knew. Eventually, ask which holds the most. Ask children to show you which of two containers holds more when they use a third container to fill each of the others. Discuss how they knew.
5–6	**Volume Quantifier** Partial understanding of cubes as filling a space. Able to estimate number of scoops needed to fill. Able to attend to both the portion of container filled and the portion remaining unfilled. Recognizes when container is half full. Exhibits initial spatial structuring. Packs box neatly and completely with cubes; may count one cube at a time, while packing, to determine total. Compares objects by physically or mentally aligning and explicitly recognizing three dimensions Initially, may count the *faces* of a cube building, possibly double counting cubes at the corners and usually not counting internal cubes. Eventually counts one cube at a time in carefully structured and guided contexts, such as packing a small box with cubes.	*Guessing Jar (Volume Quantifier)*, [LT]²: Children estimate the number of cubes in a clear container. *Exploring Rectangular Prisms*, [LT]²: Children explore rectangular prisms to determine their volume. They use cubes to fill boxes constructed so a small number of cubes fit well. They eventually predict how many cubes they will need, fill the box, and count to check. Ask children to compare the volume of objects by counting the number of cubes. Encourage them to break a larger object into smaller pieces to "see" all the cubes.

(Continued)

Table 11.2 (Cont.)

Age	Developmental Progression	Instructional Tasks
7	**Volume Unit Relater and Repeater** Uses simple units to fill containers, with accurate counting. Fills a container by repeatedly filling a unit and counting how many. Relates size and number of units explicitly; understands that fewer larger than smaller units will be needed to fill or pack a given container. Can accurately convert units in 1:2 ratio. Says "Let's use the big blocks. We don't need as many of those to fill the box."	*Comparing Juice Containers*, [LT]²: The teacher provides three half-gallon containers labeled "A," "B," and "C" in three different colors, cut to hold two, four, and eight cups, a one-cup measuring cup, and water or sand. Ask children to find the one that holds only four cups. Help them to fill to the "level top" of the measuring cup.
7	**Initial Composite 3D Structurer** Understands cubes as filling a space but does not use layers or multiplicative thinking. Moves to more accurate counting strategies. Relates number of cubes to cubic units as measured by capacity. Given a graduated cylinder marked in cubic-inch units, child understands that sand filled to the 10 in the cylinder would fill a box that holds ten 1-inch cubes. Begins to visualize and operate on composite units such as rows or columns (what we call a 1x1xn core). Iterates to pack the space completely, accounting for "internal/hidden" cubes. Decomposes space, allowing for accurate use of units and subunits. Recognizes when a box is half full, visualizes remaining rows or columns. Counts unsystematically but attempts to account for internal cubes. Counts systematically, trying to account for outside and inside cubes. Counts the numbers of cubes in one row or column of a 3D structure and uses skip counting to get the total.	*How Many Cubes? (Initial Composite 3D Structurer)*, [LT]²: Students use cubes to fill boxes constructed so a small number of cubes fit well. They eventually predict how many cubes they will need, fill the box, and count to check.
8	**3D Row and Column Structurer** Able to coordinate flexibly filling, packing, building aspects of volume. Shows a propensity for additive comparisons (e.g., "this one has 12 more") but may show some nascent multiplicative comparisons (e.g., "this one is four times as big"). Counts or computes (row by column by height) the number of cubes in one row, and then uses addition or skip counting to determine the totals. Initially counts or computes (e.g., number of rows times number of columns) the *number of cubes in one layer*, and then uses addition or skip counting by layers to determine the total volume. Eventually moves to multiplication (e.g., number of cubes in a layer times number of layers). Computes (row times column times height) the number of cubes in one row, and then multiplies by the number of layers to determine the total.	*Fill the Boat*, [LT]²: Children fill the cargo hold in a "boat" with the most wooden blocks possible. *How Many Cubes? (3D Row and Column Structurer)*, [LT]²: Children predict how many cubes will be needed to fill the box, then count and check. Students first get a net, or pattern (below on the left), and a picture. 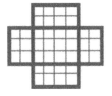

(Continued)

Table 11.2 (Cont.)

Age	Developmental Progression	Instructional Tasks
9	**3D Array Structurer** Has an abstract understanding of the rectangular prism volume formula. Shows a propensity for multiplicative comparisons, coordinates multiplicative and additive comparisons flexibly. With linear measures or other similar indications of the three dimensions, multiplicatively iterates cubes in a row, column, and/or layers to determine the area. Constructions and drawings are not necessary. In multiple contexts, children can compute the volume of rectangular prisms from its dimensions *and* explain how that multiplication creates a measure of volume.	*Measure the Boat*, [LT]²: Children measure the volume of the cargo hold from the Fill the Boat activity. *Cubes in a Box–Pictures Only!*, [LT]²: Ask students how many cubes are needed to fill *only a picture* of a box such as that above, and then just the dimensions. Later, non-integer measures should be used.

Relationships among Length, Area, and Volume

Research indicates that there is no strict developmental sequence for length, area, and volume, but overlapping progress, except in one sense. Spatial structuring appears to develop in order in one, then two, and three dimensions. So, it is reasonable to develop length first, emphasizing the iteration of a unit. Experiences with "filling" volume could be used as another domain in which to discuss the importance of basic measurement concepts (e.g., iterations of equal-size units). Informal experiences constructing arrays with a given number of objects (e.g., square tiles) could develop spatial structuring of 2D space, on which area concepts could be built. Packing volume would follow. Throughout, teachers should explicitly discuss the similarities and differences in the unit structures of length, area, and volume measurement.

Angle and Turn Measure

Methods of measuring the size of angles are based on the division of a circle. As with length and area, children need to understand concepts such as equal partitioning and unit iteration to understand angle and turn measure. In addition, there are several unique challenges in the learning of angle measure. Mathematically, angle has been defined in distinct but related ways. For example, an angle can be considered the figure formed by two rays extending from the same point *or* as the amount of turning necessary to bring one line or plane into coincidence with or parallel to another. The former involves the composition of two components, or parts, of a geometric figure and the latter—the measurement of angle size that concerns us here—involves a *relationship* between two components. Therefore, both are geometric *properties* (see Chapter 8, p. 186) and both are difficult for students to learn. They are also difficult to relate to each other. Students in the early and elementary grades often form separate concepts of angles, such as angle-as-a-shape and angle-as-movement. They also hold separate notions for different turn contexts (e.g., unlimited rotation as a fan vs. a hinge) and for various "bends" in roads, chenille sticks, or figures.

Children hold many misconceptions about angles and angle measure. For example, "straight" may mean "no bend" but also "not up and down" (vertical). Many children correctly compare

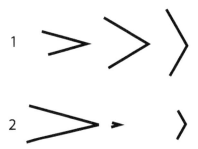

Figure 11.4 Angles with (1) the same and (2) different length line segments

angles if all the line segments are the same length (see the first part of Figure 11.4), but, when the length of the line segments are different (second part of Figure 11.4), only less than half of primary-grade students do so. Instead, they base their judgments on the length of the segments or the distance between their endpoints. Other misconceptions include children's belief that a right angle is an angle that points to the right, or that two right angles in different orientations are not equal.

Experience and Education

The difficulties children encounter might imply that angle and turn measure need not be introduced to young children. However, there are valid reasons to include these as goals for early childhood math education. First, children can and do compare angle and turn measures informally. Second, use of angle size, at least implicitly, is necessary to work with shapes; for example, children who distinguish a square from a non-square rhombus are recognizing angle size relationships, at least at an intuitive level. Third, angle measure plays a pivotal role in geometry throughout school, and laying the groundwork early is a sound curricular goal. Fourth, the research indicates that, although only a small percentage of students learn angles well through elementary school, young children *can* learn these concepts successfully.

Perhaps the most difficult step for students is to understand angle measure dynamically, as in turning. One useful instructional tool is the computer.

Certain computer environments help children quantify angles and especially turns, attaching numbers to these quantities to achieve true measurement. Here we examine two types of computer environments. The first type is computer manipulatives, perhaps the more appropriate of the two for younger children. For example, software can encourage children to use turn and flip tools meaningfully to make pictures and designs and to solve puzzles. Just using these tools helps children bring the concept of a turn to an explicit level of awareness (Sarama et al., 1996). For example, 4-year-old Leah first called the tool the "spin" tool, which made sense—she clicked it repeatedly, "spinning" the shape. Within one week, however, she called it the turn tool and used the left or right tool deliberately. Similarly, when a kindergarten boy worked off-computer, he quickly manipulated the pattern block pieces, resisting answering any questions as to his intent or his reasons. When he finally paused, a researcher asked him how he had made a particular piece fit. He struggled with the answer and then finally said that he "turned it." When working on-computer, he seemed aware of his actions, in that when asked how many times he turned a particular piece (in 30° increments), he correctly said, "Three," without hesitation (Sarama et al., 1996). A second computer environment is Logo's turtle geometry. Logo can also assist children in learning ideas of angle and turn measurement. A young child explained how she turned the turtle 45°: "I went 5, 10, 15, 20 ... 45! [*rotating her hand as she counted*]. It's like a car speedometer. You go up by fives!" (Clements & Battista, 1991). This child mathematized turning. She applied a unit to an act of turning and used her counting abilities to determine a measurement.

Logo's "turtle" needs exact turn commands, such as "RT 90" for "turn right 90 degrees." *If they work under the guidance of a teacher on worthwhile tasks, children can learn a lot about angle and turn measure by directing the Logo turtle. Discussions should focus on the difference between the angle of rotation and the angle formed as the turtle traced a path.*

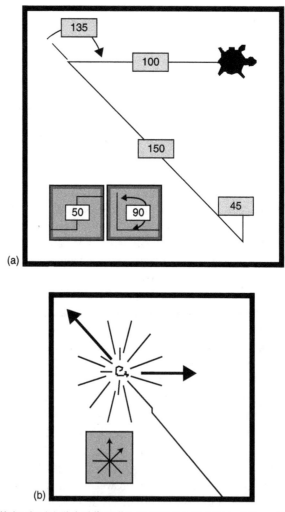

Figure 11.5 Turtle Math tools: (a) "label lines" and "label turn" (inserts) and (b) "angle measure"

For example, Figure 11.5 shows several tools. The "label turns" tool (illustrated in Figure 11.5a) shows the measure of each turn, reminding children that the command "RT 135" created an *external* angle of 135°, creating an *angle* of 45° (the *internal* angle formed by the two lines, 100 and 150 units long).

Figure 11.5b shows a tool that allows children to measure a turn they desire. These tools were built into *Turtle Math* (Clements & Meredith, 1994), but teachers using any Logo, or turtle geometry environment, should ensure students understand the relationships among these ideas. Encourage children to turn their bodies and discuss their movements, then to visualize such movements mentally, using "benchmarks" such as 90° and 45°.

Learning Trajectory for Angle and Turn Measurement

To understand angles, children must understand the various aspects of the angle concept. They must overcome difficulties with orientation, discriminate angles as critical parts of geometric figures, and represent the idea of turns and their measure. They must learn to *connect* all these ideas. This is a difficult task that might best start early, as children deal with corners of figures, comparing angle size, and turns. A learning trajectory for angle measurement is shown in Table 11.3.

Table 11.3 Learning Trajectory for Angle (And Turn) Measurement

Age (years)	Developmental Progression	Instructional Tasks
1-2	**Angle and Turn Senser: Foundations** Infants are sensitive to angles-as-turning, both turning objects and their own body. See more at the first three levels of the Spatial Orientation and the first level of Spatial Visualization.	*Going for a Walk*: Taking children for a walk is one of the first ways they develop an understanding of turning. *Note*: Also see instruction in the first three levels of the Spatial Orientation (turning one's own body) and the first level of Spatial Visualization (turning objects) in Chapter 7.

2-3	**Intuitive Angle Builder** Intuitively uses some angle measure notions in everyday settings, such as building with blocks, solving puzzles, and walking (please see the video in [LT]²).
	
	    Places blocks parallel to one another and at right angles (with the perceptual support of the blocks themselves) to build a "road."
		Around Every Corner!, [LT]²: Use the terms "turn" and "angle" to describe a variety of contexts in which angle is used.
		    Note: Use instruction from Chapter 9 and everyday navigation in Chapter 7 to also emphasize angles and turns.

4-5	**Implicit Angle User** Uses angles and, at least implicitly, some angle measure concepts, such as parallelism and perpendicularity—in physical alignment tasks, construction with blocks, or other everyday contexts (Mitchelmore, 1989, 1992; Seo & Ginsburg, 2004). May identify corresponding angles of a pair of congruent triangles using physical models. Uses the word "angle" or other descriptive vocabulary to describe some of these situations.	*Discussing Angles in Constructions*, [LT]²: Ask children who are building with blocks to describe why they placed blocks as they did, or challenge them to re-route a block "road," to help them reflect on parallelism, perpendicularity, and non-right angles. *As the World Turns (Angle User)*, [LT]²: Use the terms "turn" and "angle" to describe a variety of contexts in which angle is used, from corners of shapes to bending wire, bends in

(*Continued*)

Table 11.3 (Cont.)

Age (years)	Developmental Progression	Instructional Tasks
	Moves a long unit block to be parallel with another block after adjusting the distance between them so as to accurately place a perpendicular block across them, in anticipation of laying several other blocks perpendicularly across them.	a road, or ramps. Ask children to find and describe other things in the world that "have similar angles." Thus, children might relate a door opening to scissors opening, a ramp made with blocks to a ladder against a wall, and so forth. The focus here should be on the notion of angle and turn.
6	**Angle Matcher** Matches angles concretely. Explicitly recognizes parallels from non-parallels in specific contexts (Mitchelmore, 1992). Sorts angles into "smaller" or "larger" (but may be misled by irrelevant features, such as length of line segments). Given several non-congruent triangles, finds pairs that have one angle that is the same measure, by laying the angles on top of one another.	*Match Angles*, [LT][2]: Children find shapes that have the same angles, even if the shapes are not congruent. *Pick the Correct Rhombus*, [LT][2]: Children justify which rhombus they picked to place in a puzzle based on the angles of the shape. *Shape Composition*: Solve shape puzzles that require attention to angle size (i.e., "Shape Composer" level or above; see Chapter 9).
7	**Angle Size Comparer** Differentiates angle and angle size from shapes and contexts and compares angle sizes. Recognizes right angles, and then equal angles of other measures, in different orientations (Mitchelmore, 1989). Compares simple turns. (Note that, without instruction, this and higher levels may not be achieved even by the end of the elementary grades.) "I put all the shapes that have right angles here, and all the ones that have bigger or smaller angles over there." Turns Logo turtle, using degree measurements.	*As the World Turns (Angle Size Comparer)*, [LT][2]: Use the terms "turn" and "angle" to describe a variety of contexts in which angle is used with the focus on the *size* of the "opening" (for scissors) or angle (to the horizontal, for a ramp). Ask children to find and describe other things in the world that "have similar angles." Thus, children might relate a door opening to scissors opening, a ramp made with blocks to a ladder against a wall, and so forth. Talk about "foolers," in which an angle with a smaller measure is represented with longer line segments to address students' persistent *misconception* that the length of the segments, or the resulting length between the endpoints, is an appropriate indication of angle size. *Turtle Turns*: Children use the Logo turtle to make or follow paths and construct shapes (Clements & Meredith, 1994). Similarly, talk about turns and their measures in a variety of movement contexts, such as taking walks and making maps.
8+	**Angle Measurer** Understands angle and angle measure in both primary aspects, and can represent multiple contexts in terms of the standard, generalizable concepts and procedures of angle and angle measure (e.g., two rays, the common endpoint, rotation of one ray to the other around that endpoint, and measure of that rotation).	*As the World Turns (Angle Measurer)*, [LT][2]: Relate a variety of angle size contexts to a common metaphor, such as a clock, noting the two sides of the angle (clock "hands"), the center of rotation, and the amount of turning from one side to the other. *Turtle Turns and Angles*: Students calculate the measure (internal) of angles formed by the Logo turtle's turns (exterior angle).

What about Time, Weight, and Money?

When we were planning the National Research Council (NRC) report on early math (NRC, 2009), we confronted the common presence of the topics of time, weight, and money in state standards. After reviewing the research, we decided that these were in many cases more appropriate as science or social studies, rather than math, topics. Money is a useful representation to use in teaching and learning math, but coin recognition is, again, not math. Making change in project-based learning and so forth can be valuable math (Capraro, 2017). (These topics are mentioned in the CCSSM, but probably simply because they are in other State standards. For example, kindergartners are to "Tell and write time in hours and half-hours using analog and digital clocks" (K.MD), and second graders to "Tell and write time from analog and digital clocks to the nearest five minutes, using a.m. and p.m." and "Solve word problems involving dollar bills, quarters, dimes, nickels, and pennies, using $ and ¢ symbols appropriately. Example: If you have 2 dimes and 3 pennies, how many cents do you have?" (2.MD)). For these reasons, we provide only a brief discussion of time here, and use examples from money in other chapters.

Time is a measurement that is used to order, or sequence, events, and to compare the duration of events and the intervals between them (Burny, Valcke, & Desoete, 2009). Time can be confusing for many reasons. The nature of time still puzzles scientists and philosophers. Mathematically, time is complex with 60 seconds making a minute, 60 minutes an hour, 24 hours a day, 7 days a week, 4 weeks … think of all those number lines! Children need to possess number sense, spatial and time sense, language abilities, the ability to count, and often a beginning knowledge of fractions (halves and quarters). Finally, measuring durations or time-intervals, requires adding and subtracting skills. No wonder time is a difficult concept for all children to learn (Burny, 2012; Burny et al., 2009; Russell & Kamii, 2012).

There is a simple developmental progression for clock reading. Most preschoolers can do little more than label the hour that is linked to familiar activities such as bedtime and eating (Burny et al., 2009). Between one-third to half of 5-year-olds can read the hour and most 6-year-olds can read hours accurately. Almost all second graders can read hours and half-hours and third graders can read within an accuracy of about 5 minutes.

Even though many children do not learn to integrate time concepts until third grade, teachers of younger children can profitably emphasize the meaning of time and connections between time contexts, such as clocks and calendars (Burny, Valcke, & Desoete, 2012). Primary-grade students have greater ability to understand these concepts than some curricula would indicate, and those that teach clock-reading earlier are successful in teaching children earlier (Burny, Valcke, Desoete, & Van Luit, 2013). They should ensure that children understand the time (scientific) concepts, the math concepts, and the language (vocabulary, stories can help here). Time may involve spatial competencies as well (Burny et al., 2012). Many cultures think about time using spatial metaphors (Núñez, Cooperrider, Doan, & Wassmann, 2012). Successful instruction may involve the use of gestures and speech to annotate clock faces (Williams, 2008). Educational technology may help (Wang, Xie, Wang, Hao, & An, 2016).

Children with mathematical difficulties (see Chapter 14) perform worse on clock reading than average achieving children. They struggle with both the procedural and retrieval strategies that are needed to read complex 5- and 1-minute clock times (Burny et al., 2012).

Elapsed time is especially difficult, because students have to coordinate units of different sizes (e.g., hours and minutes). For example, students in Grades 2 and above often claim that the duration between 8:30 and 11:00 is 3 hours 30 minutes, because from 8:00 to 11:00 is 3 hours, and then they *add* 30 minutes (Kamii & Russell, 2012). Understanding these challenges and helping children think about durations in their own lives and then guiding them first to their own informal strategies may be helpful (Kamii & Russell, 2012).

Final Words

Measurement is one of the principal real-world applications of math. It also helps connect the two other critical realms of early math, geometry, and number. Chapter 12 also deals with content domains that are important in connecting math ideas and in solving real-world problems. These include patterns, structures, and early algebraic processes, and data analysis.

Note

1 We include a brief discussion of non-geometric measurement—time and weight—toward the end of this chapter.

12 Other Content Domains
Patterns, Structure, and Algebraic Thinking: Classification and Data

What math is shown in Figure 12.1?

Figure 12.1 What math have these two preschoolers used?

We have discussed most of the domains in standards such as the CCSSM, such as Counting, Number, Operations, Geometry, and Measurement. A common early childhood math topic, patterning, has not been mentioned. And in the CCSSM, the domain is "Operations *and Algebraic Thinking.*" Do patterns belong there? Also, the CCSSM includes "Measurement *and Data.*" What about data?

Patterns, Structure, and Algebraic Thinking: Descriptions and Mathematics

The breadth of ways the term "patterns" is used illustrates a main strength and weakness of the notion as a goal in mathematics. Consider some examples from other chapters:

- Perceptual patterns, such as subitized domino patterns, finger patterns, or auditory patterns (e.g., three beats) (see Chapter 2).

- Patterns in the number words of counting including counting and moving (Wu, 2011b; see also Chapter 3).
-

- The "one-more" pattern of counting (Chapter 3), which also connects counting with arithmetic.
- Numerical patterns, such as a mental representation of 3 as a triangle; or a similar pattern of 5 that can be broken into 2 and 3 and then put back together to make 5 again (see Chapters 2, 3, 5, and 6).
- Arithmetic patterns that are especially powerful and easy for children to see: doubles (3 + 3, 7 + 7), which allow access to combinations such as 7 + 8, and fives (6 made as 5 + 1, 7 as 5 + 2, etc.), which allow for decomposition into fives (see also Chapter 6, as well as other examples in Parker & Baldridge, 2004).
- Spatial patterns, such as the spatial pattern of squares (Chapter 8) or the composition of shapes (Chapter 9), including array structures (Chapter 11).

None of these examples of patterns in early math illustrates the most typical practice of "doing patterns" in early childhood classrooms. Typical practice involves activities such as making paper chains that are "red, blue, red, blue ..." and so forth. These are *repeating patterns*, cyclical repetitions of an identifiable core (Markworth, 2016). Such repeating patterns are important (Lüken, 2018; Rittle-Johnson et al., 2018b), but educators should be aware of the *role* of patterns in math and math education and of how repeated patterns such as the paper chains fit into (but certainly do not, alone, constitute) the large role of patterning and structure.

To begin, mathematician Lynne Steen referred to mathematics as the "science of patterns"—patterns in number and space (1988). The theory of mathematics, according to Steen, is built on relations among patterns and on applications derived from the fit between pattern and observations. Further, these are not "extras" in math education: Children's competencies with pattern and structure have been shown to predict and be an important component of their math learning (Lüken, 2012).

So, the concept of "pattern" goes far beyond sequential, repeating patterns. *Patterning is the search for mathematical regularities and structures*. Identifying and applying patterns helps bring order, cohesion, and predictability to seemingly unorganized situations and allows you to make generalizations beyond the information in front of you. Although it can be viewed as a "content area," *patterning is more than a content area–it is a process, a domain of study, and a habit of mind*. From this broad perspective, children begin this development from the first year of life, as previous chapters have shown. In this chapter, we focus on repeating, numerical (e.g., "growing") and arithmetic patterns. But we should not forget that this is just one small aspect of Steen's "science of patterns."

This position is also consistent with other documents. The NRC report on early math (NRC, 2004) is filled with references to patterns, not as a content area, but, rather, as a general math reasoning process (see "Looking for Patterns and Structures and Organizing Information" on p. 46). That is our main focus in this book. Similarly, two "mathematical practices" of the Common Core relate to patterning and structures: "7. Look for and make use of structure" and "8. Look for and express regularity in repeated reasoning."

The Development of Patterns, Structure, and Algebraic Thinking

From the earliest years, children are sensitive to patterns–of actions, behaviors, visual displays, and so forth. An explicit understanding of patterns develops gradually during the early childhood years. For example, about ¾ of those entering school can copy a repeating pattern, but only ⅓ can extend or explain such patterns. Preschoolers can learn to copy simple patterns and, at least by kindergarten, children can learn to extend and create patterns. Further, children learn to recognize the relationship between different representations of the same pattern (e.g., between visual and motoric, or movement, patterns; red, blue, red, blue ... and snap, clap, snap, clap ...). This is a crucial step in using patterns to make generalizations and to reveal common underlying structures. In the early years of school, children benefit from learning to identify the core unit (e.g., AB) that either repeats (ABABAB) or "grows" (ABAABAAAB), and then use it to generate both these types of patterns. Little else is known, except that patterns are one of many elements of teaching visual literacy with positive long-term impact in the Agam program (Clements et al., 2018a; Razel & Eylon, 1990).

Even though we argue that pattern and structure go far beyond simple repeating patterns, we do *not* ignore such patterning–it is important (Lüken, 2018). For example, preschoolers' repeating patterning predicts later math knowledge (even after controlling for early math knowledge, see also Rittle-Johnson et al., 2018b) although some caution that we need more evidence (Burgoyne, Witteveen, Tolan, Malone, & Hulme, 2017). Patterning is also related to the executive functions of patterning, cognitive flexibility, and working memory (Bock et al., 2015; Miller, Rittle-Johnson, Loehr, & Fyfe, 2016), and these three executive functions are related to math competencies (Schmerold et al., 2017; see also Pasnak, 2017b). Importantly, a review of research showed that learning *complex* patterning is more likely to support children's learning of math than simple repeating (or "alternating") patterns (Pasnak, 2017b, e.g., Collins & Laski, 2015). That suggests teachers must help children progress to the higher levels of the learning trajectory in Table 12.2.

Where is "algebra" in patterning? Having one thing stand for another is the beginnings of algebraic representation. Note that by the pre-K or kindergarten year, many children can name patterns with conventions such as "ABAB." This is potentially another step to algebraic thinking, as it involves using variable names (letters) to label or identify patterns that involve different physical embodiments. Such naming helps children recognize that math focuses on underlying structures, not physical appearances. Further, making a one-to-one correspondence is a primitive version of the basic algebraic notion of mapping—like a function table. Perhaps most clear is that even preschoolers and kindergartners can make certain "early algebraic generalizations," such as "subtracting zero from any number gives that number," or that "subtracting a number from itself gives zero." Such algebraic generalizations can be further developed in the primary grades, although students usually become conscious of these only with explicit guidance from the teacher.

As suggested by the notion of mapping and function tables, *functional thinking* is closely connected to such algebraic generalization. Functional thinking involves (a) generalizing relationships between covarying quantities (e.g., the more rain, the fewer people in the park); (b) representing and justifying these relationships in multiple ways using natural language, tables, and graphs; and (c) reasoning with these representations to understand and predict functional behavior (Blanton, Brizuela, Gardiner, Sawrey, & Newman-Owens, 2015). Working with Grade 1 children, the researchers identified levels of functional thinking (Blanton et al., 2015) and use of variables to represent algebraic relationships (Blanton, Brizuela, Gardiner, Sawrey, & Newman-Owens, 2017). Children worked on tasks related to two sets of data, such as the relationships between the numbers of dogs and noses (for adults, $y = x$), of feet in people's heights without or with a 1-foot or 2-foot hat ($y = x + 1$ or $y = x + 2$), or of stops a train makes and cars if it picks up 2 cars per stop ($y = x + x$ if exclude engine, or $y = x + x + 1$, see the t-chart in Table 12.1). At the earliest levels, children did not discuss relationships in the data. They then could generate a t-chart as in the left of Table 12.1, *but* didn't see relationships even within the two columns (Stops and Cars). Later they could see those relationships but did not relate one column to the other. At later levels they began to be able to do so—to actually engage in functional thinking. However, there was considerable development here too. At first, they relate the Stops to the Cars—but one case at a time (3 stops, 6 cars). They gradually come to see the relationships as a function, even eventually representing it with letters (C = S ± S, for the number of cars equal the number of stops added to itself). At the highest level, they take functions as "mental objects" that they can apply "actions" to. At that level, they see that the relation (doubling) on the left of Table 12.1 has to be altered if we could count the train's engine as a car, yielding the t-chart on the right.

This body of research on young children's understanding of patterns may be used to establish developmentally appropriate learning trajectories for pattern instruction in early math

Table 12.1 Example T-charts of the Train Problem—without considering the engine on the left, and counting the engine on the right

Stops	Cars	Stops	Cars
1	2	1	3
2	4	2	5
3	6	3	7
4	8	4	9
5	10	5	11

education, at least for simple repeating patterns. The research regarding patterning as a way of thinking is less developed, but still offers guidance. The next section includes some promising approaches.

Experience and Education: Patterns, Structure, and Algebraic Thinking

Approaches to teaching the most typical type of patterning in early childhood, repeating patterns, have been documented in several curriculum projects around the world (see Chapter 15). The learning trajectories for this type of pattern are presented in Table 12.2, developing into numerical and algebraic patterning. These activities show that, in addition to placing shapes or other objects in repeating patterns, young children can also engage in rhythmic and musical patterns. They can learn more complicated patterns than the simple ABABAB pattern. For example, they may begin with "clap, clap, slap; clap, clap slap …." They can talk about this pattern, representing the pattern with words and other motions, so that "clap, clap slap …" is transformed to "jump, jump, fall down; jump, jump, fall down …" and soon symbolized as an AABAAB pattern—discussed in that way. That is, surprisingly early, children can name a pattern as an "AABAAB" (and eventually just naming the core unit, "AAB"), which helps them see the same *structure* in patterns using different materials and solve problems more effectively (Fyfe, McNeil, & Rittle-Johnson, 2015). Several curricula have successfully taught such patterns to 4- to 5-year-olds. (For more on the role of rhythm in learning math, see Steinke, 2013.)

Young children's play and informal activities, including stories, storybooks, and songs, can be effective vehicles for learning mathematical patterning in meaningful and motivating contexts. However, teachers need to understand how to take advantage of such opportunities. One teacher, for example, asked children to make clothing patterns for a paper doll. Unfortunately, her examples were colorful, but all had complex random designs that did not include repeated patterns!

In another study, a teacher observed a child paint four iterations of a green, pink, and purple pattern core. The child said, "Look at my patterns." The teacher observed this and called out, "Looks like you are doing some lovely artwork." She did not seem to be aware of the opportunity she had missed (Fox, 2005, p. 317). In another preschool, a child was working with a hammer and nails construction kit. Chelsea was tapping shapes on to the corkboard and described it to other children at the table. "It is a necklace with diamonds—diamond, funny shape, diamond, funny shape, diamond, funny shape." The teacher questioned Chelsea about her creation. After the teacher intervened, another child, Harriet, began to use the equipment to make a repeating pattern (yellow circle—green triangle). A second child, Emma, joined the table and created a necklace utilizing an ABBA pattern. Chelsea's explicit interest in mathematical patterning, and the teacher's involvement and intervention, encouraged other children to join her in creating patterns. This was useful mathematical patterning in a play-based context (p. 318).

Extending the conclusions of these research projects, we believe that teachers need to understand the learning trajectories of patterning in all its forms and the wider implications of patterning as a habit of mind. We agree that in patterning, as in all math areas, there is a need to help teachers plan specific experiences and activities, capitalize on relevant child-initiated activities, and elicit and guide mathematically generative discussions in all settings.

Several studies and projects illustrate this approach. First graders who studied repeating patterns, but also symmetrical patterns, patterns with increasing numbers of elements, and patterns involving rotation of an object through six or eight positions, scored better in reading and math (Pasnak et al., 2012). In a related study, first graders who worked with patterns, compared to those who worked with reading or social studies, performed better on math concepts. They even outperformed those who worked directly with math on one of two assessments (Kidd et al., 2013).

Similarly, additional projects from Australia show the power of emphasizing a broad range of activities focusing on *mathematical pattern and structure*. The Pattern and Structure Mathematical Awareness Program (PASMAP) focuses on five structural groupings: sequences, structured counting, shape and alignment, equal spacing, and partitioning (Mulligan & Mitchelmore, 2018). The instructional activities developed students' visual memory as they observed, recalled and represented numerical and spatial structures in processes such as counting, partitioning, subitizing, grouping and unitizing (this implies that *many of the most important patterning activities in this book are in other chapters*, as the introduction to this chapter suggested). These activities were regularly repeated in varied form to encourage children to generalize. For example, children reproduced patterns, including repeating patterns and simple grids and arrays of varying sizes (including triangular or square numbers). They explained why patterns are "the same" and described repeating patterns with ordinal numbers (e.g., "every third block is blue"). They reproduced grid patterns when part of the pattern was hidden, or from memory.

Thus, these "pattern and structure" activities included visual structures such as those used in subitizing (Chapter 2) and spatial structuring (Chapters 7 and 11); structuring linear space (Chapter 10) and the structure of numbers connected to these (Chapters 3 to 6). Thus, this view of pattern and structure includes, but goes far beyond, simple linear patterns, and connects seemingly separate areas of math. *Children who do not develop this type of knowledge tend to make little progress in mathematics.* But all children, especially those with low entry skills, can make substantial progress quickly when provided with learning experiences focusing on pattern and structure (Mulligan, Mitchelmore, English, & Crevensten, 2012), defined broadly (e.g., not just as "alternating color"; Papic, Mulligan, & Mitchelmore, 2011). They benefit substantially by focused instruction on structure (Mulligan, English, Mitchelmore, Welsby, & Crevensten, 2011a, 2011b; Mulligan & Mitchelmore, 2018).

Moving into the elementary school years, children benefit from describing patterns with numbers. Even repeating patterns can be described as "two of something, then one of something else." The patterns of counting, arithmetic, spatial structuring, and so forth have been emphasized in other chapters and those in number and arithmetic are included in the learning trajectory here as well. For example, we re-emphasize that children should be helped to make and use arithmetic generalizations, such as the following:

- When you add zero to a number the sum is always that number.
- When you add one to a number the sum is always the next number in the counting sequence.
- When you add two numbers it does not matter which number "comes first."
- When you add three numbers it does not matter which two you add first.

For many, these are the first clear links among patterns, number, and algebra. One student's use of a strategy might prompt another student to ask why it would work, which would lead to discussions of general statements about a given operation. However, Carpenter and Levi found this did not occur regularly in first- and second-grade classrooms, so they used Bob Davis' activities from the Madison Project, in particular his activities involving true and false and open number sentences. For example, students were asked to verify the truth of "true/false number sentences" such as 22 − 12 = 10 (true or false?), and others such as 7 + 8 = 16, 67 + 54 = 571. They also solved open number sentences in a variety of forms. The open number sentences involved single variables, such as $x + 58 = 84$, multiple variables such as $x + y = 12$, and repeated variables, such as $x + x = 48$. Certain cases were selected to prompt discussion of basic properties of numerical operations and relations; for example, verifying the truth of 324 + 0 = 324 led students to generalizations about zero. (Note: when you say adding a zero to a number does not change that number, you must mean "adding just plain zero," not concatenating a zero, e.g., 10 and 0 is 100, or adding numbers that include zero, e.g., 100 + 100; Carpenter & Levi, 1999.) Students also enjoyed and benefited from creating and trading their own true/false number sentences. Another case is sentences in the form of 15 + 16 = 15 + x. This may prompt students to recognize they do not have to compute, and then to use more sophisticated strategies for problems such as 67 + 83 = x + 82, such as "I knew 83 is one more than 82, so x has to be one more than 67 to balance—68!" (Carpenter, Franke, & Levi, 2003, pp. 47–57).

These researchers also indicated several practices to *avoid* (Carpenter et al., 2003). For example, avoid using the equal sign to list objects and numbers (e.g., John = 8, Marcie = 9 ...). Do not use it to give a number in a collection (| | | = 3) or to indicate that the same number is in two collections. Finally, do not use it to represent strings of calculations, such as 20 + 30 = 50 + 7 = 57 + 8 = 65. This last one is a common, but perhaps the most egregious, case. It could be replaced with series of equations, if they are really needed, such as 20 + 30 = 50; 50 + 7 = 57; 57 + 8 = 65.

There are a few more research-based instructional suggestions on the equal sign, which is often badly taught. One project introduces it *only* in the context of finding all the decompositions for a number, and they place that number (e.g., 5) first: 5 = 5 + 0, 5 = 4 + 1, 5 = 3 + 2 (Fuson & Abrahamson, 2009). Children then write equations chains in which they write a number in many varied ways (e.g., 9 = 8 + 1 = 23 − 14 = 109 − 100 = 1 + 1 + 1 + 1 + 5 = ...). Such work helps avoid limited conceptualizations.

Another study found that kindergartners and first graders' knowledge could recognize legitimate number sentences, such as 3 + 2 = 5, but only first graders could *produce* such sentences. However, they found it more difficult to recognize number sentences such as 8 = 12 − 4. Thus, teachers need to provide a variety of examples for children, including having the operation on the right side and having multiple operations, such as 4 + 2 + 1 + 3 + 2 = 12. In all such work, discuss the nature of addition and subtraction number sentences and the different symbols, the role they play, and their defining and non-defining properties. For example, students might eventually generalize to see not just that 3 + 2 = 5 and 2 + 3 = 5, but that 3 + 2 = 2 + 3. Still, however, they might only see that the order of the numbers "does not matter"—without understanding that this is a property of *addition* (not pairs of numbers in general). Discussions can help them to understand the arithmetic operations as "things to think about" and to discuss their properties (see many examples in Kaput, Carraher, & Blanton, 2008).

Another study of third and fourth graders revealed that teaching the equal sign in equations *contrasted* with the greater than (>) and less than (<) signs helped these students understand the equal sign relational meaning (Hattikudur & Alibali, 2007). The students learned three signs in the same time that the comparison students learned just one.

Providing second graders with equations such as $2 + 5 + 1 = 3 + \square$ and giving them feedback improved their performance substantially. In this study, the type of tasks, non-symbolic, semi-symbolic, or symbolic, did not matter (Sherman, Bisanz, & Popescu, 2007). What probably does matter is whether students see such work and all arithmetic work as a sense-making activity. That is, asked to solve a problem like $8 + 4 = \square + 5$, students often put "12" in the blank space/box. Others include the 5 in their total, putting "17" in the blank space/box. Others create a running total by putting a "12" in the blank space/box and an "= 17" following the 5 (Franke, Carpenter, & Battey, 2008). As discussed, they see the equal sign as an instruction to compute, as "the answer is coming" sign. This is not its mathematical meaning.

In a later study, the type of tasks did matter. Experience with non-symbolic problems facilitated performance on symbolic problems (Sherman & Bisanz, 2009). That is, children solved problems with objects, such as what to put in the fourth tray to keep the number of objects in two pairs of trays the same: (e.g., ••••• •• | •••• ?). Such experiences helped children map their successful concepts and strategies to symbolic equivalence problems.

Solutions are facilitated when one understands the semantics—the meaning of each symbol. For example, students might think as follows:

What I face is an equation, with a number I don't know. I am supposed to find the number in the box. The two sides of the equation must be equal. I do know how to find the sum on the left-hand side of the equation: $8 + 4 = 12$. So, I can rewrite the equation as:

$12 = \square + 5$

or maybe more comfortably as:

$\square + 5 = 12.$

So, now I'm looking for the number that has the property that when I add 5 to it, I get 12. I know how to do that. The answer is 7, so 7 goes in the [blank space/]box. And, I can check: $8 + 4 = 12$ and $7 + 5 = 12$, so $8 + 4 = 7 + 5$.

(Schoenfeld, 2008)

Such solutions depend on knowing the semantics of the equation. If students see these equations in terms of their meaning, they can make sense of them and solve them. Schoenfeld argues that every problem, even $3 + 2 = 5$, is related to meaning (a group of 3 is combined with a group of 2 ...) and that the more it is explicitly connected to that meaning for students, the stronger will be both their arithmetic and early algebra competence.

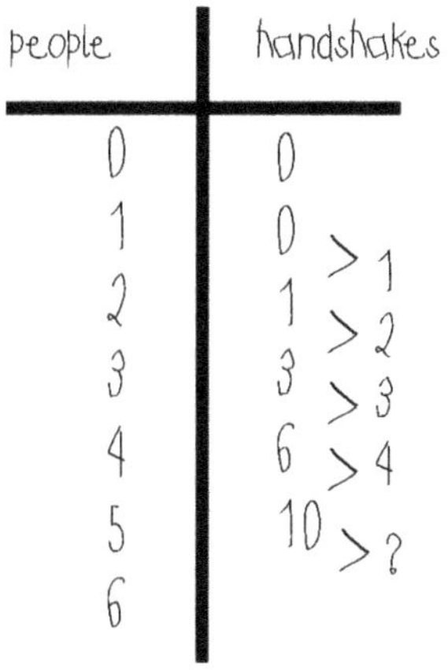

Figure 12.2 First graders solve the "Handshake Problem" with a t-chart

This means that teaching computation without attention to relational and algebraic thinking erects a roadblock to students' later progress in math. Students must see all math as a search for patterns, structure, and relationships, as a process of making and testing ideas, and, in general, making sense of quantitative and spatial situations (Schoenfeld, 2008). Only if they do so throughout their work with math will they be well prepared for later math, including algebra.

A couple of recent projects are perhaps the most surprising. The Mathematics Enhancement Project in England has developed algebra activities for preschoolers. Consider the problem of solving two simultaneous linear equations $x + y = 4$ and $x = y$. In this project, 4- to 5-year-old children color in the outlines of snails following two rules: they have to color in four snails, and the number of brown snails must equal the number of yellow snails. The materials were developed by David Burghes based on the Hungary mathematics curriculum.

Similarly, an early algebra project by Maria Blanton and others (Blanton & Kaput, 2011; Blanton et al., 2012) shows that children in pre-K to first grade can count and record patterns using objects or drawings, and by second and third grade could organize numerical-only data independently. They suggested using t-charts (teachers' name for simple function tables with a column of data for the independent variable followed by a column of data for the dependent variable) with all early grades. For example, first graders created t-charts such as shown in Figure 12.2 to record the total number of handshakes in groups of varying size. Can you figure out the pattern and extend it (and check it)?

Another study showed that 8-year-olds similarly could perform and represent functional thinking (Warren & Cooper, 2008). Finally, a recent study showed that students need to both recognize and produce number sentences in different formats to understand them in ways that supports algebraic thinking (Mark-Zigdon & Tirosh, 2017b).

Learning Trajectory for Pattern and Structure

Two reports agree with our position that patterning is a general way of thinking mathematically. In developing our report on early math (NRC, 2009), we decided that patterning should not be a content domain, but, rather, a math process (and as such, belongs in Chapter 13).

A learning trajectory for patterns is presented in Table 12.2. Remember that almost every chapter in this book contains relational thinking about the patterns and structures of math. And remember that videos for every level of the developmental progression, as well as resources, videos, and many additional activities for every level are on [LT]^2. Finally, this table also has a "forest and trees" column that encourages you to think of the *big picture*, the broad levels of thinking.

Table 12.2 Learning Trajectory for Patterns, Structure, and Algebraic Thinking

Age	Broad	Developmental Progression	Instructional Activities
0–2	Perceptual Patterner	**Intuitive Patterner: Foundations** Detects and uses patterning implicitly and intuitively, such as in movement activities or common nursery rhymes that repeat words and action. May be attentive to repeating patterns without recognizing them explicitly or accurately, often attending to individual attributes such as color. Names a striped shirt with no repeating unit a "pattern."	*Rhythmic Patterns* and *Finger Sticks Finger Play*, [LT]^2: Children learn to identify patterns by using rhythmic expressions. Emphasize the patterns in children's songs, poems, and spontaneous movements, such as dancing. *Math in Everyday Routines* and *Patterning Talk*, [LT]^2: Work with manipulatives, such as blocks or puzzles, manipulatives to order (e.g., simple materials, such as pencils of different lengths, or such commercial materials as those from the Montessori group), and discussions of regularities help children use and, eventually, recognize patterns.
2–3		**Pattern Recognizer** Recognizes a simple pattern, usually ABABAB, *as* a pattern, even if doesn't yet name or describe it. "I'm wearing a pattern" about a shirt with black, white, black, white (and so on) stripes.	*Movement Patterns*, [LT]^2: Spend only a few minutes counting with children in patterns of 2, or another appropriate even number; for example, "one, *two!*, three, *four!*, five, *six!* ...." For more fun, get a drum or use the corners of a wooden block to tap along with the counting, tapping harder for emphasis at each second beat. *Patterns in the Environment*, [LT]^2 or *Pattern Walk*: Read the book *I See Patterns*. Patterns in the world may be confusing

(Continued)

Table 12.2 (Cont.)

Age Broad	Developmental Progression	Instructional Activities
		because of all the irrelevant, distracting information available; this book will help explain and distinguish types of patterns. Then, go on a "pattern walk" and find, discuss, photograph, and draw the patterns you see. *Clothes Patterns*, [LT]²: Find repeating patterns in children's clothing colors. Encourage them to wear clothes with patterns, and to discuss the patterns they wear to school.
3-4	**Patterner AB:** Recognizes, describes, and builds repeating ABAB patterns. These involve the following, which many children learn in this order, although this can vary by the task.[1] • **Fixes AB**: Fills in missing element of an ABAB pattern. Given objects in a row with one missing, ABAB_BAB, identifies and fills in the missing element. • **Duplicates AB**: Duplicates ABABAB pattern (at first may have to work close to the model pattern, but eventually can build the same pattern away from the model pattern or when the model is out of sight). Given objects in a row, ABABAB, makes their own ABABAB row in a different location. • **Extends AB:** Extends AB patterns to add multiple units to the end of the pattern. This is easier for children if the pattern ends with a complete unit (Tsamir, Tirosh, Levenson, Barkai, & Tabach, 2017), but they eventually learn to extend those that end with a partial unit.	*Pattern Fixer with Beads*, [LT]²: Show children a pattern and chant it with them (e.g., "square, triangle, square, triangle, square, triangle," for at least three complete units of the pattern). Point to a space later in the pattern where a shape "fell off." Ask children what shape they need to fix the pattern. If children need help, have them chant the pattern as you point to each block, allowing the pattern of words to indicate the missing shape. *Pattern Strips*, [LT]²: Show children a strip of paper with a geometric pattern pictured on it and have them describe the pattern on the strip ("square, circle, square, circle, square, circle..."). • Have the children help you copy the pattern, if necessary, by placing pattern blocks directly on the pattern strip. • Have them chant the pattern as you point to each block. *Make a Longer Pattern (Patterner AB)*, [LT]²: Show children a pattern strip with an ABABAB pattern and ask them to use materials to "keep going" with the pattern. Then, discuss how they knew how to do so. *Dancing Patterns (Patterner AB)*, [LT]²: Tell the children they will be dancing patterns, and that the first one will be clap, kick; clap, kick ... Sing a song along with the pattern. Later, have them describe the pattern.
4-5	**Patterner:** Recognizes, describes, and builds repeating patterns, including AB but also patterns with core units such as AAB, ABC, and AABC. • *Fixes*: Fills in missing element of a repeating pattern.[2] • *Duplicates*: Duplicates repeating patterns.	*Note*: Most of the activities in the previous level can be used here with different core units. *Dancing Patterns (Patterner)*, [LT]²: As above. *Creative Patterns*, [LT]²: This is a good time to add pattern-creating materials to your creative area. Someone is sure to want to make a pattern they can take home.

(Continued)

Table 12.2 (Cont.)

Age	Broad	Developmental Progression	Instructional Activities
		• *Extends*: Extends repeating patterns to add multiple units to the end of the pattern. This is easier for children if the pattern ends with a complete unit (Tsamir et al., 2017), but they can learn to extend those that end with a partial unit. Given objects in a row, ABBABBABB, adds ABBABB to the end of the row.	*Make a Longer Pattern (Patterner)*, [LT]²: As above, with different core units. *Stringing Beads*, [LT]²: Following a "pattern tag" at the end of the string, children place beads on the string to extend the pattern and make a pattern necklace. *Marching Patterns 2 (and 3)–Extend*: Children extend a linear pattern of musicians by one full repetition of an entire unit. When they complete the pattern, the musicians march in a parade. The musicians are in patterns such as AAB and ABB in level 2 and ABC in level 3.  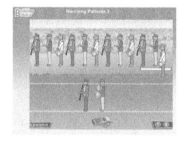
4-5	**Abstract Patterner**	**Pattern Translator and Unit Recognizer** Translates patterns into new media or using new materials; that is, abstract and generalize the pattern. Identifies the smallest core unit of a repeating pattern. (Most research indicates this develops later, Miller et al., 2016.) • *Translates Pattern*. Translates patterns into new media; that is, abstract and generalize the pattern (e.g., sees a "red, blue, purple" pattern of connecting cubes and builds the same pattern with toothpicks, –|\,–|\,–|\, naming both of them: "Those are ABC patterns."	*Pattern Strips–Extended*, [LT]²: Re-introduce "Pattern Strips," emphasizing the idea of the *core unit* of the pattern. • Show children a pattern strip and have children describe the pattern on the strip (vertical, vertical, horizontal; vertical, vertical, horizontal; vertical, vertical, horizontal; ...). • Ask them what the "core" of this pattern is ("vertical, vertical, horizontal"). • Have the children help you copy the pattern using sticks. Each child should make one copy of the core. • Ask them to "keep going" by adding additional copies of the core.

(Continued)

Table 12.2 (Cont.)

Age	Broad	Developmental Progression	Instructional Activities
		• *Recognize Core Units.* Identifies the core unit of a repeating pattern; that is, the smallest portion of the pattern that repeats to create the pattern (e.g., "red, blue, purple" in an ABCABCABC pattern). Given objects in an ABBABBABB pattern, identifies the core unit of the pattern as "ABB." In functional thinking situations (e.g., p. 282), does not yet see math relationships in sets of data (Blanton et al., 2015).	*Cube Patterns,* [LT][2]: Put a large group of cubes in the middle of the children. Show them a "tower" of cubes of two colors, such as blue, blue, yellow. • Have each child make a blue, blue, yellow tower. • Have children link them together, making a long cube pattern train! • Chant the colors as you point to each cube in the long pattern train. • Repeat with a different core tower. Scaffolding Strategies: • More help—For children who have difficulty making and extending a pattern, making cube patterns step by step may be useful. Help them to stand several towers next to each other (e.g., red cube, blue cube), and see they are all the same. "Read" the pattern, chanting each color as you read one tower after another from the bottom up. Finally, link them together and chant the pattern again. • Extra challenge—Use more complex patterns. Even try ones that end with the same item they begin with, such as a core unit of ABBCA, which produces the confusing pattern: ABBCAABBCAABBCA. *Patterns Free Explore*: Students explore patterning by creating rhythmic patterns of their own. The patterns are presented in drumbeats of two pitches and constant duration (steady beat), but also visually—emphasizing the *core unit* of the pattern. 
5-7	**Numeric Patterner**	**Numeric Patterner** Describes a pattern numerically, can translate between geometric and numeric representation of a series. In functional thinking, builds and perceives a t-chart as a sequence of particular instances (Blanton et al., 2015).	*Growing Patterns,* [LT][2]: Children observe, copy, and create patterns that grow—especially those such as the square growing pattern and triangular growing pattern—noting the geometric and numerical patterns that they embody.

(Continued)

Table 12.2 (Cont.)

Age	Broad	Developmental Progression	Instructional Activities
		Given objects in a geometric pattern, describes the numeric progression. Given a situation and asked to generate data for a t-chart, children build each column separately, by counting or skip counting.	 *Patterns on a Hundreds Chart (Numeric Patterner)*, [LT]²: Students skip count multiples of 1 to 12 to identify patterns they find on a hundreds chart. *Finding Patterns in Books*: Children's literature is filled with good texts that encourage children to be "pattern hunters" (see examples and lists of books in Whitin & Whitin, 2011). *Arithmetic and Algebraic Thinking*: See the many examples in the text (especially pp. 279–280).
	Arithmetic and Algebraic Patterner	**Beginning Arithmetic Patterner** Recognizes and uses arithmetic patterns with perceptual or pedagogical support, often first those that involve properties of zero. The child also accepts number sentences not in the form of 3 + 4 = 7 (e.g., 7 = 3 + 4, or even 3 + 4 = 2 + 5). This represents a move from an "equals-as-an answer" notion to recognizing that equals means equivalent numbers. (See Chapters 5 and 6.) In functional thinking, builds two sets (e.g., in a t-chart) following two separate general rules (Blanton et al., 2015). Given a situation and asked to generate data for a t-chart, children generalize a rule (you add 2 every time) for each column separately.	*Generating Conjectures*, [LT]²: Children discuss (after teacher models) different number sentences to develop understanding of the meaning of a conjecture about arithmetic patterns or use of arithmetic properties.
6–7		**Relational Thinker ✛** Recognizes and uses patterns that involve addition and subtraction and, understanding equality, can compare two sides of a number sentence with reasoning, and thus does not have to carry out computations. In functional thinking, creates functional relationships between two data sets but only for specific cases (Blanton et al., 2015). May use letters to represent numbers, but only as representing objects or fixed values (Blanton et al., 2017). Given a situation involving two data sets, relates the columns in a t-chart but only for one row at a time.	*True or False with Number Sentences (Relational Thinker ✛)*, [LT]²: Children determine if both sides of number sentences such as 7 + 2 = 3 + 6 will equal the same number (even without adding), that is, if the sentences are true or false in their structure. *Functions and T-charts*: Have children solve simple function problems (e.g., dogs and noses, p. 282) and discuss their t-charts.

(Continued)

Table 12.2 (Cont.)

Age	Broad	Developmental Progression	Instructional Activities

		Relational Thinker–Symbolic ➕ Recognizes and uses patterns that involve addition and subtraction and an understanding of equality. Can compare two sides of a number sentence with reasoning, even when the quantities are represented by variables, such as a + b = b + a. In functional thinking, generalizes functional relationships between two data sets, at first just noticing, and later a quantitative relationship (Blanton et al., 2015). Uses letters for unknown numbers, an initial algebraic notion.
		    Given a situation involving two data sets, relates the columns in a t-chart, describing how they added to get each number.
			True or False with Number Sentences (Symbolic ➕), [LT]²: Children determine if both sides of algebraic sentences such as a + b - b = a will equal the same number, that is, if the sentences are true or false in their structure.
			    Functions and T-charts: Have children solve simple function problems (e.g., dogs and noses or heights-with-hats, p. 282) and discuss how they created their t-charts.

6-8		**Relational Thinker with Multiplication** Recognizes and uses patterns that involve multiplication as repeated addition and use of the distributive property to partition number facts. In functional thinking, generalizes functional relationships between two data sets, using letters as variables to represent this relationship (Blanton et al., 2015).
		    Given a situation involving two data sets, relates the columns in a t-chart, describing the *specific math transformation* that would apply to each number in the first column to generate the corresponding number in the second column.
			Patterns on a Hundreds Chart (Relational Thinker with Multiplication), [LT]²: Students will skip count multiples of 1-12 to identify patterns they find on a hundreds chart.
			    Functions and T-charts: Have children solve function problems and discuss the relationships between the columns.

6-9	Functional Algebraic Thinker	**Functions-as-Objects** In functional thinking, generalizes functional relationships between two data sets, understanding the boundaries of generalizability and thus understanding the function as a math object (Blanton et al., 2015). Given a situation involving two data sets, relates the columns in a t-chart, describing the *specific math transformation* in a formula and understands that changing any conditions would change the relationship. Uses variables to show the change, such as C = S + S changed to C = S + S + 1 if the engine is counted.	*Functions and T-charts:* Have children solve function problems and discuss the relationships between the columns and how those need to change if we reconsider the situation, such as considering the train engine as a car in the "stops and cars" problem (p. 282).

The Development of Data Analysis, Classification, and Probability

This learning trajectory develops children's ability to understand, gather, and use data. In the early years, data is an important context for solving problems but data analysis itself develops slowly. Children first learn the foundational ideas and processes of *classification*, and then learn to quantify the categories, that is, tell how many in each group. Eventually children learn to gather data to answer a question or make a decision—an effective means to develop applied problem solving and number and spatial sense.

Thus, the foundations for data analysis, especially for the early years, lie in other areas, such as counting and classification. Object counting was discussed in Chapter 3. Classification is important for structuring data but also as a general process that we have discussed throughout the book (see also Chapter 13). Given its importance for data, we focus on it here. At all ages, children classify intuitively. For example, by 2 weeks of age, infants distinguish between objects they suck and those they do not. By 2 years, toddlers form sets with objects that are similar on some properties, although not necessarily identical. At about age 3 most children learn to follow verbal rules for sorting. In the preschool ages, many children learn to sort objects according to a given attribute, forming categories, although they may switch attributes during the sorting. Not until age 5 or 6 years do children usually sort consistently by a single attribute and re-classify by different attributes.

Turning to *data analysis*, development ideally begins with young children's inquiries and investigations of meaningful situations and phenomena, identifying important attributes of the phenomena), and finally organizing, structuring, visualising, and representing data (English, 2010, 2018a; Lehrer & Schauble, 2002).

Early in development, children learn to sort objects *and* quantify their groups. They might sort a collection of buttons into those with one to four holes and count to find out how many they have in each of the four groups. To do this, they focus on and describe the attributes of objects, classifying according to those attributes, and quantify the resulting categories. Children eventually became capable of simultaneously classifying and counting; for example, counting the number of colors in a group of objects.

However, in data analysis, children also have to determine *which attributes are relevant* to solving a problem and which can be disregarded. Then the process of organizing and representing the data can begin. This process, too, is developmental. Even after gathering pertinent data to answer questions, children's initial representations often do not use categories. Their interest in data is on the particulars (Russell, 1991). For example, they might simply list each child in their class and each child's response to a question. They then learn to classify these responses and represent data according to category. Finally, young children can use physical objects to make graphs (objects that are the object of attention, such as shows, then manipulatives such as connecting cubes), then picture graphs, then line plots, and, finally, bar graphs that include grid lines to facilitate reading frequencies (Friel, Curcio, & Bright, 2001). By second grade, most children should be able to organize and display data through both simple numerical summaries such as counts, tables, and tallies, and graphical displays, including picture graphs, line plots, and bar graphs (Russell, 1991). They can compare parts of the data, make statements about the data as a whole, and generally determine whether the graphs answer the questions posed initially.

To understand data analysis, students must learn the dual concepts of expectation and variation. Expectation deals with averages and probabilities (such as the mean, one measure of central tendency). Variation deals with uncertainty, "spread" of values (such as the standard deviations), outliers, and anticipated and unanticipated change. Data analysis has been called the search for signals (expectations) within the noise (variation) (Konold & Pollatsek, 2002). This research agrees that children often initially see only the *individuals* in a data display ("That's me. I liked chocolate best"). They do not "pull the pieces together" to think about the data as a whole (Watson, Callingham, & Kelly, 2007). Children in the late primary or early intermediate grades can learn to view ranges in data or view the mode (the number or range of numbers that occurs most frequently). Eventually, students can focus on features of the data set as a whole, including the relative frequencies, density ("shape"), and location (centers, such as the mean).

Probability is a difficult concept and is usually taught in later years. However, young children do have some intuitive awareness of probability and can build on it with good experiences (Falk, Yudilevich-Assouline, & Elstein, 2012). Children as young as preschoolers can discuss and even document their various strategies for solving a problem such as, "One takes two marbles out of a bag containing four (two red, two yellow) and notes the result. Which event will occur most often if the experiment is undertaken 20 times?" (Van Bommel & Palmér, 2016, p. 101). These might include playing freely chosen probability games which use dice and spinners. Such games have been promoted in early chapters as building number and arithmetic concepts, and so there is no concern of spending too much time on probability. If children are interested, alterations of the random number generated could be used to stimulate discussions, such as spinners with unequal areas for the different numbers.

A final note connects data representation and probability to the discussion of algebraic thinking. The goal of both should be making sense of quantitative situations and laying the foundation for more complex math to come. At the heart of both is the examination of *quantitative relationships* and representing those relationships to better *make sense* of them.

Experience and Education: Data Analysis, Classification, and Probability

Provide all young children with opportunities to achieve at least a minimal level of competence with classification (and seriation, see Chapter 13) before they reach the primary grades. For classification, they should at the least solve oddity problems—"one of these is not like the others." Even simple teaching strategies—demonstration, practice, and feedback with many varied concrete examples—benefit children, especially those with special needs (Lebron-Rodriguez & Pasnak, 1977b; Pasnak, 1987b). Children can be told and shown the rule but may need help figuring out rules and when to use them. Game-like instruction may help children learn to induce simple rules. Consider alternative, richer, problem-solving approaches that teach these and other competencies (see Clements, 1984; Kamii, Rummelsburg, & Kari, 2005).

When should such instruction begin? Provide informal, child-centered experiences to children younger than 3 years. Many 2½-year-old children know a rule and have relevant conceptual knowledge but fail to use it to regulate their behavior. Seemingly impervious to efforts to improve their rule use, 32-month-olds could not label pictures in terms of appropriate categories, even with varieties of extra help in sorting, including feedback and reinforcement (Zelazo, Reznick, & Piñon, 1995). Improvements in sorting by rules may require emerging control over actions. Challenge older children to label, discuss attributes, and classify objects by more than one attribute.

Turning to data representation, such as graphs, preschoolers appear to be able to understand discrete graphs as representations of numerosity based on one-to-one correspondence. Providing them with examples, motivating tasks (such as graphing their progress toward gathering all the items for a scavenger hunt), and feedback may be helpful.

The instruction in one successful exploratory study used two phases (Schwartz, 2004). Phase 1 consists of group experiences. *Selection of the topics for group graphing* is guided by children's interest and ease of collection of data ("Who are the people that live in their houses?"

or "How does each child come to school?" or "What is their favorite home activity?"). *Providing a variety of models for recording data* begins with concrete materials and extends to graphic, alphabetic, and numeric representation. Teachers pose the problem of how the group could save the information, so "we won't forget what we said." Some children suggested using concrete materials for graphing the information. Also, many had little concern for sorting the data as they recorded it. After a plan was agreed upon, children were able to help record the information. *Summarizing and interpreting the data* began with the question, "What did we find out?", which focused attention on sorting the information. If a decision had to be made, such as what kinds of cookies to purchase, children resorted. The second phase was independent data collection for those children who were interested. These experiences build upon those in phase 1, with the teacher providing tools (clipboards were popular), and working with individuals to organize, record, and communicate their findings.

Another study reported success with children working with software that develops foundational skills for data analysis (Hancock, 1995). Using "Tabletop Jr.," children make and arrange objects, such as cartoon characters, pizzas, stick figures, party hats, attribute "blocks," numerals, and abstract designs, which will be used to represent data or be the objects of the exploration. All objects are created by combining simple attributes, just as attribute blocks are structured (such blocks are one of the object sets). Children can choose the attributes for each object produced, or have them generated randomly. See Figure 12.4.

Next, they can arrange them in different ways, including using loops (Venn diagrams), bunches, stacks (picture graphs), grids, and chains. Children can make free-form arrangements

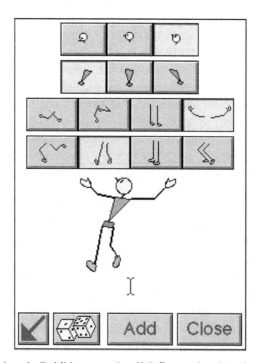

Figure 12.4 Using "Tabletop Jr.," children create stick figures by choosing attributes

manually, or they can get the objects to arrange themselves automatically, based on their attributes. The objects are animated and move across the screen to meet whatever rule of arrangement has been defined by the user. Arrangements may be treated as patterns and designs, or as plots and graphs that can help with analyzing data. Figure 12.5 is a computer-generated sort of children's hand sizes.

These tools can be used to play "guess my rule" and others that emphasize attributes, sorting, and arranging data. Anecdotal reports with children as young as 5 years of age are positive (Hancock, 1995).

As a reminder of how all this content and processes hang together, recall the early algebra project by Maria Blanton and others in the patterning section of this chapter, involving counting and organizing data (e.g., using t-charts, see p. 282-287 and Figure 12.2).

Thus, we suggest that curricula and teachers might focus on one big idea: Classifying, organizing, representing, and using information to ask and answer questions. If graphing is to be part of that type of activity, young children might use physical objects to make graphs, such as laying down "shoes or sneakers" in two columns on a square grid laid on the floor. Next, they could use manipulatives, or other discrete, physical objects such as connecting cubes. This could be represented next with picture graphs (Friel et al., 2001) and, in first grade, with simple bar graphs.

Learning Trajectory for Classification and Data

The CCSSM's goals for data analysis are shown in Table 12.3 and the two other parts of the learning trajectory in Table 12.4.

Final Words

How essential are the topics of this chapter? If viewed as "separate topics"—for example, units of instruction on different types of repeating patterns, or on graphing—they are of secondary

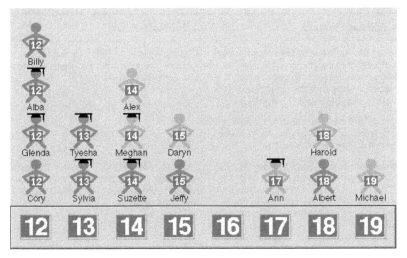

Figure 12.5 Children instruct the computer to sort their data in a pictograph

Table 12.3 Goals for Data Analysis from the CCSSM

Measurement and Data [K.MD In CCSS]

Classify Objects and Count the Number of Objects in Each Category.

1. Classify objects into given categories; count the numbers of objects in each category and sort the categories by count.

Measurement and Data [1.MD In CCSS]

Represent and Interpret Data.

1. Organize, represent, and interpret data with up to three categories; ask and answer questions about the total number of data points, how many in each category, and how many more or less are in one category than in another.

Measurement and Data [2.MD In CCSS]

Represent and Interpret Data.

1. Generate measurement data by measuring lengths of several objects to the nearest whole unit, or by making repeated measurements of the same object. Show the measurements by making a line plot, where the horizontal scale is marked off in whole-number units.
2. Draw a picture graph and a bar graph (with single-unit scale) to represent a data set with up to four categories. Solve simple put-together, take-apart, and compare problems using information presented in a bar graph.

Measurement and Data [3.MD In CCSS]

Represent and Interpret Data.

1. Draw a scaled picture graph and a scaled bar graph to represent a data set with several categories. Solve one- and two-step "how many more" and "how many less" problems using information presented in scaled bar graphs. *For example, draw a bar graph in which each square in the bar graph might represent five pets.*
2. Generate measurement data by measuring lengths using rulers marked with halves and fourths of an inch. Show the data by making a line plot, where the horizontal scale is marked off in appropriate units—whole numbers, halves, or quarters.

Table 12.4 Learning Trajectory for Classification and Data

Age	Developmental Progression	Instructional Tasks
0-1	**Foundations: Similarity Intuiter** *Classification* Intuitively recognizes objects or situations as similar in some way (objects to suck or not, 2 weeks). Places objects together that are different (6 months) and then alike (12 months). Classifies informally, for example by differentiating between objects they suck and those they do not at 2 weeks of age.	*Classifying in Play*, [LT][2]: Provide many objects to explore. Name objects and mention those that are the same and different.
1-2	**Similar/dissimilar Maker** *Classification* By 18 months, forms sets in which objects in each set are identical and objects in the other sets are different, and by 2 years, intuitively forms groups with objects that are similar on some attributes (may be mixed and inconsistent), but not necessarily identical. May use functional relationships as basis for sorting.	*Everyday Classifying*, [LT][2]: In natural situations, name objects and mention those that are the same and different and the attribute(s) on which they are the same or differ.

(Continued)

Table 12.4 (Cont.)

Age	Developmental Progression	Instructional Tasks
	In play, puts several red toy animals together, and then sees several red cats, so puts other cats with them regardless of the color.	
3	**Simple Sorter** *Classification* Follows verbal rules for sorting scaffolded by an adult. (These may be made with shifting criteria; nevertheless, they play an essential role in number, through the unitizing process.) Can "fix" a simple sort with mistakes. Told a simple rule for classifying pictures, sorts with adult assistance, such as modeling the sorting or reminding the child of the attribute.	*Sort Stuff*, [LT]²: Provide materials to think with and to sort, including by color but also by size, shape, function, and so forth. Especially look for the initial sorting that children naturally do—ask them about it and look for ways to build upon it. *Sort Race*, [LT]²: Play games that emphasize sorting. Lay out bowls and objects, such as different types of buttons, beans, or letters. To focus on color, put different colors of construction paper on the wall, and give children dot stickers to put on the same-color paper. To avoid always sorting by color, lay out the bowls and a lot of objects—all the *same* color.
4	**Sorter by Similar Attributes** *Classification* Sorts objects according to an explicit attribute (although still may decide to switch attributes during the sorting). The end result may appear to reflect adult categorizations, but often has a different basis, such as general resemblance. Can, especially if scaffolded, "hold fast" for some time to a criterion for sorting and recognize that alternative bases for classification exist. However, may switch and are still predisposed to respond in certain ways.	*Not Quite the Same*, [LT]²: Read *A Mother for Choco* by Keiko Kasza and record, on a whiteboard, children's ideas about why Choco thought different animals could be his mother. How is each the same as Choco, and different? (See Hynes-Berry & Grandau, 2019.) *Sort by One Attribute*, [LT]²: Small group lessons involving demonstration, practice, and feedback with many varied concrete examples (especially important for at-risk pre-K and kindergarten children, those with IEPs, and others, such as children with visual impairments). Remember many number and shape activities involve classification! *Sorting Books*, [LT]²: Read *How Many Snails?* (Giganti & Crews, 1994) in which children different subcategories of things, such as separate colors of flowers in the meadow. Afterwards, sort objects by an attribute such as color and then count how many of each color. Another good story is *Hannah's Collections* (Marthe, 2000). Hannah has to figure out which of her many collections to take to school. There is also a new math idea on every page, including a good introduction to "guess my rule" games. *Guess My Rule*, [LT]² games are also excellent for classifying. See Table 8.1. Giving children clues concerning, or naming and discussing, a rule enables them to represent and follow it. *Sort and Count*, [LT]²: Encourage children to sort objects and quantify their groups. They might sort a collection of buttons into those with one to four holes and count to find out how many they have in each of the four groups. To do this, they focus on and describe the attributes of objects, classifying according to those attributes, and quantify the resulting categories. *One Of These Things Is Not Like The Others*, [LT]²: Sing this song and play the game with a variety of attributes and materials.

(Continued)

Table 12.4 (Cont.)

Age	Developmental Progression	Instructional Tasks
4-6	**Consistent, Flexible Sorter** *Classification* Sorts consistently by a single attribute and re-classifies by different attributes. Sorts consistently and exhaustively by an attribute, given or created, and uses the terms "some" and "all."	*Classify with Cause*, [LT]²: Have children sort for a reason ("classification with good causation," Forman & Hill, 1984, see Chapter 13, p. 307). For example, they might discover math or science concepts by classifying three-dimensional solids to find out which will and will not roll down a ramp … and why. Or, which ones stack and which don't, *and why*. And so forth for science (which objects does a magnet attract). *Resorting to (Re-sorting)*, [LT]²: In a whole group, read *Five Creatures* by Emily Jenkins, about a girl who classifies "creatures" (family and cats!) many different ways. Then divide the children into two groups, to be sorted and sort checkers. Model one way to sort and have children act it out, with checkers checking. Then children suggest new ways. Switch roles. (See Hynes-Berry & Grandau, 2019.) *Guess My Rule*, [LT]² games are also excellent for classifying. See Table 8.1. Research suggests that if children need help, try direct verbal instruction, feedback, and modeling by peers just one level above the target child's assessed level.
4-6	**Data Case Viewer** *Data* Associates a value with an individual case. Uses numeric data to identify largest/smallest cases. May graph by listing all cases. Before this level, children may be "pointers" in which data records point to the entire event ("We talked about favorite colors"). They use it like string tied around a finger, to remember that they did something. Children may at first see only the *individuals* in a data display ("That's me. I'm turning 6 this year"). They do not "pull the pieces together" to think about the data as a whole.	*Graph with Things*, [LT]²: Work with children to use physical objects to make graphs (objects that are the object of attention, such as shoes, then manipulatives such as connecting cubes) on large grids. *Picture Graphs*, [LT]²: Construct other types of discrete (e.g., picture) graphs with children as representations of numerosity based on one-to-one correspondence. Interpret the graphs and use them to solve math problems. Provide children with examples, motivating tasks such graphing their progress toward gathering items for a scavenger hunt, and feedback, may be helpful.
5-6	**Data Classifier** *Data* Treats cases with similar values as the same. Uses to compare category frequencies (most and least popular case-types). Visually compares two graphs. Makes graphs by classifying and representing data in those categories. "More people picked red as their favorite color than any other color."	*Classifying and Graphing for the Environment*, [LT]²: A class reads *Baxter Brown's Messy Room* and helps Baxter figure out which items in his room might be recycled, which might be reused, and which should be thrown away, based on the attributes of the items. They classify pictures of the items and graph the number of each category several times, creating their own representations (for a full description, see English, 2010)
5-7	**Multiple Attribute Classifier** *Classification* Classifies objects by multiple attributes in a single sort. "I'll put the big triangles here, the little ones next to them, then the big circles there and then the little circles."	*Matrices*, [LT]²: Have children complete two-dimensional matrices, puzzles that have, for example, rows with different shapes and columns with different colors.

(Continued)

Table 12.4 (Cont.)

Age	Developmental Progression	Instructional Tasks

	Red	Green	Orange	Blue
▲			△	
▬				▭
●				

7-8 **Data Aggregater** *Data* Classifies objects that may be perceptually different by more abstract attributes such as function or conceptual attributes.

Focuses on features of the data set as a whole. Uses to describe relative frequency and density (shape), and location (centers).

Begins to understand the concepts of expectation (averages and probabilities) and variation ("spread" of values).

Reacting to a graph of the number of years families have lived in a town: "Look at that clump. Most families have lived here 1 to 6 years." "How many?" "It's 11 families out of 23–almost half."

Understands ranges in data or the mode (the number that occurs most frequently). Eventually, can focus on features of the data set as a whole, including the relative frequencies, density ("shape"), and location (centers, such as the mean).

Our Data, [LT]²: Students select a topic, decide what attributes are important, and then invent a variety of models for recording their data. After sharing and discussing they create different ways to model and interpret their data.

What Is the Chance of That?, [LT]²: In this series of investigations of probability and variation, children create their own chance experiments and independently developed core probability understandings. They record examples of events that would be certain to happen for them the following weekend, could possibly happen, and would be impossible to occur. They then play a "bingo" game where the notions of randomness and variation in chance events were experienced. Finally, they help a game-design company determine the chances of selecting various coloured counters from a mystery bag. (English, 2018a).

8 **Hierarchical Classifier** *Classification* Classifies categories and subcategories using hierarchical inclusion.

Conscientiously classifies according to multiple attributes, naming and relating the attributes, understanding that objects could belong to more than one group.

Completes two-dimensional classification matrices or forming subgroups within groups.

Matrices, [LT]²: Have children complete Venn diagrams such those in Chapter 8, Figure 8.2, or simpler ones to begin, such as this.

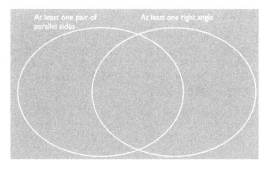

Table 12.4 (Cont.)

Age	Developmental Progression	Instructional Tasks
8+	**Data Representer** *Data* Shows an appreciation of the "center" of graphs and for their variation or spread. Compares graphs of data sets of the same size accurately. Similarly, can use other representations such as tables to detect variation in different sets, develop models of those variations, and apply them to make predictions.	*Making Licorice*, [LT][2]: Students experience the "creation of variation" as they compared "licorice sticks" they make by hand (with Play-Doh) to those factory-made (i.e., using a Play-Doh extruder kit). That is, they discuss quality control and then in small groups identify, measure, compare, and record attributes of the sticks including their mass. Each child creates their own representation of their group's data. Whole-group presentations, discussions, and a graph of all the data identify the range and "typical" masses displayed in each group model (English, 2018a). *Classy Art for Classification*, [LT][2]: Students develop a rule-based classification model of self-portraits drawn by children of different ages. That is, children identify attributes that are common among a small number of kindergarten portraits and those that are common among Grade 2 portraits. They then test their model on a larger number of self-portraits for each age, using tables and graphical representations to support their reasoning. That is, they apply their models to predict what new self-portraits are drawn by kindergartners and which by second graders (for full details, see Oslington, Mulligan, & Van Bergen, 2018b).

importance and may even take too much time away from the core instruction described in previous chapters. However, if they are viewed as fundamental processes and ways of thinking—habits of mind that seek math patterns and structure and classify math objects and ideas—they are an essential component of most early math education. (The importance of early *graphing* is unknown, and we promote it only when a real problem arises that graphs will help answer *more* than, for example, a simple table.) Similar arguments apply to the processes that are the focus of Chapter 13.

Notes

1 For example, patterns represented by two attributes of change (shape and color) are easier than those represented by just one (e.g., orientation). Further, this may be more difficult for some children or populations of children (Warren, Miller, & Cooper, 2012).
2 Fixing a pattern is easier than the other if only one item is missing but may be more difficult if more than one is missing.

13 Mathematical Processes and Practices

> Carmen had almost filled her pretend pizzas with toppings. As she got ready to roll the number cube, she said, "I'm going to get a high number and win!" "You can't," replied her friend, "You have four spaces and the number cube only has 1s, 2s, and 3s on it."

The numbers may be small, but the reasoning is impressive. *Children can reason mathematically.* Indeed, one could argue that math is essential for all thinking. That's a strong statement. How can it be true that all thinking involves math? *Logic (reasoning) is a branch of mathematics and thinking involves logic at some point.*

Consider the first vignette. Before reading further, ask yourself: What *reasoning* do you think Carmen's friend was using? In our view, Carmen's friend probably intuitively used logic that might be described as the following:

- To win, Carmen must get at least a 4.
- The number cube has only 1, 2, and 3.
- These numbers are less than 4.
- Therefore, Carmen cannot win on her next roll.

Although logic might seem like the most abstract, least likely area of math for young children to learn to use, researchers and other sensitive observers see implicit use of logic in all children. An 18-month-old child pulling a blanket to bring a toy within reach shows the beginnings of "means–end" analysis.

Children appear to be impressive problem solvers, as we've seen in every previous chapter. Here, we focus on problem solving, reasoning, and other math processes or, as the CCSS calls them, "mathematical practices" (see Table 13.1). These describe varieties of expertise that math educators at all levels should seek to develop in their students. The practices rest on two important "processes and proficiencies" with longstanding importance in math education. The first of these are the NCTM process standards of problem solving, reasoning and proof, communication, representation, and connections. The second are the strands of mathematical proficiency specified in the National Research Council's report, *Adding It Up* (Kilpatrick et al., 2001): adaptive reasoning, strategic competence, conceptual understanding (comprehension of math concepts, operations, and relations), procedural fluency (skill in carrying out procedures flexibly, accurately, efficiently, and appropriately), and productive disposition (habitual inclination to see math as sensible, useful, and worthwhile, coupled

Table 13.1 The Common Core State Standards for Mathematical Practices (abbreviated from CCSSO/NGA, 2010, Pp. 6-8) and Illustrations from Early Childhood

1. Make sense of problems and persevere in solving them

Mathematically proficient students start by explaining to themselves the meaning of a problem and looking for entry points to its solution. [...] They monitor and evaluate their progress and change course if necessary. [...] Mathematically proficient students check their answers to problems using a different method, and they continually ask themselves, "Does this make sense?" They can understand the approaches of others to solving complex problems and identify correspondences between different approaches.

Making sense of problems and *perseverance* in solving them—don't we emphasize these every day? Children *invent* solutions that are meaningful to them by thinking about all the different strategies they could use (Clements et al., 2020).

Do I have to put together two quantities, or take them apart (Chapter 5)? How can I slide, turn, or flip this shape to finish that puzzle (Chapters 7 and 9)? How can I make sure I have just the right number for my table (Chapter 4)?

2. Reason abstractly and quantitatively

Mathematically proficient students make sense of quantities and their relationships in problem situations. [...] Quantitative reasoning entails habits of creating a coherent representation of the problem at hand; considering the units involved; attending to the meaning of quantities, not just how to compute them; and knowing and flexibly using different properties of operations and objects.

We have seen children can reason quantitatively, intuitively at least, from birth! But can *young* children reason *abstractly?* Yes! Remember Abby thinking about her missing trains (Chapter 3, p. 36) or the first grader thinking about lengths saying, "If it's an inequality, then you can write four statements. If it's equal, you can only write two" (Chapter 10, p. #)? Or 4-year-olds knowing that if four are under a cloth and you put another one there, "It's 5!"

3. Construct viable arguments and critique the reasoning of others

Mathematically proficient students [...] make conjectures and build a logical progression of statements to explore the truth of their conjectures. [...] They justify their conclusions, communicate them to others, and respond to the arguments of others. [...] Elementary students can construct arguments using concrete referents such as objects, drawings, diagrams, and actions. Such arguments can make sense and be correct, even though they are not generalized or made formal until later grades. [...]

If you have ever argued with a preschooler over bedtime when the summer sun is still shining, you know their ability to make their case and critique *your* reasoning. If sharing blocks, "You got 6 and I got 4, that's *not* fair, 'cause 6 is more than 4." Or, "I think that *every* time you multiply by zero, it's got to be zero. There's none of them—zero!" Children from ages 1 to 5 years use mathematical properties in reasoning during free outdoor play (Sumpter & Hedefalk, 2015)! The beginning of real mathematics—reasoning and proof.

4. Model with mathematics

Mathematically proficient students can apply the mathematics they know to solve problems arising in everyday life, society, and the workplace. In early grades, this might be as simple as writing an addition equation to describe a situation. [...]

When they solve a problem by making sets with counters, or lay units down to compare the lengths of two objects, children are modeling with mathematics. Their models get more abstract in the primary grades. Recall the solution to the "67 + 83 = x + 82" problem: "I knew 83 is one more than 82, so x has to be one more than 67 to balance—68!"

5. Use appropriate tools strategically

Mathematically proficient students consider the available tools when

Children love to use tools. Earlier chapters show how they use all these tools. They *relate* the tools, seeing how and why laying inch-

(Continued)

Table 13.1 (Cont).

solving a mathematical problem. These tools might include pencil and paper, concrete models, a ruler, a protractor, a calculator, a spreadsheet [...]. | long objects down gives the same measure as using a ruler. Counters are tools to build solutions and justifications for solving problems. Shapes are tools for arguing that equilateral triangles cannot be used to completely fill a large square.

6. Attend to precision

Mathematically proficient students try to communicate precisely to others. They try to use clear definitions in discussion with others and in their own reasoning. [...] In the elementary grades, students give carefully formulated explanations to each other. [...] | Asking young children "How do you know?" "What if...?" and similar questions develops their ability to communicate and be precise in their argumentation. Recall the preschooler arguing with her friend who claimed a shape was "too skinny" to be a triangle: "It is a triangle. It's got three straight sides, see? One, two, three! It doesn't matter that I made it skinny." This is *justification* based on mathematical definitions and logic (Chapter 8, p. 106). In the early years, rules become increasingly important, such as in their play. And so it is with mathematics: This is the beginning of real mathematics—precision of thinking and reasoning.

7. Look for and make use of structure

Mathematically proficient students look closely to discern a pattern or structure. Young students, for example, might notice that three and seven more is the same amount as seven and three more, or they may sort a collection of shapes according to how many sides the shapes have. Later, students will see 7 × 8 equals the well-remembered 7 × 5 + 7 × 3, in preparation for learning about the distributive property. [...] | Children use structure from their earliest years, "It is too a dog, it's got four legs and barks—it's just small as a cat." The mathematical examples from the CCSSM are perfect: Commutativity (a + b = b + a), associativity: 7 + 4 + 6 = 7 + (4 + 6) = 7 + 10 = 17 are algebraic patterns that well-taught primary-grade students abstract, use, and discuss (Chapter 12).

8. Look for and express regularity in repeated reasoning

Mathematically proficient students notice if calculations are repeated and look both for general methods and for shortcuts. [...] | Similarly, children see patterns in repeated reasoning: "If you keep putting another one in there ... it's like ... just the next counting number!" "Look. This pattern is growing one more on the top and two more on the bottom. So, the top is regular counting, and the bottom is counting by twos."

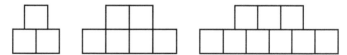

(Clements, Agodini, & Harris, 2013; Platas, 2019; Sarama & Clements, 2009c)

with a belief in diligence and one's own efficacy). Table 13.1 presents an abbreviated description of the CCSSM practices along with elaborations and illustrations of them for early childhood.

Reasoning and Problem Solving

Even though advanced mathematical reasoning would be inappropriate for most young children, you can help them develop mathematical reasoning, along with precision of thinking and definitions, *at their level*. Recall preschoolers arguing about whether a shape is a triangle, *based on its attributes and their definition of a triangle as a (closed) shape with three straight sides* (Chapter 8). Young children arguing that "we already found 5 + 2 is 7, so we *know* 2 + 5, 'cause you can always add with either number first" shows again their ability to reason from mathematical properties (Chapters 5 and 6). And they can reason with data as well (Oslington et al., 2018, Chapter 12). Children as young as 5 years can engage in all types of relational reasoning (Jablansky, Alexander, Dumas, & Compton, 2015).

Mathematical reasoning is a core process and makes a unique contribution to children's mathematical development. For example, in one study, fluid (relational) reasoning was the only consistent predictor of mathematics achievements decades later (Green, Bunge, Briones Chiongbian, Barrow, & Ferrer, 2017). Another team of researchers found that mathematical reasoning and arithmetic made separate and specific contributions to mathematical achievement (Nunes, Bryant, Barros, & Sylva, 2012). Further, *mathematical reasoning was the strongest predictor, greater than arithmetic skill and greater than general intelligence and working memory.* Training in logical reasoning increased children's mathematics achievement in a related study (Nunes et al., 2007).

Of course, children use such reasoning in solving problems. There are also additional strategies possessed by young children. Luke, 3 years old, watched his father unsuccessfully looking under the van for a washer that had fallen and suggested, "Why don't you just roll the car back, so you can find it?" Luke employed means-end analysis better than his father. This strategy involves determining the difference between the current state and the goal, and then taking action that reduces the difference between them, reasoning backward from the goal to set subgoals. Means-end problem solving may emerge between 6 and 9 months, when, as in the previous example, children learn to pull on a blanket to bring a toy into their reach.

Even young children have multiple problem-solving strategies at their disposal and the ability to choose among them. Means-end analysis is a general strategy, as are several others. Children know and prefer cognitively easier strategies. For example, in hill climbing, children reason forward from the current state in the direction of the desired goal (DeLoache, Miller, & Pierroutsakos, 1998).

Children develop such abilities from the first months of life. For example, infants are shown three crosses and one cube mixing in a machine. They are hidden. If a cube comes out, they look at it longer than if a cross emerges. Studies show that they may use logic or probabilities in estimating which is more likely (Denison & Xu, 2019). As another example, before 6 months of age, children will explore objects in a variety of ways (Sarama & Clements, 2009).

By 1 year, they respond to new objects with interest, recognizing differences, and change their actions to seek an object they want. These sorts of trial and error, with light cognitive requirements, are related to Piagetian circular reactions—trying to make an interesting sight or sound repeat. Between 1 and 2 years, they search for hidden toys and purposely experiment with the effects of new actions on objects. They try a strategy they found successful in one situation (tugging on a stuck object) in new situations. By 2 years, they vary their actions systematically, and use objects in new, creative ways to solve problems.

These strategies develop throughout the toddler and preschool years, enabling children to address problems of increasing complexity. For example, recall that kindergartners can solve a wide range of addition, subtraction, multiplication, and division problems when they are encouraged to use manipulatives or drawings to model the objects, actions, and relationships in those situations.

In summary, considering their minimal experience, young children are impressive problem solvers. They are learning to learn and learning the rules of the "reasoning game." Research on problem solving and reasoning again reveals that children are more skilled, and adults less skilled, than conventionally thought. Although domain-specific knowledge is essential (Özcan & Doğan, 2017), we should not fail to recognize that reasoning from domain-specific knowledge builds upon the basis of mindful general problem-solving and reasoning abilities that are evident from the earliest years. Helping children talk about problem solving ("vocal engagement") and make strategic plans to solve problems builds multiple abilities and reduces the risk of academic failure (McDermott et al., 2010). Notice if some children get anxious tackling difficult problems (Ho-Hong, 2017). Finally, remember that a reasoning approach also develops math knowledge—such as fluency with arithmetic combinations, better than direct instruction (Baroody et al., 2016).

The Logical Operations: Classification, Seriation, and Patterning and Algebraic Thinking

We have already discussed classification, seriation, and patterning in multiple chapters. The development of classification, for example, was described in detail in Chapter 12 ... but also, children were classifying by number, shape, and even arithmetic type throughout *all* the previous chapters. Similarly, children were seriating—putting in order—numbers and measures in multiple chapters. And we emphasize again that *patterning, writ large, is also one of the most important processes and habits of mind for mathematical thinking* (Chapter 12).

Then, why bring them up again? Because *these "logical operations" (Piaget) are general mathematical processes fundamental to children's success in mathematics ... and in school and life* (Ciancio, Rojas, McMahon, & Pasnak, 2001; Pasnak, 2017; Pasnak et al., 2015).

Experience and Education

> You present problems, and they figure out what to do. You present problems, and they figure out what to do. Then you ask what process they used. I'm amazed ... they learn to describe their processes! They'll use this knowledge to answer science questions. They really do critical thinking. Asking, "How do you know?" starting at pre-K is very powerful.
>
> (Anne, preschool teacher, Building Blocks curriculum)

The NCTM, the NAEYC, mathematicians (e.g., Wu, 2011), and research all point to the same educational goal and recommendation: essential processes, especially reasoning and problem solving, must be central to the mathematical education of students of all ages.

Reasoning

Help children develop pre-mathematical reasoning from the earliest years. Provide an environment that invites exploration and reasoning with objects such as blocks. Encourage language to support the growth of reasoning abilities. For example, labeling situations with both "Daddy/ Mommy/Baby" and "big/little/tiny" led to a 2-year age gain in reasoning with relations in 3-year-old children. As other chapters have shown, having children explain and justify their solutions to mathematical problems is an effective way to develop mathematical (and general) reasoning.

Encourage, notice, and discuss children's reasoning in play too. Consider this episode of preschoolers climbing rocks (Sumpter & Hedefalk, 2015, adapted from p. 5). The teacher, Kristina, notes, "That one, that one is pretty big. I think it is bigger than me." Kasper: "Should we measure? ... It is bigger than me anyway" [walks and stands next to the rock and looks up, using her own body as a measure]. Kristina: "Yes, it is bigger than you anyway" [directly comparing lengths, Chapter 10]. The teacher notes that the rock is not as tall as she is. The children disagree, stating they are the same, but when the teacher moves next to it, they agree it comes up to her nose. The children then climb the rock and say: "Yes, but the house is bigger than the rock." Kristina: "The house? Yes, definitely. Because the house, I can step in [the house], right?" [transitive reasoning]. The children open up the mathematical questions, but the teacher provides most of the reasoning; however, providing such models can be useful.

Later the children do the reasoning when building a tower. Sara says the tower "should be, taller than you. Then you need to look up .... It will be fat cool when we add this [a sitting pad] on top." Kasper: "Yes. But not so high" [challenging the length]. Sara: "Yes, taller than her (pointing at the observer). Taller!" [contradicting]. Sofia: "No [agreeing with Sara, not Kasper], we are going high." Kasper [clarifying/limiting]: "Not all the way up to the house." Sara [agreeing but establishing a goal]: "No, but as tall as the slide. ... Tall as Kristoffer [teacher]. So then, we need to make it as tall as the slide .... Then it is taller than Kristoffer, ok."

Sara suggested that they should increase the height by adding to the length: A + D > A. Kasper challenged the estimation and Sara, with the support of Sofia, then delivered several arguments where she narrowed the estimation, reaching a conclusion based on deductive logic: If A = B (and B > C), then A > C.

Problem Solving[1]

Children make progress when they solve many problems over the course of years. Children as young as preschoolers and kindergartners, and perhaps younger, benefit from intentional instruction (but not prescribed strategies), from a teacher who believes problem solving is important. They benefit from modeling a wide variety of situations (geometric, and, in arithmetic, varied problem types, including addition, subtraction, and, appropriately, multiplication, and division) with concrete objects, and also from drawing a representation to show their thinking, as well as from explaining and discussing their solutions.

Solving more complex word problems remains a challenge for primary-grade students. Their conceptions must move from the many messy details of a real-world situation to more abstracted (mathematized) quantitative conceptions (Fuson & Abrahamson, 2009). For example, children might read, "Mary bought 8 candies at the store, but she ate 3 on the way home. How many did she still have when she got home?" The children have to see that the store plays little part, but that it's important that there is a group of candies and some got eaten. They might then think, she had 8 but ate 3. Then, I have to find 8 take away 3. Then they might think to model this with fingers, finally putting up 8 fingers and lowering the 3 on one hand. Using "you-language" especially at first may help; "You bought 8 candies ..." (Artut, 2015). Also, recall (Chapter 5, p. 106) that asking children to explore problems, then instructing, and then having them check their answers is particularly effective (Loehr et al., 2014).

As an example sequence, start by having as many students as possible solve a problem at the chalkboard, using diagrams, numerals, and so forth, while others solve them at their seats, on student-sized chalk- or whiteboards if available. Then ask two to three to explain their solutions. Have a different group go to the chalkboard to solve the *next* problem. Eventually, all children explain their thinking on at least one problem (and explain to another student on most). English language learners (ELLs) may point to their diagram or co-present a solution with a peer. Educational technology can make multiple contributions (Herodotou, 2018; Outhwaite, Faulder, Gulliford, & Pitchford, 2019).

Progress from easier to more difficult problem types. For each problem type, move from problems with more familiar situations and language to those that are less familiar. Guide students first to use more sophisticated strategies and then to algorithms. Also, introduce problems with extra or missing information, as well as multistep problems. Use larger or more complex numbers (e.g., fractions). Combine new problem types with other problem types and practice with feedback. See p. 91 for problem types.

Problem solving is particularly important in the primary grades. For example, having first graders explain their strategies for solving problems and working on problems is related to higher math achievement (Guarino, Dieterle, Bargagliotti, & Mason, 2013). Research suggests that this process of mathematizing the story situation has a reverse process that is also important. That is, children should also *make up word problems* that fit number sentences (Fuson, 2018). Problem *posing* appears to be an effective way for children to express their creativity and integrate their learning (Brown & Walter, 1990; Kilpatrick, 1987; van Oers, 1994). Solving problems in the context of a project-based approach can be particularly motivating and beneficial.

Classification and Seriation as Logical Operations

Ideas for teaching these processes are in most chapters (e.g., classifying by number and shape, seriating by discrete number and continuous measures). Also, classification is in the learning trajectory in Table 12.3 and seriation in Chapters 4, 10, and 11. Here we simply add a few notes on these two processes as logical operations and we emphasize that these processes may best be developed as ways to solve meaningful everyday problems for the child. As Jean Piaget (1971/1974, p. 17) stated:

> The child may on occasion be interested in seriating for the sake of seriating, in classifying for the sake of classifying, etc., but, in general, it is when events or phenomena must be explained and goals attained through an organization of causes that operations [logico-mathematical knowledge] will be used [and developed] most.

For example, although many types of activities may support the learning of classification, a guideline of "classify with good causation" (Forman & Hill, 1984) indicates that children will learn from sorting shapes according to teachers' directions, but more from *also* sorting 3D objects to find out which will and will not roll down a ramp ... and *why*.

Taking a wider Piagetian view, researchers (Kamii et al., 2005) provided first graders from low-resource communities a variety of physical knowledge activities, such as bowling, balancing cubes (on a circular plate balanced on a soda bottle), and pick-up sticks, instead of typical mathematics instruction. When they showed "readiness" for arithmetic, they were given arithmetic games and word problems that stimulated the exchange of viewpoints. At the end of the year, these children outperformed others who focused narrowly on number instruction. The researchers claim that the physical knowledge activities also develop logico-mathematical knowledge, as in *classifying* the sticks to decide which stick to pick up first and *seriating* them from easiest to hardest to pick up. Effects of the physical knowledge and arithmetic activities cannot be disaggregated, and there was no random assignment, but the results are suggestive (see also Kamii & Kato, 2005).

Other research suggests that the processes of classification and seriation are related to number knowledge—but in surprising ways. Preschoolers were randomly assigned to one of three educational conditions for 8 weeks: classification and seriation, number (subitizing and counting), and control (Clements, 1984). The first two groups improved on what they were taught, but also improved on the *other* topics. Also surprisingly, the number group learned more about classification and seriation than the classification and seriation group learned about number. It may be that all number and counting implies some level of classification. For example, children might count the blue cars, the red cars, and then all the cars.

And, although these studies used physical materials, the *meaningfulness* of the representations and tasks are more important than the form of the materials; therefore, well-designed computer materials may be as or more useful than physical materials (Clements, 1999a, see also Chapter 16) for those older than 3 years. In one study, children learning from computer manipulatives learned classification and other topics as well as children learning from physical materials, but only the computer group gained significantly on seriation (Kim, 1994). Further, the computer manipulatives provided children with a more interesting learning environment that generated more time thinking mathematically.

Finally, remember that high-quality classification games can be good for mathematical practices and executive function! See *Guess My Rule* in several levels of Table 8.1.

Final Words

Children can be impressive problem solvers. They are learning to learn and learning the rules of the "reasoning game." Problem posing and problem solving are effective ways for children to express their inventiveness and integrate their learning. They develop mathematics, language, and creativity. And they build *connections* among these—the essence of learning to *think*.

Especially for younger children, mathematical topics should not be treated as isolated topics; rather, they should be connected to each other, often in the context of solving a significant problem or engaging in an interesting project. Thus, this book's main organization based on mathematical content should not be considered a de-emphasis on other aspects of mathematics, including general processes and practices, which should be interwoven throughout the teaching and learning of content.

This concludes the chapters focused on mathematical goals and specific learning trajectories. Chapter 14 begins with a discussion of cognition (thinking, understanding, and learning), affect (emotions or feelings), and equity (fairness).

Note

1 Most of the information regarding teaching problem solving is integrated within the content chapters.

14 Cognition, Affect, and Equity

Three teachers are discussing their students who are "good" and "not so good" at math:

Aretha:	Some students are just good at math and others aren't. You can't change it. You can tell just by watching them in your classroom.
Brenda:	I don't think so. Students get smarter at math by *thinking* about it. Working at it makes them smarter.
Carina:	There certainly are a few who seem to find aspects of math particularly challenging and a few who, for whatever reason, can learn new math ideas quickly. But no one's ability is fixed; they all need good experiences to learn more and those experiences make them better at … more able to learn more math.

Which teacher do you think is most accurate in her evaluation of the roles of aptitude or ability ("nature") compared to effort and experience ("nurture")? Why?

Thinking, Learning, Feeling, Teaching

The last three chapters of this book discuss issues that are important for putting learning trajectories into practice. This chapter describes how children think about math and how their feelings are involved, as well as crucial issues of equity. The next one, Chapter 15, discusses the contexts in which early childhood education occurs and the curricula that are used. We conclude with Chapter 16, which describes instructional practices and reviews research on which ones are particularly effective and for whom. The topics of these three chapters are unique to this book. Because there are no corresponding chapters in the companion book, there is more research reviewed. We have marked the final paragraph(s) in each section with tips for practitioners with the phrase ***Practical Implications*** for those who wish to focus only on these.

Learning: Processes and Issues

Cognitive Science and the Processes of Learning

At the core of our theory of hierarchic interactionalism (see our companion book), and our learning trajectories, are the learning processes of young children. This section "steps back" from the specific math topics to focus on a few important general principles of cognition and learning that you can use to better understand children's thinking and learning.

When children think and learn, they build mental representations (what we call "mental objects"). They *act* on these representations with cognitive processes ("actions on objects") and control these actions with executive function processes.

Practical Implications

Use of cognitive science to guide instruction is embedded in the very notion of learning trajectories and throughout this book. Table 14.1 lists a few specific principles as examples (for a full discussion, see Booth et al., 2017).

Executive Function (Self-regulation)

To learn and to solve problems, people need resources. Math concepts and processes are resources that we have discussed throughout this book. Another set of resources allows people to control, supervise, or regulate their own thinking, and behavior. Such executive function (EF) processes develop most rapidly in the early childhood years (the following is adapted from Clements, Sarama, & Germeroth, 2016).

Cognitive processes such as EF are palpably connected to students' achievement in school. Children need to plan ahead, focus attention, and remember past experiences. According to some, EF processes constitute "a major characteristic of productive mathematics learning" (De Corte, Mason, Depaepe, & Verschaffel, 2011, p. 155). Such EF processes support children's

Table 14.1 Guiding Principles from Cognitive Science (from Booth et al., 2017)

Principle	Description
Scaffolding	Gradually fading support enables learners to solve problems fluently and independently.
Distributed Practice	Spacing out practice is better than practicing all at once.
Feedback	Receiving informative feedback increases learning.
Worked Examples	Studying (or explaining) worked out examples plus solving problems is better for only problem solving.
Interleaving	Practicing solving different types of problems in mixed order is better than practicing the same type of problems.
Abstract and Concrete Representations	Linking abstract and concrete representations increases learning and transfer.
Error Reflection	Thinking about errors improves problem representation and increases conceptual understanding.
Analogical Comparison	Comparing and contrasting multiple instances leads to better understanding than studying one instance.

learning across subject matter areas but may be particularly important to math. As one example, when the initial reading of an arithmetic problem is not the correct one, children need to inhibit the first impulse to answer (incorrectly) and carefully examine the problem. Consider the following problem, "There were six birds in a tree. Three birds already flew away. How many birds were there from the start?" Children have to *inhibit* the immediate desire to subtract based on the phrase "flew away" and instead calculate the sum (through addition, counting on, or other strategies). Over the last 100 years, the demand for the application of such EF processes as inhibitory control has increased in math education (Baker et al., 2010). Together, these processes allow children to complete tasks even when facing difficulties in problem solving or learning, or fatigue, distraction, or decreased motivation (e.g., Blair & Razza, 2007; Neuenschwander, Röthlisberger, Cimeli, & Roebers, 2012). It is thus unsurprising that kindergarten teachers say that such EF processes (albeit not by that name) are as important as academics (Bassok, Latham, & Rorem, 2016). Most teachers rate EF components, such as inhibitory control and attention shifting, as important for math thinking and learning, and these ratings increase with teaching experience (Gilmore & Cragg, 2014).

Many studies show that EF is important, leading some to assume that EF has to be developed first, so children can learn subjects such as math. However, once early math is taken into account, EF is not a predictor of later school success (Watts, Duncan, & Quan, 2018). Instead, early math predicts later EF. So, the relationship may not be one-directional. We return to this issue, but first we describe the three major EF processes.

First, *attention shifting and cognitive flexibility* involves switching a "mental set" from one aspect of a situation to another as the situation requires. A simple example in math is counting by different units (e.g., feet and inches, to find a total length). Cognitive flexibility is similarly involved in avoiding "functional fixedness"; for example, the tendency to see represented objects only in terms of their most familiar function. An example in math of the lack of cognitive flexibility is repeating the same solution strategy even after it has failed.

Second, *inhibitory control* involves suppressing unproductive responses or strategies, such as controlling a proponent response (e.g., the first solution or answer that occurs to you, as in the "six birds in a tree" example) to think about better strategies or ideas. Ignoring irrelevant information in a mathematics word problem is another example. A non-math example is when children stop themselves from following a command in the game "Simon Says" when the command is given "Touch your head" without the necessary "Simon says 'Touch your head'."

Third, *working memory* involves a system that is responsible for the short-term holding and processing of information. Working memories are the amount of mental "space" they have to think about math and solving math problems (indeed, another useful metaphor is that working memory is children's capacity to *attend* to multiple items in memory). This allows children to consciously think about the task or problem. Working memory affects children's ability to solve problems, to learn, and to remember (Ashcraft, 2006; Gilmore, Keeble, Richardson, & Cragg, 2017). For example, working memory predicts children's knowledge of arithmetic combinations (Geary, 2011; Geary et al., 2012; Passolunghi et al., 2007, especially the executive functioning component of working memory). Processes that are slower and more complex put additional demands on working memory. Unsurprisingly, then, limits on working memory may be one cause of learning difficulties or disabilities (Geary, Hoard, & Hamson, 1999; see the section later in this chapter). On the other hand, a particularly large working memory may be one cause of superior competence in math.

The EF process emphasizes *updating* working memory as new information is processed; that is, maintaining, manipulating, and adding relevant information often while engaging in another cognitively demanding task. Students solving a measurement problem may have to keep the problem situation and their solution in mind while they perform a necessary computation, interpret the result of the computation in terms of the measurement units, and then apply that to the problem context to solve the problem.

Practical Implications

Research on EF also offers some surprising good news: *High-quality math education may have the dual benefit* of teaching math *and developing EF processes* (Clements et al., 2020). Given the precious few hours children—especially those most in need—have in early childhood settings, a strategy that develops multiple critical competencies is particularly valuable. (Working memory is particularly important to math learning, and especially for children with disabilities, Cargnelutti & Passolunghi, 2017.) Intentional use of LT-based math education contribute to both: See especially the "Math Plus" activities on [LT]² that identify ways to teach that do this—supporting math *plus* EF.

Research has also identified certain environments and teaching practices that can help (see Chapter 16). Carefully guiding children to attend to specific math features, such as the number in a collection or the corners of a polygon, is likely to improve their learning. The predisposition to spontaneously recognize number, for example (see Chapter 2), is a skill but also a *habit of mind* that includes the ability to *direct attention to number* (Lehtinen & Hannula, 2006). These habits of mind generate further development of specific math knowledge *and* the ability to direct attention to math in situations in which it is relevant; that is, to *generalize* and *transfer* knowledge to new situations.

Children develop greater working memory capacity as they age, probably due to greater self-regulation and executive control and the ability to represent content more efficiently (Cowan, Saults, & Elliott, 2002). At all ages, one way people's minds deal with limits on working memory is to make certain processes *automatic*—fast and easy. Such automatic processes do not take much working memory (Shiffrin & Schneider, 1984). Some automatic processes are "bootstrap" abilities, such as the ability to recognize faces. In math, most must be learned and experienced many times. A familiar example is knowing arithmetic combinations so well that one "just knows" and does not have to figure them out while performing a more complicated task. Such automaticity requires much practice. Such practice could be "drill," but a broader definition is *repeated experiencing*, which might include drill but also includes use of the skill or knowledge in multiple difference situations, which promotes both automaticity and transfer to new situations.

Effortful Control is also inhibitory; that is, it is the ability to suppress one response (e.g., grab a toy from another) so you can respond in a better way (ask for or share the toy). Effortful control often focuses on more emotional and motivational responses to situations involving risk and reward. Effortful control may affect learning behaviors and relationships with adults and peers. Further, the lack of such social-emotional self-regulation can stand in the way of a child's ability to have positive teacher-child interactions in kindergarten, which, in turn, predicts later poor academic performance and behavior problems (Hamre & Pianta, 2001). Similarly, children low in effortful control act disruptively and aggressively, and so receive less support from their peers, which in turn hurts their learning (Valiente et al., 2011).

Practical Implications: Effortful Control

Research has also identified certain environments and teaching practices that can help children pay attention, and grow in their ability to do so, as well as to develop general self-regulation competencies (see Chapter 16). Instructional activities in each of this book's learning trajectories have been intentionally designed to help children direct attention.

Long-term Memory and Retrieval

Long-term memory is how people store information. Concepts ("understandings") take effort and time to be built into long-term memory. People have difficulty transferring their knowledge to new situations. That is, it is easier to use knowledge within the situation which one learned it. Without conceptual knowledge, such transfer would be even more difficult.

Practical Implications

Helping children build rich representations of concepts (called "integrated-concrete knowledge"; see Chapter 16) and see how something they know can be used to solve new problems helps them remember and transfer what they have learned. Varied situations do not necessarily need to be radically different. In one study, 6- and 7-year-old children practiced using flashcards or worksheets. The two groups performed equally well if tested in the same format that they had practiced–with the group who had practiced with flashcards being tested with flashcards and the group who had practiced worksheets testing with worksheets. However, if the format was switched, their performance was significantly lower (Nishida & Lillard, 2007a).

   Although material that is easy to understand can promote fast initial learning, it does not help store knowledge in long-term memory. *Challenging materials leads to better longer-term memory*, because children have to process it and understand it more thoroughly. Their extra effort translates into more active processing, and thus more likely storage, of information. This helps children remember information longer and retrieve ("remember") it more easily. Thus, they can retrieve the information better and thus are more likely to transfer its use to new situations.

   Next we turn to the mental objects children build. They include declarative, conceptual, and procedural representations.

What Predicts Math Achievement?

Consideration of such general learning and cognitive process, including affect and motivation, raise the question: Do these, or other, competencies or dispositions, *predict* math achievement?

Best Overall Predictors of Math Achievement

Perhaps most important, the *early learning of math predicts later achievement* (e.g., Bodovski & Youn, 2012). Knowledge of math in preschool correlated 0.46 with *tenth-grade math achievement*

(Stevenson & Newman, 1986). Kindergartners' cognitive skills, such as discriminating between same and different visual stimuli and coding visual stimuli, predicted later *interest* in math (see also Curby, Rimm-Kaufman, & Ponitz, 2009). Further, the *rate of growth* of math skills is faster among those with higher, rather than lower, initial math skills (Aunola, Leskinen, Lerkkanen, & Nurmi, 2004). Researchers concluded that "by far the most powerful avenue for boosting first-grade test scores appears to be improving the basic skills of low-achieving children upon entry into kindergarten." Surprisingly, early math predicts reading, but reading does not predict math achievement (Lerkkanen, Rasku-Puttonen, Aunola, & Nurmi, 2005). Also, "soft" or social-emotional skills, such as being able to sit still in class or make friends upon school entry did *not* predict achievement (Duncan, Claessens, & Engel, 2004). The effects of early knowledge of math is unusually strong and notably persistent (Duncan, Claessens, & Engel, 2004; Duncan et al. 2007; Duncan & Magnuson, 2011; Romano, Babchishin, Pagani, & Kohen, 2010). (Important to note that this includes not just education, but stable traits of the individual, family, and community, Watts, Duncan, Clements, & Sarama, 2018.)

Several studies showed that young children's general knowledge and especially fine motor skills add to the predictive power of early math knowledge (Dinehart & Manfra, 2013; Grissmer, Grimm, Aiyer, Murrah, & Steele, 2010; Pagani & Messier, 2012). However, a close look at the assessment administration reveals that many of the items intended to capture "fine motor skills" are also well-suited to capturing *spatial or geometric* competencies (e.g., use building blocks to replicate a model, copy five figures on paper).

What Particular *Math Skills are Predictive?*

Answering this could be useful for screening, or early identification of those who might have mathematical difficulties (MD, see pp. 325–332). Some research has found support for specific tasks, such as the following:

- Early-developing representations of magnitude in the ANS, or Approximate Number System in Chapter 2 (Geary, 2013; Mazzocco et al., 2011).
- Spontaneous focusing on number, such as using subitizing independently, which predicts arithmetic but not later reading abilities (see Chapter 2, Hannula, Lepola, & Lehtinen, 2007).
- Subitizing, especially relating small quantities to numerals (Geary & vanMarle, 2016).
- Magnitude discrimination, as in naming the larger of two digits, which may relate to a weakness in spatial representations (Chard et al., 2005; Cirino, 2010; Clarke & Shinn, 2004; Gersten, Jordan, & Flojo, 2005; Jordan, Hanich, & Kaplan, 2003; Lembke & Foegen, 2008; Lembke, Foegen, Whittake, & Hampton, 2008; Geary & vanMarle, 2016).
- If children cannot compare numbers, both symbolic and non-symbolic in kindergarten, they are at risk for later mathematical disabilities (Desoete, Ceulemans, De Weerdt, & Pieters, 2012; Olkun, Altun, Göçer Şahin, & Akkurt Denizli, 2015).
- Numeral identification, such as reading numerals (really a language arts skill) (Geary & vanMarle, 2016) (Chard et al., 2005; Gersten et al., 2005; Lembke & Foegen, 2008; Lembke et al., 2008).

- Similarly, the ability to use symbols such as numerals and connect them to quantities (Kolkman, Kroesbergen, & Leseman, 2013).
- Missing number tasks, that is, naming the missing number in a series (Chard et al., 2005; Cirino, 2010; Lembke & Foegen, 2008; Lembke et al., 2008).
- Object counting and counting strategies, without errors (see Chapters 3 and 5, Cirino, 2010; Clarke & Shinn, 2004; Geary, Brown, & Samaranayake, 1991; Gersten et al., 2005; Passolunghi et al., 2007) and *especially advanced*, not basic, *counting competencies* (Nguyen et al., 2016).
- Ability to map numbers on to a number line; that is, developing an explicit understanding of the logical structure of the number system (Geary, 2013).
- A different perspective that combines several of these into a measure of "number sense"– counting knowledge and principles, number recognition, number comparisons, nonverbal calculation, story problems and number combinations (Jordan, Glutting, & Ramineni, 2009; Jordan, Glutting, Ramineni, & Watkins, 2010).
- Fluency in arithmetic combinations, such as addition "facts" (for older children, Geary et al., 1991; Gersten et al., 2005) and de/composition of number (Geary et al., 1991).
- Knowledge of patterns and math structure in kindergarten also predicts mathematical, and in particular, arithmetical competencies at the end of Grade 2; this knowledge is almost as predictive as knowledge of number (Lüken, 2012).
- Finally, *specific math language*, such as number (e.g., "more" and "less" and number words) and spatial (e.g., "behind" and "above" and shape terms) concepts is strongly related to early maths learning, even beyond oft-cited factors such as working memory and comparison abilities (Toll & Van Luit, 2014b).

Although it is important that we build our evidence base of what predicts later math abilities, caution advised, however, because both the screening measures and the predicted measure often ignore any math outside of routine numerical skills.

Other domains such as language and literacy are also related to math (Purpura, Day, Napoli, & Hart, 2017). For example, both vocabulary and knowledge of print predict later numeracy scores (Purpura, Hume, Sims, & Lonigan, 2011).

Other cognitive processes related to math for some children with MD or MLD including working memory (e.g., reverse digit span, Geary, 2003; Gersten et al., 2005; Toll, Van der Ven, Kroesbergen, & Van Luit, 2010); or general intelligence, working memory, and processing speed (Geary et al., 1991). Others have found working memory not predictive of fact fluency once attention (one of the strongest predictors) was controlled (Fuchs et al., 2005). Attention, working memory, and nonverbal problem solving predicted conceptual competence. Recall that competence with early counting, including counting confidently and accurate use of counting strategies, and magnitude comparison, appear particularly important (Gersten et al., 2005; Jordan et al., 2003).

In addition, a closer relationship with the teacher is positively related to achievement, especially for younger and at-risk children. Finally, children who were more outgoing acquired math (and reading) skills more rapidly (Burchinal, Peisner-Feinberg, Pianta, & Howes, 2002). Children who receive more instructional support from teachers show fewer task-avoidant behaviors and this in turn leads to higher levels of math skills (Pakarinen et al., 2010). Thus, warm, caring, *and* educationally supportive teachers help children learn math and more.

A common, critical, component of these studies may be engagement in mathematical thinking and learning. One large study confirmed the importance of engagement, or "approaches to learning," which was the best predictor of learning as far out as fifth grade (Bodovski & Youn, 2011). Such engagement in learning, including persistence at tasks, eagerness to learn, attentiveness, learning independence, flexibility, and organization, is especially important for girls and minority students.

A caution in drawing implications from all of the studies reviewed in this section is that they are correlational, *not* experimental. We cannot attribute causation to them. However, they are suggestive. Chapter 16 contains evidence from experiments in which we can say something about the effects of providing better early math instruction. For now, we simply make several recommendations.

Practical Implications

Teach math early. Focus on the key math topics outlined in this book. Also focus on improving self-regulation skills. Remember that the development of self-regulation and math competencies are mutually beneficial—growth in one supports the growth of the other (Van der Ven, Kroesbergen, Boom, & Leseman, 2012) and this is not true of literacy (Welsh, Nix, Blair, Bierman, & Nelson, 2010). Once again, math is a fundamental cognitive ability.

Affect (Emotion) and Beliefs (Including "Aptitude Vs. Effort") and Motivation

Given that mathematical thinking and learning is *cognitive*, does emotion play a role? Most definitely (Mercader, Miranda, Presentación, Siegenthaler, & Rosel, 2017). For example, if people are anxious about math, they may perform poorly (Pantoja et al., 2019), not necessarily because they have limited ability or skills but because nervous thoughts "push" themselves into their minds, limiting the amount of working memory available to work on math (Ashcraft, 2006; Boaler, 2014; Fritz, Haase, & Räsänen, 2019). Further, it blocks young children from even trying to use more advanced solution strategies (Ramirez, Chang, Maloney, Levine, & Beilock, 2016). In this section, we review key findings about affect.

As a culture, people in the U.S. have unfortunate emotions (negative) and beliefs about math. Indeed, all it takes to raise math anxiety in the approximately 17% of the population who suffer from this is to show them that number (Ashcraft, 2006)! Anxiety harms students' abilities to solve math problems (Cargnelutti, Tomasetto, & Passolunghi, 2017), especially those that are more demanding (Ho-Hong, 2017).

One deeply embedded belief is that achievement in math depends mostly on *aptitude* or *ability*, as Aretha illustrated at the beginning of this chapter. In contrast, people from other countries believe that achievement comes from *effort*—Brenda's view. Even more disturbing, *research shows that this U.S. belief hurts children and, further, that it is just not true*. Children who believe—or are helped to understand—that they can learn if they try, work on tasks longer and achieve better throughout their school careers than children who believe you either "have it" (or "get it") or you do not. This latter view often leads to failure and "learned helplessness." Similarly, those who have mastery-oriented goals—who try to learn and see the point of school to develop knowledge and skills—achieve more than children whose goals are directed toward high grades or outperforming others (Middleton & Spanias, 1999; NMP, 2008). They even see failure as an opportunity to learn (cf. Papert, 1980).

As Carina argued, there certainly are differences between children, as will be discussed later in this chapter. However, whether these are due to nature or nurture or an intricate combination is difficult to tell. All children can develop math competence, and even "intelligence," working in high-quality educational environments.

Fortunately, most young children have positive feelings about math and are motivated to explore numbers and shapes (Middleton & Spanias, 1999). Unfortunately, after only a couple of years in typical schools, they begin to believe that "only some people have the ability to do math." Further, by second or third grade, many experience math anxiety, especially related to more demanding calculations and problem solving (Wu, Barth, Amin, Malcarne, & Menon, 2012), and this may be worse for children who are underprepared in math (Wu et al., 2012). We believe that those who experience math as a *sense-making activity* will build positive feelings about math throughout their school careers. This is important, because there is a reciprocal relationship between math interest and math ability—each supports the development of the other (Fisher, Dobbs-Oates, Doctoroff, & Arnold, 2012).

Practical Implications: Math Anxiety

Provide meaningful tasks that make sense to children and connect with their everyday interests and lives using learning trajectories and other characteristics of high-quality teaching (e.g., Gervasoni, 2018). The right degree of challenge and novelty can promote interest and facilitating and discussing skill improvement can promote a mastery orientation. Researchers have estimated that children should be successful about 70% of the time to maximize motivation (Middleton & Spanias, 1999).

In summary, many negative beliefs are embedded in our culture. However, you can help children change them. *One of the most important ways to help them is to decrease your own math anxiety.* When early childhood and elementary female teachers are math anxious—and many are—the girls in their classrooms have worse math achievement and come to believe only boys are good at math (Beilock, Gunderson, Ramirez, & Levine, 2010).

Returning to the emotions, we see that affect plays a significant role in problem solving, involving both joys and frustrations (McLeod & Adams, 1989). Based on Mandler's theory, the source of such emotion is the interruption of a scheme. For example, if a plan is blocked, an emotion is generated, which might be negative or positive.

Practical Implications: Affect and Motivation

If children realize they are incorrect, they may believe this warrants embarrassment, but you can change that by directly assuring children that trying and discussing, including making errors and being frustrated, are part of the learning process. Also, discuss how working hard to learn and figure a problem out can make you "feel good" (Cobb, Yackel, & Wood, 1989). Hold such discussions to build positive affect and beliefs about math and math problem solving (an important, interesting activity that is an end in itself), as well as learning (e.g., emphasis on effort, not ability).

Trying hard also requires motivation. Fortunately, most children are motivated to learn. Even better, they are *intrinsically* motivated—they like to learn for the sake of learning. Such intrinsic motivation correlates with and supports academic success. However, children are not motivated equally, and such engagement predicts later school success. Indeed, in more than one study, children's motivational orientation (e.g., engagement and persistence in tasks) in preschool predicted their math knowledge from kindergarten to the primary and even intermediate grades (Fitzpatrick & Pagani, 2013; Lepola, Niemi, Kuikka, & Hannula, 2005). Further, those who begin with the lowest math knowledge have the lowest engagement in tasks (Bodovski & Farkas, 2007). Extrinsic motivation is related to performance goals (NMP, 2008) and self-regulation. Self-regulation is not just a cognitive process but also has a motivational component. Some research shows that children in classrooms with more emphasis on child-centered teaching practices show more interest in math (and reading, Lerkkanen et al., 2012). This is important, but before drawing conclusions, note that the authors' child-centered and teacher-directed practices are a strict (what we would call a *false*) dichotomy. For example, in child-centered discipline: "Conflict resolution is smooth; consequences are appropriate and apply equally" (p. 268). Teacher-directed "discipline is imposed without explanation or discussion; consequences are inconsistent." This may serve the authors' research purposes, but we believe this could lead to misinterpretations of this and many similar studies. Many teacher-guided activities are quite appropriate. Indeed, many of the activities we suggest are led by the teacher but would be coded as "child-centered" by the authors. It is always important to know the specifics. This leads us to our next point.

Practical Implications: Intention, Structured Activities, and Affect

Some worry that *structured* math activities negatively affect children's motivations or affect. No research we know of supports that concern. Research suggests the opposite (Malofeeva et al., 2004)—motivation and engagement increase with intentional, structured, appropriate math activities. Educators do have to avoid narrow views of math and learning. Teachers hamper students' learning if they define success only as fast, correct responses and accuracy in following the teacher's example (Middleton & Spanias, 1999). Finally, negative affect about math affects children with math learning disability most of all (Lebens, Graff, & Mayer, 2011). We must be especially conscientious about positive instructional practices with these children.

However, there *are ways to structure activities* to ensure they make memorable, motivating, math moments that matter to children. See Kyle Pearce and Jon Orr's website https://make mathmoments.com on their four-step "curiosity path": withholding information, anticipation, notice & wonder, and estimation.

Equity: Group and Individual Differences

Children from higher-income families (higher levels of parental education and use of progressive parenting beliefs) come to school better prepared in math than others (Burchinal et al., 2002; Duncan & Magnuson, 2011). For most children, this "achievement gap" does not close; it widens (Geary, 2006; Lee, 2002; Navarro et al., 2012). As will be discussed in the next section, this gap is more appropriately deemed a learning *opportunity gap* given its relationship to differences in children's exposure to high-quality math experiences (Clements et al., 2020; Sarama & Clements, 2018).

Opportunities to Learn: Poverty and Minority Status

Worldwide, the number of children who do not learn these basic competencies during the primary education varies from 15% in North America and Europe to about 85% in sub-Saharan Africa (Fritz et al., 2019). As mentioned in Chapter 1, children who live in poverty and who are members of linguistic and ethnic minority groups demonstrate significantly lower levels of achievement (Bowman et al., 2001; Brooks-Gunn, Duncan, & Britto, 1999; Campbell & Silver, 1999; Denton & West, 2002; Entwisle & Alexander, 1990; Halle, Kurtz-Costes, & Mahoney, 1997; Mullis et al., 2000; Natriello, McDill, & Pallas, 1990; Rouse, Brooks-Gunn, & McLanahan, 2005; Secada, 1992; Sylva, Melhuish, Sammons, Siraj-Blatchford, & Taggart, 2005; Thomas & Tagg, 2004).

If high-quality math education does not start in preschool and continue through the early years, children who have not been given opportunities to learn can be trapped in a trajectory of failure (Rouse et al., 2005). This is a crime. Children with few learning opportunities, who are from communities with fewer "charging stations" for learning math (Blevins-Knabe & Musun-Miller, 1996; Lee & Burkam, 2002), can start out behind their peers in multiple topics, numerical, arithmetic, spatial/geometric, patterning, and measurement knowledge (Sarama & Clements, 2009).

These children face other barriers, such as "stereotype threat"–the imposition of societal biases such as the prejudice that people of color or women are "not as good at math"–have a negative influence on the performance of the threatened groups (NMP, 2008).

Extra support–better "charging stations"–must be provided to those from low-resource communities and those whose home language is different from that of school. We also must meet the needs of all children, including children with disabilities.

We must take an asset-based approach. These children bring diverse experiences on which to build meaningful math learning (Moll, Amanti, Neff, & Gonzalez, 1992). An asset-based approach focuses on strengths while respecting diversity in culture, thinking, and ability as positive assets to the math learning environment. The younger the child, the more their learning is enhanced by contexts that they find relevant and meaningful. Research shows that all children can learn the math that other children learn. In our studies, *these children learned more than their more advantaged peers in the same classrooms* (Clements, Sarama, Spitler, Lange, & Wolfe, 2011; Clements, Sarama, Wolfe, & Spitler, 2013).

ELs/DLLs/ELLs

This raises the important issue of children whose first language is not English (National Academies of Sciences, 2017). Too many believe that language is less of a concern in math, compared with other subjects, because math is based on "numbers" or "symbols." This is a mistake. Children learn math mostly from oral language, rather than textbooks or math symbolism (Janzen, 2008). Challenges include technical vocabulary, some of which is similar too but distinct from everyday phrases, and the use of complex noun phrases.

There is often a gap between the achievement of children who are English Language Learners and those of children proficient in English (Wilkinson, 2017) due to the *language demands* of math tasks (Alt, Arizmendi, & Beal, 2014). However, the *risk factor of second-language learners is not their multilingualism* but rather proficiency in the language of instruction. In fact, multilingualism also provides *cognitive benefits* (Hartanto, Yang, & Yang, 2018; National Academies of Sciences, 2017; Prediger, Erath, & Opitz, 2019). Indeed, they may learn *faster* (Choi, Jeon, & Lippard, 2018; Miller & Warren, 2014). Thus, the best approach is to teach these young children in their first language (Celedón-Pattichis, Musanti, & Marshall, 2010; Espada, 2012). The long-term goal should be to help children maintain and build the first language while adding fluency and literacy skills in English, not replacing the child's home language with English (Espinosa, 2005). Minimally, bilingual teachers need to understand the linguistic characteristics of classroom language and also master ways to connect everyday language with the language of math (Janzen, 2008).

Practical Implications

Children who live in poverty and who are members of linguistic and ethnic minority groups need more math and better math programs (Rouse et al., 2005). They need programs that emphasize the higher-order concepts and skills at each level, as well as base knowledge and skills (Fryer & Levitt, 2004; Clements & Sarama, 2008). They should learn math in their native language.

What programs address these issues? Several research-based programs are discussed at length in Chapter 15. Some general guidelines are given here (from Espinosa, 2005).

There are two important and general guidelines. First, take an asset-based approach. All children can learn substantial math. All children have knowledge and skills on which to build (a fundamental principle of the learning trajectories approach). *Second, provide high-quality math education from birth through the primary grades.* Children from low-resource communities who are in high-quality care at *multiple* points in their lives from infancy through preschool *show no difference in their math knowledge* compared to those from higher-resource communities (Dearing, McCartney, & Taylor, 2009). *High-quality education matters.*

- *Provide the following for children from low-resource communities:*
  - *Positive, supporting relationships.*
  - *Strong emphasis on language development at school and home.* Families should be strongly encouraged to talk about math, especially number, arithmetic, spatial relations, and patterns, with children of all ages (Levine, Gunderson, & Huttenlocher, 2011) (Toll & Van Luit, 2014).
  - *A collaborative and respectful relationship with parents and other family members.*
  - *Small class sizes.* Each child needs to have frequent individual interactions and learning experiences that are tailored to his or her unique talents and abilities.
  - *Teams of teachers who engage in collaborative planning and reflection.*
  - *Games and activities that connect intuitive knowledge to math verbal and written symbols.* Children from low-resource communities have equal informal or intuitive number sense as more advanced peers, but may lack opportunities to link these to symbols—number words and numerals (Jordan, Huttenlocher, & Levine, 1994; Scalise, DePascale, McCown, & Ramani, 2019). Games and other activities can provide those missing links.

- *More, not different, high-quality math.* Children may need more, but not different, *high-quality* math education that is recommended for all children (Gaidoschik, 2019, cf. Burchinal, Zaslow, & Tarullo, 2016). Intensive tutoring may be called for (Barnes et al., 2016).

- *Provide the following for ELLs* (see also the "Resources" section of [LT]² for many more tips and help, including invaluable lists of Spanish cognates):

  - *Bilingual instructional support including paraprofessionals* (instructional assistant, parent volunteers, and older and more competent students).
  - *Instruction in children's home language* (Burchinal, Field, López, Howes, & Pianta, 2012) and use of cognates and other means of explaining math concepts with familiar language (Janzen, 2008). This includes educational technology in the home language, which has been proven effective (Foster et al., 2018).
  - *Systematic introduction of English during the infant, toddler, and preschool years with simultaneous maintenance of the home language* (National Academies of Sciences, 2017).
  - *Following learning pathways,* gradual progressions with modeling what is required, followed by children of similar ability working in groups, and finally children working individually (Warren & Miller, 2014).
  - *Careful development of academic language* during content area instruction including *visual and verbal supports,* as well as *movement, manipulating objects,* and so forth to make core content comprehensible (National Academies of Sciences, 2017; Warren & Miller, 2014).
  - *Substantial incorporation of children's culture, including funds of knowledge* (Murphey, Madill, & Guzman, 2017; Warren & Miller, 2014).
  - *Discussion between the children and the teacher and between children,* explaining solutions and working toward more formal math language and ideas (Warren & Miller, 2014).
  - *Simple print material in the children's home language* in learning centers and labeled objects.
  - *Strong emphasis on language development at school and home* (as above).
  - *Word problems that are created from students' personal narratives,* helping children "mathematize" situations (Janzen, 2008).
  - *Generation of math problems through storytelling.* This helps kindergartners learn problem solving (Turner, Celedón-Pattichis, & Marshall, 2008, who focused on Latinax), as does giving additional time to problem solving, posing a broad range of problems involving multiplication, division, and multiple steps, and providing consistent access to Spanish (Turner & Celedón-Pattichis, 2011).
  - *Encouragement to parents and other family members to use the home language during family activities and early literacy and math development,* as well as to visit school and share where math is used in the home and community.
  - *Age-appropriate books and stories in the child's home language* (school and loan to the home). This might include e-books (Murphey et al., 2017; Shamir & Lifshitz, 2012).
  - *Interventions in preschool through the primary grades, preferably with bilingual components* (Clements et al., 2011, 2013; Fuchs et al., 2013; Sarama, Clements, Wolfe, & Spitler, 2012) (Foster et al., 2018).

- *Encouragement for families of children with specific language impairments to talk about math, numbers, and arithmetic*, as they tend to do so less than other families (Kleemans, Segers, & Verhoeven, 2013; Prediger et al., 2019).
- *High-quality math education*, especially including conceptual understanding, procedural fluency, and math practices; high cognitive demand; and positive beliefs (Moschkovich, 2013).

Other Resources

Finally, there are Spanish resources throughout [LT]² and information for teaching those with any languages in the Resources section. Also see the DLL!Ready app for teacher support for all DLL/ELL/EL children.

Mathematical Learning Difficulties and Disabilities

Similar to those at risk for other reasons, children with disabilities (CWD) often do not fare well in the typical early childhood classroom. Many children show specific learning difficulties in math at young ages. Unfortunately, they are often not identified, or are categorized broadly with other children as "developmentally delayed." This is especially unfortunate because focused math interventions at early ages are effective (Berch & Mazzocco, 2007; Dowker, 2004).

Two Categories: MD and MLD

Children with *mathematical difficulties* (MD) are those who are struggling to learn math for any reason (Berch & Mazzocco, 2007). Often defined as all those below the 35th percentile on assessments, estimates can be as high as 40% to 48% of the population. Those with a specific *mathematics learning disability* (MLD) have some form of memory or cognitive deficit that interferes with their ability to learn concepts and/or procedures in one or more domains of math (Geary, 2004). They are, therefore, a much smaller subset of all those with MD, with estimates of 6% to 7% of the population (Berch & Mazzocco, 2007; Mazzocco & Myers, 2003). Studies have found that such classifications are not stable for many children in the early and primary grades; only 63% of those classified as MLD in kindergarten were still so classified in third grade (Mazzocco & Myers, 2003).

MLD Identifying Behaviors

Children with MLD must, by definition, have a genetic basis, but presently are defined by their behaviors. MLD in the primary grades is often characterized by developmental lags (Dowker, 2004; Jordan & Montani, 1997).[1] However, specific behaviors that define MLD—general cognitive, conceptual, skill, or some combination—is still debated (Berch & Mazzocco, 2007). For example, there is research that suggests each of the following.

- MLD results from a single underlying deficit of number sense.
- MLD results from various deficits (Moeller, Fischer, Cress, & Nuerk, 2012).
- Researchers agree that children with MLD have difficulty quickly retrieving basic arithmetic facts. Again, there are studies that suggests each of the following as the cause:

- inability to store or retrieve facts, including disruptions in the retrieval process,
- impairments in visuospatial representations (Resnick, Newcombe, & Jordan, 2019),
- deficits in working memory and speed of processing (Geary, Hoard, Byrd-Craven, Nugent, & Numtee, 2007),
- the same factors that are thought to underlie performance limitations of normally achieving children (Hopkins & Lawson, 2004), and
- impairments in the executive control of verbal material (Berch & Mazzocco, 2007) that prevent learning all the counting principles and holding an error violation in working memory, lead to long use of immature strategies such as finger counting throughout elementary school (Geary, Bow-Thomas, & Yao, 1992; Ostad, 1998), and limit subitizing (Berch & Mazzocco, 2007).

Diverse Needs

We can see that children who have MLD or MD may have quite diverse learning needs (Dowker, 2004; Gervasoni, 2005; Gervasoni, Hadden, & Turkenburg, 2007; Verschaffel et al., 2018). These findings support the need to understand, assess, and teach these children with topic-specific learning trajectories, as has been the theme of this book. That is, as the *hierarchic interactionalism* tenet of *domain specific progression* would indicate, there are many relatively independent components of arithmetical competence each of which develops along its own learning trajectory. Research on both people with brain injuries and students with MD show that it is possible to have a deficit in any of those areas independent of others (Dowker, 2004, 2005).

What do these needs include? As the list above, these may be any of the following.

- *Number sense*: number comparison, number conservation, numeral reading, nonverbal calculations, story problems, and arithmetic combinations (Aunio, Hautamäki, Sajaniemi, & Van Luit, 2008; Aunola et al., 2004; Geary et al., 1999; Gersten et al., 2005; Jordan, Kaplan, Locuniak, & Ramineni, 2006; Mazzocco & Thompson, 2005).
- *Counting*: weak conceptual knowledge and skill in certain areas of counting.
- *Subitizing*: arithmetic (Ashkenazi et al., 2013).
- *Place value and word problem solving* (Dowker, 2004).

Note that these studies often ignore math topics other than number; we will address topics beyond number in a succeeding section.

Math, Reading, and Language Learning Disabilities

Children with both MLD and reading learning disabilities (RLD) score lower on number production and comprehension tasks, such as number naming, numeral writing, and magnitude comparison, possibly due to inadequate experience with written numerals (Geary et al., 1999). They are more likely to view counting as a mechanical activity (c.f. Krajewski & Schneider, 2009; Vukovic, 2012). In contrast, MLD only and MLD/RLD children do not differ on approximate arithmetic (estimating answers to addition and subtraction problems), suggesting that it is weaknesses in *spatial* representations related to numerical magnitudes (rather than verbal representations) that underpin fact retrieval deficits (Resnick et al., 2019) (Jordan et al., 2003; Mazzocco & Myers, 2003).

In contrast, another study showed that children with MLD and MLD/RLD could compare the number in *collections* as well as their normal-developing peers, but were impaired when comparing Arabic numerals (Rousselle & Noël, 2007). Importantly, there was no difference between the MLD only and MLD/RLD groups. This suggests that, at least for some children, MLD means having difficulty in accessing number magnitude from *symbols*, rather than in processing numbers. This is significant, as difficulty attaching meaning to numerals could confound children's performance in a wide variety of tasks and be the start of many other related problems with math. Traditional teaching that separates instruction on concepts from procedures would be particularly devastating for these children. Instead, connecting concepts and procedures, concrete/visual representations and abstract symbols, would be more effective.

The *type* of RLD may matter: Children with dyslexia were weaker in math than children with reading comprehension difficulties and more likely to have deficits in math fact fluency, operations, and problem solving (Vukovic, Lesaux, & Siegel, 2010). The deficit in fluency may have something to do with problems with phonological processing, although separate numerical processing difficulties might also be involved.

Children with specific language impairments may have specific MLD, such as coordinating the items with a structure of correspondences between speech sounds and numerical relations (Donlan, 1998) (Prediger et al., 2019). For example, they may not acquire the quantifiers of their grammatical system, such as "a," "some," "few," or "two" (cf. Carey, 2004). Or, they may have difficulty relating "two, three, four, five …" to "twenty, thirty, forty, fifty …." Exact arithmetic may depend more heavily on language systems (Berch & Mazzocco, 2007). Children with specific language impairments need qualitatively rich interactions with their teachers (Prediger et al., 2019). Provide meaningful discourse, including explaining meanings of math concepts and operations and describing general patterns. Equally important is using meaningful vocabulary connected to the formal technical terms. This is most useful when it occurs in structured phrases in math talk, instead of teaching isolated terms (Prediger et al., 2019).

Other Impairments

Specific disabilities must be considered in a complete picture of infant to adult developmental trajectories. Different impairments in low-level processes may result in different difficulties in children and adults.

The most prevalent disorder in the U.S. is attention-deficit hyperactivity disorder (ADHD) (Berch & Mazzocco, 2007). These children habituate to stimuli rapidly and thus have difficulty maintaining attention, spend less time rehearsing, and make more errors. Attention to auditory processes is especially problematic. This may account for their difficulty learning basic arithmetic combinations and their difficulty with multistep problems and complex computations. Tutoring and work with computer games have shown success (Ford, Poe, & Cox, 1993; Shaw, Grayson, & Lewis, 2005; Chmiliar, 2017; Iuculano et al., 2015; Ok & Kim, 2017). Use of calculators allows some children to succeed (Berch & Mazzocco, 2007).

Most children with *Down Syndrome* could maintain one-to-one correspondence when counting, but had particular difficulties producing the count words correctly. Their errors were most often skipping words, indicating difficulty with auditory sequential memory. That is, they had inadequate connections between one number word and the next in the sequence. They also lacked approaches to problem-solving or counting strategies (Porter, 1999). Teachers of children with Down Syndrome often neglect number tasks, but this is unwise. Visually presented number sequences may help children learn to count (Porter, 1999).

Physical impairments such as *hearing difficulties* may be considered risk factors for MD. However, these children seem to learn math the same ways as their peers, and there is not a strong or necessary connection (Nunes & Moreno, 1998). Visually based interventions may be effective with children who are *deaf* (Nunes & Moreno, 2002). One study indicated that deaf/hard-of-hearing children's difficulties in math begin prior to the primary grades, so early intervention is particularly important (Pagliaro & Kritzer, 2013). The study confirmed that these children often have areas of strength, such as geometric competencies that can be used as a starting point, and also areas of challenge, including problem solving and measurement, which can be addressed throughout the early years.

Blind children cannot rely on visual-spatial strategies for object counting, instead using tactile motor systems for keeping track of which objects have been counted (Sicilian, 1988). Accurate blind counters used three sets of strategies. The following brief developmental progressions for each moves from no, to inefficient, to efficient strategies:

- Preliminary scanning strategies—no scanning (just started counting); moves the hand across objects unsystematically; moves the hand across all objects in a fixed array systematically or moves objects during counting.
- Organizing strategies—none; follows a row, circle, or array but does not use reference point to mark where started; uses reference point or moves objects during counting.
- Partitioning—no one-to-one correspondence; touches objects but no systematic partitioning, or moves objects but puts them back in same group; uses moveable partitioning system or moves objects to new location.

Children with *cerebral palsy* perform worse than their peers on math, especially word-problem solving (Jenks, van Lieshout, & de Moor, 2012). Impairments of visuospatial sketchpad and inhibitory control predicted future word-problem solving, and fact fluency and reading ability were both important for promoting word-problem solving ability for these children.

Geometry and Spatial Thinking

As we have seen, some researchers believe that a deficit in visuospatial strategies is a component of MLD because these strategies may underlie numerical thinking (e.g., Geary et al., 1991; see also Jenks et al., 2012). What about other areas of math, such as geometry, spatial reasoning, and measurement? Researchers tend to only investigate number topics, so we know little. Unsurprisingly, geometry is a more difficult area to address for children who are visually impaired. However, strategies have been proposed for specific skills, such as making distance judgments from a tactile map (Ungar, Blades, & Spencer, 1997). Students were taught to use their fingers to measure relative distances and think in terms of fractions or ratios, or at least in terms of "much longer" or "only a little bit longer." The 30-minute training helped them be as accurate as sighted children.

The discussion of the spatial thinking of blind children in Chapter 7 indicated that all students can build up spatial sense and geometric notions. Spatial knowledge *is* spatial, not "visual." Even children blind from birth are aware of spatial relationships. By age 3, they begin to learn about spatial characteristics of certain visual language (Landau, 1988). They can learn from spatial-kinesthetic (movement) practice (Millar & Ittyerah, 1992). They perform many aspects of spatial tasks similar to blindfolded sighted children (Morrongiello, Timney, Humphrey, Anderson, & Skory, 1995). Second, visual input is important, but spatial relations can be constructed without it (Morrongiello et al., 1995). People who are blind can learn to discriminate the size of objects, or their shape (circle, triangle, and square) with 80% accuracy by distinguishing echoes (Rice, 1967, as cited in Gibson, 1969). They can certainly do so through tactile explorations. For example, students who are blind have been successfully taught to seriate lengths (Lebron-Rodriguez & Pasnak, 1977). Primary-grade students can develop the ability to compare rectangular areas by tactile scanning of the two dimensions (Mullet & Miroux, 1996).

Students with low vision can often follow activities for sighted students, as long as they are provided with enlarged print, visuals, and manipulatives. Sometimes, use of low vision devices facilitates students' geometry learning. Using real objects and manipulative solids to represent 2D and 3D objects is critical for all students with visual impairments. Two-dimensional objects can be represented in tactile form on a two-dimensional plane adequately, but care should be taken that the entire presentation is not too complex. For example, the book *Let's Learn Shapes with Shapely CAL* presents tactile representations of common shapes (Keller & Goldberg, 1997).

However, 2D tactile representations are *not* adequate for representing 3D objects. Detailed, specific guidance and elaboration of the students' experiences with such objects is important. Make sure the students explore all components of the object and reflect on their relationship to each other. Students can explore and describe a 3D solid, reconstruct a solid made of components (such as with Googooplex), and construct a cube given only one edge (e.g., with D-stix).

Research with students who are deaf has indicated that both teachers and students often did not have substantial experience with geometry (Mason, 1995). Language, however, did play an important role. For example, the iconic nature of the American Sign Language (ASL) sign used for triangle is roughly equilateral or isosceles. After an 8-day geometry unit, many students spelled "triangle" instead of using signs, indicating a differentiation in their minds between their new definition of the word "triangle" and what they had previously associated with the sign "triangle" (Mason, 1995).

Given the sometimes-confusing vocabulary in geometry education, students with limited English proficiency (LEP) require special attention. One study showed that English proficient (EP) and LEP students can work together using computers to construct the concepts of reflection and rotation. Students experiencing the dynamic computer environment significantly outperformed students experiencing a traditional instructional environment on content measures of the concepts of reflection and rotation as well as on measures of 2D visualization ability. LEP students did not perform statistically significantly differently than their EP peers on any of the tests when experiencing the same instructional environments (Dixon, 1995).

Although, as stated, the research has been limited, some children appear to have difficulty with spatial organization across a wide range of tasks. Children with certain math learning difficulties may struggle with spatial relationships, visual-motor and visual-perception, and a poor sense of direction (Lerner, 1997). They may not perceive a shape as a complete and integrated entity as children without learning disabilities do. For example, a triangle may appear to them as three separate lines, as a rhombus, or even as an undifferentiated closed shape (Lerner, 1997). Children with different brain injuries show different patterns of competence. Those with right hemispheric injuries have difficulty organizing objects into coherent spatial groupings, while those with left hemispheric injuries have difficulty with local relations within spatial arrays (Stiles & Nass, 1991). Teaching with learning trajectories based on the developmental sequences described here is even more important for children with learning disabilities, as well as children with other special needs. Know the developmental sequences through which children pass as they learn geometric ideas.

As noted previously, spatial weakness may underlie children's difficulties with numerical magnitudes (e.g., knowing that 5 is greater than 4, but only by a little, whereas 12 is a lot greater than 4) and rapid retrieval of numeral names and arithmetic combinations (Jordan et al., 2003). These children may not be able to manipulate visual representations of a number line.

Similarly, due to the difficulties in perceiving shapes and spatial relationships, recognizing spatial relationships, and making spatial judgments, these children are unable to copy geometric forms, shapes, numbers, or letters. They are likely to perform poorly in handwriting as well as in arithmetic. When children cannot write numbers easily, they also cannot read and align their own numbers properly. As a result, they make errors in computation.

Summary and Policy Implications: Asset-based Approaches

There are substantial inequities in math experiences in the early years. U.S. children are educationally at risk due to a culture that devalues math, inhospitable schools, bad teaching, and textbooks that make little sense (Ginsburg, 1997). Children are considered learning disabled if they do not learn despite having experienced "conventional instruction." But that instruction is often flawed. This has led some experts to estimate that 80% of children labeled as learning disabled were labeled in error (Geary, 1990; Ginsburg, 1997).

There is no single cognitive deficit that causes MD (Dowker, 2005; Gervasoni, 2005; Gervasoni et al., 2007; Ginsburg, 1997) (Fritz, Haase, & Räsänen, 2019). Children from vulnerable populations often are deprived of adequate opportunities to learn math before school, and then attend preschools, childcare, and elementary schools that are themselves low-resourced in math! This double dilemma is then compounded as children suffer yet a third assault: Mis-identified as learning disabled, they suffer from lowered expectations from all educators they encounter. This is an educational shame. We must provide complete evaluations of the child's past experiences; present knowledge, skills, and cognitive abilities (e.g., strategic competence, attentional abilities, memorial competencies); and learning potential. If children have difficulties learning, we must determine whether they lack background information and informal knowledge, foundational concepts and procedures, or connections among these. Educative experiences—beyond those regularly provided to children—must be provided over a time frame of months to provide dynamic, formative, assessments of the children's needs (Feuerstein, Rand, & Hoffman, 1979) and the implications for instruction.

Practical Implications

Identify children with math difficulties *as early as possible* (Fritz et al., 2019, see assessments here too)—*before 3 years of age* (Hojnoski et al., 2018). Enroll them in research-based math intervention as soon as possible. Identify children who may have been miseducated and mislabeled—often high-quality education is effective (Verschaffel et al., 2018). Better educational experience, including practice, is indicated for such children. Other children who did not benefit substantially are in need of specialized instruction. Often, simple drill and practice would not be indicated.

Focus on essential areas such as components of "number sense" and "spatial sense" as described above. Some children with MLD may have difficulty maintaining one-to-one correspondence when counting or matching. They may need to physically grasp and move objects, as grasping is an earlier skill than pointing in development (Lerner, 1997). They often understand counting as a rigid, mechanical activity (Geary, Hamson, & Hoard, 2000). These children also may count objects in small sets one by one for long after their peers are strategically subitizing these amounts. Emphasizing their ability to learn to subitize the smallest number, perhaps representing them on their fingers, may be helpful. (Children who have continued difficulty perceiving and distinguishing even small numbers are at risk of severe general MD, Dowker, 2004.)

Other children may have difficulty with subitizing (Landerl, Bevan, & Butterworth, 2004), magnitude comparisons (e.g., knowing which of two digits is larger; Landerl et al., 2004; Wilson, Revkin, Cohen, Cohen, & Dehaene, 2006), and in learning and using more sophisticated counting and arithmetic strategies (Gersten et al., 2005; Wilson et al., 2006). Computer programs that help develop ANS (Chapter 2) and symbolic (counting, numerals) competencies are effective (Van Herwegen & Donlan, 2018). Children's lack of progress in arithmetic, especially in mastering arithmetic combinations, causes consistent problems; thus, early and intensive intervention is indicated. In another study children who show very low performance benefited from ANS-type *arithmetic* experiences, whereas children with higher performance benefited from symbolic (numeral identification) experiences (Szkudlarek & Brannon, 2018).

The relationship between counting and arithmetic needs further comment. Recall one behavior indicator of MLD was doing arithmetic by counting. But if children have been mis-educated, what else might they do (Gaidoschik, 2019)? Early on, meaningful counting on fingers, for example, should be encouraged, not suppressed. However, as emphasized in Chapters 2, 5, and 6, moving, as is common in East Asian countries, to derived facts and (de)composing numbers via subitizing and other strategies, is a more powerful route to arithmetic (Gaidoschik, 2019). If children do not receive such high-quality education, they may cling to counting, and be (mis)identified as MLD.

For those with MLD or MD struggling with arithmetic problem solving, schema-based approaches that give explicit attention to naming the problem type have shown to help CWD in the upper primary grades (see Chapter 5, p. 104, Jitendra, 2019; Peltier & Vannest, 2017). Young children with MLD are not accurate in evaluating the accuracy of their solutions, which has implications for asking them to "check their work" or "ask for help" (Berch & Mazzocco, 2007).

Although CWD may show weaknesses in some spatial processes, they also show strengths in others, such as mental rotation (Resnick et al., 2019). In any case, shoring up on weaknesses, such as using number lines, and building on spatial strengths will be particularly useful for CWD (Resnick et al., 2019).

There are many gaps in resources to help children with special needs. There is no widely used measure to identify specific learning difficulties or disabilities in math (Geary, 2004, but see recent efforts in Fritz et al., 2019; Olkun & Denizli, 2015). There are too few research-based programs and instructional approaches, but there are some. Those that do exist are discussed in Chapter 15. Finally, however, *the most important implication for early childhood may be to prevent most learning difficulties by providing high-quality early childhood mathematics education to all children* (Bowman et al., 2001). Equity must be complete equity, devoid of labeling, prejudice, and unequal access to opportunities to learn (see Bishop & Forgasz, 2007, for a more complete discussion). Further, it is essential to follow through on these early interventions, as MD and MLD may be more persistent even than reading disabilities (Powell, Fuchs, & Fuchs, 2013). *And these children may need more, but not fundamentally different, high-quality education that is recommended for all children* (Gaidoschik, 2019). That is, what they do not need is "different" if that means lower-level rote learning. They may need different ways of dealing with languages and cultures, adaptations for children with disabilities, and so forth.

Summarizing, follow research on what makes interventions effective, such as the following (Dowker, 2019; Hojnoski et al., 2018).

- *Start as early as possible, before 3 years of age,* with *systematic, consistent interventions* (Dennis, Bryant, & Drogan, 2015; Gersten et al., 2015; Hardy & Hemmeter, 2018; Hojnoski et al., 2018; Mononen, Aunio, Koponen, & Aro, 2014), with 2 years of high-quality preschool (Shah et al., 2017) or transitional kindergarten (Manship et al., 2017) recommended.
- *Take a learning trajectories approach* and apply knowledge of how performance and knowledge typically develop in the age group being studied (Gervasoni, 2018).
- *Assess children's level of thinking specifically,* diagnosing individual strengths and weaknesses.
- *Plan carefully,* taking availability of resources into account, and appropriate use of school staff: the best-designed program will not work if teaching staff are unavailable, excessively overburdened, or not adequately trained to deliver the program.
- *Embedded instruction across routines, activities, and environments.* Also, enhance families' awareness of the importance of early math.
- *Motivate children,* preventing or counteracting the association of math with boredom, or worse, fear and anxiety.
- *Use games,* especially with preschool and primary school children, including computer games and activities (Cascales-Martínez, Martínez-Segura, Pérez-López, & Contero, 2017; Chmiliar, 2017; Mohd Syah, Hamzaid, Murphy, & Lim, 2016; Mononen et al., 2014; Ok & Kim, 2017; Salminen, Koponen, Räsänen, & Aro, 2015).
- *Teach the processes and practices* in the previous chapters. For example, children need to develop EF, or executive function, processes. High-quality math education can contribute to this, along with other good educational practices (Clements & Sarama, 2019; Dowker, 2017; Shah et al., 2017). Recall that the resource has special "Math Plus" activities to help you teach both math and EF simultaneously.
- *Use small groups.* This is an important part of high-quality education for all children, but *especially important for CWD* because teachers can focus on children's thinking, guide their learning, and teach concepts and then let the children apply them together and individually (Aunio, 2019). *In other words, teachers can implement the learning trajectories approach fully and well.*
- *Use technology.* Computers can assist with a variety of adaptations, sensory, motoric, emotional, and cognitive. They may be especially useful in helping CWD and other special needs learn geometry (Galitskaya & Drigas, 2020, see multiple adaptations for different children).
- *Use research-validated interventions,* documented here (e.g., for children with emotional and behavior disorders, see Ralston et al., 2014).

Gifted and Talented

Although often perceived by educators as "doing just fine," children with special needs due to their exceptional potential, also do not fare well in most early childhood (and later) programs

(NMP, 2008). They actually decline in some arithmetic skills relative to others, especially in the preschool and primary grades (Mooij & Driessen, 2008). Many gifted and talented children may not be identified.

Teachers sometimes expose gifted and talented children to concepts generally introduced to older students; however, they most frequently teach concepts traditionally found in early childhood programs (Wadlington & Burns, 1993). Even though research shows that these children possess advanced knowledge of measurement, time, and fractions, such topics are rarely explored.

One Australian study showed that the kindergarten year math curriculum is most suited to the least advanced children. Talented children learned little or nothing of math throughout an entire kindergarten year (Wright, 1991). In his first year of school, Harry knew all the little math that was presented. Harry did maintain the outward semblance of being interested in the work and, at least, being willing to complete it. However, it seems that the strongest lesson he learned in his classroom math experience is that "you do not have to work hard at it" (Perry & Dockett, 2005).

This is a serious concern because the beginning of preschool and kindergarten can be a critical time for gifted children. They often cannot find peers at their level with similar interests, and become frustrated and bored (Harrison, 2004). Clearly, curricula and educators have to do better to serve the learning needs of all children.

One study showed that parents and teachers can accurately identify gifted children. The children's scores were more than one standard deviation above the mean for their age. The children tended to be almost as advanced in verbal and visual-spatial skills on psychometric measures as on measures of math skills. Although boys' level of performance was higher on measures of math skills and visual-spatial working memory span, the underlying relationships among cognitive factors were for the most part similar in girls and boys, with the exception that, for boys, the correlation between verbal and spatial factors was greater than for girls (Robinson, Abbot, Berninger, & Busse, 1996). The highest relationships overall, however, were between visual-spatial and math skills.

Gifted young children show the same characteristics as do older gifted children. They are divergent thinkers, curious, and persistent. They have exceptional memories (one 4-year-old said, "I remember things because I have pictures in my head"). They are able to make abstract connections and engage in independent investigations–formulating, researching, and testing theories. They show advanced thinking, knowledge, visual representations, and creativity. They have advanced awareness of math concepts. At 21 months, they sort out the difference between number and letters. One said, "I'll tell you what infinity is. A frog lays eggs, eggs hatch into tadpoles, the tadpole grows back legs and becomes a frog and then lays eggs again. Now that's a circle. It's infinity. Everything that's alive is infinity ..." (Harrison, 2004, p. 82).

Most children who are gifted and talented are not well served. This is especially true for young children and those from low-resource communities (Little et al., 2017). Many gifted and talented children may not be identified as such, especially the youngest. Teachers sometimes expose gifted and talented children to concepts generally introduced to older students; however, they most frequently teach concepts traditionally found in early childhood programs (Wadlington & Burns, 1993). Even though research shows that these children possess advanced knowledge of measurement, time, and fractions, such topics were rarely explored. Presently, these children are often taught through unstructured activities, discovery learning, centers, and games within small groups, strategies that are supported by research in some contexts. However, these children also need to solve engaging, difficult problems in the domains of number, operations, geometry, and spatial sense. They need to be challenged to engage in high-level math reasoning, including abstract reasoning.

When they are challenged, they make remarkable gains (Little et al., 2017).

Practical Implications

Identify children with gifts in math *as early as possible*. And note, children who are economically disadvantaged are not only at high education risk, they are also at risk of not being identified as gifted. We need to identify these children early and support their learning of challenging mathematics (Molfese et al., 2012).

Make sure they have interesting math to think about and perform. These children are often taught through unstructured activities, unguided discovery learning, centers, and games within small groups, which often are supported by research (Wadlington & Burns, 1993), although *guided* discovery is often better (Alfieri, Brooks, Aldrich, & Tenenbaum, 2010). However, they also need to solve engaging, difficult problems using manipulatives, number and spatial sense, and reasoning, including abstract reasoning. Indeed, the more teachers interacted with skilled preschool children the less they learned (Molfese et al., 2012). Why? Whereas the structure provided by teachers and staff through close attention to their interactions was helpful for low-achieving children, more advanced learners did not need that structure. Instead, they benefitted from teachers' encouragement of reasoning and other verbal skills, such as talking through or explaining their reasoning when solving a problem or puzzle. Such interactions encouraged a deeper understanding of the concepts. It may help to use gifted cluster grouping, in which a significant number of gifted children are in one or more mixed-ability classroom (Brulles, Peters, & Saunders, 2012).

One rigorous study randomly assigned equally able gifted students to a supplemental enrichment math class conducted on Saturdays over 2 years or to no treatment. The enrichment class, with 28 sessions in all, was constructivist in philosophy, "developmentally appropriate," and adhered to NCTM guidelines. Teachers created social communities that engaged in open-ended problem solving. At the end of 2 years, the participants outperformed non-participants (effect size, 0.44, which just missed statistical significance, but is moderately large, and thus remains promising). Children were not accelerated, which is a different strategy frequently used successfully with older students (NMP, 2008).

Seek out challenging but achievable tasks for these children. They need rich problems and projects (see example and a research review in Freiman, 2018). Depending on the children's age and abilities, problems might be the following. Find *all* the possibilities for dividing five counters into two groups and prove you found them all. Using square tiles, keep building larger squares and explain the pattern emerging from the number of tiles in each (Freiman, 2018).

The summer program in the study mentioned previously focused on geometry closely aligned with that in Chapters 7 through 9: the study of two-dimensional shapes, with emphasis on composing and decomposing shapes; describing, sorting, and classifying shapes; and investigating congruence and symmetry of shapes. There was also a strong emphasis on math practices, including math reasoning and communication, with specific attention to strategies for math discourse and written communication (Little et al., 2017).

Gender

> "My daughter just does not *get* numbers. I told her, 'Don't worry, honey. I was never good at math either.'" "I know," replied her friend. "Only people with special talent can really do math well."

Myths about math abound in our country. You probably recognized two in the above conversation. The first is that only a small number of "talented" people can succeed in math—we discussed that in a previous section in this chapter. The second, just as dangerous, is that women are not usually in that successful group. As early as second grade, children believe "math is for boys" even though boys and girls are achieving equally (Cvencek, Meltzoff, & Greenwald, 2011).

Findings and opinions vary widely regarding gender differences in early math. A large meta-analysis of 100 studies found that girls outperformed boys overall a negligible amount (0.05 standard deviations, Hyde, Fennema, & Lamon, 1990). On computation, 0.14; for understanding, 0.03; for complex problem solving, +0.08 (boys were slightly higher). Differences favoring men emerged in high school (+0.29) and college (+0.32). Girls are more likely than boys to be proficient in recognizing numbers and shapes, while males were more likely than females to be proficient in addition and subtraction and multiplication and division. All of these differences were small (Coley, 2002). Girls may be better at drawing tasks (Hemphill, 1987). About equal proportions of girls and boys have MD (Dowker, 2004).

One study from the Netherlands found girls having superior numerical skills (Van de Rijt & Van Luit, 1999); another found no differences (Van de Rijt, Van Luit, & Pennings, 1999). Studies of preschoolers from Singapore, Finland, and Hong Kong reported no gender differences (Aunio, Ee, Lim, Hautamäki, & Van Luit, 2004), although in another study in Finland, girls performed better on a relational, but not a counting, scale (Aunio et al., 2008). Differences were found in math self-concept among young children in Hong Kong (Cheung, Leung, & McBride-Chang, 2007). Mothers' perceived maternal support was correlated to self-concept, but only for girls.

Brain studies show differences, but they tend to be small (Waber et al., 2007). Boys performed slightly better on perceptual analysis, but girls performed a bit better on processing speed and motor dexterity.

Several studies show that boys, more than girls, are likely to be at the low or high end of math achievement (Clements, 1984; Hyde et al., 1990; Rathbun & West, 2004; Wright, 1991). This applies even to the gifted young children in the study previously discussed (Robinson et al., 1996), which reflects differences found in gifted adolescents (NMP, 2008). Some show differences in some number domains but not in geometry and measurement (Horne, 2004). The differences that were significant in one study were not present at the beginning of school but developed from kindergarten to Grade 4. This finding is consistent with studies showing that boys make slightly greater progress in math than girls (Thomas & Tagg, 2004).

One of the most consistent gender differences is in spatial abilities, especially mental rotation. Most research on gender differences in spatial skills has involved older students. Recent research, however, has identified differences in young children (Ehrlich, Levine, & Goldin-Meadow, 2006; Johnson, 1987). For example, 4- to 5-year-old males demonstrate a strong advantage on mental rotation, with girls performing at chance levels (Rosser, Ensing, Glider, & Lane, 1984). Similarly, boys showed an advantage by age 4 years 6 months on a spatial trans-formation task, with the advantage no more robust for rotation than for translation items. A comparable vocabulary task performance indicated that the boys' advantage on the spatial tasks was not attributable to overall intellectual advantage (Levine, Huttenlocher, Taylor, & Lan-grock, 1999). At least some of this is caused by lack of experience (Ebbeck, 1984). Girls tend to be more social, boys more interested in movement and action, from the first year of life (Lutch-maya & Baron-Cohen, 2002). Boys gesture more and perform better on spatial transformation tasks, providing one way to assess spatial abilities and suggesting that encouraging gesture, especially for girls, may be worthwhile (Ehrlich et al., 2006).

One observational study confirmed that boys' and girls' puzzle play was related to their mental transformation ability (McGuinness & Morley, 1991). However, parents' use of spatial lan-guage was only related to girls', not boys', mental transformation skill (controlling for the effects of parents' overall speech to children, SES, and parents' spatial abilities). Parents' spatial language may be more important for girls (Levine, Ratliff, Huttenlocher, & Cannon, 2012).

Similarly, such research suggests that intentional instruction in spatial skills may be espe-cially important for girls. The relationship between spatial skills and math achievement is higher for girls than boys (Battista, 1990; Casey, Nuttall, & Pezaris, 2001; Friedman, 1995; Kersh et al., 2008). Middle school girls who scored high on spatial tests solved math problems as well or better than the boys (Fennema & Tartre, 1985). Those girls with low spatial/high verbal scores performed most poorly. Spatial skills are stronger mediators than even math anxiety or self-confidence (Casey, Nuttall, & Pezaris, 1997). Parents' use of spatial language is related to girls', but not boys' skill at mental transformations. For example, doing puzzles, parents might talk about features, dimensions, or shapes of objects (e.g., "corner," "straight," "square"), orienta-tion and transformations (e.g., "upside down," "turn around," "flip"), spatial relations (e.g., "top," "under," "between," "near"), or part/whole relations (e.g., "whole," "half," "section"). Girls may use more verbal mediation on some tasks (Levine et al., 2012).

Boys in one study were more confident in math, but they were not accurate, as confidence did not predict math competence (Carr, Steiner, Kyser, & Biddlecomb, 2008). One important dif-ference, however, was that girls preferred using manipulatives to solve problems, but boys pre-ferred more sophisticated strategies. These cognitive strategies may influence their performance and later learning. Such difference in strategy use has been replicated repeatedly and is cause for serious concern (Carr & Alexeev, 2011; Carr & Davis, 2001; Fennema, Carpenter, Franke, & Levi, 1998). The children solved basic arithmetic problems under two conditions: a free-choice condition in which they were allowed to solve the problems any way they pre-ferred and a game condition in which the children's strategy use was constrained so that all children used the same strategies on the same arithmetic problems. Strategy use during the free-choice session replicated the findings of earlier research indicating that girls tend to use strategies utilizing manipulatives and boys tend to use retrieval. During the game condition, when we controlled the types of strategies children used on different problems, we found that boys were as able as girls to calculate solutions using manipulatives. Girls, however, were not as capable as boys in their retrieval of answers to arithmetic problems from memory. No differences were found in error rates or speed of retrieval. Gender differences were found in the variability of correct retrieval, with boys being significantly more variable than girls (Carr & Davis, 2001). Boys are more likely to take risks, trying to use retrieval, and they profit from that approach (Geary et al., 2012). Risk-takers get more practice. Also, girls with strong spatial skills are more likely to use more advanced arithmetic strategies (Laski et al., 2013).

Although the source is unknown, we know that gender differences can be minimized when all children are provided with good education, including encouraging everyone to develop more sophisticated strategies and to take risks. One study suggested that girls' strategy use is guided by classroom norms that do not actively promote the use of more mature strategies. For example, they would continue to count out manipulatives to solve problems, compared to boys who tried to use mental strategies, including fluency with arithmetic combinations. Unfortunately, this pattern resulted in the highest number of failures on the competency test for girls (Carr & Alexeev, 2011). Spatial skills also may promote more mature strategies (Carr, Shing, Janes, & Steiner, 2007).

Practical Implications

Teach spatial skills, particularly intentionally to girls, and encourage parents to do so. Encourage girls as well as boys to use sophisticated strategies, even if that means taking "risks."

Final Words

To be fully professional and effective, teachers must understand children's cognition and affect, and issues of individual differences and equity. However, this is not sufficient—we also need to understand how to use these understandings to promote thinking, positive dispositions, and fairness. Such is the intent of the next two chapters. Chapter 15 addresses the contexts of instruction—the types of settings in which children are taught, including children's first setting, their families, and their homes. It also focuses on specific curricula that are effective in helping young children learn math.

Note

1 Children who can catch up, especially with high-quality instruction, may be developmentally delayed, but not disabled. The Response to Intervention (RTI) model includes this basic idea: If children are behind because of a lack of high-quality experiences and education, *they* have no "mathematical difficulties"; their environment is to blame and must be improved.

15 Early Childhood Mathematics Education
Contexts and Curricula

> I really enjoy teaching Building Blocks. My children have shown *tremendous* growth. One child, who initially could not verbally count at all, is now able to verbally count, use one-to-one correspondence, and make sets up to 20 with confidence.
>
> (Carla F., preschool teacher)

What makes a good math curriculum for young children? How would you evaluate your own? Previous chapters discussed the roles of experience, education, and teaching for specific topics. This chapter expands that discussion to address the types of settings in which children are taught, including children's first setting—their families and their homes. We then focus on general findings regarding curricula that are effective in helping young children learn math. Again, we have marked sections with implications for practitioners with **"*Practical Implications*,"** for those who wish to focus on these.

Early Childhood Education—Where Is the Math?

Generally, children who attend preschool are better prepared for academic work in kindergarten than those who do not (Barnett, Frede, Mobasher, & Mohr, 1987; Brown & Lee, 2014; Lee, Brooks-Gunn, Schnur, & Liaw, 1990). Additionally, those who have 2 years of preschool have higher scores on both math and executive function (Shah et al., 2017). Internationally, preschools have multiple benefits for vulnerable children, such as those in high-poverty areas of rural Mozambique (Martinez, Naudeau, & Pereira, 2017), Ethiopian immigrants in Israel (Korat, Gitait, Bergman Deitcher, & Mevarech, 2017), and others.

However, benefits depend on achieving at least *minimal* standards of quality in preschool programs (Anderson & Phillips, 2017; Barnett et al., 1987; Sobayi, 2018; Yoshikawa, Weiland, & Brooks-Gunn, 2016). That is, early education *is* an effective way to enhance the lives of vulnerable children and address inequalities in educational, economic, and social outcomes. However, most public programs in the USA fail to invest sufficiently in the necessary quality and intensity to achieve this potential (Barnett & Frede, 2017). In the remainder of this section, we examine what we know about math in early childhood settings.

Math in the Primary Grades

Math in Grades 1 and 2 is driven largely by standards, curriculum, and tradition (more on this later). However, the earlier grades tend to vary. Kindergarten teachers spend an average of

39 minutes each session, for a total of 3.1 hours each week of math instruction (Hausken & Rathbun, 2004). This is about half of what they spend on reading. The time spent on math, however, might not be *well* spent. Achievement for children entering first grade is not substantially higher than the mean for those entering kindergarten (Heuvel-Panhuizen, 1996). Kindergarten and first-grade curricula may spend too much time teaching children things they already know (Engel, Claessens, & Finch, 2013), and not enough teaching them more challenging math, including problem solving (Carpenter & Moser, 1984; Engel, Claessens, Watts, & Farkas, 2016).

Math in Preschool

Preschool math also varies. An older study reported that the majority of 3-year-olds had *no* math experiences across 180 full-day observations (Tudge & Doucet, 2004). A smaller observational study revealed that little math was presented in any of the classrooms, either directly or indirectly (Graham, Nash, & Paul, 1997). Teachers stated that they believed that math was important and that they engaged in math discussions. It appears that selection of and engagement with materials and activities such as puzzles, blocks, games, songs, and finger plays constituted math for these teachers.

In a similar vein, the National Center for Early Development and Learning (NCEDL) studies report that children are not engaged in learning or constructive activities during a large proportion of the pre-K day (Early et al., 2005; Swinton et al., 2005). They spent the largest part of their day, up to 44%, in routine maintenance activities (like standing in line) and eating and about 6% to 8% of the day on average involves math activities in any form. Teachers were observed *not* interacting with children 73% of the day; another 18% of the day was spent in minimal interaction. On average, children were engaged in pre-academic experiences less than 3% of the time, and less than half the children experienced these at all (Swinton et al., 2005). However, recent studies suggest that may be changing. One found only 24 minutes of math during a whole-day observation (Piasta, Pelatti, & Miller, 2014). Variability was high, however, with some children not experiencing any math (or science).

We need to increase not just children's access to preschool, but the *quality* of it (Yoshikawa et al., 2016), and *the quality of all subsequent years of education.* Before we turn to programs and curricula that attempt to address math more adequately, we consider the first and consistently influential setting in which children learn math—the home.

Families

Of course, families also play a major role in young children's development, including their learning of math. Math in the home predicts school success in math in the U.S. (Levine, Gibson, & Berkowitz, 2019), Chile (Susperreguy, Di Lonardo Burr, Xu, Douglas, & LeFevre, 2020), China (Huang, Zhang, Liu, Yang, & Song, 2017), Finland (Sorariutta & Silvén, 2017), Germany (Niklas & Schneider, 2017), Russia (Vasilyeva, Laski, Veraksa, Weber, & Bukhalenkova, 2018), Tanzania (Sobayi, 2018), Turkey (Cosgun, Şahin, & Aydin, 2017), and other countries (see McCoy et al., 2018).

Families and Math

The level of parents' education and family factors, such as adjustment and parenting practices related to education and enrichment, are especially important to children's early math learning (Crosnoe & Cooper, 2010). Even parents' ANS is related to their children's (Navarro, Braham, & Libertus, 2018). There may be a relationship between the frequency with which parents use numbers and their children's early math performance (Blevins-Knabe & Musun-Miller, 1996), although the frequency is often so low that this relationship is not significant (Blevins-Knabe, Berghout Austin, Musun-Miller, Eddy, & Jones, 2000). There are several sociocultural barriers. For example, although parents believe that both home and school are important for reading development, they consider the school more important for math development, and they provide fewer experiences in math than in reading (Sonnenschein, Baker, Moyer, & LeFevre, 2005). They believe it is more important to help their children learn literacy than math (Cannon, Fernandez, & Ginsburg, 2005), that math is less important than social skills, general information, reading, and language skills (Blevins-Knabe et al., 2000), and that math ability is fixed (Scalise et al., 2019). These are profound differences that have severe implications.

Further, as with pre-K teachers, parents have a limited view of the breadth of math appropriate for young children (Sarama, 2002). They know more about what might be taught in language than math (Cannon et al., 2005) and are more comfortable with language (Blevins-Knabe et al., 2000). This was true regardless of what groups to which parents belong. However, cultural differences are occasionally relevant. For example, Chinese mothers are more likely than U.S. mothers to teach arithmetic calculation in their everyday involvement with children's learning, and maternal instruction was related to Chinese, but not U.S., children's learning of proportional reasoning (Pan, Gauvain, Liu, & Cheng, 2006). Comparatively, mothers in China rate math as equal in importance to reading, but mothers in the U.S. rate math as less important (Miller, Kelly, & Zhou, 2005).

Let's examine some practices in more detail. The vignette that began the section on gender in the previous chapter, regarding the mother's daughter who "just does not *get* numbers," indicates the effects—sometimes negative, but many positive—that parents and families can have on children's success in math. Research describes several, as follows.

- Prenatal alcohol exposure is associated with poorer calculation abilities (Burden, Jacobson, Dodge, Dehaene, & Jacobson, 2007). This apparently is mediated entirely by alcohol's effect on children's "number sense"—the basic quantitative bootstrap competence (e.g., Dehaene, 1997; see also Chapters 2 and 4).
- Very low birth weight may lead to less mature levels of numerical reasoning on problems with a spatial component and those that required complex problem solving; however, verbal tasks were affected more strongly by levels of parent education (Wakeley, 2005). Similarly, moderate preterm children earn lower math scores than full-term children (van Baar, de Jong, & Verhoeven, 2013). Intervention programs can be successful (Liaw, Meisels, & Brooks-Gunn, 1995).
- Poor mother-child engagement related to lower levels of academic success (Konold & Pianta, 2005).
- Mothers rating themselves as high on affection but also high on psychological control–behaviors that are intrusive and manipulative of children's thoughts, feelings, and

attachments to parents (e.g., guilt-inducing)–is predictive of their children's *slow* progress in math. Children may become "enmeshed" in family relations and less independent or may receive inconsistent messages of their mother's affection and approval and thus become more anxious about performing well.

- Parents prefer teaching language to teaching math. They are biased towards language and believe there are "universal" grounds for helping children learn language over math. They also have more nuanced beliefs about preschoolers' ability to learn language than math. For language more than math, parents believe that teaching should ensure children acquire specific knowledge, that teachers want to delve deeply into children's understanding, and that teachers should facilitate children's learning throughout the day (Cannon et al., 2005).
- Parents with "fixed" beliefs (like Aretha at the start of Chapter 14) *and* their children perform lower on some math tasks–it is a debilitating belief (Scalise et al., 2019).
- U.S. parents do not have high expectations. U.S. parents, compared to Chinese parents, set lower standards. The U.S. culture does not value diligent work, as the Chinese culture does. Chinese students' favorite saying was "Genius comes from hard work and knowledge depends on accumulation." U.S. parents said they would be satisfied with 7 points *lower* than their expectation for their children, but Chinese parents were only satisfied with 10 points *higher*.
- Recent international comparison, which shows the U.S. is behind, also documented that children of parents who engaged their children in math activities at home (and got them into high-quality early education) had higher math achievement in elementary school (Mullis et al., 2012).
- In many low-resource communities, a limited number of math activities are provided (Blevins-Knabe & Musun-Miller, 1996; Ginsburg, Klein, & Starkey, 1998; Thirumurthy, 2003). Educators should help by sharing such resources (such as [LT]^2!).
- Risk factors "mount up"–the combination of low parent education, poverty, and lack of engagement in education are especially harmful for math learning (Crosnoe & Cooper, 2010)
- One study reported that U.S. parents work less often and for less time with their children on homework (Chen & Uttal, 1988). However, another found U.S. parents more involved with school activities than Chinese parents, who stressed interest in math and the child's responsibility (Pan & Gauvain, 2007). East Asian parents also provide games, building, and paper-folding activities; U.S. parents allow children's time to be dominated by video games and television.
- In some cases, Black children may start school with similar competencies, but grow at a slower rate. Parent programs that help build bridges and prepare children for school expectations may help alleviate these difficulties (Alexander & Entwisle, 1988; Baker, 2014). Perhaps most important is to provide learning-trajectories-based math education in schools where there is evidence that Black children learn at a *faster* rate (Clements et al., 2011).
- Home numeracy activities predict numeracy skills (Blevins-Knabe, Whiteside-Mansell, & Selig, 2007; LeFevre, Polyzoi, Skwarchuk, Fast, & Sowinskia, 2010) including math talk and gestures about numbers, shapes, and space, with *less* negative affect about math (Levine et al., 2019).

- Math activities in the home, such as measuring and comparing quantities, discussing math facts, and discussing time using a clock, are closely related to girls' arithmetic skills, and mothers' spatial skills and verbal skills predicts their daughters' spatial skills (Dearing et al., 2012).
- Computers in the home predict children's entering math knowledge (Navarro et al., 2012).

One study showed the more the mother "provides behaviors," the lower the child's math ability (Christiansen, Austin, & Roggman, 2005). Too many directive behaviors might be over-stimulating. Introducing formal math was also negatively related to children's informal math knowledge. These relationships, however, appeared to hold only for boys, not girls.

Practical Implications

Schools can work to make relationships with families a positive force in children's education. For example, children learn more when parents and teachers match on their perspectives concerning child-centered beliefs, low control, and high support (Barbarin, Downer, Odom, & Head, 2010). Policies should encourage parents to be actively invested in and managing their children's education (Crosnoe & Cooper, 2010), which is more challenging for parents with lower levels of education and economic resources (Dearing et al., 2012).

Research describes several additional avenues for families to promote positive math learning ([LT]² has an entire section with resources for families):

- Interacting with, discussing, and support infants' play helps form foundations for later math learning (as well as reading, Cook, Roggman, & Boyce, 2012; Sorariutta & Silvén, 2017).
- Engaging children of all ages with math (Thompson, Napoli, & Purpura, 2017).
- Making sure children get sufficient sleep–they usually do not get at least 10 hours or more per night (Touchette et al., 2007).
- Providing learning experiences, including sensitivity, quality of assistance in problem solving, and avoiding of harsh, punitive interactions (all highly related to IQ; Brooks-Gunn et al., 1999).
- Discussing math ideas when reading storybooks (Anderson, Anderson, & Shapiro, 2004) and doing home numeracy activities of all types (LeFevre et al., 2010). Read math books ... with numbers above 10 (Powell & Nurnberger-Haag, 2015) and more interesting topics (see a comprehensive list at [LT]²).
- Talking about numbers, shapes, and space consistently, from the time children are toddlers (Gerofsky, 2015; Levine, Suriyakham, Rowe, Huttenlocher, & Gunderson, 2010a; Levine et al., 2019; Pruden, Levine, & Huttenlocher, 2011; Vasilyeva et al., 2018). The kinds of talk matters. Counting with cardinality or labeling sets of present, visible objects is related to children's later cardinal-number knowledge, just as we described in the subitizing and counting chapters (Gunderson & Levine, 2011). Number talk that refers to large sets of present objects (i.e., sets of size 4 to 10 that fall outside children's ability to track individual objects) is probably more helpful than talk about smaller sets.
- Talking about a *variety* of math topics, such *as all those in this book*, is valuable (Pruden et al., 2011; Vasilyeva et al., 2018).
- Keeping fathers involved. One study showed that fathers' teaching interactions with their 2-year-olds predicted the children's math skills at ages 5 and 7 (McKelvey et al., 2011).

A similar study of low-resource, ethnically diverse families showed that fathers' participation in learning activities with young children has long-lasting effects, including higher math achievement in Grade 5 (McFadden, Tamis-LeMonda, & Cabrera, 2011).

• Also, *talking to girls as much as to boys*. Research shows parents talk to their boys *twice as much* as they do to their girls about numbers (Chang, Sandhofer, & Brown, 2011; Gunderson, Ramirez, Levine, & Beilock, 2012). Also, the quality of fathers' support of spatial concepts during block building predicts their daughters' early math skills (Thomson et al., 2018). Similarly, the more *puzzles* children work on, the better they performed on a spatial transformation tasks (Levine et al., 2012).

• Playing math games with children. Parents should ensure they spend some time playing *only* with their young children, as positive interactions and teaching are substantially higher in this case (Benigno & Ellis, 2004).

• Cooking with children, especially using rich vocabulary such as number and measurement words (Young-Loveridge, 1989a). Contingent responses to children are more important than just using the words—giving them feedback and elaborating on their responses is more effective in building their math knowledge.

• *Coding* with children! That is, use resources below and in Chapter 16 to learn to program computers. Parent–child interaction is beneficial, although asking too many questions limits children's learning (Sheehan, Pila, Lauricella, & Wartella, 2019).

• Maintaining high to very high expectations for children (Thomson, Rowe, Underwood, & Peck, 2005). Engaging in *challenging* math at home (Ramani et al., 2015; Thompson et al., 2017), such as arithmetic problems with higher numbers (Kleemans, Segers, & Verhoeven, 2018) and different problem types (Chapter 5).

• Being willing and able to participate actively in the school's math program and training in how to effectively assist in the classroom (Thomson et al., 2005).

• Supporting and encouraging children, which is associated with children's motivation to learn (Cheung & McBride-Chang, 2008). Parents' achievement demands are correlated with actual academic performance. Children's mastery (intrinsic) motivation, not their parents' practices or beliefs, explained their perceptions of themselves as competent.

• Using the resources available on the web, such as our *Learning and Teaching with Learning Trajectories*, [LT]² (LearningTrajectories.com), and NCTM's site, (www.nctm.org/resources/families.aspx). As an example, http://bedtimemath.org provides a daily math problem for children (and adults) of all ages. See also www.figurethis.org, www.math.com/parents/family.html, and http://sv.berkeley.edu/showcase/pages/fm_act.html. Search for more.

• Using high-quality materials that provide activity ideas and guidance. Perhaps the most useful suggestion for parents is to encourage them to get and use books and other resources that provide ideas for activities that will engage their children and their whole family. A recommended list of books is at [LT]². Family Math is a well-established program with books for parents (Stenmark, Thompson, & Cossey, 1986), see www.lawrencehallofscience.org/equals/aboutfm.html. Other books include *Family Math for Young Children (Pre-K–3)*; and *Family Math for Young Children* by Brian Gothberg (also see Ginsburg, Duch, Ertle, & Noble, 2012). Searching with the phrase "family math" will yield these and other resources.

Research also provides several additional avenues for educators to help families:

*   Work closely with children's schools and teachers (Crosnoe & Cooper, 2010). Parents introduce more math in home activities such as cooking if teachers give them hints and guidance (Vandermaas-Peeler, Boomgarden, Finn, & Pittard, 2012).
*   Adapt successful programs that forge connections between homes and school (Muir, 2018; Park, Stone, & Holloway, 2017), provide parent education (Landry et al., 2017), or guide home visiting programs (Bierman, Welsh, Heinrichs, & Nix, 2018). Families engaged in school matter (Sorariutta & Silvén, 2017). Programs designed to improve home math learning have been found to be most successful when they had three components: joint and separate sessions for parents and children, a structured numeracy curriculum, and "bridging" activities for parents to develop their child's numeracy at home (Doig, McCrae, & Rowe, 2003). Interventions may address anxiety in families (Schaeffer, Rozek, Berkowitz, Levine, & Beilock, 2018).
*   Provide intense interventions for families and for children who need it (Garon-Carrier et al., 2018; Miller, Farkas, Vandell, & Duncan, 2014).
*   Use research-based programs that contain specific suggestions written for parents (Doig et al., 2003).

In working with parents, with policy-makers, and with children, early childhood math educators should be strong advocates for foundational and explicit math experiences for all children of all ages. In the earliest ages especially, these can often be seamlessly integrated with children's ongoing play and activities, but this usually requires a knowledgeable adult who creates a supportive environment and provides challenges, suggestions, tasks, and language.

Equity in Math Education

Children's learning trajectories are influenced by their first educational experiences (Barnett & Frede, 2017). Indeed, "the early grades may be precisely the time that schools have their strongest effects" (Alexander & Entwisle, 1988). Early childhood schools and teachers have the power and responsibility to have the strongest possible positive effect on math learning. As we saw, this potential is often left unrealized. Further, those children whose communities struggled to provide frequent experiences are just those who need–but do not receive–those experiences in their early childhood programs.

Children at Risk

As we saw, providing high-quality educational support to children at risk results in greater school readiness upon entry into kindergarten (Bowman et al., 2001; Magnuson & Waldfogel, 2005; Shonkoff & Phillips, 2000), because such support helps young children develop a foundation of informal math knowledge (Clements, 1984). Early knowledge has been shown to support later school math achievement, and lack of it places minorities on a path away from engagement in math and science (Campbell, Pungello, Miller-Johnson, Burchinal, & Ramey, 2001; Oakes, 1990; Tuğluk & Öcal, 2017). Longitudinal research indicates that attendance in center-based (but not other types of) care in the pre-K year is associated with higher math scores in kindergarten and (to a lesser extent) in first grade (Turner & Ritter, 2004), and that achievement in preschool is related to differences in elementary school achievement for Hispanic children (Shaw, Nelsen, & Shen, 2001). In another study, African American, Hispanic, and female children who attended an intervention preschool program had a significantly greater probability of achieving high scores in fourth grade than their peers who did not attend preschool (Roth, Carter, Ariet, Resnick, & Crans, 2000). Childcare in general can help, with greater number of hours in childcare correlating with greater quantitative skills in children from low-resource communities (Votruba-Drzal & Chase, 2004).

High-quality preschool experience is predictive of later school success in math (Campbell et al., 2001; Peisner-Feinberg et al., 2001) for many years to come (Barnett & Frede, 2017; Brooks-Gunn, 2003). Most important for the effects on math were actual classroom practices—materials, activities, and interactions. Although the size of the effects were moderate, they were significant for math (more than other subjects) *for as long as 4 years* (Peisner-Feinberg et al., 2001).

Unfortunately, children most in need of high-quality environments may not attend high-quality elementary schools, even when their preschools were high in quality. One study revealed very low correlation (0.06 to 0.15) between quality of care in pre-K and that of the elementary schools (Peisner-Feinberg et al., 2001). In other cases, some effects may even emerge *only* later ("sleeper effects," Broberg, Wessels, Lamb, & Hwang, 1997; Clements et al., 2020). Thus, for both practice and research, it is critical to evaluate children's entire educational experience.

Other research confirms the importance of high-quality schools. Oklahoma has led the nation in providing preschool education to 70% of its children and maintaining relatively high standards (Barnett, Hustedt, Hawkinson, & Robin, 2006). Two rigorous evaluations indicate substantial positive effects on achievement scores for math and literacy (although smaller effects for math). Children from all ethnic and SES groups benefited (Barnett et al., 2006; Gormley, Gayer, Phillips, & Dawson, 2005). Unfortunately, a commitment to universal pre-K, high-quality pre-K, and well-funded pre-K remain the exception, rather than the norm, in the USA (Barnett & Frede, 2017; Barnett et al., 2006; Swinton et al., 2005).

In a similar vein, state-funded preschool programs in states with high standards have been found to positively affect preschoolers' math achievement (Wong, Cook, Barnett, & Jung, 2008), more than Head Start. Similarly, the Head Start Impact Study found no significant impacts for the early math skills for 3- or 4-year-olds (DHHS, 2005; cf. Vogel, Brooks-Gunn, Martin, & Klute, 2013). So, some programs do not yet include adequate math. However, Head Start did have a compensatory effect for children from homes reporting low preacademic stimulation.

Practical Implications

Children living in poverty and those with special needs increase in math achievement after high-quality interventions focused on math (Campbell & Silver, 1999; Fuson et al., 1997; Griffin, 2004; Griffin, Case, & Capodilupo, 1995; Ramey & Ramey, 1998), which can be sustained into first (Clements et al., 2013; Rathbun & West, 2004) *to* third grade (Gamel-McCormick & Amsden, 2002).

Curricula and approaches exist that can help achieve this (Clements et al., 2013; Clements & Sarama, 2008). Importantly, multiple resources and efforts are needed for successful scale up (Sarama & Clements, 2013). Higher-quality programs result in learning benefits into elementary school, including in math (Fuson, 2004; Griffin, 2004; Karoly et al., 1998).

Do Children at Risk Already Have Substantial Math Knowledge or Not?

There appears to be a contradiction between two pictures of the math knowledge and competencies of children of different income or SES groups. On the one hand, the evidence suggests a substantive and widening gap. On the other hand, there are few, or no, differences between children from different communities in the amount of math they exhibit in their free play (Ginsburg, Ness, & Seo, 2003; Seo & Ginsburg, 2004). A possible explanation is that children from low-resource or stressed communities have not been provided with the opportunities to *reflect on* and *discuss* their pre-mathematical activity. Some children hear *60 times* as many number words as other children (Levine et al., 2010) These children may thus engage in pre-mathematical play but fail to connect this activity to school math because to do so requires the children to bring the ideas to an explicit level of awareness. One main difference between children is not their ability to perform with physical objects but to solve problems verbally (Jordan, Hanich, & Uberti, 2003) or explain their thinking (Sophian, 2002). Consider a child who turned 4 years of age. When asked to solve "How much is ten and one more," she used physical blocks, added 1 to 10, and answered, "eleven." Five minutes later, asked several times using the same wording, "How many is two and one more," the child did not respond, and, asked again, said, "fifteen" in a couldn't-care-less tone of voice (Hughes, 1981, pp. 216–217).

In summary, we believe the pattern of results suggest that, although all children have pre-mathematical knowledge, they may lack opportunities to learn the *language of math*. So, they have not been given the tools to connect their informal pre-mathematical knowledge to school math. Children must learn to mathematize their informal experiences, abstracting, representing, and elaborating them mathematically, and using math ideas and symbols to create models of their everyday activities. This includes the ability to generalize, connecting the math ideas to different situations and using the ideas and processes adaptively. In all its multifaceted forms, they lack the language of math.

Practical Implications

Begin with number tasks in which numerosities are represented with objects and model verbal descriptions, facilitating children's receptive and expressive vocabularies. From toddlerhood, naming the number in very small groups supports a variety of number competencies (Hannula, 2005). As another example, the simple task of putting blocks in and out of a box reveals that even 4-year-olds enjoy and can perform arithmetic (Hughes, 1986). (This is despite the quoted guidelines of the time that "arithmetic for this age would be ludicrous.") One child, faced with two blocks in the box (which he could not see), was asked to take out three. He replied as follows:

Richard:	You can't, can you?
MH:	Why not?
Richard:	You just have to put one in, don't you?
MH:	Put one in?
Richard:	Yea, and then you can take three out.

(p. 27)

Eventually, facilitate children's transition to using more abstract symbols, both verbal and written (e.g., numerals). In general, hold the processes of communication and representation as important, not incidental, goals of math education. These processes are not merely ways to express math, desirable but secondary accoutrements, but, rather, essential aspects of math understanding.

Connections between the development of math and literacy are numerous and bidirectional (McGraw et al., 2019; Purpura & Napoli, in press). For example, preschoolers' narrative abilities, particularly their ability to convey all the main events of the story, offer a perspective on the events in the story, and relate the main events of the story through use of conjunctions, predicts math achievement 2 years later (O'Neill, Pearce, & Pick, 2004). Rich math activities, such as discussing multiple solutions and posing and solving narrative story problems, help lay a groundwork for literacy, and rich literacy, that includes but goes beyond phonetic skills, helps lay a groundwork for the development of math. Without the language of math, children's learning suffers (Purpura et al., 2017).

The benefits of learning rich math *in simultaneously developing literacy and language skills* may seem farfetched to some readers. So, it is satisfying to say that rigorous studies support this idea. First, we conducted a randomized study of the effects of Building Blocks on pre-K children's letter recognition and oral language skills. The Building Blocks and control children performed perhaps the same on letter recognition, and on three of the oral language subscales. However, children in the Building Blocks group outperformed children in the control group on four oral language subscales: (a) ability to recall key words, (b) use of complex utterances, (c) willingness to reproduce narratives independently, and (d) inference. *These had no obvious relation to the math curriculum, but children learned important verbal language competencies.* Asking "how do you know?" and developing (Piagetian-like) logical-math abilities is cognitively fundamental. Second, a study of 5- to 7-year-olds in the U.K. showed that an early math and logical-mathematical intervention increased later scores on English by 14 percentile points (Shayer & Adhami, 2010). Even though it may "take up" school time, *language and literacy do not suffer when a math intervention is introduced; indeed, language competencies are enhanced.*

Gender

Gender equity also remains a concern, as we saw in Chapter 14. Females are socialized to view math as a male domain and themselves as having less ability. Teachers show more concern when boys, rather than girls, struggle. They call on and talk to boys more than girls. Finally, they believe success in math is due to high ability more frequently for boys than girls and view boys as the most successful students in their class. All these unintentionally undermine girls' achievement motivation (Middleton & Spanias, 1999). In more than one study, boys are more likely than girls to appear in the lowest and highest ranges of scores in math (Callahan & Clements, 1984; Rathbun & West, 2004). In addition, there was evidence of a faster growth rate for high-achieving boys (Aunola et al., 2004). Reasons for this are still unclear, but there are practical ramifications. There are also some indications that boys outperform girls as early as kindergarten on tasks that have a spatial component (Jordan, Kaplan, Oláh, & Locuniak, 2006). However, in the U.K., preschool girls scored higher than boys (Sylva et al., 2005). And most research shows that, again, if *opportunities* are equitable, so are outcomes (e.g., Korkmaz & Yilmaz, 2017; Lee & Bull, 2015).

Practical Implications

Thus, the problems are complex, and there are distinct concerns about boys and girls. Educators need to ensure everyone receives complete opportunities to learn. As a simple example, is access to and use of the blocks and computer center equitable?

Children with Special Needs—MD and MLD

As we saw in Chapter 14, some children show signs of MD and MLD at young ages. Unfortunately, they are often not identified, or are categorized broadly with other children as "developmentally delayed" (Clements et al., 2020). This is especially unfortunate because focused math interventions at early ages are effective (Dowker, 2019; Lerner, 1997). These children often have low skills and concepts in subitizing, counting, fact retrieval, and other aspects of computation. They appear not to use reasoning-based strategies and seem rigid in their use of immature problem-solving, counting, and arithmetic strategies. *Children with special needs require the earliest and most consistent interventions* (Gervasoni et al., 2007; Gervasoni, 2018).

In the primary years, because children with MLD only (not MLD/RLD) performed worse than normally developing children in timed tests, but performed just as well in untimed tests, children who have MLD only may simply need extra time studying, and extra time to complete, calculation tasks. Probably the use of a calculator and other computation aides would enable these children to concentrate on developing their otherwise good problem-solving skills (Jordan & Montani, 1997). Children with MLD/RLD may need more systematic remedial intervention aimed at problem conceptualization and the development of effective computational strategies as well as efficient fact retrieval (Jordan & Montani, 1997).

Practical Implications

Many children with special needs have quite *different* learning needs (Dowker, 2017; Gervasoni et al., 2007; Gervasoni, 2018). We *need* to individualize instruction. Moreover, it appears that no particular topic as a whole must precede another topic. For this reason, *teaching with learning trajectories is the best way to address the needs of all children, especially those with special needs*. Through formative assessment using learning trajectories, which has been featured throughout this book, is a recommended strategy for putting learning trajectories to work, especially for children with any type of special needs.

MD and MLD in the Primary Grades

Addressing these topics early is critical (Clements, Vinh, Lim, & Sarama, 2020). Strategies from family collaboration (Kritzer & Pagliaro, 2013), to direct instruction (Chandler, McLaughlin, Neyman, & Rinaldi, 2012), to distinct uses of educational technology (Chmiliar, 2017; Gay, 1989) have reported successes. Specific approaches that help children at risk include the following.

- Identify the most critical content, such as number competencies in the Common Core (Doabler et al., 2012). Target specific areas of need.

- For these goals, use learning trajectories and formative assessment (Dowker, 2004, 2017; Gervasoni & Sullivan, 2007).
- As our approach to learning trajectories always does, *take an asset-based approach. All young children have myriad competencies and resources, individual, family, and community, on which to build.*
- Ensure that all teachers get and use ongoing assessment data on their students and ongoing feedback that helps them use this data to adjust instruction (Jayanthi, Gersten, & Baker, 2008; NMP, 2008).
- Share information on their performance with students.
- Provide clear, specific feedback to parents on their children's math achievement.
- Use peers as tutors (see also Chapter 16).
- Use explicit instruction, including modeling and demonstrating. Use clear and concise language and have children actively participate in using several models for math concepts (Doabler et al., 2012; Jayanthi et al., 2008; NMP, 2008).
- Sequence instructional examples carefully (Doabler et al., 2012).
- Use multiple instructional examples (Jayanthi et al., 2008; NMP, 2008).
- Encourage students to verbalize their thinking or their strategies, or even the explicit strategies you model (Jayanthi et al., 2008; NMP, 2008).
- Encourage students to use *multiple* strategies and heuristics in solving problems (Jayanthi et al., 2008; NMP, 2008).
- Use a special tutorial intervention (one successful example for first graders used suggestions from research, including the first edition of this book; Nunes et al., 2011).
- Find other interventions that are research-based (e.g., Clements, 2000; Dowker, 2009; Dowker & Sigley, 2010; Gersten et al., 2005) and fit your needs, as not every intervention works for early math (e.g., Phillips & Meloy, 2012).
- Include individualized work, even for brief periods, as a component of such focused interventions (Dowker, 2004; Gersten et al., 2008).
- Provide students with MD specific instruction both on math and word problems and on the equal sign, as this had been shown to benefit them (Powell & Fuchs, 2010).

In general, children with MD or MLD benefit most from explicit, systematic instruction (NMP, 2008; Powell et al., 2013). This instruction involves teacher demonstration, alongside teacher-guided and independent practice, with "think-alouds" to monitor and enhance students' understanding and reasoning. Concepts, skills, and problem solving are all taught, often with the aid of visual representations, as well as explicit attention to heuristics, mnemonics, and strategies. Formative assessment is key, with teachers carefully monitoring progress along learning trajectories for major math topics.

Three useful components of such explicit instruction for children with MLD or MD are model-lead-test (or MLT), systematic error correction, and choral responding. In MLT, teachers model a new skill, lead children in responding, then allow them to try the skill independently. For example, "I'm going to count by 2s–2, 4, 6, 8, 10. Let's do it together … Your turn to count by 2s." If children make errors, the teacher corrects them. For example, if they incorrectly name a shape, the teacher might say, "This shape is a *rectangle* [*show*]. *This* is a *tri*angle [*show*]. Say 'rectangle' with me. Good. Now, everyone, what shape is this [*show a rectangle again*]?" (Kretlow, Wood, & Cooke, 2011).

Interventions are more effective the *earlier* they are started, both in building content knowledge and in preventing negative attitudes and math anxiety (Dowker, 2004). A few additional approaches for primary-grade students are described here.

Number and Arithmetic

Specific approaches that show promise include teaching *strategies* about computation, mixed with practice (which is usually less interesting and less conceptual) and using visual models and teaching children to analyze the structure of word problems. One example from the NMP studies provided explicit instruction for second graders with MLD who had not learned to "count on from larger" to solve addition problems (Tournaki, 2003):

Teacher:	When I get a problem, what do I do?
Student (*expected repetition of the rule*):	I read the problem: 5 plus 3 equals how many. Then I find the smaller number.
Teacher (*points to the number*):	3. Now I count the fingers. So how many fingers am I going to count?
Student:	3. (*and so forth …*)

After a few problems, the teacher had students solve problems while thinking aloud, that is, repeating the steps and asking themselves the questions. The teacher always provided clear, immediate feedback when students made errors. The large effect size of this study (1.61) indicates the benefit of teaching a *strategy*, not just providing more practice, especially for MLD students.

Another study included in the NMP report, classified as more implicit, examined the effects on achievement of vulnerable first graders' participation in 48 small group tutorial sessions that included the use of concrete objects to promote conceptual learning. Those randomly assigned to this intervention, compared to a control group, improved on computation, concepts/applications, and story problems, but not on fact fluency (Fuchs et al., 2005) (although children still did not catch up to their peers who were not at risk). Thus, this appears to be an early intervention for students who exhibit problems in math at the beginning of the first grade, as well as an example of how concepts, procedures, and problem solving can be taught and practiced in an intense, integrated fashion.

Two tutoring conditions, one focused on improving fluency in number combinations and one designed to teach problem solving, both improved number combination fluency (Fuchs et al., 2008). Both increased competence in procedural calculations, with the problem-solving condition having the greater effect size. Only the problem-solving condition also developed algebraic thinking and strengthened the ability to solve word problems.

Recall that explicit (or a mixture of explicit and implicit) instruction is quite distinct from older models of "direct instruction." Students are explicitly taught *strategies*, building up a repertoire a bit at a time, not just "facts" or "skills." They participate in a considerable amount of small-group interaction where children are encouraged to think aloud as they do math, receiving feedback from peers and the teacher. They are taught to solve problems, using strategies and, often, using concrete objects and visual representations in conjunction with more abstract representations to analyze the problem's structure. The teacher highlights key aspects of each type of problem (*not* "key words") and supports students' ability to discriminate one type from another. At the end of each instructional cycle, students not only practice but also are helped, explicitly, to generalize and transfer their knowledge.

Other interventions have been shown to be effective. For example, tutoring successfully remediated fact retrieval deficits, procedural computation, and computational estimation (Fuchs et al., 2008). This intervention helped all children equally (e.g., those with MD only or MD and reading difficulties). Computer programs can help children develop mastery with arithmetic combinations (Burns, Kanive, & DeGrande, 2012). However, extensive involvement by teachers is usually needed as well.

Many children with MD or MLD have difficulties related to number "sense." An intervention targeted to exactly that is "The Number Race" computer game (Wilson et al., 2006, 2006). The researchers stated that a basic deficit might be in abilities related to numerical sense, the ability to represent and manipulate numerical quantities nonverbally, emphasizing number comparison and estimation. (The authors call this "number sense," consistent with their previous usage, but to avoid confusion with the much broader math education research use of the term, which they also call number sense, we use "numerical sense" here.) The researchers hypothesize that children lack either nonverbal numerical sense or access to it due to dissociation from symbolic representations. Results of the game were promising on multiple math topics.

Other approaches have also shown promise, including those that are more reform-oriented. Even children with mental handicaps are capable of meaningful learning (Baroody, 1986b). Teachers must ensure that these children develop basic subitizing and counting skills and concepts. That is, they should avoid a narrow focus on skills when more balanced and comprehensive instruction, building on the child's strengths to shore up weaknesses, may provide better long-range results. Visual-spatial training or mass practice should not substitute for experience looking for and using patterns in learning the basic facts or learning arithmetic strategies (Baroody, 1996). Poor instruction may be the reason many children show signs of MD, and even of MLD. Helping these children build on their strengths and informal knowledge, invent counting strategies, connect concepts and procedures, and solve problems may show that many of these children can learn math successfully. Strategies and patterns may need explicit teaching, but should not be neglected (Baroody, 1996). Teachers need to carefully and sensitively assess the understanding and skills of children with mental handicaps along the relevant learning trajectories. For example, children with moderate retardation may not count *verbally* up to 5 but may count *collections* of 5 or more. They may just not be motivated to perform oral counting (Baroody, 1999). Training based on these principles showed some success, more so on near-transfer tasks (Baroody, 1996). Careful attention to tasks was helpful. For example, helping them master a few $n + 1$ tasks ($4 + 1$, $6 + 1$) helped them discover the number-after-n rule, after which children spontaneously invented counting on (realizing, e.g., that if $7 + 1$ is 8, $7 + 2$ is two count words after 7). Importantly, these children can be active learners, who, because of developing adaptive expertise, can learn to monitor their own math activity.

Spatial Thinking and Geometry

Although most researchers' intervention programs focus only on number, this is too limited for educators. The link between high-scoring children's numerical ability and their spatial and measurement ability and the lack of any growth on measurement and geometry in lower-scoring children implies that geometry and measurement must also be addressed (Stewart, Leeson, & Wright, 1997). For example, some children have difficulty with spatial organization across a wide range of tasks. Children with certain math learning difficulties may struggle with spatial relationships, visual-motor and visual-perception, and a poor sense of direction (Lerner, 1997). As discussed (pp. 329–330), they may not perceive a shape as a complete and integrated entity as children without learning disabilities do (Lerner, 1997). Children with different brain injuries show different patterns of competence. Those with right hemispheric injuries have difficulty organizing objects into coherent spatial groupings, while those with left hemispheric injuries have difficulty with local relations within spatial arrays (Stiles & Nass, 1991). Teaching with learning trajectories based on the developmental sequences described here is even more important for children with learning disabilities, as well as children with other special needs. Teachers should know the developmental sequences through which children pass as they learn geometric ideas (see [LT]²).

Spatial weakness may underlie children's difficulties with numerical magnitudes and rapid retrieval of numeral names and arithmetic combinations (Jordan et al., 2003). Similarly, due to the difficulties in perceiving shapes and spatial relationships, recognizing spatial relationships, many also cannot read and align their own numbers properly. As a result, they make errors in computation. They must learn to copy and line up numbers accurately to calculate problems in addition and subtraction, in place value, and in multiplication and division (Bley & Thornton, 1981; Thorton, Langrall, & Jones, 1997).

Other Issues

Recall the promising results of early emphases on structure and pattern (Chapter 12 and others). The Pattern and Structure Math Awareness Program (PASMAP), focused on improving students' visual memory, the ability to identify and apply patterns, and to seek structure in math ideas and representations, has shown to have positive effects on children at risk of later school failure (Fox, 2006).

Children diagnosed as autistic need structured interventions from the earliest years. They must be kept engaged with their world, including math. Use intense interests that characterize many children with autism to motivate them to study geometry and spatial structures. For example, if they enjoy construction, they might study how triangles are used in bridges. Many children with autism are visually-oriented. Manipulatives and pictures can aid children's learning of most topics, in geometry, number, and other areas. Children benefit from illustrating even verbs with dramatizations. In a related vein, teachers might break down what might have been a long verbal explanation or set of directions. About a tenth of children with autism exhibit savant (exceptional) abilities, often spatial in nature, such as art, geometry, or a particular area of arithmetic. These abilities are probably due not to a mysterious talent but from (or also from) massive engagement, the reason and motivation for which remains unknown (Ericsson et al., 1993).

Across all these children and math topics, focus is essential. To develop fundamental competencies, teachers might choose two to three learning trajectories (Common Core clusters) that
are central for the children's grade (Powell et al., 2013). Using formative assessment, find where
the children are in that learning trajectory and plan activities to move them to grade level (e.g.,
see Gervasoni et al., 2012; Sarama & Clements, 2009).

In conclusion, there is substantial evidence that early inequities in knowledge of math can
be avoided or ameliorated, but also evidence that our society has not taken the necessary
steps to do either. Interventions should start in pre-K and kindergarten (Gersten et al., 2005).
Without such interventions, children in special need are often relegated to a path of failure
(Baroody, 1999; Clements and Conference Working Group, 2004; Jordan et al., 2003; Wright,
1991; Wright, Stanger, Cowper, & Dyson, 1996).

Education for All

Specific interventions can be important, *but these should not be a replacement but an addition to children's math education*. All children learn from good math education. *If we want
to close the gap, those with low entering knowledge need more time on better math* (Perry
et al., 2008). Full-day kindergarten programs have been shown to produce greater math
learning gains than half-day programs, particularly for disadvantaged children (Bodovski &
Farkas, 2007). But if other children also participate in full-day programs, the gaps will
remain.

Children at risk or with special needs need *more* time, *more* math. Attention to children
who may lack opportunities to learn might start early, as toddlers (Reikerås, 2016). As we
saw in Chapter 14, affect and motivation are also important. Children who begin kindergarten with the least math knowledge have the most to gain (or to lose) from their engagement
with learning (see the previous section in this chapter on affect). The low engagement of
these students may be at least partly due to teachers' difficulties in engaging them or keeping them engaged. Thus, future instructional efforts with these students should focus on
innovative attempts to improve their engagement with learning. If students with few previous opportunities to learn spent some time daily in small-group instruction that covered the
basic number knowledge that they lack, engagement, and hopefully achievement, might be
accelerated. Finally, if the average beginning achievement of these children can be increased
by more intensive preschool interventions, they may be able also to increase their later
achievement growth (Bodovski & Farkas, 2007). Interventions that specifically address these
needs are discussed in a following section.

Taking a wider view, learning trajectories support children as members of their community
and as individuals, and simultaneously help teachers see and respect all children as learners
and "doers" of math, each with an important voice (Myers, Wilson, Sztajn, & Edgington, 2015).
In this way, learning trajectories can support a wider view of social justice.

Practical Implications

Use learning trajectories to promote equitable math education in all its aspects, as in Figure 15.1.
There are many other resources available to address this country's severe problems with equitable

Table 15.1 Using Learning Trajectories to Provide Equitable Math Education (adapted from Myers et al., 2015)

Access	Ensure that children at various levels have ways to enter the math activities. Use curricular materials that are aligned with LTs. Use formative assessment to understand children's level of thinking. Scaffold discussions to promote all children's participation and use knowledge of LTs to build upon ideas and to make connections among math ideas. Build upon children's level of thinking progressively, providing challenging but achievable activities.
Achievement	Set goals for children that are appropriate based on children's current understandings. Distinguish what children have already learned from what they are learning and use that understanding to design instruction to advance the children's learning. Think of a variety of ways to solicit evidence about children's understanding.
Identity	Support children's efforts and encourage movement along the learning trajectory. Create open tasks that are relevant to and affirm their children's homes and communities. Recognize, encourage, and determine the validity of a variety of strategies, algorithms, and tools to solve problems. Assist children in making not only mathematical connections, but also real-world connections (global, national, and local).
Power	Ensure all children participate, have voice, and ensure equitable ownership of the ideas and activities. Position children as experts based on their usage of certain skills or strategies. Select or create tasks that impact the communities in which children live. Recognize various mathematical ideas present in the classroom and encourage all children to present, justify, and defend their ideas. Frame *every* student as a creator of mathematical knowledge, recognize what children already know, and *self*-empower children by helping them see themselves as doers of math.

math education. See the references (and see [LT]^2, Nasir & Cobb, 2007, and our new STEM Innovation for Inclusion in Early Education, STEMI^{2}E^2, Center at https://stemie.fpg.unc.edu).

Research-based Early Childhood Math Curricula and Approaches

In Chapter 14, we saw that early knowledge predicted math achievement for years to come. Also, young children were more capable learners than previously thought and need curriculum and pedagogy that foster their potential for math thinking (Hunting & Pearn, 2003). What does this mean for curricula and approaches to teaching?

Widely Used, General Curricula are Not Effective

Many preschool settings, such as Head Start, *are* using curricula such as Creative Curriculum and Bright Beginnings. The What Works Clearinghouse is clear that high-quality research shows that these curricula were "found to have no discernible effects on oral language, print knowledge, phonological processing, or math for preschool children" (Clements & Sarama, 2013; What Works Clearinghouse, 2013, 2013). What is commonly used is *not* a valid criterion for what should be used.

As other examples, two curricula, one literacy-oriented (Bright Beginnings), and one developmentally focused (Creative Curriculum), engendered no more math instruction than a control group (Aydogan et al., 2005). Another study showed that classrooms using the OWL (Opening the World of Learning) curriculum, which was designed to develop literacy *and* math (Guisti et al., 2018), across a *360-minute day, devoted only 58 seconds to math* (Farran, Lipsey, Watson, & Hurley, 2007). There was little instruction, few opportunities for children to engage with math materials, and few opportunities for children to talk about math (or anything else, but they talked most in centers, less in small groups, and least in whole-group activities). No children gained math skills, and those beginning with higher scores *lost* math skills over the year. They did gain in literacy skills, but only modestly (Farran et al., 2007). *Most children stayed the same or lost math skills during the year.*

Even in one of the highest-quality programs recently created and run, the Abbott programs, the quality of *math* materials and teaching has been rated as very low (Lamy et al., 2004). This may be one reason that East Asian countries tend to outperform Western countries—the culture develops math ideas and skills more consistently at earlier ages (Aunio et al., 2004, 2006; Sakakibara, 2014).

Curriculum that focus on domains such as math are simply more effective than widely used whole-child curricula (Jenkins et al., 2018).

Other Curricula and Approaches are Effective

We have already described several research-based approaches with proven effectiveness. Here we describe other illuminating studies.

One compared two approaches (Clements, 1984). The first took the then popular, and still influential, position that early instruction on number skills is useless (cf. Baroody & Benson, 2001). Based on an interpretation of Piaget, this position held that if a child does not conserve number (Chapter 3)—that is, believes that changing the arrangement of a collection changes its numbers—instruction may even be harmful. If math is taught at all, it should focus on the logical foundations of classifying, ordering, and conserving. The second approach claimed that children build competency with numbers directly. That is, counting and arithmetic are themselves complex cognitive processes that play a critical and constructive role in the development of number and logical foundations in young children (Clements & Callahan, 1983). Four-year-olds were randomly assigned to one of three groups, a logical foundation group, a number group, and a control group. The group taught classifying and ordering made significant gains on those logical operations. Similarly, the group taught number concepts learned those. This is good news, but not surprising. What *is* surprising is that the logical foundations group made *small* gains on number concepts, but the number group made *large* gains on classification and orderings—matching the performance of the group taught these specific skills. The control group did not improve on any abilities. So, children benefited by engaging in meaningful number activities, many of which involved classifying and ordering.

Curriculum and approaches based on learning trajectories are effective—it's as simple as that (Clements & Sarama, 2011, 2007, 2013; Griffin, 2009; Perry et al., 2008; Young-Loveridge, 1989b, 2004; Weiland & Yoshikawa, 2012; Wright et al., 2006). As one example, our own Building Blocks curriculum (Clements & Sarama, 2013) significantly and substantially increases the math knowledge of vulnerable preschool children. Formative, qualitative research indicated that the curriculum raised achievement in a variety of math topics (Clements & Sarama, 2004; Sarama & Clements, 2002a). Summative, quantitative research confirmed these findings, with effect sizes ranging from 0.85 (Cohen's *d*) for number to 1.47 for geometry in a small-scale study (Clements & Sarama, 2007a). In a larger study involving random assignment of 36 classrooms, the Building Blocks curriculum increased the quantity and quality of the math environment and teaching, and substantially increased scores on a math achievement test. The effect size compared to the control group score was very large (*d* = 1.07) and the effect size compared to a group receiving a different and extensive math curriculum was substantial (*d* =. 47). This has been substantiated by other researchers (Weiland & Yoshikawa, 2012), even in other countries such as Ecuador (Bojorquea, Torbeyns, Van Hoof, Van Nijlen, & Verschaffel, 2018). Follow-up analyses suggest that Building Blocks changes the processes of children's development of math, helping them transfer their knowledge from one context to another (Watts et al., 2017).

Finally, large-scale implementations showed our approach could be implemented across entire urban school districts, again with large effects (Clements et al., 2013, 2011).

But do these effects last? In our study, they did decrease over time (Watts et al., 2017). Skeptics have suggested that it is not worth the effort if effects "fade." We believe that without follow-through, it is simply not realistic to expect short-term early interventions to last indefinitely (Brooks-Gunn, 2003). Our projects show that if *kindergarten and first-grade teachers also use learning trajectories in their teaching,* children retain more of their early advantage (Clements et al., 2013). That is, if all competent entering preschoolers' experience is the same old curriculum in kindergarten, their *learning trajectories will be flattened.* We see that with even a moderate follow-through, children *build* on their early gains. In our studies, this was especially true for African American children (Clements et al., 2013) because their teacher had and supported higher expectations for them with Building Blocks. And we could do much better. What should persist is not just a pre-K gain, but also a dramatic trajectory of successful learning.

Note, however, results do not fade in all cases. In a study of Building Blocks in Ecuador, benefits remained strong into first grade (Verschaffel, Bojorquea, Torbeyns, & Van Hoof, 2019).

Other evidence supports our contention that one of the reason for so-called "fade out" of the effects of early math programs is the low quality of the math children receive afterward (Carr, Mokrova, Vernon-Feagans, & Burchinal, 2019). Additional professional development helps (Jenkins et al., 2018). Also, some elementary curriculum build on early competencies; Karen Fuson's "Math Expressions" curriculum performed well in a study of primary-grade math (Agodini & Harris, 2010). A major conclusion is that *early childhood classrooms through the primary grades underestimate children's ability to learn math and are ill-suited to help them learn.* One researcher, noting that children actually *regress* on some math skills during kindergarten, said simply that sorting and classifying, and one-to-one correspondence, are just not enough (Wright et al., 1994). *We need more structured, sophisticated, and better-developed and well-sequenced math from preschool through the elementary grades.*

For CWD, the Children's School Success curriculum (Lieber, Horn, Palmer, & Fleming, 2008) uses math activities adapted from the Building Blocks curriculum (Clements & Sarama, 2013) to use Universal Design for Learning. Use of this curriculum helps preschoolers with disabilities develop in both academic and social domains. Another program helped at-risk children outperform their control counterparts on standardized measures of math achievement (Clarke et al., 2011).

Another finding from elementary curriculum, a finding that is important to teachers of any age child, is that teaching a combination of skills, concepts, and problem solving helps children learn skills about as well as if they had studied only skills. These children also learn concepts and problem solving, which children in skills-only curricula do not learn as well (e.g., Senk & Thompson, 2003).

Final Words

Understanding the contexts of instruction and curricula used are necessary to be an effective educator. The final area of professionalism deals with specific *instructional strategies*, the topic of Chapter 16.

16 Instructional Practices and Pedagogical Issues

The three friends turn to discussing how they teach math:

Aretha:	Math is different to me. The kids have to memorize specific facts and skills. It's not like language, which you can help kids develop, well, more naturally or informally. Math is something you have to teach directly.
Brenda:	Maybe, but don't you think they have to see math in their world? I mean aren't they doing math when they build with blocks?
Carina:	Both of you sound right. Does mixing those types of approaches make sense?

What do *you* think about teaching math? Should it be more teacher-directed or more child-centered? What role is there for play in early math education? What are the best strategies to meet individual children's needs? Are specific manipulatives helpful? *Should* we emphasize skills or concepts? Do children have too much technology at home? Similar to times at home, should schools keep them away from computers, or should we use good environments to show them how to use technology for *learning*? If so, what types, and how much?

This is a long chapter, because it answers these and many other critical questions. In addition to large entities such as a "program" (e.g., Head Start) or a curriculum, there are specific perspectives, approaches, and strategies for teaching math to young children that research indicates are effective. Here, we briefly describe some of the most important. Although there is research evidence for each, this evidence is in most cases qualitative and/or correlational; therefore, we cannot be certain that the specific instructional strategy caused the learning. This occurs when we cite studies that used randomized designs, because the data on specific *components* of the instruction were not randomly assigned (only the entire curriculum was). Therefore, these results are usually suggestive but not definitive. We note wherever one or more studies did rigorously evaluate a specific approach.

Teaching Beliefs and Basic Pedagogical Strategies

Teachers with certain belief systems about early childhood teaching and learning, and those who tend to use a corresponding category of instructional strategies, are more successful at promoting children's learning. For example, observations allowed researchers to reliably categorize teachers into three belief systems: transmission, discovery, and connectionist, or some combination (Askew, Brown, Rhodes, Wiliam, & Johnson, 1997). Transmission teachers believe in "teacher telling" and a view of math as a collection of separate skills. They believe in teaching primary-grade students mechanical skills with paper-and-pencil procedures. To them, learning is predominantly an individual activity in which one routine at a time is memorized, students' strategies are of little importance, and mistakes are failures to grasp correct methods. They do not expect all students to become fluent (believing that some have more "math ability").

Discovery-oriented teachers believe that children discover ideas, including those in math. They believe that children should find answers by any methods and should learn to apply math to everyday problems. They view learning as an individual activity, often involving manipulatives. They believe that children need to be "ready" to learn.

Finally, connectionist teachers value children's strategies, but also teach strategies in an attempt to establish connections between math ideas, skills, and topics. They believe in efficient methods of calculation, but also an emphasis on mental strategies, on reasoning, and on justifying results. Learning is viewed more as a social activity in which students first develop their own strategies but are helped to refine them by the teacher. Misunderstandings are discussed and worked on. All students are expected to become fluent in using and doing math.

Practical Implications

The researchers also classified the teachers' effectiveness, based on their children's actual gain scores in math over the year (Askew et al., 1997). *Those teachers with more connectionist orientations were more likely to be highly effective than teachers with strong discovery or transmission orientations*. These findings are in close agreement with our theory of hierarchic interactionalism.

It is also important that teachers have an *interest and self-efficacy* in, and *knowledge about*, math (Thomson, Rowe, Underwood, & Peck, 2005) (Şeker & Alisinanoğlu, 2015). Unfortunately, many teachers in early childhood tend to have negative views about math and about teaching math (Knaus, 2017). Often due to negative experiences they have had, such attitudes can change! For example, using children's literature (Jett, 2018) or engaging in a research project with an empirically validated curriculum (Clements, Sarama, Wolfe, & Spitler, 2015; Sarama, Clements, Wolfe, & Spitler, 2016).

Group Size and Structure

Our knowledge of what group size is most effective is limited. The previous study (Askew et al., 1997) did not find that more, compared to less, effective teachers were any more likely to use whole-class, small-group, or individualized approaches (Askew et al., 1997). However, small-group work can significantly increase children's scores on tests aligned with that work (Klein & Starkey, 2004; Klein, Starkey, & Wakeley, 1999). Children can also transfer knowledge they learned in small-group activities to tasks that they have not been taught (Clements, 1984).

Practical Implications

We suspect that small-group work, individual work at the computer, and perhaps to a lesser extent, focused whole-group activities are the main keys to the success of Building Blocks. However, our curriculum also uses centers and everyday activities (Clements & Sarama, 2007a, 2008). All activities are *active*, but we make an extra effort to ensure that the whole-group activities are active—physically ("Counting and Move"), intellectually and individually ("Snapshots" with "bunny ears"—all children are solving problems and showing their solutions individually), or socially ("talk to the person next to you about how you can figure this out")—and usually some combination of these.

Small-group work is *where formative assessment with learning trajectories works hardest* (Clements & Sarama, 2007a, 2008). One relevant finding is that these groups do not have to be small: Groups with two children may not be any more effective than those with five at a time (Clarke et al., 2017).

Observations in countries that use far more whole-group instruction with young children suggest its advantages may be overlooked in the U.S. For example, the teacher-directed, whole-class Korean approach provides a positive, nurturing environment that offers children the opportunity to develop essential pre-academic skills (French & Song, 1998).

Finally, learning centers can make valuable contributions to children's learning as well. However, as in Building Blocks, they are most effective in combination with other group sizes and structure and when they are carefully planned, introduced, and *guided* by the teacher (Uyanik Aktulun & Inal Kiziltepe, 2018).

Intentional, Planned Instruction

Intentional, planned teaching is more effective than laissez-faire approaches or teaching based on "teachable moments" (see the following section, Helenius, 2017; Knaus, 2017; Lai et al., 2018; Lehrl, Kluczniok, Rossbach, & Anders, 2017), even in play contexts, such as the block center (Schmitt et al., 2018; Trawick-Smith, Swaminathan, & Liu, 2016). This is especially true for children with disabilities (Hojnoski et al., 2018). However, compared to Chinese teachers, U.S. preschool teachers are less intentional in math teaching. For example, 27% of the U.S. participants did not set any goals for math, and 20% did not use a curriculum or any resources (Li et al., 2015). Chinese teachers were using more emergent play-based approaches in which to infuse math as well—an approach that may not be fully utilized in U.S. primary-grade classrooms.

Practical Implications

Understand the need for planned, intentional, sequenced teaching of math from the earliest years (Thomson et al., 2005). Actively engage with students (Clements & Sarama, 2008; Thomson et al., 2005).

Planned instruction does *not* have to be done in a certain way—certainly not in a rigid and boring manner. Teaching children from birth through second grade can often be play-like (see the later section on play, pp. 368-373) (Trawick-Smith, et al., 2016) and child-centered (Gervasoni, 2018). As an example, Luke, 3 years of age, was ready to produce a set, but his teacher had found him particularly uninterested in doing so during small group activities. But she knew Luke loved cars. So, she gathered up 20 paper plates and said, "Luke, let's make a huge car show! Let's put four cars on every stand!" Luke happily laid out the paper plates and proceeded to put four cars on every one. If the child won't come to you, go to the child. The activity is just (or more) meaningful and memorable and remains intentional and planned.

Teachable Moments

If play has so much potential to elicit math thinking, should educators simply use "teachable moments"? An old and honored tradition capitalizing on teachable moments is an important pedagogical strategy. The teacher carefully observes children and identifies elements in the spontaneously emerging situations that can be used to promote learning of math (Ginsburg, 2008).

However, there are serious problems with *depending* on this approach. For example, most teachers spend little time in careful observation necessary to find such moments (Ginsburg, 2008; Lee, 2004). They spend little time with the children during their free play (Seo & Ginsburg, 2004). Further, as we have seen, many teachers have a difficult time engaging children in tasks at their level (Bennett, Desforges, Cockburn, & Wilkinson, 1984). Most teachers do not have the math language and concepts at their command. For example, they do not tend to think about relational terms in math. According to researchers, teachers' language in general may influence their ability to see opportunities for teaching math throughout the curriculum (Ginsburg, 2008; Moseley, 2005). Finally, it is unrealistic to expect teachers to see opportunities for multiple children to build multiple concepts (Ginsburg, 2008).

Practical Implications

Seek and exploit teachable moments in everyday play and routines (Lehrl et al., 2017). This could be an important equity issue, so attend to all children, including very young children, who would not be seen as "doing math" (Björklund & Barendregt, 2016). However, recognize that in most situations these moments will constitute only a small portion of the math activities children need.

Using Learning Trajectories

A teacher talks about interviewing a child for report cards, and her use of *learning trajectories* to understand the child fully.

She was able to do verbal counting to 8, and then when she slowed down, she could get to 11. So, I said, "Can you make me a group of 6?" And so she did. So then I added... I asked her to make a group of 12. She couldn't do it.

Then I noted that, *so now I'm thinking in the trajectories*, I think she's a "Counter (Small Numbers)," right? She's on her way to being a "Counter (10)." She's in between the two. *I know just what to do to teach her the next level of thinking*. That's what I was thinking of as I did this.

(Pat, Anghileri, 2004)

Throughout the book we have documented how the use of learning trajectories, in creating stand-ards and curriculum, and in teaching, are useful. Even experiments that carefully tested if you *really* need to use learning trajectories indicate that approach *is* superior. For example, children randomly assigned to learn with learning trajectories performed better than children that were taught the *target* level activities. Even though they spent less time on the target levels, children who moved up the learning trajectories performed better on tasks from all levels, including the one the others had spent all their time learning (Clements et al., 2020, 2019). Math *children's way* is better for them.

Practical Implications

Engage in *intentional, planned teaching in relation to learning trajectories* (Carpenter & Moser, 1984; Clarke et al., 2002; Clements & Sarama, 2007c, 2008; Cobb et al., 1991, note that not all projects use that term—the process is the key). *Focus on key ideas* and understand how those key ideas develop in children. Using learning trajectories well, as suggested by Pat's quote above, *implies* a use of the next instructional strategy, formative assessment.

Formative Assessment

I (Sarama) often have teachers-in-training ask about tests and other assessments they give. They often say they give standardized tests and all quizzes from their textbook. I ask why; what do they do with them? They say this is for grading. I ask, how does it affect your *teaching*? This is usually met with a confused silence. In our own education, we have experienced so many tests and quizzes that we don't always think about what purpose they should serve. Perhaps the most effective use of tests is for the *teaching* strategy called "formative assessment."

Of the ten instructional practices the National Math Advisory Panel (NMAP) researched, only a few had an adequate number of rigorous studies supporting them. One of the most strongly supported was teachers' use of formative assessment (NMAP, Clements & Sarama, 2008). Formative assessment is the ongoing monitoring of student learning *to inform instruction*. One can monitor the class and individuals within it.

Although the youngest children in NMAP's rigorous studies were in the upper primary grades, other studies confirm that regular assessment and individualization are key to effective education in general (Shepard & Pellegrino, 2018) and early math education (Thomson et al., 2005) (Connor et al., 2018) in particular, including internationally (Gallego, Näslund-Hadley, & Alfonso, 2018). Teachers should observe not just answers but *strategies* as well. Second graders experiencing such individualization gained *4 months more* in achievement than those in regular classrooms (Connor et al., 2018).

Other syntheses have reported that formative assessment as an intervention has been evalu-ated to have effect sizes from 0.40 to 0.70, *larger than effects of most instructional programs* (Black & Wiliam, 1998; Shepard, 2005). It helps all children learn but helps the lower-achieving children the most. They gain the higher-order (metacognitive) skills already attained by higher-achieving children.

Of course, it is important for the assessment piece to be accurate and specific. And most early childhood teachers are neither (Kilday, Kinzie, Mashburn, & Whittaker, 2012), due to a lack of professional development. This book, and [LT]², have been designed to fill that gap.

Again, formative assessment is for everyone. In his first year of school, Harry knew all the little math that was presented. Harry gave the appearance of being interested in the work and, at least, being willing to complete it. However, the strongest lesson he learned in his kindergarten math experience is that "you do not have to work hard at it" (Perry & Dockett, 2005). Similarly, observations of early childhood teachers show they usually misjudge children's level and give practice ("more of the same") problems *even when they intend* to provide learning opportunities (challenging problems), *especially* to the highest-performing children. This is simply a reminder, discussed in Chapter 14, that it is *just as important to serve the needs of the gifted as those who are struggling* (Bennett et al., 1984). Thus, the high-performing children were the least well served–they rarely learned new math. Also mismatched were the lowest performers—teachers rarely moved to the lower levels they needed to learn.

Ability grouping should be flexible, based on formative assessment, and sensitive to children's emotional and social development. Done badly, it can lead children with lower entry skills into misbehaviors and lower their self-efficacy (e.g., Catsambis & Buttaro, 2012). Unfortunately, it is often done badly in schools that serve low SES and high-minority students, in which primary-grade teachers may use four or more groups (reducing instructional time) and spend more time with higher-performing groups (Nomi, 2010). In contrast, in advantaged schools, ability group increases achievement for all students.

Practical Implications

Use formative assessment and learning trajectories to serve the needs of all children. As with all instructional practices, formative assessment has to be done right. Ask yourself the following questions (Shepard, 2005):

- What is the key error?
- What is the probable reason the child made this error?
- How can I guide the child to avoid this error in the future?

Also, transfer is more likely when you focus your formative assessment on children's understanding of concepts and relationships. If all this seems obvious and easy, note that an analysis of the ECLS data showed that about half of kindergarten teachers report *never* using such strategies as achievement grouping in math (NRC, 2009). Few pre-K or kindergarten teachers use small groups at all–whole-group instruction dominates (see Group Size, above).

Interactions, Discussions, and Connecting Math: Math Talk

Effective teachers talk to their children about math (Clements et al., 2017a; Gervasoni & Perry, 2017; Trawick-Smith, Oski, DePaolis, Krause, & Zebrowski, 2016; Trawick-Smith, et al., 2016; Walshaw & Anthony, 2008). There are dramatic differences between the amounts of math-related talk that preschool teachers provide (Klibanoff, Levine, Huttenlocher, Vasilyeva, & Hedges, 2006). *The more teachers talk about math, the more their children develop math knowledge.* The contexts in which the talk occurred ranged from planned math instruction to everyday activities (e.g., children engaged in an art project that involved constructing a book were asked to put numbered pages in order), to incidental comments about quantity (e.g., "Can you tell me what is different about those two beads?"). A follow-up study showed that it was not the *overall* number of words but the amount of specific *math talk* that is related to children's growth in math (Ehrlich & Levine, 2007b). Another medium of communication, writing math journals, has also been found to increase children's learning of math (Kostos & Shin, 2010).

Further, children in classrooms with low teacher math talk actually *decreased* in math competence. Unfortunately, most teachers do *not* talk to their children about math, even when the children bring it up. In one study, when children made a math utterance, 60% of the time their teachers ignored it. They only responded mathematically 10% of the time (Diaz, 2008). That may be because only a quarter of the teachers thought of math beyond counting.

These studies are consistent with studies that show that children have more secure, positive relationships with teachers who set up appropriate classroom environments *and* give children high-quality feedback to stretch their emerging knowledge and skills (Howes, Fuligni, Hong, Huang, & Lara-Cinisomo, 2013). This is especially important for Latinx children (Murphey, Madill, & Guzman, 2017) and other groups. Specific math language concepts is strongly related to early maths learning, especially for children who have not had previous high-quality math learning opportunities (Toll & Van Luit, 2014).

Practical Implications

Talk about math. Effective teachers make greater use of open-ended questions than less effective teachers. Ask children, "Why?" and "How do you know?" Expect children, as young as preschool, to share strategies, explain their thinking, work together to solve problems, and listen to each other (Askew et al., 1997; Carpenter, Fennema, Franke, Levi, & Empson, 1999; Carpenter, Franke, Jacobs, Fennema, & Empson, 1998; Clarke et al., 2002; Clements & Sarama, 2007c, 2008; Cobb et al., 1991; Thomson et al., 2005) (Clements et al., 2017a, 2017b; Clements, Sarama, et al., 2019; Fuson et al., 2015).

Place a greater emphasis on summarizing key ideas at the end of any activity. Be aware of the properties and relationships of math. Highlight links and connections between math ideas and between math and everyday problems to be solved (Askew et al., 1997; Clarke et al., 2002; Clements & Sarama, 2007c, 2008).

In summary, be actively engaged in discussing math with children around planned activities. Build on and elaborate children's mathematical ideas and strategies and facilitate children's responding (Clements & Sarama, 2008). Although studies that address this specific instructional practice are correlational rather than experimental, the results are promising.

High Expectations

High expectations of what children can learn in math helps all children realize their potential (Kim, 2015), especially for subgroups such as African American children (Schenke et al., 2017).

Practical Implications

Challenge children. Effective teachers hold higher expectations of children than ineffective teachers (Clarke et al., 2002; Clements & Sarama, 2007c, 2008; Thomson et al., 2005). They hold high expectations of *all* children (Askew et al., 1997).

Developing Positive Math Attitudes and Affect

Children's math anxiety predicts future math achievement over and above cognitive math ability, especially tackling challenging problems (Pantoja et al., 2019). Surprisingly, children with high achievement and high working memory may avoid using more advanced solution strategies *due* to math anxiety (Ramirez et al., 2016). Unsurprisingly, most of these simply mirror the pedagogical strategies discussed previously, but the point here is that these have *also* been identified as improving children's attitudes and beliefs about math.

Practical Implications

Learning environments can enhance children's early development of a positive mathematical disposition (Anghileri, 2001, 2004; Cobb, 1990; Cobb et al., 1991, 1989; Fennema et al., 1996; Hiebert, 1999; Kutscher et al., 2002; McClain, Cobb, Gravemeijer, & Estes, 1999; Sarama & DiBiase, 2004). Effective strategies are *necessary* and include the following.

- Use problems that have meaning for children (both practical and mathematical).
- Expect that children will invent, explain, and critique their own solution strategies within a social context.
- Provide opportunities for both creative invention and practice.
- Use manipulatives (Liggett, 2017).
- Use technology (Sarama & Clements, 2020; Silander et al., 2016).
- Encourage and support children progressing toward increasingly sophisticated and abstract math methods and understandings, and to understand and develop more efficient and elegant solution strategies.
- Help children see connections between various types of knowledge and topics, with the goal of having each child build a well-structured, coherent knowledge of math.
- Ensure that your expectations of and interactions with girls about math are positive and equal to that with boys (Gunderson et al., 2012).

A Word on Assignments, Grading, and "Teaching Responsibility"

I (Sarama) often have graduate students ask for an extension on assignments, saying how busy they were or that there were hardships. I always say "OK," and then add, "Please do one thing in return. When *your* young students ask you for an extension, be just as understanding." This is not always obvious to teachers. I once (and only once) asked teachers what their homework policy was. We made the list, consisting often of punishments such as a zero for any assignments turned in even a day late. They claim they are teaching responsibility. I said, "That will be our homework policy for this class." They were outraged and said I didn't respect them. No one seemed to be able to reflect on the dissonance.

Remember, when a child cannot understand a math concept, we *teach* them. When a child cannot tie his shoes, we *teach* him. When a child forgets an assignment (even just forgetting to bring it in) we ... *punish*? That's not teaching.

Collaborative Learning/Peer Tutoring

The NMP's review of child- and adult-centered instruction in elementary and middle school math concluded that instruction should not be either entirely "child-centered" or "teacher-directed" (NMP, 2008). In the technique "Peer-Assisted Learning Strategies" (PALS) (http://kc. vanderbilt.edu/pals/), teachers identify children who require help on specific skills and others who might teach those skills. All pairs then study math. These pairs and the skills each pair focuses on change frequently, so that all students have the opportunity to be "coaches" and "players." The teacher circulates, observing and providing individual remedial lessons. Findings regarding this approach were promising, but not definitive. The clearest positive results were for low-achieving students on computational measures. Several studies also used a form of formative assessment, so the relative contributions of these two pedagogical strategies is not known. As an example, kindergartners worked on PALS for 15 weeks (Fuchs, Fuchs, & Karns, 2001). The control group was provided teacher-directed lessons and demonstrations. Positive and practically (but not statistically) significant effects on achievement were detected for special education students (effect size = 0.43), low-achieving students (0.37), and medium-achieving students (0.44).

A similar, class-wide peer tutoring program achieved substantial success (Greenwood, Delquadri, & Hall, 1989). This approach involves weekly pairing of the entire class into tutor-tutee pairs, with rewards for responding to the tasks. When adjustments were made for initial Grade 1 pre-test achievement and measured IQ differences, the low-SES experimental group achieved significantly greater gains in math (and literacy measures) than did the equivalent low-SES control group, which received the standard instructional program, including Title I services.

Other cooperative learning strategies have not been evaluated as consistently with rigorous designs (NMP, 2008) although results are positive (Mustafa, Omar, Shafie, & Kamarudin, 2017), particularly so for initially low-achieving children (Meloni, Fanari, Bertucci, & Berretti, 2017). However, research provides several guidelines (Clements, 1991; Johnson & Johnson, 2009; Nastasi & Clements, 1991). Children need constructive group discussions, including presentations of different views, group engagement, solicitation and provision of explanations, and shared leadership (Wilkinson, Martino, & Camilli, 1994).

Practical Implications

A recommendation for an approach designed to enhance social skills, effectance motivation, and higher-order thinking was based on an integration of the research (Clements, 1991). Groups in this approach have the following characteristics:

- *Positive group interdependence* (i.e., if you do well, I do well). Students in a group share the same goal and resources (e.g., one activity sheet for each pair of students). Each has a specific role to play, and these roles are rotated. Students talk together about the work, encouraging each other to learn.
- *Reciprocal sense-making* (i.e., build upon your partner's ideas). Students strive to understand and elaborate upon the viewpoints of their partners. They engage in a mutual process of constructing ideas.

- *Cognitive conflict, then consensus* (i.e., two heads are better than one—in fact, sometimes two wrongs can make a right!). Students learn by taking the perspective of their partners and trying to synthesize discrepant ideas to produce even better ideas. Individual accountability is maintained (i.e., all must learn). Each student is accountable for understanding the concepts.

These lead to the following responsibilities that the teacher must make clear:

- *Work together, explaining fully to each other.*
- *Try to make sense of your partner's explanations.*
- *Ask specific questions when requesting help.* When asked a question by your partner, you have a responsibility to help. Do not just give answers, give explanations. Some teachers also use the "Ask three before me" strategy. Students are not to ask the teacher a question until three other students have been asked and were not able to help.
- *Welcome conflicts of ideas; then work toward consensus.* Partners must agree before writing down the final solution. Of course, they may agree just to "try out" the ideas of one partner!
- *Encourage each other.* When disagreeing, criticize ideas, not people.

As students work together, the teacher's role is to encourage interaction and cooperation, as well as to discuss the children's solutions. For example, if one student does not respond to his or her partner, the teacher would do so to keep the discussion going. The teacher also lets students know that working to understand is more important than getting the single, correct answer. The teacher watches for situations that may be discussed profitably. For example, he/she might tell the whole class that, although a certain pair of students worked on only two problems, they learned a lot from each other by figuring out what the other person was thinking. Sometimes it is also worthwhile to have students discuss social situations that arise. For example, the teacher might ask a pair of students to tell the class how they successfully resolved a conflict over turn-taking. Within a small group, students might be encouraged to discuss and decide how task responsibilities are to be divided.

Suggestions for teachers wishing to promote the development of effective collaborative skills include the following:

- *Emphasize the importance of social support.* Encourage students to provide help for peers. Emphasize that the goal is for all students to learn and be successful.
- *Teach specific communication skills* such as active listening, asking and answering questions, providing explanations, and effective debating techniques.
- *Provide students with informational feedback and social reinforcement regarding their social interactions.* Teach students to give such feedback to each other. In addition, model appropriate interactive behavior.
- *Teach and model conflict resolution skills such as negotiation, compromise, and cooperative problem solving.*
- *Encourage perspective taking* ("put yourself in the other person's shoes") consistent with the students' developmental levels.

- In all phases, evaluate children's learning and help them reflect on what they learned and how their collaborative work helped them learn or how they could collaborate better (Johnson & Johnson, 2009).

A final suggestion from research is especially helpful to African American children and possibly other under-represented groups: Ensue active collaboration and participation, as well as expressive creativity (Waddell, 2010).

Play

Several findings support the traditional emphasis on play and child-centered experiences. In one study, children made more progress overall and specifically on math when they attended child-initiated, compared to strictly academically oriented, programs (Marcon, 1992). Evidence shows that these children's grades were higher at the end of elementary school (sixth, but not fifth grade) (Marcon, 2002). This may be consistent with some Asian countries. For example, Japanese pre-K and kindergarten education places emphasis on social-emotional, rather than academic goals (but "informal" math teaching may be ubiquitous at home and school, as we will describe later in this section). Preschoolers engage in free play most of the day. Parents interact with their children in math, usually in real life, such as counting down elevator numbers. Few parents mention workbooks (Murata, 2004). Similarly, Flemish Belgium's pre-primary education is more concerned with overall development and less concerned with teaching specific content areas than is education in the Netherlands (Torbeyns et al., 2002). Whereas Dutch children start ahead, they are met and surpassed by Flemish children in the elementary years (reasons are not clear). Finally, a cross-national study showed that preschools in which free-choice activities predominated, compared to those in which personal/social activities (personal care and group social activities) predominated, had higher language scores at age 7 (Montie, Xiang, & Schweinhart, 2006). Whole-group activities in preschool were negatively related to cognitive scores at age 7 (cognition including math-relevant content areas, including quantity, spatial relations, problem solving, and time). In contrast, in free play, 2- and 3-year-old children can learn higher-order generalizations (Sim & Xu, 2017).

However, there are cautions to those interpreting this literature (Clements & Sarama, 2014). Most are correlational—there is no way to know what caused what effects. Further, exposure to math instruction explained a substantive portion of the greater gains of young Chinese, compared to U.S. children (Geary & Liu, 1996). Perhaps most troubling to a solely "everyday-" or "play-"oriented approach to math is that many such programs show negligible gains. One analysis of the PCER math curriculum showed that teaching math indirectly through everyday activities did not predict achievement gains, whereas group work did. Nevertheless, the importance of well-planned free-choice play should not be underestimated, appropriate to the age of the children.

Perhaps the most important caution is the notion of *what is and is not an academic goal*. Japanese preschool teachers, as stated, distinguish themselves from elementary teachers as enhancing social and emotional growth. However, what they mean is that, instead of direct teaching of numbers, they prepared materials that induced quantitative thinking, such as card games, skipping ropes, scoreboards on which to write numerals, and so forth (Hatano & Sakakibara, 2004). Further, they enhanced this activity by questioning the children or participating in the activities. They invited children who revealed more advanced understanding to express their ideas as a way of stimulating the thinking of other children (Hatano & Sakakibara, 2004). Given that the broader Japanese culture puts high value on math skills and concepts, such quantitative activities are presented frequently, and attract the children. For example, during free play, a child took a few sheets of newspaper. Others wanted some, and the teacher intervened and gave "one sheet [to] each" (number). She provided two roles of tape on the combined tables of two. Some children started to create origami objects of their own, folding two edges into triangles. One child folded, saying "Fold this into half. Fold this into half" (making fourths, p. 197). The teacher participated by making slightly more advanced paper objects. Children gathered around and conversations developed about geometry and quantity. Children began to make more complex objects of their own. Composition and decompositions of specific shapes were enacted and discussed extensively. Size and measure concepts were threaded throughout the conversations. Thus, these "non-academic" teachers teach math extensively, arranging situations in which children can manipulate materials and discuss ideas; offer increasingly challenging tasks; help children through modeling, participation, and provision of guidance; and offer corrective or expanding feedback (Hatano & Sakakibara, 2004). Thus, the ubiquitous occurrence in Japanese children's homes and schools indicates that math education is emphasized, even if contrasted with the elementary schools' "academic" focus on math.

Play has several different faces in math development. "Play creates a zone of proximal development of the child. In play a child always behaves beyond his average age, above his daily behavior; in play it is as though he were a head taller than himself" (Vygotsky, 1978, p. 102). Preschoolers showed at least one sign of math thinking during 43% of the minutes of which they are observed (Ginsburg et al., 1999). Of course, this may have been just a brief episode, but this illustrates that children could be involved in math during a considerable portion of their free play. The following six categories of math content emerged from the researchers' observations (Seo & Ginsburg, 2004).

- Classification (2%) includes grouping, sorting, or categorizing by attributes. One girl, Anna, took out all the plastic bugs from the container and sorted them by type of bug and then by color.
- Magnitude (13%) includes describing or comparing the size of objects. When Brianna brought a newspaper to the art table to cover it, Amy remarked, "This isn't big enough to cover the table."
- Enumeration (12%) includes saying number words, counting, instantly recognizing a number of objects (subitizing), or reading or writing numbers. Three girls drew pictures of their families and discussed how many brothers and sisters they had and how old their siblings were.
- Dynamics (5%) includes putting things together, taking them apart, or exploring motions such as flipping. Several girls flattened a ball of clay into a disk, cut it, and made "pizza."
- Pattern and Shape (21%) includes identifying or creating patterns or shapes, or exploring geometric properties. Jennie made a bead necklace, creating a yellow-red color pattern.
- Spatial Relations (4%) includes describing or drawing a location or direction. When Teresa put a dollhouse couch beside a window, Katie moved it to the center of the living room, saying, "The couch should be in front of TV" (Seo & Ginsburg, 2004, pp. 93–94).

About 88% of children engaged in at least one such activity during their play. In comparison to some preschools in which teachers emphasize only simple verbal counting and shape recognition, this reveals a rich foundation on which to build interesting math. We consider these activities *pre-mathematical foundations*–critically important, but not yet mathematized for most children until teachers help children talk about them, reflect on them, and build on them.

How about younger children? Even toddlers show significant competencies in their play, across three main areas of math: number and counting, geometry, and problem solving (Reikerås, Løge, & Knivsberg, 2012). Observations indicate that play can support math learning if it stimulates learning and integrates both children and educators' interests (van Oers, 1994). One observational study found that spontaneous use of math in young children's (4 to 7 years) play was frequent, enough so that there were more teaching opportunities than a teacher could possibly notice, much less seize upon (van Oers, 1996). Although a different categorization scheme was used for categories of math, and just one dramatic play setting, a "shoe store," was observed, some comparisons can be made: classification (5%), counting (5%), one-to-one correspondence (4%), measuring (27%), estimating (1%), solving number problems (1%), simple arithmetic (1%), quantitative concepts (20%), number words (11%), space-time (5%), notation (7%), dimensions (5%), money (5%), and seriation and con-servation (0%). In another study, young children exposed to a play-based curriculum scored signifi-cantly higher than national norms on math. However, the findings are equivocal, as the differences declined from age 5 to 7 to insignificance, and the children scored significantly lower than these norms in literacy (van Oers, 2003, notes that the tests emphasize lower-level content).

However, teachers aware of the math and children's relationship with it can support math learning through play (e.g., Helenius et al., 2016).

Practical Implications

Teachers support math in play by providing a fertile environment and intervening appropriately (Clements & Sarama, 2014).

Types of Play

Stepping back, there are several types of play, such as sensorimotor/manipulative and symbolic/pretend (Monighan-Nourot, Scales, Van Hoorn, & Almy, 1987; Piaget, 1962). Sensorimotor play might involve rhythmic patterns, correspondences, and exploring materials such as blocks. Play in perceptually oriented toddlers is enhanced with realistic objects. All children should also play with structured, open-ended materials. In both China and America, the use of LEGOs and blocks is strongly linked with math activity in general and with pattern and shape in particular. However, U.S. preschools have many toys, some of which do not encourage math activity. Chinese preschools have only a few play objects, and blocks and LEGOs are prominent (Ginsburg et al., 2003). Again, less is more.

Symbolic play can be further classified as constructive, dramatic, or rule-governed. In con-structive play, children manipulate objects to make something. This constitutes about 40% of the play of 3-year-olds and half of the play of 4- to 6-year-olds. The power lies in children's playing with alternate ways of building something.

Materials such as sand, play dough, and blocks offer many rich opportunities for math thinking and reasoning (Perry & Dockett, 2002). Teachers might provide suggestive materials (cookie cutters), engage in parallel play with children, and raise comments or questions regarding shapes and amounts of things; for example, making multiple copies of the same shape in play dough with the cookie cutters or transforming sand or play dough objects into one another. One teacher told two boys she was "going to hide the ball" made of play dough, covered it with a flat piece, and pressed down. The boys said the ball was still there, but when she lifted the piece, the ball was "gone." This delighted them and they copied her actions and discussed that the ball was "in" the "circle" (Forman & Hill, 1984, pp. 31-32).

Such play with materials, when creative use is supported, can help children solve problems. A research review reported that children encouraged to play productively with materials before using them to solve problems were more effective at solving those problems than children who had no such experience or those taught how to use the materials (Holton, Ahmed, Williams, & Hill, 2001).

Dramatic play involves substituting some imaginary situation for the children's immediate environment. Math in constructive play is often enhanced when the dramatic is added. Two children making block buildings in parallel may begin arguing whose skyscraper is the "biggest." Similarly, sociodramatic play can be naturally mathematical with the right setting. One suite of activities in the Building Blocks curriculum revolves around a Dinosaur Shop where toys are purchased. Teachers and children put together a shop in the dramatic play area, where the shopkeeper fills orders and asks the customer for money (simply $1 for each dinosaur toy).

In one classroom, Gabi was the shopkeeper. Tamika handed her a 5 card (five dots and the numeral "5") as her order. Gabi counted out five toy dinosaurs:

Teacher (*just entering the area*):	How many did you buy?
Tamika:	Five.
Teacher:	How do you know?
Tamika:	Because Gabi counted.

Tamika was still working on her counting skills, and trusted Gabi's counting more than her own knowledge of five. The play context allowed her to develop her knowledge:

Janelle:	I'm getting a big number. She handed Gabi a 2 and a 5 card.
Gabi:	I don't have that many.
Teacher:	You could give Janelle two of one kind and five of another.

As Gabi counted out the two separate piles and put them in a basket, Janelle counted out dollars. She miscounted and gave her $6:

Gabi:	You need $7.

The sociodramatic play setting, with the teacher's help, was beneficial for children at three levels of math thinking.

In symbolic play, teachers need to structure settings, observe play for its potential, provide materials based on their observations (e.g., if children are comparing sizes, teachers might introduce objects with which to measure), highlight and discuss math as it emerges within play, and ask questions such as "How do you know?" and "Are you sure?" (about your answer or solution) (van Oers, 1996).

Games with rules involve the gradual acceptance of prearranged, often arbitrary rules (Van Herwegen & Donlan, 2018). Such games are a fertile ground for the growth of math reasoning, especially strategic reasoning, and autonomy, or independence (Griffin, 2004; Kamii, 1985). For example, games with number cards provide experiences with counting and comparison (Kamii & Housman, 1999). Card games can be used or adapted for learning math and reasoning, such as Compare ("War"), Odd Card ("Old Maid"), and Go Fish (Kamii & DeVries, 1980; Sarama, 2004). These games are often central inside of a focused, sequential curriculum.

A Special Type: Math Play

These examples bring us another type, *math play, or play with math itself* (cf. Steffe & Wiegel, 1994). For example, recall Abby playing with three of the five identical toy train engines her father had brought home. Abby said,

> I have 1, 2, 3. So [*pointing in the air*] foooour, fiiiive ... two are missing, 4 and 5. [*Pauses*] No! I want these to be [*pointing at the three engines*] 1, 3, and 5. So, 2 and 4 are missing. Still two missing, but they're numbers 2 and 4.

Abby transformed her symbolic play into playing with the idea that counting words themselves could be counted.

The following features of math play have been suggested: (a) it is a solver-centered activity with the solver in charge of the process; (b) it uses the solver's current knowledge; (c) it develops links between the solver's current schemes while the play is occurring; (d) it will, via "c," reinforce current knowledge; (e) it will assist future problem-solving/math activity as well as it enhances future access to knowledge; and (f) these behaviors and advantages are irrespective of the solver's age (Holton et al., 2001).

The Need for Guided Play

Children can draw abstractions from their play, but to be educationally useful, teachers must introduce interesting problems into their play and provide feedback regarding the meaning of children's actions (Pound, 2017) (van Oers & Poland, 2012). For example, if the children play in a zoo setting, the teacher might say how interesting it would be to have a map of the zoo for visitors. Once they begin making a map, the teacher can discuss it and ask questions about how to represent objects, distances, and directions (see Chapter 7).

This is the notion of *guided play*. Play is fun, flexible, voluntary, and intrinsically motivated; it involves active engagement and often incorporates make believe. Guided play maintains the joyful child-directed aspects of free play, maintaining child agency, *and* adds a focus on learning goals through gentle adult scaffolding (Hassinger-Das et al., 2017).

Play "versus" Academics: A False and Harmful Dichotomy (Clements & Sarama, 2014; Merkley & Ansari, 2018): Some argue that all math learning should be through play and suggest that "academic" approaches and play approaches are in conflict (Fisher, Hirsh-Pasek, & Golinkoff, 2012). However, they also say (p. 87) that Building Blocks is a play-based learning program. We agree—if you define "play" broadly and refuse to accept that academics and play are in conflict.

Although math can and should be playful and joyous, this does not mean that "letting children play" provides high-quality, or even barely adequate, math education (Sarama & Clements, 2012 and see "teachable moments" on p. 361). "Free play" classrooms have the lowest gains in math (Chien et al., 2010). Children, especially those at risk, need intentional and sequenced instruction. Traditional approaches to early childhood, such as "developmentally appropriate practice" (DAP) have not been shown to increase children's learning (Van Horn, Karlin, Ramey, Aldridge, & Snyder, 2005). Programs based only on an "everyday" or "play" approach to math education frequently show negligible gains. In comparison, more academic approaches have strong, consistent, positive effects (Fuller et al., 2017) with no harm to social-emotional development (Le at al., 2019).

We need ways to keep the probable benefits of DAP, such as socio-emotional growth (Van Horn et al., 2005; Curby, Brock, & Hamre, 2013), and yet infuse the young child's day with interesting, equally appropriate, opportunities to engage in math thinking (Lange, Meaney, Riesbeck, & Wernberg, 2013) (Peisner-Feinberg et al., 2001). In another study, teaching math indirectly through everyday activities did not predict achievement gains, whereas sequential, intentional group work did (Klein, Starkey, Clements, Sarama, & Iyer, Clements & Sarama, 2008). Mathematization is requisite to basic math ability. Adults must help children discuss and think about the math they learn in their play. Further, math is a hierarchical subject. Intentional teaching using a sequenced math curriculum is an essential complement to rich, scaffolded free play. This is especially important for children from low-resource communities.

In summary, high-quality, explicit, and sequential teaching should be the core of children's math experiences. This helps children learn, helps teachers see the math potential of other, everyday activities, and—this is important—such math promotes higher-quality play. *Really?* Yes: Children in classrooms with stronger emphasis on math were more likely to be engaged at a higher-quality level during free-choice (play) time (Aydogan et al., 2005). Thus, high-quality instruction in math and high-quality free play do not have to "compete" for time in the classroom. Doing both makes each richer, and children benefit in every way. Unfortunately, many adults believe that "open-ended free play" is good and "lessons" in math are not (Sarama, 2002; Sarama & DiBiase, 2004). They do not believe that preschoolers need specific math teaching. They do not realize that they are depriving their children both of the joy and fascination of math and of higher-quality free play as well. Everyone wins.

Direct Instruction, Child-centered Approaches, Discovery Learning, and Play—How to Develop Math Knowledge and Self-regulation Skills

We have seen research supporting explicit instruction (especially for those with few previous opportunities to learn), *and* some evidence for child-centered approaches. Other studies have indicated that direct instruction techniques may affect achievement, especially in the short term, but more child-centered techniques favor overall intelligence in the long term (Schweinhart & Weikart, 1988, 1997). What are educators to conclude? In this section, we synthesize research to provide clear recommendations.

The term "child-centered approaches" has been the catch-all for everything from a laissez-faire classroom where teachers do not teach anything to well-planned teacher–child interactions that lead the child toward the development of more mature levels of underlying skills such as self-regulation. No wonder those considering only laissez-faire approaches conclude that child-centered approaches are not effective. Likewise, "teacher-directed" has meant everything from appropriately scaffolded activities to prison-like rigidity (Lerkkanen et al., 2012). Again, no wonder some considering only rigid drill reject teacher-guided work.

As we just saw, child-centered activities, such as play, *when planned and implemented carefully*, can support the development of underlying cognitive and social-emotional skills necessary for school readiness and performance on academic tasks. Specific child-centered pedagogical strategies can build the essential competence of self-regulation and executive function. Encouraging children to talk to each other in solving a problem in small-group or large-group settings ("turn to your partner and figure out what you think the number will be") facilitates this development. Promoting high-level sociodramatic play is one way to develop self-regulation, as children have to negotiate roles and rules—and keep to them, if they want to be included. Equally important is eliminating the dead times, dull routines, and overly authoritarian environments that do not develop children's self-regulation. Such strategies have been proven successful in improving young children's self-regulation competencies and academic achievement (e.g., Bodrova & Leong, 2006). Used as a part of a comprehensive preschool curriculum as well as a part of an early literacy intervention, these strategies may be useful in improving young children's self-regulation and academic achievement (Barnett, Yarosz, Thomas, & Hornbeck, 2006; Bodrova & Leong, 2001; Bodrova, Leong, Norford, & Paynter, 2003; Diamond, Barnett, Thomas, & Munro, 2007). However, a recent research symposium presented four separate studies (including one of our own with Bodrova and Leong) in which teachers used the play-based strategy with good fidelity, but found *no* gains in executive function (Society for Research on Educational Effectiveness Annual Conference, Washington, DC, March 7, 2012). Therefore, this approach is useful, but not sufficient. It may be that the benefits that do occur have more to do with improving classroom management, reducing children's problem behaviors, and reducing children's stress, which leads to gains in self-regulation and achievement (Raver et al., 2011, 2009). Effective models for developing these teacher competencies exist (Fox, 2006; Hsieh, Hemmeter, McCollum, & Ostrosky, 2009).

Recent research indicates that a key way that children develop executive function abilities such as attention is interacting with adults who provide guidance. This can be done in a variety of settings, such as small groupwork music training, or special training in focusing attention (Neville et al., 2008). *And also high-quality math activities* (Clements et al., 2020).

Also, unfortunately, much of the research against direct instruction (Schweinhart & Weikart, 1988, 1997) may not be reliable. Results are mostly non-significant, the approaches used in different groups were not as different as one might suppose, numbers are very small, and so forth (Bereiter, 1986; Gersten, 1986; Gersten & White, 1986). Finally, research supports *certain types* of explicit instruction, as we saw previously.

Research indicates that curricula designed to improve self-regulation skills *and* enhance early academic abilities are most effective in helping children succeed in school (e.g., Blair & Razza, 2007). Further, research has shown that children in classrooms with intentional focus on math do better in math, but that is not all. *Children in classrooms with math content are more likely to engage at high-quality level during free play* (Aydogan, Plummer, Kang, Bilbrey, Farran, & Lipsey, 2005).

Finally, what about *direct* versus *discovery* instruction? The findings of a large meta-analysis of many studies agree with our perspective. First, unassisted discovery tasks are ineffective. However, *enhanced* or *guided* discovery was generally better than all others: direct teaching, providing explanations, or unassisted discovery learning. That is, children learn best when they construct their own explanations and participate in guided discovery. Such enhanced discovery tasks require children to be actively engaged for their learning to be optimized. "Unassisted discovery does not benefit learners, whereas feedback, worked examples, scaffolding, and elicited explanations do" (Alfieri et al., 2010, p. 1). (Baroody et al., 2015) (Levesque, 2010, found similar results.)

Practical Implications

Our conclusions from these diverse bodies of research are as follows:

- When explicit content-oriented instruction is mistakenly implemented as (only) direct instruction activities at the expense of engaging children in activities of their choice, children practice being "teacher-regulated" and are not given an opportunity to develop self-regulated behaviors which affect their ability to later engage in learning behaviors of their own accord. *The dichotomy between explicit instruction and a child-centered approach is a false one, and high-quality early math programs combine an explicit focus on content with equally explicit focus on promoting play and self-regulatory behaviors.*
- Child-centered approaches, such as the implementation of dramatic, make-believe play, and the use of small-group discussions (including pairs of children discussing solutions during whole-group time) make a valuable contribution to a child's development, *when well-structured and guided by the teacher.*
- Curricula designed *both* to improve self-regulation skills *and* to enhance early academic abilities are most effective in helping children succeed in school.
- *Children learn better from instruction when they explore problems first.* For example, if second graders tried to solve problems such as 3 + 5 = 4 + _ *before* they were instructed, they learned better than when they followed the typical "instruction-then-practice" sequence. Exploration helped children more accurately gauge their own understanding and competence, encouraged them to try a larger variety of strategies, and directed them to the important features of the problems (DeCaro & Rittle-Johnson, 2012).

- *A combination of teaching strategies, emphasizing guided discovery, is beneficial.* Scaffold children's engagement in guided tasks. Have and help children to explain their own ideas and ensure that these ideas are accurate by providing timely feedback and math vocabulary and ideas. Provide worked examples of how to succeed in the tasks (Alfieri et al., 2010; Baroody et al., 2006).
- *Math curricula and approaches that teach a combination of skills, concepts, and problem solving help children learn skills about as well as if they had studied only skills, but also concepts and problem solving, which children in skills-only curricula do not* (e.g., Senk & Thompson, 2003).

Projects

Math should be gleaned from myriad everyday situations, including play, but going beyond it as well. For example, a group of young children in Reggio Emilia investigated many measurement ideas as they attempted to draw plans for a carpenter, so that he could build them a new table (Malaguzzi, 1997). Preschoolers learned STEM making a skyscraper (McCormick & Twitchell, 2017).

However, the PCER studies found no differences in children's development of math in project approach, compared to control, classrooms. Was the problem that the teachers did not or could not implement their projects well? Or was it that project-based programs are not effective in supporting long-term, comprehensive growth of math skills and ideas? It is not clear. We need research to see if rich environments such as Reggio Emilia and project-based programs can be implemented well at scale and what the benefits are. We do know that the use of a variety of pedagogical approaches based on learning trajectories, *culminating* in a project, is promising (Sarama, et al., 2017)

Time ("on Task")

Generally, the more time they spend learning, the more children learn. Children spent more time on math in full-day compared to half-day programs (Lee, Burkam, Ready, Honigman, & Meisels, 2006; Walston & West, 2004; Anghileri, 2004), although the effects may not persist to Grade 3 (Walston, West, & Rathbun, 2005). Further, average-quality centers may have negative impact on social-emotional development. Attending more than 15–30 hours may benefit children from low-resource communities, but not those from higher-resource communities. Children gained the most if they entered centers between the ages of 2 and 3 years (Loeb et al., 2007; Clements & Sarama, 2008). Remember that these studies involve large numbers of children but are correlational only.

Similarly, the more time in the school day children spent on math, and the more math activities in which they engaged (up to about 20–30 minutes per day in pre-K), the more they learn—without harming their development in other areas (Clements & Sarama, 2008). In a single but provocative study, preschoolers benefited more not from more *time* on task so much as the *number of* math activities they engaged in (Sarama et al., 2012). Children learn better from a variety of activities emphasizing the same level of thinking. They may learn concepts more readily from generalizing math structures from different situations that require the same concepts and processes (e.g., mental actions-on-objects).

Class Size and Teachers' Aides

A meta-analysis found that small class size might have the greatest positive effects on reading and math achievement and on students in grades K-3. This is especially so when the class size was 22 or fewer students, and when students were economically disadvantaged or belonged to a racial/ethnic minority group (Robinson, 1990). The Project STAR studies, large-scale randomized experiments (Finn & Achilles, 1990; Finn, Gerber, Achilles, & Boyd-Zaharias, 2001; Finn, Pannozzo, & Achilles, 2003), indicated that at every grade, K-3 students who attended smaller classes outperformed students who attended regular-size classrooms or regular-size classrooms with aides on every academic measure (Finn & Achilles, 1990; Finn et al., 2001). The greatest benefits were to students who started attending small classes in the earliest grades, and who attended small classes for more years.

Less attention has been given to *why* small classes are helpful. Some studies suggest that teacher morale is improved, teachers spend more time in direct instruction and less on mere management, there are fewer discipline problems, students' engaging in learning is increased, and in-grade retentions and drop-outs are reduced (Finn, 2002). Thus, teachers may teach more effectively. In addition, students may become better students. They may be more engaged, exhibiting more pro-learning and pro-social behaviors and fewer anti-social behaviors (Finn et al., 2003).

There are at least two policy pitfalls, or "how to do small classes the wrong way" (Finn, 2002). First, administrators might overlook the need for expert teachers (California reduced class sizes so quickly that it accepted many low-quality teachers who lacked credentials—STAR had all credentialed teachers). Second, they might confuse student–teacher ratios (two adults in a classroom with 30 children has a small ratio but a large class size—and the research is on *class size*). Just reducing class size without planning will likely make no difference (Milesi & Gamoran, 2006).

Practical Implications

In summary, there are benefits of smaller classes, *especially* for younger students, and especially for children at risk for school failure (Finn, 2002; Finn et al., 2001). They are not a "cause" of better teaching and learning but an opportunity for both to be more effective. Project STAR had no additional intervention. One could hope for larger-effect sizes when teachers had been engaged in professional development specifically designed to show them how to use innovative curriculum and formative assessment effectively in the context of the smaller classes.

Another surprising result from these studies is that the presence of teacher aides makes little difference in learning (Finn, 2002; see also NMP, 2008). Funding might be better spent on additional teachers and/or additional professional development (see Chapter 14 of the companion book). And *just doing more advanced math* may yield similar gains for virtually no extra expense (Engel et al., 2016).

Practice, or Repeated Experiencing

For young children learning knowledge that needs to be practiced, such as subitizing, counting, comparing number, shape naming, or arithmetic combinations, research has some clear guidelines. *Substantial practice is required.* We prefer the term *repeated experience* because it suggests many contexts and different types of activities, none of which has to be "drill" for young children and because varying contexts support generalization and transfer. Also, *distributed, spaced practice is better than massed* (all in one session, repetition of the same item over and over) practice (Cepeda, Pashler, Vul, Wixted, & Rohrer, 2006). Because we want such knowledge available quickly throughout the student's life, short, frequent practice sessions of facts and skills *whose conceptual foundations have been well learned and understood* are recommended.

Manipulatives and "Concrete" Representations

The notion of "concrete," from concrete manipulatives to pedagogical sequences such as "concrete to abstract," is embedded in educational theories, research, and practice, especially in math education. Although widely accepted notions often have a good deal of truth behind them, they can also become immune from critical reflection (Sarama & Clements, 2016).

Generally, students who use manipulatives in their math classes outperform those who do not (Driscoll, 1983; Guarino et al., 2013; Johnson, 2000; Raphael & Wahlstrom, 1989; Sowell, 1989; Suydam, 1986; Thompson, 2012). These benefits hold across grade level, ability level, and topic, given that the use of a manipulative "makes sense" for that topic. Manipulative use also increases scores on retention and problem-solving tests. Attitudes toward math are improved when students have instruction with concrete materials provided by teachers knowledgeable about their use (Sowell, 1989). As an example, using cubes increased math scores of second graders (Liggett, 2017).

However, manipulatives do not guarantee success (Baroody, 1989). One study showed that classes not using manipulatives outperformed classes using manipulatives on a test of transfer (Fennema, 1972). Second graders were taught multiplication as repeated addition with manipulatives (colored rods) or symbolically (e.g., 2 + 2 + 2). Both groups learned multiplication, but the symbolic group scored higher on a transfer test. All teachers in this study emphasized learning with understanding whether using manipulatives, mental math, or paper and pencil.

Another study revealed that there is often a lack of connection between children's representations, such as with manipulatives or paper and pencil. For example, they found that some students who performed subtraction best with manipulatives were the worst with paper and pencil, *and vice versa* (Resnick & Omanson, 1987). The researchers explored the benefit of "mapping instruction," designed to help children link their "concrete" knowledge shown by their use of manipulatives to symbolic work with numerals. Although this sounded reasonable, it had limited benefit. "Concrete" experience did not help—it was attention to *quantities.* In contrast, students sometimes learn to use manipulatives only in a rote manner. For example, a student working on place value with beans and beansticks used the (one) bean as ten and the beanstick (with ten beans on it) as one (Hiebert & Wearne, 1992). The lesson? *Manipulatives do not "carry" mathematical ideas.* To understand the role of concrete manipulatives and any concrete-to-abstract pedagogical sequence, we must further define what we mean by "concrete."

Most practitioners and researchers argue that manipulatives are effective because they are concrete. By "concrete," most mean physical objects that students can grasp with their hands. This sensory nature ostensibly makes manipulatives "real," connected with one's intuitively meaningful personal self, and therefore helpful. There are, however, problems with this view.

First, students cannot necessarily "read off" math ideas from manipulatives. Working with Cuisenaire rods, John Holt said that he and his fellow teacher …

> were excited about the rods because we could see strong connections between the world of rods and the world of numbers. We therefore assumed that children, looking at the rods and doing things with them, could *see* how the world of numbers and numerical operations worked. The trouble with this theory is that [my colleague] and I *already* knew how the numbers worked. We could say, 'Oh, the rods behaved just the way numbers do.' But if we *hadn't* known how numbers behaved, would looking at the rods enable us to find out? Maybe so, maybe not.
>
> (Holt, 1982, pp. 138-139)

Second, even if children begin to make connections between manipulatives and nascent ideas, physical actions with certain manipulatives may suggest different mental actions than those we wish students to learn. For example, researchers found a mismatch among students using the number line to perform addition. When adding 6 + 3, the students located 6, counted "one, two, three" and read the answer as "9." This did not help them solve the problem mentally, for to do so they have to count "seven, eight, nine" and at the same time *count the counts*—7 is 1, 8 is 2, and so on. These actions are quite different (Gravemeijer, 1991). These researchers also found that students' external actions on an abacus do not always match the mental activity intended by the teacher. Indeed, some authors believe that the number line model does not help young children learn addition and subtraction, and that, certainly, using the number line model to assess children's knowledge of arithmetic makes several important assumptions about what *else* they know (Ernest, 1985). In any case, the number line cannot be viewed as a "transparent" model (Núñez, Cooperrider, & Wassmann, 2012); if used, it must be *taught*.

Similarly, second graders did not learn more sophisticated strategies (e.g., adding 34 and 52 by counting by tens: "34, 44, 54 …") using a hundreds board, because it did not correspond to students' activity or help them to build useful imagery that supported creation of abstract composite units of ten (Cobb, 1995).

Therefore, although manipulatives have an important place in learning, their *physicality does not carry—and may not even be essential in supporting—the meaning of the mathematical idea.* Students may require concrete materials to build meaning initially, but they must *reflect on their actions* with manipulatives, *thinking conceptually*, to do so. They need teachers who can reflect on their students' representations for math ideas and help them develop increasingly sophisticated math representations.

> Although kinesthetic experience can enhance perception and thinking, understanding does not travel through the fingertips and up the arm.
>
> (Ball, 1992, p. 47)

Further, when we speak of concrete understanding, we are not always referring to physical objects. Teachers of later grades expect students to have a concrete understanding that goes beyond manipulatives. For example, we like to see that numbers—as mental objects ("I can think of 43 + 26")–are "concrete" for older students. *It appears that there are different ways to think about "concrete."*

We have "sensory-concrete knowledge" when we need to *use* sensory material to make sense of an idea. For example, at early stages, children cannot count, add, or subtract meaningfully unless they have actual things. Remember the story of Brenda (see p. 41). The interviewer had covered four of seven squares with a cloth, told Brenda that four were covered, and asked how many in all. Brenda tried to raise the cloth but was thwarted by the interviewer. She then counted the three visible squares.

Brenda's attempt to lift the cloth indicates that she was aware of the hidden squares and wanted to count the collection. This did not lead to counting because she could not yet coordinate saying the number word sequence with items that she only imagined. She needed physically present items to count. This does not mean that manipulatives were the *root* of the idea (Gelman & Williams, 1997). However, there appears to be a level of thinking when children can solve tasks with physical objects that they cannot solve without such objects. For example, consider asking a girl who just turned 4 years of age to add small numbers with and without blocks ("bricks") (Hughes, 1981).

(1)

> E: Let's just put one more in (*does so*). Ten and one more, how many's that?
> C: Err … (*thinks*) eleven!
> E: Yes, very good. Let's just put one more in (*does so*). Eleven and one more, how many's that?
> C: Twelve!

Five minutes later, with the bricks put away:
(2)

> E: I'm just going to ask you some questions, OK? How many is two and one more?
> C: (*No response.*)
> E: Two and one more, how many's that?
> C: Err … makes …
> E: Makes … how many?
> C: Err … fifteen (*in couldn't-care-less tone of voice*).
>
> (pp. 216–217)

The following involved a slightly older boy.

> E: What's three and one more? How many is three and one more?
> C: Three and what? One what? Letter–I mean number? (*We had earlier been playing a game with magnetic numbers, and he is presumably referring to them here.*)

E: How many is three and one more?
C: One more what?
E: Just one more, you know?
C: I *don't* know (*disgruntled*).

(p. 218)

This is consistent with research showing that most children do not solve larger-number problems without the support of concrete objects until 5 + years of age (Levine, Jordan, & Huttenlocher, 1992) but have also developed the ability to convert verbal number words to quantitative meaning (cf. the ordinal-to-cardinal shift in Fuson, 1992a). Preschoolers are more successful solving arithmetic problems when they have blocks available (Carpenter & Moser, 1982) and may not be able to solve even the simplest of problems without such physical, concrete support (Baroody, Eiland, Su, & Thompson, 2007).

At an even younger age, researchers argue that children have a relatively concrete understanding of number until they learn number words. At that point, they gain a more abstract understanding (Spelke, 2003).

In summary, those with sensory-concrete knowledge need to *use* or at least *refer directly to* sensory material to make sense of a concept or procedure (Jordan et al., 1994). Such material often facilitates children's development of math operations by serving as material support for children's action schemes (Correa, Nunes, & Bryant, 1998). This does not mean that their understanding is only concrete; even infants make and use abstractions in thinking (Gelman, 1994). As another example, preschoolers understand—at least as "theories in action"—principles of geometric distance and do not need to depend on concrete, perceptual experience to judge distances (Bartsch & Wellman, 1988).

Concrete "Versus" Abstract?

What about abstraction? Some worry that "abstract" knowledge is developmentally inappropriate. They are probably thinking of what results from inappropriate (limited) teaching. Almost 90 years ago Vygotsky warned that:

Direct teaching of concepts is impossible and fruitless. A teacher who tries to do this usually accomplishes nothing but empty verbalism, a parrot-like repetition of words by the child, simulating a knowledge of the corresponding concepts but actually covering up a vacuum.

(Vygotsky, 1934/1986, p. 150)

This is *abstract-only* knowledge.

However, abstraction is not to be avoided, at any age. Math is *about* abstraction and generalization. "Two"—as a concept—is an abstraction. Further, even infants use conceptual categories that are abstract as they classify things (Lehtinen & Hannula, 2006; Mandler, 2004), including by quantity. These are enabled by innately specified knowledge-rich predispositions that give children a head start in constructing knowledge. These are "abstractions-in-action," not represented explicitly by the child but used to build knowledge (Karmiloff-Smith, 1992). When an infant says "two doggies," she is using abstraction structures of numerosity to label a concrete situation. Thus, the situation is analogical to Vygotsky's (1934/1986) formulation of spontaneous ("concrete") versus scientific ("abstract") concepts in that abstractions-in-action guide the development of concrete knowledge and eventually, depending largely on social mediation, become explicated as linguistic abstractions. We discuss this type of knowledge, a synthesis of concrete and abstract understandings, next.

Integrated-concrete Knowledge

"Integrated-concrete" knowledge is knowledge that is *connected* in special ways. This is the root of the word concrete—"to grow together." What gives sidewalk concrete its strength is the combination of separate particles in an interconnected mass. What gives integrated-concrete thinking its strength is the combination of many separate ideas in an interconnected structure of knowledge. For students with this type of interconnected knowledge, physical objects, actions performed on them, and abstractions are all interrelated in a strong mental structure. Ideas such as "75," "3/4," and "rectangle" become as real, tangible, and strong as a concrete sidewalk. Each idea is as concrete as a wrench is to a plumber—an accessible and useful tool. Knowledge of money was in the process of becoming such a tool for him.

Therefore, an idea is not simply concrete or not concrete. Depending on what kind of *relationship* you have with the knowledge (Wilensky, 1991), it might be "sensory-concrete," "abstract" only, or "integrated-concrete." Further, we as educators cannot engineer math into sensory-concrete materials because ideas such as number are not "out there." As Piaget has shown us, they are constructions—reinventions—of each human mind. "Fourness" is no more "in" four blocks than it is "in" a picture of four blocks. The child creates "four" by building a representation of number and connecting it with either physical or pictured blocks (Battista, 1990; Clements, 1989; Kamii, 1973, 1985, 1986). As Piaget's collaborator, Hermine Sinclair says, "… numbers are *made* by children, not *found* (as they may find some pretty rocks, for example) or *accepted* from adults (as they may accept and use a toy)" (Sinclair, Forward, in Steffe & Cobb, 1988, p. v).

What, ultimately, makes math ideas integrated-concrete is not their physical characteristics. Indeed, physical knowledge is a different kind of knowledge than logical/mathematical knowledge, according to Piaget (Kamii, 1973). Also, some research indicates that pictures are as effective for learning as physical manipulatives (Scott & Neufeld, 1976). What makes ideas integrated-concrete is how "meaning-full"—connected to other ideas and situations—they are. John Holt reported that children who already understood numbers could perform the tasks with or without the blocks.

But children who could not do these problems without the blocks didn't have a clue about how to do them with the blocks.… They found the blocks … as abstract, as disconnected from reality, mysterious, arbitrary, and capricious as the numbers that these blocks were supposed to bring to life.

(Holt, 1982, p. 219)

Good uses of manipulatives are those that aid students in building, strengthening, and connecting various representations of math ideas. Older students' greater facility with math may stem from their greater knowledge or procedures or strategies. However, sometimes younger children *do* possess the relevant knowledge but cannot effectively create a mental representation of the necessary information (Greeno & Riley, 1987). This is where good manipulatives can play a role.

Comparing the two levels of concrete knowledge, we see a shift in what the adjective "concrete" describes. "Sensory-concrete" refers to knowledge that demands the support of concrete objects and children's knowledge of manipulating these objects. "Integrated-concrete" refers to knowledge that is "concrete" at a higher level because it connected to other knowledge, both physical knowledge that has been abstracted and thus distanced from concrete objects and abstract knowledge of a variety of types. Such knowledge consists of units that "are primarily *concrete*, embodied, incorporated, lived" (Varela, 1999, p. 7). Ultimately, these are descriptions of changes in the configuration of knowledge as children develop. Consistent with other theoreticians (Anderson, 1993), we do not believe there are fundamentally different, incommensurable types of knowledge, such as "concrete" versus "abstract" or "concrete" versus "symbolic."

Practical Implications: Use of Manipulatives

Justification for using manipulatives is that they are "concrete" and thus understandable. We have seen, however, that—like beauty—"concrete" is, quite literally, in the mind of the beholder. What role *should* manipulatives play? Research offers some guidelines:

- *Model with manipulatives.* We noted that young children can solve problems and, at the earliest ages, appear to need concrete manipulatives—or, more precisely, sensory-concrete support—to do so. One study showed higher achievement in children who used manipulatives for counting tasks (Guarino et al., 2013). However, the key is that children are successful because they can model the situation (Carpenter, Ansell, Franke, Fennema, & Weisbeck, 1993; Outhred & Sardelich, 1997). Nevertheless, early number recognition, counting, and arithmetic may require (recall Brenda), or benefit from, the use of sensory-concrete support, *if they help children investigate and understand the math structures and processes* (Griffiths, Back, & Gifford, 2017). For example, children benefit more from using chenille sticks ("pipe cleaners") than pictures to make non-triangles into triangles (Martin, Lukong, & Reaves, 2007). They merely drew on top of the pictures, but they transformed the non-triangles made with chenille sticks, which is more likely to expand the actions and their thinking. One study showed that 3-year-olds who used more "interesting" manipulatives (fruit instead of plain blocks) were more likely to accurately identify numbers in a recall task and answer subtraction questions correctly (Nishida & Lillard, 2007b).
- *Ensure manipulatives serve as symbols.* Recall the work on models and maps (DeLoache, 1987). Multiple studies such as this (Björklund, 2014) (Munn, 1998; Uttal, Scudder, &

DeLoache, 1997) and research reviews (Griffiths et al., 2017) support this guideline: Physical "concreteness" is not necessarily an instructional advantage. This "concreteness" can physically make it difficult for children to use a manipulative as a symbol. To be useful, children must interpret the manipulative as representing a math idea. A second example comes from early introduction of algebraic thinking. When the goal is abstraction, concrete materials may not help. For example, working with differences in children's heights (e.g., Mary is 4 inches taller than Tom), agreeing that Tom's height would be T, children resisted representing Mary's height as "T + 4," preferring "M" (Schliemann, Carraher, & Brizuela, 2007). Others solved some problems but still said "T" stood for "tall" or "ten." Also, students tended to think of the differences in height as the (absolute) heights. Part of their difficulty was thinking of any letter as a variable amount when the concrete situations used in the instruction implied that there was a particular quantity—unknown, perhaps, but not one that varies. That is, children could think of the value of a height, or the amount of money in a wallet as unknown, or a "surprise," but had difficulty thinking of it as a range of values. In contrast, they learned more playing activities such as "guess my rule," in which the context was simply math, not with physical manipulatives, objects, or settings. The pure number activities were meaningful and had advantages in helping children from a low-performing school to think about numerical relationships and to use algebraic notations.

- *Children must be able to see the manipulative as a symbol for a math idea.* The relationship of manipulatives to the concepts they are to represent is not transparent to children (Uttal, Marzolf et al., 1997; Schweinhart & Weikart, 1997). In addition, in some contexts the physicality of a manipulative may interfere with students' math development, and other representations may be more effective for learning. Further, active teaching must guide children to make, maintain, and use manipulatives as symbols or tools for doing math. As we describe in more detail in a subsequent section, *connecting* manipulative work (e.g., place value blocks) with verbal and representations can build both concepts and skills successfully (Brownell & Moser, 1949; Fuson & Briars, 1990; Hiebert & Wearne, 1993) (Griffiths et al., 2017).

In summary, children must construct, understand, and use the structural similarities between any representation and the problem situation to use objects as tools for thinking. When children do not see those similarities, manipulatives may fail to help, and many even hinder, problem solving and learning (Outhred & Sardelich, 1997). As we saw in the previous section, if they do not mirror the mental actions we wish children to develop, their use could be a waste of time or even counterproductive. Manipulatives, drawings, and other representations should, as far as possible, be used instructionally in ways consistent with the mental actions on objects that students are to develop (Figure 16.1).

- *Encourage <u>appropriate</u> play with manipulatives* (Griffiths et al., 2017). Is it good to let children play with manipulatives? Usually yes, sometimes no. Most teachers recognize that if young children have not explored a manipulative on their own (say, toy dinosaurs), getting them to address the teacher's agenda (say, counting) can be at best

Figure 16.1 Effective teachers use manipulatives and discussion to build integrated-concrete
knowledge

inefficient, and at worst, near impossible. Further, children can and do learn pre-
mathematical foundations through their self-directed play, especially with structured
manipulatives, such as pattern blocks or building blocks (Griffiths et al., 2017) (Seo & Ginsburg, 2004). However, these experiences are rarely mathematical without teacher guidance.
Counterintuitively, play can sometimes be counterproductive. When a physical object is
intended to serve as a symbol, playing with the object can interfere with understanding. For
example, having children play with a model of a room decreased young children's success in
using it as a symbol in a map search task, and eliminating any interaction increased their success (Bryant, 1997). Thus, the purpose and intended learning with the manipulatives must be
considered carefully.

• *Use few manipulatives well.* Some research indicates the more manipulatives used, the
better. However, U.S. teachers tend to use *different* manipulatives to increase "motivation" and "make math more fun" (Moyer, 2000; Uttal, Marzolf et al., 1997; Schweinhart &
Weikart, 1997). Further, Dienes' "multiple embodiment" theory suggests that to truly
abstract a math concept, students need to experience it in more than one context. However, there are opposing practices and evidence. For example, too many attributes can
distract young children (Björklund, 2014). Successful teachers in Japan tend to reuse the
same manipulatives repeatedly (Uttal, Marzolf et al., 1997; Schweinhart & Weikart, 1997).
Research indicates that deeper experience with one manipulative is more productive than
equivalent experiences using various manipulatives (Hiebert & Wearne, 1996). A synthesis
seems to indicate that multiple representations are useful (e.g., a manipulative, drawings,
verbalizations, symbols), but many different manipulatives may be less useful. These
manipulatives should be used for multiple tasks, so children do not view them as objects
to play with but tools for thinking (Björklund, 2014) (Sowell, 1989).

- *Use caution in beginning with "prestructured" manipulatives*. We must be wary of using "prestructured" manipulatives—ones where the math is built in by the manufacturer, such as base-ten blocks (as opposed to interlocking cubes). They can be as colored rods for John Holt's students—"another kind of numeral, symbols made of colored wood rather than marks on paper" (Holt, 1982). Sometimes the simpler the better. For example, educators from the Netherlands found students did not learn well using base-ten blocks and other structured base-ten materials. There may have been a mismatch between trading one base-ten block for another and the actions of mentally separating a ten into ten ones or thinking of the same quantity simultaneously as "one ten" and "ten ones." The Netherlands' students were more successful hearing a story of a sultan who often wants to count his gold. The setting of the story gave students a reason for counting and grouping: The gold had to be counted, packed, and sometimes unwrapped—and an inventory constantly maintained (Gravemeijer, 1991). So, students might best start using manipulatives with which they create and break up groups of tens into ones (e.g., interlocking cubes) rather than base-ten blocks (Baroody, 1990). Settings that provide reasons for grouping are ideal.
- *Use drawings, visualizations, and symbols—move away from manipulatives, at least for number and operations, as soon as possible* (Griffiths et al., 2017). Children using manipulatives in second grade to do arithmetic tend to do so even in fourth grade (Carr & Alexeev, 2011). That is a failure to move along the learning trajectory. Although modeling necessitates manipulatives at some early levels of thinking, even preschoolers and kindergartners can use other representations, such as drawings and symbols, with, or instead of, physical manipulatives (Carpenter et al., 1993; Outhred & Sardelich, 1997; van Oers, 1994). Even for children as young as 5 years of age, *physical* manipulatives may play a surprisingly small role. For example, in one study there was no significant difference in the accuracy or in the discovery of arithmetic strategies between kindergartners given and not given manipulatives (Grupe & Bray, 1999). The similarities go on: Children without manipulatives used their fingers on 30% of all trials, while children with manipulatives used the bears on 9% of the trials but used their fingers on 19% of trials for a combined total of 28%. Finally, children stopped using external aids approximately halfway through the 12-week study. Physical objects can make an important contribution, but are not guaranteed to help (Baroody, 1989; Clements, 1999a). Drawings can include models, such as the "empty number line" approach (Klein, Beishuizen, & Treffers, 1998; see Chapter 5). Another consideration is children's use of images. High-achieving children build images that have a spectrum of quality and a more conceptual and relational core. They are able to link different experiences and abstract similarities. Low-achieving children's images tended to be dominated by surface features. Instruction might help these children develop more sophisticated images (Gray & Pitta, 1999).

With both physical and computer manipulatives, we should choose meaningful representations in which the objects and actions available to the student parallel the math objects (ideas) and actions (processes or algorithms) we wish the students to learn. We then need to guide students to make connections between these representations (Fuson & Briars, 1990; Lesh, 1990).

Technology—Computers (iPads, Tablets, Phones, Etc.) and TV

Kindergartner Chris is making shapes with a simplified version of Logo (Clements et al., 2001). He has been typing "R" (for rectangle) and then two numbers for the side lengths. This time he chooses 9 and 9. He sees a square and laughs.

> Adult: Now, what do the two nines mean for the rectangle?
> Chris: I don't know, now! Maybe I'll name this a square rectangle!

Chris uses his invented terminology of "square rectangle" repeatedly on succeeding days.

Appropriateness of Technology

In Clements, 1995, we argued that "we no longer need to ask whether the use of technology is 'appropriate'" in early childhood education (Clements & Swaminathan, 1995). The research supporting that statement was, and remains, convincing. However, misunderstandings and unfounded criticisms of computers in early childhood continue to be published (e.g., Cordes & Miller, 2000). This is important, because some teachers retain a bias against computers that contradicts research evidence:

> I just hate computers for children this age... It's just too removed, too far removed from the senses.... There's no thought involved. It's totally just pressing buttons. If this doesn't work right with one button, they just randomly press another button. There's no thinking, there's no process involved. There's no logical analysis of anything going on there.
>
> I think that computers tend to just block in one child at a time. I mean, maybe it'll take in two or three, doing group activity. But it kind of isolates the child. I really don't think that computers have a place in early childhood.
>
> (Lee & Ginsburg, 2007, p. 15)

We have countered such criticisms elsewhere (Clements & Sarama, 2003b) (Sarama & Clements, 2019). Here, we simply summarize some basic findings from research on young children and computers (Clements & Sarama, 2010) (Sarama & Clements, 2019) in the U.S. and across the world (e.g., the Latin America and the Caribbean, Sarama & Clements, 2020).

- Children overwhelmingly display positive emotions when using computers (Ishigaki, Chiba, & Matsuda, 1996; Shade, 1994). They show higher positive affect and interest when they use the computer together (Shade, 1994) and prefer to work with a peer rather than alone (Lipinski, Nida, Shade, & Watson, 1986; Rosengren, Gross, Abrams, & Perlmutter, 1985; Swigger & Swigger, 1984). Further, working on the computer can instigate new instances and forms of collaborative work such as helping or instructing, and discussing and building upon each other's ideas (Clements, 1994).

- Children who had access to a computer at home performed better on measures of school readiness and cognitive development, controlling for children's developmental stage and family socioeconomic status (Li & Atkins, 2004). Computers in the home predict children's entering math knowledge (Navarro et al., 2012). "Screen time" may not be the issue—the *type* of activity is—TV viewing might *decrease* executive function, but high-quality, interactive programs *increase* executive function (Huber et al., 2018).

- The addition of a computer center does not disrupt ongoing play or social interaction but facilitates extensive positive social interaction, cooperation, and helping behaviors (Binder & Ledger, 1985; King & Alloway, 1992; Rhee & Chavnagri, 1991; Rosengren et al., 1985). Even in the preschool classroom, a computer center fosters a positive climate characterized by praise and encouragement of peers (Klinzing & Hall, 1985).

- Computers may represent an environment in which both cognitive and social interactions simultaneously are encouraged, each to the benefit of the other (Clements, 1986; Clements & Nastasi, 1985).

- Computers can motivate academic work (see the many references in Clements & Sarama, 2003b). Children are energized. They are active and take charge of their learning processes. Those behind in other areas excelled at computer learning (Primavera, Wiederlight, & DiGiacomo, 2001).

- Technology can support children often denied opportunities (Outhwaite, Gulliford, & Pitchford, 2017), such as children of immigrants (Moon & Hofferth, 2018) and CWD (Ok & Kim, 2017).

- Computers can engender creativity, including creative mathematical thinking (Clements, 1986, 1995; Clements & Sarama, 2003b).

- Teachers need and deserve support to realize these benefits for their children (Urbina & Polly, 2017).

This last point is most directly relevant to this book, so we will elaborate on it especially.

Computer Aided Instruction (CAI)

Even children as young as 2 or 3 years of age can benefit from technology-assisted instruction (TAI) to develop math skills and concepts, in subitizing, counting, addition, and other topics. One review of rigorous studies indicated that TAI applications that are well designed and implemented could have a positive impact on math performance (National Mathematics Advisory Panel, 2008), and recent studies support this conclusion across math topics and age, especially pre-K through the primary grades (Foster, Anthony, Clements, & Sarama, 2016; Moradmand, Datta, & Oakley, 2013; Nusir, Alsmadi, Al-Kabi, & Sharadgah, 2013; Outhwaite et al., 2019; Reeves, Gunter, & Lacey, 2017; Schacter & Jo, 2016; Thompson & Davis, 2014; van der Ven, Segers, Takashima, & Verhoeven, 2017; Van Herwegen & Donlan, 2018; Zaranis, 2018a, 2018b) and for DLLs (Foster et al., 2018). Another recent review concluded that there are positive effects, although they are modest (e.g., effect size of +.15 standard deviations, Cheung & Slavin, 2013). This review also suggested differences due to the model of TAI used. Supplemental TAI had the largest effect, at a size of +0.18. The other two interventions, technology-management learning and comprehensive programs, which integrated TAI and traditional instruction, had a smaller effect size, +0.08 and +0.07, respectively. However, another meta-analysis of educational technology for early math found a moderate effect size of .48 (.53 for number sense; .42 for operations; .57 for word problems; and .59 for geometry and measurement) (Harskamp, 2015). Individual research-based programs, however, have shown high effect sizes, including more than 1 SD (Aragón-Mendizábal, Aguilar-Villagrán, Navarro-Guzmán, & Howell, 2017). And a recent study in the U.K. showed strong effects of math apps compared to standard practice for 4- and 5-year-olds, on everything from basic facts and concepts to higher-level math reasoning and problem-solving skills (Outhwaite et al., 2019).

Practice/Repeated Experiencing

A common use of TAI is to provide practice; for example, TAI has produced significant increases in skills such as sorting and counting for children as young as 3 years (Clements & Nastasi, 1993), as well as addition facts and computational estimation (Fuchs et al., 2006, 2008; Salminen et al., 2015). Indeed, some reviewers claim that the largest gains in the use of TAI have been in practicing math for lower-primary-grade students (Fletcher-Flinn & Gravatt, 1995), especially in compensatory education programs (Clements & Nastasi, 1993). About 10 minutes per day proved to be sufficient time for significant gains; 20 minutes was even better (note that research suggests short repeated sessions, so for young children, 5 to 15 minutes in a session is suggested). Another program showed good effects in arithmetic fluency for a first grader who practiced for 15 minutes three times per week for 4 months (Smith, Marchand-Martella, & Martella, 2011). Similarly, first-grade students improved their learning of whole-number concepts in skills working with TAI for 48 15-minute sessions (Fien et al., 2016). Preschoolers using Math Shelf as a supplement to their regular curriculum for 15 weeks made sizable gains (> 1 SD) compared to control children (Schacter & Jo, 2016). Kindergarteners learned more math than their peers using the Building Blocks software for 21 weeks (Foster et al., 2016). Geometry and spatial reasoning via TAI is also more effective than traditional approaches in school (Lin & Chen, 2016; Lin & Hou, 2016; Zaranis & Synodi, 2017) and home (Silander et al., 2016).

The practical goal of these studies was to address equity issues, such as closing early learning opportunity gaps. Others have addressed similar equity problems with different populations, and again there are many advantages of technology if used well (Clements & Sarama, 2017; Fien et al., 2016). Children with special needs also benefit from TAI, more so than other approaches (Cascales-Martínez et al., 2017). For instance, technology practice can be especially helpful for children who have mathematical difficulties (MD) or mathematical learning disabilities (MLD) (Harskamp, 2015; Mohd Syah et al., 2016). However, this must come at the right point in the learning trajectory (see below) and it should be the right kind of practice. For example, "bare bones" practice, such as repeated, speed-based, *drill* in arithmetic "facts," does not help children who are at the level of more immature counting strategies. Instead, research suggests practice that helps them understand concepts and learn arithmetic facts before any time-pressured drills (Clements & Sarama, 2017).

Also, practice that teaches fluency and cognitive strategies is more effective than either alone especially for boys (Carr, Taasoobshirazi, Stroud, & Royer, 2011). After 40 30-minute sessions, the combination of these was most effective (effect size, .53 compared to the control group). However, boys seemed to benefit more on the use of the strategies and on fluency. Girls tended to continue to use simple counting; they improved, but did not use more sophisticated strategies, perhaps because the boys had more number sense at pre-test (Carr et al., 2011). Both technology and non-technology approaches may need to better support girls' development. Finally, *make sure that children practice on paper as well as computers.* Practicing on only paper or only computers does not generalize as well as practice on both (Rich et al., 2017).

Research has shown that technology applications, not even necessarily designed for this purpose, can help children with attention-deficit hyperactivity disorder (ADHD). One study showed a substantial improvement in first graders' logic, math and concentration skills, problem solving, and sometimes even the stoppage of involuntary tics (Zaretsky, 2017). There are promising findings also for children who are dual language learners (DLLs) (Lysenko et al., 2016). Technology use for math was associated with a reduced gap in math achievement between native English-speaking and DLL students (Kim & Chang, 2010). Use of Building Blocks software (Clements & Sarama, 2007/2018) as a supplement significantly improved the math competencies of Hispanic dual language learners from low-income backgrounds (Foster et al., 2016).

A caveat is that drills should be used carefully and usually in moderation, especially with the youngest children, whose creativity may be harmed by a consistent diet of drills (Haugland, 1992). Some students may be less motivated to perform academic work or less creative following a steady diet of only drills (Clements & Nastasi, 1993). There is also a possibility that children will be less motivated to perform academic work following drills and that drills on computers alone may not generalize as well as paper-and-pencil work (Clements & Nastasi, 1993; Duhon, House, & Stinnett, 2012). Having children practice about 20% of the time on paper and pencil seems to solve that generalization limitation (Rich et al., 2017). In contrast, practice that encourages the development and use of strategies, provides different contexts (supporting generalization), and promotes problem solving may be more appropriate than drills, or may be best used in combination with it. To be effective, all types of practice must follow and be consistent with Phase 1 and Phase 2 instruction, and appropriate for the children's culture.

Practice does not have to be restricted to routine drills. Deliberate practice is more intentional, involving thinking, problem solving, and reflection for analyzing, conceptualizing, and cultivating one's strategies and understandings (Lehtinen, Hannula- Sormunen, McMullen, & Gruber, 2017). TAI can include such deliberate practice. For example, the Number Navigation Game (NNG) is based on research on adaptive arithmetic strategies and principles of deliberate practice (Lehtinen et al., 2015). Children create their own calculation strategies to progress, with the tasks and constraints becoming gradually more demanding, requiring more and more advanced numerical strategies. The game provides strategic scaffolding and continuous feedback (Lehtinen et al., 2015). NNG achieves its goals and, with teacher support, can be transferred to pre-algebraic skills (Lehtinen et al., 2017). We return to the use of games in a later section. Another example is the use of Realistic Mathematics Education with learning trajectories, a well-established approach, to teach arithmetic by using stories that presents arithmetic problems (Zaranis, 2017). Kindergartners engaged in this approach, which combined non-computer contexts as introductions followed by similar work on computers, learned substantially more arithmetic than children who followed the regular school program (including some simple software).

Other TAI models include and often combine approaches that also go beyond simple practice. In one study, combinations of problem solving, stories, and practice taught preschoolers number concepts and natural science (solubility and recycling). Further, measurement concepts provided through the use of tutorials or video models have taught length to preschoolers (Aladé, Lauricella, Beaudoin-Ryan, & Wartella, 2016) and area to primary-grade students (Clements et al., 2018).

Successes have been reported for other research-based programs. For example, TAI, even with minimal scaffolding, has been found to be a feasible means of helping at-risk first graders discover the add-1 rule (adding one is the same as "counting one more") by way of pattern detection (Baroody et al., 2015). The software might pose, "What number comes after three when we count?" and then was immediately followed by answering a related addition question, "3 + 1 = ?" Also, an "add-zero" item and an addition item (with both addends greater than one) served as nonexamples of the add-1 rule to discourage overgeneralizing this rule. A similar technology program that combined fluency and cognitive strategy use helped second graders, especially boys, improve their arithmetic achievement (Carr et al., 2011).

Different types and different ways of using TAI can achieve different goals. For example, all kindergartners working in multimedia environments improved their math skills more than those not working with any technology environment. Those working individually performed at the highest level, while those working cooperatively increased their positive attitude about cooperative learning (Weiss, Kramarski, & Talis, 2006). Finally, longer tutorials are rare in early math, but some programs are developing new approaches. One program used collaborative multimedia environments with problems that children (4 to 7 years old) solved cooperatively with feedback (Kramarski & Weiss, 2007). These children outperformed those who worked collaboratively but without the multimedia environment. In another approach, children created digital images that represented a person or character and used that character to share thoughts and ideas through typed text or the computer microphone (Cicconi, 2014).

Games and Exploratory Environments

Properly chosen, *technology games* are effective, facilitating both greater skills and conceptual change (Ketamo & Kiili, 2010). Second graders with an average of 1 hour of interaction with a technology game over a 2-week period responded correctly to twice as many items on an addition facts speed test as did students in a control group (Kraus, 1981). Even younger children benefit from a wide variety of technology-based as well as non-technology games (Clements & Sarama, 2008). For example, in one simple game, young children place finger combinations on an iPad to play a game of recognizing and representing numbers before time runs out. Early pilot work with this novel interface, which also promotes use of children's most accessible manipulative, their fingers, is promising (Barendregt et al., 2012). Even a popular game, Angry Birds, has been shown to help 4- and 5-year-olds learn science concepts such as projectile motion (Herodotou, 2018). Interactive 3D visualization helps second graders learn about the Earth-Sun-Moon system by allowing them to observe the space objects moving in the virtual space. This technology provided a hands-on experience that may support young children's ability to view phenomena that could typically demand direct, long-term observations in outer space (Isik-Ercan, Zeynep Inan, Nowak, & Kim, 2014). And exploratory environments can engage young children in investigations of symmetry (Chorney & Sinclair, 2018; Seloraji & Eu, 2017).

Game-based learning also shows promise for children with disabilities, as well as migrant children, because they attract children with imaginary worlds, interesting stories, and shared experiences with peers. They also may offer a variety of new affordances to explore and play with (Kankaanranta, Koivula, Laakso, & Mustola, 2017). Moreover, well-designed games can facilitate the development of a wide range of skills such as phonological awareness, memory enhancement strategies, motor skills and coordination, and logical and math competencies (Peirce, 2013).

Newer technology games can take quite different forms and can target different areas of a child's learning. For example, the robot Nao promotes engagement, social interaction, and geometry learning through social games and activities (Keren & Fridin, 2014). The robot pictured on a screen identifies a shape and asks children to find and touch the same shape on the physical robot. Evaluations revealed that these experiences improved both geometric thinking and meta-cognitive tasks in kindergartners (Keren & Fridin, 2014). Geometry education benefits from technology in many ways, providing technological supports on visualization, manipulation, cognitive tools, discourse promoters, and ways of thinking (Crompton, Grant, & Shraim, 2018). Thus, games and exploratory environments, again *of high quality*, can make unique contributions to STEM learning, and a greater variety are sure to be invented. The following sections discuss other approaches to educational technology.

Programming, Coding, and Robotics

Programming, or coding—instructing a computer to follow a set of commands—is possible for children as young as preschoolers, with the proper technology environment and guidance from teachers (Gedik, Çetin, & Koca, 2017). Lower-primary-grade children have shown greater explicit awareness of the properties of shapes and the meaning of measurements after programming a robotic turtle to move and draw shapes with Logo. They learn about the measurement of length and angle (Sarama et al., 2003) and competencies such as sequencing (Kazakoff, Sullivan, & Bers, 2013). Especially now with new versions of computer languages, such as Scratch Jr. (Flannery et al., 2013; Portelance, Strawhacker, & Bers, 2016), young children can learn related language and can transfer their knowledge to other tasks, such as map reading and interpreting the right and left rotation of objects. For example, first grader Ryan wanted to turn the turtle to point into his rectangle. He asked the teacher, "What's half of 90?" After she responded, he typed RT 45 (for "right turn 45°"). When the turtle said nothing, Ryan said, "Oh, I went the wrong way," while keeping his eyes on the screen. "Try LEFT 90," he said at last. This inverse operation produced exactly the desired effect. These effects are not limited to small studies. A major evaluation of a coding-based geometry curriculum included 1,624 students and their teachers (Clements et al., 2001).

The original Logo turtle was a robot that moved about on the floor. Computer coding of more modern robotics environments have even stronger focus on engineering, including LEGO-Logo and robots (Keren & Fridin, 2014; Palmér, 2017). In LEGO-Logo, children create LEGO structures, including lights, sensors, motors, gears, and pulleys, and they control their structures through computer codes. Another study shows how students 5 to 7 years of age learned modeling, exploring, and evaluating building and programming LEGO robots in Australia (McDonald & Howell, 2012). Such studies show that technological and hands-on learning environments complement each other. For example, second graders who acted out programming commands with their bodies demonstrated better problem-solving skills than a group who planned only with paper and pencil (Sung, Ahn, Kai, & Black, 2017), one more validation of Papert's notion of "body synchrony" (Papert, 1980, see also Sarama & Clements, 2016). Such experiences can positively affect math and science achievement and competencies in higher-order thinking skills (Sarama & Clements, 2020), especially for students at risk for academic failure (Day, 2002). This approach addresses equity concerns in other ways as well. If started as young as kindergarten, few differences appear between boys and girls, and both benefit from work with robots (Sullivan & Bers, 2013).

Younger children can meaningfully and joyfully play with programmable digital toys such as Beebot, but explicit scaffolding may be important to have them think about the sequencing that defines "programming" (Newhouse, Cooper, & Cordery, 2017; Palmér, 2017). From directing robots to carry, push, and/or sort recyclable materials found in the classroom (Sullivan, Kazakoff, & Bers, 2013) to learning more advanced geometry, programming and robotics are accessible, engaging, and beneficial for young children. Recent projects have created and evaluated new environments for young children's coding, such as tablet environments with appealing contexts, such as dinosaurs, for 4- and 5-year-olds (Sheehan et al., 2019), as well as explicit instruction in programming for CWD (Taylor, 2017).

Children with disabilities (CWD) can fully participate in programming and learn computational thinking (Israel, Jeong, Ray, & Lash, 2020). Research suggests that supports that CWD needed were not CT-specific, but rather they needed the same supports, specific to each child, that were successful in other educational areas (Snodgrass, Israel, & Reese, 2016). For one child, for example, that included access to materials, verbal directions about what to do and how to do it, models of problem-solving techniques (e.g., watching the researcher try different combinations of programming code), and models of how to complete the assigned task (e.g., watching the researcher complete an activity while the computer stayed in front of the child).

Computer Manipulatives

Even if we agree that "concrete" cannot simply be equated with physical manipulatives as we discussed earlier in this chapter, we might have difficulty accepting objects on the computer screen as valid manipulatives. However, computers might provide representations that are just as personally meaningful to students as physical objects. Paradoxically, research indicates that computer representations are more manageable, "clean," flexible, and extensible than their physical counterparts. For example, one group of young students learned number concepts with a computer environment. They constructed "bean-stick pictures" by selecting and arranging beans, sticks, and number symbols. Compared to a physical bean-stick environment, this computer environment offered equal, and sometimes greater, control and flexibility to students (Char, 1989).

The computer manipulatives were just as meaningful and easier to use for learning. Both computer and physical manipulatives are worthwhile. However, addressing the issues of pedagogical sequencing, work with one did not need to precede work with the other. In a similar vein, students who used physical and software manipulatives demonstrated a much greater sophistication in classification and logical thinking than did a control group that used physical manipulatives only (Olson, 1988). Other studies support the use of both physical and concrete manipulatives (Thompson, 2012) (Tucker et al., 2017).

The reason partially lies in the ways that computer manipulatives can follow the guidelines described in the previous section. These and other potential advantages of using computer manipulatives are summarized in two broad categories: those that offer mathematical or psychological benefits to the student and teacher, and those that offer practical and pedagogical benefits.

1. ***Mathematical/psychological benefits***. Perhaps the most powerful feature of the software is that the actions possible with the software embody the processes we want children to develop and internalize as mental actions:

    *   *Bringing math ideas and processes to conscious awareness.* Most students can use physical manipulatives to perform motions such as slides, flips, and turns; however, they make intuitive movements and corrections without being aware of these geometric motions. Even young children can move puzzle pieces into place without conscious awareness of the geometric motions that can describe these physical movements. Our research has shown that using computer tools to manipulate shapes brings those geometric motions to an explicit level of awareness (Sarama et al., 1996). For example, pre-K children working on pattern block puzzles off-computer were unable to explain the motions needed to make the pieces fit. On-computer, the children were quickly able to adapt to the tools and were able to explain to peers what they needed to do: "You need to click there. You need to turn it."

    *   *Encouraging and facilitating complete, precise, explanations.* Compared to students using paper and pencil, students using computers work with more precision and exactness (Clements et al., 2001; Gallou-Dumiel, 1989; Johnson-Gentile, Clements, & Battista, 1994).

    *   *Supporting mental "actions on objects."* The flexibility of computer manipulatives allows them to mirror mental "actions on objects" better than physical manipulatives. For example, physical manipulations can become so disconnected that students see only the trees—manipulations of many pieces—and miss the forest—place value ideas. In addition, students can break computer base-ten blocks into ones, or glue ones together to form tens. Such actions are more in line with the *mental actions* that we want students to learn. Geometric tools can encourage composition and decomposition of shapes (Clements & Sarama, 2007; Sarama et al., 1996). As an example, Mitchell started making a hexagon out of triangles (Sarama et al., 1996). After placing two, he counted with his finger on the screen around the center of the incomplete hexagon, imaging the other triangles. He announced that he would need four more. After placing the next one, he said, "Whoa! Now, three more!" Whereas off-computer, Mitchell had to check each placement with a physical hexagon, the intentional and deliberate actions on the computer lead him to form mental images (decomposing the hexagon imagistically) and predict each succeeding placement. Further, composing shapes can encourage children to build units of units in their tilings and patterning. Teachers can help by discussing the unit of units that forms the core of such structures. If included in the software, teachers can also show children how the glue tool can be used to actually make such a unit and then copy, slide, turn, and flip it as a unit.

- It also makes building such patterns much easier (and more elegant). Sets of grouped shapes turn, flip, and otherwise act *as a unit*. Thus, the actions children perform on the computer are a reflection of the mental operations we wish to help children develop. Actions on computer manipulatives can include precise decompositions that cannot easily be duplicated with manipulatives; for example, cutting a shape (e.g., a regular hexagon) into other shapes (e.g., not only into two trapezoids but also two pentagons and a variety of other combinations). Computer manipulatives have supported dramatic gains in this competency (Clements, Battista, Sarama, & Swaminathan, 1997; Clements & Sarama, 2007c; Sarama et al., 1996).

- *Changing the very nature of the manipulative.* In a similar vein, computer manipulatives' flexibility allows children to explore geometric figures in ways not available with physical shape sets. For example, children can change the size of the computer shapes, altering all shapes or only some. Matthew wanted to make an all-blue man and recognized that he could overlap the computer rhombuses to exactly cover a triangle space. In a study of patterning, researchers stated that the computer manipulative's flexibility had several positive effects on kindergartners' patterning (Moyer, Niezgoda, & Stanley, 2005). They made a greater number of patterns and used more elements in their patterns with computer manipulatives than with physical manipulatives or drawing. Finally, only when working on the computer did they create new shapes (by partial occlusion).

- *Symbolizing and making connections.* Computer manipulatives can also serve as symbols for math ideas, often better than physical manipulatives. For example, the manipulative can have just the math features that we wish it to have, and just the actions on it that we wish to promote, and not additional properties that may be distracting.

- *Linking the concrete and the symbolic with feedback.* Closely related, the computer can link manipulatives to symbols—the notion of multiple linked representations. For example, the number represented by the base-ten blocks is dynamically linked to the students' actions on the blocks, so that when the student changes the blocks the number displayed is automatically changed as well. This can help students make sense of their activity and the numbers. Is it too restrictive or too hard to have to operate on symbols rather than directly on the manipulatives? Ironically, less "freedom" might be *more* helpful. In a study of place value, one group of students worked with a computer base-ten manipulative. The students could not move the computer blocks directly. Instead, they had to operate on symbols (Thompson, 1992; Thompson & Thompson, 1990). Another group of students used physical base-ten blocks. Although teachers frequently guided students to see the connection between what they did with the blocks and what they wrote on paper, the physical blocks group did not feel constrained to write something that represented what they did with blocks. Instead, they appeared to look at the two as separate activities. In comparison, the computer group used symbols more meaningfully, tending to connect them to the base-ten blocks. In computer environments such as computer base-ten blocks or computer programming, students cannot overlook the consequences of their actions, whereas that is possible to do with physical manipulatives. So, computer manipulatives can help students build on their physical experiences, tying them tightly to symbolic representations. In this way, computers help students link sensory-concrete and abstract knowledge so they can build inte-grated-concrete knowledge.

- *Recording and replaying students' actions.* Computers allow us to store more than static configurations. Once we finish a series of actions, it's often difficult to reflect on them. But computers have the power to record and replay *sequences* of our actions on manipulatives. We can record our actions and later replay, change, and view them. This encourages real math exploration. Computer games such as "Tetris" allow students to replay the same game. In one version, *Tumbling Tetrominoes* (Clements, Russell, Tierney, Battista, & Meredith, 1995), students try to cover a region with a random sequence of tetrominoes. If students believe they could improve their strategy, they can elect to receive the same tetrominoes in the same order and try a new approach.

2. **Practical/pedagogical benefits.** This group includes advantages that help students in a practical manner or provide pedagogical opportunities for the teacher:

- *Providing another medium, one that can store and retrieve configurations.* Shape software can serve as another medium for building, especially one in which careful development can take place day after day (i.e., physical blocks have to be put away most of the time—on the computer, they can be saved and worked on again and again, and there's an infinite supply for all children). We observed this advantage when a group of children were working on a pattern with physical manipulatives. They wanted to move it slightly on the rug. Two girls (four hands) tried to keep the design together, but they were unsuccessful. Marissa told Leah to fix the design. Leah tried, but in recreating the design, she inserted two extra shapes and the pattern wasn't the same. The girls experienced considerable frustration at their inability to get their "old" design back. Had the children been able to save their design, or had they been able to move their design and keep the pieces together, their group project would have continued.
- *Providing a manageable, clean, flexible manipulative.* Shapes manipulatives are more manageable and clean than their physical counterparts. For example, they always snap into correct position even when filling an outline and—also unlike physical manipulatives—they stay where they are put. If children want them to stay where they're put no matter what, they can "freeze" them into position. We observed that while working on the *Shapes* software, children quickly learned to glue the shapes together and move them as a group when they needed more space to continue their designs.
- *Providing an extensible manipulative.* Certain constructions are easier to make with the software than with physical manipulatives, for example, trying to build triangles from different classes. That is, we have observed children making non-equilateral triangles by partially occluding shapes with other shapes, creating many different types of triangle. Making right angles by combining and occluding various shapes is a similar example.
- *Recording and extending work.* The printouts make instant record-your-work, take-it-home paper copies. (Although we are also in favor of kids recording their work with templates and/or cut-outs, this is time-consuming and should not be required all the time.)

Computers encourage students to make their knowledge explicit, which helps them build integrated-concrete knowledge. Using both computer and physical manipulatives is better than using no manipulatives or using just one or the other (Lane, 2010).

Computers and Play

Research shows that the dynamic aspects of the computer often engage children in math play more so than do physical manipulatives or paper media (Steffe & Wiegel, 1994). For example, two preschoolers were playing with the free explore level of a set of activities called "Party Time" from the Building Blocks project (Sarama, 2004) in which they could put out any number of items that the computer then counted and labeled for them. "I have an idea!" said one girl, clearing off all the items and dragging placemats to every chair. "You have to put out cups for everybody. But first you have to tell me how many cups that'll be." Before her friend could start counting, she interrupted—"And everyone needs one cup for milk and one for juice!" The girls worked hard cooperatively, at first trying to find cups in the house center, but finally counting two times on each placemat on the screen. Their answer—initially 19—wasn't exact, but they were not upset to be corrected when they actually placed the cups and found they needed 20. These children played with the math in the situation, with solutions, as they played with each other.

Math can be intrinsically interesting to children if they are building ideas while engaged in math play (Steffe & Wiegel, 1994). To do so, the materials, physical, on a computer, or just verbal, must be of high quality.

Practical Implications: Effective Teaching with Computers

Initial adult support helps young children use computers to learn (Rosengren et al., 1985; Shade, Nida, Lipinski, & Watson, 1986). With such help, children can often use computers independently. Still, children are more attentive, more engaged, and less frustrated when an adult is nearby (Binder & Ledger, 1985). One implication of research, therefore, is that teachers make the computer one of many choices, placed where they or other adults can supervise and assist children (Sarama & Clements, 2002b).

In this section, we provide more details on research implications regarding arranging and managing the classroom, choosing software, strategies for interacting with children in computer environments, and supporting children with special needs:

- *Arranging the classroom.* The physical arrangement of the computers in the classroom can enhance their social use (Davidson & Wright, 1994; Shade, 1994). The parts of the computer with which the children interact, the keyboard, mouse or trackpad, and monitor, should be at the children's eye level, on a low table or even on the floor. Software might be changed, along with other centers, to match educational themes. The other parts should be out of children's reach. All parts can be stabilized and locked down as necessary. If computers are to be shared, rolling carts might be used.
- *Placing two seats in front of the computer and one at the side for the teacher encourages positive social interaction.* If more than two children work with a computer, they assert the right to control the keyboard frequently (Shrock, Matthias, Anastasoff, Vensel, & Shaw,

1985). Placing computers close to each other can facilitate the sharing of ideas among children. Computers that are centrally located in the classroom invite other children to pause and participate in the computer activity. Such an arrangement also helps keep teacher participation at an optimum level. Teachers are nearby to provide supervision and assistance as needed (Clements, 1991). Other factors, such as the ratio of computers to children, may also influence social behaviors. Less than a 10:1 ratio of children to computers might ideally encourage computer use, cooperation, and equal access to girls and boys (Lipinski et al., 1986; Yost, 1998). Cooperative use of computers raises achievement (Xin, 1999); a mixture of use in pairs and individual work may be ideal (Shade, 1994).

- *Encouraging children to connect off- and on-computer experiences by placing print materials, manipulatives, and real objects next to the computer* (Hutinger & Johanson, 2000). This also provides good activities for children who are observing or waiting for their turn.

- *Managing the computer center.* As you might with any center, teach children proper computer use and care, and post signs to remind them of the rules (e.g., no liquids, sand, food, or magnets near computers). Using a child-oriented utility that helps children find and use the programs they want and prevents them from inadvertently harming other programs or files makes everyone's life easier.

- *Monitoring the time children spend on computers and giving everyone fair access.* However, at least one study has found that rigid time limits generated hostility and isolation instead of social communication (Hutinger & Johanson, 2000). A better idea is flexible time with sign-up lists that encourage children to manage themselves. The sign-up list itself can have a positive effect on preschoolers' emergent literacy (Hutinger & Johanson, 2000).

- *Introducing computer work gradually.* Provide substantial support and guidance initially, even sitting with children at the computer to encourage turn-taking. Gradually foster self-directed and cooperative learning. When necessary, teach children effective collaboration, for example, communication and negotiation skills. For young children, this might include such matters as what constitutes a "turn" in a particular game or free explore environment. However, do not mandate sharing the computer all the time. Especially with construction-oriented programs such as manipulatives, free explore environments, or Logo, children sometimes need to work alone. If possible, make at least two computers available so that peer teaching and other kinds of interaction can take place, even if children are working on one computer.

- *Providing enough guidance, but not too much, especially after children are working independently.* Intervening too much or at the wrong times can decrease peer tutoring and collaboration (Bergin, Ford, & Mayer-Gaub, 1986; Emihovich & Miller, 1988; Riel, 1985). On the other hand, without any teacher guidance, children tend to "jockey" for position at the computer and use the computer in the turn-taking, competitive manner of video games (Lipinski et al., 1986; Silvern, Countermine, & Williamson, 1988).

- *Planning carefully to use only computer programs that will substantially benefit children.* Research shows that the introduction of a microcomputer often places many additional demands on the teacher (Shrock et al., 1985). The computer should not be an end unto itself. Computers can help children learn and should be used reflectively by both children and their teachers. Children should learn to understand how and why the programs they use work the way they do (Turkle, 1997).

- *Using effective teaching strategies.* Critical to effective use of computers is teacher planning, participation, and support. Optimally, the teacher's role should be that of a facilitator of children's learning. Such facilitation includes not only physical structuring of the environment but also establishing standards for and supporting specific types of learning environments. When using open-ended programs, for example, considerable support may need to precede independent use. Other important aspects of support include structuring and discussing computer work to help children form viable concepts and strategies, posing questions to help children reflect on these concepts and strategies, and "building bridges" to help children connect their computer and non-computer experiences. Ideally, the computer software should be closely aligned with the rest of the curriculum.

- *Staying actively involved.* Across the educational goals, we find that teachers whose children benefit significantly from using computers are always active. Such active mentoring has significant positive effects on children's learning with computers (Primavera et al., 2001). These teachers closely guide children's learning of basic tasks, and then encourage experimentation with open-ended problems. They are frequently encouraging, questioning, prompting, and demonstrating without offering unnecessary help or limiting children's opportunity to explore (Hutinger & Johanson, 2000). They redirect inappropriate behaviors, model strategies, and give children choices (Hutinger et al., 1998). Such scaffolding leads children to reflect on their own thinking behaviors and brings higher-order thinking processes to the fore. Such metacognitively oriented instruction includes strategies of identifying goals, active monitoring, modeling, questioning, reflecting, peer tutoring, discussion, and reasoning (Elliott & Hall, 1997; Schweinhart & Weikart, 1997).

- *Making the subject matter to be learned clear and extending the ideas children encounter.* Teachers focus attention on critical aspects and ideas of the activities. When appropriate, they facilitate disequilibrium by using the computer feedback to help children reflect on and question their ideas and eventually strengthen their concepts. Teachers also help children build links between computer and non-computer work. Whole-group discussions that help children communicate about their solution strategies and reflect on what they've learned are also essential components of good teaching with computers (Galen & Buter, 1997). Effective teachers avoid overly directive teaching behaviors (except as necessary for some populations and on topics such as using the computer equipment), and, as has been stated, strict time limits (which generate hostility and isolation instead of social communication), and offering unnecessary help without allowing children the opportunity to explore (Hutinger et al., 1998). Instead, teachers prompt children to teach each other by physically placing one child in a teaching role or verbally reminding a child to explain his or her actions and respond to specific requests for help (Paris & Morris, 1985).

- *Remembering that preparation and follow-up are as necessary for computer activities as they are for any other.* Do not omit critical whole-group discussion sessions following computer work. Consider using a single computer with a large screen or with a projector.

- *Supporting DLL/ELL/EL children.* Remember the many resources throughout [LT]² and in its Resources section. Also remember the DLL!Ready app for teacher support for all DLL/ELL/EL children.

- *Supporting children with special needs.* Even critics of technology support its use in supporting young children with special needs. Used well, technology can increase children's ability to function in diverse and less restrictive settings. Computers' unique advantages include (Fritz, Haase, & Räsänen, 2019) (Schery & O'Connor, 1997): assessing children's level of thinking, being patient and non-judgmental, providing undivided attention, proceeding at the child's pace, and providing immediate reinforcement. These advantages lead to significant improvements for children with special needs. Teachers should attempt to ensure that they select such software and guide children with special needs to use it successfully. However, we should be careful not to limit children with special needs to "compensatory" software. They also can benefit from exploratory and problem-solving software. For example, several studies reveal that Logo is a particularly engaging activity to young children, fostering higher-order thinking in children from preschool through the primary grades, including special needs students (Battista, 1990; Clements & Nastasi, 1988; Degelman, Free, Scarlato, Blackburn, & Golden, 1986; Lehrer, Harckham, Archer, & Pruzek, 1986; Nastasi, Clements, & Battista, 1990).

- *Using high-quality software.* One of the most important guidelines is to use high-quality software with empirical evidence of its effectiveness. Recall that the Building Blocks and TRIAD evaluations showed that teachers' use of the software increased children's learning. Even independent evaluations of the software *alone* show increased math achievement (Clements & Sarama, 2011).
- *Considering the full range of technologies.* Computers are in tablets, tables, phones, and so forth. All types of technologies provide a wide range of tools. For example, having young children record experiences with widely available cameras can be effective in promoting their learning of math (Northcote, 2011).

Software can help, but we could do better. Few software programs are designed based on explicit (i.e., published) theoretical and empirical research foundations (but see Clements, 2007; Clements & Sarama, 2007c; Ritter, Anderson, Koedinger, & Corbett, 2007). More continuous, committed, iterative research and development projects are needed in this area. Research-based iterative cycles of evaluation and development, fine-tuning software's math and pedagogy within each cycle, can make a substantial difference in learning (e.g., see Aleven & Koedinger, 2002; Clements & Battista, 2000; Clements et al., 2001; Laurillard & Taylor, 1994; Steffe & Olive, 2002). Such research could identify how and why software designs could be improved (NMP, 2008).

We mentioned that high-quality, interactive programs can *increase* executive function but viewing cartoons on TV might *decrease* it (Huber et al., 2018). What else do we know about TV?

TV

There is even more debate in the early childhood field about the influences—positive and especially negative—of television. There is an extensive literature (see Clements & Nastasi, 1993). The following summarize key findings:

- Content matters—violent TV can lead to aggressiveness, but educational programming can lead to prosocial behaviors.
- Many experts advise no TV for children less than 3 years of age (and some advise none until the primary school years).

- Educational TV such as *Sesame Street*, *Blue's Clues*, and *Peep and the Big Wide World* have positive effects on learning and continue to be updated in content and pedagogy. *Watching educational programs predicts school readiness at age 5.*
- Longitudinal studies show that *high school students who watched educational television have higher grades* than those who did not. This is probably due to the *early learning model*—learning leads to success in the first grades of school, which leads to positive motivation, perceptions of teachers of competence, placement in higher-ability groups, receiving more attention, and thus continuous success in school.
- Children's learning is increased when adults mediate the children's use of TV (as well as other media). Parents might watch educational TV with their children and discuss what is viewed. They might involve the child in active engagement with the material, following suggestions from the show or creating their own.
- Providing parents with print materials or in-person workshops on how to follow up on media is necessary and helpful.

One disturbing result is that preschoolers from high-resource communities understand the math ideas presented on *Sesame Street* better than their counterparts from lower-resource communities. Also, the better the vocabulary and math understanding the child has, the better that child can comprehend the math presented on the screen (Morgenlander, 2005). Another finding that "the rich get richer" presents a challenge to educators and the society as a whole.

Integrate Teaching of Concepts, Skills, and Problem Solving

The National Math Panel concluded, "The curriculum must simultaneously develop conceptual understanding, computational fluency, and problem-solving skills." The debate about whether teachers should concentrate on "skills" or "ideas" should end—both are needed, and both should be developed at the same time, in an integrated fashion (Gilmore et al., 2017; Özcan & Doğan, 2017). As just one example, second-grade classes were randomly assigned to one of two instructional programs. The first was a reformed-based program based on "Realistic Math Education," in which students create and discuss their solution procedure. From the beginning of instruction, this program emphasized developing both conceptual understanding simultaneously with procedural skill, and flexible application of multiple strategies. These students outperformed those in a traditional textbook program that focused on mastery of procedures initially, and varied application of strategies only toward the end of instruction. The reform group children more often selected strategies related to the number properties of the problems and used strategies more adaptively, such as solving problems with an integer ending with the digit 8 with compensation strategies. That is, flexible problem solvers are those who can adapt their strategies to the number characteristics of the problem at hand; for example, solving $62 - 49$ as $62 - 50 = 12$, $12 + 1 = 13$, but solving $62 - 44$ as $44 + 6 = 50$, $50 + 10 = 60$, $60 + 2 = 62$, and $6 + 10 + 2 = 18$. Such flexible use indicates both conceptual understanding and procedural skill. The traditional group did not use the procedures flexibly, even after months of instruction in that program emphasized such flexible use. The reform group scored higher on three measures, showing superior conceptual understanding. Children in both groups developed conceptual understanding before achieving procedural skill, but the two domains were more interconnected for the reform group (Blöte, Van der Burg, & Klein, 2001).

Other studies send the same message. For example, low-SES, urban first and second graders benefit when taught conceptually, by connecting place value block and written representations (Fuson & Briars, 1990). A far older study had similar conclusions. Second graders taught mechanically were faster and more accurate on an immediate post-test, but those taught meaningfully were better able to explain why the algorithm worked, scored better on the retention test, and transferred their knowledge more successfully (Brownell & Moser, 1949). A third study similarly showed the benefits of conceptual instruction (Hiebert & Wearne, 1993), bringing low-achieving children up to the level of their high-achieving peers. Each of these has limitations but the pattern is clear: Good conceptual and procedural instruction is superior to mechanical instruction in helping children achieve today's math goals (Hiebert & Grouws, 2007).

A final study found that, unlike the usual "skills" approach, poor children benefit more from a greater emphasis on meaning, understanding, and problem solving (Knapp, Shields, & Turnbull, 1992). Such an approach is more effective at building advanced skills and is more—or at least as—effective at teaching basic skills. Further, it engages children more extensively in academic learning.

For the least to the most able children, studies show that the foundation of flexible and creative use of math procedures is *conceptual understanding*. Children's knowledge must connect procedures to ideas, to everyday experiences, to analogies, and to other skills and concepts (Baroody & Dowker, 2003).

Practical Implications

Teach students conceptually to help them build skills *and* ideas, helping them use skills *adaptively*. Students then have *fluent* and *adaptive* expertise rather than mere efficiency (Baroody, 2003). Pose problems, make connections, and then work out these problems in ways that make the connections visible, playing both more and less active roles.

Final Words

Teachers matter more than other factors, and teachers in the early years matter the most (Tymms, Jones, Albone, & Henderson, 2009). So, teachers of early math have to use the best pedagogical strategies.

Teaching techniques are tools, and as such, must be used carefully, thoughtfully, and appropriately. Every strategy, from play to direct instruction, can be educative or mis-educative. "Any experience is mis-educative that has the effect of arresting or distorting the growth of further experience" (Dewey, 1938/1997, p. 25). For example, mis-educative experiences resulting from inappropriate direct teaching may decrease sensitivity to the wide range of applications of math ideas or develop automatic skill but narrow the range of further experience with the idea underlying the skill. Conversely, child-centered education that totally rejects the structures or sequencing of subject matter content may be motivating to children at the time yet be so disconnected as to limit later integrative experiences. "High-quality learning results from formal and informal experiences during the preschool years. 'Informal' does not mean unplanned or haphazard" (NCTM, 2000, p. 75). As Dewey said, "Just because traditional education was a matter of routine in which the plans and programs were handed down from the past, it does not follow that progressive education is a matter of planless improvisation" (p. 28). Such every-day activities have been shown to effectively raise math knowledge in Head Start classrooms (Arnold, Fisher, Doctoroff, & Dobbs, 2002).

In summary, in this new educational arena, we know mainly that several approaches, if performed in high-quality settings, can be effective. Most successful pedagogical strategies, even those with focused goals, include play or play-like activities. All approaches have a shared core of concern for children's interest and engagement and content matched to children's cognitive level. Although some studies support general, play-oriented approaches, learning math seems to be a distinct process, even in preschool (Day, Engelhardt, Maxwell, & Bolig, 1997), and approaches focused on math have been successful.

Regardless of instructional approach or strategy, educators must remember that the ideas young children construct can be uniquely different from those of adults (e.g., Piaget & Inhelder, 1967; Steffe & Cobb, 1988). Early childhood teachers must be particularly careful not to assume that children "see" situations, problems, or solutions as adults do. Successful teachers interpret what the child is doing and thinking and attempt to see the situation from the child's point of view. Based on their interpretations, teachers conjecture what the child might be able to learn or abstract from his or her experiences. Similarly, when they interact with the child, they also consider their own actions from the child's point of view. This makes early childhood teaching both demanding and rewarding.

Not only are children's conceptions uniquely different from those of adults, they are the best foundation on which to build subsequent learning. Research and expert practice agree that children should learn skills in conjunction with learning the corresponding concepts—indeed, learning skills before developing understanding can lead to learning difficulties (Baroody, 2004a; 2004b; Fuson, 2004; Kilpatrick et al., 2001; Sophian, 2004; Steffe, 2004). Successful innovative curricula and teaching build directly on students' thinking (the understandings and skills they possess), provide opportunities for both invention and practice, and ask children to explain their various strategies (Hiebert, 1999). Such programs facilitate conceptual growth and higher-order thinking without sacrificing the learning of skills.

In all their interactions with children, teachers should help children develop strong relationships between concepts and skills because skill development is promoted by a strong conceptual foundation. They should encourage children to create and describe their own solution methods and encourage methods found to be effective, introducing them when appropriate. They should encourage children to describe and compare different solution methods. Research indicates that instruction that views children as active learners with relevant initial knowledge and that provides substantial support during learning is superior to traditional instruction that lacks these characteristics (Fuson, 2004). Teachers need to consistently integrate real-world situations, problem solving, and math content (Fuson, 2004). This integration is more than a pedagogical strategy; it is necessary to achieve both sense-making and the development of skills such as computational fluency. It supports transfer to future learning and out-of-school contexts.

Math itself involves a vast web of connections among concepts and topics (NCTM, 2000). Programs for prekindergarten through the primary grades should interweave real-world, meaningful contexts; problem solving; and math concepts and skills. Such programs have a good chance of countering the unfortunate pattern in U.S. math education, in which young children who are initially motivated to explore math (Perlmutter, Bloom, Rose, & Rogers, 1997) come to "learn" that effort does not matter and that only a select few are "talented" at math (Middleton & Spanias, 1999). Teachers should use inquiry-based and discourse-rich approaches (Walshaw & Anthony, 2008), emphasize working hard to understand math (rather than "finishing" or "correctness"), and focus on intrinsic motivation. Making connections to real-life situations may also enhance children's knowledge and beliefs about math (Perlmutter et al., 1997).

Nevertheless, early competence still reflects limited understanding. Varied reasons account for this. Expectations have risen. Only a few hundred years ago, college-level work in math involved simple arithmetic. Cultural tools for math have multiplied. Most instruction in the U.S. is not based on awareness of these tools and/or of the power of children's thinking and the necessity of plumbing the depths of that thinking, engendering children's inventions, leading to our final point.

Teachers are critical but cannot do it alone. The **system** *needs to change* (Bodovski, Nahum-Shani, & Walsh, 2013). *We need to work at all levels, federal to the individual child,* **to integrate research-validated approaches to goals, curriculum, assessments, and professional development—all based on learning trajectories** (Hiebert & Stigler, 2017).

We believe that the knowledge we have tried to help you develop through this book and [LT]^2 will empower you to be a truly effective, professional educator who works for a better system and a better education for every child.

References

Agodini, R., & Harris, B. (2010). An experimental evaluation of four elementary school math curricula. *Journal of Research on Educational Effectiveness, 3*(3), 199-253. doi: 10.1080/19345741003770693

Akers, J., Battista, M. T., Goodrow, A., Clements, D. H., & Sarama, J. (1997). *Shapes, halves, and symmetry: Geometry and fractions*. Dale Seymour.

Aksoy, A. B., & Aksoy, M. K. (2017). The role of block play in early childhood. In I. Koleva & G. Duman (Eds.), *Educational research and practice* (pp. 104-113). Sofia, Bulgaria: St. Kliment Ohridski University Press.

Aktas-Arnas, Y., & Aslan, D. (2004). The development of geometrical thinking in 3 to 6 years old children group. In O. Ramazan, K. Efe, & G. Güven (Eds.), *1st international pre-school education conference* (Vol. I, pp. 475-494). İstanbul, Turkey: Ya-Pa Yayıncılık.

Aladé, F., Lauricella, A. R., Beaudoin-Ryan, L., & Wartella, E. (2016). Measuring with Murray: Touchscreen technology and preschoolers' STEM learning. *Computers in Human Behavior, 62*, 433-441. doi: 10.1016/j.chb.2016.03.080

Aleven, V. A. W. M. M., & Koedinger, K. R. (2002). An effective metacognitive strategy: Learning by doing and explaining with a computer-based Cognitive Tutor. *Cognitive Science, 26*(2), 147-179.

Alexander, K. L., & Entwisle, D. R. (1988). Achievement in the first 2 years of school: Patterns and processes. *Monographs of the Society for Research in Child Development, 53*(2), 1-157.

Alfieri, L., Brooks, P. J., Aldrich, N. J., & Tenenbaum, H. R. (2010). Does discovery-based instruction enhance learning? *Journal of Educational Psychology, 103*(1), 1-18. doi: 10.1037/a0021017

Alt, M., Arizmendi, G. D., & Beal, C. R. (2014). The relationship between mathematics and language: Academic implications for children with specific language impairment and English language learners. *Lang Speech Hear Serv Sch, 45*(3), 220-233. doi: 10.1044/2014_LSHSS-13-0003

Alvarado, M. (2015). The utility of written numerals for preschool children when solving additive problems/La utilidad de los numerales escritos en la resolución de problemas aditivos en niños preescolares. *Estudios De Psicología, 36*(1), 92-112. doi: 10.1080/02109395.2014.1000026

Anantharajan, M. (2020). teacher noticing of mathematical thinking in young children's representations of counting. *Journal for Research in Mathematics Education, 51*(3), 268-300. www.jstor.org/stable/10.5951/jresemtheduc-2019-0068

Anderson, A., Anderson, J., & Shapiro, J. (2004). Mathematical discourse in shared storybook reading. *Journal for Research in Mathematics Education, 35*(1), 5-33.

Anderson, J. R. (Ed.). (1993). *Rules of the mind*. Hillsdale, NJ: Lawrence Erlbaum Associates.

Anderson, S., & Phillips, D. (2017). Is pre-K classroom quality associated with kindergarten and middle-school academic skills? *Developmental Psychology, 53*(6), 1063. doi: 10.1037/dev0000312

Anghileri, J. (2001). What are we trying to achieve in teaching standard calculating procedures? In M. V. D. Heuvel-Panhuizen (Ed.), *Proceedings of the 25th Conference of the International Group for the Psychology in Mathematics Education* (Vol. 2, pp. 41-48). Utrecht, The Netherlands: Freudenthal Institute.

Anghileri, J. (2004). Disciplined calculators or flexible problem solvers? In M. J. Høines & A. B. Fuglestad (Eds.), *Proceedings of the 28th Conference of the International Group for the Psychology in Mathematics Education* (Vol. 2, pp. 41-46). Bergen, Norway: Bergen University College.

Angier, N. (2018). Many animals can count, some better than you, *The New York Times*. Retrieved from www.nytimes.com/2018/02/05/science/animals-count-numbers.html?hp&action=click&pgtype=Homepage&clickSource=story-heading&module=second-column-region&region=top-news&WT.nav=top-news

Anthony, J., Hecht, S. A., Williams, J., Clements, D. H., & Sarama, J. (2011a). Efficacy of computerized Earobics and Building Blocks instruction for kindergarteners from low SES, minority and ELL backgrounds: Year 2 results. *Paper presented at the Institute of Educational Sciences Research Conference*, Washington, DC.

Arditi, A., Holtzman, J. D., & Kosslyn, S. M. (1988). Mental imagery and sensory experience in congenital blindness. *Neuropsychologia, 26*(1), 1-12.

Aragón-Mendizábal, E., Aguilar-Villagrán, M., Navarro-Guzmán, J. I., & Howell, R. (2017). Improving number sense in kindergarten children with low achievement in mathematics. *Anales de Psicología, 33*(2), 311-318. doi: 10.6018/analesps.33.2.239391

Arnold, D. H., Fisher, P. H., Doctoroff, G. L., & Dobbs, J. (2002). Accelerating math development in Head Start classrooms: Outcomes and gender differences. *Journal of Educational Psychology, 94*(4), 762-770.

Artut, P. D. (2015). Preschool children's skills in solving mathematical word problems. *Educational Research and Reviews, 10*(18), 2539-2549. doi: 10.5897/ERR2015.2431

Ashcraft, M. H. (2006, November). Math performance, working memory, and math anxiety: Some possible directions for neural functioning work. *Paper presented at the Neural Basis of Mathematical Development*, Nashville, TN.

Ashkenazi, S., Mark-Zigdon, N., & Henik, A. (2013). Do subitizing deficits in developmental dyscalculia involve pattern recognition weakness? *Developmental Science, 16*(1), 35-46. doi: 10.1111/j.1467-7687.2012.01190.x

Askew, M., Brown, M., Rhodes, V., Wiliam, D., & Johnson, D. (1997). Effective teachers of numeracy in UK primary schools: Teachers' beliefs, practices, and children's learning. In M. V. D. Heuvel-Panhuizen (Ed.), *Proceedings of the 21st Conference of the International Group for the Psychology of Mathematics Education* (Vol. 2, pp. 25-32). Utrecht, The Netherlands: Freudenthal Institute.

Aslan, D. (2004). *The investigation of 3 to 6 year-olds preschool children's recognition of basic geometric shapes and the criteria they employ in distinguishing one shape group from the other (Anaokuluna devam eden 3-6 yas grubu çocuklarina temel geometrik sekilleri tanimalari ve sekilleri ayirtetmede kullandiklari kriterlerin incelenmesi).* (Masters), Adana, Turkey: Cukurova University.

Aslan, D., & Aktas-Arnas, Y. (2007). Three-to six-year-old children's recognition of geometric shapes. *International Journal of Early Years Education, 15*(1), 81-101.

Aubrey, C. (1997). Children's early learning of number in school and out. In I. Thompson (Ed.), *Teaching and learning early number* (pp. 20-29). Philadelphia, PA: Open University Press.

Aunio, P. (2019). Small group interventions for children aged 5-9 years old with mathematical learning difficulties. In A. Fritz, V. G. Haase & P. Räsänen (Eds.), *International handbook of mathematical learning difficulties: From the laboratory to the classroom* (pp. 709-731). Cham, Switzerland: Springer.

Aunio, P., Ee, J., Lim, S. E. A., Hautamäki, J., & Van Luit, J. E. H. (2004). Young children's number sense in Finland, Hong Kong and Singapore. *International Journal of Early Years Education, 12*(3), 195-216.

Aunio, P., Hautamäki, J., Sajaniemi, N., & Van Luit, J. E. H. (2008). Early numeracy in low-performing young children. *British Educational Research Journal, 35*(1), 25-46.

Aunio, P., Korhonen, J., Bashash, L., & Khoshbakht, F. (2014). Children's early numeracy in Finland and Iran. *International Journal of Early Years Education*, 1-18. doi: 10.1080/09669760.2014.988208

Aunio, P., Niemivirta, M., Hautamäki, J., Van Luit, J. E. H., Shi, J., & Zhang, M. (2006). Young children's number sense in China and Finland. *Scandinavian Journal of Psychology, 50*(5), 483-502.

Aunio, P., & Räsänen, P. (2015a). Core numerical skills for learning mathematics in children aged five to eight years - A working model for educators. *European Early Childhood Education Research Journal*, 1-21. doi: 10.1080/1350293x.2014.996424

Aunio, P., & Räsänen, P. (2015b). Core numerical skills for learning mathematics in children aged five to eight years - A working model for educators. *European Early Childhood Education Research Journal*, 1-21. doi: 10.1080/1350293x.2014.996424

Aunola, K., Leskinen, E., Lerkkanen, M.-K., & Nurmi, J.-E. (2004). Developmental dynamics of math performance from preschool to grade 2. *Journal of Educational Psychology, 96*(4), 699-713.

Aydogan, C., Plummer, C., Kang, S. J., Bilbrey, C., Farran, D. C., & Lipsey, M. W. (2005, June 5-8). An investigation of prekindergarten curricula: Influences on classroom characteristics and child engagement. *Paper presented at the NAEYC*, Washington, DC.

Bachman, H. J., Votruba-Drzal, E., El Nokali, N. E., & Castle Heatly, M. (2015). Opportunities for learning math in elementary school: Implications for SES disparities in procedural and conceptual math skills. *American Educational Research Journal, 52*(5), 894-923. doi: 10.3102/0002831215594877

Bagiati, A., & Evangelou, D. (2018). Identifying engineering in a prek classroom: An observation protocol to support guided project-based instruction. In L. D. English & T. Moore (Eds.), *Early engineering learning* (pp. 83–111). Gateway East, Singapore: Springer.

Baker, C. E. (2014). Does parent involvement and neighborhood quality matter for African American boys' kindergarten mathematics achievement? *Early Education and Development, 26*(3), 342–355. doi: 10.1080/10409289.2015.968238

Baker, D., Knipe, H., Collins, J., Leon, J., Cummings, E., Blair, C. B., & Gramson, D. (2010). One hundred years of elementary school mathematics in the United States: A content analysis and cognitive assessment of textbooks from 1900 to 2000. *Journal for Research in Mathematics Education, 41*(4), 383–423.

Ball, D. L. (1992). Magical hopes: Manipulatives and the reform of math education. *American Educator, 16*(2), 14; 16–18; 46–47.

Banse, H. W., Clements, D. H., Sarama, J., Day-Hess, C. A., Simoni, M., Ratchford, J., & Pugia, A. (2020). *What teaching moves support young children's in-the-moment understanding of early addition and subtraction?* Manuscript submitted for publication.

Baratta-Lorton, M. (1976). *Mathematics their way: An activity-centered mathematics program for early childhood education.* Menlo Park, CA: Addison-Wesley.

Barbarin, O. A., Downer, J. T., Odom, E., & Head, D. (2010). Home–school differences in beliefs, support, and control during public pre-kindergarten and their link to children's kindergarten readiness. *Early Childhood Research Quarterly, 25*(3), 358–372. doi: 10.1016/j.ecresq.2010.02.003

Barendregt, W., Lindström, B., Rietz-Leppänen, E., Holgersson, I., & Ottosson, T. (2012). Development and evaluation of Fingu: A mathematics iPad game using multi-touch interaction. *Paper presented at the Proceedings of the 11th International Conference on Interaction Design and Children*, Bremen, Germany.

Barnett, W. S., & Frede, E. C. (2017). Long-term effects of a system of high-quality universal preschool education in the United States. In H. P. Blossfeld, N. Kulic, J. Skopek, & M. Triventi (Eds.), *Childcare, Early Education and Social Inequality: An International Perspective* (pp. 152–172). Cheltenham, UK: Edward Elgar Publishing.

Barnett, W. S., Frede, E. C., Mobasher, H., & Mohr, P. (1987). The efficacy of public preschool programs and the relationship of program quality to efficacy. *Educational Evaluation and Policy Analysis, 10*(1), 37–49.

Barnett, W. S., Hustedt, J. T., Hawkinson, L. E., & Robin, K. B. (2006). *The state of preschool 2006: State preschool yearbook.* New Brunswick, NJ: National Institute for Early Education Research (NIEER).

Barnett, W. S., Yarosz, D. J., Thomas, J., & Hornbeck, A. (2006). *Educational effectiveness of a Vygotskian approach to preschool education: A randomized trial.* New Brunswick, NJ: National Institute of Early Education Research (NIEER).

Barnes, M. A., Klein, A., Swank, P., Starkey, P., McCandliss, B., Flynn, K., … Roberts, G. (2016). Effects of tutorial interventions in mathematics and attention for low-performing preschool children. *Journal of Research on Educational Effectiveness, 9*(4), 577–606. doi: 10.1080/19345747.2016.1191575

Baroody, A. J. (1986b). Counting ability of moderately and mildly handicapped children. *Education and Training of the Mentally Retarded, 21*(4), 289–300.

Baroody, A. J. (1987a). *Children's mathematical thinking.* New York, NY: Teachers College.

Baroody, A. J. (1987b). The development of counting strategies for single-digit addition. *Journal for Research in Mathematics Education, 18*, 141–157.

Baroody, A. J. (1989). Manipulatives don't come with guarantees. *Arithmetic Teacher, 37*(2), 4–5.

Baroody, A. J. (1990). How and when should place value concepts and skills be taught? *Journal for Research in Mathematics Education, 21*, 281–286.

Baroody, A. J. (1996). An investigative approach to the mathematics instruction of children classified as learning disabled. In D. K. Reid, W. P. Hresko, & H. L. Swanson (Eds.), *Cognitive approaches to learning disabilities* (3rd ed., pp. 547–615). Austin, TX: Pro-Ed.

Baroody, A. J. (1999). The development of basic counting, number, and arithmetic knowledge among children classified as mentally handicapped. In L. M. Glidden (Ed.), *International review of research in mental retardation* (Vol. 22, pp. 51–103). New York, NY: Academic Press.

Baroody, A. J. (2003). The development of adaptive expertise and flexibility: The integration of conceptual and procedural knowledge. In A. J. Baroody & A. Dowker (Eds.), *The development of arithmetic concepts and skills: Constructing adaptive expertise* (pp. 1–33). Mahwah, NJ: Lawrence Erlbaum Associates.

Baroody, A. J. (2004a). The developmental bases for early childhood number and operations standards. In D. H. Clements, J. Sarama, & A.-M. DiBiase (Eds.), *Engaging young children in mathematics: Standards for early childhood mathematics education* (pp. 173–219). Mahwah, NJ: Lawrence Erlbaum Associates.

Baroody, A. J. (2004b). The role of psychological research in the development of early childhood mathematics standards. In D. H. Clements, J. Sarama, & A.-M. DiBiase (Eds.), *Engaging young children in mathematics: Standards for early childhood mathematics education* (pp. 149–172). Mahwah, NJ: Lawrence Erlbaum Associates.

Baroody, A. J. (2016). Curricular approaches to introducing subtraction and fostering fluency with basic differences in grade 1. In R. Bracho (Ed.), *The development of number sense: From theory to practice. Monograph of the Journal of Pensamiento Numérico y Algebraico (Numerical and Algebraic Thought)* (Vol. 10, pp. 161–191). University of Granada.

Baroody, A. J., Bajwa, N. P., & Eiland, M. (2009). Why can't Johnny remember the basic facts? *Developmental Disabilities, 15*(1), 69–79.

Baroody, A. J., & Benson, A. P. (2001). Early number instruction. *Teaching Children Mathematics, 8*(3), 154–158.

Baroody, A. J., & Dowker, A. (2003). *The development of arithmetic concepts and skills: Constructing adaptive expertise*. Mahwah, NJ: Erlbaum.

Baroody, A. J., Eiland, M., Su, Y., & Thompson, B. (2007). Fostering at-risk preschoolers' number sense. *Paper presented at the American Educational Research Association*.

Baroody, A. J., Eiland, M. D., Purpura, D. J., & Reid, E. E. (2012). Fostering at-risk kindergarten children's number sense. *Cognition and Instruction, 30*(4), 435–470. doi: 10.1080/07370008. 2012.720152

Baroody, A. J., Eiland, M. D., Purpura, D. J., & Reid, E. E. (2013). Can computer-assisted discovery learning foster first graders' fluency with the most basic addition combinations? *American Educational Research Journal, 50*(3), 533–573. doi: 10.3102/0002831212473349

Baroody, A. J., Lai, M.-L., & Mix, K. S. (2005, December). Changing views of young children's numerical and arithmetic competencies. *Paper presented at the National Association for the Education of Young Children*, Washington, DC.

Baroody, A. J., Lai, M.-L., & Mix, K. S. (2006). The development of young children's number and operation sense and its implications for early childhood education. In B. Spodek & O. N. Saracho (Eds.), *Handbook of research on the education of young children* (pp. 187–221). Mahwah, NJ: Lawrence Erlbaum Associates.

Baroody, A. J., Li, X., & Lai, M.-L. (2008). Toddlers' spontaneous attention to number. *Mathematical Thinking and Learning, 10*(3), 240–270.

Baroody, A. J., & Purpura, D. J. (2017). Number and operations. In J. Cai (Ed.), *Handbook for research in mathematics education* (pp. 308–354). Reston, VA: National Council of Teachers of Mathematics (NCTM)

Baroody, A. J., Purpura, D. J., Eiland, M. D., & Reid, E. E. (2015). The impact of highly and minimally guided discovery instruction on promoting the learning of reasoning strategies for basic add-1 and doubles combinations. *Early Childhood Research Quarterly, 30, Part A*(0), 93–105. doi: 10.1016/j.ecresq. 2014.09.003

Baroody, A. J., Purpura, D. J., Eiland, M. D., Reid, E. E., & Paliwal, V. (2016). Does fostering reasoning strategies for relatively difficult basic combinations promote transfer by K-3 students? *Journal of Educational Psychology, 108*(4), 576–591.

Baroody, A. J., & Rosu, L. (2004, April). Adaptive expertise with basic addition and subtraction combinations—The number sense view. *Paper presented at the American Educational Research Association*, San Francisco, CA.

Baroody, A. J., & Tiilikainen, S. H. (2003). Two perspectives on addition development. In A. J. Baroody & A. Dowker (Eds.), *The development of arithmetic concepts and skills: Constructing adaptive expertise* (pp. 75–125). Mahwah, NJ: Lawrence Erlbaum Associates.

Barrett, J. E., Clements, D. H., & Sarama, J. (2017). Children's measurement: A longitudinal study of children's knowledge and learning of length, area, and volume. In B. Herbel-Eisenmann (Ed.), *Journal for Research in Mathematics Education* (Vol. 16). Reston, VA: National Council of Teachers of Mathematics.

Bartsch, K., & Wellman, H. M. (1988). Young children's conception of distance. *Developmental Psychology, 24*(4), 532–541.

Bassok, D., Latham, S., & Rorem, A. (2016). Is kindergarten the new first grade? How early elementary school is changing in the age of accountability. *AERA Open, 1*(4), 1–31. doi: 10.1177/2332858 415616358

Batchelor, S., & Gilmore, C. (2015). Magnitude representations and counting skills in preschool children. *Mathematical Thinking and Learning, 17*(2-3), 116–135. doi: 10.1080/10986065.2015. 1016811

Battista, M. T. (1990). Spatial visualization and gender differences in high school geometry. *Journal for Research in Mathematics Education, 21*(1), 47–60.

Beilin, H. (1984). Cognitive theory and mathematical cognition: Geometry and space. In B. Gholson & T. L. Rosenthal (Eds.), *Applications of cognitive-developmental theory* (pp. 49–93). New York, NY: Academic Press.

Beilock, S. L., Gunderson, E. A., Ramirez, G., & Levine, S. C. (2010). Female teachers' math anxiety affects girls math achievement. *Proceedings of the National Academy of Sciences, 107*(5), 1860–1863.

Benigno, J. P., & Ellis, S. (2004). Two is greater than three: Effects of older siblings on parental support of preschoolers' counting in middle-income families. *Early Childhood Research Quarterly, 19*(1), 4-20.

Bennett, N., Desforges, C., Cockburn, A., & Wilkinson, B. (1984). *The quality of pupil learning experiences.* Hillsdale, NJ: Lawrence Erlbaum Associates.

Berch, D. B., & Mazzocco, M. M. M. (Eds.). (2007). *Why is math so hard for some children? The nature and origins of mathematical learning difficulties and disabilities.* Baltimore, MD: Paul H. Brooks.

Bereiter, C. (1986). Does direct instruction cause delinquency? Response to Schweinhart and Weikart. *Educational Leadership, 44*(3), 20-21.

Bergin, D. A., Ford, M. E., & Mayer-Gaub, G. (1986). *Social and motivational consequences of microcomputer use in kindergarten.* San Francisco, CA: American Educational Research Association.

Bierman, K. L., Welsh, J., Heinrichs, B. S., & Nix, R. L. (2018). Effect of preschool home visiting on school readiness and need for services in elementary school: A randomized clinical trial. *JAMA Pediatrics*, e181029. doi: 10.1001/jamapediatrics.2018.1029

Binder, S. L., & Ledger, B. (1985). *Preschool computer project report.* Oakville, Ontario, Canada: Sheridan College.

Bishop, A. J. (1980). Spatial abilities and mathematics education–A review. *Educational Studies in Mathematics, 11*(3), 257-269.

Bishop, A. J. (1983). Space and geometry. In R. A. Lesh & M. S. Landau (Eds.), *Acquisition of mathematics concepts and processes* (pp. 7-44). New York, NY: Academic Press.

Bishop, A. J., & Forgasz, H. J. (2007). Issues in access and equity in mathematics education. In F. K. Lester, Jr. (Ed.), *Second handbook of research on mathematics teaching and learning* (pp. 1145-1167). New York, NY: Information Age Publishing.

Björklund, C. (2012). What counts when working with mathematics in a toddler-group? *Early Years, 32*(2), 215-228. doi: 10.1080/09575146.2011.652940

Björklund, C. (2014). Less is more-mathematical manipulatives in early childhood education. *Early Child Development and Care, 184*(3), 469-485.

Björklund, C. (2015). Pre-primary school teachers' approaches to mathematics education in Finland. *Journal of Early Childhood Education Research, 4*(2), 69-92.

Björklund, C., & Barendregt, W. (2016). Teachers' pedagogical mathematical awareness in diverse child-age-groups. *Nordic Studies in Mathematics Education, 21*(4), 115-133.

Björklund, C. (2018). Powerful frameworks for conceptual understanding. In V. Kinnear, M. Y. Lai, & T. Muir (Eds.), *Forging connections in early mathematics teaching and learning.* Gateway East, Singapore: Springer.

Black, P., & Wiliam, D. (1998). Assessment and classroom learning. *Assessment in Education: Principles, Policy & Practice, 5*(1), 7-76.

Blair, C., & Razza, R. P. (2007). Relating effortful control, executive function, and false belief understanding to emerging math and literacy ability in kindergarten. *Child Development, 78*(2), 647-663.

Blanton, M., Brizuela, B. M., Gardiner, A. M., Sawrey, K., & Newman-Owens, A. (2015). A learning trajectory in 6-year-olds' thinking about generalizing functional relationships. *Journal for Research in Mathematics Education, 46*, 511-558. doi: 10.5951/jresematheduc.46.5.0511

Blanton, M., Brizuela, B. M., Gardiner, A. M., Sawrey, K., & Newman-Owens, A. (2017). A progression in first-grade children's thinking about variable and variable notation in functional relationships. *Educational Studies in Mathematics, 95*(2), 181-202. doi: 10.1007/s10649-016-9745-0

Blanton, M. L., & Kaput, J. J. (2011). Functional thinking as a route into algebra in the elementary grades. In J. Cai & E. J. Knuth (Eds.), *Early algebraization: A global dialogue from multiple perspectives* (pp. 5-23). New York, NY: Springer.

Blanton, M. L., Stephens, A. C., Knuth, E. J., Gardiner, A. M., Isler, I., Marum, T. et al. (2012). *The development of children's algebraic thinking using a learning progressions approach.* Paper presented at the Research Presession of the 2012 Annual Meeting of the National Council of Teachers of Mathematics, Philadelphia, PA.

Blevins-Knabe, B., Berghout Austin, A., Musun-Miller, L., Eddy, A., & Jones, R. M. (2000). Family home care providers' and parents' beliefs and practices concerning mathematics with young children. *Early Child Development and Care, 165*(1), 41-58. doi: 10.1080/0300443001650104

Blevins-Knabe, B., & Musun-Miller, L. (1996). Number use at home by children and their parents and its relationship to early mathematical performance. *Early Development and Parenting, 5*(1), 35-45.

Blevins-Knabe, B., Whiteside-Mansell, L., & Selig, J. (2007). Parenting and mathematical development. *Academic Exchange Quarterly, 11*, 76-80.

Bley, N. S., & Thornton, C. A. (1981). *Teaching mathematics to the learning disabled.* Rockville, MD: Aspen Systems Corporation.

Blöte, A. W., Van der Burg, E., & Klein, A. S. (2001). Students' flexibility in solving two-digit addition and subtraction problems: Instruction effects. *Journal of Educational Psychology, 93* (3), 627-638.

Boaler, J. (2014). Research suggests that timed tests cause math anxiety. *Teaching Children Mathematics, 20*(8), 469-474.

Bock, A., Cartwright, K. B., Gonzalez, C., O'Brien, S., Robinson, M. F., Schmerold, K., ... Pasnak, R. (2015). The role of cognitive flexibility in pattern understanding. *Journal of Education and Human Development, 4*(1). doi: 10.15640/jehd. v4n1a3

Bodovski, K., & Farkas, G. (2007). Mathematics growth in early elementary school: The roles of beginning knowledge, student engagement, and instruction. *The Elementary School Journal, 108* (2), 115-130.

Bodovski, K., Nahum-Shani, I., & Walsh, R. (2013). School climate and students' early mathematics learning: Another search for contextual effects. *American Journal of Education, 119*(2), 209-234. doi: 10.1086/667227

Bodovski, K., & Youn, M.-J. (2011). The long term effects of early acquired skills and behaviors on young children's achievement in literacy and mathematics. *Journal of Early Childhood Research, 9*(1), 4-19.

Bodovski, K., & Youn, M.-J. (2012). Students' mathematics learning from kindergarten through 8th grade: The long-term influence of school readiness. *International Journal of Sociology of Education, 1*(2), 97-122. doi: 10.4471/rise.2012.07

Bodrova, E., & Leong, D. J. (2001). *The tools of the mind: A case study of implementing the Vygotskian approach in American early childhood and primary classrooms.* Geneva, Switzerland: International Bureau of Education.

Bodrova, E., & Leong, D. J. (2006). Self-regulation as a key to school readiness: How can early childhood teachers promote this critical competency? In M. Zaslow & I. Martinez-Beck (Eds.), *Critical issues in early childhood professional development* (pp. 203-224). Baltimore, MD: Brookes Publishing.

Bodrova, E., Leong, D. J., Norford, J. S., & Paynter, D. E. (2003). It only looks like child's play. *Journal of Staff Development, 24*(2), 47-51.

Bofferding, L., & Alexander, A. (2011). Nothing is something: First graders' use of zero in relation to negative numbers. *Paper presented at the American Educational Research Association,* New Orleans, LA.

Bojorquea, G., Torbeyns, J., Van Hoof, J., Van Nijlen, D., & Verschaffel, L. (2018). Effectiveness of the Building Blocks program for enhancing Ecuadorian kindergartners' numerical competencies. *Early Childhood Research Quarterly, 44*(3), 231-241. doi: 10.1016/j.ecresq.2017.12.009

Bonny, J. W., & Lourenco, S. F. (2013). The approximate number system and its relation to early math achievement: Evidence from the preschool years. *Journal of Experimental Child Psychology, 114*(3), 375-388. doi: 10.1016/j.jecp.2012.09.015

Bower, C., Zimmermann, L., Verdine, B. N., Toub, T. S., Islam, S. S., Foster, L., ... Hirsh-Pasek, K. (2020). Piecing together the role of a spatial assembly intervention in preschoolers' spatial and mathematics learning: Influences of gesture, spatial language, and socioeconomic status. *Developmental Psychology, 56*(4), 686-698. doi: 10.1037/dev0000899

Bowman, B. T., Donovan, M. S., & Burns, M. S. (Eds.). (2001). *Eager to learn: Educating our preschoolers.* Washington, DC: National Academy Press.

Brendefur, J. L., Strother, S., & Rich, K. (2018). Building place value understanding through modeling and structure. *Journal of Mathematics Education, 11*(1), 31-45. doi: 10.26711/00757715 2790017

Broberg, A. G., Wessels, H., Lamb, M. E., & Hwang, C. P. (1997). Effects of day care on the development of cognitive abilities in 8-year-olds: A longitudinal study. *Developmental Psychology, 33*(1), 62-69.

Brooks-Gunn, J. (2003). Do you believe in magic? What we can expect from early childhood intervention programs. *Social Policy Report, 17*(1), 1, 3-14.

Brooks-Gunn, J., Duncan, G. J., & Britto, P. R. (1999). Are socioeconomic gradients for children similar to those for adults? In D. P. Keating & C. Hertzman (Eds.), *Developmental health and the wealth of nations* (pp. 94-124). New York, NY: Guilford Press.

Brosnan, M. J. (1998). Spatial ability in children's play with LEGO blocks. *Perceptual and Motor Skills, 87*(1), 19-28. doi: 10.2466/pms.1998. 87.1.19

Brown, S. I., & Walter, M. I. (1990). *The art of problem posing.* Mahwah, NJ: Lawrence Erlbaum Associates.

Brownell, W. A., & Moser, H. E. (1949). *Meaningful vs. mechanical learning: A study in grade III subtraction.* Durham, NC: Duke University Press.

Bruce, C. D., Flynn, T. C., & Bennett, S. (2015). A focus on exploratory tasks in lesson study: The Canadian 'Math for Young Children' project. *ZDM Mathematics Education.* doi: 10.1007/ s11858-015-0747-7

Brulles, D., Peters, S. J., & Saunders, R. (2012). Schoolwide mathematics achievement within the gifted cluster grouping model. *Journal of Advanced Academics*, *23*(3), 200-216. doi: 10.1177/1932202x12451439

Bryant, P. E. (1997). Mathematical understanding in the nursery school years. In T. Nunes & P. Bryant (Eds.), *Learning and teaching mathematics: An international perspective* (pp. 53-67). East Sussex, England: Psychology Press.

Burchinal, M. R., Field, S., López, M. L., Howes, C., & Pianta, R. (2012). Instruction in Spanish in pre-kindergarten classrooms and child outcomes for English language learners. *Early Childhood Research Quarterly*, *27*(2), 188-197. doi: 10.1016/j. ecresq.2011.11.003

Burchinal, M. R., Zaslow, M., & Tarullo, L. (2016). *Quality thresholds, features, and dosage in early care and education: Secondary data analyses of child outcomes*. Monographs of the Society for Research in Child Development.

Burchinal, M. R., Peisner-Feinberg, E., Pianta, R., & Howes, C. (2002). Development of academic skills from preschool through second grade: Family and classroom predictors of developmental trajectories. *Developmental Psychology*, *40*(5), 415-436.

Burden, M. J., Jacobson, S. W., Dodge, N. C., Dehaene, S., & Jacobson, J. L. (2007). Effects of prenatal alcohol and cocaine exposure on arithmetic and "number sense." *Paper presented at the Society for Research in Child Development*.

Burger, W. F., & Shaughnessy, J. M. (1986). Characterizing the van Hiele levels of development in geometry. *Journal for Research in Mathematics Education*, *17*(1), 31-48.

Burgoyne, K., Witteveen, K., Tolan, A., Malone, S., & Hulme, C. (2017). Pattern understanding: Relationships with arithmetic and reading development. *Child Development Perspectives*. doi: 10.1111/ cdep.12240

Burns, M. K., Kanive, R., & DeGrande, M. (2012). Effect of a computer-delivered math fact intervention as a supplemental intervention for math in third and fourth grades. *Remedial and Special Education*, *33*(3), 184-191. doi: 10.1177/07419325 10381652

Burny, E. (2012). Towards an understanding of children's difficulties with conventional time systems. In *Time-related competences in primary education* (Chapter 2), doctoral dissertation. Belgium: Ghent University.

Burny, E., Valcke, M., & Desoete, A. (2009). Towards an agenda for studying learning and instruction focusing on time-related competences in children. *Educational Studies*, *35*(5), 481-492. doi: 10.1080/ 03055690902879093

Burny, E., Valcke, M., & Desoete, A. (2012). Clock reading: An underestimated topic in children with mathematics difficulties. *Journal of Learning Disabilities*, *45*(4), 351-360. doi: 10.1177/00222194 11407773

Burny, E., Valcke, M., Desoete, A., & Van Luit, J. E. H. (2013). Curriculum sequencing and the acquisition of clock-reading skills among Chinese and Flemish children. *International Journal of Science and Mathematics Education*, *11*, 761-785.

Butterworth, B. (2010). Foundational numerical capacities and the origins of dyscalculia. *Trends in Cognitive Sciences*, *14*, 534-541.

Callahan, L. G., & Clements, D. H. (1984). Sex differences in rote counting ability on entry to first grade: Some observations. *Journal for Research in Mathematics Education*, *15*, 378-382.

Campbell, F. A., Pungello, E. P., Miller-Johnson, S., Burchinal, M., & Ramey, C. T. (2001). The development of cognitive and academic abilities: Growth curves from an early childhood educational experiment. *Developmental Psychology*, *37*, 231-242.

Campbell, P. F., & Silver, E. A. (1999). *Teaching and learning mathematics in poor communities*. Reston, VA: National Council of Teachers of Mathematics.

Cannon, J., Fernandez, C., & Ginsburg, H. P. (2005, April). Parents' preference for supporting preschoolers' language over mathematics learning: A difference that runs deep. *Paper presented at the Biennial Meeting of the Society for Research in Child Development*, Atlanta, GA.

Canobi, K. H., Reeve, R. A., & Pattison, P. E. (1998). The role of conceptual understanding in children's addition problem solving. *Developmental Psychology*, *34*, 882-891.

Capraro, K. (2017). "Making change" in second grade: Exploring money through project-based learning. *YC Young Children*, *72*(3), 30-36.

Carey, S. (2004). Bootstrapping and the origin of concepts. *Daedulus*, *133*(1), 59-68.

Carpenter, T. P., Ansell, E., Franke, M. L., Fennema, E. H., & Weisbeck, L. (1993). Models of problem solving: A study of kindergarten children's problem-solving processes. *Journal for Research in Mathematics Education*, *24*, 428-441.

Carpenter, T. P., Coburn, T., Reys, R. E., & Wilson, J. (1976). Notes from National Assessment: Recognizing and naming solids. *Arithmetic Teacher*, *23*, 62-66.

Carpenter, T. P., Fennema, E. H., Franke, M. L., Levi, L., & Empson, S. B. (1999). *Children's mathematics: Cognitively guided instruction*. Portsmouth, NH: Heinemann.

Carpenter, T. P., Fennema, E. H., Franke, M. L., Levi, L., & Empson, S. B. (2014). *Children's mathematics: Cognitively guided instruction* (2nd ed.). Portsmouth, NH: Heinemann.

Carpenter, T. P., Franke, M. L., Jacobs, V. R., Fennema, E. H., & Empson, S. B. (1998). A longitudinal study of invention and understanding in children's multidigit addition and subtraction. *Journal for Research in Mathematics Education, 29*, 3-20.

Carpenter, T. P., Franke, M. L., & Levi, L. (2003). *Thinking mathematically: Integrating arithmetic and algebra in elementary school.* Portsmouth, NH: Heinemann.

Carpenter, T. P., & Levi, L. (1999). *Developing conceptions of algebraic reasoning in the primary grades.* Montreal, Canada: American Educational Research Association.

Carpenter, T. P., & Moser, J. M. (1982). The development of addition and subtraction problem solving skills. In T. P. Carpenter, J. M. Moser, & T. A. Romberg (Eds.), Addition and subtraction: A cognitive perspective (pp. 9-24). Erlbaum.

Carpenter, T. P., & Moser, J. M. (1984). The acquisition of addition and subtraction concepts in grades one through three. *Journal for Research in Mathematics Education, 15*, 179-202.

Carper, D. V. (1942). Seeing numbers as groups in primary-grade arithmetic. *The Elementary School Journal, 43*, 166-170.

Carr, M., & Alexeev, N. (2011). Fluency, accuracy, and gender predict developmental trajectories of arithmetic strategies. *Journal of Educational Psychology, 103*(3), 617-631.

Carr, M., & Davis, H. (2001). Gender differences in arithmetic strategy use: A function of skill and preference. *Contemporary Educational Psychology, 26*, 330-347.

Carr, M., Shing, Y. L., Janes, P., & Steiner, H. H. (2007). Early gender differences in strategy use and fluency: Implications for the emergence of gender differences in mathematics. *Paper presented at the Society for Research in Child Development.*

Carr, M., Steiner, H. H., Kyser, B., & Biddlecomb, B. (2008). A comparison of predictors of early emerging gender differences in mathematics competence. *Learning and Individual Differences, 18*, 61-75.

Carr, M., Taasoobshirazi, G., Stroud, R., & Royer, M. (2011). Combined fluency and cognitive strategies instruction improves mathematics achievement in early elementary school. *Contemporary Educational Psychology, 36*, 323-333.

Carr, M., Alexeev, N., Wang, L., Barned, N., Horan, E., & Reed, A. (2018). The development of spatial skills in elementary school students. *Child Development, 89*(2), 446-460. doi: 10.1111/cdev.12753

Carr, R. C., Mokrova, I. L., Vernon-Feagans, L., & Burchinal, M. R. (2019). Cumulative classroom quality during pre-kindergarten and kindergarten and children's language, literacy, and mathematics skills. *Early Childhood Research Quarterly, 47*, 218-228.

Cargnelutti, E., & Passolunghi, M. C. (2017). Cognitive and affective factors in second-grade children with math difficulties. *Perspectives on Language and Literacy, 43*(1), 41.

Cargnelutti, E., Tomasetto, C., & Passolunghi, M. C. (2017). The interplay between affective and cognitive factors in shaping early proficiency in mathematics. *Trends in Neuroscience and Education, 8-9*, 2836. doi: 10.1016/j.tine.2017.10.002

Cascales-Martínez, A., Martínez-Segura, M.-J., Pérez-López, D., & Contero, M. (2017). Using an augmented reality enhanced tabletop system to promote learning of mathematics: A case study with students with special educational needs. *EURASIA Journal of Mathematics, Science & Technology Education, 13*(2), 355-380.

Casey, B. M., Paugh, P., & Ballard, N. (2002). *Sneeze builds a castle.* Bothell, WA: The Wright Group/McGraw-Hill.

Casey, B., Andrews, N., Schindler, H., Kersh, J. E., Samper, A., & Copley, J. (2008a). The development of spatial skills through interventions involving block building activities. *Cognition and Instruction, 26*(3), 1-41.

Casey, B., Erkut, S., Ceder, I., & Young, J. M. (2008). Use of a storytelling context to improve girls' and boys' geometry skills in kindergarten. *Journal of Applied Developmental Psychology, 29*(1), 29-48.

Casey, B., Nuttall, R. L., & Pezaris, E. (1997). Mediators of gender differences in mathematics college entrance test scores: A comparison of spatial skills with internalized beliefs and anxieties. *Developmental Psychology, 33*(4), 669-680.

Casey, B., Nuttall, R. L., & Pezaris, E. (2001). Spatial-mechanical reasoning skills versus mathematics self-confidence as mediators of gender differences on mathematics subtests using cross-national gender-based items. *Journal for Research in Mathematics Education, 32*(1), 28-57.

Casey, B. M., Andrews, N., Schindler, H., Kersh, J. E., Samper, A., & Copley, J. V. (2008b). The development of spatial skills through interventions involving block building activities. *Cognition and Instruction, 26*, 1-41.

Catsambis, S., & Buttaro, A., Jr. (2012). Revisiting "Kindergarten as academic boot camp": A nationwide study of ability grouping and psycho-social development. *Social Psychology of Education, 15*(4), 483–515. doi: 10.1007/s11218-012-9196-0

CCSSO/NGA. (2010). *Common core state standards for mathematics.* Washington, DC: Council of Chief State School Officers and the National Governors Association Center for Best Practices.

Celedón-Pattichis, S., Musanti, S. I., & Marshall, M. E. (2010). Bilingual elementary teachers' reflections on using students' native language and culture to teach mathematics. In M. Q. Foote (Ed.), *Mathematics teaching & learning in K-12: Equity and professional development* (pp. 7–24). New York, NY: Palgrave Macmillan.

Cepeda, N. J., Pashler, H., Vul, E., Wixted, J. T., & Rohrer, D. (2006). Distributed practice in verbal recall tasks: A review and quantitative synthesis. *Psychological Bulletin, 132,* 354–380.

Chalufour, I., Hoisington, C., Moriarty, R., Winokur, J., & Worth, K. (2004). The science and mathematics of building structures. *Science and Children, 41*(4), 30–34.

Chandler, A., McLaughlin, T. F., Neyman, J., & Rinaldi, L. (2012). The differential effects of direct instruction flashcards with and without a shorter math racetrack to teach numeral identification to preschoolers: A failure to replicate. *Academic Research International, 2*(3), 308–313.

Chang, A., Sandhofer, C. M., & Brown, C. S. (2011). Gender biases in early number exposure to preschool-aged children. *Journal of Language and Social Psychology, 30*(4), 440–450.

Chang, A., Zmich, K. M., Athanasopoulou, A., Hou, L., Golinkoff, R. M., & Hirsh-Pasek, K. (2011). Manipulating geometric forms in two-dimensional space: Effects of socio-economic status on preschoolers' geometric-spatial ability. *Paper presented at the Society for Research in Child Development*, Montreal, Canada.

Char, C. A. (1989). *Computer graphic feltboards: New software approaches for young children's mathematical exploration.* San Francisco, CA: American Educational Research Association.

Chard, D. J., Clarke, B., Baker, S., Otterstedt, J., Braun, D., & Katz, R. (2005). Using measures of number sense to screen for difficulties in mathematics: Preliminary findings. *Assessment for Effective Intervention, 30*(2), 3–14.

Chen, C., & Uttal, D. H. (1988). Cultural values, parents' beliefs, and children's achievement in the United States and China. *Human Development, 31,* 351–358.

Cheng, Y.-L., & Mix, K. S. (2012). Spatial training improves children's mathematics ability. *Journal of Cognition and Development, 15*(1), 2–11. doi: 10.1080/15248372.2012.725186

Cheung, C., Leung, A., & McBride-Chang, C. (2007). Gender differences in mathematics self concept in Hong Kong children: A function of perceived maternal academic support. *Paper presented at the Society for Research in Child Development.*

Cheung, A. C. K., & Slavin, R. E. (2013). The effectiveness of educational technology applications for enhancing mathematics achievement in K-12 classrooms: A meta-analysis. *Educational Research Review, 9*(1), 88–113. doi: 10.1016/j.edurev.2013.01.001

Cheung, C., & McBride-Chang, C. (2008). Relations of perceived maternal parenting style, practices, and learning motivation to academic competence in Chinese children. *Merrill-Palmer Quarterly, 54*(1), 1–22.

Chien, N. C., Howes, C., Burchinal, M. R., Pianta, R. C., Ritchie, S., Bryant, D. M., Clifford, R. M. … Barbarin, O. A. (2010). Children's classroom engagement and school readiness gains in prekindergarten. *Child Development, 81*(5), 1534–1549. doi: 10.1111/j.1467-8624.2010.01490.x

Chmiliar, L. (2017). Improving learning outcomes: The iPad and preschool children with disabilities. *Frontiers in Psychology, 8,* 1–11. doi: 10.3389/fpsyg.2017.00660

Choi, J. Y., Jeon, S., & Lippard, C. (2018). Dual language learning, inhibitory control, and math achievement in Head Start and kindergarten. *Early Childhood Research Quarterly, 42*(Supplement C), 66–78. doi: 10.1016/j.ecresq.2017.09.001

Chorney, S., & Sinclair, N. (2018). Fingers-on geometry: The emergence of symmetry in a primary school classroom with multi-touch dynamic geometry. In N. Calder, K. Larkin, & N. Sinclair (Eds.), *Using mobile technologies in the teaching and learning of mathematics* (pp. 213–230). Cham, Switzerland: Springer.

Christiansen, K., Austin, A., & Roggman, L. (2005, April). Math interactions in the context of play: Relations to child math ability. *Paper presented at the Biennial Meeting of the Society for Research in Child Development*, Atlanta, GA.

Ciancio, D. S., Rojas, A. C., McMahon, K., & Pasnak, R. (2001). Teaching oddity and insertion to Head Start children: An economical cognitive intervention. *Journal of Applied Developmental Psychology, 22,* 603–621.

Cicconi, M. (2014). Vygotsky meets technology: A reinvention of collaboration in the early childhood mathematics classroom. *Early Childhood Education Journal, 42*(1), 57–65. doi: 10.1007/s10643-013-0582-9

Cirino, P. T. (2010). The interrelationships of mathematical precursors in kindergarten. *Journal of Experimental Child Psychology, 108*(4). doi: 10.1016/j.jecp.2010.11.004

Clarke, B., Doabler, C. T., Kosty, D., Nelson, E. K., Smolkowski, K., Fien, H., & Turtura, J. (2017). Testing the efficacy of a kindergarten mathematics intervention by small group size. *AERA Open*, *3*(2), 1-16. doi: 10.1177/2332858417706899

Clarke, B., & Shinn, M. R. (2004). A preliminary investigation into the identification and development of early mathematics curriculum-based measurement. *School Psychology Review*, *33*(2), 234-248.

Clarke, B., Smolkowski, K., Baker, S., Fien, H., Doabler, C. T., & Chard, D. (2011). The impact of a comprehensive Tier I core kindergarten program on the achievement of students at risk in mathematics. *Elementary School Journal*, *111*(4), 561-584.

Clarke, B. A., Clarke, D. M., & Horne, M. (2006). A longitudinal study of children's mental computation strategies. In J. Novotná, H. Moraová, M. Krátká, & N. Stehlíková (Eds.), *Proceedings of the 30th Conference of the International Group for the Psychology in Mathematics Education* (Vol. 2, pp. 329-336). Prague, Czech Republic: Charles University.

Clarke, D. M., Cheeseman, J., Gervasoni, A., Gronn, D., Horne, M., McDonough, A., Montgomery, P. ... Rowley, G. (2002). *Early numeracy research project: Final report*. Melbourne, Victoria, Australia: Department of Education, Employment and Training, the Catholic Education Office, and the Association of Independent Schools.

Clements, D. H. (1984). Training effects on the development and generalization of Piagetian logical operations and knowledge of number. *Journal of Educational Psychology*, *76*, 766-776.

Clements, D. H. (1986). Effects of Logo and CAI environments on cognition and creativity. *Journal of Educational Psychology*, *78*, 309-318.

Clements, D. H. (1989). *Computers in elementary mathematics education*. Englewood Cliffs, NJ: Prentice-Hall.

Clements, D. H. (1991). Current technology and the early childhood curriculum. In B. Spodek & O. N. Saracho (Eds.), *Yearbook in early childhood education, Volume 2: Issues in early childhood curriculum* (pp. 106-131). New York, NY: Teachers College Press.

Clements, D. H. (1994). The uniqueness of the computer as a learning tool: Insights from research and practice. In J. L. Wright & D. D. Shade (Eds.), *Young children: Active learners in a technological age* (pp. 31-50). Washington, DC: National Association for the Education of Young Children.

Clements, D. H. (1995). Teaching creativity with computers. *Educational Psychology Review*, *7*(2), 141-161.

Clements, D. H. (1999a). "Concrete" manipulatives, concrete ideas. *Contemporary Issues in Early Childhood*, *1*(1), 45-60.

Clements, D. H. (1999b). Subitizing: What is it? Why teach it? *Teaching Children Mathematics*, *5*, 400-405.

Clements, D. H. (1999c). Teaching length measurement: Research challenges. *School Science and Mathematics*, *99*(1), 5-11.

Clements, D. H. (2000). Translating lessons from research into mathematics classrooms: Mathematics and special needs students. *Perspectives*, *26*(3), 31-33.

Clements, D. H. (2001). Mathematics in the preschool. *Teaching Children Mathematics*, *7*, 270-275.

Clements, D. H., & Conference Working Group. (2004). Part one: Major themes and recommendations. In D. H. Clements, J. Sarama, & A.-M. DiBiase (Eds.), *Engaging young children in mathematics: Standards for early childhood mathematics education* (pp. 1-72). Mahwah, NJ: Lawrence Erlbaum Associates.

Clements, D. H. (2007). Curriculum research: Toward a framework for "research-based curricula". *Journal for Research in Mathematics Education*, *38*, 35-70.

Clements, D. H., & Sarama, J. (2008). Mathematics and technology: Supporting learning for students and teachers. In O. N. Saracho & B. Spodek (Eds.), *Contemporary perspectives on science and technology in early childhood education* (pp. 127-147). Charlotte, NC: Information Age.

Clements, D. H., Agodini, R., & Harris, B. (2013). Instructional practices and student math achievement: Correlations from a study of math curricula. Retrieved from NCEE (National Center for Education Evaluation and Regional Assistance) website: http://ies.ed.gov/ncee/pubs/20134020/

Clements, D. H., & Sarama, J. (2014, March 3, 2014). Play, mathematics, and false dichotomies [Blog post]. Preschool matters...today! (New Brunswick NJ: National Institute for Early Education Research (NIEER) at Rutgers University). Retrieved from http://preschoolmatters.org/2014/03/03/play-mathematics-and-false-dichotomies/

Clements, D. H., Sarama, J., Wolfe, C. B., & Spitler, M. E. (2015). Sustainability of a scale-up intervention in early mathematics: Longitudinal evaluation of implementation fidelity. *Early Education and Development*, *26*(3), 427-449. doi: 10.1080/10409289.2015.968242

Clements, D. H., Sarama, J., & Germeroth, C. (2016). Learning executive function and early mathematics: Directions of causal relations. *Early Childhood Research Quarterly*, *36*(3), 79-90. doi: 10.1016/j.ecresq.2015.12.009

Clements, D. H., & Sarama, J. (2017). Valid issues but limited scope: A response to Kitchen and Berk's research commentary on educational technology. *Journal for Research in Mathematics Education*, *48*(5), 474–482.

Clements, D. H., & Sarama, J. (2007/2018). *Building Blocks Software [Computer software]*. Columbus, OH: McGraw-Hill Education.

Clements, D. H., & Sarama, J. (2019). Executive function and early mathematical learning difficulties. In A. Fritz, V. G. Haase & P. Räsänen (Eds.), *International handbook of mathematical learning difficulties: From the laboratory to the classroom* (pp. 755–771). Cham, Switzerland: Springer.

Clements, D. H., Sarama, J., Baroody, A. J., Joswick, C., & Wolfe, C. B. (2019). Evaluating the efficacy of a learning trajectory for early shape composition. *American Educational Research Journal*, *56*(6), 2509–2530. doi: 10.3102/0002831219842788

Clements, D. H., Vinh, M., Lim, C.-I., & Sarama, J. (2020). STEM for inclusive excellence and equity. *Early Education and Development*. doi: 10.1080/10409289.2020.1755776

Clements, D. H., & Battista, M. T. (1990). Constructivist learning and teaching. *Arithmetic Teacher*, *38*(1), 34–35.

Clements, D. H., & Battista, M. T., (Artist). (1991). *Logo geometry*. Morristown, NJ: Silver Burdett & Ginn.

Clements, D. H., & Battista, M. T. (1992). Geometry and spatial reasoning. In D. A. Grouws (Ed.), *Handbook of research on mathematics teaching and learning* (pp. 420–464). New York, NY: Macmillan.

Clements, D. H., & Battista, M. T. (2000). Designing effective software. In A. E. Kelly & R. A. Lesh (Eds.), *Handbook of research design in mathematics and science education* (pp. 761–776). Mahwah, NJ: Lawrence Erlbaum Associates.

Clements, D. H., Battista, M. T., & Sarama, J. (1998). Students' development of geometric and measurement ideas. In R. Lehrer & D. Chazan (Eds.), *Designing learning environments for developing understanding of geometry and space* (pp. 201–225). Mahwah, NJ: Lawrence Erlbaum Associates.

Clements, D. H., Battista, M. T., & Sarama, J. (2001). Logo and geometry. *Journal for Research in Mathematics Education Monograph Series*, *10*.

Clements, D. H., Battista, M. T., Sarama, J., & Swaminathan, S. (1997). Development of students' spatial thinking in a unit on geometric motions and area. *The Elementary School Journal*, *98*, 171–186.

Clements, D. H., Battista, M. T., Sarama, J., Swaminathan, S., & McMillen, S. (1997). Students' development of length measurement concepts in a Logo-based unit on geometric paths. *Journal for Research in Mathematics Education*, *28*(1), 70–95.

Clements, D. H., & Callahan, L. G. (1983). Number or prenumber experiences for young children: Must we choose? *The Arithmetic Teacher*, *31*(3), 34–37.

Clements, D. H., & Callahan, L. G. (1986). Cards: A good deal to offer. *The Arithmetic Teacher*, *34*(1), 14–17.

Clements, D. H., Dumas, D., Dong, Y., Banse, H. W., Sarama, J., & Day-Hess, C. A. (2020). Strategy diversity in early mathematics classrooms. *Contemporary Educational Psychology*, *60*. doi: 10.1016/j.cedpsych.2019.101834

Clements, D. H., Fuson, K. C., & Sarama, J. (2017a). The research-based balance in early childhood mathematics: A response to Common Core criticisms. *Early Childhood Research Quarterly*, *40*, 150–162.

Clements, D. H., Fuson, K. C., & Sarama, J. (2017b). What is developmentally appropriate teaching? *Teaching Children Mathematics*, *24*(3), 179–188. doi: 10.5951/teacchilmath.24.3.0178

Clements, D. H., Fuson, K. C., & Sarama, J. (2019). Critiques of the Common Core in early math: A research-based response. *Journal for Research in Mathematics Education*, *50*(1), 11–22. doi: 10.5951/jresematheduc.50.1.0011

Clements, D. H., & Meredith, J. S. (1993). Research on Logo: Effects and efficacy. *Journal of Computing in Childhood Education*, *4*, 263–290.

Clements, D. H., & Meredith, J. S. (1994). *Turtle math [Computer software]*. Montreal, Quebec: Logo Computer Systems, Inc. (LCSI).

Clements, D. H., & Nastasi, B. K. (1985). Effects of computer environments on social-emotional development: Logo and computerassisted instruction. *Computers in the Schools*, *2*(2–3), 11–31.

Clements, D. H., & Nastasi, B. K. (1988). Social and cognitive interactions in educational computer environments. *American Educational Research Journal*, *25*, 87–106.

Clements, D. H., & Nastasi, B. K. (1993). Electronic media and early childhood education. In B. Spodek (Ed.), *Handbook of research on the education of young children* (pp. 251–275). New York, NY: Macmillan.

Clements, D. H., Russell, S. J., Tierney, C., Battista, M. T., & Meredith, J. S. (1995). *Flips, turns, and area*. Cambridge, MA: Dale Seymour Publications.

Clements, D. H., & Sarama, J. (1996). Turtle Math: Redesigning Logo for elementary mathematics. *Learning and Leading with Technology*, *23*(7), 10–15.

Clements, D. H., & Sarama, J. (1997). Research on Logo: A decade of progress. *Computers in the Schools*, *14*(1-2), 9–46.

Clements, D. H., & Sarama, J. (2003a). Strip mining for gold: Research and policy in educational technology—A response to "Fool's Gold". *Educational Technology Review*, 11(1), 7–69.

Clements, D. H., & Sarama, J. (2003c). Young children and technology: What does the research say? *Young Children*, 58(6), 34–40.

Clements, D. H., & Sarama, J. (2004). Building Blocks for early childhood mathematics. *Early Childhood Research Quarterly*, 19, 181–189.

Clements, D. H., & Sarama, J. (2007a). Effects of a preschool mathematics curriculum: Summative research on the *Building Blocks* project. *Journal for Research in Mathematics Education*, 38(2), 136–163. doi: 10.2307/748360

Clements, D. H., & Sarama, J. (2007b). *Building Blocks—SRA Real Math, Teacher's Edition, Grade PreK*. Columbus, OH: SRA/McGraw-Hill.

Clements, D. H., & Sarama, J. (2008). Experimental evaluation of the effects of a research-based preschool mathematics curriculum. *American Educational Research Journal*, 45(2), 443–494. doi: 10.3102/0002831207312908

Clements, D. H., & Sarama, J. (2010). Technology. In V. Washington & J. Andrews (Eds.), *Children of 2020: Creating a better tomorrow* (pp. 119–123). Washington, DC: Council for Professional Recognition/National Association for the Education of Young Children.

Clements, D. H., & Sarama, J. (2011). Early childhood mathematics intervention. *Science*, 333(6045), 968–970. doi: 10.1126/science.1204537

Clements, D. H., & Sarama, J. (2013). *Building Blocks (Volumes 1 and 2)*. Columbus, OH: McGraw-Hill Education.

Clements, D. H., Sarama, J., Baroody, A. J., & Joswick, C. (2020). Efficacy of a learning trajectory approach compared to a teach-to-target approach for addition and subtraction. *ZDM Mathematics Education*. doi: 10.1007/s11858-019-01122-z

Clements, D. H., Sarama, J., Baroody, A. J., Joswick, C., & Wolfe, C. B. (2019). Evaluating the efficacy of a learning trajectory for early shape composition. *American Educational Research Journal*, 56(6), 2509–2530. doi: 10.3102/0002831219842788

Clements, D. H., Sarama, J., Barrett, J. E., Van Dine, D. W., Cullen, C. J., Hudyma, A., ... Eames, C. L. (2018). Evaluation of three interventions teaching area measurement as spatial structuring to young children. *The Journal of Mathematical Behavior*, 50, 23–41. doi: 10.1016/j.jmathb.2017.12.004

Clements, D. H., Sarama, J., & DiBiase, A.-M. (2004). *Engaging young children in mathematics: Standards for early childhood mathematics education*. Mahwah, NJ: Lawrence Erlbaum Associates.

Clements, D. H., Sarama, J., Layzer, C., Unlu, F., & Fesler, L. (2020). Effects on mathematics and executive function of a mathematics and play intervention versus mathematics alone. *Journal for Research in Mathematics Education*, 51(3), 301–333. doi: 10.5951/jresemtheduc-2019-0069

Clements, D. H., Sarama, J., & MacDonald, B. L. (2019). Subitizing: The neglected quantifier. In A. Norton & M. W. Alibali (Eds.), *Constructing number: Merging perspectives from psychology and mathematics education* (pp. 13–45). Gateway East, Singapore: Springer.

Clements, D. H., Sarama, J., Spitler, M. E., Lange, A. A., & Wolfe, C. B. (2011). Mathematics learned by young children in an intervention based on learning trajectories: A large-scale cluster randomized trial. *Journal for Research in Mathematics Education*, 42(2), 127–166. doi: 10.5951/jresematheduc.42.2.0127

Clements, D. H., Sarama, J., Swaminathan, S., Weber, D., & Trawick-Smith, J. (2018). Teaching and learning Geometry: Early foundations. *Quadrante*, 27(2), 7–31.

Clements, D. H., Sarama, J., Wolfe, C. B., & Spitler, M. E. (2013). Longitudinal evaluation of a scale-up model for teaching mathematics with trajectories and technologies: Persistence of effects in the third year. *American Educational Research Journal*, 50(4), 812–850. doi: 10.3102/0002831212469270

Clements, D. H., & Stephan, M. (2004). Measurement in pre-K-2 mathematics. In D. H. Clements, J. Sarama, & A.-M. DiBiase (Eds.), *Engaging young children in mathematics: Standards for early childhood mathematics education* (pp. 299–317). Mahwah, NJ: Lawrence Erlbaum Associates.

Clements, D. H., & Swaminathan, S. (1995). Technology and school change: New lamps for old? *Childhood Education*, 71, 275–281.

Clements, D. H., Swaminathan, S., Hannibal, M. A. Z., & Sarama, J. (1999). Young children's concepts of shape. *Journal for Research in Mathematics Education*, 30, 192–212.

Clements, D. H., Vinh, M., Lim, C.-I., & Sarama, J. (2020). STEM for inclusive excellence and equity. *Early Education and Development*. doi: 10.1080/10409289.2020.1755776

Cobb, P. (1990). A constructivist perspective on information-processing theories of mathematical activity. *International Journal of Educational Research*, 14, 67–92.

Cobb, P. (1995). Cultural tools and mathematical learning: A case study. *Journal for Research in Mathematics Education*, 26, 362–385.

Cobb, P., Wood, T., Yackel, E., Nicholls, J., Wheatley, G., Trigatti, B., Perlwitz, M. (1991). Assessment of a problem-centered second-grade mathematics project. *Journal for Research in Mathematics Education, 22*(1), 3-29.

Cobb, P., Yackel, E., & Wood, T. (1989). Young children's emotional acts during mathematical problem solving. In D. B. McLeod & V. M. Adams (Eds.), *Affect and mathematical problem solving: A new perspective* (pp. 117-148). New York, NY: Springer-Verlag.

Codding, R. S., Hilt-Panahon, A., Panahon, C. J., & Benson, J. L. (2009). Addressing mathematics computation problems: A review of simple and moderate intensity interventions. *Education and Treatment of Children, 32*(2), 279-312.

Cohen, L. E., & Emmons, J. (2017). Block play: Spatial language with preschool and school-age children. *Early Child Development and Care, 187*(5-6), 967-977.

Cohen, L. E., & Uhry, J. (2007). Young children's discourse strategies during block play: A Bakhtinian approach. *Journal of Research in Childhood Education, 21*(3), 302-315.

Colburn, W. (1849). *Colburn's first lessons: Intellectual arithmetic upon the inductive method of instruction.* William J. Reynolds.

Coley, R. J. (2002). *An unequal start: Indicators of inequality in school readiness.* Princeton, NJ: Educational Testing Service.

Collins, M. A., & Laski, E. V. (2015). Preschoolers' strategies for solving visual pattern tasks. *Early Childhood Research Quarterly, 32*, 204-214. doi: 10.1016/j.ecresq.2015.04.004

Confrey, J., Maloney, A. P., Nguyen, K. H., & Rupp, A. A. (2014). Equipartitioning: A foundation for rational number reasoning. Elucidation of a learning trajectory. In A. P. Maloney, J. Confrey, & K. H. Nguyen (Eds.), *Learning over time: Learning trajectories in mathematics education* (pp. 61-96). New York, NY: Information Age Publishing.

Connor, C. M., Mazzocco, M. M. M., Kurz, T., Crowe, E. C., Tighe, E. L., Wood, T. S., & Morrison, F. J. (2018). Using assessment to individualize early mathematics instruction. *Journal of School Psychology, 66*, 97-113. doi: 10.1016/j.jsp.2017.04.005

Crompton, H., Grant, M. R., & Shraim, K. Y. H. (2018). Technologies to enhance and extend children's understanding of geometry: A configurative thematic synthesis of the literature. *Educational Technology & Society, 21*(1), 59-69.

Cook, G. A., Roggman, L. A., & Boyce, L. K. (2012). Fathers' and mothers' cognitive stimulation in early play with toddlers: Predictors of 5th grade reading and math. *Family Science, 2*, 131-145.

Cooper, R. G., Jr. (1984). Early number development: Discovering number space with addition and subtraction. In C. Sophian (Ed.), *Origins of cognitive skills* (pp. 157-192). Mahwah, NJ: Lawrence Erlbaum Associates.

Cordes, C., & Miller, E. (2000). *Fool's gold: A critical look at computers in childhood.* Retrieved November 7, 2000, from www.allianceforchildhood.net/projects/computers/computers_reports.htm

Correa, J., Nunes, T., & Bryant, P. (1998). Young children's understanding of division: The relationship between division terms in a noncomputational task. *Journal of Educational Psychology, 90*, 321-329.

Cosgun, A. A., ahin, F. T., & Aydin, Z. N. (2017). Role of family in promoting math skills in early childhood. In R. Efe, E. Atasoy, I. Koleva, & V. Kotseva (Eds.), Current Trends in Educational Sciences (pp. 635-646). Sofia, Bulgaria: St. Kliment Ohridski University Press.

Cowan, N., Saults, J. S., & Elliott, E. M. (2002). The search for what is fundamental in the development of working memory. *Advances in Child Development and Behavior, 29*, 1-49.

Crollen, V., & Noël, M.-P. (2015). The role of fingers in the development of counting and arithmetic skills. *Acta Psychologica, 156*(0), 37-44. doi: 10.1016/j.actpsy.2015.01.007

Crosnoe, R., & Cooper, C. E. (2010). Economically disadvantaged children's transitions into elementary school: Linking family processes, school contexts, and educational policy. *American Educational Research Journal, 47*, 258-291.

Curby, T. W., Brock, L. L., & Hamre, B. K. (2013). Teachers' emotional support consistency predicts children's achievement gains and social skills. *Early Education & Development, 24*(3), 292-309. doi: 10.1080/10409289.2012.665760

Curby, T. W., Rimm-Kaufman, S. E., & Ponitz, C. C. (2009). Teacher-child interactions and children's achievement trajectories across kindergarten and first grade. *Journal of Educational Psychology, 101*(4), 912-925. doi: 10.1037/a0016647

Curtis, R. P. (2005). Preschoolers' counting in peer interaction. *Paper presented at the American Educational Research Association*, New Orleans, LA.

Cvencek, D., Meltzoff, A. N., & Greenwald, A. G. (2011). Math-gender stereotypes in elementary school children. *Child Development, 82*(3), 766-779. doi: 10.1111/j.1467-8624.2010.01529.x

Davenport, L. R., Henry, C. S., Clements, D. H., & Sarama, J. (2019a). *No more math fact frenzy.* Portsmouth, NH: Heinemann.

Davenport, L. R., Henry, C. S., Clements, D. H., & Sarama, J. (2019b). *No more math fact frenzy.* Portsmouth, NH: Heinemann.

Davidson, J., & Wright, J. L. (1994). The potential of the microcomputer in the early childhood classroom. In J. L. Wright & D. D. Shade (Eds.), *Young children: Active learners in a technological age* (pp. 77–91). Washington, DC: National Association for the Education of Young Children.

Day, S. L. (2002). Real kids, real risks: Effective instruction of students at risk of failure. *Bulletin*, 86(682). doi: https://doi.org/10.1177/019263650208663203

Duhon, G. J., House, S. H., & Stinnett, T. A. (2012). Evaluating the generalization of math fact fluency gains across paper and computer performance modalities. *Journal of School Psychology*, 50, 335–345. doi: 10.1016/j.jsp.2012.01.003

Davis, R. B. (1984). *Learning mathematics: The cognitive science approach to mathematics education.* Norwood, NJ: Ablex.

Dawson, D. T. (1953). Number grouping as a function of complexity. *The Elementary School Journal*, 54, 35–42.

Day, J. D., Engelhardt, J. L., Maxwell, S. E., & Bolig, E. E. (1997). Comparison of static and dynamic assessment procedures and their relation to independent performance. *Journal of Educational Psychology*, 89(2), 358–368.

Dearing, E., Casey, B. M., Ganley, C. M., Tillinger, M., Laski, E., & Montecillo, C. (2012). Young girls' arithmetic and spatial skills: The distal and proximal roles of family socioeconomics and home learning experiences. *Early Childhood Research Quarterly*, 27, 458–470.

DeCaro, M. S., & Rittle-Johnson, B. (2012). Exploring mathematics problems prepares children to learn from instruction. *Journal of Experimental Child Psychology*, 113(4), 552–568. doi: 10.1016/j.jecp.2012.06.009

De Corte, E., Mason, L., Depaepe, F., & Verschaffel, L. (2011). Self-regulation of mathematical knowledge and skills. In B. J. Zimmerman & D. H. Schunk (Eds.), *Handbook of self-regulation of learning and performance* (pp. 155–172). New York: Routledge.

Degelman, D., Free, J. U., Scarlato, M., Blackburn, J. M., & Golden, T. (1986). Concept learning in preschool children: Effects of a short-term Logo experience. *Journal of Educational Computing Research*, 2(2), 199–205.

Dehaene, S. (1997). *The number sense: How the mind creates mathematics.* New York, NY: Oxford University Press.

Dearing, E., McCartney, K., & Taylor, B. A. (2009). Does higher-quality early child care promote low-income children's math and literacy achievement in middle childhood? *Child Development*, 80(5),

1329–1349. doi: 10.1111/cdev.2009.80.issue-5.10.1111/j.1467-8624.2009.01336.x

Dennis, M. S., Bryant, B. R., & Drogan, R. (2015). The impact of Tier 2 mathematics instruction on second graders with mathematics difficulties. *Exceptionality*, 23(2), 124–145. doi: 10.1080/09362835.2014.986613

DeLoache, J. S. (1987). Rapid change in the symbolic functioning of young children. *Science*, 238, 1556–1557.

DeLoache, J. S., Miller, K. F., & Pierroutsakos, S. L. (1998). Reasoning and problem solving. In D. Kuhn & R. S. Siegler (Eds.), *Handbook of child psychology: Vol. 2. Cognition, perception, & language* (5th ed.) (pp. 801–850). New York, NY: Wiley.

DeLoache, J. S., Miller, K. F., Rosengren, K., & Bryant, N. (1997). The credible shrinking room: Very young children's performance with symbolic and nonsymbolic relations. *Psychological Science*, 8, 308–313.

Denison, S., & Xu, F. (2019). Infant statisticians: The origins of reasoning under uncertainty. *Perspectives on Psychological Science*, 14(4), 499–509. doi: 10.1177/1745691619847201

Denton, K., & West, J. (2002). *Children's reading and mathematics achievement in kindergarten and first grade.* from http://nces.ed.gov/pubsearch/pubsinfo.asp?pubid=2002125.

Desoete, A., Ceulemans, A., De Weerdt, F., & Pieters, S. (2012). Can we predict mathematical learning disabilities from symbolic and non-symbolic comparison tasks in kindergarten? Findings from a longitudinal study. *British Journal of Educational Psychology*, 82(1), 64–81. doi: 10.1348/2044-8279.002002

Dewey, J. (1938/1997). *Experience and education.* New York, NY: Simon & Schuster.

DHHS. (2005). *Head Start impact study: First year findings.* Washington, DC: U.S. Department of Health and Human Services; Administration for Children and Families.

Diamond, A., Barnett, W. S., Thomas, J., & Munro, S. (2007). Preschool program improves cognitive control. *Science*, 318, 1387–1388.

Diaz, R. M. (2008). *The role of language in early childhood mathematics: A parallel mixed method study. Doctoral dissertation, Florida International University.* Retrieved from http://search.proquest.com/docview/304815869.

Dindyal, J. (2015). Geometry in the early years: A commentary. *ZDM Mathematics Education*, 47(3), 519–529.

Dinehart, L., & Manfra, L. (2013). Associations between low-income children's fine motor skills in preschool and academic performance in second grade. *Early Education & Development*, *24*(2), 138-161. doi: 10.1080/10409289.2011.636729

Dixon, J. K. (1995). Limited English proficiency and spatial visualization in middle school student's construction of the concepts of reflection and rotation. *The Bilingual Research Journal*, *19*(2), 221-247.

Doabler, C. T., Cary, M. S., Jungjohann, K., Clarke, B., Fien, H., Baker, S., Smolkowski, K., Chard, D. (2012). Enhancing core mathematics instruction for students at risk for mathematics disabilities. *Teaching Exceptional Children*, *44*(4), 48-57.

Doig, B., McCrae, B., & Rowe, K. (2003). *A good start to numeracy: Effective numeracy strategies from research and practice in early childhood*. Canberra ACT, Australia: Australian Council for Educational Research.

Donlan, C. (1998). Number without language? Studies of children with specific language impairments. In C. Donlan (Ed.), *The development of mathematical skills* (pp. 255-274). East Sussex, UK: Psychology Press.

Dowker, A. (2004). *What works for children with mathematical difficulties? (Research Report No. 554)*. Nottingham, UK: University of Oxford/DfES.

Dowker, A. (2005). Early identification and intervention for students with mathematics difficulties. *Journal of Learning Disabilities*, *38*, 324-332.

Dowker, A. (2009). *What works for children with mathematical difficulties? The effectiveness of intervention schemes*. Nottingham, England: DCSF Publications.

Dowker, A. (2017). Interventions for primary school children with difficulties in mathematics. *Advances in Child Development and Behavior*, *53*, 255-287. doi: 10.1016/bs.acdb.2017.04.004

Dowker, A. (2019). Children's mathematical learning difficulties: Some contributory factors and interventions. In A. Fritz, V. G. Haase, & P. Räsänen (Eds.), *International handbook of mathematical learning difficulties: From the laboratory to the classroom* (pp. 773-787). Cham, Switzerland: Springer.

Dowker, A., & Sigley, G. (2010). Targeted interventions for children with arithmetical difficulties. *British Journal of Educational Psychology Monographs*, *II*(7), 65-81.

Downs, R. M., & Liben, L. S. (1988). Through the map darkly: Understanding maps as representations. *The Genetic Epistemologist*, *16*, 11-18.

Downs, R. M., Liben, L. S., & Daggs, D. G. (1988). On education and geographers: The role of cognitive developmental theory in geographic education. *Annals of the Association of American Geographers*, *78*, 680-700.

Draisma, J. (2000). Gesture and oral computation as resources in the early learning of mathematics. In T. Nakahara & M. Koyama (Eds.), *Proceedings of the 24th Conference of the International Group for the Psychology in Mathematics Education* (Vol. 2, pp. 257-264).

Driscoll, M. J. (1983). *Research within reach: Elementary school mathematics and reading*. St. Louis: CEMREL, Inc.

Dumas, D., McNeish, D., Sarama, J., & Clements, D. (2019). Preschool mathematics intervention can significantly improve student learning trajectories through elementary school. *AERA Open*, *5*(4), 1-5. doi: 10.1177/2332858419879446

Duncan, G. J., Claessens, A., & Engel, M. (2004). *The contributions of hard skills and socio-emotional behavior to school readiness*. Evanston, IL: Northwestern University.

Duncan, G. J., Dowsett, C. J., Claessens, A., Magnuson, K., Huston, A. C., Klebanov, P. Pagani, L. ... Japel, C. (2007). School readiness and later achievement. *Developmental Psychology*, *43*(6), 1428-1446.

Duncan, G. J., & Magnuson, K. (2011). The nature and impact of early achievement skills, attention skills, and behavior problems. In G. J. Duncan & R. Murnane (Eds.), *Whither opportunity? Rising inequality and the uncertain life chances of low-income children* (pp. 47-70). New York, NY: Russell Sage Press.

Duran, C. A. K., Byers, A., Cameron, C. E., & Grissmer, D. (2018). Unique and compensatory associations of executive functioning and visuomotor integration with mathematics performance in early elementary school. *Early Childhood Research Quarterly*, *42*, 21-30. doi: 10.1016/j.ecresq.2017.08.005

Duval, R. (2014). The first crucial point in geometry learning: Visualization. *Mediterranean Journal for Research in Mathematics Education*, *13*, 1-28.

Early, D., Barbarin, O., Burchinal, M. R., Chang, F., Clifford, R., Crawford, G., Weaver, W. ... Barnett, W. S. (2005). *Pre-kindergarten in eleven states: NCEDL's multi-state study of pre-kindergarten & study of State-Wide Early Education Programs (SWEEP)*. Chapel Hill, NC: University of North Carolina.

Ebbeck, M. (1984). Equity for boys and girls: Some important issues. *Early Child Development and Care*, *18*, 119-131.

Eberle, R. S. (2014, September). The role of children's mathematical aesthetics: The case of tessellations. *The Journal of Mathematical Behavior*, *35*, 129-143. doi: 10.1016/j.jmathb.2014.07.004

Ebersbach, M., Luwel, K., & Verschaffel, L. (2015). The relationship between children's familiarity with numbers and their performance in bounded and unbounded number line estimations. *Mathematical*

Thinking and Learning, 17(2-3), 136-154. doi: 10.1080/10986065.2015.1016813

Edens, K. M., & Potter, E. F. (2013). An exploratory look at the relationships among math skills, motivational factors and activity choice. *Early Childhood Education Journal, 41*(3), 235-243. doi: 10.1007/s10643-012-0540-y

Edwards, C., Gandini, L., & Forman, G. E. (1993). *The hundred languages of children: The Reggio Emilia approach to early childhood education.* Norwood, N.J.: Ablex Publishing Corp.

Ehrlich, S. B., & Levine, S. C. (2007, April). The impact of teacher "number talk" in low-and middle-SES preschool classrooms. *Paper presented at the American Educational Research Association*, Chicago, IL.

Ehrlich, S. B., Levine, S. C., & Goldin-Meadow, S. (2006). The importance of gesture in children's spatial reasoning. *Developmental Psychology, 42* (6), 1259-1268. doi: 10.1037/0012-1649.42.6.1259

Eimeren, L. V., MacMillan, K. D., & Ansari, D. (2007, April). The role of subitizing in childrens development of verbal counting. *Paper presented at the Society for Research in Child Development*, Boston, MA.

Elia, I. (2018). Observing the use of gestures in young children's geometric thinking. In I. Elia, J. Mulligan, A. Anderson, A. Baccaglini-Frank, & C. Benz (Eds.), *Contemporary Research and Perspectives on Early Childhood Mathematics Education* (pp. 159-182). Cham: Springer International Publishing.

Elia, I., Gagatsis, A., & Demetriou, A. (2007). The effects of different modes of representation on the solution of one-step additive problems. *Learning and Instruction, 17*, 658-672.

Elia, I., van den Heuvel-panhuizen, M., & Gagatsis, A. (2018). Geometry learning in the early years: Developing understanding of shapes and space with a focus on visualization. In V. Kinnear, M. Y. Lai, & T. Muir (Eds.), *Forging connections in early mathematics teaching and learning* (pp. 73-95). Gateway East, Singapore: Springer.

Elliott, A., & Hall, N. (1997). The impact of self-regulatory teaching strategies on "at-risk" preschoolers mathematical learning in a computer-mediated environment. *Journal of Computing in Childhood Education, 8*(2/3), 187-198.

Emihovich, C., & Miller, G. E. (1988). Talking to the turtle: A discourse analysis of Logo instruction. *Discourse Processes, 11*, 183-201.

Engel, M., Claessens, A., & Finch, M. A. (2013). Teaching students what they already know? The (mis) alignment between mathematics instructional content and student knowledge in kindergarten.

Educational Evaluation and Policy Analysis, 35(2), 157-178. doi: 10.3102/0162373712461850

Engel, M., Claessens, A., Watts, T., & Farkas, G. (2016). Mathematics content coverage and student learning in kindergarten. *Educational Researcher, 45* (5), 293-300. doi: 10.3102/0013189x16656841

English, L. D. (2010). Young children's early modelling with data. *Mathematics Education Research Journal, 22*(2), 24-47.

English, L. D. (2018a). Young children's statistical literacy in modelling with data and chance. In A. Leavy, M. Meletiou-Mavrotheris, & E. Paparistodemou (Eds.), *Statistics in early childhood and primary education* (pp. 295-313). Springer doi: 10.1007/978-981-13-1044-7_17.

English, L. D. (Ed.). (2018b). *Early engineering learning.* Gateway East, Singapore: Springer.

Entwisle, D. R., & Alexander, K. L. (1990). Beginning school math competence: Minority and majority comparisons. *Child Development, 61*, 454-471.

Ericsson, K. A., Krampe, R. T., & Tesch-Römer, C. (1993). The role of deliberate practice in the acquisition of expert performance. *Psychological Review, 100*, 363-406.

Ernest, P. (1985). The number line as a teaching aid. *Educational Studies in Mathematics, 16*, 411-424.

Espada, J. P. (2012). The native language in teaching kindergarten mathematics. *Journal of International Education Research, 8*(4), 359-366.

Espinosa, L. M. (2005). Curriculum and assessment considerations for young children from culturally, linguistically, and economically diverse backgrounds. *Psychology in the Schools, 42*(8), 837-853. doi: 10.1002/pits.20115

Evans, D. W. (1983). *Understanding infinity and zero in the early school years.* Unpublished doctoral dissertation, University of Pennsylvania.

Falk, R., Yudilevich-Assouline, P., & Elstein, A. (2012). Children's concept of probability as inferred from their binary choices—revisited. *Educational Studies in Mathematics, 81*(2), 207-233. doi: 10.1007/s10649-012-9402-1

Farran, D. C., Lipsey, M. W., Watson, B., & Hurley, S. (2007). Balance of content emphasis and child content engagement in an early reading first program. *Paper presented at the American Educational Research Association*.

Fennema, E. H. (1972). The relative effectiveness of a symbolic and a concrete model in learning a selected mathematics principle. *Journal for Research in Mathematics Education, 3*, 233-238.

Fennema, E. H., Carpenter, T. P., Frank, M. L., Levi, L., Jacobs, V. R., & Empson, S. B. (1996). A longitudinal study of learning to use children's thinking in mathematics instruction. *Journal for Research in Mathematics Education, 27*, 403-434.

Fennema, E. H., Carpenter, T. P., Franke, M. L., & Levi, L. (1998). A longitudinal study of gender differences in young childrens mathematical thinking. *Educational Researcher, 27,* 6-11.

Fennema, E. H., & Tartre, L. A. (1985). The use of spatial visualization in mathematics by girls and boys. *Journal for Research in Mathematics Education, 16,* 184-206.

Feuerstein, R., Rand, Y. A., & Hoffman, M. B. (1979). *The dynamic assessment of retarded performers: The Learning Potential Assessment Device, theory, instruments, and techniques.* Baltimore, MD: University Park Press.

Finn, J. D. (2002). Small classes in American schools: Research, practice, and politics. *Phi Delta Kappan, 83,* 551-560.

Finn, J. D., & Achilles, C. M. (1990). Answers and questions about class size. *American Educational Research Journal, 27*(3), 557-577.

Finn, J. D., Gerber, S. B., Achilles, C. M., & Boyd-Zaharias, J. (2001). The enduring effects of small classes. *Teachers College Record, 103*(2), 145-183.

Finn, J. D., Pannozzo, G. M., & Achilles, C. M. (2003). The "why's" of class size: Student behavior in small classes. *Review of Educational Research, 73,* 321-368.

Fisher, K., Hirsh-Pasek, K., & Golinkoff, R. M. (2012). Fostering mathematical thinking through playful learning. In S. Suggate & E. Reese (Eds.), *Contemporary Debates in Childhood Education and Development* (pp. 81-91). New York, NY: Routledge.

Fisher, K. R., Hirsh-Pasek, K., Golinkoff, R. M., & Newcombe, N. (2013). Taking shape: Supporting preschoolers acquisition of geometric knowledge through guided play. *Child Development, 84*(6), 1872-1878.

Fisher, P. H., Dobbs-Oates, J., Doctoroff, G. L., & Arnold, D. H. (2012). Early math interest and the development of math skills. *Journal of Educational Psychology, 104*(3), 673-681. doi: 10.1037/a0027756

Fitzpatrick, C., & Pagani, L. S. (2013). Task-oriented kindergarten behavior pays off in later childhood. *Journal of Developmental & Behavioral Pediatrics, 34*(2), 94-101. doi: 10.1097/DBP.0b013e 31827a3779

Fletcher-Flinn, C. M., & Gravatt, B. (1995). The efficacy of computer assisted instruction (CAI): A meta-analysis. *Journal of Educational Computing Research, 12,* 219-242.

Flevares, L. M., & Schiff, J. R. (2014). Learning mathematics in two dimensions: A review and look ahead at teaching and learning early childhood mathematics with children's literature. *Frontiers in Psychology, 5*(459), 1-12. doi: 10.3389/fpsyg.2014.00459

Flexer, R. J. (1989). Conceptualizing addition. *Teaching Exceptional Children, 21*(4), 21-25.

Fluck, M. (1995). Counting on the right number: Maternal support for the development of cardinality. *Irish Journal of Psychology, 16,* 133-149.

Fluck, M., & Henderson, L. (1996). Counting and cardinality in English nursery pupils. *British Journal of Educational Psychology, 66,* 501-517.

Ford, M. J., Poe, V., & Cox, J. (1993). Attending behaviors of ADHD children in math and reading using various types of software. *Journal of Computing in Childhood Education, 4,* 183-196.

Forman, G. E., & Hill, F. (1984). *Constructive play: Applying Piaget in the preschool* (rev. ed.). Menlo Park, CA: Addison Wesley.

Foster, M. E., Anthony, J. L., Clements, D. H., Sarama, J., & Williams, J. J. (2018). Hispanic dual language learning kindergarten students' response to a numeracy intervention: A randomized control trial. *Early Childhood Research Quarterly, 43,* 83-95. doi: 10.1016/j.ecresq.2018.01.009

Fien, H., Doabler, C. T., Nelson, N. J., Kosty, D. B., Clarke, B., & Baker, S. K. (2016). An examination of the promise of the Numbershire level 1 gaming intervention for improving student mathematics outcomes. *Journal of Research on Educational Effectiveness, 9*(4), 635-661. doi: 10.1080/19345747.2015.1119229

Flannery, L. P., Silverman, B., Kazakoff, E. R., Bers, M. U., Bonta, P., & Resnick, M. (2013). Designing ScratchJr: Support for early childhood learning through computer programming. Paper presented at the Proceedings of the 12th International Conference on Interaction Design and Children, New York, New York. http://dl.acm.org/citation.cfm?id=2485785

Foster, M. E., Anthony, J. L., Clements, D. H., & Sarama, J. (2016). Improving mathematics learning of kindergarten students through computer assisted instruction. *Journal for Research in Mathematics Education, 47*(3), 206-232. doi: https://doi.org/10.5951/jresematheduc.47.3.0206

Fuller, B., Bein, E., Bridges, M., Kim, Y., & Rabe-Hesketh, S. (2017). Do academic preschools yield stronger benefits? Cognitive emphasis, dosage, and early learning. *Journal of Applied Developmental Psychology, 52,* 1-11. doi: 10.1016/j.appdev.2017.05.001

Fox, J. (2005). Child-initiated mathematical patterning in the pre-compulsory years. In H. L. Chick & J. L. Vincent (Eds.), *Proceedings of the 29th Conference of the International Group for the Psychology in Mathematics Education* (Vol. 2, pp. 313-320). Melbourne, AU: PME.

Fox, J. (2006). A justification for mathematical modelling experiences in the preparatory classroom.

In P. Grootenboer, R. Zevenbergen, & M. Chinnappan (Eds.), *Proceedings of the 29th annual conference of the Mathematics Education Research Group of Australia* (pp. 221-228). Canberra, Australia: MERGA.

Franke, M. L., Carpenter, T. P., & Battey, D. (2008). Content matters: Algebraic reasoning in teacher professional development. In J. J. Kaput, D. W. Carraher, & M. L. Blanton (Eds.), *Algebra in the early grades* (pp. 333-359). Mahwah, NJ: Lawrence Erlbaum Associates.

Freiman, V. (2018). Complex and open-ended tasks to enrich mathematical experiences of kindergarten students. In F. M. Singer (Ed.), *Mathematical creativity and mathematical giftedness: enhancing creative capacities in mathematically promising students* (pp. 373-404). Cham: Springer International Publishing.

French, L., & Song, M.-J. (1998). Developmentally appropriate teacher-directed approaches: Images from Korean kindergartens. *Journal of Curriculum Studies, 30,* 409-430.

Friedman, L. (1995). The space factor in mathematics: Gender differences. *Review of Educational Research, 65*(1), 22-50.

Friel, S. N., Curcio, F. R., & Bright, G. W. (2001). Making sense of graphs: Critical factors influencing comprehension and instructional implications. *Journal for Research in Mathematics Education, 32,* 124-158.

Fritz, A., Haase, V. G., & Räsänen, P. (Eds.). (2019). *International handbook of mathematical learning difficulties: From the laboratory to the classroom.* Cham, Switzerland: Springer.

Frontera, M. (1994). On the initial learning of mathematics: Does schooling really help? In J. E. H. Van Luit (Ed.), *Research on learning and instruction of mathematics in kindergarten and primary school* (pp. 42-59). Doetinchem, The Netherlands: Graviant.

Fryer, J., & Levitt, S. D. (2004). Understanding the Black-White test score gap in the first two years of school. *The Review of Economics and Statistics, 86*(2), 447-464.

Fuchs, L. S., Compton, D. L., Fuchs, D., Paulson, K., Bryant, J. D., & Hamlett, C. L. (2005). The prevention, identification, and cognitive determinants of math difficulty. *Journal of Educational Psychology, 97,* 493-513.

Fuchs, L. S., Fuchs, D., Hamlett, C. L., Powell, S. R., Capizzi, A. M., & Seethaler, P. M. (2006). The effects of computer-assisted instruction on number combination skill in at-risk first graders. *Journal of Learning Disabilities, 39,* 467-475.

Fuchs, L. S., Fuchs, D., & Karns, K. (2001). Enhancing kindergartners' mathematical development:

Effects of peer-assisted learning strategies. *Elementary School Journal, 101,* 495-510.

Fuchs, L. S., Geary, D. C., Compton, D. L., Fuchs, D., Schatschneider, C., Hamlett, C. L., DeSelms, J., ... Changas, P. (2013). Effects of first-grade number knowledge tutoring with contrasting forms of practice. *Journal of Educational Psychology, 105* (1), 58-77. doi: 10.1037/a0030127.supp

Fuchs, L. S., Powell, S. R., Cirino, P. T., Fletcher, J. M., Fuchs, D., & Zumeta, R. O. (2008). Enhancing number combinations fluency and math problem-solving skills in third-grade students with math difficulties: A field-based randomized control trial. *Paper presented at the Institute of Education Science 2007 Research Conference.*

Fuchs, L. S., Powell, S. R., Hamlett, C. L., Fuchs, D., Cirino, P. T., & Fletcher, J. M. (2008). Remediating computational deficits at third grade: A randomized field trial. *Journal of Research on Educational Effectiveness, 1,* 2-32.

Fuchs, L. S., Powell, S. R., Seethaler, P. M., Cirino, P. T., Fletcher, J. M., Fuchs, D. Hamlett, C. L. (2010). The effects of strategic counting instruction, with and without deliberate practice, on number combination skill among students with mathematics difficulties. *Learning and Individual Differences, 20*(2), 89-100. doi: 10.1016/j.lindif.2009.09.003

Fuhs, M. W., McNeil, N. M., Kelley, K., O'Rear, C., & Villano, M. (2016). The role of non-numerical stimulus features in approximate number system training in preschoolers from low-income homes. *Journal of Cognition and Development, 17*(5), 737-764. doi: 10.1080/15248372.2015.1105228

Fuson, K. C. (1988). *Children's counting and concepts of number.* New York, NY: Springer-Verlag.

Fuson, K. C. (1992a). Research on learning and teaching addition and subtraction of whole numbers. In G. Leinhardt, R. Putman, & R. A. Hattrup (Eds.), *Handbook of research on mathematics teaching and learning* (pp. 53-187). Mahwah, NJ: Lawrence Erlbaum Associates.

Fuson, K. C. (1992b). Research on whole number addition and subtraction. In D. A. Grouws (Ed.), *Handbook of research on mathematics teaching and learning* (pp. 243-275). New York, NY: Macmillan.

Fuson, K. C. (2003). Developing mathematical power in whole number operations. In J. Kilpatrick, W. G. Martin, & D. Schifter (Eds.), *A research companion to Principles and Standards for School Mathematics* (pp. 68-94). Reston, VA: National Council of Teachers of Mathematics.

Fuson, K. C. (2004). Pre-K to grade 2 goals and standards: Achieving 21st century mastery for all. In D. H. Clements, J. Sarama, & A.-M. DiBiase (Eds.), *Engaging young children in mathematics:*

Standards for early childhood mathematics education (pp. 105-148). Mahwah, NJ: Lawrence Erlbaum Associates.

Fuson, K. C. (2009). *Mathematically-desirable and accessible whole-number algorithms: Achieving understanding and fluency for all students.* Chicago, IL: Northwestern University.

Fuson, K. C. (2018). Building on Howe's three pillars in kindergarten to grade 6 classrooms. In Y. Li, W. J. Lewis, & J. J. Madden (Eds.), *Mathematics matters in education: Essays in honor of Roger E. Howe* (pp. 185-207). Cham: Springer International Publishing.

Fuson, K. C. (2020). The best multidigit computation methods: A cross-cultural cognitive, empirical, and mathematical analysis. *Universal Journal of Educational Research, 8*(4), 1299-1314. doi: 10.13189/ujer.2020.080421

Fuson, K. C., & Abrahamson, D. (2009). *Word problem types, numerical situation drawings, and a conceptual -phase model to implement an algebraic approach to problem-solving in elementary classrooms.* Chicago, IL: Northwestern University.

Fuson, K. C., & Briars, D. J. (1990). Using a base-ten blocks learning/teaching approach for first- and second-grade place-value and multidigit addition and subtraction. *Journal for Research in Mathematics Education, 21,* 180-206.

Fuson, K. C., Clements, D. H., & Sarama, J. (2015). Making early math education work for all children. *Phi Delta Kappan, 97,* 63-68.

Fuson, K. C., Perry, T., & Kwon, Y. (1994). Latino, Anglo, and Korean childrens finger addition methods. In J. E. H. Van Luit (Ed.), *Research on learning and instruction of mathematics in kindergarten and primary school* (pp. 220-228). Doetinchem, The Netherlands: Graviant.

Fuson, K. C., Smith, S. T., & Lo Cicero, A. (1997). Supporting Latino first graders' ten-structured thinking in urban classrooms. *Journal for Research in Mathematics Education, 28,* 738-760.

Fuson, K. C., Wearne, D., Hiebert, J. C., Murray, H. G., Human, P. G., Olivier, A. I., Carpenter, T. P., Fennema, E. H. (1997). Children's conceptual structures for multidigit numbers and methods of multidigit addition and subtraction. *Journal for Research in Mathematics Education, 28,* 130-162.

Fyfe, E. R., McNeil, N. M., & Rittle-Johnson, B. (2015). Easy as ABCABC: Abstract language facilitates performance on a concrete patterning task. *Child Development, 86*(3), 927-935. doi: 10.1111/cdev.12331

Galitskaya, V., & Drigas, A. (2020). Special education: Teaching geometry with ICTs. *International Journal of Emerging Technologies in Learning (iJET), 15*(06). doi: 10.3991/ijet.v15i06.11242

Gadanidis, G., Hoogland, C., Jarvis, D., & Scheffel, T.-L. (2003). Mathematics as an aesthetic experience. In *Proceedings of the 27th Conference of the International Group for the Psychology in Mathematics Education* (Vol. 1, p. 250). Honolulu, HI: University of Hawai'i.

Gallego, F. A., Näslund-Hadley, E., & Alfonso, M. (2018). *Tailoring instruction to improve mathematics skills in preschools [IDB Working Paper Series ; 905].* Inter-American Development Bank. www.povertyactionlab.org/sites/default/files/publications/613_1026_Tailoring-Instructions-to-Improve-Mathematics-Skills-in-PreSchool_June2017.pdf

Gedik, N., Çetin, M., & Koca, C. (2017). Examining the experiences of preschoolers on programming via tablet computers. *Mediterranean Journal of Humanities, 7*(1), 193-203. doi: 10.13114/mjh.2017.330

Gervasoni, A., & Perry, B. (2017). Notice, explore and talk about mathematics: Making a positive difference for preschool children, educators and families in Australian communities that experience multiple disadvantages. *Advances in Child Development and Behavior, 53,* 169-225. doi: 10.1016/bs.acdb.2017.03.002

Griffiths, R., Back, J., & Gifford, S. (2017). Using manipulatives in the foundations of arithmetic. Retrieved from University of Leicester website: www.nuffieldfoundation.org/sites/default/files/files/Nuffield%20Main%20Report%20Mar%202017web(1).pdf

Gaidoschik, M. (2019). Didactics as a source and remedy of mathematical learning difficulties. In A. Fritz, V. G. Haase & P. Räsänen (Eds.), *International handbook of mathematical learning difficulties: From the laboratory to the classroom* (pp. 73-89). Cham, Switzerland: Springer.

Gagatsis, A., & Elia, I. (2004). The effects of different modes of representation on mathematical problem solving. In M. J. Høines & A. B. Fuglestad (Eds.), *Proceedings of the 28th Conference of the International Group for the Psychology in Mathematics Education* (Vol. 2, pp. 447-454). Bergen, Norway: Bergen University College.

Gagatsis, A., & Patronis, T. (1990). Using geometrical models in a process of reflective thinking in learning and teaching mathematics. *Educational Studies in Mathematics, 21,* 29-54.

Galen, F. H. J., & Buter, A. (1997). De rol van interactie bij leren rekenen met de computer [Computer tasks and classroom discussions in mathematics]. *Panama-Post. Tijdschrift Voor Nascholing En Onderzoek Van Het Reken-w Iskundeonderwijs, 16*(1), 11-18.

Gallou-Dumiel, E. (1989). Reflections, point symmetry and Logo. In C. A. Maher, G. A. Goldin, & R. B. Davis

(Eds.), *Proceedings of the eleventh annual meeting, North American Chapter of the International Group for the Psychology of Mathematics Education* (pp. 149-157). New Brunswick, NJ: Rutgers University.

Gamel-McCormick, M., & Amsden, D. (2002). *Investing in better outcomes: The Delaware early childhood longitudinal study*. New Castle, DE: Delaware Interagency Resource Management Committee and the Department of Education.

Garon-Carrier, G., Boivin, M., Lemelin, J.-P., Kovas, Y., Parent, S., Séguin, J., ... Dionne, G. (2018). Early developmental trajectories of number knowledge and math achievement from 4 to 10 years: Low-persistent profile and early-life predictors. *Journal of School Psychology, 68*, 84-98. doi: 10.1016/j.jsp.2018.02.004

Gathercole, S. E., Tiffany, C., Briscoe, J., Thorn, A., & The, A. T. (2005). Developmental consequences of poor phonological short-term memory function in childhood: A longitudinal study. *Journal of Child Psychology and Psychiatry, 46*(6), 598-611. doi: 10.1111/j.1469-7610.2004.00379.x

Gavin, M. K., Casa, T. M., Adelson, J. L., & Firmender, J. M. (2013). The impact of challenging geometry and measurement units on the achievement of grade 2 students. *Journal for Research in Mathematics Education, 44*(3), 478-509.

Gay, P. (1989). Tactile turtle: Explorations in space with visually impaired children and a floor turtle. *British Journal of Visual Impairment, 7*(1), 23-25. doi: https://doi.org/10.1177/026461968900700106

Geary, D. C. (1990). A componential analysis of an early learning deficit in mathematics. *Journal of Experimental Child Psychology, 49*, 363-383.

Geary, D. C. (1994). *Children's mathematical development: Research and practical applications*. Washington, DC: American Psychological Association.

Geary, D. C. (2003). Learning disabilities in arithmetic: Problem solving differences and cognitive deficits. In H. L. Swanson, K. Harris, & S. Graham (Eds.), *Handbook of learning disabilities* (pp. 199-212). New York, NY: Guilford Press.

Geary, D. C. (2004). Mathematics and learning disabilities. *Journal of Learning Disabilities, 37*, 4-15.

Geary, D. C. (2006). Development of mathematical understanding. In D. Kuhn, R. S. Siegler, W. Damon, & R. M. Lerner (Eds.), *Handbook of child psychology: Volume 2–Cognition, perception, and language* (6th ed.) (pp. 777-810). Hoboken, NJ: Wiley.

Geary, D. C. (2011). Cognitive predictors of achievement growth in mathematics: A 5-year longitudinal study. *Developmental Psychology, 47*(6), 1539-1552. doi: 10.1037/a0025510

Geary, D. C. (2013). Early foundations for mathematics learning and their relations to learning disabilities. *Current Directions in Psychological Science, 22*(1), 23-27. doi: 10.1177/0963721412469398

Geary, D. C., Bow-Thomas, C. C., & Yao, Y. (1992). Counting knowledge and skill in cognitive addition: A comparison of normal and mathematically disabled children. *Journal of Experimental Child Psychology, 54*, 372-391.

Geary, D. C., Brown, S. C., & Samaranayake, V. A. (1991). Cognitive addition: A short longitudinal study of strategy choice and speed-of-processing differences in normal and mathematically disabled children. *Developmental Psychology, 27*(5), 787-797.

Geary, D. C., Hamson, C. O., & Hoard, M. K. (2000). Numerical and arithmetical cognition: A longitudinal study of process and concept deficits in children with learning disability. *Journal of Experimental Child Psychology, 77*, 236-263.

Geary, D. C., Hoard, M. K., Byrd-Craven, J., Nugent, L., & Numtee, C. (2007). Cognitive mechanisms underlying achievement deficits in children with mathematical learning disability. *Child Development, 78*, 1343-1359.

Geary, D. C., Hoard, M. K., & Hamson, C. O. (1999). Numerical and arithmetical cognition: Patterns of functions and deficits in children at risk for a mathematical disability. *Journal of Experimental Child Psychology, 74*, 213-239.

Geary, D. C., Hoard, M. K., & Nugent, L. (2012). Independent contributions of the central executive, intelligence, and in-class attentive behavior to developmental change in the strategies used to solve addition problems. *Journal of Experimental Child Psychology, 113*(1), 49-65. doi: 10.1016/j.jecp.2012.03.003

Geary, D. C., & Liu, F. (1996). Development of arithmetical competence in Chinese and American children: Influence of age, language, and schooling. *Child Development, 67*(5), 2022-2044.

Geary, D. C., van Marle, K., Chu, F. W., Rouder, J., Hoard, M. K., & Nugent, L. (2017). Early conceptual understanding of cardinality predicts superior school-entry number-system knowledge. *Psychological Science, 29*(2), 191-205. doi: 10.1177/0956797617729817

Geary, D. C., & vanMarle, K. (2016). Young children's core symbolic and nonsymbolic quantitative knowledge in the prediction of later mathematics achievement. *Dev Psychol, 52*(12), 2130-2144. doi: 10.1037/dev0000214

Gebuis, T., & Reynvoet, B. (2011). Generating nonsymbolic number stimuli. *Behavior Research Methods, 43*(4), 981-986. ·

Gelman, R. (1994). Constructivism and supporting environments. In D. Tirosh (Ed.), *Implicit and explicit knowledge: An educational approach* (Vol. 6, pp. 55–82). Norwood, NJ: Ablex.

Gelman, R., & Williams, E. M. (1997). Enabling constraints for cognitive development and learning: Domain specificity and epigenesist. In D. Kuhn & R. Siegler (Eds.), *Cognition, perception, and language. Vol. 2: Handbook of Child Psychology* (5th ed., pp. 575–630). New York, NY: John Wiley & Sons.

Gerofsky, P. R. (2015). Why Asian preschool children mathematically outperform preschool children from other countries. *Western Undergraduate Psychology Journal, 3*(1). Retrieved from http://ir.lib.uwo.ca/wupj/vol3/iss1/11

Gersten, R. (1986). Response to "consequences of three preschool curriculum models through age 15." *Early Childhood Research Quarterly, 1,* 293–302.

Gersten, R., Chard, D. J., Jayanthi, M., Baker, M. S., Morpy, S. K., & Flojo, J. R. (2008). *Teaching mathematics to students with learning disabilities: A meta-analysis of the intervention research.* Portsmouth, NH: RMC Research Corporation, Center on Instruction.

Gersten, R., Jordan, N. C., & Flojo, J. R. (2005). Early identification and interventions for students with mathematical difficulties. *Journal of Learning Disabilities, 38,* 293–304.

Gersten, R., Rolfhus, E., Clarke, B., Decker, L. E., Wilkins, C., & Dimino, J. (2015). Intervention for first graders with limited number knowledge: Large-scale replication of a randomized controlled trial. *American Educational Research Journal, 52*(3), 516–546. doi: 10.3102/0002831214565787

Gersten, R., & White, W. A. T. (1986). Castles in the sand: Response to Schweinhart and Weikart. *Educational Leadership, 44*(3), 19–20.

Gervasoni, A. (2005). The diverse learning needs of children who were selected for an intervention program. In H. L. Chick & J. L. Vincent (Eds.), *Proceedings of the 29th Conference of the International Group for the Psychology in Mathematics Education* (Vol. 3, pp. 33–40). Melbourne, Australia: PME.

Gervasoni, A. (2018). The impact and challenges of early mathematics intervention in an Australian context. In G. Kaiser, H. Forgasz, M. Gravenm, A. Kuzniak, E. Simmt, & B. Xu (Eds.), *13th International Congress on Mathematical Education* (pp. 115–133). Cham: Springer International Publishing.

Gervasoni, A., Hadden, T., & Turkenburg, K. (2007). Exploring the number knowledge of children to inform the development of a professional learning plan for teachers in the Ballarat Diocese as a means of building community capacity. In J. Watson & K. Beswick (Eds.), *Mathematics: Essential research, essential practice* (Proceedings of the 30th Annual Conference of the Mathematics Education Research Group of Australasia) (Vol. 3, pp. 305–314). Hobart, Australia: MERGA.

Gervasoni, A., Parish, L., Hadden, T., Livesey, C., Bevan, K., Croswell, M., Turkenburg, K. (2012). The progress of grade 1 students who participated in an extending mathematical understanding intervention program. In J. Dindyalm, L. P. Cheng, & S. F. Ng (Eds.), *Mathematics education research group of Australasia* (pp. 306–313). M. Evans and Company.

Gervasoni, A., & Sullivan, P. (2007). Assessing and teaching children who have difficulty learning arithmetic. *Educational & Child Psychology, 24*(2), 40–53.

Gibson, E. J. (1969). *Principles of perceptual learning and development.* New York, NY: Appleton-Century-Crofts, Meredith Corporation.

Giganti, P., Jr., & Crews, D. (1994). *How Many Snails?* New York, NY: Harper Trophy.

Gilligan, K. A., Flouri, E., & Farran, E. K. (2017). The contribution of spatial ability to mathematics achievement in middle childhood. *Journal of Experimental Child Psychology, 163,* 107–125. doi: 10.1016/j.jecp.2017.04.016

Gilmore, C., & Cragg, L. (2014). Teachers' understanding of the role of executive functions in mathematics learning. *Mind, Brain, and Education, 8*(3), 132–136. doi: 10.1111/mbe.12050

Gilmore, C., Keeble, S., Richardson, S., & Cragg, L. (2017). The interaction of procedural skill, conceptual understanding and working memory in early mathematics achievement. *Journal of Numerical Cognition, 3*(2), 400–416. doi: 10.5964/jnc.v3i2.51

Gilmore, C. K., & Papadatou-Pastou, M. (2009). Patterns of individual differences in conceptual understanding and arithmetical skill: A meta-analysis. *Mathematical Thinking and Learning, 10,* 25–40.

Ginsburg, H. P. (1977). *Children's arithmetic.* Austin, TX: Pro-Ed.

Ginsburg, H. P. (1997). Mathematics learning disabilities: A view from developmental psychology. *Journal of Learning Disabilities, 30,* 20–33.

Ginsburg, H. P. (2008). Mathematics education for young children: What it is and how to promote it. *Social Policy Report, 22*(1), 1–24.

Ginsburg, H. P., Duch, H., Ertle, B., & Noble, K. G. (2012). How can parents help their children learn math? In B. H. Wasik (Ed.), *Handbook of family literacy* (2nd ed., p. 496). New York, NY: Routledge.

Ginsburg, H. P., Inoue, N., & Seo, K.-H. (1999). Young children doing mathematics: Observations of everyday activities. In J. V. Copley (Ed.), *Mathematics in the early years* (pp. 88–99). Reston, VA: National Council of Teachers of Mathematics.

Ginsburg, H. P., Klein, A., & Starkey, P. (1998). The development of children's mathematical thinking: Connecting research with practice. In W. Damon, I. E. Sigel, & K. A. Renninger (Eds.), *Handbook of child psychology. Volume 4: Child psychology in practice* (pp. 401–476). New York, NY: John Wiley & Sons.

Ginsburg, H. P., Ness, D., & Seo, K.-H. (2003). Young American and Chinese children's everyday mathematical activity. *Mathematical Thinking and Learning, 5*, 235–258.

Gold, Z. S. (2017). *Engineering play: Exploring associations with executive function, mathematical ability, and spatial ability in preschool.* (THESIS. DEGREE), Purdue University, Ann Arbor.

Goldschmeid, E., & Jackson, S. (1994). *People under three: Young children in daycare.* London, UK: Routledge.

Gormley, W. T., Jr., Gayer, T., Phillips, D., & Dawson, B. (2005). The effects of universal pre-Kon cognitive development. *Developmental Psychology, 41*, 872–884.

Graham, T. A., Nash, C., & Paul, K. (1997). Young children's exposure to mathematics: The child care context. *Early Childhood Education Journal, 25*, 31–38.

Granrud, C. E. (1987). Visual size constancy in newborn infants. *Investigative Ophthalmology & Visual Science, 28*(Suppl. 5), 5.

Gravemeijer, K. P. E. (1990). Realistic geometry instruction. In K. P. E. Gravemeijer, M. van den Heuvel, & L. Streefland (Eds.), *Contexts free productions tests and geometry in realistic mathematics education* (pp. 79–91). Utrecht, The Netherlands: OW&OC.

Gravemeijer, K. P. E. (1991). An instruction-theoretical reflection on the use of manipulatives. In L. Streefland (Ed.), *Realistic mathematics education in primary school* (pp. 57–76). Utrecht, The Netherlands: Freudenthal Institute, Utrecht University.

Gray, E. M., & Pitta, D. (1997). Number processing: Qualitative differences in thinking and the role of imagery. In L. Puig & A. Gutiérrez (Eds.), *Proceedings of the 20th Annual Conference of the Mathematics Education Research Group of Australasia* (Vol. 3, pp. 35–42).

Gray, E. M., & Pitta, D. (1999). Images and their frames of reference: A perspective on cognitive development in elementary arithmetic. In O. Zaslavsky (Ed.), *Proceedings of the 23rd Conference of the International Group for the Psychology of Mathematics Education* (Vol. 3, pp. 49–56). Haifa, Israel: Technion.

Green, C. T., Bunge, S. A., Briones Chiongbian, V., Barrow, M., & Ferrer, E. (2017). Fluid reasoning predicts future mathematical performance among children and adolescents. *Journal of Experimental Child Psychology, 157*, 125–143. doi: 10.1016/j.jecp.2016.12.005

Greeno, J. G., & Riley, M. S. (1987). Processes and development of understanding. In R. E. Weinert & R. H. Kluwe (Eds.), *Metacognition, motivation, and understanding* (pp. 289–313). Mahwah, NJ: Lawrence Erlbaum Associates.

Greenwood, C. R., Delquadri, J. C., & Hall, R. V. (1989). Longitudinal effects of classwide peer tutoring. *Journal of Educational Psychology, 81*, 371–383.

Griffin, S. (2004). Number Worlds: A research-based mathematics program for young children. In D. H. Clements, J. Sarama, & A.-M. DiBiase (Eds.), *Engaging young children in mathematics: Standards for early childhood mathematics education* (pp. 325–342). Mahwah, NJ: Lawrence Erlbaum Associates.

Griffin, S. (2009). Learning sequences in the acquisition of mathematical knowledge: Using cognitive developmental theory to inform curriculum design for pre-K-6 mathematics education. *Mind, Brain & Education, 3*(2), 96–107.

Griffin, S., Case, R., & Capodilupo, A. (1995). Teaching for understanding: The importance of the Central Conceptual Structures in the elementary mathematics curriculum. In A. McKeough, J. Lupart, & A. Marini (Eds.), *Teaching for transfer: Fostering generalization in learning* (pp. 121–151). Mahwah, NJ: Lawrence Erlbaum Associates.

Griffin, S., Case, R., & Siegler, R. S. (1994). Rightstart: Providing the central conceptual prerequisites for first formal learning of arithmetic to students at risk for school failure. In K. McGilly (Ed.), *Classroom lessons: Integrating cognitive theory and classroom practice* (pp. 25–49). Cambridge, MA: MIT Press.

Grissmer, D., Grimm, K. J., Aiyer, S. M., Murrah, W. M., & Steele, J. S. (2010). Fine motor skills and early comprehension of the world: Two new school readiness indicators. *Developmental Psychology, 46*(5), 1008–1017. doi: 10.1037/a0020104.supp

Grissmer, D., Mashburn, A. J., Cottone, E., Chen, W. B., Brock, L. L., Murrah, W. M., & Cameron, C. E. (2013). Play-based after-school curriculum improves measures of executive function, visuospatial and math skills and classroom behavior for high risk K-1 children. *Paper presented at the Society for Research in Child Development*, Seattle, WA.

Grupe, L. A., & Bray, N. W. (1999). *What role do manipulatives play in kindergartners' accuracy and strategy use when solving simple addition problems?* Albuquerque, NM: Society for Research in Child Development.

Guarino, C., Dieterle, S. G., Bargagliotti, A. E., & Mason, W. M. (2013). What can we learn about effective early mathematics teaching? A framework for estimating causal effects using longitudinal survey data. *Journal of Research on Educational Effectiveness, 6*, 164-198.

Guisti, J., Hinkle, K., Oldenburg, G., Paul, H., Vlasie, J., Lincoln, B., & Moulton, C. (2018). Critique of the OWL curriculum. *University of Montana Journal of Early Childhood Scholarship and Innovative Practice, 2*(1), 1-9.

Gunderson, E., Ramirez, G., Levine, S., & Beilock, S. (2012). The role of parents and teachers in the development of gender-related math attitudes. *Sex Roles, 66*(3-4), 153-166. doi: 10.1007/s11199-011-9996-2

Gunderson, E. A., & Levine, S. C. (2011). Some types of parent number talk count more than others: Relation between parents' input and children's number knowledge. *Developmental Science, 14*(5), 1021-1032. doi: 10.1111/j.1467-7687.2011.01050.x

Gunderson, E. A., Ramirez, G., Beilock, S., & Levine, S. C. (2012). The relation between spatial skill and early number knowledge: The role of the linear number line. *Developmental Psychology, 48*(5), 1229-1241. doi: 10.1037/a0027433

Gupta, D. (2014). *Early elementary students' fractional understanding: examination of cases from a multi-year longitudinal study* Baylor University]. Curriculum & Instruction. http://hdl.handle.net/2104/9162

Halle, T. G., Kurtz-Costes, B., & Mahoney, J. L. (1997). Family influences on school achievement in low-income, African American children. *Journal of Educational Psychology, 89*, 527-537.

Hamdan, N., & Gunderson, E. A. (2017). The number line is a critical spatial-numerical representation: Evidence from a fraction intervention. *Developmental Psychology, 53*(3), 587-596. doi: 10.1037/dev0000252

Hamre, B. K., & Pianta, R. C. (2001). Early teacher-child relationships and the trajectory of children's school outcomes through eighth grade. *Child Development, 72*, 625-638.

Hancock, C. M. (1995). Das Erlernen der Datenanalyse durch anderweitige Beschäftigungen: Grundlagen von Datencompetenz bei Schülerinnen und Schülern in den klassen 1 bis 7. [Learning data analysis by doing something else: Foundations of data literacy in grades 1-7]. *Computer Und Unterricht, 17*(1), 33-39.

Hannibal, M. A. Z., & Clements, D. H. (2010). Young children's understanding of basic geometric shapes. Manuscript submitted for publication.

Hannula, M. M. (2005). *Spontaneous focusing on numerosity in the development of early mathematical skills*. Turku, Finland: University of Turku.

Hannula, M. M., Lepola, J., & Lehtinen, E. (2007). Spontaneous focusing on numerosity at Kindergarten predicts arithmetical but not reading skills at grade 2. *Paper presented at the Society for Research in Child Development*.

Hannula-Sormunen, M. M., Lehtinen, E., & Räsänen, P. (2015). Children's spontaneous focusing on numerosity, subitizing, and counting skills as predictors of their mathematical performance seven years later at school. *Mathematical Thinking and Learning, 17*(2-3), 155-177. doi: 10.1080/10986065.2015.1016814

Hardy, J. K., & Hemmeter, M. L. (2018). Systematic instruction of early math skills for preschoolers at risk for math delays. *Topics in Early Childhood Special Education*. doi: 10.1177/0271121418792300

Hartanto, A., Yang, H., & Yang, S. (2018). Bilingualism positively predicts mathematical competence: Evidence from two large-scale studies. *Learning and Individual Differences, 61*, 216-227. doi: 10.1016/j.lindif.2017.12.007

Harris, L. J. (1981). Sex-related variations in spatial skill. In L. S. Liben, A. H. Patterson, & N. Newcombe (Eds.), *Spatial representation and behavior across the life span* (pp. 83-125). New York, NY: Academic Press.

Harrison, C. (2004). Giftedness in early childhood: The search for complexity and connection. *Roeper Review, 26*(2), 78-84.

Hassidov, D., & Ilany, B.-S. (2017). Between natural language and mathematical symbols (<,>,=): The comprehension of pre-service and preschool teachers-perspective of numbers. *Creative Education, 8*, 1903-1911. doi: 10.4236/ce.2017.812130

Hassinger-Das, B., Hirsh-Pasek, K., & Golinkoff, R. M. (2017). The case of brain science and guided play: A developing story. *Young Children, 72*(2), 45.

Hatano, G., & Sakakibara, T. (2004). Commentary: Toward a cognitive-sociocultural psychology of mathematical and analogical development. In L. D. English (Ed.), *Mathematical and analogical reasoning of young learners* (pp. 187-200). Mahwah, NJ: Lawrence Erlbaum Associates.

Hattikudur, S., & Alibali, M. (2007). Learning about the equal sign: Does contrasting with inequalities help? *Paper presented at the Society for Research in Child Development*.

Haugland, S. W. (1992). Effects of computer software on preschool children's developmental gains. *Journal of Computing in Childhood Education, 3* (1), 15–30.

Hausken, E. G., & Rathbun, A. (2004). Mathematics instruction in kindergarten: Classroom practices and outcomes. *Paper presented at the American Educational Research Association.*

Hawes, Z., LeFevre, J.-A., Xu, C., & Bruce, C. D. (2015). Mental rotation with tangible three-dimensional objects: A new measure sensitive to developmental differences in 4- to 8-year-old children. *Mind, Brain, and Education, 9*(1), 10–18. doi: 10.1111/mbe.12051

Hawes, Z., Moss, J., Caswell, B., Naqvi, S., & MacKinnon, S. (2017). Enhancing children's spatial and numerical skills through a dynamic spatial approach to early geometry instruction: Effects of a 32-week intervention. *Cognition and Instruction, 35*(3), 236–264. doi: 10.1080/07370008.2017.1323902

Hegarty, M., & Kozhevnikov, M. (1999). Types of visual-spatial representations and mathematical problems-solving. *Journal of Educational Psychology, 91*, 684–689.

Hemmeter, M. L., Ostrosky, M. M., & Fox, L. (2006). Social emotional foundations for early learning: A conceptual model for intervention. *School Psychology Review, 35*, 583–601.

Hemphill, J. A. R. (1987). *The effects of meaning and labeling on four-year-olds' ability to copy triangles.* Columbus, OH: The Ohio State University.

Henry, V. J., & Brown, R. S. (2008). First-grade basic facts: An investigation into teaching and learning of an accelerated, high-demand memorization standard. *Journal for Research in Mathematics Education, 39*(2), 153–183.

Herodotou, C. (2018). Young children and tablets: A systematic review of effects on learning and development. *Journal of Computer Assisted Learning, 34*(1), 1–9.

Herzog, M., Ehlert, A., & Fritz, A. (2019). Development of a sustainable place value understanding. In A. Fritz, V. G. Haase, & P. Räsänen (Eds.), *International handbook of mathematical learning difficulties: From the laboratory to the classroom* (pp. 561–579). Cham, Switzerland: Springer.

Heuvel-Panhuizen, M. V. D. (1996). *Assessment and realistic mathematics education.* Utrecht, The Netherlands: Freudenthal Institute, Utrecht University.

Hickendorff, M., Torbeyns, J., & Verschaffel, L. (2019). Multi-digit addition, subtraction, multiplication, and division strategies. In A. Fritz, V. G. Haase, & P. Räsänen (Eds.), *International handbook of mathematical learning difficulties:*

From the laboratory to the classroom (pp. 543–560). Cham, Switzerland: Springer.

Hiebert, J. C. (1999). Relationships between research and the NCTM Standards. *Journal for Research in Mathematics Education, 30*, 3–19.

Hiebert, J. C., & Grouws, D. A. (2007). The effects of classroom mathematics teaching on students' learning. In F. K. Lester, Jr. (Ed.), *Second handbook of research on mathematics teaching and learning* (Vol. 1, pp. 371–404). New York, NY: Information Age Publishing.

Hiebert, J. C., & Wearne, D. (1992). Links between teaching and learning place value with understanding in first grade. *Journal for Research in Mathematics Education, 23*, 98–122.

Hiebert, J. C., & Wearne, D. (1993). Instructional tasks, classroom discourse, and student learning in second-grade classrooms. *American Educational Research Journal, 30*, 393–425.

Hiebert, J. C., & Wearne, D. (1996). Instruction, understanding, and skill in multidigit addition and subtraction. *Cognition and Instruction, 14*, 251–283.

Ho-Hong, C. B. (2017). Mathematics anxiety and working memory: Longitudinal associations with mathematical performance in Chinese children. *Contemporary Educational Psychology, 51*, 99–113. doi: 10.1016/j.cedpsych.2017.06.006

Hojnoski, R. L., Caskie, G. I. L., & Miller Young, R. (2018). Early numeracy trajectories: Baseline performance levels and growth rates in young children by disability status. *Topics in Early Childhood Special Education, 37*(4), 206–218. doi: 10.1177/0271121417735901

Holt, J. (1982). *How children fail.* New York, NY: Dell.

Holton, D., Ahmed, A., Williams, H., & Hill, C. (2001). On the importance of mathematical play. *International Journal of Mathematical Education in Science and Technology, 32*, 401–415.

Harskamp, E. (2015). The effects of computer technology on primary school students' mathematics achievement: A meta-analysis. In S. Chinn (Ed.), *The Routledge international handbook of dyscalculia* (pp. 383–392). Abingdon, Oxon, UK: Routledge.

Helenius, O. (2017). Theorizing professional modes of action for teaching preschool mathematics. Paper presented at the Nordic Conference on Mathematics Education, NORMA 17, Stockholm, Sweeden.

Helenius, O., Johansson, M. L., Lange, T., Meaney, T., & Wernberg, A. (2016). Measuring temperature within the didactic space of preschool. *Nordic Studies in Mathematics Education, 21*(4), 155–176.

Hiebert, J., & Stigler, J. W. (2017). Teaching versus teachers as a lever for change: Comparing a Japanese and a U.S. perspective on improving instruction. *Educational Researcher*, *46*(4), 169-176. doi: 10.3102/0013189X17711899

Huber, B., Yeates, M., Meyer, D., Fleckhammer, L., & Kaufman, J. (2018). The effects of screen media content on young children's executive functioning. *Journal of Experimental Child Psychology*, *170*, 72-85. doi: 10.1016/j.jecp.2018.01.006

Hopkins, S. L., & Lawson, M. J. (2004). Explaining variability in retrieval times for addition produced by students with mathematical learning difficulties. In M. J. Høines & A. B. Fuglestad (Eds.), *Proceedings of the 28th Conference of the International Group for the Psychology in Mathematics Education* (Vol. 3, pp. 57-64). Bergen, Norway: Bergen University College.

Horne, M. (2004). Early gender differences. In M. J. Høines & A. B. Fuglestad (Eds.), *Proceedings of the 28th Conference of the International Group for the Psychology in Mathematics Education* (Vol. 3, pp. 65-72). Bergen, Norway: Bergen University College.

Howe, R. E. (2018). Cultural knowledge for teaching mathematics. In Y. Li, W. J. Lewis, & J. J. Madden (Eds.), *Mathematics matters in education: Essays in honor of Roger E. Howe* (pp. 19-39). Cham: Springer International Publishing.

Howes, C., Fuligni, A. S., Hong, S. S., Huang, Y. D., & Lara-Cinisomo, S. (2013). The preschool instructional context and child-teacher relationships. *Early Education & Development, 24*(3), 273-291. doi: 10.1080/10409289.2011.649664

Hsieh, W.-Y., Hemmeter, M. L., McCollum, J. A., & Ostrosky, M. M. (2009). Using coaching to increase preschool teachers' use of emergent literacy teaching strategies. *Early Childhood Research Quarterly, 24*, 229-247.

Huang, Q., Zhang, X., Liu, Y., Yang, W., & Song, Z. (2017). The contribution of parent-child numeracy activities to young Chinese children's mathematical ability. *British Journal of Educational Psychology, 87*(3), 328-344. doi: 10.1111/bjep.12152

Hudson, T. (1983). Correspondences and numerical differences between disjoint sets. *Child Development, 54*, 84-90.

Hughes, M. (1981). Can preschool children add and subtract? *Educational Psychology, 1*, 207-219.

Hughes, M. (1986). *Children and number: Difficulties in learning mathematics*. Oxford, England: Basil Blackwell.

Humphrey, G. K., & Humphrey, G. K. (1995). The role of structure in infant visual pattern perception. *Canadian Journal of Psychology, 43*(2), 165-182.

Hunting, R., & Davis, G. (Eds.). (1991). *Early fraction learning*. New York, NY: Springer-Verlag.

Hunting, R. P. (2003). Part-whole number knowledge in preschool children. *The Journal of Mathematical Behavior, 22*, 217-235.

Hunting, R., & Pearn, C. (2003). The mathematical thinking of young children: Pre-K–2. In N. S. Pateman, B. J. Dougherty, & J. Zilliox (Eds.), *Proceedings of the 27th Conference of the International Group for the Psychology in Mathematics Education* (Vol. 1, p. 187). Honolulu, HI: University of Hawai'i.

Hurst, M., Monahan, K. L., Heller, E., & Cordes, S. (2014). 123s and ABCs: Developmental shifts in logarithmic-to-linear responding reflect fluency with sequence values. *Developmental Science.* doi: 10.1111/desc.12165

Hutinger, P. L., Bell, C., Beard, M., Bond, J., Johanson, J., & Terry, C. (1998). *The early childhood emergent literacy technology research study. Final report.* Macomb, IL: Western Illinois University.

Hutinger, P. L., & Johanson, J. (2000). Implementing and maintaining an effective early childhood comprehensive technology system. *Topics in Early Childhood Special Education, 20*(3), 159-173.

Huttenlocher, J., Jordan, N. C., & Levine, S. C. (1994). A mental model for early arithmetic. *Journal of Experimental Psychology: General, 123*, 284-296.

Huttenlocher, J., Levine, S. C., & Ratliff, K. R. (2011). The development of measurement: From holistic perceptual comparison to unit understanding. In N. L. Stein & S. Raudenbush (Eds.), *Developmental science goes to school: Implications for education and public policy research* (pp. 175-188). New York, NY: Taylor and Francis.

Huttenlocher, J., Newcombe, N. S., & Sandberg, E. H. (1994). The coding of spatial location in young children. *Cognitive Psychology, 27*(2), 115-147.

Hyde, J. S., Fennema, E. H., & Lamon, S. J. (1990). Gender differences in mathematics performance: A meta-analysis. *Psychological Bulletin, 107*, 139-155.

Hynes-Berry, M., & Grandau, L. (2019). *Where's the math?* Washington, DC: National Association for the Education of Young Children.

Irwin, K. C., Vistro-Yu, C. P., & Ell, F. R. (2004). Understanding linear measurement: A comparison of Filipino and New Zealand children. *Mathematics Education Research Journal, 16*(2), 3-24.

Ishigaki, E. H., Chiba, T., & Matsuda, S. (1996). Young children's communication and self expression in the technological era. *Early Childhood Development and Care, 119*, 101-117.

Isik-Ercan, Z., Zeynep Inan, H., Nowak, J. A., & Kim, B. (2014). "We put on the glasses and moon comes closer!" Urban second graders exploring the earth, the sun and moon through 3d technologies in a science and literacy unit. *International Journal of Science Education, 36*(1), 129-156.

Israel, M., Jeong, G., Ray, M., & Lash, T. (2020). Teaching elementary computer science through universal design for learning. Paper presented at the Proceedings of the 51st ACM Technical Symposium on Computer Science Education.

Iuculano, T., Rosenberg-Lee, M., Richardson, J., Tenison, C., Fuchs, L. S., Supekar, K., & Menon, V. (2015). Cognitive tutoring induces widespread neuroplasticity and remediates brain function in children with mathematical learning disabilities. *Nat Commun, 6*, 8453. doi: 10.1038/ncomms9453

Jablansky, S., Alexander, P. A., Dumas, D., & Compton, V. (2015). Developmental differences in relational reasoning among primary and secondary school students. *Journal of Educational Psychology Advanced Online Publication* 18. doi: 10.1037/edu0000070

Janzen, J. (2008). Teaching English language learners. *Review of Educational Research, 78*, 1010-1038.

Jayanthi, M., Gersten, R., & Baker, S. (2008). *Mathematics instruct ion for students with learning disabilities or difficulty learning mathematics: A guide for teachers.* Portsmouth, NH: RMC Research Corporation, Center on Instruction.

Jenkins, J. M., Duncan, G. J., Auger, A., Bitler, M. P., Domina, T., & Burchinal, M. R. (2018). Boosting school readiness: Should preschool teachers target skills or the whole child? *Economic of Education Review, 65*, 107-125. doi: 10.1016/j.econedurev.2018.05.001

Jenkins, J. M., Watts, T. W., Magnuson, K. A., Gershoof, E., Clements, D. H., Sarama, J., & Duncan, G. J. (2018). Do high quality kindergarten and first grade classrooms mitigate preschool fadeout? *Journal of Research on Educational Effectiveness, 11*(3), 339-374. doi: 10.1080/19345747.2018.1441347

Jenks, K. M., van Lieshout, E. C. D. M., & de Moor, J. M. H. (2012). Cognitive correlates of mathematical achievement in children with cerebral palsy and typically developing children. *British Journal of Educational Psychology, 82*(1), 120-135. doi: 10.1111/j.2044-8279.2011.02034.x

Jett, C. (2018). The effects of children's literature on preservice early childhood mathematics teachers' thinking. *Journal of the Scholarship of Teaching and Learning, 18*(1), 96-114. doi: 10.14434/josotl.v18i1.20722

Jitendra, A. K. (2019). Using schema-based instruction to improve students' mathematical word problem solving performance. In A. Fritz, V. G. Haase, & P. Räsänen (Eds.), *International handbook of mathematical learning difficulties:*

From the laboratory to the classroom (pp. 595-609). Cham, Switzerland: Springer.

Johnson, D. W., & Johnson, R. T. (2009). An educational psychology success story: Social interdependence theory and cooperative learning. *Educational Researcher, 38*(5), 365-379.

Johnson, M. (1987). *The body in the mind.* Chicago: The University of Chicago Press.

Johnson, V. M. (2000). *An investigation of the effects of instructional strategies on conceptual understanding of young children in mathematics.* New Orleans, LA: American Educational Research Association.

Johnson-Gentile, K., Clements, D. H., & Battista, M. T. (1994). The effects of computer and noncomputer environments on student's conceptualizations of geometric motions. *Journal of Educational Computing Research, 11*, 121-140.

Jordan, K. E., Suanda, S. H., & Brannon, E. M. (2008). Intersensory redundancy accelerates preverbal numerical competence. *Cognition, 108*, 210-221.

Jordan, N. C., Glutting, J., & Ramineni, C. (2009). The importance of number sense to mathematics achievement in first and third grades. *Learning and Individual Differences, 22*(1), 82-88.

Jordan, N. C., Glutting, J., Ramineni, C., & Watkins, M. W. (2010). Validating a number sense screening tool for use in kindergarten and first grade: Prediction of mathematics proficiency in third grade. *School Psychology Review, 39*(2), 181-195.

Jordan, N. C., Hanich, L. B., & Kaplan, D. (2003). A longitudinal study of mathematical competencies in children with specific mathematics difficulties versus children with comorbid mathematics and reading difficulties. *Child Development, 74*, 834-850.

Jordan, N. C., Hanich, L. B., & Uberti, H. Z. (2003). Mathematical thinking and learning difficulties. In A. J. Baroody & A. Dowk-er (Eds.), *The development of arithmetic concepts and skills: Constructing adaptive expertise* (pp. 359-383). Mahwah, NJ: Lawrence Erlbaum Associates.

Jordan, N. C., Huttenlocher, J., & Levine, S. C. (1994). Assessing early arithmetic abilities: Effects of verbal and nonverbal response types on the calculation performance of middle- and low-income children. *Learning and Individual Differences, 6*, 413-432.

Jordan, N. C., Kaplan, D., Locuniak, M. N., & Ramineni, C. (2006). Predicting first-grade math achievement from developmental number sense trajectories. *Learning Disabilities Research and Practice, 22*(1), 36-46.

Jordan, N. C., Kaplan, D., Oláh, L. N., & Locuniak, M. N. (2006). Number sense growth in kindergarten:

A longitudinal investigation of children at risk for mathematics difficulties. *Child Development, 77*, 153-175.

Jordan, N. C., & Montani, T. O. (1997). Cognitive arithmetic and problem solving: A comparison of children with specific and general mathematics difficulties. *Journal of Learning Disabilities, 30*, 624-634.

Kankaanranta, M., Koivula, M., Laakso, M.-L., & Mustola, M. (2017). Digital games in early childhood: Broadening definitions of learning, literacy, and play. In M. Ma & A. Oikonomou (Eds.), *Serious Games and Edutainment Applications : Volume II* (pp. 349-367). Cham: Springer International Publishing.

Kazakoff, E., Sullivan, A., & Bers, M. (2013). The effect of a classroom-based intensive robotics and programming workshop on sequencing ability in early childhood. *Early Childhood Education Journal, 41*(4), 245-255. doi: 10.1007/s10643-012-0554-5

Ketamo, H., & Kiili, K. (2010). Conceptual change takes time: Game based learning cannot be only supplementary amusement. *Journal of Educational Multimedia and Hypermedia, 19*(4), 399-419.

Kilday, C. R., Kinzie, M. B., Mashburn, A. J., & Whittaker, J. V. (2012). Accuracy of teachers' judgments of preschoolers' math skills. *Journal of Psychoeducational Assessment, 30*(2), 48-158. doi: 10.1016/j.ecresq.2014.06.007

Kim, H. (2015). Foregone opportunities: Unveiling teacher expectancy effects in kindergarten using counterfactual predictions. *Social Psychology of Education*, 1-24. doi: 10.1007/s11218-014-9284-4

Kim, S., & Chang, M. (2010). Does computer use promote the mathematical proficiency of ELL students? *Journal of Educational Computing Research, 42*, 285-305.

Knaus, M. J. (2017). Supporting early mathematics learning in early childhood settings. *Australasian Journal of Early Childhood, 42*(3), 4-13. doi: 10.23965/AJEC.42.3.01

Kramarski, B., & Weiss, I. (2007). Investigating preschool children's mathematical engagement in a multimedia collaborative environment. *Journal of Cognitive Education and Psychology, 6*, 411-432.

Kraus, W. H. (1981). Using a computer game to reinforce skills in addition basic facts in second grade. *Journal for Research in Mathematics Education, 12*, 152-155.

Kamii, C. (1973). Pedagogical principles derived from Piaget's theory: Relevance for educational practice. In M. Schwebel & J. Raph (Eds.), *Piaget in the classroom* (pp. 199-215). New York, NY: Basic Books.

Kamii, C. (1985). *Young children reinvent arithmetic: Implications of Piaget's theory*. New York, NY: Teaching College Press.

Kamii, C. (1986). Place value: An explanation of its difficulty and educational implications for the primary grades. *Journal of Research in Childhood Education, 1*, 75-86.

Kamii, C. (1989). *Young children continue to reinvent arithmetic: 2nd grade. Implications of Piaget's theory*. New York, NY: Teaching College Press.

Kamii, C., & DeVries, R. (1980). *Group games in early education: Implications of Piaget's theory*. Washington, DC: National Association for the Education of Young Children.

Kamii, C., & Dominick, A. (1997). To teach or not to teach algorithms. *Journal of Mathematical Behavior, 16*, 51-61.

Kamii, C., & Dominick, A. (1998). The harmful effects of algorithms in grades 1-4. In L. J. Morrow & M. J. Kenney (Eds.), *The teaching and learning of algorithms in school mathematics* (pp. 130-140). Reston, VA: National Council of Teachers of Mathematics.

Kamii, C., & Housman, L. B. (1999). *Young children reinvent arithmetic: Implications of Piaget's theory* (2nd ed.). New York, NY: Teachers College Press.

Kamii, C., & Kato, Y. (2005). Fostering the development of logico-mathematical knowledge in a card game at ages 5-6. *Early Education & Development, 16*, 367-383.

Kamii, C., Miyakawa, Y., & Kato, Y. (2004). The development of logico-mathematical knowledge in a block-building activity at ages 1-4. *Journal of Research in Childhood Education, 19*, 13-26.

Kamii, C., Rummelsburg, J., & Kari, A. R. (2005). Teaching arithmetic to low-performing, low-SES first graders. *Journal of Mathematical Behavior, 24*, 39-50.

Kamii, C., & Russell, K. A. (2012). Elapsed time: Why is it so difficult to teach? *Journal for Research in Mathematics Education, 43*(3), 296-315.

Kaput, J. J., Carraher, D. W., & Blanton, M. L. (Eds.). (2008). *Algebra in the early grades*. Mahwah, NJ: Lawrence Erlbaum Associates.

Karmiloff-Smith, A. (1992). *Beyond modularity: A developmental perspective on cognitive science*. Cambridge, MA: MIT Press.

Karoly, L. A., Greenwood, P. W., Everingham, S. S., Houbé, J., Kilburn, M. R., Rydell, C. P., Sanders, M., Chiesa, J. (1998). *Investing in our children: What we know and don't know about the costs and benefits of early childhood interventions*. Santa Monica, CA: Rand Education.

Kawai, N., & Matsuzawa, T. (2000). Numerical memory span in a chimpanzee. *Nature, 403*, 39-40.

Keller, S., & Goldberg, I. (1997). *Let's Learn Shapes with Shapely-CAL*. Great Neck, NY: Creative Adaptations for Learning, Inc.

Keren, G., & Fridin, M. (2014). Kindergarten social assistive robot (KindSAR) for children's geometric thinking and metacognitive development in preschool education: A pilot study. *Computers in Human Behavior*, 35, 400-412. doi: 10.1016/j.chb.2014.03.009

Kersh, J., Casey, B. M., & Young, J. M. (2008). Research on spatial skills and block building in girls and boys: The relationship to later mathematics learning. In B. Spodek & O. N. Saracho (Eds.), *Contemporary perspectives on mathematics in early childhood education* (pp. 233-251). Charlotte, NC: Information Age Publishing.

Kidd, J. K., Carlson, A. G., Gadzichowski, K. M., Boyer, C. E., Gallington, D. A., & Pasnak, R. (2013). Effects of patterning instruction on the academic achievement of 1st-grade children. *Journal of Research in Childhood Education*, 27(2), 224-238. doi: 10.1080/02568543.2013.766664

Kilpatrick, J. (1987). Problem formulating: Where do good problems come from? In A. H. Schoenfeld (Ed.), *Cognitive science and mathematics education* (pp. 123-147). Hillsdale, NJ: Lawrence Erlbaum Associates.

Kilpatrick, J., Swafford, J., & Findell, B. (Eds.) (2001). *Adding it up: Helping children learn mathematics*. Washington, DC: Mathematics Learning Study Committee, National Research Council; National Academies Press.

Kim, B., Pack, Y. H., & Yi, S. H. (2017). Subitizing in children and adults, depending on the object individuation level of stimulus: Focusing on performance according to spacing, color, and shape of objects. *Family and Environment Research*, 55(5), 491-505. doi: 10.6115/fer.2017.036

Kim, S.-Y. (1994). The relative effectiveness of hands-on and computer-simulated manipulatives in teaching seriation, classification, geometric, and arithmetic concepts to kindergarten children. *Dissertation Abstracts International*, 54/09, 3319.

King, J. A., & Alloway, N. (1992). Preschooler's use of microcomputers and input devices. *Journal of Educational Computing Research*, 8, 451-468.

Kinnear, V., & Wittmann, E. C. (2018). Early mathematics education: A plea for mathematically founded conceptions. In V. Kinnear, M. Y. Lai, & T. Muir (Eds.), *Forging connections in early mathematics teaching and learning* (pp. 17-35). Gateway East, Singapore: Springer.

Kleemans, T., Segers, E., & Verhoeven, L. (2013). Relations between home numeracy experiences and basic calculation skills of children with and without specific language impairment. *Early Childhood Research Quarterly*, 28(2), 415-423. doi: 10.1016/j.ecresq.2012.10.004

Kleemans, T., Segers, E., & Verhoeven, L. (2018). Individual differences in basic arithmetic skills in children with and without developmental language disorder: Role of home numeracy experiences. *Early Childhood Research Quarterly*, 43(2), 62-72. doi: 10.1016/j.ecresq.2018.01.005

Klein, A., & Starkey, P. (2004). Fostering preschool children's mathematical development: Findings from the Berkeley Math Readiness Project. In D. H. Clements, J. Sarama, & A.-M. DiBiase (Eds.), *Engaging young children in mathematics: Standards for early childhood mathematics education* (pp. 343-360). Mahwah, NJ: Lawrence Erlbaum Associates.

Klein, A., Starkey, P., Clements, D. H., Sarama, J., & Iyer, R. (2008). Effects of a pre-kindergarten mathematics intervention: A randomized experiment. Journal of Research on Educational Effectiveness, 1 (2), 155-178. doi: 10.1080/19345740802114533

Klein, A., Starkey, P., & Wakeley, A. (1999). Enhancing pre-kindergarten children's readiness for school mathematics. *Paper presented at the American Educational Research Association*.

Klein, A. S., Beishuizen, M., & Treffers, A. (1998). The empty number line in Dutch second grades: Realistic versus gradual program design. *Journal for Research in Mathematics Education*, 29, 443-464.

Klibanoff, R. S., Levine, S. C., Huttenlocher, J., Vasilyeva, M., & Hedges, L. V. (2006). Preschool children's mathematical knowledge: The effect of teacher "math talk". *Developmental Psychology*, 42, 59-69.

Klim-Klimaszewska, A., & Nazaruk, S. (2017). The scope of implementation of geometric concepts in selected kindergartens in Poland. *Problems of Education in the 21st Century*, 75(4), 345-353.

Klinzing, D. G., & Hall, A. (1985). *A study of the behavior of children in a preschool equipped with computers*. Chicago: American Educational Research Association.

Knapp, M. S., Shields, P. M., & Turnbull, B. J. (1992). *Academic challenge for the children of poverty*. Washington, DC: U.S. Department of Education.

Kolkman, M. E., Kroesbergen, E. H., & Leseman, P. P. M. (2013). Early numerical development and the role of non-symbolic and symbolic skills. *Learning and Instruction*, 25(165), 95-103. doi: 10.1016/j.learninstruc.2012.12.001

Konold, C., & Pollatsek, A. (2002). Data analysis as the search for signals in noisy processes. *Journal for Research in Mathematics Education*, 33, 259-289.

Konold, T. R., & Pianta, R. C. (2005). Empirically-derived, person-oriented patterns of school readiness in typically- developing children: Description and prediction to first-grade achievement. *Applied Developmental Science, 9,* 174–187.

Koontz, K. L., & Berch, D. B. (1996). Identifying simple numerical stimuli: Processing inefficiencies exhibited by arithmetic learning disabled children. *Mathematical Cognition, 2,* 1–23.

Koponen, T., Salmi, P., Eklund, K., & Aro, T. (2013). Counting and RAN: Predictors of arithmetic calculation and reading fluency. *Journal of Educational Psychology, 105*(1), 162–175. doi: 10.1037/a0029285

Korat, O., Gitait, A., Bergman Deitcher, D., & Mevarech, Z. (2017). Early literacy programme as support for immigrant children and as transfer to early numeracy. *Early Child Development and Care, 187*(3), 18.

Korkmaz, H. ., & Yilmaz, A. (2017). Investigating kindergartners geometric and spatial thinking skils: In context of gender and age. *European Journal of Education Studies, 3*(9), 55–69. doi: 10.5281/zenodo.845498

Kostos, K., & Shin, E.-K. (2010). Using math journals to enhance second graders' communication of mathematical thinking. *Early Childhood Education Journal, 38*(3), 223–231.

Krajewski, K., & Schneider, W. (2009). Exploring the impact of phonological awareness, visual–spatial working memory, and preschool quantity–number competencies on mathematics achievement in elementary school: Findings from a 3-year longitudinal study. *Journal of Experimental Child Psychology, 103*(4), 516–531 doi: 10.1016/j.jecp.2009.03.009

Kretlow, A. G., Wood, C. L., & Cooke, N. L. (2011). Using in-service and coaching to increase kindergarten teachers' accurate delivery of group instructional units. *The Journal of Special Education, 44*(4), 234–246.

Kritzer, K. L., & Pagliaro, C. M. (2013). An intervention for early mathematical success: Outcomes from the hybrid version of the Building Math Readiness Parents as Partners (MRPP) project. *Journal of Deaf Studies and Deaf Education, 18*(1), 30–46. doi: 10.1093/deafed/ens033

Kutscher, B., Linchevski, L., & Eisenman, T. (2002). From the Lotto game to subtracting two-digit numbers in first-graders. In A. D. Cockburn & E. Nardi (Eds.), *Proceedings of the 26th Conference of the International Group for the Psychology in Mathematics Education* (Vol. 3, pp. 249–256). University of East Anglia.

Lai, Y., Carlson, M. A., & Heaton, R. M. (2018). Giving reason and giving purpose. In Y. Li, W. J. Lewis, & J. J. Madden (Eds.), *Mathematics matters in education: Essays in honor of Roger E. Howe* (pp. 149–171). Cham: Springer International Publishing.

Lamy, C. E., Frede, E., Seplocha, H., Strasser, J., Jambunathan, S., Juncker, J. A., Jambunathan, S. ... Wolock, E. (2004). Inch by inch, row by row, gonna make this garden grow: Classroom quality and language skills in the Abbott Preschool Program [Publication]. Retrieved September 29, 2007, from http://nieer.org/docs/?DocID=94

Landau, B. (1988). The construction and use of spatial knowledge in blind and sighted children. In J. Stiles-Davis, M. Kritchevsky, & U. Bellugi (Eds.), *Spatial cognition: Brain bases and development* (pp. 343–371). Mahwah, NJ: Lawrence Erlbaum Associates.

Landerl, K., Bevan, A., & Butterworth, B. (2004). Developmental dyscalculia and basic numerical capacities: A study of 8-9-year-old children. *Cognition, 93,* 99–125.

Landry, S. H., Zucker, T. A., Williams, J. M., Merz, E. C., Guttentag, C. L., & Taylor, H. B. (2017). Improving school readiness of high-risk preschoolers: Combining high quality instructional strategies with responsive training for teachers and parents. *Early Childhood Research Quarterly, 40,* 38–51. doi: 10.1016/j.ecresq.2016.12.001

Lane, C. (2010). *Case study: The effectiveness of virtual manipulatives in the teaching of primary mathematics.* (Master thesis), University of Limerick, Limerick, UK. Retrieved from http://digitalcommons.fiu.edu/etd/229

Langhorst, P., Ehlert, A., & Fritz, A. (2012). Non-numerical and numerical understanding of the part–whole concept of children aged 4 to 8 in word problems. *Journal Für Mathematik-Didaktik, 33*(2), 233–262. doi: 10.1007/s13138-012-0039-5

Lansdell, J. M. (1999). Introducing young children to mathematical concepts: Problems with "new" terminology. *Educational Studies, 25,* 327–333.

Larson, L. C., & Rumsey, C. (2018). Bringing stories to life: Integrating literature and math manipulatives. *The Reading Teacher, 71*(5), 589–596. doi: 10.1002/trtr.1652

Laski, E. V., Casey, B. M., Yu, Q., Dulaney, A., Heyman, M., & Dearing, E. (2013). Spatial skills as a predictor of first grade girls' use of higher level arithmetic strategies. *Learning and Individual Differences, 23*(1), 123–130. doi: 10.1016/j.lindif.2012.08.001

Laski, E. V., & Siegler, R. S. (2014). Learning from number board games: You learn what you encode. *Developmental Psychology, 50*(3), 853. doi: 10.1037/a0034321

Laski, E. V., & Yu, Q. (2014). Number line estimation and mental addition: Examining the potential roles of language and education. *Journal of Experimental Child Psychology, 117,* 29–44.

Laurillard, D., & Taylor, J. (1994). Designing the Stepping Stones: An evaluation of interactive media in the classroom. *Journal of Educational Television, 20,* 169–184.

Leavy, A., Pope, J., & Breatnach, D. (2018). From cradle to classroom: Exploring opportunities to support the development of shape and space concepts in very young children. In V. Kinnear, M. Y. Lai, & T. Muir (Eds.), *Forging Connections in Early Mathematics Teaching and Learning* (pp. 115-138). Singapore: Springer Singapore.

Lebens, M., Graff, M., & Mayer, P. (2011). The affective dimensions of mathematical difficulties in schoolchildren. *Education Research International, 2011,* 1-13.

Lebron-Rodriguez, D. E., & Pasnak, R. (1977). Induction of intellectual gains in blind children. *Journal of Experimental Child Psychology, 24,* 505-515.

Lee, J. (2002). Racial and ethnic achievement gap trends: Reversing the progress toward equity? *Educational Researcher, 31,* 3-12.

Lee, J. (2004). Correlations between kindergarten teachers' attitudes toward mathematics and teaching practice. *Journal of Early Childhood Teacher Education, 25*(2), 173-184.

Lee, J. S., & Ginsburg, H. P. (2007). What is appropriate mathematics education for four-year-olds? *Journal of Early Childhood Research, 5*(1), 2-31.

Lee, K., & Bull, R. (2015). Developmental changes in working memory, updating, and math achievement. *Journal of Educational Psychology, 108*(6), 869-882.

Lee, S. A., Spelke, E. S., & Vallortigara, G. (2012). Chicks, like children, spontaneously reorient by three-dimensional environmental geometry, not by image matching. *Biology Letters, 8*(4), 492-494. doi: 10.1098/rsbl.2012.0067

Lee, V. E., Brooks-Gunn, J., Schnur, E., & Liaw, F.-R. (1990). Are Head Start effects sustained? A longitudinal follow-up comparison of disadvantaged children attending Head Start, no preschool, and other preschool programs. *Child Development, 61,* 495-507.

Lee, V. E., & Burkam, D. T. (2002). *Inequality at the starting gate.* Washington, DC: Economic Policy Institute.

Lee, V. E., Burkam, D. T., Ready, D. D., Honigman, J. J., & Meisels, S. J. (2006). Full-day vs. half-day kindergarten: In which program do children learn more? *American Journal of Education, 112,* 163-208.

Leeson, N. (1995). Investigations of kindergarten student's spatial constructions. In B. Atweh & S. Flavel (Eds.), *Proceedings of 18th Annual Conference of Mathematics Education Research Group of Australasia* (pp. 384–389). Darwin, AU: Mathematics Education Research Group of Australasia.

Leeson, N., Stewart, R., & Wright, R. J. (1997). Young children's knowledge of three-dimensional shapes: Four case studies. In F. Biddulph & K. Carr (Eds.), *Proceedings of the 20th Annual Conference of the Mathematics Education Research Group of Australasia* (Vol. 1, pp. 310-317). Hamilton, New Zealand: MERGA.

LeFevre, J.-A., Polyzoi, E., Skwarchuk, S.-L., Fast, L., & Sowinskia, C. (2010). Do home numeracy and literacy practices of Greek and Canadian parents predict the numeracy skills of kindergarten children? *International Journal of Early Years Education, 18*(1), 55-70.

Lehrer, R. (2003). Developing understanding of measurement. In J. Kilpatrick, W. G. Martin, & D. Schifter (Eds.), *A Research companion to Principles and Standards for School Mathematics* (pp. 179-192). Reston, VA: National Council of Teachers of Mathematics.

Lehrer, R., Harckham, L. D., Archer, P., & Pruzek, R. M. (1986). Microcomputer-based instruction in special education. *Journal of Educational Computing Research, 2,* 337-355.

Lehrer, R., Jacobson, C., Thoyre, G., Kemeny, V., Strom, D., Horvarth, J., Gance, S.& Koehler, M. (1998). Developing understanding of geometry and space in the primary grades. In R. Lehrer & D. Chazan (Eds.), *Designing learning environments for developing understanding of geometry and space* (pp. 169-200). Mahwah, NJ: Lawrence Erlbaum Associates.

Lehrer, R., Jenkins, M., & Osana, H. (1998). Longitudinal study of children's reasoning about space and geometry. In R. Lehrer & D. Chazan (Eds.), *Designing learning environments for developing understanding of geometry and space* (pp. 137-167). Mahwah, NJ: Erlbaum.

Lehrer, R., & Pritchard, C. (2002). Symbolizing space into being. In K. P. E. Gravemeijer, R. Lehrer, B. Van Oers, & L. Verschaffel (Eds.), *Symbolizing, modeling and tool use in mathematics education* (pp. 59-86). Dordrecht: Kluwer Academic Publishers.

Lehrer, R., & Schauble, L. (Eds.). (2002). *Investigating real data in the classroom: Expanding children's understanding of math and science.* New York, NY: Teachers College Press.

Lehrer, R., Strom, D., & Confrey, J. (2002). Grounding metaphors and inscriptional resonance: Children's emerging understandings of mathematical similarity. *Cognition and Instruction, 20*(3), 359-398.

Lehtinen, E., & Hannula, M. M. (2006). Attentional processes, abstraction and transfer in early mathematical development. In L. Verschaffel, F. Dochy, M. Boekaerts, & S. Vosniadou (Eds.), *Instructional psychology: Past, present and future trends. Fifteen essays in honour of Erik De Corte* (Vol. 49, pp. 39–55). Amsterdam, The Netherlands: Elsevier.

Leibovich, T., Katzin, N., Harel, M., & Henik, A. (2016). From 'sense of number' to 'sense of magnitude'–The role of continuous magnitudes in numerical cognition. *Behavioral and Brain Sciences In Press*, 60. doi: 10.1017/S0140525X1600096

Lembke, E. S., & Foegen, A. (2008). *Identifying indicators of performance in early mathematics for kindergarten and grade 1 students*. Submitted for publication.

Lembke, E. S., Foegen, A., Whittake, T. A., & Hampton, D. (2008). Establishing technically adequate measures of progress in early numeracy. *Assessment for Effective Intervention*, *33*(4), 206–210.

Lange, T., Meaney, T., Riesbeck, E., & Wernberg, A. (2014). Mathematical teaching moments: between instruction and construction. In C. Benz, B. Brandt, U. Kortenkamp, G. Krummheuer, S. Ladel, & R. Vogel (Eds.), *Early mathematics learning: Selected papers of the POEM 2012 conference* (pp. 37–54). Springer. https://doi.org/10.1007/978-1-4614-4678-1_4

Le, V.-N., Schaack, D., Neishi, K., Hernandez, M. W., & Blank, R. K. (2019). Advanced content coverage at kindergarten: Are there trade-offs between academic achievement and social-emotional skills? *American Educational Research Journal*, *56*(4). doi: 10.3102/0002831218813913

Lehrl, S., Kluczniok, K., Rossbach, H.-G., & Anders, Y. (2017). Longer-term effects of a high-quality preschool intervention on childrens mathematical development through age 12: Results from the German model project Kindergarten of the Future in Bavaria. *Global Education Review*, *4*(3), 70–87.

Lehtinen, E., Brezovszky, B., Rodríguez-Aflecht, G., Lehtinen, H., Hannula-Sormunen, M. M., McMullen, J., ... Jaakkola, T. (2015). Number Navigation Game (NNG): Design principles and game description *Describing and Studying Domain-Specific Serious Games* (pp. 45–61).

Lehtinen, E., Hannula- Sormunen, M. M., McMullen, J., & Gruber, H. (2017). Cultivating mathematical skills: From drill-and-practice to deliberate practice. *ZDM Mathematics Education*. doi: 10.1007/s11858-017-0856-6

Lepola, J., Niemi, P., Kuikka, M., & Hannula, M. M. (2005). Cognitive-linguistic skills and motivation as longitudinal predictors of reading and arithmetic achievement: A follow-up study from kindergarten to grade 2. *International Journal of Educational Research*, *43*, 250–271.

Lerkkanen, M.-K., Kiuru, N., Pakarinen, E., Viljaranta, J., Poikkeus, A.-M., Rasku-Puttonen, H. Siekkinen, M., & Nurmi, J.-E. (2012). The role of teaching practices in the development of children's interest in reading and mathematics in kindergarten. *Contemporary Educational Psychology*, *37*(4), 266–279. doi: 10.1016/j.cedpsych.2011.03.004

Lerkkanen, M.-K., Rasku-Puttonen, H., Aunola, K., & Nurmi, J.-E. (2005). Mathematical performance predicts progress in reading comprehension among 7-year-olds. *European Journal of Psychology of Education*, *20*(2), 121–137.

Lerner, J. (1997). *Learning disabilities*. Boston, MA: Houghton Mifflin Company.

Lesh, R. A. (1990). Computer-based assessment of higher order understandings and processes in elementary mathematics. In G. Kulm (Ed.), *Assessing higher order thinking in mathematics* (pp. 81–110). Washington, DC: American Association for the Advancement of Science.

Levesque, A. (2010). *An investigation of the conditions under which procedural content enhances conceptual self-explanations in mathematics*. Master's thesis, Concordia University. Available from ProQuest Dissertations and Theses database (UMI no. MR67234). Retrieved from http://proquest.umi.com/pqdlink?did=2191474161&Fmt=7&clientId=39334&RQT=309&VName=PQD

Levine, S. C., Gibson, D. J., & Berkowitz, T. (2019). Mathematical development in the early home environment. In D. C. Geary, D. B. Berch, & K. M. Koepke (Eds.), *Cognitive foundations for improving mathematical learning* (Vol. 5, pp. 107–142). San Diego, CA: Academic Press (an Elsevier imprint).

Levine, S. C., Gunderson, E., & Huttenlocher, J. (2011). Mathematical development during the preschool years in context: Home and school input variations. In N. L. Stein & S. Raudenbush (Eds.), *Developmental Science Goes to School: Implications for Education and Public Policy Research* (pp. 190–202). New York, NY: Taylor and Francis.

Levine, S. C., Huttenlocher, J., Taylor, A., & Langrock, A. (1999). Early sex differences in spatial skill. *Developmental Psychology*, *35*(4), 940–949.

Levine, S. C., Jordan, N. C., & Huttenlocher, J. (1992). Development of calculation abilities in young children. *Journal of Experimental Child Psychology*, *53*, 72–103.

Levine, S. C., Ratliff, K. R., Huttenlocher, J., & Cannon, J. (2012). Early puzzle play: A predictor of preschoolers' spatial transformation skill. *Developmental Psychology, 48*(2), 530–542. doi: 10.1037/a0025913

Levine, S. C., Suriyakham, L. W., Rowe, M. L., Huttenlocher, J., & Gunderson, E. A. (2010). What counts in the development of young children's number knowledge? *Developmental Psychology, 46*(5), 1309-1319. doi: 10.1037/a0019671

Li, X., Chi, L., DeBey, M., & Baroody, A. J. (2015). A study of early childhood mathematics teaching in the United States and China. *Early Education and Development, 26*(3), 450–478. doi: 10.1080/10409289.2015.994464

Li, Z., & Atkins, M. (2004). Early childhood computer experience and cognitive and motor development. *Pediatrics, 113*, 1715-1722.

Liaw, F.-R., Meisels, S. J., & Brooks-Gunn, J. (1995). The effects of experience of early intervention on low birth weight, premature children: The Infant Health and Development program. *Early Childhood Research Quarterly, 10*, 405-431.

Liben, L. S. (2008). Understanding maps: Is the purple country on the map really purple? *Knowledge Question, 36*, 20-30.

Libertus, M. E. (2019). Understanding the link between the approximate number system and math abilities. In D. C. Geary, D. B. Berch, & K. M. Koepke (Eds.), *Cognitive foundations for improving mathematical learning* (Vol. 5, pp. 91-106). San Diego, CA: Academic Press (an Elsevier imprint).

Libertus, M. E., Feigenson, L., & Halberda, J. (2011a). Preschool acuity of the Approximate Number System correlates with math abilities. *Developmental Science, 14*(6), 1292-1300. doi: 10.1111/j.1467-7687.2011.080100x

Libertus, M. E., Feigenson, L., & Halberda, J. (2011b). Effects of approximate number system training for numerical approximation and school math abilities. *Poster presented at NICHD Math Cognition Conference*, Bethesda, MD.

Libertus, M. E., Feigenson, L., & Halberda, J. (2013, May). Effects of approximate number system training for numerical approximation and school math abilities. *Paper presented at the NICHD Mathematics Meeting*, Bethesda, MD.

Lieber, J., Horn, E., Palmer, S., & Fleming, K. (2008). Access to the general education curriculum for preschoolers with disabilities: Children's School Success. *Exceptionality, 16*(1), 18-32. doi: 10.1080/09362830701796776

Liggett, R. S. (2017). The impact of use of manipulatives on the math scores of grade 2 students. *Brock Education Journal, 26*(2), 87-101.

Lin, C.-H., & Chen, C.-M. (2016). Developing spatial visualization and mental rotation with a digital puzzle game at primary school level. *Computers in Human Behavior, 57*, 23-30. doi: 10.1016/j.chb.2015.12.026

Lin, G. (2020a). *Circle! sphere!* Watertown, MA: Charlesbridge Publishing.

Lin, G. (2020b). *The last marshmallow [math notes by Douglas H. Clements]*. Watertown, MA: Charlesbridge Publishing.

Lin, Y.-H., & Hou, H.-T. (2016). Exploring young children's performance on and acceptance of an educational scenario-based digital game for teaching route-planning strategies: A case study. *Interactive Learning Environments, 24*(8), 1967-1980.

Link, T., Moeller, K., Huber, S., Fischer, U., & Nuerk, H.-C. (2013). Walk the number line – An embodied training of numerical concepts. *Trends in Neuroscience and Education, 2*(2), 74-84.

Linnell, M., & Fluck, M. (2001). The effect of maternal support for counting and cardinal understanding in pre-school children. *Social Development, 10*, 202-220.

Lipinski, J. M., Nida, R. E., Shade, D. D., & Watson, J. A. (1986). The effects of microcomputers on young children: An examination of free-play choices, sex differences, and social interactions. *Journal of Educational Computing Research, 2*, 147-168.

Lippard, C. N., Riley, K. L., & Lamm, M. H. (2018). Encouraging the development of engineering habits of mind in prekindergarten learners. In L. D. English & T. Moore (Eds.), *Early engineering learning* (pp. 19-36). Gateway East, Singapore: Springer.

Little, C. A., Adelson, J. L., Kearney, K. L., Cash, K., & O'Brien, R. (2017). Early opportunities to strengthen academic readiness: Effects of summer learning on mathematics achievement. *Gifted Child Quarterly, 62*(1), 83-95. doi: 10.1177/0016986217738052

Loeb, S., Bridges, M., Bassok, D., Fuller, B., & Rumberger, R. (2007). How much is too much? The influence of preschool centers on children's development nationwide. *Economics of Education Review, 26*, 52-56.

Loehr, A. M., Fyfe, E. R., & Rittle-Johnson, B. (2014). Wait for it. delaying instruction improves mathematics problem solving: Classroom study. *The Journal of Problem Solving, 7*(1). doi: 10.7771/1932-6246.1166

Lüken, M. M. (2012). Young children's structure sense. *Journal Für Mathematik-Didaktik, 33*(2), 263-285. doi: 10.1007/s13138-012-0036-8

Lüken, M. M. (2018). Repeating pattern competencies in three- to five-year old kindergartners: A closer look at strategies. In I. Elia, J. Mulligan, A. Anderson, A. Baccaglini-Frank, & C. Benz

(Eds.), *Contemporary Research and Perspectives on Early Childhood Mathematics Education* (pp. 35–53). Cham: Springer International Publishing.

Lutchmaya, S., & Baron-Cohen, S. (2002). Human sex differences in social and non-social looking preferences, at 12 months of age. *Infant Behavior and Development, 25*, 319–325.

Lyons, I. M., Bugden, S., Zheng, S., De Jesus, S., & Ansari, D. (2018). Symbolic number skills predict growth in nonsymbolic number skills in kindergarteners. *Developmental Psychology, 54* (3), 440–457. doi: 10.1037/dev0000445

Lysenko, L., Rosenfield, S., Dedic, H., Savard, A., Idan, E., Abrami, P. C., … Naffi, N. (2016). Using interactive software to teach foundational mathematical skills. *Journal of Information Technology Education: Innovations in Practice, 15*, 19–34.

MacDonald, B. L. (2015). Ben's perception of space and subitizing activity: A constructivist teaching experiment. *Mathematics Education Research Journal, 27*(4), 563–584. doi: 10.1007/s13394-015-0152-0

MacDonald, B. L., & Shumway, J. F. (2016). Subitizing games: Assessing preschool children's number understanding. *Teaching Children Mathematics, 22*(6), 340–348.

MacDonald, B. L., & Wilkins, J. L. M. (2017). Amy's subitizing activity relative to number understanding and item orientation. *Manuscript submitted for publication.*

Magargee, S. D. (2017). *An exploration of the math names for numbers: An early childhood mathematics intervention*. (Doctoral dissertation), University of the Incarnate Word, Ann Arbor. ProQuest Dissertations & Theses Global database.

Magnuson, K. A., Meyers, M. K., Rathbun, A., & West, J. (2004). Inequality in preschool education and school readiness. *American Educational Research Journal, 41*, 115–157.

Magnuson, K. A., & Waldfogel, J. (2005). Early childhood care and education: Effects on ethnic and racial gaps in school readiness. *The Future of Children, 15*, 169–196.

Malaguzzi, L. (1997). *Shoe and meter*. Reggio Emilia, Italy: Reggio Children.

Malofeeva, E., Day, J., Saco, X., Young, L., & Ciancio, D. (2004). Construction and evaluation of a number sense test with Head Start children. *Journal of Education Psychology, 96*, 648–659.

Mandler, J. M. (2004). *The foundations of mind: Origins of conceptual thought*. New York, NY: Oxford University Press.

Manginas, J., Nikolantonakis, C., & Papageorgioy, A. (2017). Cognitive skills and mathematical performance, memory (short-term, long-term, working) mental performance and their relationship with mathematical performance of pre-school students. *European Journal of Education Studies, 3*(12). doi: 10.5281/zenodo.1098252

Manship, K., Holod, A., Quick, H., Ogut, B., de los Reyes, I. B., Anthony, J., … Keuter, S. (2017). The impact of transitional kindergarten on California students: Final report from the study of California's transitional kindergarten program. Retrieved from American Institutes for Research website: www.air.org

Marcon, R. A. (1992). Differential effects of three preschool models on inner-city 4-year-olds. *Early Childhood Research Quarterly, 7*, 517–530.

Marcon, R. A. (2002). Moving up the grades: Relationship between preschool model and later school success. *Early Childhood Research & Practice*. Retrieved from http://ecrp.uiuc.edu/v4n1/marcon.html

Mari i, S. M., & Stamatovi, J. D. (2017). The effect of preschool mathematics education in development of geometry concepts in children. *Eurasia Journal of Mathematics, Science and Technology Education, 13*(9), 6175–6187. doi: 10.12973/eurasia.2017.01057a

Mark, W., & Dowker, A. (2015a). Linguistic influence on mathematical development is specific rather than pervasive: Revisiting the Chinese number advantage in Chinese and English children. *Acta Psychologica, 6*, 203. doi: 10.3389/fpsyg.2015.00203

Markovits, Z., & Hershkowitz, R. (1997). Relative and absolute thinking in visual estimation processes. *Educational Studies in Mathematics, 32*, 29–47.

Markworth, K. A. (2016). A repeat look at repeating patterns. *Teaching Children Mathematics, 23*(1), 22–29. doi: 10.5951/teacchilmath.23.1.0022

Mark-Zigdon, N., & Tirosh, D. (2017). What is a legitimate arithmetic number sentence? The case of kindergarten and first-grade children. In J. J. Kaput, D. W. Carraher, & M. L. Blanton (Eds.), *Algebra in the early grades* (pp. 201–210). Mahwah, NJ: Erlbaum.

Marthe, J. (2000). *Hannah's collections*. New York, NY: Dutton Children's Books.

Martin, R. B., Cirino, P. T., Sharp, C., & Barnes, M. A. (2014). Number and counting skills in kindergarten as predictors of grade 1 mathematical skills. *Learning and Individual Differences, 34*, 12–23. doi: 10.1016/j.lindif.2014.05.006

Martin, T., Lukong, A., & Reaves, R. (2007). The role of manipulatives in arithmetic and geometry tasks. *Journal of Education and Human Development, 1*(1), 27–50. doi: 10.1080/07370008.2015.1124882.

Martinez, S., Naudeau, S., & Pereira, V. A. (2017). Preschool and child development under extreme poverty: Evidence from a randomized experiment in rural Mozambique. *World Bank Policy Research Working Paper No. 8290.*

Mason, M. M. (1995). Geometric knowledge in a deaf classroom: An exploratory study. *Focus on Learning Problems in Mathematics, 17*(3), 57-69.

Mazzocco, M. M. M., Feigenson, L., & Halberda, J. (2011). Preschoolers' precision of the approximate number system predicts later school mathematics performance. *PLoS ONE, 6*(9), e23749. doi: 10.1371/journal.pone.0023749.t001

Mazzocco, M. M. M., & Myers, G. F. (2003). Complexities in identifying and defining mathematics learning disability in the primary school-age years. *Annals of Dyslexia, 53,* 218-253.

Mazzocco, M. M. M., & Thompson, R. E. (2005). Kindergarten predictors of math learning disability. *Quarterly Research and Practice, 20,* 142-155.

McClain, K., Cobb, P., Gravemeijer, K. P. E., & Estes, B. (1999). Developing mathematical reasoning within the context of measurement. In L. V. Stiff & F. R. Curcio (Eds.), *Developing mathematical reasoning in grades K-12* (pp. 93-106). Reston, VA: National Council of Teachers of Mathematics.

McCormick, K. K., & Twitchell, G. (2017). A preschool investigation: The skyscraper project. *Teaching Children Mathematics, 23*(6), 340-348.

McCoy, D. C., Salhi, C., Yoshikawa, H., Black, M., Britto, P., & Fink, G. (2018). Home- and center-based learning opportunities for preschoolers in low- and middle-income countries. *Children and Youth Services Review, 88,* 44-56. doi: 10.1016/j.childyouth.2018.02.021

McCoy, D. C., Yoshikawa, H., Ziol-Guest, K. M., Duncan, G. J., Schindler, H. S., Magnuson, K., ... Shonkoff, J. P. (2017). Impacts of early childhood education on medium- and long-term educational outcomes. *Educational Researcher, 46*(8), 474-487. doi: 10.3102/0013189x17737739

McCrink, K., & de Hevia, M. D. (2018). From innate spatial biases to enculturated spatial cognition: The case of spatial associations In number and other sequences. *Frontiers in Psychology, 9*(Article 415). doi: 10.3389/fpsyg.2018.00415

McDermott, P. A., Fantuzzo, J. W., Warley, H. P., Water Man, C., Angelo, L. E., Gadsden, V. L., & Sekino, Y. (2010). Multidimensionality of teachers graded responses for preschoolers' stylistic learning behavior: The learning-to-learn scales. *Educational and Psychological Measurement, 71* (1), 148-169. doi: 10.1177/0013164410387351

McDonald, S., & Howell, J. (2012). Watching, creating and achieving: Creative technologies as a conduit for learning in the early years. *British Journal of Educational Technology, 43*(4), 641-651. doi: 10.1111/j.1467-8535.2011.01231.x

McFadden, K. E., Tamis-LeMonda, C. S., & Cabrera, N. J. (2011). Quality matters: Low-income fathers engagement in learning activities in early childhood predict children's academic performance in fifth grade. *Family Science, 2,* 120-130.

McGarvey, L. M., Luo, L., & Hawes, Z., & Spatial Reasoning Study Group. (2018). Spatial skills framework for young engineers. In L. D. English & T. Moore (Eds.), *Early engineering learning* (pp. 53-81). Gateway East, Singapore: Springer.

McGee, M. G. (1979). Human spatial abilities: Psychometric studies and environmental, genetic, hormonal, and neurological influence? *Psychological Bulletin, 86,* 889-918.

McGraw, A. L., Ganley, C. M., Powell, S. R., Purpura, D. J., Schoen, R. C., & Schatschneider, C. (2019, March). An investigation of mathematics language and its relation with mathematics and reading. *2019 SRCD Biennial Meeting,* Baltimore, MD.

McGuinness, D., & Morley, C. (1991). Gender differences in the development of visuospatial ability in pre-school children. *Journal of Mental Imagery, 15,* 143-150.

McKelvey, L. M., Bokony, P. A., Swindle, T. M., Conners-Burrow, N. A., Schiffman, R. F., & Fitzgerald, H. E. (2011). Father teaching interactions with toddlers at risk: Associations with later child academic outcomes. *Family Science, 2,* 146-155.

McLeod, D. B., & Adams, V. M. (Eds.). (1989). *Affect and mathematical problem solving.* New York, NY: Springer-Verlag.

McMullen, J., Hannula-Sormunen, M. M., & Lehtinen, E. (2014). Spontaneous focusing on quantitative relations in the development of children's fraction knowledge. *Cognition and Instruction, 32*(2), 198-218.

McNeil, N. M. (2008). Limitations to teaching children 2 + 2 = 4: Typical arithmetic problems can hinder learning of mathematical equivalence. *Child Development, 79*(5), 1524-1537.

McNeil, N. M., Fyfe, E. R., & Dunwiddie, A. E. (2015). Arithmetic practice can be modified to promote understanding of mathematical equivalence. *Journal of Educational Psychology, 107*(2), 423-436. doi: 10.1037/a0037687

McNeil, N. M., Fyfe, E. R., Petersen, L. A., Dunwiddie, A. E., & Brletic-Shipley, H. (2011). Benefits of practicing 4 = 2 + 2: Nontraditional problem formats facilitate children's understanding of mathematical equivalence. *Child Development, 82*(5), 1620-1633.

Meaney, T. (2016). Locating learning of toddlers in the individual/society and mind/body divides. *Nordic Studies in Mathematics Education, 21*(4), 5-28.

Meloni, C., Fanari, R., Bertucci, A., & Berretti, S. (2017). *Impact of early numeracy training on kindergarteners from middle-income families*. Paper presented at the 14th International Conference on Cognition and Exploratory Learning in Digital Age.

Mercader, J., Miranda, A., Presentación, M. J., Siegenthaler, R., & Rosel, J. F. (2017). Contributions of motivation, early numeracy skills, and executive functioning to mathematical performance. A longitudinal study. *Frontiers in Psychology*, *8*. doi: 10.3389/fpsyg.2017.02375

Merkley, R., & Ansari, D. (2018). *Foundations for learning: Guided play for early years maths education*. Chartered College of Teaching. https://impact.chartered.college/article/merkley-ansari-learning-guided-play-early-years-maths/

Methe, S., Kilgus, S., Neiman, C., & Chris Riley-Tillman, T. (2012). Meta-analysis of interventions for basic mathematics computation in single-case research. *Journal of Behavioral Education*, *21*(3), 230–253. doi: 10.1007/s10864-012-9161-1

Middleton, J. A., & Spanias, P. (1999). Motivation for achievement in mathematics: Findings, generalizations, and criticisms of the research. *Journal for Research in Mathematics Education*, *30*, 65–88.

Milesi, C., & Gamoran, A. (2006). Effects of class size and instruction on kindergarten achievement. *Education Evaluation and Policy Analysis*, *28*(4), 287–313.

Millar, S., & Ittyerah, M. (1992). Movement imagery in young and congenitally blind children: Mental practice without visuospatial information. *International Journal of Behavioral Development*, *15*, 125–146.

Miller, E. B., Farkas, G., Vandell, D. L., & Duncan, G. J. (2014). Do the effects of Head Start vary by parental pre-academic stimulation? *Child Development*, *85*, 1385–1400. doi: 10.1111/cdev.12233

Miller, K. F. (1984). Child as the measurer of all things: Measurement procedures and the development of quantitative concepts. In C. Sophian (Ed.), *Origins of cognitive skills: The eighteenth annual Carnegie symposium on cognition* (pp. 193–228). Hillsdale, NJ: Erlbaum.

Miller, K. F. (1989). Measurement as a tool of thought: The role of measuring procedures in children's understanding of quantitative invariance. *Developmental Psychology*, *25*, 589–600.

Miller, K. F., Kelly, M., & Zhou, X. (2005). Learning mathematics in China and the United States: Cross-cultural insights into the nature and course of preschool mathematical development. In J. I. D. Campbell (Ed.), *Handbook of mathematical cognition* (pp. 163–178). New York, NY: Psychology Press.

Miller, K. F., Smith, C. M., Zhu, J., & Zhang, H. (1995). Preschool origins of cross-national differences in mathematical competence: The role of number-naming systems. *Psychological Science*, *6*, 56–60.

Miller, M. R., Rittle-Johnson, B., Loehr, A. M., & Fyfe, E. R. (2016). The influence of relational knowledge and executive function on preschoolers' repeating pattern knowledge. *Journal of Cognition and Development*, *17*(1), 85–104. doi: 10.1080/15248372.2015.1023307

Miller, J., & Warren, E. (2014). Exploring ESL students' understanding of mathematics in the early years: Factors that make a difference. *Mathematics Education Research Journal*. doi: 10.1007/s13394-014-0121-z

Mitchelmore, M. C. (1989). The development of children's concepts of angle. In G. Vergnaud, J. Rogalski, & M. Artique (Eds.), *Proceedings of the 13th Annual Conference of the International Group for the Psychology of Mathematics Education* (Vol. 2, pp. 304–311). Paris, France: City University.

Mitchelmore, M. C. (1992). Children's concepts of perpendiculars. In W. Geeslin & K. Graham (Eds.), *Proceedings of the 16th Annual Conference of the International Group for the Psychology in Mathematics Education* (Vol. 2, pp. 120–127). Durham, NH: Program Committee of the 16th PME Conference.

Mitchelmore, M. C. (1993). The development of pre-angle concepts. In A. R. Baturo & L. J. Harris (Eds.), *New directions in research on geometry* (pp. 87–93). Centre for Mathematics and Science Education, Queensland University of Technology.

Mitchelmore, M. C., & White, P. (1998). Development of angle concepts: A framework for research. *Mathematics Education Research Journal*, *10*, 4–27.

Mix, K. S., Levine, S. C., Cheng, Y. L., Young, C., Hambrick, D. Z., Ping, R., & Konstantopoulos, S. (2016). Separate but correlated: The latent structure of space and mathematics across development. *Journal of Experimental Psychology*, *145*(9), 1206–1227. doi: 10.1037/xge0000182.

Mix, K. S., Levine, S. C., & Huttenlocher, J. (1997). Early fraction calculation ability. *Developmental Psychology*, *35*, 164–174.

Mix, K. S., Moore, J. A., & Holcomb, E. (2011). One-to-one play promotes numerical equivalence concepts. *Journal of Cognition and Development*, *12*(4), 463–480.

Mix, K. S., Smith, L. B., & Crespo, S. (2019). Leveraging relational learning mechanisms to improve place value instruction. In A. Norton & M. W. Alibali (Eds.), *Constructing number: Merging perspectives from psychology and mathematics education* (pp. 87–121). Springer. https://doi.org/10.1007/978-3-030-00491-0

Moeller, K., Fischer, U., Cress, U., & Nuerk, H.-C. (2012). Diagnostics and intervention in developmental dyscalculia: Current issues and novel perspectives. In Z. Breznitz, O. Rubinsten, V. J. Molfese, & D. L. Molfese (Eds.), *Reading, writing, mathematics and the developing brain: Listening to many voices* (Vol. 6, pp. 233–275). The Netherlands: Springer.

Mohd Syah, N. E., Hamzaid, N. A., Murphy, B. P., & Lim, E. (2016). Development of computer play pedagogy intervention for children with low conceptual understanding in basic mathematics operation using the dyscalculia feature approach. *Interactive Learning Environments, 24*(7), 1477–1496. doi: 10.1080/10494820.2015.1023205

Molfese, V. J., Brown, T. E., Adelson, J. L., Beswick, J., Jacobi-Vessels, J., Thomas, L., Ferguson, M., & Culver, B. (2012). Examining associations between classroom environment and processes and early mathematics performance from pre-kindergarten to kindergarten. *Gifted Children, 5*(2), article 2. Retrieved from http://docs.lib.purdue.edu/giftedchildren/vol5/iss2/2

Moll, L. C., Amanti, C., Neff, D., & Gonzalez, N. (1992). Funds of knowledge for teaching: Using a qualitative approach to connect homes and classrooms. *Theory into Practice, 31*, 132–141.

Monighan-Nourot, P., Scales, B., Van Hoorn, J., & Almy, M. (1987). *Looking at children's play: A bridge between theory and practice*. New York, NY: Teachers College.

Mononen, R., Aunio, P., Koponen, T., & Aro, M. (2014). A review of early numeracy interventions for children at risk in mathematics. *International Journal of Early Childhood Special Education, 6*(1), 25–54.

Montie, J. E., Xiang, Z., & Schweinhart, L. J. (2006). Preschool experience in 10 countries: Cognitive and language performance at age 7. *Early Childhood Research Quarterly, 21*, 313–331.

Mooij, T., & Driessen, G. (2008). Differential ability and attainment in language and arithmetic of Dutch primary school pupil? *British Journal of Educational Psychology, 78*(Pt 3), 491–506. doi: 10.1348/000709907X235981

Moomaw, S. (2015). Assessing the difficulty level of math board games for young children. *Journal of Research in Childhood Education, 29*(4), 17. doi: 10.1080/02568543.2015.1073201

Moon, U. J., & Hofferth, S. (2018). Change in computer access and the academic achievement of immigrant children. *Teachers College Record, 120*(4).

Moradmand, N., Datta, A., & Oakley, G. (2013). My maths story: An application of a computer-assisted

framework for teaching mathematics in the lower primary years. Paper presented at the Society for Information Technology & Teacher Education International Conference 2013, New Orleans, Louisiana, United States. Conference paper retrieved from www.editlib.org/p/48603

Morgenlander, M. (2005). *Preschoolers' understanding of mathematics presented on Sesame Street*. Paper presented at the American Educational Research Association, New Orleans, LA.

Morrongiello, B. A., Timney, B., Humphrey, G. K., Anderson, S., & Skory, C. (1995). Spatial knowledge in blind and sighted children. *Journal of Experimental Child Psychology, 59*, 211–233.

Moseley, B. (2005). Pre-service early childhood educators' perceptions of math-mediated language. *Early Education & Development, 16*(3), 385–396.

Moschkovich, J. (2013). Principles and guidelines for equitable mathematics teaching practices and materials for English language learners. *Journal of Urban Mathematics Education, 6*(1), 45–57.

Moss, J., Hawes, Z., Naqvi, S., & Caswell, B. (2015). Adapting Japanese Lesson Study to enhance the teaching and learning of geometry and spatial reasoning in early years classrooms: A case study. *ZDM Mathematics Education, 47*(3), 1–14. doi: 10.1111/mono.12280

Moyer, P. S. (2000). Are we having fun yet? Using manipulatives to teach "real math". *Educational Studies in Mathematics: An International Journal, 47*(2), 175–197.

Moyer, P. S., Niezgoda, D., & Stanley, J. (2005). Young children's use of virtual manipulatives and other forms of mathematical representations. In W. Masalski & P. C. Elliott (Eds.), *Technology-supported mathematics learning environments: 67th Yearbook* (pp. 17–34). Reston, VA: National Council of Teachers of Mathematics.

Moyer-Packenham, P. S., Shumway, J. F., Bullock, E., Tucker, S. I., Anderson-Pence, K. L., Westenskow, A., … Jordan, K. (2015). Young children's learning performance and efficiency when using virtual manipulative mathematics iPad apps. *Journal of Computers in Mathematics and Science Teaching, 34*(1), 41–69.

Muir, T. (2018). Using mathematics to forge connections between home and school. In V. Kinnear, M. Y. Lai, & T. Muir (Eds.), *Forging connections in early mathematics teaching and learning* (pp. 173–190). Gateway East, Singapore: Springer.

Mullet, E., & Miroux, R. (1996). Judgment of rectangular areas in children blind from birth. *Cognitive Development, 11*, 123–139.

Mulligan, J., English, L. D., Mitchelmore, M. C., Welsby, S., & Crevensten, N. (2011). An evaluation of the pattern and structure mathematics awareness program in the early school years. In J. Clark, B. Kissane, J. Mousley, T. Spencer, & S. Thornton (Eds.), *Proceedings of the AAMT-MERGA Conference 2011, The Australian Association of Mathematics Teachers Inc. & Mathematics Education Research Group of Australasia* (pp. 548-556). Alice Springs, Australia.

Mulligan, J., & Mitchelmore, M. (2018). Promoting early mathematical structural development through an integrated assessment and pedagogical program. In I. Elia, J. Mulligan, A. Anderson, A. Baccaglini-Frank, & C. Benz (Eds.), *Contemporary Research and Perspectives on Early Childhood Mathematics Education* (pp. 17-33). Cham: Springer International Publishing.

Mulligan, J., Mitchelmore, M., English, L. D., & Crevensten, N. (2012). *Evaluation of the "reconceptualising early mathematics learning" project.* Paper presented at the AARE APERA International Conference, Sydney.

Mulligan, J., Prescott, A., Mitchelmore, M. C., & Outhred, L. (2005). Taking a closer look at young students' images of area measurement. *Australian Primary Mathematics Classroom, 10*(2), 4-8.

Mulligan, J., Verschaffel, L., Baccaglini-Frank, A., Coles, A., Gould, P., He, S., ... Yang, D.-C. (2018). Whole number thinking, learning and development: Neuro-cognitive, cognitive and developmental approaches. In M. G. Bartolini Bussi & X. H. Sun (Eds.), *Building the Foundation: Whole Numbers in the Primary Grades: The 23rd ICMI Study* (pp. 137-167). Cham: Springer International Publishing.

Mulligan, J. T., English, L. D., Mitchelmore, M. C., Welsby, S. M., & Crevensten, N. (2011b). *Developing the Pattern and Structure Assessment (PASA) interview to inform early mathematics learning.* Paper presented at the AAMT-MERGA Conference 2011, Alice Springs, Australia.

Mullis, I. V. S., Martin, M. O., Foy, P., & Arora, A. (2012). *TIMSS 2011 International Results in Mathematics.* Chestnut Hill, MA: TIMSS & PIRLS International Study Center, Lynch School of Education, Boston College.

Mullis, I. V. S., Martin, M. O., Gonzalez, E. J., Gregory, K. D., Garden, R. A., O'Connor, K. M., Chrostowski, S. J., & Smith, T. A. (2000). *TIMSS 1999 international mathematics report.* Boston: The International Study Center, Boston College, Lynch School of Education.

Munn, P. (1998). Symbolic function in pre-schoolers. In C. Donlan (Ed.), *The development of mathematical skills* (pp. 47-71). East Sussex, England: Psychology Press.

Murata, A. (2004). Paths to learning ten-structured understanding of teen sums: Addition solution methods of Japanese Grade 1 students. *Cognition and Instruction, 22*, 185-218.

Murata, A. (2008). Mathematics teaching and learning as a mediating process: The case of tape diagrams. *Mathematical Thinking and Learning, 10*, 374-406.

Murata, A., & Fuson, K. C. (2006). Teaching as assisting individual constructive paths within an interdependent class learning zone: Japanese first graders learning to add using 10. *Journal for Research in Mathematics Education, 37*(5), 421-456. doi: 10.2307/30034861

Murphey, D., Madill, R., & Guzman, L. (2017). Making math count more for young Latinos. *The Education Digest, 83*(1), 8-14.

Mussolin, C., Nys, J., Content, A., & Leybaert, J. (2014). Symbolic number abilities predict later approximate number system acuity in preschool children. *PLoS ONE, 9*(3), e91839. doi: 10.1371/journal.pone.0091839

Mustafa, N. A., Omar, S. S. S., Shafie, N., & Kamarudin, M. F. (2017). *Understanding preschool children's skill in subtraction using cooperative learning.* Paper presented at the International Scientific and Professional Conference, Opatija, Croatia.

Myers, M., Wilson, P. H., Sztajn, P., & Edgington, C. (2015). From implicit to explicit: Articulating equitable learning trajectories based instruction. *Journal of Urban Mathematics Education, 8*(2), 11-22.

Nanu, C. E., McMullen, J., Munck, P., & Hannula-Sormunen, M. M. (2018). Spontaneous focusing on numerosity in preschool as a predictor of mathematical skills and knowledge in the fifth grade. *Journal of Experimental Child Psychology, 169*, 42-58. doi: 10.1016/j.jecp.2017.12.011

Nasir, N. I. S., & Cobb, P. (2007). *Improving access to mathematics: Diversity and equity in the classroom.* New York, NY: Teachers College Press.

Nastasi, B. K., & Clements, D. H. (1991). Research on cooperative learning: Implications for practice. *School Psychology Review, 20*, 110-131.

Nastasi, B. K., Clements, D. H., & Battista, M. T. (1990). Social-cognitive interactions, motivation, and cognitive growth in Logo programming and CAI problem-solving environments. *Journal of Educational Psychology, 82*, 150-158.

National Academies of Sciences, E., and Medicine. (2017). *Promoting the educational success of children and youth learning English: Promising futures.* Washington, DC: The National Academies Press.

National Mathematics Advisory Panel. (2008). *Foundations for success: The final report of the National Mathematics Advisory Panel.* Washington,

DC: U.S. Department of Education, Office of Planning, Evaluation and Policy Development.

National Research Council. (2009). *Mathematics learning in early childhood: Paths toward excellence and equity*. Washington, DC: National Academy Press.

Natriello, G., McDill, E. L., & Pallas, A. M. (1990). *Schooling disadvantaged children: Racing against catastrophe*. New York, NY: Teachers College Press.

Navarro, J. I., Aguilar, M., Marchena, E., Ruiz, G., Menacho, I., & Van Luit, J. E. H. (2012). Longitudinal study of low and high achievers in early mathematics. *British Journal of Educational Psychology, 82*(1), 28–41. doi: 10.1111/j.2044-8279.2011.02043.x

Navarro, M. G., Braham, E. J., & Libertus, M. E. (2018). Intergenerational associations of the approximate number system in toddlers and their parents. *British Journal of Developmental Psychology, 36*(4), 521–539. doi: 10.1111/bjdp.12234

NCTM. (2000). *Principles and standards for school mathematics*. Reston, VA: National Council of Teachers of Mathematics.

NCTM. (2006). *Curriculum focal points for prekindergarten through grade 8 mathematics: A quest for coherence*. National Council of Teachers of Mathematics.

Nes, F. T. v. (2009). *Young children's spatial structuring ability and emerging number sense*. Doctoral dissertation, de Universtiteit Utrecht, Utrecht, The Netherlands.

Neuenschwander, R., Röthlisberger, M., Cimeli, P., & Roebers, C. M. (2012). How do different aspects of self-regulation predict successful adaptation to school? *Journal of Experimental Child Psychology, 113*(3), 353–371. doi: 10.1016/j.jecp.2012.07.004

Neville, H., Andersson, A., Bagdade, O., Bell, T., Currin, J., Fanning, J., & Yamada, Y. (2008). Effects of music training on brain and cognitive development in under-privileged 3- to 5-year-old children: Preliminary results. In C. Asbury & B. Rich (Eds.), *Learning, Arts, & the Brain* (pp. 105–116). New York/Washington, DC: Dana Press.

Newcombe, N. (2010). Picture this: Increasing math and science learning by improving spatial thinking. *American Educator, 34*(2), 29–35.

Newcombe, R. S., & Huttenlocher, J. (2000). *Making space: The development of spatial representation and reasoning*. Cambridge, MA: MIT Press.

Newhouse, C. P., Cooper, M., & Cordery, Z. (2017). Programmable toys and free play in early childhood classrooms. *Australian Educational Computing, 32*(1), 14.

Ng, S. N. S., & Rao, N. (2010). Chinese number words, culture, and mathematics learning. *Review of Educational Research, 80*(2), 180–206.

Nguyen, T., Watts, T. W., Duncan, G. J., Clements, D. H., Sarama, J., Wolfe, C. B., & Spitler, M. E. (2016). Which preschool mathematics competencies are most predictive of fifth grade achievement? *Early Childhood Research Quarterly, 36*, 550–560. doi: 10.1016/j.ecresq.2016.02.003

Nieuwoudt, H. D., & van Niekerk, R. (1997, March). The spatial competence of young children through the development of solids. *Paper presented at the American Educational Research Association*, Chicago, IL.

Niklas, F., & Schneider, W. (2017). Home learning environment and development of child competencies from kindergarten until the end of elementary school. *Contemporary Educational Psychology, 49*, 263–274. doi: 10.1016/j.cedpsych.2017.03.006

Nishida, T. K., & Lillard, A. S. (2007a, April). *From flashcard to worksheet: Children's inability to transfer across different formats*. Paper presented at the Society for Research in Child Development, Boston, MA.

Nishida, T. K., & Lillard, A. S. (2007b, April). *Fun toy or learning tool?: Young children's use of concrete manipulatives to learn about simple math concepts*. Paper presented at the Society for Research in Child Development, Boston, MA.

NMP. (2008). *Foundations for success: The final report of the National Mathematics Advisory Panel*. Washington, DC: U.S. Department of Education, Office of Planning, Evaluation and Policy Development.

Nomi, T. (2010). The effects of within-class ability grouping on academic achievement in early elementary years. *Journal of Research on Educational Effectiveness, 3*, 56–92.

Northcote, M. (2011). Step back and hand over the cameras! Using digital cameras to facilitate mathematics learning with young children in K-2 classrooms. *Australian Primary Mathematics Classroom, 16*(3), 29–32.

NRC. (2004). *On evaluating curricular effectiveness: Judging the quality of K-12 mathematics evaluations*. Washington, DC: Mathematical Sciences Education Board, Center for Education, Division of Behavioral and Social Sciences and Education, National Academies Press.

NRC. (2009). *Mathematics in early childhood: Learning paths toward excellence and equity*. Washington, DC: National Academy Press.

Nührenbörger, M. (2001). Insights into children's ruler concepts–Grade-2 students conceptions and knowledge of length measurement and paths of development. In M. V. D. Heuvel-Panhuizen (Ed.), *Proceedings of the 25th Conference of the International Group for the Psychology in Mathematics*

Education (Vol. 3, pp. 447–454). Utrecht, The Netherlands: Freudenthal Institute.

Nunes, T., Bryant, P., Evans, D., & Bell, D. (2010). The scheme of correspondence and its role in children's mathematics. *British Journal of Educational Psychology, 2*(7), 83–99. doi: 10.1348/97818543370009x12583699332537

Nunes, T., Bryant, P., Evans, D., Bell, D., & Barros, R. (2011). Teaching children how to include the inversion principle in their reasoning about quantitative relations. *Educational Studies in Mathematics, 79*(3), 371–388. doi: 10.1007/s10649-011-9314-5

Nunes, T., Bryant, P., Evans, D., Bell, D., Gardner, S., Gardner, A., & Carraher, J. (2007). The contribution of logical reasoning to the learning of mathematics in primary school. *British Journal of Developmental Psychology, 25*(1), 147–166. doi: 10.1348/026151006x153127

Nunes, T., Bryant, P. E., Barros, R., & Sylva, K. (2012). The relative importance of two different mathematical abilities to mathematical achievement. *British Journal of Educational Psychology, 82*(1), 136–156. doi: 10.1111/j.2044-8279.2011.02033.x

Nunes, T., Bryant, P. E., Burman, D., Bell, D., Evans, D., & Hallett, D. (2009). Deaf children's informal knowledge of multiplicative reasoning. *Journal of Deaf Studies and Deaf Education, 14*(2), 260–277.

Nunes, T., Bryant, P. E., Evans, D., & Barros, R. (2015). Assessing quantitative reasoning in young children. *Mathematical Thinking and Learning, 17*(2–3), 178–196. doi: 10.1080/10986065.2015.1016815

Nunes, T., Dorneles, RB. V., Lin, P.-J., & Rathgeb-Schnierer, E. (2016). *Teaching and learning about whole numbers in primary school*. Springer. doi: 10.1007/978-3-319-45113-8_1

Nunes, T., & Moreno, C. (1998). Is hearing impairment a cause of difficulties in learning mathematics? In C. Donlan (Ed.), *The development of mathematical skills* (Vol. 7, pp. 227–254). Hove, UK: Psychology Press.

Nunes, T., & Moreno, C. (2002). An intervention program for promoting deaf pupil's achievement in mathematics. *Journal of Deaf Studies and Deaf Education, 7*(2), 120–133.

Núñez, R., Cooperrider, K., Doan, D., & Wassmann, J. (2012). Contours of time: Topographic construals of past, present, and future in the Yupno valley of P. N. Guinea. *Cognition, 124*(1), 25–35. doi: 10.1016/j.cognition.2012.03.007

Núñez, R., Cooperrider, K., & Wassmann, J. (2012). Number concepts without number lines in an indigenous group of Papua New Guinea. *PLoS ONE, 7*(4), 1–8. doi: 10.1371/journal.pone.0035662

Núñez, R., Doan, D., & Nikoulina, A. (2011). Squeezing, striking, and vocalizing: Is number representation fundamentally spatial? *Cognition, 120*(2), 225–235. doi: 10.1016/j.cognition.2011.05.001

Núñez, R. E. (2011). No innate number line in the human brain. *Journal of Cross-cultural Psychology, 42*(4), 651–668. doi: 10.1177/0022022111406097

Nurnberger-Haag, J. (2016). A cautionary tale: How children's books (mis)teach shapes. *Early Education and Development, 28*(4), 415–440. doi: 10.1080/10409289.2016.1242993

Nusir, S., Alsmadi, I., Al-Kabi, M., & Sharadgah, F. (2013). Studying the impact of using multimedia interactive programs on children's ability to learn basic math skills. *E-Learning and Digital Media, 10*(3), 305–319.

Ok, M. W., & Kim, W. (2017). Use of iPads and iPods for academic performance and engagement of prek-12 students with disabilities: A research synthesis. *Exceptionality, 25*(1), 54–75.

O'Neill, D. K., Pearce, M. J., & Pick, J. L. (2004). Preschool children's narratives and performance on the Peabody Individualized Achievement Test Revised: Evidence of a relation between early narrative and later mathematical ability. *First Language, 24*(2), 149–183.

Oakes, J. (1990). Opportunities, achievement, and choice: Women and minority students in science and mathematics. In C. B. Cazden (Ed.), *Review of research in education* (Vol. 16, pp. 153–222). Washington, DC: American Educational Research Association.

Obersteiner, A., Reiss, K., & Ufer, S. (2013). How training on exact or approximate mental representations of number can enhance first-grade students' basic number processing and arithmetic skills. *Learning and Instruction, 23*(1), 125–135. doi: 10.1016/j.learninstruc.2012.08.004

OECD. (2014). *Strong performers and successful reformers in education - Lessons from PISA 2012 for the United States*. OECD Publishing. doi: 10.1787/9789264207585-en

Olkun, S., Altun, A., Göçer ahin, S., & Akkurt Denizli, Z. (2015). Deficits in basic number competencies may cause low numeracy in primary school children. *Ted Eğitim Ve Bilim, 40*(177). doi: 10.15390/eb.2015.3287

Olkun, S., & Denizli, Z. A. (2015). Using basic number processing tasks in determining students with mathematics disorder risk. *Dusunen Adam: The Journal of Psychiatry and Neurological Sciences*, 47–57. doi: 10.5350/dajpn2015280105

Olson, J. K. (1988). *Microcomputers make manipulatives meaningful*. Budapest, Hungary: International Congress of Mathematics Education.

Örnkloo, H., & von Hofsten, C. (2007). Fitting objects into holes: On the development of spatial cognition skills. *Developmental Psychology, 43* (2), 404-416. doi: 10.1037/0012-1649.43.2.404

Oslington, G., Mulligan, J. T., & Van Bergen, P. (2018). Young children's reasoning through data exploration. In V. Kinnear, M. Y. Lai, & T. Muir (Eds.), *Forging Connections in Early Mathematics Teaching and Learning* (pp. 191-212). Singapore: Springer Singapore.

Ostad, S. A. (1998). Subtraction strategies in developmental perspective: A comparison of mathematically normal and mathematically disabled children. In A. Olivier & K. Newstead (Eds.), *Proceedings of the 22nd Conference for the International Group for the Psychology of Mathematics Education* (Vol. 3, pp. 311-318). Stellenbosch, South Africa: University of Stellenbosch.

Outhred, L. N., & Sardelich, S. (1997). Problem solving in kindergarten: The development of representations. In F. Biddulph & K. Carr (Eds.), *People in Mathematics Education. Proceedings of the 20th Annual Conference of the Mathematics Education Research Group of Australasia* (Vol. 2, pp. 376-383). Rotorua, New Zealand: Mathematics Education Research Group of Australasia.

Outhwaite, L. A., Faulder, M., Gulliford, A., & Pitchford, N. J. (2019). Raising early achievement in math with interactive apps: A randomized control trial. *Journal of Educational Psychology, 111,* 284-298. doi: 10.1037/edu0000286

Outhwaite, L. A., Gulliford, A., & Pitchford, N. J. (2017). Closing the gap: Efficacy of a tablet intervention to support the development of early mathematical skills in UK primary school children. *Computers & Education, 108,* 43-58. doi: 10.1016/j.compedu.2017.01.011

Owens, K. (1992). Spatial thinking takes shape through primary-school experiences. In W. Geeslin & K. Graham (Eds.), *Proceedings of the 16th Conference of the International Group for the Psychology in Mathematics Education* (Vol. 2, pp. 202-209). Durham, NH: Program Committee of the 16th PME Conference.

Özcan, Z. Ç., & Doğan, H. (2017). A longitudinal study of early math skills, reading comprehension and mathematical problem solving. *Pegem Eğitim Ve Öğretim Dergisi, 8*(1), 1-18. doi: 10.14527/pegegog.2018.001

Pagani, L., & Messier, S. (2012). Links between motor skills and indicators of school readiness at kindergarten entry in urban disadvantaged children. *Journal of Educational and Developmental Psychology, 2*(1), 95. doi: 10.5539/jedp.v2n1p95

Pagliaro, C. M., & Kritzer, K. L. (2013). The math gap: A description of the mathematics performance of preschool-aged deaf/hard-of-hearing children. *Journal of Deaf Studies and Deaf Education, 18* (2), 139-160. doi: 10.1093/deafed/ens070

Pakarinen, E., Kiuru, N., Lerkkanen, M.-K., Poikkeus, A.-M., Ahonen, T., & Nurmi, J.-E. (2010). Instructional support predicts children's task avoidance in kindergarten. *Early Childhood Research Quarterly, 26*(3), 376-386. doi: 10.1016/j.ecresq.2010.11.003

Paliwal, V., & Baroody, A. J. (2020). Cardinality principle understanding: The role of focusing on the subitizing ability. *ZDM Mathematics Education.* doi: 10.1007/s11858-020-01150-0

Palmér, H. (2017). Programming in preschool: With a focus on learning mathematics. *International Research in Early Childhood Education, 8*(1), 75-87.

Pan, Y., & Gauvain, M. (2007). *Parental involvement in children's mathematics learning in American and Chinese families during two school transitions.* Paper presented at the Society for Research in Child Development.

Pan, Y., Gauvain, M., Liu, Z., & Cheng, L. (2006). American and Chinese parental involvement in young children's mathematics learning. *Cognitive Development, 21,* 17-35.

Pantoja, N., Rozek, C. S., Schaeffer, M. W., Berkowitz, T., Beilock, S. L., & Levine, S. C. (2019, March). Children's math anxiety predicts future math achievement over and above cognitive math ability. Paper presented at the 2019 SRCD Biennial Meeting, Baltimore, MD.

Papert, S. (1980). *Mindstorms: Children, computers, and powerful ideas.* New York, NY: Basic Books.

Papic, M. M., Mulligan, J. T., & Mitchelmore, M. C. (2011). Assessing the development of preschoolers' mathematical patterning. *Journal for Research in Mathematics Education, 42*(3), 237-269. doi: 10.5951/jresematheduc.42.3.0237

Paris, C. L., & Morris, S. K. (1985). *The computer in the early childhood classroom: Peer helping and peer teaching.* Cleege Park, MD: MicroWorld for Young Children Conference.

Park, J., Bermudez, V., Roberts, R. C., & Brannon, E. M. (2016). Non-symbolic approximate arithmetic training improves math performance in preschoolers. *Journal of Experimental Child Psychology, 152,* 278-293. doi: 10.1016/j.jecp.2016.07.011

Park, S., Stone, S. I., & Holloway, S. D. (2017). School-based parental involvement as a predictor of achievement and school learning environment: An elementary school-level analysis. *Children and Youth Services Review, 82*(Supplement C), 195-206. doi: 10.1016/j.childyouth.2017.09.012

Parker, T. H., & Baldridge, S. J. (2004). *Elementary mathematics for teachers.* Quebecor World, MI: Sefton-Ash Publishing.

Pasnak, R. (1987). Accelerated cognitive development of kindergartners. *Psychology in the Schools,*

28(4), 358-363. doi: 10.1002/1520-6807(198710) 24:4<358::AID-PITS2310240410>3.0.CO;2-Q

Pasnak, R. (2017). Empirical studies of patterning. *Psychology*, 8(13), 2276-2293. doi: 10.4236/ psych.2017.813144

Pasnak, R., Kidd, J. K., Gadzichowski, K. M., Gallington, D. A., Schmerold, K. L., & West, H. (2015). Abstracting sequences: Reasoning that is a key to academic achievement. *The Journal of Genetic Psychology*, 176(3), 171-193. doi: 10.1080/ 00221325.2015.1024198

Pasnak, R., Kidd, J. K., Gadzichowski, M., Gallington, D. A., McKnight, P., Boyer, C. E., & Carlson, A. (2012). *An efficacy test of patterning instruction for first grade*. Fairfax, VA: George Mason University.

Passolunghi, M. C., Vercelloni, B., & Schadee, H. (2007). The precursors of mathematics learning: Working memory, phonological ability and numerical competence. *Cognitive Development*, 22(2), 165-184. doi: 10.1016/j.cogdev.2006.09.001

Peisner-Feinberg, E. S., Burchinal, M. R., Clifford, R. M., Culkins, M. L., Howes, C., Kagan, S. L., & Yazejian, N. (2001). The relation of preschool child-care quality to children's cognitive and social developmental trajectories through second grade. *Child Development*, 72, 1534-1553.

Peltier, C., & Vannest, K. J. (2017). The effects of schema-based instruction on the mathematical problem solving of students with emotional and behavioral disorders. *Behavioral Disorders*, 43(2), 277-289. doi: 10.1177/0198742917704647

Perlmutter, J., Bloom, L., Rose, T., & Rogers, A. (1997). Who uses math? Primary children's perceptions of the uses of mathematics. *Journal of Research in Childhood Education*, 12(1), 58-70.

Perry, B., & Dockett, S. (2002). Young children's access to powerful mathematical ideas. In L. D. English (Ed.), *Handbook of International Research in Mathematics Education* (pp. 81-111). Mahwah, NJ: Lawrence Erlbaum Associates.

Perry, B., & Dockett, S. (2005). "I know that you don't have to work hard": Mathematics learning in the first year of primary school. In H. L. Chick & J. L. Vincent (Eds.), *Proceedings of the 29th Conference of the International Group for the Psychology in Mathematics Education* (Vol. 4, pp. 65-72). Melbourne, Australia: PME.

Perry, R., & Lewis, C. C. (2017). Lesson study to scale up research-based knowledge: A randomized, controlled trial of fractions learning. *Journal for Research in Mathematics Education*, 48(3), 261-299.

Perry, B., Young-Loveridge, J. M., Dockett, S., & Doig, B. (2008). The development of young children's mathematical understanding. In H. Forgasz, A. Barkatsas, A. Bishop, B. A. Clarke, S. Keast, W. T. Seah et al. (Eds.), *Research in mathematics education in Australasia 2004-2007* (pp. 17-40). Rotterdam, The Netherlands: Sense Publishers.

Phillips, D., & Meloy, M. (2012). High-quality school-based pre-K can boost early learning for children with special needs. *Exceptional Children*, 78(4), 471-490.

Piaget, J. (1962). *Play, dreams and imitation in childhood*. New York, NY: W. W. Norton.

Piaget, J. (1971/1974). *Understanding causality*. New York, NY: W. W. Norton.

Piaget, J., & Inhelder, B. (1967). *The child's conception of space*. New York, NY: W. W. Norton.

Piasta, S. B., Pelatti, C. Y., & Miller, H. L. (2014). Mathematics and science learning opportunities in preschool classrooms. *Early Education and Development*, 25(4), 445-468.

Peirce, N. (2013). Digital game-based learning for early childhood. Retrieved from Learnovate Centre website: www.learnovatecentre.org/wp-content/ uploads/2013/05/Digital_Game-based_Learning_ for_Early_Childhood_Report_FINAL.pdf

Platas, L. M. (2019). Practicing the mathematical practices DREME TE. Retrieved from https:// dreme.stanford.edu/people/linda-platas

Pollio, H. R., & Whitacre, J. D. (1970). Some observations on the use of natural numbers by preschool children. *Perceptual and Motor Skills*, 30, 167-174.

Portelance, D. J., Strawhacker, A. L., & Bers, M. U. (2016). Constructing the ScratchJr programming language in the early childhood classroom. *International Journal of Technology and Design Education*, 26(4), 489-504.

Porter, J. (1999). Learning to count: A difficult task? *Down Syndrome Research and Practice*, 6(2), 85-94.

Portsmore, M., & Milto, E. (2018). Novel engineering in early elementary classrooms. In L. D. English & T. Moore (Eds.), *Early engineering learning* (pp. 203-223). Gateway East, Singapore: Springer.

Pound, L. (2017). Count on play: The importance of play in making sense of mathematics. In G. Goodliff, N. Canning, J. Parry & L. Miller (Eds.), *Young Children's Play and Creativity: Multiple Voices* (pp. 220-228). Abingdon, Oxon & New York, NY: Routledge.

Powell, S. R., & Fuchs, L. S. (2010). Contribution of equal-sign instruction beyond word-problem tutoring for third-grade students with mathematics difficulty. *Journal of Educational Psychology*, 102 (2), 381-394.

Powell, S. R., Fuchs, L. S., & Fuchs, D. (2013). Reaching the mountaintop: Addressing the common core standards in mathematics for students with mathematical disabilities. *Learning Disabilities Research & Practice, 28*(1), 38-48. doi: 10.1111/ldrp.12001

Powell, S. R., & Nurnberger-Haag, J. (2015). Everybody counts, but usually just to 10! A systematic analysis of number representations in children's books. *Early Education and Development, 26*(3), 377-398. doi: 10.1080/10409289.2015.994466

Pratt, C. (1948). *I learn from children.* New York, NY: Simon and Schuster.

Prediger, S., Erath, K., & Opitz, E. M. (2019). The language dimension of mathematical difficulties. In A. Fritz, V. G. Haase & P. Räsänen (Eds.), *International handbook of mathematical learning difficulties: From the laboratory to the classroom* (pp. 437-455). Cham, Switzerland: Springer.

Primavera, J., Wiederlight, P. P., & DiGiacomo, T. M. (2001, August). *Technology access for low-income preschoolers: Bridging the digital divide.* Paper presented at the American Psychological Association, San Francisco, CA.

Pruden, S. M., Levine, S. C., & Huttenlocher, J. (2011). Children's spatial thinking: Does talk about the spatial world matter? *Developmental Science, 14* (6), 1417-1430. doi: 10.1111/j.1467-7687.2011.01088.x

Purpura, D. J., Day, E., Napoli, A. R., & Hart, S. A. (2017). Identifying domain-general and domain-specific predictors of low mathematics performance: A classification and regression tree analysis. *Journal of Numerical Cognition, 3*(2), 365-399. doi: 10.5964/jnc.v3i2.53

Purpura, D. J., Hume, L. E., Sims, D. M., & Lonigan, C. J. (2011). Early literacy and early numeracy: The value of including early literacy skills in the prediction of numeracy development. *Journal of Experimental Child Psychology, 110,* 647-658. doi: 10.1016/j.jecp.2011.07.004

Purpura, D. J., & Napoli, A. R. (2015). Early numeracy and literacy: Untangling the relation between specific components. *Mathematical Thinking and Learning, 17*(2-3), 197-218. doi: 10.1080/10986065.2015.1016817

Ralston, N. C., Benner, G. J., Tasai, S.-F., Riccomini, P. C., & Nelson, J. R. (2014). Mathematics instruction for students with emotional and behavioral disorders: A best-evidence synthesis. *Preventing School Failure, 58*(1), 1-16.

Ramani, G. B., Rowe, M. L., Eason, S. H., & Leech, K. A. (2015). Math talk during informal learning activities in Head Start families. *Cognitive Development, 35,* 15-33. doi: 10.1016/j.cogdev.2014.11.002

Ramani, G. B., Siegler, R. S., & Hitti, A. (2012). Taking it to the classroom: Number board games as a small group learning activity. *Journal of Educational Psychology, 104*(3), 661-672. doi: 10.1037/a0028995.supp

Ramey, C. T., & Ramey, S. L. (1998). Early intervention and early experience. *American Psychologist, 53,* 109-120.

Ramirez, G., Chang, H., Maloney, E. A., Levine, S. C., & Beilock, S. L. (2016). On the relationship between math anxiety and math achievement in early elementary school: The role of problem solving strategies. *Journal of Experimental Child Psychology, 141,* 83-100. doi: doi:10.1016/j.jecp.2015.07.014

Raphael, D., & Wahlstrom, M. (1989). The influence of instructional aids on mathematics achievement. *Journal for Research in Mathematics Education, 20,* 173-190.

Rathbun, A., & West, J. (2004). *From kindergarten through third grade: Children's beginning school experiences.* Washington, DC: U.S. Department of Education, National Center for Education Statistics.

Rathé, S., Torbeyns, J., De Smedt, B., & Verschaffel, L. (2019). Spontaneous focusing on Arabic number symbols and its association with early mathematical competencies. *Early Childhood Research Quarterly, 48,* 111-121. doi: 10.1016/j.ecresq.2019.01.011

Rathé, S., Torbeyns, J., Hannula-Sormunen, M., De Smedt, B., & Verschaffel, L. (2016). Spontaneous focusing on numerosity: A review of recent research. *Mediterranean Journal for Research in Mathematics Education, 15,* 1-25.

Raver, C. C., Jones, S. M., Li-Grining, C., Zhai, F., Bub, K., & Pressler, E. (2011). CSRP's impact on low-income preschoolers preacademic skills: Self-regulation as a mediating mechanism. *Child Development, 82*(1), 362-378. doi: 10.1111/j.1467-8624.2010.01561.x

Raver, C. C., Jones, S. M., Li-Grining, C., Zhai, F., Metzger, M. W., & Solomon, B. (2009). Targeting children's behavior problems in preschool classrooms: A cluster-randomized controlled trial. *Journal of Consulting and Clinical Psychology, 77* (2), 302-316. doi: 10.1037/a0015302

Razel, M., & Eylon, B.-S. (1986). Developing visual language skills: The Agam program. *Journal of Visual Verbal Languaging, 6*(1), 49-54.

Razel, M., & Eylon, B.-S. (1990). Development of visual cognition: Transfer effects of the Agam program. *Journal of Applied Developmental Psychology, 11,* 459-485.

Razel, M., & Eylon, B.-S. (1991, July). Developing mathematics readiness in young children with the Agam program. *Paper presented at the Fifteenth Conference of the International Group for the Psychology of Mathematics Education,* Genoa, Italy.

Reardon, S. F. (2011). The widening academic achievement gap between the rich and the poor: New evidence and possible explanations. In G. J. Duncan & R. Murnane (Eds.), *Whither*

Opportunity? *Rising Inequality, Schools, and Children's Life Chances* (pp. 91–116). New York, NY: Russell Sage Foundation.

Reeves, J. L., Gunter, G. A., & Lacey, C. (2017). Mobile learning in pre-kindergarten: Using student feedback to inform practice. *Educational Technology & Society, 20*(1), 37–44.

Reikerås, E. (2016). Central skills in toddlers' and pre-schoolers' mathematical development, observed in play and everyday activities *Nordic Studies in Mathematics Education, 21*(4), 57–77.

Reikerås, E., Løge, I. K., & Knivsberg, A.-M. (2012). The mathematical competencies of toddlers expressed in their play and daily life activities in Norwegian kindergartens. *International Journal of Early Childhood, 44*(1), 91–114. doi: 10.1007/s13158-011-0050-x

Resnick, I., Newcombe, N. S., & Jordan, N. C. (2019). The relation between spatial reasoning and mathematical achievement in children with mathematical learning difficulties. In A. Fritz, V. G. Haase & P. Räsänen (Eds.), *International handbook of mathematical learning difficulties: From the laboratory to the classroom* (pp. 423–435). Cham, Switzerland: Springer.

Resnick, L. B., & Omanson, S. (1987). Learning to understand arithmetic. In R. Glaser (Ed.), *Advances in instructional psychology* (pp. 41–95). Hillsdale, NJ: Lawrence Erlbaum Associates.

Resnick, L. B., & Singer, J. A. (1993). Protoquantitative origins of ratio reasoning. In T. P. Carpenter, E. H. Fennema, & T. A. Romberg (Eds.), *Rational numbers: An integration of research* (pp. 107–130). Erlbaum.

Rhee, M. C., & Chavnagri, N., (Cartographer). (1991). *Four-year-old children's peer interactions when playing with a computer.* ERIC Document No. ED342466. Wayne State University

Rich, S. E., Duhon, G. J., & Reynolds, J. (2017). Improving the generalization of computer-based math fluency building through the use of sufficient stimulus exemplars. *Journal of Behavioral Education, 26*(2), 123–136.

Richardson, K. (2004). Making sense. In D. H. Clements, J. Sarama, & A.-M. DiBiase (Eds.), *Engaging young children in mathematics: Standards for early childhood mathematics education* (pp. 321–324). Mahwah, NJ: Lawrence Erlbaum Associates.

Riel, M. (1985). The Computer Chronicles Newswire: A functional learning environment for acquiring literacy skills. *Journal of Educational Computing Research, 1*, 317–337.

Ritchie, S. J., & Bates, T. C. (2013). Enduring links from childhood mathematics and reading achievement to adult socioeconomic status. *Psychological Science, 24*, 1301–1308. doi: 10.1177/0956797612466268

Ritter, S., Anderson, J. R., Koedinger, K. R., & Corbett, A. (2007). Cognitive Tutor: Applied research in mathematics education. *Psychonomics Bulletin & Review, 14*(2), 249–255.

Rittle-Johnson, B., Fyfe, E. R., & Zippert, E. (2018). The roles of patterning and spatial skills in early mathematics development. *Early Childhood Research Quarterly.* doi: 10.1016/j.ecresq.2018.03.006

Robinson, G. E. (1990). Synthesis of research on effects of class size. *Educational Leadership, 47*(7), 80–90.

Robinson, N. M., Abbot, R. D., Berninger, V. W., & Busse, J. (1996). The structure of abilities in math-precocious young children: Gender similarities and differences. *Journal of Educational Psychology, 88*(2), 341–352.

Rogers, A. (2012). *Steps in developing a quality whole number place value assessment for years 3-6: Unmasking the "experts."* Paper presented at the Mathematics Education Research Group of Australasia, Singapore.

Romano, E., Babchishin, L., Pagani, L. S., & Kohen, D. (2010). School readiness and later achievement: Replication and extension using a nationwide Canadian survey. *Developmental Psychology, 46*(5), 995–1007. doi: 10.1037/a0018880

Rosengren, K. S., Gross, D., Abrams, A. F., & Perlmutter, M. (1985). *An observational study of preschool children's computing activity.* Austin, TX: "Perspectives on the Young Child and the Computer" conference, University of Texas at Austin.

Rosser, R. A., Ensing, S. S., Glider, P. J., & Lane, S. (1984). An information-processing analysis of children's accuracy in predicting the appearance of rotated stimuli. *Child Development, 55*, 2204–2211.

Rosser, R. A., Horan, P. F., Mattson, S. L., & Mazzeo, J. (1984). Comprehension of Euclidean space in young children: The early emergence of understanding and its limits. *Genetic Psychology Monographs, 110*, 21–41.

Roth, J., Carter, R., Ariet, M., Resnick, M. B., & Crans, G. (2000, April). *Comparing fourth-grade math and reading achievement of children who did and did not participate in Florida's statewide Prekindergarten Early Intervention Program.* Paper presented at the American Educational Research Association, New Orleans, LA.

Rouse, C., Brooks-Gunn, J., & McLanahan, S. (2005). Introducing the issue. *The Future of Children, 15*, 5–14.

Rousselle, L., & Noël, M.-P. (2007). Basic numerical skills in children with mathematics learning disabilities: A comparison of symbolic vs. non-symbolic number magnitude processing. *Cognition, 102,* 361-395.

Russell, K. A., & Kamii, C. (2012). Children's judgements of durations: A modified republication of Piaget's study. *School Science and Mathematics, 112*(8), 476-482.

Russell, S. J. (1991). Counting noses and scary things: Children construct their ideas about data. In D. Vere-Jones (Ed.), *Proceedings of the Third International Conference on Teaching Statistics* (pp. 158-164). Dunedin, New Zealand: International Statistical Institute.

Sæbbe, P.-E., & Mosvold, R. (2016). Initiating a conceptualization of the professional work of teaching mathematics in kindergarten in terms of discourse. *Nordic Studies in Mathematics Education, 21*(4), 79-93.

Sakakibara, T. (2014). Mathematics learning and teaching in Japanese preschool: Providing appropriate foundations for a elementary schooler's mathematics learning. *International Journal of Educational Studies in Mathematics, 1*(1), 16-26.

Salminen, J., Koponen, T., Räsänen, P., & Aro, M. (2015). Preventive support for kindergarteners most at-risk for mathematics difficulties: Computer-assisted intervention. *Mathematical Thinking and Learning, 17*(4), 273-295. doi: 10.1080/10986065.2015.1083837

Sandhofer, C. M., & Smith, L. B. (1999). Learning color words involves learning a system of mappings. *Developmental Psychology, 35,* 668-679.

Sarama, J. (2002). Listening to teachers: Planning for professional development. *Teaching Children Mathematics, 9,* 36-39.

Sarama, J. (2004). Technology in early childhood mathematics: "Building Blocks" as an innovative technology-based curriculum. In D. H. Clements, J. Sarama, & A.-M. DiBiase (Eds.), *Engaging young children in mathematics: Standards for early childhood mathematics education* (pp. 361-375). Mahwah, NJ: Lawrence Erlbaum Associates.

Sarama, J., Brenneman, K., Clements, D. H., Duke, N. K., & Hemmeter, M. L. (2017). Interdisciplinary teaching across multiple domains: The C4L (Connect4Learning) Curriculum. In L. B. Bailey (Ed.), *Implementing the Common Core State Standards across the early childhood curriculum* (pp. 1-53). New York, NY: Routledge.

Sarama, J., & Clements, D. H. (2016). Physical and virtual manipulatives: What is "concrete"? In P. S. Moyer-Packenham (Ed.), *International perspectives on teaching and learning mathematics with virtual manipulatives* (Vol. 3, pp. 71-93). Switzerland: Springer International Publishing.

Sarama, J., & Clements, D. H. (2020). Promoting a good start: Technology in early childhood

mathematics. In E. Arias, J. Cristia & S. Cueto (Eds.), *Learning mathematics in the 21st Century: Adding technology to the equation* (pp. 181-223). Washington, DC: Inter-American Development Bank.

Sarama, J., Clements, D. H., Wolfe, C. B., & Spitler, M. E. (2016). Professional development in early mathematics: Effects of an intervention based on learning trajectories on teachers' practices. *Nordic Studies in Mathematics Education, 21*(4), 29-55.

Sarama, J., & Clements, D. H. (2002a). Building Blocks for young children's mathematical development. *Journal of Educational Computing Research, 27*(1&2), 93-110.

Sarama, J., & Clements, D. H. (2002b). Learning and teaching with computers in early childhood education. In O. N. Saracho & B. Spodek (Eds.), *Contemporary Perspectives on Science and Technology in Early Childhood Education* (pp. 171-219). Greenwich, CT: Information Age Publishing, Inc.

Sarama, J., & Clements, D. H. (2003). *Building Blocks* of early childhood mathematics. *Teaching Children Mathematics, 9*(8), 480-484.

Sarama, J., & Clements, D. H. (2009). *Early childhood mathematics education research: Learning trajectories for young children.* New York, NY: Routledge.

Sarama, J., & Clements, D. H. (2012). Mathematics for the whole child. In S. Suggate & E. Reese (Eds.), *Contemporary debates in childhood education and development* (pp. 71-80). New York, NY: Routledge.

Sarama, J., & Clements, D. H. (2013). Lessons learned in the implementation of the TRIAD scale-up model: Teaching early mathematics with trajectories and technologies. In T. G. Halle, A. J. Metz, & I. Martinez-Beck (Eds.), *Applying implementation science in early childhood programs and systems* (pp. 173-191). Baltimore, MD: Brookes.

Sarama, J., & Clements, D. H. (2018). Promoting positive transitions through coherent instruction, assessment, and professional development: The TRIAD scale-up model. In A. J. Mashburn, J. LoCasale-Crouch & K. Pears (Eds.), *Kindergarten transition and readiness: Promoting cognitive, social-emotional, and self-regulatory development* (pp. 327-348). Cham, Switzerland: Springer International Publishing.

Sarama, J., & Clements, D. H. (2019). Technology in early childhood education. In O. N. Saracho (Ed.), *Handbook of research on the education of young children* (Vol. 4, pp. 183-198). New York, NY: Routledge.

Sarama, J., Clements, D. H., Barrett, J. E., Cullen, C. J., & Hudyma, A. (2019). Length measurement in the early years: Teaching and learning with learning trajectories. *Submitted for publication.*

Sarama, J., Clements, D. H., Barrett, J. E., Van Dine, D. W., & McDonel, J. S. (2011). Evaluation of a learning trajectory for length in the early years. *ZDM-The International Journal on Mathematics Education, 43*, 667-680. doi: 10.1007/s11858-011-0326-5

Sarama, J., Clements, D. H., Swaminathan, S., McMillen, S., & González Gómez, R. M. (2003). Development of mathematical concepts of two-dimensional space in grid environments: An exploratory study. *Cognition and Instruction, 21*, 285-324.

Sarama, J., Clements, D. H., & Vukelic, E. B. (1996). The role of a computer manipulative in fostering specific psychological/mathematical processes. In E. Jakubowski, D. Watkins, & H. Biske (Eds.), *Proceedings of the 18th Annual Meeting of the North America Chapter of the International Group for the Psychology of Mathematics Education* (Vol. 2, pp. 567-572). Columbus, OH: ERIC Clearinghouse for Science, Mathematics, and Environmental Education.

Sarama, J., Clements, D. H., Wolfe, C. B., & Spitler, M. E. (2012). Longitudinal evaluation of a scale-up model for teaching mathematics with trajectories and technologies. *Journal of Research on Educational Effectiveness, 5*(2), 105-135.

Sarama, J., & DiBiase, A.-M. (2004). The professional development challenge in preschool mathematics. In D. H. Clements, J. Sarama, & A.-M. DiBiase (Eds.), *Engaging young children in mathematics: Standards for early childhood mathematics education* (pp. 415-446). Mahwah, NJ: Lawrence Erlbaum Associates.

Sarama, J., Lange, A., Clements, D. H., & Wolfe, C. B. (2012). The impacts of an early mathematics curriculum on emerging literacy and language. *Early Childhood Research Quarterly, 27*(3), 489-502. doi: 10.1016/j.ecresq.2011.12.002

Sariba , ., & Arnas, Y. A. (2017). Which type of verbal problems do the teachers and education materials present to children in preschool period? *Necatibey Faculty of Education Electronic Journal of Science and Mathematics Education, 11*(1), 81-100.

Scalise, N. R., DePascale, M., McCown, C., & Ramani, G. B. (2019, March). "My child's math ability will never change": Relations between parental beliefs and preschoolers' math skills. Paper presented at the 2019 SRCD Biennial Meeting, Baltimore, MD.

Schacter, J., & Jo, B. (2016). Improving low-income preschoolers mathematics achievement with Math Shelf, a preschool tablet computer curriculum. *Computers in Human Behavior, 55*(A), 223-229. doi: 10.1016/j.chb.2015.09.013

Schaeffer, M. W., Rozek, C. S., Berkowitz, T., Levine, S. C., & Beilock, S. L. (2018). Disassociating the relation between parents' math anxiety and children's math achievement: Long-term effects of a math app intervention. *Journal of Experimental Psychology General, 147*(12), 1782-1790. doi: 10.1037/xge0000490

Schenke, K., Watts, T. W., Nguyen, T., Sarama, J., & Clements, D. H. (2017). Differential effects of the classroom on African American and non-African American's mathematics achievement. *Journal of Educational Psychology, 109*(6), 794-811.

Schery, T. K., & O'Connor, L. C. (1997). Language intervention: Computer training for young children with special needs. *British Journal of Educational Technology, 28*, 271-279.

Schliemann, A. C. D., Carraher, D. W., & Brizuela, B. M. (2007). *Bringing out the algebraic character of arithmetic.* Mahwah, NJ: Lawrence Erlbaum Associates.

Schmerold, K. L., Bock, A., Peterson, M., Leaf, B., Vennergrund, K., & Pasnak, R. (2017). The relations between patterning, executive function, and mathematics. *Journal of Psychology: Interdisciplinary and Applied, 151*(2), 207-228. doi: 10.1080/00223980.2016.1252708

Schmitt, S. A., Korucu, I., Napoli, A. R., Bryant, L. M., & Purpura, D. J. (2018). Using block play to enhance preschool children's mathematics and executive functioning: A randomized controlled trial. *Early Childhood Research Quarterly, 44*, 181-191. doi: 10.1016/j.ecresq.2018.04.006

Schoenfeld, A. H. (2008). Early algebra as mathematical sense making. In J. J. Kaput, D. W. Carraher, & M. L. Blanton (Eds.), *Algebra in the early grades* (pp. 479-510). Mahwah, NJ: Lawrence Erlbaum Associates.

Schumacher, R. F., & Fuchs, L. S. (2012). Does understanding relational terminology mediate effects of intervention on compare word problems? *Journal of Experimental Child Psychology, 111*(4), 607-628. doi: 10.1016/j.jecp.2011.12.001

Schwartz, S. (2004). Explorations in graphing with prekindergarten children. In B. Clarke (Ed.), *International perspectives on learning and teaching mathematics* (pp. 83-97). Gothenburg, Sweden: National Centre for Mathematics Education.

Schweinhart, L. J., & Weikart, D. P. (1988). Education for young children living in poverty: Child-initiated learning or teacher-d automatic human infordirected instruction? *The Elementary School Journal, 89*, 212-225.

Schweinhart, L. J., & Weikart, D. P. (1997). The High/Scope curriculum comparison study through age

23. *Early Childhood Research Quarterly, 12,* 117-143.

Scott, L. F., & Neufeld, H. (1976). Concrete instruction in elementary school mathematics: Pictorial vs. manipulative. *School Science and Mathematics, 76,* 68-72.

Secada, W. G. (1992). Race, ethnicity, social class, language, and achievement in mathematics. In D. A. Grouws (Ed.), *Handbook of research on mathematics teaching and learning* (pp. 623-660). New York, NY: Macmillan.

Sedaghatjou, M., & Campbell, S. R. (2017). Exploring cardinality in the era of touchscreen-based technology. *International Journal of Mathematical Education in Science and Technology, 48*(8), 1225-1239.

eker, P. T., & Alisinano lu, F. (2015). A survey study of the effects of preschool teachers' beliefs and self-efficacy towards mathematics education and their demographic features on 48-60-month-old preschool children's mathematic skills. *Creative Education, 06*(03), 405-414. doi: 10.4236/ce.2015.63040

Sella, F., Berteletti, I., Lucangeli, D., & Zorzi, M. (2016). Spontaneous non-verbal counting in toddlers. *Development of Science, 19*(2), 329-337. doi: 10.1111/desc.12299

Seloraji, P., & Eu, L. K. (2017). Students' performance in geometrical reflection using GeoGebra. *Malaysian Online Journal of Educational Technology, 5* (1), 65-77.

Senk, S. L., & Thompson, D. R. (2003). *Standards-based school mathematics curricula. What are they? What do students learn?* Mahwah, NJ: Lawrence Erlbaum Associates.

Seo, K.-H., & Ginsburg, H. P. (2004). What is developmentally appropriate in early childhood mathematics education? In D. H. Clements, J. Sarama, & A.-M. DiBiase (Eds.), *Engaging young children in mathematics: Standards for early childhood mathematics education* (pp. 91-104). Mahwah, NJ: Lawrence Erlbaum Associates.

Shade, D. D. (1994). Computers and young children: Software types, social contexts, gender, age, and emotional responses. *Journal of Computing in Childhood Education, 5*(2), 177-209.

Shade, D. D., Nida, R. E., Lipinski, J. M., & Watson, J. A. (1986). Microcomputers and preschoolers: Working together in a classroom setting. *Computers in the Schools, 3,* 53-61.

Shah, H. K., Domitrovich, C. E., Morgan, N. R., Moore, J. E., Rhoades, B. L., Jacobson, L., & Greenberg, M. T. (2017). One or two years of participation: Is dosage of an enhanced publicly funded preschool program associated with the academic and executive function skills of low-income children in early elementary school? *Early Childhood Research Quarterly, 40,* 123-137. doi: 10.1016/j.ecresq.2017.03.004

Shahbari, J. A. (2017). Mathematical and pedagogical knowledge amongst first-and second-grade inservice and preservice mathematics teachers. *International Journal for Mathematics Teaching and Learning, 18*(1), 41-65.

Shamir, A., & Lifshitz, I. (2012). E-books for supporting the emergent literacy and emergent math of children at risk for learning disabilities: Can metacognitive guidance make a difference? *European Journal of Special Needs Education, 28*(1), 33-48. doi: 10.1080/08856257.2012.742746

Shaw, K., Nelsen, E., & Shen, Y.-L. (2001, April). *Preschool development and subsequent school achievement among Spanish-speaking children from low-income families.* Paper presented at the American Educational Research Association, Seattle, WA.

Shaw, R., Grayson, A., & Lewis, V. (2005). Inhibition, ADHD, and computer games: The inhibitory performance of children with ADHD on computerized tasks and games. *Journal of Attention Disorders, 8,* 160-168.

Shayer, M., & Adhami, M. (2010). Realizing the cognitive potential of children 5-7 with a mathematics focus: Post-test and longterm effects of a 2-year intervention. *British Journal of Educational Psychology, 80*(3), 363-379.

Sheehan, K. J., Pila, S., Lauricella, A. R., & Wartella, E. A. (2019). Parent-child interaction and children's learning from a coding application. *Computers & Education, 140.* doi: 10.1016/j.compedu.2019.103601

Shepard, L. (2005). Assessment. In L. Darling-Hammond & J. Bransford (Eds.), *Preparing teachers for a changing world* (pp. 275-326). San Francisco, CA: Jossey-Bass.

Shepard, L., & Pellegrino, J. W. (2018). Classroom assessment principles to support learning and avoid the harms of testing. *Educational Measurement: Issues and Practice, 37*(1), 52-57.

Sherman, J., & Bisanz, J. (2009). Equivalence in symbolic and non-symbolic contexts: Benefits of solving problems with manipulatives *Journal of Educational Psychology, 101*(1), 88-100.

Sherman, J., Bisanz, J., & Popescu, A. (2007, April). *Tracking the path of change: Failure to success on equivalence problems.* Paper presented at the Society for Research in Child Development, Boston, MA.

Shiakalli, M. A., & Zacharos, K. (2014). The contribution of external representations in pre-school mathematical problem solving. *International Journal of Early Years Education, 20*(4), 315-331.

Shiffrin, R. M., & Schneider, W. (1984). Controlled and automatic human information processing: II. Perceptual learning, automatic attending, and a general theory. *Psychological Review, 84,* 127–190.

Shonkoff, J. P., & Phillips, D. A. (Eds.). (2000). *From neurons to neighborhoods: The science of early childhood development.* Washington, DC: National Academy Press.

Shrock, S. A., Matthias, M., Anastasoff, J., Vensel, C., & Shaw, S. (1985). *Examining the effects of the microcomputer on a real world class: A naturalistic study.* Anaheim, CA: Association for Educational Communications and Technology.

Sicilian, S. P. (1988). Development of counting strategies in congenitally blind children. *Journal of Visual Impairment & Blindness, 82*(8), 331–335. doi: 10.1177/0145482X8808200811

Siegler, R. S. (1993). Adaptive and non-adaptive characteristics of low income children's strategy use. In L. A. Penner, G. M. Batsche, H. M. Knoff, & D. L. Nelson (Eds.), *Contributions of psychology to science and mathematics education* (pp. 341–366). Washington, DC: American Psychological Association.

Siegler, R. S. (1995). How does change occur: A microgenetic study of number conservation. *Cognitive Psychology, 28,* 255–273. doi: 10.1006/cogp.1995.1006

Siegler, R. S. (2017). Fractions: Where it all goes wrong. *Scientfic American.* www.scientificamerican.com/article/fractions-where-it-all-goes-wrong/

Siegler, R. S., & Booth, J. L. (2004). Development of numerical estimation in young children. *Child Development, 75,* 428–444.

Silander, M., Moorthy, S., Dominguez, X., Hupert, N., Pasnik, S., & Llorente, C. (2016). Using digital media at home to promote young children's mathematics learning: Results of a randomized controlled trial. Retrieved from Society for Research on Educational Effectiveness. 2040 Sheridan Road, Evanston, IL 60208. website: https://search.proquest.com/docview/1871568227?accountid=14608

Silverman, I. W., York, K., & Zuidema, N. (1984). Area-matching strategies used by young children. *Journal of Experimental Child Psychology, 38,* 464–474.

Silvern, S. B., Countermine, T. A., & Williamson, P. A. (1988). Young children's interaction with a microcomputer. *Early Child Development and Care, 32,* 23–35.

Sim, Z. L., & Xu, F. (2017). Learning higher-order generalizations through free play: Evidence from 2- and 3-year-old children. *Developmental Psychology, 53* (4), 642–651. doi: 10.1037/dev0000278

Simmons, F. R., Willis, C., & Adams, A.-M. (2012). Different components of working memory have different relationships with different mathematical skills. *Journal of Experimental Child Psychology, 111*(2), 139–155. doi: 10.1016/j.jecp.2011.08.011

Skoumpourdi, C. (2010). Kindergarten mathematics with 'Pepe the Rabbit': How kindergartners use auxiliary means to solve problems. *European Early Childhood Education Research Journal, 18* (3), 149–157.

Slater, A., Mattock, A., & Brown, E. (1990). Size constancy at birth: Newborn infants' responses to retinal and real size. *Journal of Experimental Child Psychology, 49,* 314–322.

Slovin, H. (2007, April). *Revelations from counting: A window to conceptual understanding.* Paper presented at the Research Presession of the 85th Annual Meeting of the National Council of Teachers of Mathematics, Atlanta, GA.

Smith, L. B., Jones, S. S., Landau, B., Gershkoff-Stowe, L., & Samuelson, L. (2002). Object name learning provides on-the-job training for attention. *Psychological Science, 13,* 13–19.

Smith, C. R., Marchand-Martella, N. E., & Martella, R. C. (2011). Assessing the effects of the *Rocket Math* program with a primary elementary school student at risk for school failure: A case study. *Education and Treatment of Children, 34,* 247–258.

Snodgrass, M. R., Israel, M., & Reese, G. C. (2016). Instructional supports for students with disabilities in K-5 computing: Findings from a cross-case analysis. *Computers & Education, 100,* 1–17. doi: 10.1016/j.compedu.2016.04.011

Sobayi, C. (2018). The role of parents and pre-primary education in promoting early numeracy development to young children in Dar es Salaam. *Papers in Education and Development*(35).

Solem, M., Huynh, N. T., & Boehm, R. (Eds.). (2015). *Learning progressions for maps, geospatial technology, and spatial thinking: A research handbook.* Washington, DC: National Center for Research in Geography Education.

Sonnenschein, S., Baker, L., Moyer, A., & LeFevre, S. (2005, April). *Parental beliefs about children's reading and math development and relations with subsequent achievement.* Paper presented at the Biennial Meeting of the Society for Research in Child Development, Atlanta, GA.

Sophian, C. (2002). Learning about what fits: Preschool children's reasoning about effects of object size. *Journal for Research in Mathematics Education, 33,* 290–302.

Sophian, C. (2004). A prospective developmental perspective on early mathematics instruction. In D. H. Clements, J. Sarama, & A.-M. DiBiase (Eds.), *Engaging young children in mathematics: Standards for early childhood mathematics education* (pp. 253-266). Mahwah, NJ: Lawrence Erlbaum Associates.

Sophian, C. (2013). Vicissitudes of children's mathematical knowledge: Implications of developmental research for early childhood mathematics education. *Early Education & Development, 24*(4), 436-442. doi: 10.1080/10409289.2013.773255

Sophian, C., & Adams, N. (1987). Infants' understanding of numerical transformations. *British Journal of Educational Psychology, 5,* 257-264.

Sorariutta, A., & Silvén, M. (2017). Maternal cognitive guidance and early education and care as precursors of mathematical development at preschool age and in ninth grade. *Infant and Child Development, 27*(2). doi: 10.1002/icd.2069

Sorariutta, A., & Silvén, M. (2018). Quality of both parents' cognitive guidance and quantity of early childhood education: Influences on pre-mathatical development. *British Journal of Educational Psychology, 88*(2), 192-215. doi: 10.1111/bjep.12217

Soto-Calvo, E., Simmons, F. R., Willis, C., & Adams, A.-M. (2015, December). Identifying the cognitive predictors of early counting and calculation skills: Evidence from a longitudinal study. *Journal of Experimental Child Psychology, 140,* 16-37. doi: 10.1016/j.jecp.2015.06.011

Sowder, J. T. (1992a). Estimation and number sense. In D. A. Grouws (Ed.), *Handbook of research on mathematics teaching and learning* (pp. 371-389). New York, NY: Macmillan.

Sowder, J. T. (1992b). Making sense of numbers in school mathematics. In G. Leinhardt, R. Putman, & R. A. Hattrup (Eds.), *Analysis of arithmetic for mathematics teaching* (pp. 1-45). Mahwah, NJ: Lawrence Erlbaum Associates.

Sowell, E. J. (1989). Effects of manipulative materials in mathematics instruction. *Journal for Research in Mathematics Education, 20,* 498-505.

Spaepen, E., Coppola, M., Spelke, E. S., Carey, S. E., & Goldin-Meadow, S. (2011). Number without a language model. *Proceedings of the National Academy of Sciences, 108*(8), 3163-3168. doi: 10.1073/pnas.1015975108

Spaepen, E., Gunderson, E. A., Gibson, D., Goldin-Meadow, S., & Levine, S. C. (2018). Meaning before order: Cardinal principle knowledge predicts improvement in understanding the successor principle and exact ordering. *Cognition, 180,* 59-81. doi: 10.1016/j.cognition.2018.06.012

The Spatial Reasoning Study Group. (2015). *Spatial reasoning in the early years: Principles, assertions, and speculations.* New York, NY: Routledge.

Spelke, E. S. (2003). What makes us smart? Core knowledge and natural language. In D. Genter & S. Goldin-Meadow (Eds.), *Language in mind* (pp. 277-311). Cambridge, MA: MIT Press.

Spelke, E. S. (2008). Effects of music instruction on developing cognitive systems at the foundations of mathematics and science. In C. Asbury & B. Rich (Eds.), *Learning, Arts, & the Brain* (pp. 17-49). New York/Washington, DC: Dana Press.

Starkey, P., Klein, A., Chang, I., Qi, D., Lijuan, P., & Yang, Z. (1999, April). *Environmental supports for young children's mathematical development in China and the United States.* Paper presented at the Society for Research in Child Development, Albuquerque, NM.

Starr, A., Libertus, M. E., & Brannon, E. M. (2013). Infants show ratio-dependent number discrimination regardless of set size. *Infancy, 18*(6), 927-941. doi: 10.1111/infa.12008

Steen, L. A. (1988). The science of patterns. *Science, 240,* 611-616.

Steffe, L. P. (1991). Operations that generate quantity. *Learning and Individual Differences, 3,* 61-82.

Steffe, L. P. (2004). PSSM from a constructivist perspective. In D. H. Clements, J. Sarama, & A.-M. DiBiase (Eds.), *Engaging young children in mathematics: Standards for early childhood mathematics education* (pp. 221-251). Mahwah, NJ: Lawrence Erlbaum Associates.

Steffe, L. P., & Cobb, P. (1988). *Construction of arithmetical meanings and strategies.* New York, NY: Springer-Verlag.

Steffe, L. P., & Olive, J. (2002). Design and use of computer tools for interactive mathematical activity (TIMA). *Journal of Educational Computing Research, 27*(1&2), 55-76.

Steffe, L. P., & Olive, J. (2010). *Children's fractional knowledge.* Springer. doi: 10.1007/978-1-4419-0519-8

Steffe, L. P., Thompson, P. W., & Richards, J. (1982). Children's counting in arithmetical problem solving. In T. P. Carpenter, J. M. Moser, & T. A. Romberg (Eds.), *Addition and subtraction: A cognitive perspective* (pp. 83-97). Mahwah, NJ: Lawrence Erlbaum Associates.

Steffe, L. P., & Wiegel, H. G. (1994). Cognitive play and mathematical learning in computer MicroWorlds. *Journal of Research in Childhood Education, 8*(2), 117-131.

Steinke, D. (2013) *Rhythm and number sense: How music teaches math.* Lafayette, CO: NumberWorks.

Stenmark, J. K., Thompson, V., & Cossey, R. (1986). *Family math.* Berkeley, CA: Lawrence Hall of Science, University of California.

Stephan, M., & Clements, D. H. (2003). Linear, area, and time measurement in prekindergarten to grade 2. In D. H. Clements (Ed.), *Learning and teaching measurement: 65th Yearbook* (pp. 3-16). Reston, VA: National Council of Teachers of Mathematics.

Stevenson, H. W., & Newman, R. S. (1986). Long-term prediction of achievement and attitudes in mathematics and reading. *Child Development, 57*, 646-659.

Stewart, R., Leeson, N., & Wright, R. J. (1997). Links between early arithmetical knowledge and early space and measurement knowledge: An exploratory study. In F. Biddulph & K. Carr (Eds.), *Proceedings of the Twentieth Annual Conference of the Mathematics Education Research Group of Australasia* (Vol. 2, pp. 477-484). Hamilton, New Zealand: MERGA.

Stigler, J. W., Fuson, K. C., Ham, M., & Kim, M. S. (1986). An analysis of addition and subtraction word problems in American and Soviet elementary mathematics textbooks. *Cognition and Instruction, 3*, 153-171.

Stiles, J., & Nass, R. (1991). Spatial grouping activity in young children with congenital right or left hemisphere brain injury. *Brain and Cognition, 15*, 201-222.

Stock, P., Desoete, A., & Roeyers, H. (2009). Mastery of the counting principles in toddlers: A crucial step in the development of budding arithmetic abilities? *Learning and Individual Differences, 19* (4), 419-422. doi: 10.1016/j.lindif.2009.03.002

Sullivan, A., & Bers, M. (2013). Gender differences in kindergarteners' robotics and programming achievement. *International Journal of Technology & Design Education, 23*(3), 691-702. doi: 10.1007/s10798-012-9210-z

Sullivan, A., Kazakoff, E. R., & Bers, M. U. (2013). The wheels on the bot go round and round: Robotics curriculum in pre-kindergarten. *Journal of Information Technology Education: Innovations in Practice, 12*, 203-219.

Sumpter, L., & Hedefalk, M. (2015). Preschool children's collective mathematical reasoning during free outdoor play. *The Journal of Mathematical Behavior, 39*, 1-10. doi: 10.1016/j.jmathb.2015.03.006

Sung, W., Ahn, J.-H., Kai, S. M., & Black, J. (2017). Effective planning strategy in robotics education: An embodied approach. Paper presented at the Society for Information Technology & Teacher Education International Conference 2017, Austin, TX, United States. www.learntechlib.org/p/177387

Sun Lee, J., & Ginsburg, H. P. (2009). Early childhood teachers' misconceptions about mathematics education for young children in the United States. *Australasian Journal of Early Childhood, 34*(4), 37-45.

Susperreguy, M. I., Di Lonardo Burr, S., Xu, C., Douglas, H., & LeFevre, J. A. (2020). Children's home numeracy environment predicts growth of their early mathematical skills in Kindergarten. *Child Development*. doi: 10.1111/cdev.13353

Suydam, M. N. (1986). Manipulative materials and achievement. *Arithmetic Teacher, 33*(6), 10, 32.

Swigger, K. M., & Swigger, B. K. (1984). Social patterns and computer use among preschool children. *AEDS Journal, 17*, 35-41.

Swinton, P. J., Buysse, V., Bryant, D., Clifford, D., Early, D., & Little, L. (2005). NCEDL Pre-kindergarten study. *Early Developments, 9*(1).

Sylva, K., Melhuish, E., Sammons, P., Siraj-Blatchford, I., & Taggart, B. (2005). *The effective provision of pre-school education [EPPE] project: A longitudinal study funded by the DfEE (1997-- 2003)*. London, England: EPPE Project, Institute of Education, University of London.

Szkudlarek, E., & Brannon, E. M. (2018). Approximate arithmetic training improves informal math performance in low achieving preschoolers. *Frontiers in Psychology*, in press. doi: 10.3389/fpsyg. 2018.00606

Taylor, M. (2017). *Computer programming with early elementary students with and without intellectual disabilities.* (Doctoral Dissertation), University of Central Florida. Retrieved from http://purl.fcla. edu/fcla/etd/CFE0006807

Tharp, R. G., & Gallimore, R. (1988). *Rousing minds to life: Teaching, learning, and schooling in social contexts.* New York, NY: Cambridge University Press.

Thirumurthy, V. (2003). *Children's cognition of geometry and spatial thinking--A cultural process.* Unpublished doctoral dissertation, University of Buffalo, State University of New York.

Tierney, C., & Berle-Caman, M. (1997). *Fair shares.* Dale Seymour.

Thom, J. S., & McGarvey, L. M. (2015). The act and artifact of drawing(s): Observing geometric thinking with, in, and through children's drawings. *ZDM Mathematics Education, 47*(3), 465-481. doi: 10.1007/s11858-015-0697-0

Thomas, B. (1982). *An abstract of kindergarten teachers' elicitation and utilization of children's prior knowledge in the teaching of shape concepts.* Unpublished manuscript, School of Education, Health, Nursing, and Arts Professions, New York University.

Thomas, G., & Tagg, A. (2004). *An evaluation of the Early Numeracy Project 2003.* Wellington, Australia: Ministry of Education.

Thommen, E., Avelar, S., Sapin, V. R. Z., Perrenoud, S., & Malatesta, D. (2010). Mapping the journey from home to school: A study on children's representation of space. *International Research in Geographical and Environmental Education, 19*(3), 191-205.

Thompson, A. C. (2012). *The effect of enhanced visualization instruction on first grade students'* scores on the North Carolina standard course assessment. (Dissertation), Liberty University, Lynchburg, VA.

Thompson, P. W. (1992). Notations, conventions, and constraints: Contributions to effective use of concrete materials in elementary mathematics. *Journal for Research in Mathematics Education, 23*, 123-147.

Thompson, C. J., & Davis, S. B. (2014). Classroom observation data and instruction in primary mathematics education: Improving design and rigour. *Mathematics Education Research Journal, 26*(2), 301-323. doi: 10.1007/s13394-013-0099-y

Thompson, P. W., & Thompson, A. G. (1990). Salient aspects of experience with concrete manipulatives. In F. Hitt (Ed.), *Proceedings of the 14th Annual Meeting of the International Group for the Psychology of Mathematics* (Vol. 3, pp. 337-343). Mexico City, Mexico: International Group for the Psychology of Mathematics Education.

Thompson, R. J., Napoli, A. R., & Purpura, D. J. (2017). Age-related differences in the relation between the home numeracy environment and numeracy skills. *Infant and Child Development, 26* (5), 1-13. doi: 10.1002/icd.2019

Thomson, D., Casey, B. M., Lombardi, C. M., & Nguyen, H. N. (2018). Quality of fathers' spatial concept support during block building predicts their daughters' early math skills – But not their sons'. *Early Childhood Research Quarterly*. doi: 10.1016/j.ecresq.2018.07.008

Thomson, S., Rowe, K., Underwood, C., & Peck, R. (2005). *Numeracy in the early years: Project Good start*. Camberwellm Victoria, Australia: Australian Council for Educational Research.

Thorton, C. A., Langrall, C. W., & Jones, G. A. (1997). Mathematics instruction for elementary students with learning disabilities. *Journal of Learning Disabilities, 30*, 142-150.

Titeca, D., Roeyers, H., Josephy, H., Ceulemans, A., & Desoete, A. (2014). Preschool predictors of mathematics in first grade children with autism spectrum disorder. *Research in Developmental Disabilities, 35*(11), 2714-2727. doi: 10.1016/j.ridd.2014.07.012

Tirosh, D., Tsamir, P., Levenson, E. S., & Barkai, R. (2020). Setting the table with toddlers: A playful context for engaging in one-to-one correspondence. *ZDM*. doi: 10.1007/s11858-019-01126-9

Toll, S. W. M., Van der Ven, S., Kroesbergen, E., & Van Luit, J. E. H. (2010). Executive functions as predictors of math learning disabilities. *Journal of Learning Disabilities, 20*(10), 1-12. doi: 10.1177/0022219410387302

Toll, S. W. M., & Van Luit, J. E. H. (2014). Explaining numeracy development in weak performing kindergartners. *Journal of Experimental Child Psychology, 124C*, 97-111. doi: 10.1016/j.jecp.2014.02.001

Toll, S. W. M., Van Viersen, S., Kroesbergen, E. H., & Van Luit, J. E. H. (2015). The development of (non-)symbolic comparison skills throughout kindergarten and their relations with basic mathematical skills. *Learning and Individual Differences, 38*, 10-17. doi: 10.1016/j.lindif.2014.12.006

Torbeyns, J., van den Noortgate, W., Ghesquière, P., Verschaffel, L., Van de Rijt, B. A. M., & van Luit, J. E. H. (2002). Development of early numeracy in 5- to 7-year-old children: A comparison between Flanders and the Netherlands. *Educational Research and Evaluation. An International Journal on Theory and Practice, 8*, 249-275.

Touchette, E., Petit, D., Séguin, J. R., Boivin, M., Tremblay, R. E., & Montplaisir, J. Y. (2007). Associations between sleep duration patterns and behavioral/cognitive functioning at school entry. *Sleep, 30*, 1213-1219.

Tournaki, N. (2003). The differential effects of teaching addition through strategy instruction versus drill and practice to students with and without learning disabilities. *Journal of Learning Disabilities, 36*(5), 449-458.

Trawick-Smith, J., Oski, H., DePaolis, K., Krause, K., & Zebrowski, A. (2016). Naptime data meetings to increase the math talk of early care and education providers. *Journal of Early Childhood Teacher Education, 37*(2), 157-174. doi: 10.1080/10901027.2016.1165762

Trawick-Smith, J., Swaminathan, S., & Liu, X. (2016). The relationship of teacher child play interactions to mathematics learning in preschool. *Early Child Development and Care, 186*(5), 716-733. doi: 10.1080/03004430.2015.1054818

Tsamir, P., Tirosh, D., Levenson, E. S., Barkai, R., & Tabach, M. (2017). Repeating patterns in kindergarten: Findings from children's enactments of two activities. *Educational Studies in Mathematics, 96*(1), 83-99. doi: 10.1007/s10649-017-9762-7

Tudge, J. R. H., & Doucet, F. (2004). Early mathematical experiences: Observing young Black and White children's everyday activities. *Early Childhood Research Quarterly, 19*, 21-39.

Tu luk, M. N., & Öcal, S. M. (2017). Examination of STEM education and its effect on economy: Importance of early childhood education. In I. Koleva & G. Duman (Eds.), *Educational research and practice* (pp. 362-370). Sofia, Bulgaria: St. Kliment Ohridski University Press.

Tucker, S. I., Lommatsch, C. W., Moyer-Packenham, P. S., Anderson-Pence, K. L., & Symanzik, J. (2017). Kindergarten children's interactions with touchscreen mathematics virtual manipulatives:

An innovative mixed methods analysis. *International Journal of Research in Education and Science, 3*(2), 646-665.

Turkle, S. (1997). Seeing through computers: Education in a culture of simulation. *The American Prospect, 31*, 76-82.

Turner, E. E., & Celedón-Pattichis, S. (2011). Problem solving and mathematical discourse among Latino/a kindergarten students: An analysis of opportunities to learn. *Journal of Latinos and Education, 10*(2), 146-169.

Turner, E. E., Celedón-Pattichis, S., & Marshall, M. E. (2008). Cultural and linguistic resources to promote problem solving and mathematical discourse among Hispanic kindergarten students. In R. S. Kitchen & E. A. Silver (Eds.), *Promoting high participation and success in mathematics by Hispanic students: Examining opportunities and probing promising practices* (Vol. 1, pp. 19-42). Tempe, AZ: TODOS: Mathematics for ALL.

Turner, R. C., & Ritter, G. W. (2004, April). *Does the impact of preschool childcare on cognition and behavior persist throughout the elementary years?* Paper presented at the American Educational Research Association, San Diego, CA.

Tymms, P., Jones, P., Albone, S., & Henderson, B. (2009). The first seven years at school. *Educational Assessment and Evaluation Accountability, 21*, 67-80.

Tzur, R., & Lambert, M. A. (2011). Intermediate participatory stages as zone of proximal development correlate in constructing counting-on: A plausible conceptual source for children's transitory "regress" to counting-all. *Journal for Research in Mathematics Education, 42*, 418-450.

Tzuriel, D., & Egozi, G. (2010). Gender differences in spatial ability of young children: The effects of training and processing strategies. *Child Development, 81*(5), 1417-1430.

Ungar, S., Blades, M., & Spencer, C. (1997). Teaching visually impaired children to make distance judgments from a tactile map. *Journal of Visual Impairment and Blindness, 91*, 163-174.

Urbina, A., & Polly, D. (2017). Examining elementary school teachers' integration of technology and enactment of TPACK in mathematics. *The International Journal of Information and Learning Technology, 34*(5), 439-451. doi: 10.1108/IJILT-06-2017-0054

Uttal, D. H., Marzolf, D. P., Pierroutsakos, S. L., Smith, C. M., Troseth, G. L., Scudder, K. V., & DeLoache, J. S. (1997). Seeing through symbols: The development of children's understanding of symbolic relations. In O. N. Saracho & B. Spodek (Eds.), *Multiple perspectives on play in early childhood education* (pp. 59-79). Albany: State University of New York Press.

Uttal, D. H., Meadow, N. G., Tipton, E., Hand, L. L., Alden, A. R., Warren, C., & Newcombe, N. S. (2013). The malleability of spatial skills: A meta-analysis of training studies. *Psychological Bulletin, 139*(2), 352-402. doi: 10.1037/a0028446

Uttal, D. H., Scudder, K. V., & DeLoache, J. S. (1997). Manipulatives as symbols: A new perspective on the use of concrete objects to teach mathematics. *Journal of Applied Developmental Psychology, 18*, 37-54.

Uyanik Aktulun, O., & Inal Kiziltepe, G. (2018). Using learning centers to improve the language and academic skills of preschool children. *World Journal of Education, 8*(6). doi: 10.5430/wje.v8n6p32

Valiente, C., Eisenberg, N., Haugen, R., Spinrad, T. L., Hofer, C., Liew, J., & Kupfer, A. S. (2011). Children's effortful control and academic achievement: Mediation through social functioning. *Early Education & Development, 22*(3), 411-433. doi: 10.1080/10409289.2010.505259

Vallortigara, G. (2012). Core knowledge of object, number, and geometry: A comparative and neural approach. *Cognitive Neuropsychology, 29*(1-2), 213-236. doi: 10.1080/02643294.2012.654772

Vallortigara, G., Sovrano, V. A., & Chiandetti, C. (2009). Doing Socrates [sic] experiment right: Controlled rearing studies of geometrical knowledge in animals. *Current Opinion in Neurobiology, 19*(1), 20-26. doi: 10.1016/j.conb.2009.02.002

van Baar, A. L., de Jong, M., & Verhoeven, M. (2013). Moderate preterm children born at 32-36 weeks gestational age around 8 years of age: Differences between children with and without identified developmental and school problems. In O. Erez (Ed.), *Preterm Birth* (pp. 175-189). Rijeka, Croatia: In Tech Europe.

Van Bommel, J., & Palmér, H. (2016). Young children exploring probability – With focus on their documentations. *Nordic Studies in Mathematics Education, 21*(4), 95-114.

van der Ven, F., Segers, E., Takashima, A., & Verhoeven, L. (2017). Effects of a tablet game intervention on simple addition and subtraction fluency in first graders. *Computers in Human Behavior, 72*, 200-207. doi: 10.1016/j.chb.2017.02.031

Van de Rijt, B. A. M., & Van Luit, J. E. H. (1999). Milestones in the development of infant numeracy. *Scandinavian Journal of Psychology, 40*, 65-71.

Van de Rijt, B. A. M., Van Luit, J. E. H., & Pennings, A. H. (1999). The construction of the Utrecht early mathematical competence scales. *Educational and Psychological Measurement, 59*, 289-309.

Van den Heuvel-panhuizen, M., Elia, I., & Robitzsch, A. (2015). Kindergartners' performance in two types of imaginary perspective-taking. *ZDM Mathematics Education, 47*(3), 345-362. doi: 10.1111/bjet.12320

Van der Ven, S. H. G., Kroesbergen, E. H., Boom, J., & Leseman, P. P. M. (2012). The development of executive functions and early mathematics: A dynamic relationship. *British Journal of Educational Psychology, 82*(1), 100-119. doi: 10.1111/j.2044-8279.2011.02035.x

Van Herwegen, J., & Donlan, C. (2018). *Improving preschoolers' number foundations*. London, England: Kingston University. www.nuffieldfoundation.org/sites/default/files/files/Van%20Herwegen%2041669%20-%20Main%20report_Improving%20Preschoolers%20Number%20Foundations%20(Mar18).pdf

Van Luit, J. E. H., & Van der Molen, M. J. (2011). The effectiveness of Korean number naming on insight into numbers in Dutch students with mild intellectual disabilities. *Research in Developmental Disabilities, 32*, 1941-1947.

van Oers, B. (1994). Semiotic activity of young children in play: The construction and use of schematic representations. *European Early Childhood Education Research Journal, 2*, 19-33.

van Oers, B. (1996). Are you sure? Stimulating mathematical thinking during young children's play. *European Early Childhood Education Research Journal, 4*, 71-87.

van Oers, B. (2003). Learning resources in the context of play. Promoting effective learning in early childhood. *European Early Childhood Education Research Journal, 11*, 7-25.

van Oers, B., & Poland, M. (2012). Promoting abstract thinking in young children's play. In B. van Oers (Ed.), *Developmental Education for Young Children* (Vol. 7, pp. 121-136). The Netherlands: Springer.

Vanbinst, K., Ghesquiere, P., & Smedt, B. D. (2012). Numerical magnitude representations and individual differences in children's arithmetic strategy use. *Mind, Brain, and Education, 6*(3), 129-136. doi: 10.1111/j.1751-228X.2012.01148.x

Vandermaas-Peeler, M., Boomgarden, E., Finn, L., & Pittard, C. (2012). Parental support of numeracy during a cooking activity with four-year-olds. *International Journal of Early Years Education, 20*(1), 78-93. doi: 10.1080/09669760.2012.663237

Van Horn, M. L., Karlin, E. O., Ramey, S. L., Aldridge, J., & Snyder, S. W. (2005). Effects of developmentally appropriate practices on children's development: A review of research and discussion of methodological and analytic issues. Elementary School Journal, 105(4), 325-351.

Varela, F. J. (1999). *Ethical know-how: Action, wisdom, and cognition*. Stanford, CA: Stanford University Press.

Vasilyeva, M., Laski, E., Veraksa, A., Weber, L., & Bukhalenkova, D. (2018). Distinct pathways from parental beliefs and practices to children's numeric skills. *Journal of Cognition and Development, 19*(4), 345-366. doi: 10.1080/15248372.2018.1483371

Verdine, B. N., Golinkoff, R. M., Hirsh-Pasek, K., & Newcombe, N. S. (2017). Links between spatial and mathematical skills across the preschool years. *Monographs of the Society for Research in Child Development, 82*(1, Serial No. 324). doi: 10.1111/mono.12280

Verdine, B. N., Lucca, K. R., Golinkoff, R. M., Newcombe, N. S., & Hirsh-Pasek, K. (2016). The shape of things: The origin of young children s knowledge of the names and properties of geometric forms. *The Journal of Cognition and Development, 17*(1), 142-161. doi: 10.1080/15248372.2015.1016610

Vergnaud, G. (1978). The acquisition of arithmetical concepts. In E. Cohors-Fresenborg & I. Wachsmuth (Eds.), *Proceedings of the 2nd Conference of the International Group for the Psychology of Mathematics Education* (pp. 344-355). Osnabruck, Germany: International Group for the Psychology of Mathematics Education.

Verschaffel, L., Baccaglini-Frank, A., Mulligan, J., van den Heuvel-Panhuizen, M., Xin, Y. P., & Butterworth, B. (2018). Special needs in research and instruction in whole number arithmetic. In M. G. Bartolini Bussi & X. H. Sun (Eds.), *Building the Foundation: Whole Numbers in the Primary Grades: The 23rd ICMI Study* (pp. 375-397). Cham: Springer International Publishing.

Verschaffel, L., Bojorquea, G., Torbeyns, J., & Van Hoof, J. (2019). *Persistence of the Building Blocks' impact on Ecuadorian children's early numerical abilities* EARLI 2019, Aachen University, Germany. https://doi.org/10.1016/j.ecresq.2017.12.009

Verschaffel, L., Greer, B., & De Corte, E. (2007). Whole number concepts and operations. In F. K. Lester, Jr. (Ed.), *Second handbook of research on mathematics teaching and learning* (pp. 557-628). New York, NY: Information Age Publishing.

Vogel, C., Brooks-Gunn, J., Martin, A., & Klute, M. M. (2013). Impacts of early Head Start participation on child and parent outcomes at ages 2, 3, and 5. *Monographs of the Society for Research in Child Development, 78*(1), 36-63. doi: 10.1111/j.1540-5834.2012.00702.x

Votruba-Drzal, E., & Chase, L. (2004). Child care and low-income children's development: Direct and moderated effects. *Child Development, 75*, 296-312.

Vukovic, R. K. (2012). Mathematics difficulty with and without reading difficulty: Findings and implications from a four-year longitudinal study. *Exceptional Children, 78*, 280-300.

Vukovic, R. K., & Lesaux, N. K. (2013). The language of mathematics: Investigating the ways language counts for children's mathematical development. *Journal of Experimental Child Psychology, 115*(2), 227-244. doi: 10.1016/j.jecp.2013.02.002

Vukovic, R. K., Lesaux, N. K., & Siegel, L. S. (2010). The mathematics skills of children with reading difficulties. *Learning and Individual Differences, 20*(6), 639-643.

Vurpillot, E. (1976). *The visual world of the child.* New York, NY: International Universities Press.

Vygotsky, L. S. (1934/1986). *Thought and language.* Cambridge, MA: MIT Press.

Vygotsky, L. S. (1978). Internalization of higher psychological functions. In M. Cole, V. John-Steiner, S. Scribner, & E. Souberman (Eds.), *Mind in society* (pp. 52-57). Cambridge, MA: Harvard University Press.

Waber, D. P., de Moor, C., Forbes, P., Almli, C. R., Botteron, K., Leonard, G., Milovan, D. … Rumsey, J.. (2007). The NIH MRI study of normal brain development: Performance of a population based sample of healthy children aged 6 to 18 years on a neuropsychological battery. *Journal of the International Neuropsychological Society, 13* (5), 729-746.

Waddell, L. R. (2010). How do we learn? African American elementary students learning reform mathematics in urban classrooms. *Journal of Urban Mathematics Education, 3*(2), 116-154.

Wadlington, E., & Burns, J. M. (1993). Instructional practices within preschool/kindergarten gifted programs. *Journal for the Education of the Gifted, 17*(1), 41-52.

Wakeley, A. (2005, April). *Mathematical knowledge of very low birth weight pre-kindergarten children.* Paper presented at the Biennial Meeting of the Society for Research in Child Development, Atlanta, GA.

Walshaw, M., & Anthony, G. (2008). The teacher's role in classroom discourse: A review of recent research into mathematics classrooms. *Review of Educational Research, 78*, 516-551.

Walston, J. T., & West, J. (2004). *Full-day and half-day kindergarten in the United States: Findings from the "Early childhood longitudinal study, kindergarten class 1998-99" (NCES 2004-2078).* Washington, DC: U.S. Department of Education, Institute of Education Sciences, National Center for Education Statistics.

Walston, J. T., West, J., & Rathbun, A. H. (2005). *Do the greater academic gains made by full-day kindergarten children persist through third grade?* Paper presented at the Annual Meeting of the American Educational Research Association, Montreal, Canada.

Wang, F., Xie, H., Wang, Y., Hao, Y., & An, J. (2016). Using touchscreen tablets to help young children learn to tell time. *Frontiers in Psychology, 7* (1800). doi: 10.3389/fpsyg.2016.01800

Wang, J. J., Odic, D., Halberda, J., & Feigenson, L. (2016). Changing the precision of preschoolers' approximate number system representations changes their symbolic math performance. *The Journal of Experimental Child Psychology, 147*, 82-99. doi: 10.1016/j.jecp.2016.03.002

Wang, M., Resnick, L. B., & Boozer, R. F. (1971). The sequence of development of some early mathematics behaviors. *Child Development, 42*, 1767-1778.

Warren, E., & Cooper, T. (2008). Generalising the pattern rule for visual growth patterns: Actions that support 8 year olds' thinking. *Educational Studies in Mathematics, 67*, 171-185. doi: 10.1007/sl0649-007-9092-2

Warren, E., Miller, J., & Cooper, T. J. (2012). Repeating patterns: Strategies to assist young students to generalise the mathematical structure. *Australasian Journal of Early Childhood, 37*(3), 111-120.

Warren, E., & Miller, J. (2014). Supporting English second-language learners in disadvantaged contexts: Learning approaches that promote success in mathematics. *International Journal of Early Years Education.* doi: 10.1080/09669760.2014.969200

Watson, J. M., Callingham, R. A., & Kelly, B. A. (2007). Students' appreciation of expectation and variation as a foundation for statistical understanding. *Mathematical Thinking and Learning, 9*, 83-130.

Watts, T. W., Clements, D. H., Sarama, J., Wolfe, C. B., Spitler, M. E., & Bailey, D. H. (2017). Does early mathematics intervention change the processes underlying children's learning? *Journal of Research on Educational Effectiveness, 10*(1), 96-115. doi: 10.1080/19345747.2016.1204640

Watts, T., Duncan, G. J., Chen, M., Claessens, A., Davis-Kean, P. E., Duckworth, K., Engel, M., Siegler, R. S., & Susperreguy, M. I. (2015). Self-concepts, school placements, executive function, and fractions knowledge as mediators of links between early and later school achievement. *Child Development, 86*(6), 1892-1907. doi: 10.1111/cdev.12416

Watts, T. W., Duncan, G. J., Clements, D. H., & Sarama, J. (2018). What is the long-run impact of learning mathematics during preschool? *Child Development, 89*(2), 539-555. doi: 10.1111/cdev.12713

Watts, T. W., Duncan, G. J., Siegler, R. S., & Davis-Kean, P. E. (2014). What's past is prologue:

Relations between early mathematics knowledge and high school achievement. *Educational Researcher*. doi: 10.3102/0013189X14553660

Watts, T. W., Duncan, G. J., & Quan, H. (2018). Revisiting the marshmallow test: A conceptual replication investigating links between early delay of gratification and later outcomes. *Psychological Science*, 1-9. doi: 10.1177/0956797618761661

Weiland, C., & Yoshikawa, H. (2012). *Impacts of BPS K1 on children's early numeracy, language, literacy, executive functioning, and emotional development*. Paper presented at the School Committee, Boston Public Schools, Boston, MA.

Weiss, I., Kramarski, B., & Talis, S. (2006). Effects of multimedia environments on kindergarten children's mathematical achievements and style of learning. *Educational Media International*, 43(1), 3-17. doi: 10.1080/09523980500490513

Wellman, H. M., & Miller, K. F. (1986). Thinking about nothing: Development of concepts of zero. *British Journal of Developmental Psychology*, 4, 31-42.

Welsh, J. A., Nix, R. L., Blair, C., Bierman, K. L., & Nelson, K. E. (2010). The development of cognitive skills and gains in academic school readiness for children from low-income families. *Journal of Educational Psychology*, 102(1), 43-53.

What Works Clearinghouse. (2013). *Bright beginnings WWC Intervention Report*. Princeton, NJ: Author.

Wheatley, G. (1996). *Quick draw: Developing spatial sense in mathematics*. Tallahassee, FL: Mathematics Learning.

Whitin, P., & Whitin, D. J. (2011, May). Mathematical pattern hunters. *Young Children*, 66(3), 84-90.

Wiegel, H. G. (1998). Kindergarten students' organizations of counting in joint counting tasks and the emergence of cooperation. *Journal for Research in Mathematics Education*, 29, 202-224.

Wilensky, U. (1991). Abstract mediations on the concrete and concrete implications for mathematics education. In I. Harel & S. Papert (Eds.), *Constructionism* (pp. 193-199). Norwood, NJ: Ablex.

Wilkerson, T. L., Cooper, S., Gupta, D., Montgomery, M., Mechell, S., Arterbury, K., Moore, S., Baker, B. R., & Sharp, P. T. (2014). An investigation of fraction models in early elementary grades: A mixed-methods approach. *Journal of Research in Childhood Education*, 29(1), 1-25. doi: 10.1080/02568543.2014.945020

Wilkinson, S. (2017). *Mathematics development in Spanish-speaking English language learners*. (Doctoral Dissertation), University of Iowa. Retrieved from http://ir.uiowa.edu/etd/5878

Wilkinson, L. A., Martino, A., & Camilli, G. (1994). Groups that work: Social factors in elementary students mathematics problem solving. In J. E. H. van Luit (Ed.), *Research on learning and instruction of mathematics in kindergarten and primary school* (pp. 75-105). Doetinchem, The Netherlands: Graviant Publishing Company.

Williams, R. F. (2008). Guided conceptualization? Mental spaces in instructional discourse. In T. Oakley & A. Hougaard (Eds.), *Mental spaces in discourse and interaction* (pp. 209-234). Amsterdam, The Netherlands: John Benjamins Publishing Company.

Wilson, A. J., Dehaene, S., Pinel, P., Revkin, S. K., Cohen, L., & Cohen, D. K. (2006). Principles underlying the design of "The Number Race", an adaptive computer game for remediation of dyscalculia. *Behavioral and Brain Functions*, 2, 19.

Wilson, A. J., Revkin, S. K., Cohen, D. K., Cohen, L., & Dehaene, S. (2006). An open trial assessment of "The number race," an adaptive computer game for remediation of dyscalculia. *Behavioral and Brain Functions*, 2, 20.

Wing, R. E., & Beal, C. R. (2004). Young children's judgments about the relative size of shared portions: The role of material type. *Mathematical Thinking and Learning*, 6, 1-14.

Wolfgang, C. H., Stannard, L. L., & Jones, I. (2001). Block play performance among preschoolers as a presdictor of later school achievement in mathematics. *Journal of Research in Childhood Education*, 15, 173-180.

Wong, V. C., Cook, T. D., Barnett, W. S., & Jung, K. (2008). An effectiveness-based evaluation of five state pre-kindergarten programs. *Journal of Policy Analysis and Management*, 27(1), 122-154.

Wright, B. (1991). What number knowledge is possessed by children beginning the kindergarten year of school? *Mathematics Education Research Journal*, 3(1), 1-16.

Wright, R. J., Stanger, G., Cowper, M., & Dyson, R. (1994). A study of the numerical development of 5-year-olds and 6-year-olds. *Educational Studies in Mathematics*, 26, 25-44.

Wright, R. J., Stanger, G., Cowper, M., & Dyson, R. (1996). First-graders' progress in an experimental mathematics recovery program. In J. Mulligan & M. Mitchelmore (Eds.), *Research in early number learning* (pp. 55-72). Adelaide, Australia: AAMT.

Wright, R. J., Stanger, G., Stafford, A. K., & Martland, J. (2006). *Teaching number in the classroom with 4-8 year olds*. London, England: Paul Chapman Publications/Sage Publications.

Wu, -H.-H. (2011). *Understanding numbers in elementary school mathematics*. Providence, RI: American Mathematical Society.

Wu, S. S., Barth, M., Amin, H., Malcarne, V., & Menon, V. (2012). Math anxiety in second and third graders and its relation to mathematics achievement. *Frontiers in Psychology, 3*(162), 1–11. doi: 10.3389/fpsyg.2012.00162

Wynn, K. (1992). Addition and subtraction by human infants. *Nature, 358,* 749–750.

Xin, J. F. (1999). Computer-assisted cooperative learning in integrated classrooms for students with and without disabilities. *Information Technology in Childhood Education Annual, 1*(1), 61–78.

Yackel, E., & Wheatley, G. H. (1990). Promoting visual imagery in young pupils. *Arithmetic Teacher, 37* (6), 52–58.

Yin, H. S. (2003). Young children's concept of shape: Van Hiele visualization level of geometric thinking. *The Mathematics Educator, 7*(2), 71–85.

Yoshikawa, H., Weiland, C., & Brooks-Gunn, J. (2016). When does preschool matter? *The Future of Children, 26*(2), 21–35.

Yost, N. J. M. (1998). Computers, kids, and crayons: A comparative study of one kindergarten's emergent literacy behaviors. *Dissertation Abstracts International, 59–08,* 2847.

Young-Loveridge, J. M. (1989a). The number language used by preschool children and their mothers in the context of cooking. *Australian Journal of Early Childhood, 21,* 16–20.

Young-Loveridge, J. M. (1989b). The development of children's number concepts: The first year of school. *New Zealand Journal of Educational Studies, 24*(1), 47–64.

Young-Loveridge, J. M. (2004). Effects on early numeracy of a program using number books and games. *Early Childhood Research Quarterly, 19,* 82–98.

Young-Loveridge, J. M., & Bicknell, B. (2018). Making connections using multiplication and division contexts. In V. Kinnear, M. Y. Lai, & T. Muir (Eds.), *Forging Connections in Early Mathematics Teaching and Learning* (pp. 259–272). Singapore: Springer Singapore.

Zacharos, K., & Kassara, G. (2012). The development of practices for measuring length in preschool education. *Skholê, 17,* 97–103.

Zaranis, N. (2017). Does the use of information and communication technology through the use of Realistic Mathematics Education help kindergarten students to enhance their effectiveness in addition and subtraction? *Preschool & Primary Education, 5*(1), 46–62. doi: 10.12681/ppej.9058

Zaranis, N. (2018a). Comparing the effectiveness of using ICT for teaching geometrical shapes in kindergarten and the first grade. *International Journal of Web-Based Learning and Teaching Technologies (IJWLTT), 13*(1), 50–63. doi: 10.4018/IJWLTT.2018010104

Zaranis, N. (2018b). Comparing the effectiveness of using tablet computers for teaching addition and subtraction *Learning Strategies and Constructionism in Modern Education Settings* (pp. 131–151): IGI Global.

Zaranis, N., & Synodi, E. (2017). A comparative study on the effectiveness of the computer assisted method and the interactionist approach to teaching geometry shapes to young children. *Education and Information Technologies, 22*(4), 1377–1393.

Zaretsky, E. (2017). The impact of using logic patterns on achievements in mathematics through application-games. In J. Horne (Ed.), *Philosophical Perceptions on Logic and Order* (pp. 73–95). IGI Global. https://doi.org/10.4018/978-1-5225-2443-4.ch002

Zelazo, P. D., Reznick, J. S., & Piñon, D. E. (1995). Response control and the execution of verbal rules. *Developmental Psychology, 31,* 508–517.

Zhang, X., & Lin, D. (2015). Pathways to arithmetic: The role of visual-spatial and language skills in written arithmetic, arithmetic word problems, and nonsymbolic arithmetic. *Contemporary Educational Psychology, 41,* 188–197. doi: 10.1016/j.cedpsych.2015.01.005

Zur, O., & Gelman, R. (2004). Young children can add and subtract by predicting and checking. *Early Childhood Research Quarterly, 19,* 121–137.

INDEX

Locators in *italics* refers to figures and those in **bold** to tables.

CPSIA information can be obtained
at www.ICGtesting.com
Printed in the USA
LVHW020419181022
730896LV00006B/433

9 780367 521974